WORLD POLITICS SINCE 1945

WORLD POLITICS SINCE 1945

SIXTH EDITION

PETER CALVOCORESSI

LONGMAN
LONDON AND NEW YORK

Longman Group UK Limited
Longman House, Burnt Mill, Harlow,
Essex CM20 2JE, England
and Associated Companies throughout the world.

Published in the United States of America
by Longman Inc., New York

© Peter Calvocoressi 1968, 1971, 1977, 1982, 1987, 1991

First published 1968
Second edition 1971
Third edition 1977
Fourth edition 1982
Fifth edition 1987
Sixth edition 1991
Second impression 1992

British Library Cataloguing in Publication Data
Calvocoressi, Peter
  World politics since 1945. — 6th ed.
  I. Title
  327.09

  ISBN 0–582–07379–0

Library of Congress Cataloging in Publication Data
applied for

Set in 10 on 12pt Bembo Roman

Produced by Longman Singapore Publishers (Pte) Ltd.
Printed in Singapore

CONTENTS

LIST OF MAPS

FOREWORD TO THE THIRD EDITION

This book now covers a period of thirty years since the end of the Second World War. Much of the international map has changed little in these years. The USA and the USSR remain in conflict, mainly because they are still powers of a different order from every other. The essence of this conflict is the clash of power, although its nature and course have been affected by ideology, particularly on the American side, for whereas the USSR has used its power – in Europe and thereafter in the Middle East and at sea – in ways and for purposes which have been standard European power practice for centuries, the USA's major display of strength – in Vietnam – owed a great deal to the view that Russian and Chinese power must be checked because they are communist. Europe remained divided. Despite periodic reminders of the hazards of the new European order, for example in Czechoslovakia in 1968, this division acquired a certain normality and even the continuing and confirmed division of Germany itself (which would not have surprised Henry the Fowler) has been absorbed into the larger division around it. The longevity of Tito has kept Yugoslavia where it is, but the mortality of Franco began the shift of Spain out of its straitjacket and the neighbouring dictatorship was cracked by Portugal's impossible policies in Africa. Middle Eastern affairs have been persistently dominated throughout these thirty years by the Arab–Israeli fight for Palestine, the increasing appetite of the rest of the world for oil, and the uneasy and unsure manoeuvrings of the superpowers in an area which has continued to hypnotize everybody. The British empire has all but completely vanished away, leaving Britain with major problems of readjustment and vast areas of Asia and Africa (where the French, Belgian, Dutch, Portuguese and Spanish empires also dissolved) with responsibility for their own problems relieved only by the meagre help which they could wring from the rich either directly or through such bodies as the UN, the World Bank or the EEC – the last a phenomenon which seemed at first to mark a major change in the world's pattern but by 1975 faced the question whether the change was major or minor. Latin America has remained a byword for instability and inequality. There has been a lot of fighting and killing in the world but none of it nuclear. It has become accepted that the major concern of superpowers is to seek to control the nuclear arms race and this is perhaps the most significant feature of the world political map, even though the hideous complexity of the matter has prevented this mood from being transformed into more than very partial agreements. The third superpower, China, recognized as such by Roosevelt before 1945 if by few others, has displayed a reticence which should probably be attributed to greatness of a different kind, namely its great size which has enormously complicated the business of organizing the country after a major revolution which itself came at the end of a century of wars and decay. Next to the threat of nuclear catastrophe, and for most of the human race, a more present threat has been poverty, squalor and starvation aggravated for many by the helpless beholding of plenty not far away and corruption even nearer. The jarring injustices of racial discrimination have been reduced by decolonization and by changes in mood but not yet eliminated from a world in which so elementary an evil as slavery still persists.

For this edition I have brought all sections of the book up to date while trying to make it not too much longer. The principal changes are these. In Part One I have added a new chapter on post-war Japan and have carried the story of arms control forward to the end of SALT 1 and into the incomplete SALT 2 negotiations. In Part Two I have essayed an appreciation of the cohesion of the two halves of Europe, the eastern after the invasion of Czechoslovakia in 1968 and in the light of economic stringencies and choices among the members of Comecon, the western in terms of the addition of three new members to the EEC and proposals to make it yet larger. The principal additions to Part Three concern the Arab–Israeli war of 1973 and the destruction of Lebanon. The end of American intervention in Vietnam and the secession of Bangladesh from Pakistan provide most of the new material in Part Four and the end of Portuguese empire and its consequences do the same for Part Five. Finally, to Part Six I have made few additions but have appended an overall view of Latin America in terms which have emerged from further thought about its problems. The arrival of man on the moon falls outside the scope of this book.

The main purpose of a book of this kind is to order a mass of factual detail and in that way offer explanations of what has happened: the danger is that it will ignore the general currents which are difficult to discern in a period so short as thirty years and so recent. Nevertheless some currents in which later historians may discern lasting significance may tentatively be indicated.

While war has never been absent from the annals of man (except, I believe, among Eskimos) there have been periods which in retrospect appear remarkably pacific and others which appear remarkably sanguinary. Unquestionably war has in the twentieth century been enormously discussed as well as diastrously waged, and its causes sedulously dissected by academic and other writers while the horrible facts of war have been witnessed directly or through photography by vaster audiences than ever before. Whether warmaking has been commensurately diminished by this specialist enquiry or general impact is another matter, over which it is worth pausing briefly.

When the Second World War ended there was, first of all, an attempt to prevent its repetition by constitutional means – through the Charter of the United Nations and the obligations and institutions thereby created. Yet – and partly because the UN was not so much a new venture as a second attempt – the aspirations invested in the UN were muted from the start and the organs of the UN soon became little more than functional additions to the established machinery of international relations. More or less contemporaneously a second view about the prevention of war emerged. This was to the effect that war had become so destructive and uncontrollable that major powers, remembering the fable of the sorcerer's apprentice, would eschew it on a calculation of expediency, let alone human revulsion: that war had ruled itself out. This was the balance of terror argument which meant that no superpower could expect to defeat another without itself being laid in ruins. But this argument, which still prevails, had a serious flaw. It rested on the presumed nature of nuclear war and applied therefore to nuclear powers only. In order to broaden the argument it was necessary to add a new factor: that non-nuclear wars too would be interdicted because the nuclear powers, fearing that a non-nuclear war might develop into a war involving themselves and their nuclear armouries, would prevent lesser states from making wars or at worst stop them almost as soon as they started (thus in effect transferring to lesser power the blitzkrieg reasoning of the twenties and thirties). The spread of nuclear weapons and, more important, of nuclear technology and capacity has eroded the credibility of this theory which in any case presumed an overriding common purpose and joint action by the superpowers. It required in effect a new kind of international police function – the policing of international disputes not by the UN or by a single world power such as Britain had been but by a combination of two, perhaps later more, powers who must in the nature of things be distrustful of one another, understand one another less than perfectly and communicate with one another with all manner of hampering reservations.

There were therefore no solid grounds for supposing the elimination or significant reduction of war as a regulator of international conflict. New constitutional apparatus, however useful, was an adjunct of an international system which included war as part of the system; this apparatus was not the instrument of a new and more pacific system. In nuclear powers *raison d'état* would, in their relations with one another, take account of the destructiveness of nuclear weapons, but for the great majority of non-nuclear states the conduct of international relations remained much as it had been since the emergence of the nation-state system. In addition groups or movements which lacked the trappings of a duly constituted state were claiming, where they could, some of the prerogatives of the state, notably diplomatic recognition and the right to make war and kill people just like states do (including the age-old practice of resorting to war without a declaration of war).

But what about the impact of war on human sensibilities? This is shaky ground. Since however it is observable that the ravages of war have been unevenly spread over the centuries, it is legitimate to try to discern why this should have been so and why in particular mankind has experienced a relative immunity from war at certain times. One such period in Europe was the age which succeeded the wars of religion, an age which certainly did not see the abolition of war but did see the exercise of more control over its initiation and conduct. One explanation which has been offered for this more benign state of affairs is that the excesses of the wars of religion, culminating in the appalling devastation of the Thirty Years War, so sickened observers and survivors that for a time war became rarer and milder. If there is anything in this argument, then there are grounds for hoping that the concluding decades of the twentieth century may follow this example, since the recent past has provided devastation enough. The peoples of the USSR suffered in the forties death and destruction on an appalling scale; the Japanese suffered the unprecedented shock of two nuclear bombs; China had lived through a century of mounting upheavals; and finally the United States, hitherto immune from the worst horrors of wars even though taking part in them, became involved in and responsible for the slaughter and wasting of Vietnam with retributive – and perhaps not wholly transient – humiliation and demoralization. Were these experiences of the world's leading states enough to put them off war and make them use their skills and strengths to stop other people's wars too?

There is, finally, another strand in the history of these thirty years which deserves an oblique glance. This is the feminist movement which, in various parts of the world, was marked by the advent of women to positions of power and a more general increase in the influence of women at many levels of public affairs. There are precedents for this phenomenon. In the later Middle Ages in Europe – particularly in France, England and Naples – queens became more than the consorts of kings and women have been credited with the softening of manners which changed a warrior world of straw-littered castle halls full of roistering illiterates into a gentler, more decent, more private, more considerate society prepared to give a higher place to the practice of the arts and the play of the mind. But whether women are nicer than men in these respects only when subject to men and without the temptations of power is a question which, so far as I know, remains unanswered.

Peter Calvocoressi
September 1976

PREFACE TO THE SIXTH EDITION

The first function of successive editions of this book is to bring it up to date. The second is to take the opportunity to review past topics and to address some of them from a new angle. Thus I added in the fourth edition a survey of Russian – and to a lesser extent Chinese – activities in Africa since the end of the Second World War and I also consolidated in a new chapter various hitherto scattered aspects of the development, or plight, of the Third World and the emergence of a Fourth. For the fifth edition I gave special thought and space to the Israeli invasion of Lebanon and its consequences, and to the contorted affairs of Central America.

These and other themes are pursued in this sixth edition, but in the five years now covered for the first time (1986–90) all else is overshadowed by the helter-skelter collapse of communist rule in central and eastern Europe and the travails of the USSR itself as, like all empires before it but more precipitately, it loses imperial status and becomes something different. Since convulsions habitually attract a maybe undue share of attention, China and South Africa figure dramatically in this quinquennium, the one balefully, the other with hope. So too does the spasm produced by Iraq's invasion and annexation of Kuwait. By contrast with these stirring events I have included an extended review of the progress of the European Community which may, in the eyes of history, turn out as significant as more turbulent contemporary chronicles.

The more often I prepare a new edition of this book the more do I feel a need to warn readers to be on the look-out for matters which, because they are too speculative for a work of this kind, do not figure in it. Of these the most puzzling is the role in world affairs of nuclear weapons which, although utterly destructive and so unprecedented, are also unusable for military or political purposes. It appears that the aggression hitherto inseparable from states and their intercourse has to find means of expression other than war. This is a notion not easily assimilated.

Peter Calvocoressi
January 1991

PART ONE

WORLD POWERS

1 THE SUPERPOWERS

THE COLD WAR

The Cold War of the two postwar superpowers was not an episode like other wars which have beginnings and ends, winners and losers. The term 'cold war' was invented to describe a state of affairs. The principal ingredient in this state of affairs was the mutual hostility and fears of the protagonists. These emotions were rooted in their several historical and political differences and were powerfully stimulated by myths which at times turned hostility into hatred. The Cold War dominated world affairs for a generation and more.

In American eyes the USSR was dedicated to the conquest of Europe and the world for itself and for communism and was capable of achieving, or at least initiating, this destructive and evil course by armed force abetted by subversion. Seen from Moscow the western world (which included half of Europe as well as the United States) was inspired by capitalist values which demanded the destruction of the USSR and the extirpation of communism by any means available but above all by force or the threat of irresistible force. Both these appreciations were absurd. When the Second World War ended the USSR was incapable of further military exertion, while the communist parties beyond its immediate sphere were unable to achieve anything of significance. The western powers, while profoundly mistrustful of the USSR and hostile to its system and beliefs, had no intention of attacking it and were not even prepared to disturb the dominance of central and eastern Europe secured by its armies in the last year of the war. Each side armed itself to win a war which it expected the other to begin but for which it had no stomach and no plans.

The focus of the Cold War was Germany where confrontation over Berlin in 1948–49 came close to armed conflict but ended in victory for the western side without a military engagement. This controlled trial of strength stabilized Europe which became the world's most stable area for several decades, but hostilities were almost simultaneously carried into Asia, beginning with the triumph of communism in China and

war in Korea. These events led in turn to an acceleration of the
independence and rearmament of west Germany within a new Euro-
American alliance and to a succession of conflicts in Asia, of which the
Vietnam War was the most devastating. At no point did the
protagonists directly engage each other but both sought to extend their
influence and win territorial advantage in adjacent parts of the world,
notably the Middle East and – after its decolonization – Africa. None of
these excursions was decisive and for nearly half a century the chief
outward expression of the Cold War was not advances or retreats but
the accumulation and refinement of the means by which the two sides
tried to intimidate each other: that is to say, their arms race. The
slackening of the Cold War resulted from the combined effect of the
huge cost of these armaments and the gradual waning of the myths
which underlay it.

In the summer of 1945 it was known both in Washington and
Moscow that Japan was ready to acknowledge defeat and abandon the
war which it had begun by the attack on Pearl Harbor in 1941. In July
the Americans experimentally exploded the first nuclear weapon in the
history of mankind and in August they dropped two bombs on
Hiroshima and Nagasaki. Japan surrendered forthwith and this
clinching of the imminent American victory deprived the Russians of
all but a token share in the postwar settlement in the Far East. The
Second World War ended with an act which contained the two central
elements in the Cold War: the advent of nuclear weapons and Russo-
American rivalry.

In the European theatre this conflict remained for a short time veiled.
The organs and habits of wartime collaboration were to be adapted to
the problems of peace, not discarded. The Russian spring offensive of
1944 had set the USSR on the way to military dominance and political
authority in Europe unequalled since Alexander I had ridden into Paris
in 1814 with plans for a concert of victors which would order the affairs
of Europe and keep them ordered. The nature of mid-twentieth century
great power control was a matter for debate – how far the powers were
collectively to order the whole world, how far each was to dominate a
sector. The Russians and the British, with the reluctant assent of
President Franklin D. Roosevelt (and the dissent of his Secretary of
State, Cordell Hull), discussed the practical aspects of an immediate
division of responsibilities, and in October 1944, at a conference in
Moscow which the president was unable to attend owing to the
American election campaign, these dispositions were expressed in
numerical terms. About western Europe no questions arose because
western control was uncontested. Poland was not included because, in
parts effectively, in parts imminently, it was under Stalin's military
control. Elsewhere the realities were expressed as percentages. The
Russian degree of influence in Romania was described as 90, in Bulgaria

and Hungary as 80, in Yugoslavia 50, in Greece 10. In practice these figures, although expressed as a bargain, described a situation: 90 and 10 were polite ways of saying 100 and 0, and the diagnosis in the two extreme cases of Romania and Greece was confirmed when the British took control in Greece without Russian protest and the USSR installed a pro-communist regime in Romania with only perfunctory British protest. Bulgaria and Hungary went the same was as Romania for military reasons. Yugoslavia appeared to fall within the Russian sphere but soon fell out of it. Europe became divided into two segments appertaining to the two principal victors, the United States and the USSR. These two powers continued for a while to talk in terms of alliance, and they were specifically pledged to collaborate in the governance of the German and Austrian territories which they and their allies had conquered.

The position of the USSR in these years was one of great weakness. For the USSR the war had been a huge economic disaster accompanied by loss of life so grievous that its full extent was probably not disclosed. The Russian state was a land power which had expanded generation by generation within a zone which presented a persistent German threat. In the Soviet phase of history Russian external politics were further characterized by a diplomacy which led to isolation and so, in 1941, to the threshold of total military defeat. The USSR had been saved by its extraordinary geographical and spiritual resources and by the concurrent war in the west in which the Germans were already engaged before they attacked the USSR and which became graver for them when, shortly afterwards, Hitler gratuitously declared war on the United States of America. For Stalin, however, the anti-fascist alliance of 1941–45 can hardly have appeared to be more than a marriage of convenience and limited span; nor did it look any different when seen from the western end, at any rate by governments, if not in the popular view. With the war over, the purpose of the alliance had been achieved, and there was little in the mentalities and traditions of the allies to encourage the idea that it might be converted into an entente: on the contrary, the diplomatic history of all parties up to 1941 and their respective attitudes to international political, social and economic problems suggest exactly the reverse.

The elimination, permanent or temporary, of the German threat coincided with the explosion of the first American nuclear bombs. For the first time in the history of the world one state had become more powerful than all other states put together. The USSR, no less than the most trivial state, was at the mercy of the Americans if they should be willing to do to Moscow and Leningrad what they had done to Hiroshima and Nagasaki. There were reasons for supposing that they were not so willing, but no government in the Kremlin could responsibly proceed upon this assumption. Stalin's only prudent course

1.1   The Cold War division of Europe

1.2 The Union of Soviet Socialist Republics, showing location of the fifteen Union Republics in this bitterly disappointing situation was to combine the maximum strengthening of the USSR with a nice assessment of the safe level of provocation of the United States, and to subordinate everything, including postwar reconstruction, to catching up with the Americans in military technology. He possessed a large army, he had occupied large areas of eastern and central Europe, and he had natural allies and servants in communists in various parts of the world.

At home his tasks were immense: they included the safeguarding of the USSR against a repetition of the catastrophe of 1941–45, and the resurrection of the USSR from the catastrophe which had cost something like 25 million lives, the destruction or displacement of a large part of its industry and the distortion of its industrial pattern to the detriment of all except war production, and the devastation and depopulation of its cultivated land so that food production was almost halved. To a man with Stalin's past and temperament the tasks of restitution included the reassertion of party rule and communist orthodoxy and the reduction therefore of the prominence of the army and other national institutions and the reshackling of all modes of thinking outside the prescribed doctrinal run. In matters of national security, in economic affairs and in the life of the spirit the outlook was grim. At home artists and intellectuals were regimented, victorious marshals were slighted and the officer class persistently if quietly purged, while the first postwar five-year plan prescribed strenuous tasks for heavy industry and offered little comfort to a war-weary populace.

Externally Stalin made it clear that the protective acquisitions of 1939–40 were not for disgorging (the three Baltic states, the eastern half of Poland which the Russians called Western Ukraine and Western Byelorussia, Bessarabia and northern Bukovina, and the territory exacted from Finland after the winter war); elsewhere in eastern and central Europe all states must have governments well disposed to the USSR, a vague formula which seemed to mean governments which could be relied upon never again to give facilities to a German aggressor and which came after 1947 or thereabouts to mean governments reliably hostile to the United States in the Cold War. Such governments must be installed and maintained by whatever means might be necessary. During the wartime conferences between Stalin, Roosevelt and Churchill parts of the USSR were still occupied by German forces, and during the war and its psychological aftermath (a period of indefinable duration) Stalin was no doubt obsessed with his German problem. The Cold War first substituted the Americans for the Germans as the main enemy but then, after the rearmament of Western Germany, combined the two threats as a new American–German one. These developments, to which Stalin himself contributed by his actions in eastern and central Europe, may nevertheless have been a disappointment to him if, as seems possible, he had entertained at one time a very different prospect of Russo–American relations.

To Stalin during the war the Americans were personified by President Franklin D. Roosevelt who made no secret of his desire to get on well with the USSR or of his distrust of British and other western imperialisms. Moreover Roosevelt wanted a Russian alliance against Japan and did not seem at all likely to do the one thing which Stalin would have feared; namely, to keep troops permanently in Europe and make the United States a European power. On the contrary, Roosevelt was not much interested in postwar Europe and showed, for example, little of Churchill's concern about what was going to happen in Poland and Greece. Whereas Russo–British relations came near to breaking-point over Poland, Russo–American relations did not; and Stalin, whether out of genuine lack of interest or calculated diplomacy, avoided serious disagreement with Roosevelt over problems of world organization (such as the representation of Soviet republics in the UN) in which Roosevelt was seriously interested. On the basis that the United States would be remote from Europe and in some degree friendly towards the USSR Stalin was prepared to moderate his support for European communists in order not to alarm the United States. He did not foresee that by abandoning Greece to Britain he was preparing the way for the transfer of Greece to the United States within three years. His failure to help the Greek communists may have been principally a result of a calculation that they were not worth helping, but he may also have reflected that helping them would alarm and irritate Americans in Roosevelt's entourage. He was continuing a line of policy applied in Yugoslavia during the war when he restrained the Yugoslav communists' desire to plan and prosecute their social revolution while the war was still in progress, and urged them to co-operate with other parties, even monarchists. Again he persuaded the Italian communists to be less anti-monarchical than the non–communist Action Party; it was the communist leader Palmiro Togliatti who proposed, after the fall of Mussolini, that the future of the Italian monarchy should remain in abeyance until the war was finished. By that time, however, Roosevelt was dead and whatever Stalin's policies towards the United States may have been, they could no longer be based on his relations with Roosevelt and his estimate of Roosevelt's intentions. Even if Roosevelt had survived, his policies might have been radically altered – as Truman's were – by the successful explosion of two nuclear bombs and by the evolution of Stalin's policies in Europe.

For Stalin, confronted in August 1945 with the evidence from Hiroshima and Nagasaki, the outstanding fact was that the USSR possessed no strategic air force and could not deliver a direct attack on the United States. The best that Stalin could do was to pose a threat to western Europe which might deter the Americans from attacking the

USSR. The Russian armies were not demobilized and they were not withdrawn from the areas which they had occupied in the last campaigns of the war and which included the historic capitals of Budapest, Prague, Vienna and Berlin. Thus Stalin created a glacis in advance of his vulnerable heartlands and at the same time scared the exhausted and tremulous Europeans and their American protectors to ask themselves whether the Russian advance had really been halted by the German surrender or might be resumed until Paris and Milan, Brest and Bordeaux, were added to the Russian bag. But by keeping a huge army in being and reducing most of central and eastern Europe to vassalage while Russian money and Russian brains were producing the Russian bomb, Stalin accentuated the American hostility which he had cause to fear.

Nuclear parity was an almost inescapable objective for the Kremlin after 1945, but there was in theory an alternative which some Americans tried to bring within the scope of practical politics. This was to sublimate or internationalize atomic energy and so remove it from inter-state politics. One of the first actions of the United Nations was to create in 1946 an Atomic Energy Commission. At the first meeting of this commission Bernard M. Baruch presented on behalf of the United States a plan for an international Atomic Development Authority which would have exclusive control and ownership in all potential warmaking nuclear activities and would also have the right to inspect all other atomic activities. Upon the inauguration of effective international control the United States would stop making nuclear weapons and destroy existing stocks. But the United States could not destroy its advanced technological knowledge and it would therefore retain a huge advantage over the USSR which, by accepting the Baruch plan, would inhibit its own advances in nuclear physics. In addition the USSR disliked the plan because it involved the abrogation in this field of the veto, the principal symbol and guarantee of national sovereignty as opposed to international government, which the USSR was even less disposed to countenance than any other state. A. A. Gromyko proposed instead a treaty banning the use of nuclear weapons, the destruction of existing stocks, and an international control commission subordinate to the Security Council (and therefore subject to the veto); he opposed the creation of a new international authority and was only prepared to allow international inspection of those plants which had been declared to have ceased nuclear production and were offered for inspection by the government of the country in which they were situated. These positions were irreconcilable and although the debate continued for a while the UN Atomic Energy Commission eventually decided in 1948 to adjourn indefinitely. The Russian rejection of the Baruch Plan was an additional factor in persuading the administration of Harry S. Truman, who had become president on the death of

Roosevelt in April 1945, that the USSR was no longer an ally but an adversary.

American policy-makers had more freedom of choice than their Russian counterparts. The nuclear bomb was a military weapon which had been used to bring the war with Japan to an end in a particular way and it was also a political weapon which was used to shackle Russian power. The war left the United States a major power in Europe with considerable military forces in Europe and nuclear weapons in the background. Endowed with mighty technical superiority, which they may have regarded as permanent, the Americans were in a position in which they could strike or threaten or wait and see. To strike – to start a preventive war – was in practice impossible because they were unable to summon up the will to do so. A preventive war is a war undertaken to remove a threat by a people which feels threatened, and the Americans were not threatened by the Russians and did not feel threatened by them. In these circumstances a preventive war by the Americans was an abstract intellectual concept. (For the Russians it was substantive but also suicidal.) The Americans therefore pursued policies which combined threats with waiting to see.

All weapons have political implications and the biggest weapons have the biggest implications. A weapon which is too frightful to use – or turns out to be, in military terms, useless except in the most exceptional circumstances – has the most implications, since its possessors will want to put it to political use in order to compensate for the anomalous limitations on its military usefulness. Truman's position was automatically different from Roosevelt's as soon as Hiroshima had been destroyed. The question was not whether he was to make political use of the new weapon, but to what political end he should use it. The relationship between the United States and the USSR had been altered: how should this alteration be exploited? The context in which this question first arose was not Asian but European, for it was in Europe that the principal political issues were arising. The United States, unlike the USSR and Britain, disliked the idea of spheres of influence. It also disliked the prospect of exclusive Russian control over half Europe and believed that the Russians were moving towards such control in contravention of pledges to install democratic governments in the countries liberated from German rule. Since Russian designs were uncertain – Stalin seemed content at first to accept coalition government in these countries and to interpret democratic as meaning anything which excluded fascists (only a moderately ambiguous term in the prevailing circumstances) – the United States wished to exert pressure on Moscow in two directions: to make the coalitions more rather than less democratic in the sense of being proportionately representative of the popular will, and to allow American and British representatives on the Control Commissions in liberated countries to have more rather than less authority in relation to their Russian colleagues. And the pressure to be used in the pursuit of these aims included the fact that the nuclear bomb should make Russian leaders think twice before adopting opposite policies.

On the American side that intangible but none the less real factor called the climate of opinion was changing at this juncture for more reasons than the accretion of nuclear power. New men impart new ideas and new ways of handling existing problems. Truman was a very different man from Roosevelt and conscious of the differences: an American of some eminence but in no sense a world figure, a man respected for the qualities which go with simpleness and directness rather than with subtlety, a man in whom political courage would have to take the place of political sophistication, a man typically American in his attachment to a few basic principles and ideologies where the less typical Roosevelt had generally preferred the modes of thought of the pragmatist. Truman in the last resort played politics by precept and not by ear, and where Roosevelt had been concerned with the problem of relations between two great powers Truman was more influenced by the conflict between communism and an even vaguer entity called anti-communism. Again, so far as these generalizations are pardonable, Truman was the more representative American of the late forties and more inclined to regard the meeting of Americans and Russians in the middle of Europe as a confrontation of systems and civilizations rather than of states. Reports of indiscipline and barbarities by Russian troops, often described in this context as Asian or mongoloid, increased this propensity. (Europeans, too, if they had to choose between a host of rapists and a host of seducers, not only preferred the latter but also stood in fear of the former as something alien as well as terrifying.)

The United States had some cause to hope that the moderating implications of Hiroshima for Europe were not lost on the Russians. Elections in Hungary in October and November 1945 were held without coercion and gave the communists only a minor share in the government of the capital and the state. Elections in Bulgaria were postponed on American insistence and against Russian wishes. In Romania the United States aligned itself with the anti-communists and the king against the prime minister, Petru Groza, whom the Russians had installed when they entered the country in 1944. But the crucial testing ground was Poland where coalition government, under a socialist prime minister, was maintained until 1947 but gradually transformed in that and the following year – the years which saw the prevailing of the east wind over the west in central and eastern Europe, the failure of the American attempt to resist the partition of Europe into spheres of influence and the formalization of the Cold War.

In these years American policy veered away from the attempt to maximize American influence throughout Europe in favour of the lesser aim of giving the USSR to understand that further territorial advances in Europe were forbidden. This prohibition was to be enforced and institutionalized by a series of open political arrangements, backed by military dispositions. The overwhelming power of the United States would be used obstructively but not destructively. In so far as the USSR presented a material menace, it would be contained by physical barriers; in so far as it presented an ideological menace, it would be countered by democratic example, money and the seeds of decay which westerners discerned in the communist system (as Marxists did in capitalism). American policy was also constructive and reconstructive. The UN Relief and Reconstruction Agency (UNRRA) was mainly financed by American money; its help was enormous, especially to the USSR and Yugoslavia. In March 1947 the United States took over Britain's traditional and now too costly role of keeping the Russians out of the eastern Mediterranean: Truman took Greece and Turkey under the American wing and promised material aid to states threatened by communism. Three months later the United States inaugurated the Marshall Plan to avert an economic collapse of Europe which could, it was feared, leave the whole continent helplessly exposed to Russian power and communist lures. The offer of American economic aid was made to the whole of Europe including the USSR but Moscow refused for itself and for its satellites. For a second time – the Baruch Plan being the first – the Russians rejected a generous overture from Washington rather than accept collaboration which would have enabled Americans and others to go up and down in the USSR and observe its true plight. Separate development of western and eastern Europe was affirmed and the American initiative in restoring western Europe killed Russian hopes (if any) of victories in the west.

Thus a line was drawn. The coup which substituted communist for coalition rule in Prague the next year made it starker. Gloom and fear descended upon European politics. Although there was no fighting except of a local, sporadic and unacknowledged kind, everybody concurred in describing the situation as a war. Then, in Germany, where the major powers had joined hands in 1945 and had established a joint administration, the struggle for the only important piece of Europe outside the two camps produced a challenge and a counter-challenge which seemed bound to lead to shooting.

At the end of the war the United States, the USSR and Britain were in apparent agreement on two fundamental propositions about Germany, both of which they failed to maintain. The first of these was that Germany should be kept under constraint, and the second was that it should remain a single unit. Within a decade Germany became divided into two separate states, each – particularly the western one – playing an increasingly effective part in international politics. The reasons for this outcome included the inability of the victors to agree on other aspects of the German problem, the intrinsic importance of Germany itself, and external circumstances, of which the Korean War was the most important. So Germany too was partitioned, like Europe as a whole, as a consequence of Russo–American rivalry in the conference chamber and on the ground in Europe and beyond. The bipolarity of postwar power politics led inevitably to delineation and demarcation – even, in a celebrated and late episode, to the building of a wall, a tactic reminiscent of such antique devices as the attempt to bar the Golden Horn to ships or the isthmus of Corinth to armies.

The principal victors were initially agreed that Germany should be disarmed and denazified, divided administratively into zones of occupation but treated economically as a single unit which would pay for imported necessities out of current production. Dismemberment, which had been discussed and may have lingered on in some French minds, was tacitly abandoned without being officially repudiated, and the territorial amputations suffered by Germany were the loss of east Prussia to the USSR and of all other territories beyond the Oder and Western Neisse rivers which were left under Polish administration pending the final delimitation of the German state by the peace conference which never took place. Churchill opposed the designation of the Western as opposed to the Eastern Neisse as the western limit of Poland's sphere (the Western Neisse flows northward into the Oder at a point where the upstream line of the Oder turns sharply eastward) but he felt unable to persist in a seemingly anti–Polish attitude. The Potsdam decision on Germany's frontiers, although expressed in provisional terms, was in reality a victory for the Russians. Germany lost nearly one quarter of its pre-1938 territory.

The victors were divided in their views on the economic policy of the occupation and on the future structure of the German state. The general principles of economic unity and the balancing of imports and production, adopted at Potsdam, were traversed by the problem of reparations which had been inconclusively discussed at Yalta and then shelved at Potsdam. It was agreed at Yalta that the sum of $20,000 million should be taken as a basis for further discussions, half of this sum being claimed by the USSR for itself and Poland. At Potsdam the Russians, whose need for reparations in kind or cash was intense, secured agreement for removals from their zone of occupation to meet Russian and Polish reparation claims but nothing was settled about the extent of these claims. The western allies were likewise to be entitled to dismantle and remove property in their zones in order to meet their claims and those of the remaining allies. This arrangement was bound to make nonsense of the principle of economic unity since the various zones were economically dissimilar both in regard to manufactures and to agricultural production. It also made nonsense of the principle of paying for imports out of current production, since it permitted the occupiers to destroy the sources of production. Germany could be looted or milked, but it could not for long be both looted and milked. The western allies soon found that dismantling left them with an obligation to provide their zones with imported goods which had to be paid for by their own taxpayers since German production was unable to foot the bill. Moreover, Russian dismantling and removals on a vast scale, coupled with severe shortages in the USSR itself, placed upon the western occupiers and their taxpayers the additional burden of supplying the Russian zone with essential foods and goods. Although the Americans might have been willing to help the Russians directly with equipment for reconstruction, they resented the roundabout way in which the Russians helped themselves to German equipment at eventual American expense, while for their part the Russians were happy to take from Germany what their *amour propre* prevented them from accepting from the Americans.

This conflict was accompanied by related disagreements about the political structure of Germany and, subsequently, about its political attachments. The British were pragmatically predisposed in favour of a unitary rather than a federal structure, for economic rather than political reasons. The main Russian concern was strategic: to maintain their position in eastern Germany. This was the essential minimum to which they subsequently adhered unfalteringly. It was strengthened, in November 1945, by the first significant political event in the reviving postwar Europe – the elections in Austria in which the communists were decisively defeated. If, compatibly with the aim of holding fast to eastern Germany, Russian power could be extended to the whole of Germany, so much the better; but this wider aim can never have seemed more than problematical after the first few disordered months of peace. So long, however, as it remained a possibility, the Russians favoured a strong central government for Germany in the hope that it would be captured by the Socialist Unity Party (SED – an attempt to create a left-wing party under communist control and prevent the operation of a distinct socialist party). They only abandoned this sub-policy after it became evident that a united Germany would no more be a communist Germany in the 1940s than it had been after 1918. They thereupon switched not to a federal solution for Germany as a whole but to a two-Germanies policy.

The supporters of federation, meaning a federation with a weak central government, were the French. Incapable themselves of imposing any control over Germany and dubious of their allies' capacity to do so for long, the French wanted a weak German state, disarmed and disabled by internal political fragmentation. They also wanted coal for their own reconstruction plans and the Saar. Their changes in policy came in stages: first, Georges Bidault, when foreign minister, reluctantly acknowledged the hostility between the USSR and the western allies, threw France's lot in with the latter and accepted the establishment of a new western German state, including the French zone; next, Robert Schuman sought, in a wider European context, to win German friendship rather than insure against German hostility, and René Pleven, in the same context, accepted a modified rearmament of Germany; finally de Gaulle, developing Schuman's policy of reconciliation without the European framework, concluded with Schuman's old colleague, Konrad Adenauer, a bilateral Franco–German alliance.

In the three years after the Potsdam conference the occupiers, having failed to produce a coherent German policy, drifted away from the notion of Germany as something to be constrained to the notion of Germany as something to be acquired, from a basically collaborative to a basically competitive position. Two conferences of foreign ministers in 1947, at Moscow in March and at London in November, failed to elaborate the peace treaty which was supposed to emerge. In the same year, which was also the year of the Truman Doctrine and the Marshall Plan, the American and British zones were fused (January) and endowed with an economic council of fifty-four members (May). In the next year the Americans and the British moved determinedly towards turning their joint zone into a solvent and autonomous parliamentary democracy. The economic council was doubled in size and given a second chamber; a plan was produced for the internationalization of the Ruhr in order to counter the fears of those who found it difficult to stomach the reappearance of a sovereign German state; in June the Americans and the British devalued the mark in their zones, a long discussed and necessary reform which the Russians had obstructed by appealing to the principle of economic unity; in September a constituent assembly met in Bonn. These steps were supplemented in April 1949 when the French zone was joined with the Anglo–American. The western occupiers invigorated this joint zone (and embryonic state) with American financial aid and a reform of its currency; and they prepared to extend the new mark to their sectors of Berlin. At this point the Russians decided to challenge the whole western policy of separate development of a western German state. They chose Berlin where their position was special and strong.

Berlin had been excluded from the zonal system and placed under a separate, joint allied authority, the Kommandatura. For practical purposes the city was divided into four sectors but these sectors did not have the administrative autonomy of the zones. But the Russian position in Berlin was distinct for two reasons. It was the Russians who first entered the city, occupying it a few days before the German surrender and setting about the business of clearing rubble, organizing rations, installing new local authorities and establishing a police force before the arrival of American or British units; and secondly, the drawing of the zonal boundaries left Berlin an enclave within the

Russian zone and separated by 260 km from the nearest point under British control. Subsequently there was much debate about the lack of foresight and political sense of the western allies in allowing the Russians to reach Berlin first and in accepting the virtual isolation of the city without even securing clearly and formally defined rights of access to it. Although something must be allowed for the temper and exigencies of wartime collaboration (which had to be preserved to the last at almost any cost), there can be little doubt that the Americans and the British would have driven a different bargain if they had realized that they were in effect handing Berlin over to the Russians subject only to the right to be imprisoned within it.

Berlin was the central point of a Russian attempt to gain control of Germany which, having started with auspicious expedition, quickly ran into trouble. The socialists refused to submerge themselves in a single party with the communists and promoted instead an anti-Russian coalition which, in elections in October 1946, thwarted the Russian design to place the city's administration in communist hands. In 1947 Ernst Reuter, an ex-communist socialist, was elected mayor in a symbolic contest in which the non-Russian occupiers were clearly, if still discreetly, aligned with Reuter against the Russians and the communists. The independent political life of the city had revived before the Russians had been able to impose a throttling substitute so that, while the Russian strategic position remained strong, the Russian political position had not thriven commensurately and the western occupiers found themselves indebted to the anti-Russian activities of Berliners. In return for this uncovenanted aid the western occupiers later felt obliged to commit themselves to the maintenance of the independence of Berlin from the Russian zone and its successor, the East German state or German Democratic Republic.

The steps taken by the western occupiers in 1947–48 to establish a West German state threatened the Russian ambition to keep Germany whole and turn it communist. They also foreshadowed the revival of an independent German power in world politics, armed and hostile to the USSR. The Russians decided to make a major issue of these developments and to resort to force to stop them. They cut the road, rail and water routes by which the western occupiers communicated with Berlin and stopped food, electricity, gas and other necessities from being supplied regularly to the western sectors from the east. The legal right to use the routes uninterruptedly was vague – and also irrelevant in what was clearly a trial of strength. The western occupiers, having considered and rejected the possibility of asserting their rights by sending an armed convoy to force its way along the road from the British zone to the boundary of the city decided instead to pierce the Russian siege by air, thus placing the Russians in the position of having to fire a first shot. They also imposed a counterblockade on the Russian zone, and the Americans moved part of their long range bomber force to airfields in England. Between July 1948 and May 1949 the American and British air forces carried over 1.5 million tons of food, fuel and other goods into Berlin (the highest load in one day exceeded 12,000 tons), thus ensuring the needs of the entire civilian population of the blockaded sectors as well as their western guardians. This doubly extraordinary feat – extraordinary for what it did and extraordinary for doing it without leading to open hostilities – defeated the Russians, who abandoned the blockade in May after 318 days in return for a promise of one more conference on Germany, which was held in Paris but achieved nothing.

The western victory over Berlin was followed by the transformation of the western zone of Germany into a sovereign state and an armed member of the Euro–American alliance against the USSR. After elections in August the German Federal Republic came into being on 20 September 1949 with its capital in Bonn and Dr Konrad Adenauer as its chancellor. Adenauer thereby tacitly agreed to postpone German reunification by joining the western camp. An occupation statute and a series of agreements (the Petersburg agreements) defined the relations between the new state and the western powers and imposed certain restrictions on its sovereignty, but these detailed provisions were of no importance compared with the transcendent fact that the greater part of Germany had been removed from the joint control of its conquerors and attached to a new anti–communist western alliance. Exactly a year after the inauguration of the Federal Republic its rearmament became a live issue: as a result of the outbreak of war in Korea in June 1950 the Americans persuaded themselves and, with more difficulty, their British and French allies and Adenauer (who was initially opposed) that the Federal Republic should contribute to the armament of the west. The western alliance which was created to wage the Cold War came into existence on 4 April 1949, during the blockade of Berlin. Two years earlier such an alliance would have seemed to most Europeans and Americans impossible because of the strength of the communist parties of France and Italy, but during 1947 communists were excluded from the government of these two countries and the belief that they were ungovernable without communist participation was proved false. The North Atlantic Treaty was an association of twelve states which declared that an armed attack on any one of them in Europe or North America would be regarded as an attack on them all, and that each would in such an event go to the help of the ally attacked by taking such action, including the use of force, as it deemed necessary. The area covered by the treaty was defined as the territories of any signatory in Europe or North America, Algeria and islands, vessels or aircraft of any signatory in the Atlantic north of the tropic of Cancer; the treaty would also be brought into operation by an attack on the occupation forces of any signatory in Europe. Greece and Turkey joined the alliance in 1952 and the German Federal Republic in 1955. The creation of Nato was an affirmation of the dissolution of the wartime alliance. It was a defensive gesture by the principal western powers based on fear of Russian aggression, revulsion against the fact and the nature of Russian domination in eastern Europe, frustration turning to hostility in German affairs, the exposure of western Europe as a result of war damage and demobilization, and the failure to internationalize the control of atomic energy.

In 1945 the American warmaking capacity had been supreme even without nuclear weapons, but in the next years a new pattern was created by American demobilization. While American supremacy was guaranteed by the nuclear bomb, the Russians, by not demobilizing, established a superiority in mobilized land power in Europe. Thus, all future attempts to disarm were bedevilled by the impossibility of comparing like with like; the defence of western Europe became dependent on nuclear power and nuclear strategy and ultimately the collective defence of western Europe provoked dissension about inter-allied control over nuclear weapons. Whereas in 1945 there had been some qualms and, on the Russian side, some hopes of an American retreat from Europe, four years later the United States was formally committed to a dominant role in European affairs for the next twenty years. Realizing too late what had been brought about, Stalin proposed in 1948 the withdrawal of all foreign troops from Germany, but his offer was regarded as a mere device to make the Americans take a long journey from which they would not return while the Russians remained within striking distance of Germany. So long as Germany was debatable ground the United States would remain on it. Hence western Germany's eventual place in Nato alongside its recent enemies.

The Cold War was a short episode in the history of Europe but it assumed at the time an air of permanence owing to the metaphors of frigidity and rigor in which it was discussed. Its two principal features were apparent in 1946 in the speeches by Churchill at Fulton, Missouri, in February in Truman's presence and by Truman's Secretary of State, James F. Byrnes, at Stuttgart in September. These speeches showed that the tripartite wartime alliance was being replaced by a new pattern of two against one and that the United States, so far from turning its back on Europe (and in spite of the reduction of American forces in Europe from 2.5 million men to fewer than half a million at the date of the Fulton speech), regarded Europe as an essential American sphere of influence. Although Truman had to accept virtual exclusion from central and eastern Europe, he secured by the Truman Doctrine of March 1947 a foothold in the Balkans and the Middle East at the time when he was preparing to consolidate anti-communist and anti-Russian positions in western Europe by a combination of economic aid and military alliance – embodied in the Marshall Plan and the North Atlantic Treaty. These were the beginnings of the policy of containment, designed to curb Russian power and change the Russian mood, but little more than a year after the signing of the North Atlantic Treaty this essentially European policy was complicated by a distant event, the outbreak of war in Korea, which became a drain on the forces available for containment in Europe and converted containment from a European to a more nearly global policy.

The Korean War also embittered the atmosphere. In the United States it was treated as evidence to fortify the myth of a masterly communist conspiracy to conquer the world. Senator Joseph McCarthy, alleging that this conspiracy extended into the United States government itself and other centres of influence, conducted a buoyant and repellent smear campaign in which he and his associates intimidated important segments of the public service by denouncing as communists (or homosexuals) anybody who did not subscribe to their extreme views of how loyal Americans ought to think: a number of Americans were driven into exile and some to suicide, and the formulation and conduct of American external policies were corrupted and demoralized before McCarthyism was anaesthetized by a few bold individuals, by its own excesses and by the residual good sense of the American people – without much help from their more supine elected leaders. This atmospheric pressure affected the American election campaign of 1952 in which the Republicans, in their bid to recapture the presidency for the first time since 1932, adopted General Eisenhower as their candidate. The principal Republican spokesman on foreign affairs was John Foster Dulles, soon to be Secretary of State.

McCarthyism apart there were grounds for questioning the Democrats' foreign policies. The United States was engaged in a grievous war; the USSR was not; containment seemed to mean peace for the Russians who, although prevented from expanding, remained unconstrained in their treatment of their satellites, whose fate bore uneasily on the American conscience. In his election speeches Dulles gave the impression that the Republicans would come to the aid of the enslaved people of eastern Europe and somehow liberate them from Russian domination. Containment was decried as negative and immoral. The Republicans won the election and the policy of liberation was rapidly forgotten. Instead Dulles proceeded with the policy of containment, filling the gap between Nato and the American position in Japan by fostering Seato (the South East Asia Treaty Organization) and the Baghdad Pact. He also tried to escape from the frustrations of containment, which he had criticized for being a series of responses to Russian initiatives, by evolving a strategy of massive retaliation to be applied at times and places of American choosing. But when in Indo–China in 1954 the United States had the choice between massive retaliation and acquiescence in an ally's defeat it chose the latter and so acknowledged that massive retaliation contained a large element of bluff.

In Europe the United States, having successfully annexed western Germany to Nato, accepted as a corollary the impossibility of dislodging the Russians from eastern Germany, which was turned into a satellite communist adjunct of the Russian empire in Europe. After passing through similar stages – an economic council, a parliament, a constitution, the election of a president (Wilhelm Pieck) and prime minister (Otto Grotewohl) – the eastern zone became in March 1954 a separate state under the name of the German Democratic Republic. The integration of western Germany into the western camp involved the end of the occupation and the negotiation of agreements which would both ally the Federal Republic with other western states and allow the latter some control over German rearmament. The three principal western powers offered to terminate their occupation of the Federal Republic if it would join a European Defence Community in which national forces would be subject to international contorl, and in May 1952 a convention was signed at Bonn ending the occupation and a European Defence Treaty was signed the next day. Elections in 1953 gave Adenauer's Christian Democratic Union and its Bavarian counterpart the Christian Social Union, a two to one victory and in 1954 the Federal Republic ratified the European Defence Treaty. The French parliament, however, refused to ratify a treaty which restored German military might without a countervailing British commitment, whereupon Britain jettisoned part of its traditional aversion to meaningful peacetime associations and promoted the Western European Union – WEU – concluded by the Treaty of Paris in October 1954 and comprising Britain, France and the Benelux countries (which had been associated by treaty since 1948 together with Italy and the Federal Republic). The end of the occupation of West Germany was confirmed and the Federal Republic joined Nato. With the ratification of these agreements in May 1955 the Federal Republic became an almost fully fledged member of the western alliance. It forswore the manufacture of nuclear, bacteriological and chemical weapons and accepted a form of inspection over industrial concerns. In return it got a reiterated pledge on reunification, the recognition of the government in Bonn as the government of the whole of Germany, and the privilege of contributing twelve divisions to Nato's forces.

These developments were strenuously opposed by the Russians who tried a variety of expedients to prevent the adherence of the Federal Republic to Nato. In 1952 they were willing to accept a degree of German rearmament if it were accompanied by neutralization; they proposed, to a sceptical west, a mutual withdrawal from Germany. In June 1953, however, shortly after Stalin's death, risings in the eastern sector of Berlin and in cities in the eastern zone, directed against too much work for too little pay and against political imprisonments, found the east German régime so helpless that it had to be helped and preserved by Russian troops. The USSR became therefore committed to the maintenance of the men whom it had salvaged, and the rising and its suppression strengthened the argument for holding on to what it had.

Upon Stalin's death in March 1953 Churchill thought he saw an opportunity to arrest the collision course of the two alliances. In keeping with his own predilections in international diplomacy he proposed a personal meeting of heads of government, but the temper of the times was inimical, the Americans (and many in Britain) were cool, the West Germans suspicious, and Churchill himself soon afterwards suffered a stroke. The riots in eastern Germany in June encouraged those in the west who preferred to wait for the USSR to get into deeper trouble, while in the USSR Stalin's death was followed by an interlude of three years.

The communist party had held its nineteenth congress in the previous year after an unconstitutional delay of thirteen years, probably occasioned by the simple fact that the party leaders needed time after the war to set many houses in order. Although nobody knew how nearly Stalin's death was approaching, the succession was inevitably uppermost in all minds. By his handling of the congress's business Stalin indicated a definite preference for G. M. Malenkov who, having outlived A. A. Zhdanov, looked like outpointing his most serious rival N. S. Khrushchev. Zhdanov's death in 1948 had been followed in 1949 by a purge of his associates; the older men had been regressing for some years and the two most eminent among them, Molotov and Mikoyan, had lost their ministerial posts (though not their other positions) in 1949; Lavrenti Beria too, the police chief, seemed somewhat less favoured and less powerful in the early fifties despite his control over a police force of 1.5 million men and a militia of 300,000. Then in January 1953 nine doctors, seven of them Jews, were accused of complicity in the death of Zhdanov. This so-called doctors' plot, which was itself declared to be a baseless plot after Stalin's death, combined anti-Semitism with an attack on Zhdanov's enemies, and it was no secret that Zhdanov's principal enemy was the man who had most markedly profited by his death, Malenkov. When therefore Stalin died in March Malenkov's position was less promising than it had seemed a year earlier, but it was still strong enough to ensure his succession to the top posts in both government and party. The evidence suggests that Malenkov's initial victory was secured in alliance with Beria but it did not last long. Malenkov and Beria may have had some similar ideas, notably in helping the consumer industries at the expense of heavy and armaments industries, but Beria was an exceptionally unpopular and dangerous man, personally and *ex officio*, and for Malenkov the support of the country's chief policeman was offset by the hostility of the armed services which disliked both Beria's private army and Malenkov's economic policy: Beria was judicially murdered in December.

Soon after the end of the war Stalin, who did not see himself as a Bonaparte and did not want any Bonapartes around, had set about putting the army and its leaders safely back in a position of subordination to the civil power but in the struggle for power after his death the army was inevitably a major counter and Khrushchev, who had military friends from his days as a commissar on the Stalingrad front, decided to use it. At first he did not have to. The devolution of Stalin's entire position on any one man was more than any of the principal civilian leaders, except Malenkov himself and possibly Beria, was prepared to tolerate. Power was almost immediately divided. Malenkov was forced to choose between being head of the government and head of the party. He chose the former and ceded the latter post to Khrushchev. The antagonism of the two men was thus institutionalized. Two teams of five faced each other. Malenkov and four others formed the top layer of government while Khrushchev and four others constituted the party secretariat. This position lasted until 1955 when Khrushchev defeated Malenkov, partly by reviving rumours of Malenkov's complicity in Zhdanov's death and the subsequent purge and by accusing Malenkov of conspiring with Beria to establish personal instead of collective rule on Stalin's death – charges which alienated party feeling from Malenkov – and partly by manufacturing a war scare which created the alliance between himself and the army. In February 1955 Khrushchev secured the removal of Malenkov and the substitution at the head of the government of Bulganin who was destined to stay there as long as Khrushchev felt it inopportune to claim the post for himself. Bulganin was succeeded at the ministry of defence by Marshal G. K. Zhukhov. Other changes were made at top ministerial level where there seemed to be a shift from political veterans to technical experts, although the chopping and changing of these years more probably reflected uncertainties and inconsistencies in economic planning.

Khrushchev's personal pre-eminence lasted from 1957 to 1964 but was never as secure as it seemed to outsiders. It was won in spite of mistakes which were not forgotten, notably his failure when put in charge of agriculture by Stalin. His policy of exploiting virgin lands in Kazakhstan was radical and sound but disastrously applied in the short run. His political acumen and agility enabled him to survive this setback and, for some years thereafter, the disfavour and machinations of his colleagues who, after forcing Malenkov into the shadows, discovered that Khrushchev was at least as keen on personal authority and impatient with the committee system. But when the elder statesmen in the party tried in 1957 to remove him, he outwitted them and strengthened his own position until he forfeited it through inexperience and waywardness.

In external affairs Khrushchev's term consisted of a short and emollient prelude when he was manoeuvring against domestic rivals and a longer period which displayed his erratic, if agreeably extrovert, temperament. This latter period included major events: risings in Poland and Hungary, the launching of the first sputnik, the building of the Berlin wall, irremediable quarrels with China and his attempt to install nuclear missiles in Cuba.

In the uncertain years immediately after Stalin's death Russian foreign policy was cautious and comparatively amiable. The German and Austrian problems were brought to the conference table, as were also Korea, where an armistice had been signed in July 1953, and Indo-China. Bulganin and Khrushchev made their peace with Tito, surrendered Porkkala in Finland and Port Arthur, put forward new disarmament proposals, visited India, Burma, Afghanistan (the first non-communist recipient of Russian aid) and Britain, and repaired in July 1955 to a meeting at Geneva with the American president and the British and French prime ministers. This meeting was a demonstration in favour of relaxing the Cold War. It produced some euphoric notions – a non-aggression treaty between Nato and the Warsaw Pact, proposed by the USSR; a free-inspection zone, proposed by Eden; and an open-skies survey, proposed by Eisenhower. An ancillary conference of foreign ministers, designed to give point and precision to the Geneva atmosphere, was a failure and this first attempt to thaw the Cold War was brought to nought by the Polish and Hungarian revolts of 1956. But the leaders had met and had set an example of decent manners and the pursuit of tolerance. In the late fifties the Russian armed forces were cut from 5.8 to 3.6 million. A further cut of 1.2 million, announced in 1960, was postponed, presumably as a result of military pressure which became more potent after the failure of the summit conference in Paris in 1960.

In relation to Germany Stalin's successors toyed with schemes for reunification, evacuation and neutralization, but in the knowledge that the Americans were committed to two propositions unacceptable to the USSR: reunification by means of free elections and not by sticking the two Germanies together (which the Russians wanted and which entailed treating the Federal Republic and the much smaller and undemocratically constituted Democratic Republic as equals), and freedom for the reunified state to make alliances (namely, to join Nato). At a conference in Berlin at the beginning of 1954 Eden and Molotov produced plans which demonstrated the impossibility of reaching agreement. Eden proposed reunification in five stages: free elections, a constituent assembly, a constitution, an all-German government and a peace treaty. Molotov seemed ready to agree to elections on certain conditions but wanted also a fifty-year European security treaty (with, it was later explained, the United States as a party) with a ban on joining other alliances; that is to say, he dropped the earlier Russian method of reunification in a bid to secure the dissolution of Nato. When this plan failed the USSR even suggested that it should join Nato. In 1955 Bulganin and Khrushchev agreed to the evacuation and neutralization of Austria, and by the State Treaty of that year Austria recovered its full sovereignty within its January 1938 borders, subject only to two prohibitions: no *Anschluss* with Germany and no alliance with either side in the Cold War. (Since by the Warsaw treaty of the same year the USSR acquired the right to station troops in Hungary and Romania, it lost nothing strategically by renouncing its postwar rights in occupied Austria and the concomitant rights of access through adjacent territories.) But Bulganin and Khrushchev secured no comparable arrangement for Germany, even though they recognized the Federal Republic and exchanged ambassadors with it. The attempt to stop the rearmament of the Federal Republic as a part of the anti-Russian alliance had failed. In the same year the Russians created a counterpart to Nato by the Warsaw treaty and in 1956 the German Democratic Republic became a member of it.

In the same year the congress of the Communist Party of the Soviet Union, assembled for its twentieth session, was astonished to hear, first from Mikoyan and then from Khrushchev, wide-ranging and vehement denunciations of Stalin and Stalinism reaching back to what Lenin's wife had said more than thirty years earlier and to the murder of Kirov in 1934. This repudiation of the past, which did not long remain secret and included a specific undertaking to revise the USSR's relations with its satellite neighbours, encouraged anti-Russian feeling and contributed to risings in Poland and Hungary. In Poznan there were strikes for better wages in June and admissions of social unrest. At the same time a conflict arose within the Polish Communist Party between the faction of Boleslaw Bierut, who had died earlier in the year, and the more nationalist or Titoist faction led by Wladyslaw Gomulka, who had recently been released from a prison to which he had been consigned after being disgraced in 1949. In July Khrushchev, Bulganin and other Russian leaders went suddenly to Warsaw and vehemently invaded discussions in the central committee of the Polish party. They were, however, unable to prevent the victory of the Gomulka faction. Gomulka was appointed first secretary and the Russians, discovering that they must choose between allowing Gomulka to take over the government and using force to prevent it, chose the former course and accepted changes which included the dismissal of the defence minister, the Russian Marshal Rokossovsky.

In Hungary the nature of the disturbances and their outcome were different. In July the established rulers, Matyas Rakosi and Erno Gerö, went to Moscow to urge reforms in order to forestall trouble. In October demonstrators demanded better wages and liberty. Hungarian police and Russian troops failed to prevent these demonstrations from turning into an anti-communist revolution. Imre Nagy, who had been prime minister from Stalin's death to 1955, was reinstated. Mikoyan and Suslov arrived from Moscow to direct operations and decided to back Janos Kadar, the reasonably well-regarded first secretary of the Communist Party who represented a compromise between the Rakosi/Gerö team and Nagy, but the revolution gained strength and at the same time the Russians found themselves confronted with the risks and opportunities of a war in the Middle East provoked by the Anglo–French attack on Nasser. After withdrawing their troops from Budapest for tactical reasons they resorted to full-scale military measures to suppress the revolution. Faced with this turn of events Kadar sided with the Russians while Nagy named a new coalition government, promised free elections, proposed to take Hungary out of the Warsaw Pact and appealed to the outside world for help. With the western powers enmeshed at Suez and the USSR vetoing UN action, the revolution was extinguished in the first week of November. The reality of Russian power was underlined by the fact that the American administration not only took no action but never looked as though it might.

These events were a setback both for Khrushchev and for the policy of east–west *rapprochement*. Both, however, recovered. In June 1957 Khrushchev was attacked by Malenkov in the presidium of the Communist Party and defeated on a vote, but he resiliently summoned a meeting of the central committee which expelled Malenkov from the presidium and, for good measure, disgraced the veteran Voroshilov and Kaganovich and virtually exiled even Molotov, the oldest of the old bolsheviks and the man who had been second only to Stalin among the civilians who had directed the war against the Germans. In October Zhukov too was removed and replaced by Marshal Malinovsky. This year saw the triumph of Khrushchev over his adversaries and over the doctrine of collective leadership. In March 1958 he became prime minister as well as first secretary and he remained predominant until his unexpected fall in October 1964. He reaped the benefit, in external affairs, of the dramatic appearance – in August and October 1957 – of the first intercontinental ballistic missile and the first earth satellite (sputnik). From a platform thus fortified, and observing the alarm in the United States at the thought that the American technological lead had been eliminated, Khrushchev adopted peaceful coexistence as a general description of his intentions. Peaceful coexistence was a benevolent and reassuring (but not new) political slogan of vague import and useful variability. By it Khrushchev reverted to the belief that communism, while remaining unshakeably hostile to capitalism, would prevail over it without war. (The reassertion of this doctrine was intended, among other things, to enlist the sympathies of the emerging Third World.)

Khrushchev's problems in central Europe in 1956 and at home in 1957 were peripheral to the Cold War but they were followed by critical developments in Germany and in Sino–Soviet relations which were directly pertinent to it. Throughout 1958 exchanges about and between the two Germanies had been clouding the atmosphere and the Poles were urging the USSR to find a way of preventing the Federal Republic from becoming a nuclear power and from making mischief in central Europe in association with Nato. Khrushchev was anxious to secure wider international recognition for the German Democratic Republic in order to stabilize the map of Europe and his own frontiers and so facilitate the reduction of the USSR's costly military commitments abroad and pursue his policy of *rapprochement*. He chose to begin with threats and when these did not work reverted to blandishments. He threatened in November 1958 to transfer the USSR's authority in Berlin to the German Democratic Republic unless a solution of the German problems were found within six months, but when the western occupiers contented themselves with controverting the USSR's right to act as it proposed, Khrushchev toned down his ultimatum and then let it die at the end of May. The failure of this gambit, coupled with Khrushchev's growing conviction that the United States did not intend to attack the USSR, and with the presentation to the twenty-first congress of the Communist Party in January 1959 of a seven-year economic plan which depended on switching funds from guns to butter, led to the second serious attempt to thaw the Cold War. After a visit to Moscow by Vice-President Richard Nixon, Khrushchev visited the United States, conferred privately with Eisenhower at Camp David, presented a plan for general and complete disarmament in four years to the General Assembly of the UN, and announced the second major cut in Russian military manpower. The centrepiece of the détente of 1959–60 was to have been a second summit conference in May 1960 but it was ruined by the shooting down of an American reconnaissance aircraft over Russian territory on 1 May. Reconnaissance flights by U-2 aircraft flying at great heights between bases in Norway and Pakistan provided the United States with militarily valuable information at no political risk so long as the aircraft were not intercepted and their missions not made public by either side. The American president either did not know about the flights or had not thought of cancelling them in the pre-conference weeks, and the Russian government either had not thought of telling its defences to stop trying to shoot them down in this delicate period or – a plausible alternative view – had ordered them to do so. False statements in Washington about the aircraft's mission only compounded the American discomfiture because they were quickly exposed by the Russians who had captured the pilot alive and with his spy kit.

After the consequent failure of the Paris conference Khrushchev repeated, in Warsaw and Moscow, his belief in the policy of *rapprochement*, but for the time being practical progress had been halted by the U-2 as surely as it had been halted in 1956 by the Hungarian revolution and it was arguable that Khrushchev had deliberately engineered this stop on his own policies, possibly in response to pressures from military and pro-Chinese lobbies. His *rapprochement* with the United States affronted the Chinese, who did not share his view about American aggressive intentions, resented and feared Russo–American confabulations, and refused to be mollified when he went to Beijing on his return from the United States. These views found some echo in the Kremlin. Further, Khrushchev's defence policy of relying on nuclear missiles and cutting non-nuclear forces was too bold for some of his colleagues and advisers. Although a Rocket Force Command was established under Marshal Nedelin (later succeeded by Marshal Moskalenko), the second cut was cancelled and at the twenty-first congress in October 1961 Malinovsky stated that he did not see eye to eye with Khrushchev. (This tussle was resumed in 1963–64 when cuts were again proposed and again opposed: Khrushchev was forced to promise that the cuts would be reasonable but this persistence was probably one of the causes of his downfall.) Finally, Khrushchev had discovered that his attempt to secure recognition of the German Democratic Republic by raising the Berlin question could be turned against him by the Americans, who proceeded to couple a settlement in Berlin with a general Russian withdrawal in Europe for which neither Khrushchev himself nor the ruling group in Moscow as a whole was yet ready.

After the dismal experiences of the fifties the next decade opened with mixed signals. The Russo–Chinese quarrel had become public property (see Chapter 3) and was held to be an incentive to Russo–American accords. In Washington the Eisenhower era closed and was succeeded by the short presidency of John F. Kennedy, whose youth and intellect seemed to promise that the sixties would be different from the fifties and less grim. A cease-fire was arranged in Laos, but in an encounter with Khrushchev in Vienna Kennedy made no great mark and may even have left Khrushchev with the impression that the omens were propitious for an anti-American stroke. At any rate Khrushchev gave permission for a new essay in Berlin.

The government of the German Democratic Republic was threatened with collapse. Its citizens were escaping from it at the rate of 1,000 a day, which was economically and psychologically ruinous. Its boss, Walter Ulbricht, had to act urgently in order to maintain his régime, while Khrushchev was probably persuaded that if he did not support Ulbricht the crisis in the German Democratic Republic would lead to a war in Germany. He accordingly gave his consent to the erection of a wall between the eastern sector and western sector in Berlin so that the eastern sector should become a part of the German Democratic Republic and the western sector might be made too uncomfortable for continued western occupation. In the night of 12–13 August the wall was built and the flow of refugees virtually stopped. Kennedy had told Khrushchev a few weeks earlier in Vienna that the United States remained committed to the use of all necessary forces to defend the status and freedom of Berlin. The building of the wall was a provocative act which the United States accepted and which may have influenced Khrushchev's estimate of how far it was safe to provoke the United States: he himself was to venture much further than the east Germans in the next year in Cuba.

Kennedy inherited from his predecessor a Cuban problem which was initially a chapter in the relations between the United States and Latin America but not a chapter in the Cold War. Its origins are described in Part Six of this book. In April 1961 Kennedy, pursuing a venture designed by the Eisenhower régime, aided an attempt by refugees to invade Cuba and overthrow Fidel Castro. It was immediately and totally unsuccessful. At some point thereafter Khrushchev, who was already giving Castro financial and diplomatic aid, decided on an audacious throw. Instead of merely helping Castro to remain in power, he decided to use Cuba to help the USSR, to convert it into a Russian base directly threatening the United States with Russian missiles. Surface-to-air missiles were despatched in the summer of 1962, followed by MiG 21 fighters, Il. 28 jet nuclear bombers and ground-to-ground (that is, offensive) missiles, of which forty-two out of a projected sixty-four arrived in late September or early October. The installation of these weapons put the United States for the first time under fire from close range and would have nearly doubled the number of bases or cities threatened by the USSR. Within three weeks of the beginning of the operation the Americans became aware of it, although it was not at first clear to them that the Russians were doing more than strengthening the defence of Cuba. The Russians assured Washington that this was indeed the case and that they had no offensive intentions, and in spite of disturbing tales from refugees close reconnaissance produced no contraverting evidence until the middle of October. On 14 October photographs showed a launching pad and one missile. Kennedy decided at once on his objective: the complete removal of Russian nuclear weapons from Cuba. The vital problem was how to achieve this objective without starting a nuclear war. It was assumed in Washington that action must be taken within about ten days. The obvious retort was an air strike but the objections were serious. Apart

1.3   Cuba and its relationship to the United States and Jamaica from the strong disinclination to open hostilities by using nuclear weapons in whatever circumstances, the president and his advisers were heavily conscious of the dangers of escalation and also of a Russian counterstroke against Berlin. Many of the Russian weapons were still on their way to Cuba by sea, and the secretary of defence, Robert McNamara, supported by the attorney-general, Robert Kennedy, proposed a naval blockade to prevent them reaching their destination and to force the Russians to remove what had already arrived. After long debate this plan, which had immediately appealed to the president, was adopted. It was explained by him to the public in a televised address and to his allies by special emissaries, and American ships of war moved into the path of the vessels bearing the Russian missiles westward. The first Russian response was to repeat that the weapons were defensive and to denounce the blockade. A clash seemed imminent. Then the president, on the suggestion of his close friend the British ambassador, Lord Harlech, moved his line of interceptors southward in order to give Khrushchev a little extra time to think and act. Khrushchev decided not to accept the challenge. The leading ships were reported slackening speed. One innocuous tanker was allowed to pass through the line unsearched and proceed upon its way. The other ships turned back. In the Security Council Adlai Stevenson confronted the Russian and other delegates with photographic proof of the threat against which the United States had acted. On the high seas and in the council chambers of the world the triumph of the United States was complete. The Secretary-General of the UN, U Thant, played a significant part in allaying the crisis but was content to remain inconspicuous.

In his choice of method and in the ensuing diplomatic exchanges Kennedy was careful to leave Khrushchev the openings for the retreat which the Americans aimed to enforce. The dramatic element was intense to the end. Khrushchev signified his surrender in a letter to Kennedy in which he averred once more that the deliveries of arms were a defensive measure; he said that they had been completed and that, if the United States would promise not to invade Cuba and would raise the blockade, the USSR would see no need for a Russian presence in Cuba. Here was the recognition of the Monroe Doctrine which the Americans wanted. But almost at once a second message arrived from Moscow. In it Khrushchev demanded not only an American undertaking not to attack Cuba but also the removal of American missiles from Turkey in return for the removal of Russian missiles from Cuba. Kennedy wanted no bargaining, only a clear-cut decision on the Cuban issue in isolation. After a brief period of consternation the attorney-general suggested that the second letter was in reality an earlier one which had got delayed and should be ignored. The president accordingly replied to the first letter, accepting its general tenor and agreeing to open negotiations on the basis that all construction work in Cuba be stopped. This message, sent on 27 October, was accepted on the next day by Khrushchev who agreed to ship the Russian missiles back to the USSR.

The clash off Cuba, like the conflict over Berlin sixteen years earlier, brought the protagonists in the Cold War face to face and once again no shot was fired. Khrushchev's attempt to leap into equality failed because it was insane and he himself was ousted, peaceably, by his own colleagues. The United States was becoming drawn deeply into Vietnam following the Bay of Tonking incident in August. From the mid-sixties the Cold War relapsed into a matter of static postures, marginally shaken by peripheral adventures (in Ethiopia, in Afghanistan) and maintained by the arms race.

THE ARMS RACE

In 1946 the United States propounded the Baruch Plan for the complete international ownership and control of the sources of nuclear energy and the transfer of American stocks to an international body. The UN Atomic Energy Committee reported that such a plan was technically practicable. It was, however, politically unattainable. The USSR presented counter-proposals for a ban on the manufacture and use of nuclear weapons and the immediate destruction of existing ones (which were exclusively American). The Russian demand for immediate destruction was unacceptable to the Americans who insisted that the creation of international machinery must come first. The American and Russian plans were also irreconcilable in other respects. The USSR accepted the principle of international control but rejected international ownership. The USSR conceded that an international authority created to supervise international control should proceed in some matters by majority vote and without a veto, but it insisted that any proposed enforcement action must be subject to a veto. In the Russian view an international convention should be reinforced by domestic legislation in each of the states signing the treaty but not by any transfer of sovereign powers to an international organ empowered to carry out inspections and to observe whether the convention was being honoured. Inspection was not entirely ruled out by the USSR but was to be limited to the inspection of proclaimed nuclear establishments, excluding any search for clandestine activities. These attitudes reflected the strategic realities of the moment. So did contemporary controversy over the reduction of non-nuclear weapons, the United States wishing to link disarmament of this kind with an agreement on nuclear weapons, while the USSR urged a proportionate reduction of forces (by one-third) which would alter the level of armaments without disturbing the relative strengths of states in these types of armament.

In 1949, the year of the conclusion of the North Atlantic Treaty, the USSR exploded its first nuclear weapon and in the next year it abandoned the UN Disarmament Commission (created in 1948 by fusing the Atomic Energy and Conventional Armaments Committees). In 1952–53 the United States and the USSR exploded their first thermonuclear or hydrogen bombs within nine months of each other. Both rapidly developed their means of delivery so that mutual deterrence ruled by the end of the fifties, and in 1961 both powers put a man into space – the Russian Yuri Gagarin leading the American John Glenn by six months. American stocks were at all times much greater than Russian stocks and American superiority was enhanced in the early sixties as Polaris and Minuteman missiles came into service. Unfounded American fears of a missile gap in the USSR's favour had the effect of spurring the United States into extending what was a gap in its own favour.

The Baruch Plan was soon, if tacitly, dropped. The USSR continued to maintain its opposition to anything which could be construed as international intervention in its affairs and to cling to its advantage in non-nuclear weaponry. The United States, Britain and France proposed in 1952 quantitative limits for the armed manpower of all states, and two years later Britain and France produced a new graduated plan which was designed to reconcile the differing American and Russian priorities in a step-by-step disarmament process. The USSR countered with a programme which began with a reduction in conventional forces and then in nuclear stocks and led to the elimination of bases on foreign soil, a cut-off in nuclear weapons production and a conference on a test ban treaty. The USSR also accepted quantitative manpower ceilings, thereby embarrassing the United States whose worldwide commit-ments demanded larger forces than those envisaged. The United States proposed in return higher ceilings (which would nevertheless have required some reduction in American forces) and an 'open skies' inspection licence whereby each side would keep the other under permanent observation from aircraft or satellites in orbit round the globe, but continued to press for an international control organ – even if subject to a veto – and rejected the idea of a ban on the use of nuclear weapons and destruction of existing stocks. In the American view the time for prohibiting the use of nuclear weapons had gone by. The attempt, initiated by the Baruch Plan, to insulate the science of war from the latest advances in physics had to be abandoned.

The pretence that these disarmament plans were serving any useful or practical purpose wore thin and palliatives were sought in schemes for disengagement, demilitarization and other forms of arms control. Disengagement – that is, putting a distance between opposing war machines by a mutual retreat from advanced positions – was attractive for a variety of reasons: it might minimize the risk of unpremeditated clashes, it might prove to be a successful experiment in local disarmament which could be repeated on a larger scale, and it might lessen political tensions in the centre of Europe and so lead towards a solution of the German problem. In 1955 Eden proposed limitations on forces in Germany and (unnamed) neighbouring states together with a system of inspection and verification controlled by a reunited German state and its four previous occupiers. Eden also proposed a European experiment in demilitarization, beginning with a zone along Germany's eastern borders, and added a few days later as an experiment in arms control a plan for mixed inspection teams on both sides of the division between eastern and western Europe. These ideas were not well received by the Americans or the West Germans whom Eden apparently failed to consult in advance and who objected to the implied recognition of the German Democratic Republic. Russian proposals presented by Gromyko in 1956 and 1957 for a zone of limitation and inspection were rejected on the same grounds. Similar plans were advanced by the leader of the British parliamentary opposition, Hugh Gaitskell. He proposed a gradual thinning out of foreign forces in the two Germanies, Poland, Czechoslovakia and Hungary and a ban on nuclear weapons throughout the same zone; the two Germanies would be reunited, the Federal Republic would withdraw from Nato and the three eastern states from the Warsaw military alliance. Finally, in 1957 the Polish foreign minister Adam Rapacki, with Russian backing, proposed at the General Assembly (and later elaborated in written form) a plan to prohibit the manufacture and presence of nuclear weapons in both Germanies. He promised that Poland would follow suit, and the Czechoslovak government promised to do so too. The Rapacki plan dealt only with nuclear weapons in a specified area and did not overtly attack the surrounding political issues – the reunification of Germany, the freedom of Germany to join alliances, the presence of considerable American and Russian forces in central European states, the balance of American and Russian power in Europe which would be unsettled by the removal of American nuclear forces without a corresponding withdrawal of Russian non-nuclear forces. It was rejected by the United States in May 1958. Disengagement was thereupon dropped from the political agenda. It had been defeated by the entirely opposite trend of arming the two Germanies as separate contributions to the strength of the forward positions of the two rival blocs, by western fears of the USSR's large non-nuclear forces, by the Nato policy of putting nuclear weapons into forward positions, and by inexperience and distrust of methods of inspection and verification. The fortification of the alliances had priority over the dismantling of them.

There was, however, some mutual inclination to restrict nuclear tests. The development of varieties of nuclear weapons, large and small, substantiated the need for tests, and these tests produced worldwide alarm about the effects of radioactive fall-out, especially after American tests in the Pacific in 1954 which were believed to have killed some Japanese fishermen, poisoned vast numbers of fish and infected an area of 18,000 sq. km. In 1957 there was a cessation of nuclear tests by tacit agreement – partly a consequence of the conclusion of series of American and Russian tests at this time – and some preliminary examination of the possibility of a more formal and permanent ban. But there was a serious gap between what was acceptable to the United States and what to the USSR: on the constitution of a control organ and the voting within it, on the manning of control posts by observers of foreign nationality, and on the number of on-site inspections to be carried out in any year in a specified area in order to ensure compliance with the ban. On all these matters the gaps between the protagonists were narrowed during discussions in 1958–60 but insufficiently to produce agreement before the destruction of the American U-2 reconnaissance aircraft over the USSR in May 1960 and the abandonment of the summit conference of that month temporarily ruffled the Russo–American *rapprochement*.

Less fruitfully, although with every appearance of seriousness, both the United States and the USSR sponsored unreal plans for general and complete disarmament and spent much time talking about them. The Russian proposals focused on such favourite objectives as the withdrawal of foreign troops and bases rather than on the less spectacular topics of control and verification with which American and British negotiators were more particularly concerned. The Russian plan, presented by Khrushchev to the General Assembly of the UN in September 1959, was followed in March and June 1960 by two American statements. A ten-nation disarmament conference at Geneva in 1960 was short-lived but also the occasion for a joint Russo-American initiative in the shape of a series of recommendations elaborated by John J. McCloy and V. Zorin. No conference was held in 1961. The Americans and Russians agreed a set of principles but failed to agree on a statement about controls submitted by the Americans; both sides produced draft treaties on general and complete disarmament (the Russian was a revision of an earlier draft) in time for the autumn session of the General Assembly.

The high-water mark of these negotiations was the McCloy–Zorin recommendations. These consisted of a set of principles to govern continuing disarmament negotiations, beginning with the acceptance of general and complete disarmament as an ultimate goal. This document was in effect an agreed statement of what had to be agreed. It clarified the issues but did not resolve them. It predicated the need to establish reliable procedures for the peaceful settlement of disputes and the maintenance of peace; the retention by each state of adequate non-nuclear forces for the preservation of law and order; the disbanding of superfluous forces and the elimination of all nuclear, chemical and bacteriological weapons, all means of delivering weapons of mass destruction, all military training institutions and all military budgets; an agreed sequence of stages in the disarmament process, subject to verification at the conclusion of each stage; balanced measures to ensure that neither side secured a temporary advantage as disarmament proceeded; and strict and effective international control of the process and thereafter through an International Disarmament Organization within the framework of the UN. This visionary package required agreement on the order in which different operations would be carried out, agreement on the equivalence of different types of armament, and agreement on the nature and modes of operation of an inspectorate. Agreement on these and other points required a degree of trust which no political leader felt or could perhaps have evinced without incurring plausible charges of gambling with national security. The Russians, for example, accepted at one stage the principle of inspection, but it transpired that what was to be inspected was weapons destroyed and not weapons surviving; they were reluctant to disclose what was left through fear of having it attacked and destroyed. Ingenious schemes for circumventing this difficulty, such as Professor Louis Sohn's proposal to divide national territory into zones and give inspectors the right to search only a limited number of zones at defined intervals, did not suffice to overcome nationalist conservatism.

The crucial feature of the revived disarmament discussion was the problem of inspection and verification (an element which had not obtruded in earlier negotiations such as those which preceded the Washington Treaty of 1922, though it had engaged the attention of the disarmament conference of 1932, which proposed a Permanent Disarmament Commission with powers of inspection but no powers of enforcement). The evolution of nuclear weapons had enormously increased the dangerous consequences of allowing a party to a disarmament agreement to cheat and to conceal; he might by doing so gain the mastery of the world. But concealment was also regarded as one of the conditions of survival. To any power inspectors were potential spies who were licensed to discover and might then reveal how the inspected territory could be denuded of its defences at a blow. The impulses of politicians who took up disarmament for one reason or another were therefore continually countered by more cautious and short-term questionings which prevented the conclusion of any except partial agreements.

Partial agreements were, however, made. The cessation of nuclear tests in the atmosphere was an early example, which was matched in the same year by an agreement to neutralize the Antarctic continent.

Tests were resumed by the Russians unilaterally in September 1961, chiefly because they had proceeded to a point at which they had something new which needed testing, but 1963 produced a new and more extensive test ban agreement (as well as the installation of a direct and permanently open, or 'hot', line of communication between the White House and the Kremlin). When the Russians announced the resumption of tests, the Americans and British offered to conclude a treaty banning atmospheric tests without any provision for inspection, but the Russians were not to be deterred from their new series of tests and shortly afterwards the Americans resumed testing too. At the end of the year the Russians proposed a treaty banning all tests, subterranean as well as atmospheric, without inspection; this proposal was immediately rejected, and the three powers reported to the UN their failure to agree and the abandonment of their attempts to do so.

Alarmed by this breakdown the UN resolved to convene yet another disarmament conference, this time with eighteen members, including eight neutrals, an innovation in as much as neutrals had not previously participated in test ban discussions but only in discussions on general and complete disarmament. The French, who were in the earlier stages of developing a nuclear armoury of their own and had therefore no wish to ban tests, took no part in the proceedings, but the neutrals (Brazil, Burma, Egypt, Ethiopia, India, Mexico, Nigeria, Sweden) proved themselves valuably persistent in devising compromises and keeping the discussions going. The debate on inspection was resumed between the nuclear powers and was narrowed down to a question of numbers, the western powers ultimately refusing to go below seven a year and the Russians refusing to concede more than two or three. In the early part of 1963 the failure of the talks was generally expected but was avoided and then converted into success largely by the unobtrusive pertinacity of the British prime minister Harold Macmillan. Early in July Khrushchev hinted in a public speech that a partial ban might be agreed, and later in that month Averell Harriman and Lord Hailsham went to Moscow, where the three powers agreed on the terms of a treaty banning nuclear tests in the atmosphere, in outer space and under water for an unlimited period but subject to the right of any party to withdraw from its undertakings if its supreme interests were jeopardized by extraordinary events connected with the subject matter of the treaty. Many other states adhered to the treaty. They did not include China or France.

The conclusion of this treaty raised the question of what to try next. It gave a fillip to the partial approach and therefore to the search for parts ripe for tackling. Lyndon B. Johnson, who had become president in the United States upon the assassination of Kennedy in November 1963, listed some topics early in the next year. They included an anti-proliferation programme to include a total ban on nuclear tests, a ban on the transfer of nuclear materials to non-nuclear states and inspection of peaceful nuclear activities; a chain of observer posts to guard against surprise attack; a verified freeze on missiles; a verified cessation of the production of fissile material; and a ban on the use of force to alter boundaries or otherwise transfer territory from one state's control to another. Proposals from other quarters included a bomber bonfire (applying to B-47s and Tu-16s) and percentage cuts in military budgets. In Poland Gomulka recast and revived the Rapacki plan by proposing, in December 1963, a nuclear freeze in Europe, which, however, the Americans disliked partly because they attached little value to controls over the location of weapons unaccompanied by controls over their production and partly out of deference to the suspicions of their German allies.

These plans bore no immediate fruit for three reasons. First, the achievement of the test ban treaty was as much as the leaders on either side could for the time being digest and make palatable in their own countries. More might become possible, but not too soon. Secondly, discussions within Nato about joint control over nuclear dispositions and nuclear weapons roused eastern fears of a nuclear Germany. The United States was caught between the desire for a continuing dialogue and *rapprochement* with the USSR and the desire to accord to its most effective continental ally the status and the authority in allied councils and operations which its material contributions to the alliance warranted. To the Russians the proposed Nato multilateral force (MLF – see Chapter 6) was a form of proliferation of nuclear weapons, although the Americans had devised it as an anti-proliferation policy to satisfy the Federal Republic and also France with something less than independent nuclear forces. And thirdly, the increasing American involvement in Vietnam put an additional strain on Russo–American relations. The American attempt to buttress an independent and non-communist South Vietnamese state entailed war against the Vietcong which ranked in communist terminology as a national liberation movement, and war against the communist state of North Vietnam, and something like war against the vastly more important communist state of China. For the Russians to fail to support President Ho Chi Minh of North Vietnam would be a betrayal of communist solidarity, dangerous at any time to Russian standing in the communist world and doubly dangerous at a time when Russian pre-eminence and doctrinal purity were being assailed by the Chinese. Further, for the Russians to fail to support the Vietcong was again doubly dangerous, for if the Vietcong lost communists would blame the Russians, whereas if the Vietcong won without Russian help Chinese influence might rout Russian influence in Asia and the Chinese would be proved right in their contention, against the Russians, that wars of national liberation could be fought without escalation into nuclear war. When by 1965 the Americans had become unconcealed principals in the war and not merely adjutants of the South Vietnamese, the scale and the nature of the fighting were changed and the Americans had to face worldwide protests against the ensuing horrors. The Russians joined in the outcry. Although, therefore, the evolution of nuclear strategies and the resurgence of China and the passage of time had combined to put an end to the bipolar Cold War, the principal adversaries were prevented by particular crisis and by habit from acknowledging the fact and acting on it more than very tentatively; only de Gaulle did both.

Nevertheless, whether by understanding or as a result of blinder forces, a significant degree of stability and tolerance had evolved on the biggest question of the time: whether the Cold War would engender a nuclear war. In the nuclear age peace could be preserved so long as each side relied on the threat of retaliation to keep the other side from attacking first. But one side might conclude that the only way to avert an attack was to attack first. It would then, using the modern version of the pre-nuclear blitzkrieg, adopt a counter-force strategy and build up, advertise and possibly use its power to destroy the enemy's warmaking capacity at a single blow. In order to neutralize this strategy it was necessary to protect aircraft and missiles sites so effectively as to make it incredible that they could all be destroyed by a first-strike surprise attack. Their protection by anti-aircraft and fighter defences had been rendered obsolete by the enormous increase in the destructive power of each single bomb and by the vastly increased speed of missiles. In its place two new and extremely expensive forms of defence were developed: missiles were placed in dispersed, hardened sites and, in the case of Polaris, under the sea in submarines; and an early warning system gave the defence enough time to get aircraft into the air and to save them from being destroyed on the ground. Before the appearance of the intercontinental missile an early warning of two to three hours was achieved by the Americans, and when this was rendered inadequate it was improved to half an hour, at which point a part of the bomber force was kept always in the air and a part at fifteen minutes' readiness on the ground. These measures to ensure the survival of an effective part of the retaliatory force, bombers and missiles, caused both antagonists to concentrate on second-strike strategies as a means of security. It was essential to the success of this attitude that each side should be seen by the other to have adopted it, and it was a consoling feature of the later years of the Cold War that each side succeeded (with the help of the fact that a first-strike force differed in size and composition from a retaliatory force) in transmitting to the other tacit messages to this effect. The probability of a surprise attack diminished.

Nuclear forces could, however, also be used in reply to a non-nuclear attack. The use of nuclear weapons was not ruled out by the reticence and deterrence of the two principal nuclear powers in relation to each other. Both could and did threaten to use them offensively in other contexts. In January 1954 Eisenhower and Dulles spoke on separate occasions of massive and instant retaliation. The last phase of the French war in Vietnam had begun and the Americans were faced with a choice between helping the French by a nuclear strike or letting them be finally beaten. The Americans tried to make political use of their nuclear armoury while knowing that they would not use it militarily; in a display of brinkmanship Dulles used tough language in order to scare the Russians and the Chinese and prevent them moving into the battle area – and perhaps in order to scare the British too and so get them to restrain him from a course from which he wanted to be diverted in any case. In 1956 Khrushchev, faced simultaneously with a war in the Middle East and a revolution in Hungary, made vague threats of using nuclear weapons in unspecified places in order to terrify the British and French governments and peoples and gain credit in the Arab world, and after the U–2 episode in 1960 he threatened smaller nations with nuclear attack if they facilitated American reconnaissance activities. But in the event both sides reserved their nuclear armaments for each other and became increasingly concerned not merely to keep nuclear weapons out of use but also to keep them out of other nations' hands. Yet one of the more sinister consequences of the Cold War was the postponement, throughout the fifties and into the sixties, of the realization of this common interest until after two other powers, France and China, had become nuclear powers and a number of others had acquired the capability and, in the absence of an international control system, were also developing the will to follow suit. During the Cold War the two protagonists had developed an increasing sobriety in relation to one another, and even a sort of fearful intimacy. There was, however, no reason to suppose that other possessors of nuclear weapons would acquire sobriety with might, or – if, for example, they were Israel, Egypt or Iraq – would develop this intimate understanding of the permitted limits of nuclear politics; nor was there reason to suppose that the two giant powers would find it as easy to control the conflicts of others as to control their own.

These two problems – how to prevent a nuclear war between nuclear powers and how to prevent more states graduating to the nuclear élite – were aspects of the wider problem of arms control which superseded more traditional approaches to disarmament during the sixties. Arms control, the regulation as opposed to the elimination of the use of weapons of war, was not new. It had been applied particularly to naval weapons by, for example, the Rush–Bagot treaty of 1817 which barred navies from the Great Lakes, and by the Washington treaties of 1922 and 1930 which sought to limit the naval power of one state in proportion to that of another. Interest in similar schemes was revived in the 1960s by scepticism about general disarmament, and academic discussion of arms control was taken up by politicians in Washington and Moscow who were feeling the need to communicate with one another (as in the Cuba missiles crisis) or to co-operate with one another (as in the Middle East crises of the decade). The idea that major powers had more in common than the need to avoid mutual annihilation was further fortified by their common interest in their own superiority. Neither of them wanted to see nuclear weapons in any other states' armouries and in 1968 they, together with Britain, concluded a Nuclear Non-Proliferation Treaty to which they invited all other states to adhere. The object of this treaty was to freeze the existing nuclear hierarchy, keeping France and China in the grade of second-rate nuclear powers and every other state permanently excluded from acquiring nuclear weapons. France and China predictably refused to sign. From the non-nuclear but potentially nuclear states there were sounds of discontent. Before subscribing to such an act of abnegation they objected that they should not be asked to forgo modern weapons without a better prospect of escaping embroilment in a nuclear war and they urged the nuclear powers to balance their enthusiasm for non-proliferation by a more serious attempt to control their own arms race.

The treaty came into force in 1970 and review conferences were held quinquennially, ineffective and acrimonious. In 1989 119 states had signed the treaty, but more significant were the number and identity of those which had not. They included France and China, which were certainly nuclear powers; South Africa and Israel, which were generally thought to be; and India and Pakistan, Argentina and Brazil, all of them some way along the road. At this date there were in the world several hundred nuclear reactors, including some which produced plutonium as a by-product of their relatively inoffensive activities. A small proportion of this material sufficed to make a bomb a year and newer techniques – in, for example, the enrichment of uranium to weapons-grade standards and the production of plutonium in fast-breeder reactors – were facilitating the manufacture of nuclear weapons. In these circumstances advanced powers which were helping developing states to build reactors were inevitably engaging in proliferation and so were in breach of the treaty, as were all nuclear powers which had failed to make serious efforts to reduce their nuclear armouries. Hopes for a more comprehensive ban were vain so long as the principal nuclear powers continued to develop new weapons which they needed to test. Progress was limited to an agreement between the superpowers, concluded in 1974 but not ratified until 1990, limiting the scale of underground tests, and a further agreement of 1976, also ratified in 1990.

Alarm at the spread of nuclear weapons was accompanied by alarm at the development of weapons technology. The MIRV (multiple independent re-entry vehicle), whose separately controlled multiple warheads greatly increased the threat from each missile; and ABM (anti-ballistic missile) systems, which could counter a first strike and so destroy the deterrent stability which rested upon the presumptive efficacy of first strike, were enormously increasing the cost of the arms race. At the same time the deadliness of new missiles which were alleged to be capable of landing within a few dozen yards of a target, combined with new defences which could destroy incoming missiles only at the cost of removing the deterrent factor which was designed to prevent their discharge in the first place, inclined the superpowers to talk about the control of the use and development, as well as the proliferation, of nuclear weapons. Strategic arms limitation talks (SALT) were begun in 1969.

Strategic arms may be defined in this context as weapons which can reach targets in an adversary's territory from bases or launching sites in one's own territory or on the high seas. They include missiles or bombs carried by long-range aircraft as well as missiles launched from static or mobile land sites or submarines. The category of strategic arms is therefore a complex one and it is further complicated by the fact that a single missile with many warheads, each of which can be independently directed to a different target, is far from being the equivalent of a missile with a single warhead that can hit one target only. There are furthermore two distinct and incompatible ways of calculating the effectiveness of a nation's strategic armoury. On the one hand it may be assessed by the number of enemy targets theoretically vulnerable, an assessment which involves counting the number of independently targeted warheads deployed; on the other hand it may be assessed by the weight of explosive which can be delivered by all available launchers and aircraft on a single occasion. Finally, the category of strategic arms is not a closed one since there is argument about whether to include nuclear weapons of shorter range which are nevertheless brought within range of the enemy by being based on intermediate territory or capable of being sent there at short notice.

Given these complexities it is remarkable that, by an exercise of political will over technical intractabilities, two agreements were signed in May 1972 (and two minor agreements in the previous year). In negotiations in 1970 at Vienna and Helsinki, which occupied five months of the year, the Americans took the initiative by proposing a total ban on mobile land sites, a special limitation on particularly potent weapons and an overall numerical limit on the sum of the land and sea sites and bombers which either country might possess. Next year the two countries reached agreement on a Seabed Treaty banning the placing of nuclear weapons on the ocean floor (the treaty to be open for signature universally) and updated their agreement of 1963 for a hot line between Washington and Moscow by modifying it to take account of the new means of communication by satellites. The United States then proposed a standstill on the deployment of intercontinental land-based missiles and all submarine-based missiles. Concurrently the negotiators tackled the defensive as distinct from the offensive aspects of strategic nuclear war by trying to set limits to the deployment of anti-ballistic missile (ABM) systems, but the familiar problem of distinguishing a defensive from an offensive weapon bedevilled progress for a time as it was impossible to say that every missile or launcher in an ABM system could never be used except for defensive purposes.

Notwithstanding these conundrums an ABM treaty and an interim agreement on offensive missiles were concluded in 1972, thus marking some progress in the regulation of both defensive and offensive weapons systems. The USSR had at this point an incomplete ABM system round Moscow and the United States was planning two systems for the protection of its intercontinental launching sites. The ABM treaty, of indefinite duration although subject to quinquennial review, permitted each party to deploy two systems, the one for the defence of its capital and the other for the defence of some part of its intercontinental missiles, the centres of the two systems to be not less than 1,300 kilometres apart and the radius of each no more than 150 kilometres; each system might contain 100 launchers, all of them static and capable of firing one warhead only. The agreement on offensive missiles was much barer. It was of limited duration, would expire in 1977 and did no more than impose a freeze on new construction subject to a proviso permitting the substitution of more modern for obsolescent equipment on land and in submarines. The United States and the USSR also agreed to begin in November a second round of SALT talks.

SALT 2 was to be concerned with what had been omitted from the 1972 agreements. This was much. The United States maintained its plea, rejected by the USSR, to ban mobile land-based launchers totally. The Russians had tried but failed to include in the interim agreement specific provisions about long-range bomber aircraft which were still a significant part of the American armoury, although not of the Russian: the Americans had over 500 such aircraft and the Russians, who wanted each aircraft to count as one launcher in an overall total, had 140. There had been no agreement about shorter-range aircraft based outside the United States: the Americans had about 1,300 such aircraft, capable of carrying nuclear weapons, 500 of them in Europe. Above all there was the problem of MIRVs. The USSR had, so far as was known, no operational MIRVs, although it had a larger total than the United States of intercontinental missiles. The United States, however, had begun deploying MIRVs on land (Minuteman 3) in 1970 and at sea (Poseidon) in 1971. By 1972 the USSR was believed to have 2,090 strategic missiles capable of hitting that number of targets, whereas the United

States had 1,710 such missiles capable of reaching 3,550 targets and, within a few years as re-equipment with MIRVs proceeded, over 7,000 targets. The Russians were expected to begin deploying MIRVs on their operational sites in 1975, at which point the effectiveness of the Russian force in terms of targets reachable would begin to multiply while the American, already largely re-equipped, would be becoming static. So in order to retain their superiority and match the expanding number of warheads sprouting from Russian launchers the Americans would have to increase the number of their launchers above the total frozen by the interim agreement. If they did not do this after 1977 the Russians would, it was assumed, have almost twice as many American targets in their sights by 1980 as the Americans had Russian. The Americans therefore were primarily concerned to set limits to the land-based missile capacity of each side. The Russians countered by proposing the elimination of American forward bases (aircraft bases in Europe and submarine bases in Spain and Scotland), a limitation on the number of aircraft carriers to be permitted in European waters (the Russians had no carriers of the conventional type but only carriers with helicopters or vertical take-off aircraft), and the relegation of nuclear-armed submarines to parts of the ocean from which they could not hit enemy territory. Progress in SALT 2 was in consequence laborious and negligible until Nixon visited Moscow in mid-1974 when the impasse was slightly shifted by three minor accords: a modification of the ABM treaty, an agreement to ban underground weapons tests of 150 kilotons and over from March 1976, and agreement that a new SALT treaty would extend to 1985. This last agreement was reflected in November when Gerald Ford, who had stepped into the presidency when Nixon resigned in August, met Brezhnev at Vladivostok in an attempt to prevent the steam from going out of Russo–American détente in general and SALT in particular. Ford and Brezhnev agreed that the talks should continue on the basis that each side might have up to 2,400 strategic launchers of all kinds (a somewhat high ceiling) of which no more than 1,320 might be fitted with MIRVs. The next year was devoted to the attempt to transpose this core into a formal agreement but with no success. The political will was there, fortified by the wish of both leaders to reach agreement before, in Brezhnev's case, the twenty-fifth congress of the Communist Party of the Soviet Union in February 1976 and, in Ford's, the presidential campaign which would take up most of that year. But the complexities and technicalities, themselves in constant flux, overpowered the negotiators. Discussions broke down early in 1977 but a new president, Jimmy Carter, tabled fresh proposals later in the year and then put a stop to the development of the neutron warhead and the long range B-1 bomber. In 1979 a SALT 2 treaty was signed.

It was to run to 1985 when a third treaty was intended to continue the process. It contained significant limitations. At its core was the restriction of nuclear delivery systems to 2,400 on each side, declining to 2,250 in 1985. Within this overall limitation there were interlocking sub-limitations in more precisely defined categories: MIRV'd systems together with aircraft carrying cruise missiles; land-based and sea-based MIRV'd missiles; and land-based MIRV'd missiles alone. Missiles over a certain size, of which the United States had none and the USSR had 308, were banned. There was a further ban on air-launched missiles delivered otherwise than from aircraft. Limits were set on the number of warheads per missile and the number of cruise missiles per aircraft. It was agreed that any launcher which fired a MIRV'd missile remained, for the purpose of the treaty, a MIRV'd launcher whatever weapons might be fixed to it. Restrictions, albeit modest, were placed on the modernization of weapons; they affected neither submarine delivery systems nor land-based intercontinental ballistic missiles and so permitted the deployment, on the American side, of Trident 1 and 2 and the MX mobile missile system, and their rough Russian equivalents. The parties to the treaty undertook to give notification of certain tests and stocks. A non-circumvention clause aimed to prevent either side from using a third party to get round its treaty obligations; this clause alarmed European members of Nato who feared that the United States might interpret it as a prohibition on the transfer of new technology. A protocol to the treaty pointed the way towards further restrictions on the deployment, although not on the testing, of new and improved weapons: for example, cruise missiles (other than cruise missiles delivered from aircraft) with an extended range. That these provisions were more effective than cosmetic was proved by the opposition which they provoked among those on either side who put the preservation or attainment of military preponderance ahead of the control of the arms race. In the United States the Senate Foreign Relations Committee recommended ratification of the treaty but public protest and expert disquiet (which concentrated on what the treaty did not secure) and then the Russian invasion of Afghanistan killed it. Non-ratification was a prominent feature in Ronald Reagan's successful bid for the presidency in 1980.

The political atmosphere had become uncongenial to such agreements. The late seventies were a time of increasing mistrust. On the American side the Russo–Cuban intervention in Angola in 1975 began a series of Russian moves – Ethiopia, Vietnam and Afghanistan were other and widely separated theatres of menacing Russian activity – which hardened American distrust and sharpened the American concern for rearmament rather than arms control. At this time too official American estimates of the size of the Russian defence budget were drastically increased. The passage of the warship *Kiev* from the Black Sea to the Mediterranean, an incident which would hardly have ruffled the waters a few years earlier, led to charges that the USSR had broken the Montreux Convention of 1936 (on the assumption, which was contested, that the *Kiev* was an aircraft-carrier within the meaning of that instrument). In 1979 a more serious scare was caused, and deliberately publicized, by the discovery of a Russian brigade in Cuba. President Carter had stopped American intelligence flights over Cuba as a conciliatory gesture, but these were resumed when Cuba was suspected of taking a hand in revolution in Nicaragua. What they revealed was a Russian training unit which had been in Cuba for some years, but the temper of the times converted it into a new threat to the United States.

On the Russian side the flourishing entente between the United States and China, and Deng Xiaoping's attempt to turn it into a triple alliance with Japan, aggravated Moscow's enduring fears of encirclement, which became more acute as the USSR became increasingly dependent on American grains to feed its beasts and so its peoples. The USSR alleged, and perhaps believed, that its troubles in Afghanistan and Poland were accentuated by American undercover interference. Its ageing leadership (procedures for an orderly succession had never been evolved) was plagued at home by an economy which failed to secure basic amenities and was consigning perhaps 20 per cent of GNP to armaments and defence.

Concurrently with this worsening of the political climate were technical advances which were altering the nature of the arms race. The nuclear deterrent had been a crude and inflexible weapon, whose effectiveness depended on its crudeness and inflexibility. It was aimed at cities and their inhabitants. On the American side there were until the late seventies only two courses that an American president could take in an emergency. He could order an attack on all the targets on which his weapons were trained; or he could order the destruction of all these targets except Moscow. He had no third choice, and because he had none his armoury posed a most fearful threat to the USSR. It was an effective deterrent – so long as it was possible to believe that the president would use it.

But during the seventies this credibility began to wear thin. Would a president nerve himself unhesitatingly to order so vast a massacre within the minutes available to him for a decision? The very question undermined the strategy of deterrence. It also revived American fears that the USSR would be tempted to revert to a first-strike strategy. At the same time the refinement of, in particular, targeting techniques enabled strategists to think once more in terms of waging war instead of deterring it. The aggressor might attack a single pinpointed military target, such as a missile site or a command headquarters or a bunker containing a head of state; each side might then exchange attacks on such single targets and carry on a war for weeks or months. Surviving a war, even winning a war – concepts which had seemed nonsense in the nuclear age – became possibilities.

A special element in the contest between the superpowers, making that contest global, was the growth of Russian naval power in the seventies. If a great power is a power that can act in any quarter of the globe – and that is as good a definition as any – then sea power is crucial. The United States was without question a great naval power capable of sailing all the world's oceans and of commanding passage through all but the most private waterways. The USSR was not such a power but was determined to become one. Because it was aiming to be what it was not, its efforts roused considerable alarm. The world was not used to seeing Russian fleets in many oceans, but the universalization of Russian power required this to happen. On land the USSR had advanced little since 1945. Its hold on eastern Europe, although sometimes troubled, remained undisputed and with it the power to pose a threat to western Europe whose credibility was a constant conundrum. It had established in the fifties its rights to be considered a power in the Middle East, although in the seventies the limits of this power were exposed by its eviction from Egypt and by its negative role in the diplomacy that followed the war of 1973. Its sallies into the Congo in 1960 and the Caribbean in 1962 were failures, its role in the wars in South-east Asia marginal, the poor performances of communists in Portugal and Greece in 1974 disappointing, the illness and absences of Brezhnev and the uncertainty of the succession a source of hesitations. Its economy and the quality of life of its peoples remained vulnerable to the vagaries of the weather and of an unwieldy bureaucratic system, both of which could perpetrate massive shocks. For all its vast armed strength the USSR was in one vital respect a power of a different kind from the United States, a power still confined whereas American power roamed free. The seaways, and the underseaways, offered one escape from this inferiority.

By the mid-seventies the Russian navy far surpassed the American in the number of its submarines but was distinctly inferior in every other respect. American naval manpower, including marines, was 733,000 against 500,000 Russian equivalents. The United States had 15 aircraft-carriers, the USSR none other than helicopter-carriers; of cruisers and destroyers with nuclear weapons the United States had 110 and the USSR 79. But the USSR had 265 submarines against 75, albeit that in nuclear-powered submarines the balance was more even at 75 Russian to 64 American. Such figures ignore a great deal, and a closer comparison of the two navies would have to take account of the age of vessels, their armaments, each nation's reserves, research expenditure and other indicators of comparative effectiveness. Political effectiveness moreover is not the same as military effectiveness. What would happen if the two navies engaged each other in combat was a nearly academic question, but the effect of the appearance of a Russian flotilla of any size in, for example, the Mediterranean was not. This fleet varied between twenty-five and sixty surface and submarine vessels, sometimes larger in numbers and sometimes smaller than the US Sixth Fleet but without air cover, smaller than the French, much smaller than the Italian and trivial beside the combined forces of Nato in this theatre. It was none the less a portent and it made a political point. It had its effect on the conduct of relations between the USSR and Algeria and Libya, two strategically placed anti-western but not pro-Russian states. It reminded western governments that their fears, acute in the late forties, of Russian bases in Yugoslavia and Albania might yet one day be realized, with incalculable consequences for Mediterranean politics. A foretaste of these consequences was provided by the prime minister of Malta, Dom Mintoff, whose search for money for his impoverished island led him to demand from Britain greatly increased fees for the use of Malta's harbour, with more than a hint that if Britain did not care to use it at the going price the Russians would. As a result Mintoff secured in 1972 a rental of £14 million a year for seven years, of which Britain's Nato partners were to provide £8.74 million, and additional lump sums of £2.5 million from Italy and £7 million from other members of Nato.

The election of Ronald Reagan to the presidency of the United States in 1980 owed a great deal to the feeling that the United States ought to be making better use of its power instead of striking deals with an adversary who was getting stronger and was not to be trusted. Reagan was not the choice of the nation's political leaders. He was the choice, in the first place, of a group of reactionary conservatives with enough money to buy for him the candidature of the Republican Party and, secondly, of the people at large who liked his personality and simplicity and responded to his forthright reduction of public issues to contests between good and evil in which it behoved the good to exert themselves with more faith than calculation. Reagan retained his popularity and won re-election in 1984 by a landslide. He had powerful support in western Europe which likewise moved to the right in the early eighties. In Britain Thatcher's electoral victory in 1979 brought to power a prime minister who was temperamentally in favour of tough talking and acting (and was also committed to monetarist economic policies which she believed to be the same as his); her success at the polls was repeated in 1983, when the Labour Party's espousal of unilateral disarmament was a major element in a disastrous campaign, and again in 1987. In West Germany conservatives triumphed when Helmut Kohl ended thirteen years of socialist rule in 1982 and won further convincing victories in 1983 and 1987. Left-wing parties lost power in Norway and Belgium (1981) and the Netherlands (1982) and although France elected a socialist president in 1981 François Mitterrand proved to be more explicit than his predecessor in his support for the deployment of Cruise and Pershing II missiles in Europe, even though he was also critical of American policies in Africa and Central America and went so far as to give encouragement to Reagan's enemies in Nicaragua. Until the unforeseen advent of Gorbachev in 1985 therefore the western alliance was at least superficially united behind the tough attitudes expressed by Reagan, and disarmament at all levels from the SALT process to non-nuclear forces appeared to be stalled.

But these were currents of a different kind. The shift to the right in Europe cleared the ground on the left for criticism of American policies more trenchant than left-wing parties were wont to express when in government. Reagan's intemperate bellicosity towards the USSR, however congenial in the United States at this stage, found fewer echoes among Europeans who, much as they disliked and distrusted the USSR, were convinced of the need for a *modus vivendi* with it and did not believe that the threats and abuse to which the president seemed naturally drawn were a sensible way forward. They consorted ill with his affirmation of a two-track policy – strength plus negotiation – with the result that his readiness to negotiate was regarded as shallow and insincere, particularly after his unbridled speech at Orlando, Florida, in March 1985 when he stigmatized the USSR as an evil empire destined for the dustbin of history. His apparent belief that the USSR could be forced to disarm by an escalation of American armaments – a bigger Trident programme, the resurrection of the discarded B-1 bomber, MX missiles, all of which were approved by Congress and, in the case of MX, later expanded – dismayed many among his allies as both dangerous and silly, his espousal of his 'Star Wars' programme doubly so. The United States was also developing to the point of production a greatly more potent anti-tank weapon, the Enhanced Radiation Warhead (or neutron bomb), which would be able to devastate a Russian armoured advance, while in the background were laser beams, chemical weapons and other alternatives to nuclear weapons.

To these complexities were added political and economic squabbles within the western alliance and difficulties of a more technical kind between the two alliances, Nato and the Warsaw Pact. Both trends hampered the pursuit of agreements on disarmaments and arms control.

The politico-economic difficulties were transient. When General Jaruzelski imposed martial law in Poland and imprisoned many of his political opponents Reagan, treating Jaruzelski as a mere Kremlin puppet, imposed sanctions on the USSR as well as Poland and did so without consulting his European allies who regarded these moves as ineffective or worse. He in his turn regarded them as soft on the USSR and their proposals for a mere freeze on Polish borrowing as ludicrously feeble. A more serious conflict arose when Reagan moved to obstruct the building of a pipeline for conveying gas from the USSR to Europe – a project of significance for western Europe as well as the

USSR but regarded in the United States as malign strengthening of the USSR, which would double its exports of gas by the end of the century and so earn much needed foreign currency. In using events in Poland to impose sanctions against the USSR Reagan threatened those European businesses which were participating in the construction of the pipeline and had subsidiaries or operations in the United States. This threat to extend the effects of sanctions to European firms was resented as impertinent and illegal. A compromise was reached at Versailles in June 1982 but it immediately broke down, whereupon Reagan – against the advice of his secretary of state, Alexander Haig, who resigned – imposed sanctions which the Europeans ignored. By the end of that year the affair had fizzled out, governments on both sides of the Atlantic being concerned to secure the planned deployment of Cruise and Pershing without too much fuss. For the same reason – the solidarity of the alliance – disagreements over other matters were kept down to the muttering level (over American partiality for South Africa and the consequent stalling of negotiations on Namibia, over American policies in the Middle East and Central America), and even the American invasion without notice of a member of the Commonwealth, Grenada, was handled by Thatcher with decorous restraint.

The second complicating factor was the more technical. It had been convenient to keep discussions on nuclear and non-nuclear weapons separate, and to divide nuclear weapons into distinct categories – long-range, intermediate and battlefield. But this way of handling the broad field of disarmament was proving unreal. At the core of SALT was the attempt to set limits to the delivery systems which either side might possess. The fixing of numbers was a matter for haggling. More difficult was the definition of the systems which the treaty should cover. The weapons on either side were not precisely comparable, nor was it any longer easy to agree which were strategic and which not. The Americans wanted the treaty to include the Russian Backfire bomber which, with its in-air refuelling service, was arguably a strategic weapon capable of hitting American cities; and also those categories of mobile missile which, although classified as intermediate, were easily convertible into an SS.16 strategic missile. The Russians were, in the nature of the case, as much concerned about Nato's intermediate-range weapons in Europe as with the ultimate deterrent based in the United States. The USSR was deploying SS.20s targeted on European cities at the rate of about one a week and striving to delay the renovation of Nato's counter-weapons in the European theatre. Thus the limitation of strategic arms – the province of the bilateral SALT talks – could no longer be divorced from the development and deployment of theatre weapons, which involved all the Nato allies and not merely the United States. The regulation of intermediate weapons (INF) became therefore interlocked with the SALT process, now renamed START. It also assumed from the mid-eighties a greater momentum because it offered better prospects of agreement.

Throughout the seventies Nato's nuclear capacity in Europe lay largely in its aircraft delivering air-to-ground missiles – the British Vulcan and the American F.111 – but in the face of the deployment of the SS.20 Nato resolved in 1979 to deploy new intermediate weapons (464 Cruise missiles, non-ballistic, low-flying and very accurate, and 108 Pershing II ballistic missiles) in five European countries, thereby reducing by a factor of five the time needed for a retaliatory strike against targets in the USSR. This decision, urged on the Americans by the Europeans and particularly by West Germany, was to some extent a miscalculation. The SS.20, which began to replace the SS.4 and SS.5 from 1976, was a mobile launcher with three warheads and a range of 5,000 km: the SS.4 and SS.5, in service from 1959 to 1961 respectively, had single warheads with ranges of 2,000 and 4,000 km. Together with the TU-26 (the Backfire) aircraft the SS.20 greatly strengthened the Russian position in Europe. The European members of Nato wanted a similar weapon within the theatre in order to square up to the SS.20, re-assert the credibility of Nato's strategy in Europe and re-knit the Euro–American linkage which, Europeans feared, was becoming frayed. But European leaders underestimated the opposition of their electorates to this proliferation of nuclear weapons and the USSR was able to play on this dissension in the hope of getting Nato's 1979 resolve reversed. In 1981 Nato, in order to placate the critics in its midst, adopted the 'zero option' for INF – that is to say, their total elimination – in the conviction that the USSR would reject it, which it immediately did. The manoeuvring continued with an offer by Moscow to withdraw SS.20s in return for the abandonment of the Cruise/Pershing II deployment and a later offer to destroy considerable numbers of them for the same consideration. The key to the manoeuvring was in Bonn and it ended when the Bundestag confirmed the acceptance of West Germany's quota of Pershing IIs. Their arrival at the end of 1983 marked the failure of the Russian attempt to stop the programme. Moscow strengthened its nuclear forces in East Germany and Czechoslovakia and broke off all negotiations, including the START talks on strategic weapons as well as the INF negotiations.

At this point the USSR was confronted with a fresh development which it was even more anxious to obstruct than the deployment of Cruise and Pershing II. This was Reagan's Strategic Defence Initiative (SDI), unveiled in 1982. SDI emphasized the distinction between offensive and defensive nuclear weapons. It consisted of startling new proposals for defence against nuclear attack which, if practicable, would destroy nuclear missiles after they had been fired and so provide invulnerability against a first strike. The president proposed to spend $26,000 million on research over an initial five years. This stupendous cost and the implications for the American economy and budget (which the president had promised to reduce) added to the air of fantasy implicit in its nickname of Star Wars. There were also more sober doubts. Many experts thought the proposals intrinsically unworkable or even absurd. They were certainly untestable to any precise degree except in war. They were open to the objection that by the time they were developed counter-measures would also have been developed. They seemed to entail contravention or denunciation of the ABM treaty of 1972 or a request to amend it which would give the USSR a chance, by refusing, to provoke fresh friction in the relations between the United States and its European allies. (Washington began at this time to claim, correctly, that the ABM treaty had already been broken by the USSR.) Most important: the SDI aimed to replace deterrence by defence and so was bound to undermine the deterrence which, however crude and unappealing, had greatly helped to keep the peace between the superpowers for a long generation. In western Europe governments were unwilling to be too openly critical, partly because they did not want to add to discord within Nato but also because Reagan invited them to share in the research and they sensed, mistakenly, that there was a great deal of money to be made by accepting.

The disarmament scene was transformed by a change in leadership in Moscow and a change of heart in Washington. Gorbachev was a new broom who needed above all to cut costs in order to save the USSR from catastrophe and Reagan, whether coincidentally or not, decided to exchange the role of Great Scourge for that of Great Peacemaker. In 1985 the two leaders met in Geneva. Nothing of great consequence was agreed but they met and – as when Napoleon and Alexander met on their raft at Tilsit – there was a kind of humanity about the mere event which cheered onlookers and was deemed to be a part of statecraft. More potent was the stark fact that the USSR was incapable of financing the Cold War and the United States too was heading towards insolvency. As both superpowers took account of the depreciation of their super-status in the world, they were forced to acknowledge the need to disarm. Nor were they any longer prevented by *raison d'état* from doing so. The myths which had played a major part in inflaming the Cold War and sustaining it were grown stale and threadbare. Hostility remained but fear had receded.

The position on disarmament when Gorbachev came to power in 1985 was as follows. The reduction of non-nuclear forces in Europe had been under discussion in Vienna since 1974 between all the members (twenty-two) of Nato and the Warsaw Pact. These discussions were designated MBFR (Mutual and Balanced Force Reductions). Proposals for thinning out conventional forces in central Europe were first made by Nato in 1969 and 1970, and in 1973 Nato proposed a 15 per cent cut by both sides in the central sector to be followed by a reduction to

700,000, which proportionately would be a bigger cut by the Warsaw alliance than by Nato. The Warsaw Pact responded by proposing initial cuts of 20,000 by both sides, followed by a 5 per cent reduction and then a 10 per cent reduction. This scheme, more proportional than numerical, reflected the Warsaw Pact's advantage in numbers, which it designed to keep. Nato on the other hand favoured a mainly numerical approach leading to a parity in numbers which it did not possess. After these opening gambits nothing much happened and nobody seemed to be in a hurry that it should, until 1979 when Brezhnev – possibly in order to sow doubts among the Nato allies about the wisdom of Nato's programme for modernising its theatre weapons – announced the impending withdrawal of 1,000 tanks and 20,000 men from East Germany. The talks continued, however, to be bedevilled by inadequate and suspect statistics and by the problem of verification. They were wound up in 1989 after nearly 500 sessions and were submerged in a new Vienna colloquy in which all European states were involved and the subject matter was extended to the entire area from the Atlantic to the Urals. This successor conference was dubbed CFE (Conventional Forces in Europe). An even larger group of thirty-five states – thirty-three in Europe plus the United States and Canada – deriving from the Helsinki Final Act in 1975 and its review conference had since 1983 been discussing security and co-operation in Europe (CSCE) and it convoked in 1986 in Stockholm a Conference on Confidence- and Security-Building Measures and Disarmament in Europe (CDE). Whereas the function of the MBFR/CFE negotiations was to reduce the size of the armed forces of Nato and the Warsaw Pact in central Europe and beyond, the CDE was concerned with the movements of these forces and the framing of rules to obviate surprise attack (and the fear of surprise attack) through such measures as advance notification of movements involving more than a given number of men or tanks. Both the CFE and CDE negotiations made satisfactory progress in the closing years of the decade.

In the nuclear field both strategic and intermediate weapons were under discussion, the former wholly, the latter primarily, in the province of the superpowers. At their first meeting, at Geneva, Reagan and Gorbachev had declared themselves in favour of halving their long-range or strategic nuclear weaponry and finding an interim agreement on INF. Gorbachev had inherited his predecessors' failure to prevent the deployment of new Nato INF in Europe. He was anxious to use his bargaining position over strategic weapons to halt Reagan's SDI. After Geneva he tried to accelerate the disarmament process with a surprising proposal for the elimination of all nuclear weapons of all categories by the year 2000. The United States responded with a mixed package which repeated the Geneva target on strategic weapons and coupled it with the removal of all INF from Europe in three years and the continuing attempt to remove the imbalances in the two sides' conventional forces. Gorbachev declared himself flexible on INF and willing to accept a reduced cut in strategic weapons – 30 per cent instead 50 per cent – and he also modified his tactics on SDI by implying that some research might be permissible provided the United States undertook to observe strictly the ABM treaty for the next fifteen to twenty years. He thereby set the development of SDI firmly within the existing ABM regime and argued for a precise term during which it might not be amended. The United States, while maintaining the proposal to reduce strategic weapons by half, proposed that the ABM treaty be guaranteed for seven and a half years on condition that SDI weapons might be deployed from 1992 (they could not in fact be ready for deployment before that date) and that after 1992 SDI technology would be shared with the USSR. The essence of the American position was to secure freedom of action after a given period during which the constraints in the ABM treaty would be observed. This was the position when Reagan and Gorbachev met again at Reykjavik in Iceland.

Reagan went to Reykjavik in order to affirm and broaden the goodwill established at Geneva. Gorbachev had precise plans: to stop SDI; affirm the strict letter of the ABM treaty for a fixed term and, if possible, strengthen its provisions on testing by getting the United States to agree that while laboratory tests might be permissible, tests in space were not; remove all INF from Europe; and negotiate the reduction of strategic weapons by 50 per cent or at least 30 per cent. He was prepared to limit INF in Asia to 100, and to discuss – and meanwhile freeze – short-range weapons (less than 500 kilometres). He rejected Reagan's offer to share SDI technology. On his side Reagan wanted all INF to be eliminated in Asia as well as Europe. He was not prepared to yield anything on SDI. Surprise at the progress marked by these exchanges was turned to astonishment by a new proposal which appeared to be approved by both leaders, although some doubt was later cast on Reagan's endorsement of it. This proposal was for the complete elimination of nuclear weapons of all kinds in ten years, this process to be geared to the elimination of 50 per cent of strategic weapons in the first five years and the remaining 50 per cent in the next five. The confused euphoria emanating from Reykjavik was dampened when it became apparent that without concessions on SDI Gorbachev would sign nothing. He had failed in his main aim.

He returned to the attack in 1987 by repeating his Reykjavik offer on INF (zero in Europe, 100 in Asia) but without linking it to agreement on SDI, to which the United States replied by agreeing on condition that the USSR's surviving INF should be out of range of western Europe and Japan. This *rapprochement* brought up the question of short-range weapons which had been skirted at Reykjavik, and Gorbachev sprang another surprise by proposing their total elimination (the 'third zero'). He also agreed to forgo the 100 INF in Asia. The outcome was an INF treaty concluded in Washington at the end of the year, and in force from June 1988, for the destruction of all INF weapons by 1991, the USSR being thereby required to destroy more than twice as many missiles and launchers as Nato. The Washington meeting also recorded some progress towards agreement on strategic weapons but none on the interlocking questions of SDI and the ABM treaty. The problems on strategic weapons were remitted to the START conference in Geneva which laboriously elaborated agreements on enough matters to justify the preparation of a START treaty, while leaving the more intractable issues – notably on sea-launched cruise missiles – to a second round and a START II treaty. The principal areas of agreement embraced considerable cuts in ballistic missile warheads and launchers, limits for land-based cruise missiles, and detailed provisions for inspection and verification backed by exchanges of information.

The arms race was an economic catastrophe sustained by the psychology of the Cold War. Economic catastrophe had struck the USSR and was lapping round the western camp too. But the psychology of the Cold War could not be stilled in a matter of a few years and one by-product of the Reagan–Gorbachev meetings was uneasiness in Nato on account both of some of the decisions announced by the leaders of the superpowers and of the way in which the United States proceeded with scant or belated attention to its allies in the front line. The trend set by the superpowers undermined the credibility of Nato's strategy. In its first, formative years Nato had adopted, at Lisbon in 1952, a programme to create forces, including German units, capable of fighting a prolonged non-nuclear war, but these forces never came into existence and Nato was refashioned as a link in a chain or ladder whose credibility depended on the existence in the chain of nuclear weapons of rising malignity. This doctrine of flexible response went through a number of phases. The invention of short-range nuclear weapons enabled Nato to plan for smaller forces with more ferocious weapons but once again the targets (set in 1957) were not reached. Nato's role was, however, set as the role of a delaying agency. Whether with non-nuclear weapons or short-range nuclear weapons or inter-mediate nuclear weapons Nato would resist an attack and cause the attacker to think again before carrying on with his operations. Although this vision of a future conflict was not demonstrably ridiculous it was difficult to see a war developing in this way and Nato's military function was therefore always ambiguous. It relied on the assumption that the aggressor's first step or steps would be taken without much thought but that the same thoughtless aggressor would quickly be made to think better. But whatever the practicalities were likely to be, the theory demanded a graduated response which, given

Nato's make-up, was a graduated nuclear response. When Reagan was persuaded at Reykjavik to approve zero options for both INF and strategic weapons he was removing the steps in the ladder – and at the same time dismantling the American strategic nuclear umbrella which Europeans had learnt to regard as the ultimate guarantee of their security. The European dilemma was intensified when Gorbachev proposed to apply the zero option to short-range or battlefield nuclear weapons also. The response could no longer be flexible and a Russian attack would start with considerable advantages, offset only by the counter-fear of an all-out American riposte with what might be left of the strategic missile force. The reversal of the arms race, coupled with the simultaneous disappearance of the Warsaw Pact, left Nato without a strategy, without an obvious foe and perhaps without a purpose. It left the superpowers still very heavily armed, although determined to be less so. Substantial cuts in conventional weapons, embodied in a treaty signed at the end of 1990 by the twenty-two members of the opposing alliances, and the prospect of a further bilateral agreement in the next year on nuclear forces, kept the ebb tide flowing.

THE DEPRECIATION OF THE SUPERPOWERS

The 1980s were the decade in which the superpowers ceased to be regarded as so far above and beyond all other states as to constitute a distinct species. This was pre-eminently true of the USSR which no longer looked like a match for the United States, was no longer able to dominate central or eastern Europe, was in acute economic decline and was threatened with disintegration. The depreciation of the United States, although of a very different order, was hardly less startling, given its unchallenged superiority over the past generation and its continuing massive resources and massive industrial and agricultural output.

The decline in American power and prestige was self-inflicted, a consequence of mistakes and misjudgments in economic management and external policies. Fumbling in foreign affairs was most unhappily displayed in Central America, where Reagan failed in his declared intention to pacify the small republic of El Salvador and make it safe for a decent right-wing democracy. In Panama the United States subsidized a known drug dealer and, when his crimes became too blatant, failed to unseat him by bribery and resorted to a military invasion on a flimsy pretext. In Nicaragua Reagan failed to overthrow the Sandinista régime in spite of waging an expensive vicarious war and resorting to clear breaches of international law, for which the United States was censured by the International Court of Justice; the government of President Daniel Ortega was later defeated not by arms but by the economic sanctions which led Nicaraguans to vote against Ortega in elections of surprising democratic rectitude. (For these matters see Chapter 27.) These failures against weak neighbours in the American continent itself betokened an inadequate grasp on the uses of power. The United States was the world's greatest military and industrial power and yet unable to operate efficiently as a regional power.

In economic affairs the Reagan administration was notable for the decline of the United States' unique position in the world and its inability either to regulate the international system devised by itself at the end of the war or to provide decently for the bulk of its own people. Reagan's determination to boost American pride and self-confidence to his own cheery level was accompanied by an equal determination to reduce taxes. Since his way to pride was papered with unprecedentedly costly expenditure on weapons of war his term of office was marked by massive borrowing and the neglect of social services. His promise on entering the White House to balance the budget was even rasher than such promises usually are. He seemed to believe that the gap between spending and revenue would evaporate because lower taxes, in association with monetarist controls, would produce higher profits and so higher tax yields to bridge the gap. But low taxes and tight money did not lay these golden eggs, deficits grew both absolutely and as a percentage of GNP, after 1982 monetary constraints were relaxed and interest rates lowered, growth continued but so too did the gap, and the only salvation lay in pulling in foreign money to finance current government spending and domestic investment. The dollar was allowed to rise but rose so strongly that its exchange value ceased to be credible and it fell even more spectacularly than it had risen. When Reagan left office in 1989 the United States had swung in less than a decade from being the world's biggest creditor to being its biggest debtor; its external debt, which exceeded $660,000 million, had risen by 25 per cent in a single year; external deficits reached $12,000 million a month and interest on external was costing $50,000 million a year; export business was crippled and foreign assets were being sold off. Within the United States capital resources shrank by $500,000 million as shares in corporations were extinguished or replaced by debt (particularly through the invention of junk bonds); half the population was worse off in real terms than it had been in 1980; personal savings had fallen below 15 per cent (half the Japanese rate); higher education in technology and science was in decline; the economic infrastructure was in decay and so were inner cities where housing and infant mortality approximated to the black spots of the Third World and crime and drugs were alarmingly prevalent; corruption in the public sector was widespread up to the level of the cabinet. These ills were remediable but they required a stark reversal of attitudes and a robust exercise of political will. Given the strength of manufacturing industry, budget deficits could be handled by modest increases in taxation; social decay could be tackled by abandoning Reagan's view that government must be minimized – itself an abdication of responsibility. For the time being, however, the United States seemed to be no longer the sole front-runner in a world in which Japan and the European Community were the thrusting societies. The confidence which Reagan had given Americans through military might and talk was being jeopardized by economic and social malfunction and mediocre leadership. Reagan armed the United States against the USSR but disarmed it against Japan, an equally aggressive adversary although one whose weapons were not military.

In Reagan's two terms of office one episode did particular damage both at home and abroad. This was the Iran–Contra affair. The damage was more to appearance than to substance since it eroded respect and confidence rather than power (leaving open the perennial question how far prestige is an element in power). It resulted from the simultaneous pursuit of two ventures, the one hypocritical and the other illicit. The one was the attempt to secure the release of Americans held hostage in the Middle East, while keeping up the pretence that the United States would do no deal with terrorists. This attempt was allied with a policy of repairing relations with Iran and the belief – or delusion – that the ruling group in Teheran included so-called moderates who would genuinely welcome and be able to engineer better political and commercial relations with the United States. The second and associated venture arose from the determination to go on arming and funding the Contra opposition to the Nicaraguan government covertly and in defiance of the Boland amendment whereby in 1984 Congress had resolved against providing further military aid. The approach to Iran, pursued in collaboration with Israeli and other arms dealers, involved supplying Iran with weapons with which to wage its war with Iraq; no arms would go directly to Iran from the United States but from stocks in Israel which the United States would then replenish. Senior American officials travelled in secret to Teheran with a consignment of parts for missile launchers. But both sides were expecting more than they could reasonably hope to get. Iran raised its demands not only for weaponry but also for political concessions such as an Israeli withdrawal from southern Lebanon and the Golan heights and the release of prisoners held in Kuwait on charge of terrorism in Lebanon. One American hostage was released in exchange for more spare parts, a second for yet more weapons. There were many clandestine meetings and much mutual deception by overstatement. The proceedings became public knowledge. Reagan dismissed his national security adviser, Admiral John Poindexter, and his principal subordinate in these matters, Colonel Oliver North, who managed to destroy much documentation before quitting his office. Reagan's first public statements were untrue, and although he knew that the Boland amendment was being bypassed in numerous ways his positive knowledge of the Iran–Contra operations remained unproved throughout the remainder of his presidency. In later testimony he more than a hundred times pleaded an inability to remember crucial matters, so that it was not clear whether he had not been told or had not understood or whether neither of these evasions was valid. His reputation for straightforwardness, competence and application to business did not recover. The importance of the Iran–Contra affair was not that it weakened the United States militarily but that it caught the attention of the world and raised questions about the dependability of the United States in world affairs. The smell of scandal was the more harmful since it came not much more than a decade after the astonishing behaviour of Richard Nixon who had been forced in 1974 by the exposure of his chicanery and mendacity to resign the presidency and transfer it to a congressman of mediocre capacity, Gerald Ford, in exchange for exemption from impeachment.

For the Euro–American alliance three American shortcomings were troubling since the position of the United States in the alliance was uniquely important: no anti-Russian alliance without the United States was conceivable so long as the Cold War prevailed. The alliance had always suffered strains, although these were usually repaired by the crassness of Russian policies (before the advent of Gorbachev) in Europe and beyond. The most serious rift in the sixties was the Franco–American acerbity which half-removed France from the alliance, but soon after the departure of de Gaulle French units again took part in Nato's naval exercises in the Mediterranean (1970). The seventies were nevertheless often uneasy. Nato was no longer a preponderantly American host with European facilities: in European theatres and waters the European allies were providing 75 per cent of the air forces, 80 per cent of naval forces and 90 per cent of land forces. The American contribution was symbolic and financially crucial, so that Americans were moved to argue that Europe could not have this costly American military umbrella and at the same time obstruct American policies in other directions. The war in Vietnam had been fiercely criticized in Europe, but the war in the Middle East in 1973 raised ill will to governmental level. The United States was angered by European refusals to permit the use of airfields for the air lift to Israel and by their hurried truckling to Arab threats of an oil boycott. Europeans retorted by pointing out that they depended on the Middle East for 80 per cent of their oil, the United States for 5 per cent, and by chiding Washington for making policy on the Middle East without consulting its allies and then expecting these to assist it. Europeans were further estranged when Washington appeared to be toying with schemes for assuring the flow of oil by force of arms and they were reluctant to attend a consumers' conference proposed by the United States as a way of putting pressure on Arab producers. For similar reasons France refused to join an Energy Authority created within the OECD or to take part in a consumers' oil-sharing agreement. Europeans preferred a conference between consumers and producers, negotiation rather than confrontation.

At this point the alliance was virtually in abeyance and matters were not improved by the Turkish invasion of Cyprus in 1974. Greece, blaming the United States for not taking a firmer stand against Turkey's excessive exploitation of the Greek dictatorship's inept interference in Cyprus, withdrew from active participation in Nato operations – a protest caused by events in Cyprus but also grounded in a more pervasive anti-Americanism which had grown with American benevolence towards the dictators throughout 1967–74. This Greek hostility was not offset by any countervailing Turkish sentiment, since the US Congress, taking the Greek side, voted in December 1974 to cut off aid to Turkey whereupon the Turkish government took control of twenty-four American military installations in Turkey, concluded a treaty of friendship with the USSR and accepted a large Russian loan.

At the diametrically opposite corner of Nato's territory two other members were engaged in a different conflict which too had implications for Nato installations. In 1972 the Icelandic parliament resolved to extend fishing limits to 50 miles. The act, which particularly affected Britain and West Germany, was a unilateral alteration of treaty dispositions of 1961. At the same time the Althing rejected in advance recourse to the International Court of Justice (which however ruled in August 1972 that British and West German vessels had the right to fish to a 12 miles limit). West Germany and Iceland compromised the resulting dispute in 1975 but with Britain, whose interests were more severely affected, Iceland's action led to armed clashes as Britain provided its fishing vessels with naval protection against the armed Icelandic coastguards trying to drive them away or destroy their gear. A two-year agreement was reached at the end of 1973, limiting the areas in which British vessels might fish and the type of vessel that might be used. This was a way of limiting the catch. Iceland, however, also declared that in 1975 it would extend its exclusive fishing rights to 200 miles. The dispute remained legally unresolved but the tensions were reduced in 1976 by a considerable British abandonment of reasonably well-founded rights. For Iceland the episode was an unyielding assertion of vital economic claims assisted by the advantages of operating in home waters; the real embarrassment of the British as a whole (as opposed to the fishing community); the likelihood that the current conference on the law of the sea would in any case recommend substantial extensions of normally accepted fishing limits; and the Nato connection which could be used to bring pressure on Britain by the United States which did not wish to see Nato's strategic installations in the northern sector imperilled by Icelandic action like that of Greece or Turkey.

In the midst of these aggravating conflicts and policy disputes Nixon upbraided his allies for ganging up on the United States. Kissinger, no less irritated but more constructive, proposed in 1973 a new Atlantic Charter to define the common aims of the United States, western Europe and Japan (added because of the economic conflicts which the United States had with both Europeans and Japanese). The United States, Kissinger said, was prepared to defend western Europe and continued to approve European unity, but it objected to Europeans concerting, among themselves and without consulting Washington, policies objectionable to the United States – which was pretty much what Europeans were objecting to in reverse. The seventies closed with the Russian invasion of Afghanistan which evoked in Washington proposals for action which many Europeans regarded as futile, while in relation to the Middle East European leaders, sceptical about the Camp David accords, set themselves to devise a European policy which, although expressed as a sequel to Camp David, was more precisely an alternative to an American policy which had in their eyes failed.

Then there was the question of paying for the alliance. For years the United States had borne a heavily disproportionate share of the costs and had regarded this burden as both inevitable and just so long as Europe was prostrate after the Second World War, but Europe recoverd (with massive American aid) while the United States began to feel the unfamiliar pains of economic overstrain. The Europeans had to acknowledge the unfairness of the economic burden-sharing but when in 1977 Nato resolved that all members should increase their defence spending by 3 per cent a year in real terms many of the Europeans failed to live up to their promises. In this context the question of leadership was an added irritant. There could be only one leader – the president of the United States. But respect for the presidency was calamitously impaired when Lyndon Johnson decided not to run for a further term because he felt that he had failed. Every president after Johnson contributed, sometimes powerfully, to the decline in the standing of the presidency among Europeans and so boosted the latent anti-Americanism which lay not far beneath the surface of European opinion. Yet this anti-Americanism was not so much a foundation for an alternative policy as an emotional luxury.

In retrospect the Helsinki conference of 1972–75 on Security and Co-operation in Europe (CSCE) proved a significant twist in the pattern of European affairs. It was attended by thirty-five states, including the United States and Canada which were accepted as rightful and essential members of the European polity. When the conference ended it was projected forward by providing for periodic reassembly in review conferences. Its participants wanted different things but got enough of what they wanted to give this wide forum – much the most comprehensive assembled in Europe since the war – a semi-permanency which presented a challenge to the prevailing bipolarity fashioned by the superpowers and to the exceptional position of each superpower *in suo orbe*.

The instigator of the Helsinki conference was the USSR. The west concurred after insisting on the inclusion of the United States and Canada. The Russian purpose was to secure general endorsement of the post-Hitlerian frontiers in Europe which no peace conference had ever ratified; and, secondly, to discuss security in terms of military bases and troop levels. The western approach to the conference was at first a mixture of boredom and cynicism, but towards the end it decided to use the occasion to exact conditions from the USSR. The west and the neutrals combined to reject a Russian proposal to declare Europe's frontiers immutable; the conference declared only that they should not be altered by force. Further, the west and the neutrals insisted on a wider interpretation of security, embracing not only military dispositions but also mutual understanding. Consequently the Helsinki Final Act contained declarations – not legally binding but nevertheless formal and normative – concerning governmental and non-governmental contacts for economic, social and technical co-operation and what was called co-operation in humanitarian fields. This phrase opened the door to discussion about human rights and breaches thereof. A Russian attempt to limit the ambit of these declarations to discussions between systems, as opposed to states, was defeated. Had it been accepted, the Final Act would have permitted abstract debate about the relative merits and vices of the capitalist and communist systems but not criticism of the policies and practices of particular states. The USSR, which had initiated the Helsinki conference, was out-manoeuvred at it and came to regret that it had ever set this particular ball rolling.

The Helsinki conference also provided for periodic reviews of the implementation of its undertakings. The first review took place in Belgrade in 1977 in a climate of considerable animosity. It achieved nothing except agreement to meet again. This next meeting began in Madrid in 1980 after protracted Russian attempts to abort it. The west predictably made great play with the Russian invasion of Afghanistan and the plight of dissidents in the USSR. France proposed yet another conference on disarmament in Europe and Brezhnev spoke warmly of confidence-building measures which he was willing to extend to all Europe up to the Urals. There was nothing new in any of these proposals which evinced only a determination to keep talking and to find something to say. But Helsinki's greater effect was outside these review conferences, for the Helsinki process coincided with a ferment in central Europe, amounting in Poland to a political revolution. The Helsinki declarations and the Helsinki watch committees set up in many countries (including the USSR) to monitor the behaviour of the signatories, contributed to this turbulence of hopes, unquantifiably but far from insignificantly, and after 1989 the CSCE became the pan-European forum which was felt to be needed after the demolition of Russian and communist power in central and eastern Europe and the consequent confusion over the continuing purposes and usefulness of Nato. In 1990 the CSCE participants (reduced to thirty-four by the extinction of the east German state) established a standing headquarters as a step away from armed bipolarity and towards a new, if dimly perceived, order in which confrontation between Europeans and also between the superpowers in Europe would be relegated, if not to the dustbin, at any rate to the pages of history.

There was at this time some confusion, at home and abroad, over the question whether a Bush administration was a coda to the Reagan era or a fresh start. The new administration began with a rare rebuff when the Senate refused to approve the president's choice for the office of Secretary of Defense, and in 1990 in the months preceding mid-term elections the president became seriously and damagingly embroiled with both parties in the Congress over ways of reducing the frightening budget deficit. Added to the kinds of conflict which stirred sharp emotions – drugs and crime, abortion, ethics in government – the crisis over the budget demonstrated not merely Bush's own vacillating character but also the fact, little appreciated outside the United States, that although the American president was commonly described as the most powerful man in the world, the American constitution provided that power and decision were to be shared between the president and the representatives of the people: that the American president had, within his own democracy, less power than many heads of government in other democracies.

The problems of the other superpower, the USSR, were very different from those of the United States. Its economic problems were of a different order of hopelessness, its society more corrupt, cruel and inefficient, its very existence as a union in question. After Khrushchev's dismissal in 1964 Leonid Brezhnev had emerged as his successor and remained at the head of affairs until he died in 1982 after a long but – in domestic matters – stagnant term and a slow personal decline. He had three successors in three years: Yuri Andropov who died in 1984, Konstantin Chernenko who died in 1985 and Mikhail Gorbachev with whom the long-awaited next generation at last reached the top. By this time the USSR no longer even looked like a match for the United States. Its empire in central and eastern Europe was unsustainable and the Union itself was threatened with disintegration on all sides of its Slav core. It was not without material resources but, mismanaged and under-equipped (except in certain heavy industries), they sufficed neither to feed its people or provide an acceptable standard of living, nor to make the USSR a world power. Gorbachev – intelligent, courageous and politically exceptionally agile – embarked upon a revolutionary course of economic and political reforms under the twin banners of *glasnost* and *perestroika*: *glasnost*, meaning openness and in particular an end to the pervasive falsification of economic performance; *perestroika*, meaning the restructure of the economy in the broadest sense of that word. He insisted that *perestroika* was not to be achieved without *glasnost* and that *glasnost* entailed not only inroads on censorship and habits of subservience but also reform of the entire political system, including the abolition of the Communist Party's monopoly of power and its control over the institutions of the state and the machinery of the economy. *Glasnost*, however unpalatable to some, was easy to understand. *Perestroika*, however, was a more ambiguous concept since it betokened change without specifying the pace of change or defining the new system into which the old system was to be changed. First steps included greater independence for co-operatives and for the managers of state enterprises, and the introduction of regulation by market forces to some extent. Even if it were agreed (which it was not) that there was a wrong system and a right one, there would still be difficulties in getting from the one to the other. How far, for example, should prices be allowed to find their own levels, if that meant that they would soar, putting goods out of reach of purchasers and leaving producers without a market? Should the prices of some things – food, for example – be controlled and, if so, by whom and on what principles and for how long? The government was caught between conflicting needs to let prices rip and to moderate their inevitable rise. While there was all but universal agreement on the need for a new economic order, there was no agreement on what it was to be: Lenin's New Economic Policy (which promoted small retailers and businesses in the hope of attracting foreign capital and skills), or the state of affairs before the NEP, or a new mixture of private capitalism and free trading and state socialism, or a plunge into something hardly distinguishable from western capitalism. The development of *perestroika* was therefore tentative and shapeless. It was contested in varying degrees; was obstructed by the thousands of people whose posts were likely to be put at risk by it; and was further complicated by the state of the economy which continued to go generally backward and was as fit for surgery as a patient with a weak heart. The economy suffered adventitious blows from the slump in the price of oil, the disaster to the nuclear reactor at Chernobyl in 1986 and an exceptionally grim earthquake in Armenia in 1988.

A first basic law for economic reform in 1987 began the process of decentralization, deregulation of prices, and financial rewards for enterprises but gave industry little freedom to shop around for its supplies and made little alteration to the discredited system of central targeting. These partial measures were extended a year later, although still in a tentative and experimental mode and limited to special zones and undertakings below a prescribed size. They were hampered by the lack of trained managers and by the inertia or opposition of the *nomenklatura*, the privileged and ossified administrators who, having survived the Brezhnev years, were in no mood to lose their jobs and perks in the aftermath.

Gorbachev's political aims did not include diminished executive authority at the centre. The road to power in the USSR might be made freer but the power at the end of the road was to be no less comprehensive and perhaps more so. As with the development of *perestroika* in industry and commerce, so with the accompanying political reforms, Gorbachev was not so much a strategic thinker as a nimble tactician who remained in control of the processes which he inaugurated by quick perception and quick moves which kept him ahead – if only just ahead – of events. At an extraordinary party conference in 1988 he promised to convoke a Congress of People's Deputies of 2,250 members, some chosen by special groups of which the Communist Party was one but the greater number (1,500) in territorial constituencies where the voters were promised a choice of candidates. All candidates were required to issue election manifestos. In elections which followed in the next year there was no contest in 384 constituencies, while in 271 no candidate got half the votes cast. The Congress elected a smaller Supreme Soviet of 750 members which met when the Congress dispersed. At the same time and by something like a coup Gorbachev secured the disappearance of hundreds of party regulars likely to obstruct his plans, purged the Central Committee of the Communist Party and had himself elected president of the USSR in the place of Andrei Gromyko who obligingly resigned. His powers as president were to be considerable but not absolute. The Supreme Court might declare his acts to be unconstitutional; two-thirds of the Supreme Soviet might override a presidential veto of new laws. Although he side-lined the Communist Party, he was obliged to accord prominence at the centre to the republics by instituting a Council of the Federation consisting of himself and all the presidents of the fifteen republics, and by abolishing the Council of Ministers – stronghold of centripetalism – and replacing it by a less prestigious and less powerful cabinet of experts. The resignation at the end of 1990 of his foreign minister Eduard Shevardnadze – a close colleague, successful minister and known advocate of liberal reforms – weakened Gorbachev and reinforced suspicions that he was being forced to veer to the conservative side and might even be becoming a captive of military leaders fearful of losing essential defence installations in dissident republics: the armed forces were, with the KGB, the principal outward and visible sign of centralised power as opposed to the centrifugal ambitions of Baltic and other dissidents or the champions of greater autonomy in the Russian republic (RSFSR) and the Ukraine. Gorbachev's weakened position was exposed when, seeking approval for his nominee for the new post of vice-president of the Union – for which Shevardnadze had seemed destined – his candidate was rejected by the Congress of Peoples Deputies and only subsequently approved after a second, strictly unconstitutional, vote.

None of these shifts and changes produced an economic policy. As the economy crumbled two competing strategies imposed themselves: to move fast or very fast. To the bolder or more desperate spirits the situation required a dash for change, damning the consequences and hoping for the best. The protagonists of this strategy produced a 500-day plan for installing a mixed economy in four stages. The first comprised selling government and Communist Party properties and enterprises, dissolving all state and collective farms, giving occupiers their plots or apartments, and cutting the budget by 5 million roubles in three months (including sharp cuts in the costs of defence and the KGB). The prime aim of this stage was to get hoarded money – money hoarded because there was nothing on which to spend it – into circulation and to do so before prices were freed and massive inflation let loose. In the second stage prices would be gradually freed and interest rates raised, but the prices of basic foods would remain controlled. In the third and longest stage (days 250–400) half the manufacturing and service enterprises would be sold and a stock exchange and other exchanges would be established. Finally, all these measures would be accelerated and 90 per cent of retail business would be put up for sale. This programme was opposed by, among others, the prime minister Nicolai Ryzhkov on the grounds that the time limits were too rigid and unreal; that more palliatives were needed for the poorer classes, for pensioners and students; and that the bureaucratic machinery for doing so much so quickly did not exist with the result that there would be more chaos than reform. The objectors argued also that the economic disruption which they foresaw would add to the anarchic forces which were threatening to dissolve the Union. Gorbachev, who seemed to favour first one side and then the other and who did not want to lose his prime minister, tried to force the discordant groups to find a compromise. He failed. The Supreme Soviet preferred to give him emergency powers, shuffling off to the presidency the task of finding an answer and imposing it by decree. The outcome was a new plan, duly endorsed by the Supreme Soviet but so vague as to leave the future not only hazardously obscure but apparently beyond the control of the government. There were rival schemes but no coherent policy.

The political and economic transformation of the USSR was bedevilled by the simultaneous upsurge of dissidence, amounting in places to separatism. Of the USSR's fifteen republics (see Map 1.2, p. 8) only three were preponderantly Slav: the Russian (which included Siberia), the Ukraine and White Russia (Byelorussia). Ethnic Slavs accounted for not much more than half the population, and the solidarity of the Ukraine with other Slavs could not be taken for granted since the Ukraine had a history of oscillating between subjection to Moscow (or Warsaw or Vilna) and bouts of asserting its independence up to and into the twentieth century. The remaining twelve republics – three Baltic republics, Moldavia, three in the Caucasus and five in central Asia – all had grievances and disruptive separatist aspirations. Discontent in the Muslim republics surfaced in riots in 1986 in Uzbekistan, notorious for corruption in the days of Brezhnev and his son-in-law Yuri Churbanov. In Georgia, where an earlier upheaval in 1972 had brought Eduard Shevardnadze to power, anti-Russian demonstrations were suppressed by Moscow with considerable, probably unnecessary, force which prompted speculation that army officers hostile to Gorbachev had deliberately inflamed the situation at a moment when Gorbachev was out of the USSR. There was also endemic conflict between Georgians and Abkhazian Turks in Georgia. Elections in 1990 produced a victory for partisans of independence. In the two neighbouring republics Azerbaijanis (Turks) and Armenians fought each other, particularly over control of the mainly Armenian district of Nagorno Karabakh which was an enclave in the Azerbaijani republic: both sides blamed Moscow for their troubles. Turkish peoples in the Caucasus, as well as the more remote, if more numerous, Turks in central Asia were natural cynosures for pan-Turanians in Turkey who dreamed dreams of a revived Turkish empire or confederation. In the Moldavian republic the extreme unpleasantness of Ceaucescu's Romania deterred the Romanians of the republic from agitating for reunion with Romania, but within the republic three separate groups – Romanian, Russian, Gagauz Turks – demonstrated for independence from one another or the USSR. There were other discontented minorities. The Crimean Tatars, deported *en masse* during the Second World War, had been cleared in 1967 of the charge of collaboration with the German invaders but their autonomous province (allotted to the Ukraine in 1954) had not been restored and some 300,000–400,000 of them remained in exile from their ancestral lands.

The most urgent problem arose in the Baltic republics which began to glimpse the recovery of their prewar independence and to claim it. In Lithuania the Sajudis movement came into being in 1988 and, like similar movements in Czechoslovakia, Hungary and elsewhere, evolved from a popular movement into a political party. Its aims were simple: independence. Together with Latvia and Estonia, Lithuania had been overrun by Stalin's armies in 1944–45 and incorporated into the USSR. Many Lithuanians had fled westward, others – perhaps a quarter of a million – were deported or killed. In the Lithuanian republic thus formed, Poles and Russians came to number a fifth of the population of 3.7 million. (In Latvia and Estonia, with 2.7 and 1.5 million, Russians numbered about one third.) Economically Lithuania's chief features were, on the one hand, an exportable agricultural surplus and, on the other, all but total dependence on the USSR for oil and gas. The economy as a whole suffered from the malformation, stultification and corruption which characterized the USSR. In 1990 elections were held for the republic's Supreme Soviet. Candidates approved by Sajudis won a majority which immediately declared Lithuania independent, repeating the similar declaration of 1918. To Gorbachev this was a challenge which had to be resisted because of its repercussions not only in the other Baltic republics but in all parts of the USSR. He was prepared to give the republics greater freedom in a relaxed USSR, to give them the constitutional right to secede, but he was not prepared to accept a unilateral act which could destroy the Union before he had had time to reform it. In addition, the Baltic republics formed part of an overall defensive system which neither Gorbachev nor his military chiefs could afford to dismantle in a hurry. Gorbachev sent troops into Lithuania and imposed an economic blockade which forced Lithuania's new leaders to moderate, if not their aims, at least their timetable – but not before they had found allies in the heart of the Union, in Moscow itself, where Gorbachev's principal Russian antagonist Boris Yeltsin had won control of the vast Russian republic (RSFSR) and was pressing Gorbachev for more radical economic and political measures and also for greater autonomy for the republics. In the second most important republic, the Ukraine, separatists turned the government out of office and asserted rights of autonomy barely distinguishable from independence – for example, a refusal to allow Ukrainians in the armed forces to serve outside the republic without its government's consent.

The Soviet Union was simultaneously threatened with economic chaos, political discord and constitutional disintegration. Its unique political force, the Communist Party, was becoming disowned by many of its chiefs and more of its followers. Radicals like Yeltsin wanted to transform the Union from an association of republics linked by a constitution into an association of states loosely linked by a treaty and were prepared to use economic sanctions to coerce the central government. The non-Slavs wanted to go further, whether immediately as did the Baltic peoples or more circumspectly as the remoter and economically more dependent Asians might be forced to do. The Union created in 1923, six years after the Bolshevik revolution, was ceasing to be and Gorbachev himself risked being squeezed into impotence between a conservative reaction powered by the armed forces and the KGB and on the other hand champions of drastic economic and political reform epitomized by Yeltsin.

2 JAPAN

The postwar history of Japan is an object lesson in what international politics are really about. In 1945 Japan was prostrate, with its military power annihilated and its national symbol, the emperor, nullified. Within a generation Japan regained the status of a great power and it did so not by replacing its armouries but by rebuilding its industries, regaining its foreign trade and reconstituting its reserves of cash and currencies. Only after these achievements did it begin to contemplate and then to refashion its lost military might. It was the one power in the world that could be referred to as a great power but had no nuclear capacity and it was evidently more powerful than some powers – Britain, France, India – which had made nuclear explosions.

Furthermore Japan in this period lacked not only the military trappings with which states are wont to make their mark in the world; it was also conspicuously short of primary resources. It had no – or virtually no – oil, uranium, aluminium or nickel; very little coal, iron ore, copper or natural gas; only half its requirements of lead and zinc. These shortages were made all the more acute by the great expansion of industry, an expansion which paradoxically was both essential to Japan's recovery and yet exacerbated its dependence on foreign materials. This need to secure primary products, whether by participating in exploration or by establishing commercial-political control in the places where they lay, became a major guideline of Japanese foreign policy.

In the immediate postwar years the most striking things about Japan were the physical devastation of a number of its cities, unemployment somewhere between 10 and 15 million, the almost total inadequacy of ordinary means of transport, and the American occupation.

The American share in the defeat of Japan had been so overwhelming that the United States could reduce postwar allied co-operation in the occupation to a not very polite figment. Two bodies were created: the Allied Council for Japan, located in Tokyo and consisting of the United States, the USSR, China and a representative of Britain and the Pacific members of the Commonwealth; and the Far Eastern Commission, located in Washington, with eleven members. But in fact Japan was

2.1 Japan and its neighbours, showing the disputed territories ruled by the supreme commander, who was General MacArthur and whose ways of treating associates, subjects and problems were a cross between those of the shoguns and Lord Curzon. Retribution took the form of disarmament, demilitarization and trials of war criminals. Then came a new constitution, administrative and social reforms, and attempts to alter the industrial and cultural patterns of the country on the basis, however, of the retention of imperial rule and the emperor himself (who lived on until 1989). The MacArthur régime was an exemplar of autocratic efficiency with an increasing touch of bene-volence as rehabilitations took the place of demilitarization. The new constitution, drafted and imposed by the occupiers, was to a large extent backward-looking in that its authors tried to identify and eliminate factors in Japanese history that had led Japan into error. The emperor was cut down to human size, over 200,000 (mostly military) persons were barred from public life, the prime minister and all his colleagues were to be civilians, the great financial conglomerates or *zaibatsu* were to be broken up. More forward-looking was the American programme of land reform, again imposed from outside and one of the few examples of its kind in the twentieth century anywhere in the world to eventuate in practice as well as on paper.

None of this stood in the way of revival when the opportunity came, and much of it was helpful. The purge may have eliminated a number of able men but it cleared the way to the top for many more who, without the purge, would not have got there so quickly: some European bureaucracies and businesses would have benefited from such a purge. The elimination of big, often absentee, landowners facilitated the modernization and re-equipment of agriculture, established a rich rural sector alongside the reviving industrial and commercial sectors, and gave Japan the efficient food production which was vital for so densely populated a country. At the same time a new abortion law halved the birthrate over a period of five years and stabilized the population. As in Germany, the Americans were quickly converted from exacting reparations to repairing the Japanese economy, first in the general Cold War context of anti-communism and then more specifically and far more vigorously by the Korean War. Above all war in Asia – the Korean War and later the wars in Vietnam – gave Japan the opportunity and the boost which transformed its fortunes in an astonishingly short time. Like the United States during the Second World War, Japan became an arsenal of war and a war-fuelled economy with the added advantage that it was not itself a belligerent. Europe in the same period saw nothing like the revival of Japan because hot war is better than cold war for making the wheels go round. What happened was no miracle but an unexpected opportunity allied with the determination and discipline of the Japanese people; the autocratic rule of General MacArthur, who permitted no interference by strikes or unions to the process of making goods and money; a form of central planning which regulated priorities and the allocation of resources without seeking to control operations; and a harsh capitalist competition which sent the weak to the wall but encouraged that adventurousness and vision which had characterized the nineteenth-century English merchant and industrialist before he was turned into a conservative twentieth-century financier. Finally, it was a condition of Japan's success that its new leaders should co-operate closely with the Americans who ruled in Tokyo and Washington.

'New' is hardly the word to describe the first of Japan's postwar prime ministers, Shigeru Yoshida, who was already 70 when he was installed in 1948 in the office which he held for six years, but Yoshida understood the constraints and the possibilities and had no inhibitions about tackling Japan's alarming postwar inflation by the most familiar deflationary devices, killing off weak businesses and adding to the unemployed. His overall purpose was to restore Japan's power in the world but not the power of the military in Japan. He struck lucky. The Korean War came (1950–53) and prosperity bloomed. MacArthur was removed by Truman but Dulles took charge of the business of turning the occupation of a defeated foe into a Japanese–American alliance. In 1951 the United States organized a peace treaty which was signed by the two countries and forty-seven others – the USSR, China, India and Burma being among the absentees. By the treaty of Portsmouth Japan renounced Korea, which it had ruled since 1910; Taiwan and the Pescadores, which had been Japanese for over half a century; the islands in the Pacific which had been administered under mandate since the end of the First World War, after being seized from Germany; all its rights and claims in China and Antarctica; and southern Sakhalin and the Kuriles. The status of these last territories remained ambiguous because the USSR, which had occupied them in 1945, was not a party to the treaty. They were formed in 1947 into a distract or *oblast* of the Russian Soviet Federal Socialist Republic: the island of Sakhalin, stretching northward from Japan's northern tip, runs offshore of the RSFSR for nearly 970 km; the Kurile archipelago, comprising thirty comparatively large volcanic islands and as many smaller ones, runs north east from Japan to the Kamchatka peninsula. The Ryuku islands (including Okinawa) and the Bonins, which had been annexed by Japan at the end of the nineteenth century and were occupied by the United States during and after the Second World War, were gradually recovered by Japan in 1968–72 subject to the continuing presence of American troops and military installations.

Japan's territorial losses were considerable but it was not required to pay any war reparations and it suffered nothing like the bisection of Germany's heartlands. On the same day as the signing of the peace treaty Japan and the United States signed a security treaty which gave the latter the right to station forces throughout Japan for purposes defined as the maintainance of international peace and security in the Far East, the defence of Japan against external aggression and the suppression of rebellion or disorders instigated by an outside power. No such rights were to be accorded to any other state except with American consent. The American occupation came formally to an end in April 1952. What had begun as a crusade to make Japan safe for democracy in the western style was superseded by the recruitment of Japan to the anti-communist side in the Cold War.

Japan's constitution forbade the creation of armed forces but this ban had already been partially circumvented in 1950 by the creation of a National Police Reserve and Self Defence Forces which looked and lived very like an army. These forces gradually expanded to the comparatively modest figure of 250,000 where they stayed. Defence expenditure was kept below 1 per cent of GNP (which was however rising steeply) and around 6 to 7 per cent of government expenditure, again a comparatively modest figure. By the seventies there were the beginnings of a debate about whether Japan should go nuclear: its weight in the world pointed affirmatively in that direction but there were special political as well as the constitutional obstacles. Japan signed the Partial Test Ban Treaty – although this was an act of supererogation if the constitution were to be taken at its face value – and public opinion in the land of Hiroshima and Nagasaki was ultra-sensitive to the exercise of the nuclear option. An incident in 1954 had dramatized these feelings. In March of that year a Japanese fishing vessel, the *Fukuryu Maru* or *Fortunate Dragon*, a few miles outside an area closed to fishing on account of American nuclear tests on the island of Bikini was caught in the fall-out of an H-bomb. Before this terrifying fact was realized the *Fukuryu Maru* had returned to port and sold part of its catch. Panic followed. One member of the crew died. Later the United States paid $2 million by way of damages or conscience money for this terrible accident. It also had to pay a political price as Japanese opinion gathered hostility to the United States and to Yoshida as the symbol of the Japanese–American alliance.

This episode coincided with the conclusion in March 1954 of new defence, financial and commercial agreements between the United States and Japan, which included a Mutual Defence Agreement providing for mutual assistance against communism and an expansion and reorganization of Japan's pseudo-military forces. In April Yoshida, whose régime was disfigured by scandals as well as charges of undue subservience to Washington, suffered a parliamentary defeat which he refused to recognize as such. He set out on a tour of western Europe, Canada and the United States, but on his return rifts in his own party had grown too large for repair and in December he was replaced by an old rival, Ichiro Hatoyama, whose foreign minister Mamoru Shigemitsu expressed the intention to restore normal relations with the USSR and China. But Hatoyama did not last long and was succeeded by Nobusuke Kishi, another of the Liberal Democratic Party's numerous but not harmonious chiefs. Kishi preferred to pursue the policy, initiated by his predecessors, of restoring relations with Japan's former enemies in South-east Asia rather than the Hatoyama–Shigemitsu approach to the USSR and China which, in view of Japan's continuing attachment to the United States, was still too hot a potato. Kishi also negotiated in 1960 a revised version of the Security Treaty of 1951, but the new treaty – and especially a clause making it last for ten years – was unpopular. The government was accused of involving Japan in the Cold War by allowing American nuclear weapons to be held on Japanese territory. This criticism was given point by the notorious flight of the U-2 reconnaissance aircraft which was shot down by the Russians in May. There were disorderly scenes in the Japanese parliament and outside it, and although the new treaty was ratified in June a projected visit by Eisenhower had to be cancelled and Kishi resigned before the end of the year.

The sixties were the years when Japan impressed itself on the rest of the world by annual growth rates of 10 per cent or more; when the alternation of boom and slump which had characterized the fifties seemed to have gone for good; when the new shape of Japanese industry with its emphasis on heavy goods and chemicals in place of textiles became apparent; when Japan's investment and performance in the most advanced technology captivated the world; and when its admission to the ranks of the OECD publicly designated it as one of the world's economic heavyweights. In 1962 Japan concluded with China a five-year commercial agreement on a barter basis. The vastness of China and its population mesmerized some Japanese industrialists but the government remained inhibited by Washington's hostility to China and in any case the present gains to be made in trade with China were small. Japan's trade with Taiwan was substantially larger and the 1962 agreement was no more than a gesture towards a vague future. More concretely Japan embarked on a policy of creating a region of economic co-operation in South-east Asia and the Pacific rimlands. Already in the fifties Japan had paved the way with agreements for the payment of reparations to Burma (1956), the Philippines (1956) and Indonesia (1958), and in 1967 the prime minister, Eisaku Sato, undertook a major tour of South-east Asian capitals, preceded and followed by visits to South Korea, Australia and New Zealand. He was the first Japanese prime minister to visit these last two countries. Japan's course was not easy. Besides being a former imperialist aggressor with an unforgotten reputation for peculiar cruelty, Japan was a rapidly developing country in a largely underdeveloped region. Sato lavished loans for development and, in the case of Vietnam, for postwar reconstruction, while by supporting ventures such as the Asian Development Bank and the Agricultural Fund for South-east Asia he hoped to stress Japan's pacific amiability in contrast not only to its past but also to the militaristic policies of the United States evinced by the Seato alliance and the war in Vietnam. Japan was at pains to supply its poorer neighbours with high-grade capital and consumer goods rather than drain them of their natural resources in the classical colonial mode. Further afield, in Australia, Japan became the leading purveyor of investment funds exceeding the sum of British, American and German funds; Australia was by the mid-sixties importing more goods from Japan than from Britain and selling more of its mineral and agricultural products (including wool) to Japan than to any other country. In its smaller way New Zealand was turning in the same direction. Even Canada, another Pacific state, although more firmly fixed in the North American economy, considerably increased its trade with Japan and its loans to and investment in the South-east Asian sector of what was becoming a vast Asian–Pacific economic zone dominated by Japan. The achievements of the 1960s were fittingly crowned by a spectacular demonstration in Tokyo in 1970 called Expo 70.

But shortly after Expo 70 Japan suffered two serious setbacks. Its industrial recovery and commercial expansion had depended on a strong dollar (which made Japanese exports to its largest market exceptionally profitable) and cheap oil. In 1971 Nixon devalued the dollar and in 1973 war in the Middle East created an economic crisis in Japan. Japan relied entirely on imported oil, 85 per cent of which was imported from the Middle East. The war so reduced supply that Japanese stocks were reduced to a few days' consumption and when the flow was resumed by urgent, even grovelling, diplomacy the price had quadrupled. Ruthless economies cut consumption by half but many businesses went under, unemployment rose sharply and the employed had to accept strict wage restraint. A second oil shock occurred a few years later with the fall of the shah in Iran in 1979 but in the interval Japan, uniquely among industrialized countries, had regained its economic health. It did so by abandoning old and moribund industries without compunction and by experimenting and investing in automation and robots, learning from (mainly) American researchers, applying the lessons with a massive investment of funds provided to industry at cheap rates by the Japanese government, and extensive retraining of the workforce again with government funds. In the next decade the same combination of industrialists, experts and government seized for Japan the world's leading place in electronics. In the same period the United States was applying its knowledge and its funds in going to the moon and creating huge, but largely useless, armaments.

Japan's prosperity made it a voracious consumer of the world's products: one estimate in the seventies had it that by 1981 Japan would need one-tenth of the world's total exports and in oil more than one-tenth of the world's total production. But Japan had no sure way of securing its needs. Britain in the nineteenth century and then the United States had had a similar problem and had solved it by a variety of means which go under the name of imperialism. The essence of imperialism from this viewpoint was not the domination of an area for glory's sake but domination in order to secure materials, whether by taking them, or by ensuring that the producers go on producing them and not something else, or by encouraging a bigger output. The means included investment and so partial or total ownership of minerals, crops or manufacturing enterprises. Japan had plenty of money to invest but there were difficulties about investing it. Apart from its specially delicate standing in the region the whole idea of foreign investment had become suspect. However welcome investment funds might be in purely financial terms, there was a wide and nervous awareness of possible conflicts of interest between investor and recipient and a legacy of hostility to the foreign investor who was presumed to be distorting and retarding a developing economy and indeed to be intent on doing so. In the special case of oil Japan's problem was aggravated by the fact that most known investment opportunities had been pre-empted by the United States or western Europeans. Nevertheless Japan, accelerating in the seventies a trend begun in the sixties, placed considerable sums abroad, particularly in Malaysia, Indonesia, Thailand and the Philippines. Anxious to reduce its dependence on Middle Eastern oil it engaged in exploration or investment in Indonesia, New Guinea, Australia and Nigeria. Japan's vulnerability in terms of oil was compounded by the fact that Middle Eastern oil bound for Japan passed through the narrow Malacca Strait and so was at the mercy of any unfriendly power in Malaya or Sumatra. The oil hunger of these years focused attention on certain small islands in the South China Sea: the Paracels, seized by China in 1974 by evicting a small South Vietnamese force, and the Spratlys further south which were claimed by China, Vietnam, the Philippines, the Netherlands and France and some of which were occupied by China in 1988.

Besides his devaluations of the dollar in 1971 Nixon shocked Japan when, without warning to Tokyo, he announced that he had accepted an invitation to visit China. The Japanese government, whose policies had been moulded and constricted by the American alliance and by American policies which, in Asia, were based on hostility to China, was seized with equal astonishment and resentment. What seemed to the rest of the world a sensible move to take some heat out of an overheated quarrel betokened in Japan a reversal of alliances not unconnected with commercial and economic rivalry. Japan feared not only a political *volte face* by Washington but also the closing of American markets to Japanese goods, partly at the instance of the

American textile lobby but more generally too in order to check the big Japanese surplus in the balance of trade between the two countries. Proposals by Japan to restrict Japanese exports to the United States had produced no result and Nixon then took unilateral action, including a 10 per-cent surcharge designed primarily to hit Japanese trade. Japanese anger was increased when it became apparent that the rate of growth in 1971 had been reduced to 6 per cent, and this interruption in Japan's expansion was blamed on American policy and ill will. The undervalued yen, a source of complaint from all Japan's trading partners, was allowed to float in August 1971 and was in consequence revalued by 16 per cent by the end of the year. Relations between Japan and the United States became, temporarily, bad. They were not sensibly improved by the return of Okinawa to Japanese sovereignty as the agreement to do this set no limit on the use of the island by American troops and was imprecise about its use as a nuclear base. The emperor visited the United States, his first journey outside Japan since 1921, but the visit was treated as a curiosity rather than a political event. Japan joined the United States' attempt to get the United Nations to retain Taiwan as a separate member when China was admitted, but the attempt failed and Japan's part in it seemed to many Japanese to be misplaced loyalty to a shifty ally. Nevertheless the drama of Nixon's visit to Beijing exceeded its immediate consequences and neither Tokyo nor Washington wished their economic disagreements to degenerate into serious political conflict. New trade agreements were signed in 1972 and in September President Nixon and Prime Minister Eisaku Sato met at Honolulu and Japan promised to make massive purchases of American (and other foreign) goods to redress the imbalance in its foreign trade. Japan's balance of payments and reserves rose again in 1972.

Sato did not long survive the Honolulu meeting. Brother to Kishi and no less pro-American he had suffered a serious decline in favour, in the country and in his party, as a result of the buffetings of the previous year and he gave way to Kakuei Tanaka who immediately went to Beijing and restored diplomatic relations with China. This was no reversal of policy, for Tanaka was doing only what the United States had done the previous year and many other countries were hastening to copy. China was neither a possible ally for Japan nor a substitute for the United States as a trading partner; nor was Tanaka markedly pro-Chinese. He was in fact too unpopular to carry through new policies. He retired temporarily into the background during 1972 and was forced to resign in 1974 on being implicated in scandals surrounding the bribery of high government personages by the Lockheed Aviation Corporation. His successor Takeo Miki survived only until 1976 when the Liberal Democratic Party (LDP) lost for the first time its overall majority in parliament. Miki's vociferous condemnation of corruption –

by implication, of his rivals – made him few friends in the party and the 71-year-old Takeo Fukuda took his place. But Miki got his revenge two years later when the party deposed Fukuda and installed Masayoshi Ohira. In an election in 1979 Ohira disappointed the party but survived the vengeful intrigues of its other chieftains for a short space. In 1980 the party found yet another leader in Zenko Suzuki. Throughout these baronial feudings the party retained its dominant position. What made Japan uniquely strange in this generation was the combination of its worldwide economic thrust with static, geriatric political leadership embodied in the LDP.

That direction continued through the next decade in spite of rebuffs: a decline in electoral favour, severe financial scandals, conflict over fiscal reforms, some sparring with the United States, and a diminution of Japan's hitherto unquenchable economic expansion. Elections in 1983, which registered some reverses for the LDP, were followed three years later by a triumphant campaign under the leadership of Yasuhiro Nakasone who was in consequence accorded an extended hold on the premiership. He was succeeded at the end of 1987 by Noboru Takeshita who, unlike Nakasone, succeeded in imposing on an unwilling parliament a series of reforms to an obsolete tax system – in particular an unpopular consumption tax (3 per cent) – with the aim of redressing the fiscal balance to the advantage of the urban middle class. Simultaneously scandals exploded over the exceptionally lavish bribery of political parties and personalities by the real-estate conglomerate Recourse Cosmos, and in 1989 Takeshita was forced to resign. His immediate successor quickly fell victim to scandals of a more personal nature but the party succeeded in finding in Toshiki Kaifu a prime minister – the thirteenth since the end of the American occupation – sufficiently reputable to hold at bay the challenge of the Japanese Socialist Party (JSP) led by Takako Doi. In elections in 1989 the LDP lost for the first time its majority in the upper house but since only half of the seats were in issue it remained the largest party, with 109 seats out of 252. The JSP won 67 seats. In the next year the LDP retained its majority in the lower house. Kaifu, more durable than had been expected, rebuilt the party's traditional base among farmers, small businesses and women, with the help of a new boom and continuing surpluses in overseas trade.

The comparatively extrovert Nakasone had been second only to Thatcher in praise of Ronald Reagan, but he also visited Moscow, took the initiative in soothing anti-Japanese susceptibilities in South Korea, increased Japan's aid to the Third World and cancelled some of its more intractable debts. Positive changes in external affairs were, however, small. A soothing speech by Gorbachev in Vladivostok in 1986 and two visits by Shevardnadze to Tokyo in 1986 and 1988 produced no more than talk about a willingness to talk about a formal resolution of the disputed Northern Territories. In response to American criticism of its trading practices and threats of retaliation Japan modified some import barriers and eased some of the obstacles in the way of foreign bids for construction contracts in Japan, but the balance of trade between the two countries remained above $50,000 million. Under the Omnibus Trade and Competitiveness Act of 1988 the US Congress gave the president authority to designate foreign countries as 'unfair traders' and required him to negotiate the removal of unfair practices and, if he failed, to retaliate. These measures were an indication of persistent American irritation with Japan and also of the fear that Japan's surging pre-eminence in industries from automobiles to computers was being extended into super-conductors and the defence industries. But so long as the Reagan and Bush administrations failed to balance government spending by cutting programmes or raising taxes they remained dependent on heavy borrowing, and since Japan was much the biggest lender American threats of commercial retaliation had limited substance.

Japan's relatively disarmed condition held great advantages and great risks. On the credit side was an enormous saving: even as late as 1980 Japan's defence spending was less than 1 per cent of GNP (but Japan's GNP was not only one of the largest in the world but also growing by 10 per cent a year). It was also a significant factor in Japan's phenomenal industrial success, since the absence of pressures from military quarters enabled Japan to plan its industrial production and training without the distortions introduced – in the United States, for example, and the USSR – by military exigencies. Within Japan's military-industrial complex the emphasis was more industrial than military. Japan was naturally reluctant to change a pattern which was making it the world's leading economic power, overtaking the United States in much the same way as the United States had overtaken Britain a hundred years earlier. By 1980 Japan had not only surpassed West Germany and Switzerland in many of their leading products but was making more steel and cars than the United States and, by installing more modern equipment, had achieved twice the American output per man.

But these triumphs of planning, education and performance rested upon the American alliance which provided the security behind which Japan's energies could be concentrated on the creation of wealth. The efficacy of that alliance was called in question by the American defeat in Vietnam and by Washington's evident incapacity (sometimes interpreted as failure of will) to redeem its hostages in Iran. Self-defence, militarily adequate in the context of the alliance, had to be re-examined. It was in effect reinterpreted. Already in the fifties the concept of self-defence had been held to include the pursuit of an enemy to his bases and attacks on those bases. It was also extended to the protection of vital sea routes and, in 1980, to joint naval exercises with other powers. Self-defence was adjudged to be a relative term whose meaning changed with the development of an enemy's military technology and one's own strategic needs. Although Japan's revulsion against nuclear arms was confirmed by its adherence in 1970 to the Nuclear Non-Proliferation Treaty of 1968, the passing of the generation which had known war and defeat was marked by growing support for larger defence budgets. The crisis caused by Iraq's annexation of Kuwait in 1990 gave a precise focus to the debate about Japan's responsibilities in world affairs. A purely financial contribution to the international muster against Iraq seemed unheroic, but a military contribution was unconstitutional and unpopular and Kaifu was obliged to abandon an attempt to change the constitution to permit it.

Japan's commanding position in the world depended on a novel use of economic strength, little of which was invested in armaments. Sensational boom was checked in the eighties when economic growth relapsed to 3–4 per cent a year, but Japan remained a formidable financial and industrial power able, if it so wished, to conduct aggressive foreign policies through buying and lending instead of through physical threat or bludgeon.

3 CHINA

THE TRIUMPH OF MAO

In 1949, a little over a quarter of a century after its birth, the Communist Party of China won the ancient capital city of Beijing. A movement had become a government. The defeated Kuomintang was reduced to the island of Taiwan where its leader Jiang Kaishek, like the last of the Ming emperors 300 years earlier, clothed himself with imperial pretences reminiscent of the French nobles and Italian bankers who wandered round western Europe in the later Middle Ages calling themselves emperors of Byzantium. The new lord of China, Mao Zedong was able to declare in January 1950 with only slight exaggeration that all China was his except Tibet.

The vast lands and imperial traditions which fell to Mao after the Second World War had been going begging since just before the First. The decline of the last (Manchu) dynasty, which had exposed China to foreign intervention and had almost occasioned its partition in the latter part of the nineteenth century, had culminated in the revolution of 1911. Revolutionary groups and secret societies, partly indigenous and partly fomented among overseas Chinese, effected the disintegration of the *ancien régime*. Faced thereafter with the task of re-establishing the cohesion, dignity and power of China they failed, so that fifty years later China was still potentially a great power but not actually one.

The most notable of these successor groups was that of Sun Yat-sen (died 1925), a nationalist, a democrat and a socialist who wanted to reform China through his instrument the Kuomintang. The Kuomintang established a government in the southern capital of Nanking but it never succeeded in bringing the whole country under its obedience. The collapse of the old régime was followed, especially in the north, by the appearance of war lords who created autonomous fiefs for themselves and engaged in civil wars. Even in the south, where the Kuomintang imposed a degree of order and stability, the huge tasks of administrative reform and modernization were tackled but not mastered.

The Kuomintang looked around for outside help and accepted from the new and no less revolutionary government of the USSR the advisory services of Michael Borodin. Under the pressure of circumstances the Kuomintang began to adopt in its fight against the war lords some of the methods (the organization of the party and of party–state relations), though not the doctrines, of European communism, and it also entered into an alliance with the Chinese Communist Party which had been founded in Shanghai in 1922. The communists consisted of small groups in certain southern provinces. They became a part of the Kuomintang under the overall leadership of Jiang Kaishek, but disputes between communist and other Kuomintang leaders (and between left and right non-communist factions within the Kuomintang) were endemic. There was also confusion among the communists themselves because communist committees in Shanghai gave ill-judged instructions to leaders active in the countryside, and still more because Moscow attempted to direct matters without adequate knowledge of Chinese history and conditions. At one moment Moscow had different emissaries in China advocating incompatible policies. In this atmosphere Mao Zedong gradually became one of the principal leaders in the countryside, often at odds with his superiors in Shanghai on political and military tactics and himself still evolving and changing his own ideas on these subjects. Disputes between communists and non-communists led to fighting. In 1931 the Japanese attack in Manchuria forced Jiang Kaishek to send troops to the north, but the confusion in the communists' ranks prevented them from taking advantage of this distraction of the non-communists and in 1934 they were decisively defeated as a result of adopting ill-chosen tactics which Mao had argued against. The communists set out on their strenuous and myth-making Long March from south-eastern China, first westward and then northward to the province of Yenan in the far north-west, where they preserved their movement and bided their time. It was during the Long March that Mao rose to ultimate authority. He had been moving away from the classic Marxist strategy of achieving power by fighting the battles of the industrial proletariat and towards annexing communism to peasant indignation (periodically a mighty subversive force in Chinese history); he proposed to set up a small peasant republic and to create peasant armies which would one day be strong enough to seize towns.

Meanwhile the Kuomintang, having disposed of the communists and made headway against the war lords (it took Peking in 1928 and secured Manchuria the next year by agreement with General Chang Hsueh-liang, the Young Marshal), was attacked by Japan, first in Manchuria in 1931 and then in China proper in 1937. From this date until 1945 the Kuomintang and the communists were rivals for the honours of effecting the revival of China as a great power and for the prize of ruling it after the Japanese had been defeated. The communist remnants which had reached Yenan grew rapidly into an army of about 100,000, attracting recruits from the peasantry and from youth generally on a nationalist anti-Japanese ticket. In 1941 the Japanese attack on the United States at Pearl Harbor merged this Far Eastern war into a general war which temporarily overlaid China's civil discords. The Kuomintang acquired powerful allies, but its fortunes were not destined to revive. It had failed to arrest economic collapse, its leadership remained narrow and cliquish, its administration became corrupt, high-handed and over-reliant on secret police, and finally its armies disintegrated. By contrast the communists rose in popular esteem. Their sojourn in the wilderness had given them glamour and concealed the seamy side of their own methods of rule. They had the reputation of fighting the Japanese more seriously than the Kuomintang and when the war ended they were ready to return from the outskirts to the centre. Only a few years later they were the government of China.

When Jiang Kaishek was chased out of China a generation of civil conflict came to an end and the communists were presented with the opportunity to do what no faction had been able to do since the fall of the empire, and what the empire itself had failed in and been reproached for: to make China strong and healthy enough to maintain its integrity and independence. In the past, threats to the integrity of China had come from the imperial powers of western Europe sailing across the seas, from the Russians approaching over land, and from the Japanese. By 1945 the western European powers were no longer in a position to menace anybody in the Far East, and Japan had been all but annihilated. The Russians, however, had just reappeared on the scene, while the Americans, traditional upholders of the integrity of China against interlopers, were despairing of the Kuomintang and were about to revert to an Asian policy centred on Japan such as they had pursued at the opening of the century.

The history of continuous Russian expansion into Asia begins after the Crimean War. That defeat in Europe inaugurated essays in liberalism at home and in Far Eastern adventure, both of which were sporadic. The tsars were more or less permanently preoccupied with the problems of Poland, the Balkans and the Straits, but there was also a party at St Petersburg which made a speciality of the Far East. The 1860s and 1870s were a period of expansion; the great Russian pro-consul Muraviev established the Amur and Maritime provinces in 1858 and 1860 respectively; Vladivostok was founded in 1861; Sakhalin was acquired (but Alaska sold); the Kazakhs and the central Asian Khanates were subjected. By the eighties Russia, having reached the borders of Persia and Afghanistan, had been brought face to face with the British in India, while further north a warm water Pacific port and a share in the China trade stimulated imperial and financial imaginations.

SOVIET UNION

MONGOL

Urumqi

AFGHANISTAN

PAKISTAN

TIBET

Lhasa

NEPAL

BHUTAN

INDIA

BANGLADESH

MYANMAR
(BURMA)

0   500   1000 km

THAILAN

3.1 China and neighbouring countries

War between the Japanese and the Chinese in Korea in 1894–95 brought Japan considerable gains (including Taiwan, the Pescadores and, temporarily, the Shantung peninsula and Port Arthur) and served noticed of the decline of Chinese power. Russia, France and Germany intervened in defence of China, although Britain, suspicious of the Russian advance in Asia, now began its pro-Japanese policy as a counter. The Russians, having with the French helped China to pay its war indemnity to Japan, entered into an alliance with China, took Port Arthur and planned the Chinese Eastern and South Manchurian railways. The Russians and the Japanese were now vying with each other for Manchuria. In 1904 Japan attacked Port Arthur and in the ensuing Russo–Japanese War the Russians were defeated and forced back into Manchuria and Mongolia. Japan's standing in Asia and the world was immensely increased and the Russian advance across the top of Asia was checked by a Japanese counter-force in Manchuria. The First World War temporarily eliminated Russian power, effected no Chinese revival, distracted other Europeans from Asian affairs, and left Japan in a situation where, far from curbing the Russians, it had itself to be curbed – and could be curbed by no power except the United States. The Russians recovered positions in Outer Mongolia and Central Asia in the twenties and came once more into conflict with the Japanese in Manchuria in the thirties, but they did not seriously return to the struggle for Manchuria until the final week of the Second World War.

For most of the war years Stalin was too much occupied with the Germans to pay much attention to Asia, let alone intervene there. The USSR had signed a neutrality pact with Japan in 1941 and before Pearl Harbor Japan sought and received assurances that the Russians would abide by this pact. Up to the Tehran conference of 1943 Stalin asked for nothing in the east, being in no position to ask for prizes until he was ready to give a helping hand against Japan. At the Moscow conference in October 1944 there were hints of a change in the Russian attitude, and at Yalta in 1945 Stalin's terms were set out and accepted by allies who were anxious to avoid quarrels, still overrated Japan's will and capacity to fight on, and were – except for a few initiates – ignorant of the nuclear weapons about to be used. Stalin asked his allies to reverse the verdict of the Russo–Japanese War of 1904–5 and also to guarantee him certain positions at the expense not of Japan but of China. The positions lost by the Russians in Manchuria and Sakhalin in 1905 were to be restored; the Kuriles were to go to the USSR too; and the USSR's virtual annexation of Outer Mongolia was to be recognized.

Stalin's policy in Asia was to nibble at the Chinese circumference and to prevent the establishment of any powerful central Chinese government. By declaring war on Japan he secured rights, and planted troops, in Manchuria. He was also able to carry off Japanese industrial plant, although not without incurring Chinese resentment. He had already engineered an anti–Chinese revolt in the Ili valley in Xinjiang (Sinkiang), where a secessionist republic of Eastern Turkestan sprouted under Russian protection in 1944. Outer Mongolia, nominally under Chinese suzerainty but effectively in the Russian sphere since 1921 and conceded to the USSR by the western allies at Yalta, was abandoned by the Chinese (who had no choice in the matter) by the Russo–Chinese treaty of August 1945. It was not recovered for China when Mao succeeded Jiang in 1949.

Stalin's declaration of war on Japan had one further notable consequence in the bisection of Korea, for when the Japanese surrendered it was arranged, as a matter of convenience, that Japanese forces north of the 38th parallel should surrender to the Russians and those south of that line to the Americans.

Russian intervention in the Far East was nicely timed. As the Russians knew, the Japanese were anxious for peace; they were taking soundings in Moscow in the hope of securing Russian mediation to end the war. The first nuclear bomb was dropped on 6 August 1945 on Hiroshima by the Americans who also knew that there was an active peace party in the Japanese cabinet. The Russian declaration of war followed two days later. On 9 August the second bomb was dropped on Nagasaki. Hostilities ended on 15 August (on which day the Russians signed their treaty with Jiang Kaishek).

Whereas Stalin wanted a weak China, worked to that end and may well have considered himself successful until the eve of his death, the Americans wanted a strong China, failed through no fault of their own during the years of transition from war to peace, and later began to see the prospect of China strong indeed but not at all to their liking.

American policies in the Far East, which began to take shape at the beginning of the century, were conditioned at the start by the acquisition of the Philippine Islands from Spain in 1898 and by suspicion of the European powers which, having turned most of Southeast Asia into colonial terrain, seemed about to carve up China too. With its interests and its moral sense in happy accord Washington claimed for itself any rights or privileges which any European power succeeded in extracting from the Chinese (the policy of the open door, that is, no commercial preferences between foreigners from different states) and stood up at the same time for the integrity and independence of China.

The American entry on this scene was unexpected and unpremeditated. The war of 1898 against Spain, which began in a muddled way in Cuba, had the incidental result of substituting American for Spanish rule in the Philippines. There ensued a considerable public debate on the politics and morality of expansionism, with the lurking background knowledge that if the United States did not assert its power in the Pacific, either the British or the

Germans or the Japanese would. This debate coincided with the manifest decline of China.

The British, alarmed by the trend towards annexations, leases and special commercial privileges for particular groups of foreigners, had sought American co-operation to put a stop to this colonialist rat race in China, but Washington was not at this point interested and the British thereupon entered a game which they despaired of preventing and began themselves to mark out enclaves and take leases.

The change in the American attitude came at the end of the nineteenth century with the appointment of John Hay as secretary of state. Hay's first set of notes, condemning spheres of influence and advocating the open door, had little practical effect, although they were popular in the United States; a second set, at the time of the Boxer rebellion and the allied intervention under German command to which the rebellion gave rise in 1900, testified to increasing American concern; so did Washington's mediation in the Russo–Japanese War and the signing of the treaty of Portsmouth on American soil. But it was some time before American and British policies were brought into harmony. Britain, seeking an ally in eastern waters and apparently rebuffed by the United States, had turned to Japan, while the United States was becoming increasingly the protector of China and the enemy at sea of Japan. This discrepancy continued, not without damage to Anglo–American relations, until after the First World War when the Washington treaties of 1921–22 in effect eliminated the Anglo–Japanese alliance, established a three-power naval ratio of 5:5:3, and secured a nine-power guarantee of the integrity of China and the open door. (At the London conference of 1930 the Japanese ratio was raised from 3 to 3.5.) In addition Secretary of State Charles Evans Hughes forced the Japanese to withdraw their troops from the Shantung peninsula and Siberia, but in the thirties the Americans, undecided whether strong action would check or strengthen the expansionist factions in Japanese politics, became less effective and there was little reaction from Washington to the Japanese conquest of Manchuria, the proclamation of the state of Manchukuo in 1932 or even to the Japanese occupation of Shanghai later in the same year. Japan withdrew from the Washington and London naval treaties at the end of 1936, claiming parity with the United States and Britain, and embarked on full-scale war with China in 1937. At the same time Japan challenged the European powers by propounding a 'new order' for all eastern Asia, and when the Europeans (western and Russian) had made it plain that they wanted no troubles in the east, Washington began to negotiate with Tokyo.

The outbreak of war in Europe in 1939 gave Japan a freer hand against China and new opportunities in South-east Asia. A new and more bellicose government, installed in 1940, decided to attack Indo–China as a first step but hoped to avoid American intervention. This government fell when Hitler attacked the USSR. The foreign minister, Yosuke Matsuoka, who wanted to join in the attack, was dropped, and General Hideki Tojo, who wanted to attack the United States, became the most influential member of the cabinet. He also became prime minister in October 1941 and gave the order for the attack on Pearl Harbor in December.

Until the turn of the tide in the middle of 1943 the Americans were in danger of being evicted from the Far East altogether, but the turning point of the Battle of Midway and the final victory over Japan in 1945 brought them back with a unique preponderance such as no power had ever previously enjoyed.

The war forced Washington to reconsider its Far Eastern policy. Everything combined to make Americans pro-Chinese – traditional policies, missionary connections, Japanese behaviour, and the appealing (in both senses) Madame Jiang – but the Kuomintang government was not successful and was ceasing to be worthy. Nevertheless Washington, which renounced extraterritorial rights in China in 1943 as a gesture, determined that China should emerge from the war fully sovereign in the full extent of its ancient territories (including Manchuria, Taiwan and the Pescadores) and a major power with a permanent place in the Security Council.

China was to be the United States of the Asian continent, a vast, united and liberal-democratic power: a view which Churchill, among others, regarded as romantic moonshine. When the shortcomings of the Kuomintang became more and more obvious, General Joseph Stilwell was sent to keep an eye on Jiang Kaishek and to bolster and, if possible, reform the Kuomintang, but the general's comments on the Kuomintang were so critical that he was recalled in October 1944 at the instance of Jiang's friends. General Patrick Hurley, who had been sent to China in August as President Roosevelt's personal representative with the Generalissimo, became the principal vehicle of American policy with the new task of bringing the Kuomintang and the communists together again in a coalition. General Hurley and General George C. Marshall, who succeeded him in November 1945, made only slight headway. The Kuomintang and the communists were ineradicably suspicious of each other – the communists had had earlier experience of the Kuomintang attacking them under cover of a truce – and discussions for an accommodation broke down on the issue of the amalgamation of their two armies. When the Japanese surrendered the Americans lifted Kuomintang forces by air to take control in north-eastern China (in the event a strategic mistake), while the Russians who had just entered Manchuria gave the communists arms and opportunities in that area. Until the latter part of 1947 there was an uneasy truce, but civil war was only suspended. The Americans, by now thoroughly distrustful of the Kuomintang, withdrew their units from China but were uncertain whether to withdraw all forms of support. General Albert C. Wedemeyer, sent to China in July 1947, recommended in September extensive American aid on the basis that the Kuomintang should introduce extensive reforms under American supervision, but by this time China was approaching economic and financial collapse and rioting was becoming common. Nevertheless interim aid to China was approved before the end of the year and the China Aid Act was passed in April 1948. This was supplemented by a Sino–American agreement and the Kuomintang made a belated effort to put its house in order.

But it was too late. The communists were winning battles in steady succession. All Manchuria was theirs by the end of 1948 and the next year became a roll-call of famous cities conquered for communism. Washington at last wrote off the Kuomintang. Jiang, who had made the characteristic blunder of over-committing himself in the last stages of the civil war, resigned the presidency at the beginning of 1949 and the Kuomintang asked – in vain – for mediation by the United States, the USSR, Britain and France. The communists had no further interest in coalitions or accommodations. A People's Republic was proclaimed in September. On 18 December 1949 Mao arrived in Moscow as a head of state.

The victory of the Chinese communists created problems for both the Americans and the Russians. During the remainder of 1949 and the first half of 1950 the Americans were moving towards diplomatic recognition of the new régime, but possible negotiations to this end were first held up by the arrest of the American consul-general in Mukden and his imprisonment with four of his colleagues for a month at the end of 1949, and were then rendered impossible by war in Korea. At some point in this period the United States decided that Taiwan was a necessary part of a line of strategic bases and must therefore not be allowed to fall into communist hands. This decision was made public and it combined with the Korean War to make the United States keep Mao's régime out of the Chinese seat at the UN and to make the Chinese believe, first, that Taiwan was being held as a temporary refuge for Jiang Kaishek pending an attempted reconquest of the mainland and, secondly, that the UN was an American tool. The Korean War also led the Chinese into an over-confident assessment of their military strength, expressed in the picturesque but inaccurate description of the United States as a paper tiger.

Mao's victory soon proved as awkward for the Russians as for the Americans. The world at large supposed that the interests and policies of the two principal communist powers must be closely allied. This assumption owed something to the Cold War, in which context the new communist state came to birth; it was strengthened by the incidence of the war in Korea in 1950–54 between communists and anti-communists; and it led to bewilderment and amazement when it transpired a few years later that Moscow and Beijing were quarrelling bitterly. In fact the interests of the USSR and China were partly congruent and partly conflicting, and the communist parties of the two countries had no close emotional bonds; in Moscow moreover the Chinese party may well have been regarded as only doubtfully communist in its doctrine and in its loyalty to the world movement dominated by the Russians. After the death of Stalin the divergence in policies became more obvious, partly because of the removal of the undoubted leader of the communist world and partly because the passage of time allowed the differences in the circumstances of the two countries to make themselves increasingly felt.

Stalin, as already stated, wanted no powerful China. So long as the government of China was non-communist it was comparatively easy for him to pursue a policy of alliance coupled with pinpricks. The treaty of August 1945 with Jiang had pins stuck into it, since the Kuomintang acknowledged in effect the absorption of Outer Mongolia into the Soviet sphere and failed to regain in Manchuria rights which now passed from Japan to the USSR. The Chinese communists were, for Stalin, another pin with which to lacerate the Kuomintang, until in 1949 they took the place of the Kuomintang and so ceased to be a mere pin. When Mao arrived in Moscow, Stalin had to devise a completely new China policy which would take into account both the USSR's desire to dominate the Asian heartlands and the inescapable expectation of fraternal love and assistance between communist parties. Given the size and potentialities of China, this was a problem which had never previously come up in Moscow.

Mao had to learn too. He had had no first-hand experience of the USSR before his visit to Moscow, which lasted two months. Its first fruits were a new Russo–Chinese treaty, concluded on 15 February 1950. This was a business measure dealing with railways, credits and similar matters. The Russians gave the Chinese a handsome present consisting of the Changchun railway and its installations. The Chinese also acquired the right to administer Dalny, though the ultimate fate of this port was to be reconsidered upon the conclusion of a treaty of peace with Japan. The USSR provided China with a credit of $300 million over five years at 1 per cent interest and repayable in 1954–63. Further agreements were concluded a month later for joint exploitation of oil in Sinkiang and joint operation of air routes in central Asia, and a general commercial agreement was signed in April. These agreements were the start of co-operation between the two countries which lasted until the late fifties and were of vital importance to China during the years of experiment and incipient modernization. They were confirmed during a visit to Moscow by Zhou Enlai in August–September 1952 shortly before the announcement of China's first five-year plan, the formation of a powerful National Planning Commission under Gao

Gang and the creation of a Ministry of Higher Education (all in November–December of that year). With the plan, the commission and the drive for higher education the Russo–Chinese agreements were an integral part of Mao's design for a new China.

CHINA AND THE SUPERPOWERS

Nine months after the proclamation of the new Chinese republic war broke out in Korea. This unforeseen and, for the Chinese, extremely inopportune event had a deep effect on Asian politics and on the relations between Asians and non-Asians involved in Far Eastern affairs. It forced the Chinese to look to their defences when they should have been concentrating on their internal affairs; it dominated American policy at a moment when that policy was in the making; it raised questions concerning consultation and co-operation between the principal communist powers; it threatened to import a cold war into Asia, boosted Indian neutralism and caused Americans for a while to equate neutralism and pacifism with indifferentism and moral perversion.

The history of Korea is like the history of any small country which finds itself wedged between more powerful neighbours. Korea is a peninsula which stretches into the sea from the south-eastern corner of Manchuria until it nearly reaches the southernmost of Japan's principal islands. For a thousand years it was ruled by two dynasties separated by a brief Mongol conquest. It suffered Japanese and Manchu incursions in the sixteenth and seventeenth centuries but survived until the end of the nineteenth, by which time it had become a pawn in Sino–Japanese–Russian conflicts. Japan's victories in the war with China in 1894–95 and with Russia in 1904–5 gave Japan a free hand in Korea which was annexed in 1910. It failed in 1919 to recover its independence although a provisional government was established under the presidency of Syngman Rhee, a Korean who had acquired a doctorate in philosophy at Princeton. Independence was, however, promised by the Cairo declaration of 1943 by Roosevelt, Churchill and Jiang Kaishek.

When therefore the war came to an end in 1945 there was no dispute over the status of Korea, but at the moment of independence an accident deprived it of unity. The Japanese having surrendered partly to the Americans and partly to the Russians, Korea was divided into two pieces along the 38th parallel. This famous line came into existence as a result of negotiations between army officers of relatively junior rank; it was not a creation of ministerial decisions. But administrative convenience hardened into political fact and thereafter all attempts to equip Korea with a single government failed. The cause of this failure was the presence of Russian as well as American troops. Contemporaneously in Poland, for which rival governments also contended, there was only one occupying army and so only one possible answer. In Korea there were two armies and so no answer.

In 1947 the United States took the problem to the United Nations which appointed a commission (UN Temporary Commission on Korea – UNTCOK) to effect unity through elections. Elections were held in the south in May 1948 but the commission was prevented from operating in the north and the result of its activities was the creation of a government which claimed to be the government of all Korea but had in fact no authority or existence north of the 38th parallel. The head of this government was Syngman Rhee, now an elderly, rough, reactionary but legendarily essential and, as it turned out, almost irremovable father figure. In 1949 the Russians (who had nurtured a rival government in the north) and the Americans both withdrew their armed forces. Korea was now a country with two governments, overhung by the Russians in Manchuria and Siberia and by the Americans in Japan and vaguely conscious of the emergence of a new China on its borders.

The first half of 1950 was occupied by new elections in South Korea and propaganda in North Korea for reunification either by elections throughout the country (from which Syngman Rhee and others were to be debarred) or by a merger of the two parliaments. When it became apparent that these gambits were unavailing northern troops crossed the border on 25 June, capturing the southern capital of Seoul the next day. It is doubtful in the extreme whether North Korean troops would have taken this action if Dean Acheson had not, in January, excluded Korea (and Taiwan) from the defence perimeter which, by implication, the United States was ready to fight to retain, and it is also extremely doubtful whether the North Koreans would have crossed the parallel without feeling assured of Russian approbation. What was perhaps unforeseeable in June was that the American attitude of January would be immediately reversed by the invasion and that South Korea and Taiwan would prove to be parts of the American defence perimeter after all.

The Security Council met at once at the request of the United States and passed, in the absence of the Russian member, a resolution requiring a cease-fire and the return of northern troops to their own side of the border. All members of the UN were asked to support these measures and President Truman thereupon instructed General Douglas MacArthur in Tokyo to give support to the South Koreans. The President also ordered the US Seventh Fleet to insulate Taiwan. Two days later (27 June) a second resolution of the Security Council called on all members to help South Korea to repel the attack made upon it and to restore international peace. This resolution proceeded upon the basis, subsequently challenged by the Russians, that the fighting between north and south was an international threat, although it was not made clear whether it was international because north and south were two different states or because an admittedly internal and civil war was deemed to have international repercussions. On 6 July China protested against illegal intervention in Korean affairs.

At first the fighting went rapidly in favour of the North. The South Koreans and the UN forces which came to their help were driven to the very tip of the Korean peninsula, but in September General MacArthur, who was in command of the UN forces, landed troops at Inchon 240 km to the north and as a result of this bold stroke South Korean and other units crossed the 38th parallel in October and pressed on to the Manchurian border. The war seemed to be over. President Truman flew to Wake Island to congratulate and confer with General MacArthur who gave his opinion that neither the Russians nor the Chinese would intervene. He was right about the Russians, who were now anxious to discountenance the war, but wrong about the Chinese, who attacked on 26 November. Exactly a month later they were across the 38th parallel and the South Koreans and their allies were once more in full retreat.

The Chinese attack was a forestalling action. The Chinese, who remembered the Japanese attack on their country via Korea in 1931, had reason to suspect that the new American power in Japan was about to repeat that performance. American aid to Jiang under the China Aid Act, General MacArthur's visit to Jiang on Taiwan soon after the outbreak of war in Korea, the crossing of the 38th parallel by the Americans in October and their approach to the Yalu River, the open debate on American strategic interests in the Pacific islands and on the possibility of a return by Jiang to the mainland – all these things combined to alert the new régime in Beijing and persuade it that the Americans intended an anti-communist campaign like the similar, albeit unsuccessful, anti-communist interventions in Russia after the 1917 revolution. So the Chinese struck first.

Chinese intervention altered the nature of the war and gave rise to a fierce debate about how it ought to be prosecuted. From the end of June to the end of November the war, although waged on one side primarily by the Americans, could be represented as an international punitive expedition. After November it became more and more a Sino–American conflict. General MacArthur wished to recognize this fact and to wage open war on China, using the most relevant and effective military means. This meant, in particular, following Chinese aircraft across the Manchurian frontier instead of breaking off pursuit when this line was reached in combat, and it meant also bombing Chinese fixed installations on the Yalu River and elsewhere. Logically this attitude to

3.2 Korea showing division between North and South.

the war could lead to the use of nuclear bombs in the heart of China itself.

But General MacArthur's views did not carry conviction in Washington. The chiefs of staff shrank from the prospect of embarking on a war with China which might drag on for years, while the president and his civilian advisers were extremely loath to re-enter Chinese politics (from which the United States had very recently extracted itself) and well aware of an almost worldwide disapproval of any such adventure. Washington's allies became alarmed (Attlee flew to Washington to express this alarm, especially about the possible use of nuclear bombs in Asia for a second time) and the neutrals began to give neutralism a markedly anti-American inclination; distrust of the United States in world affairs received in these months a fillip which was very slow to fade away.

As early as July 1950 Nehru, whose government had supported both the Security Council's resolutions, made approaches to Stalin and Acheson to put a stop to the fighting. His intervention was received with bare courtesy but in December India and other neutrals appealed to both sides not to cross the 38th parallel and during that month the Indian representative at the UN, Sir Benegal Rau, had a series of conversations in New York with an emissary from Beijing, General Wu Xiuquan. The latter, however, left New York before the end of the year with nothing achieved; a UN cease-fire committee was rebuffed by Beijing; the time for mediation was not yet.

On the first day of 1951 the Chinese launched their second offensive. UN forces were quickly forced out of Seoul and a fresh UN appeal for a cease-fire was rejected. But the Chinese advance petered out. At the UN China was declared an aggressor and in Washington in March a telegram from General MacArthur was read to the Senate in which the general in effect urged the United States to strike at China and not simply to accept the re-establishment of the 38th parallel as a boundary line. These were the alternatives, and both the declared aims of the UN and the arbitrament of war favoured the second. But it was now the Chinese turn to retreat, the UN recovered Seoul on 14 March and the South Koreans once more crossed the 38th parallel on the twenty-fifth. General MacArthur took the opportunity to issue on his own initiative a peremptory challenge to his adversaries to accept an armistice, coupled with an implied threat of massive retaliation if they did not. The challenge was ignored and President Truman warned General MacArthur that he had exceeded his powers and pursued a policy not approved by his government and commander-in-chief; he was told to stick to his own business. By way of reply the general tried once more to appeal to the Congress and people of the United States over the heads of his military and civilian superiors. He sent to the Republican leader in the House of Representatives, Joseph W. Martin, a letter which was read in the House and which recommended the strongest measures against China, including the use of Jiang's troops. On 11 April he was dismissed by President Truman.

The dramatic dismissal of General MacArthur caused such a stir that its significance was not immediately assimilated. What it meant was that the Korean War had to be brought to an end by compromise and mediation. The American government rejected the alternative of complete victory obtainable only by the military defeat of China. Yet it took more than two years more of fighting and negotiation before an armistice was eventually signed in July 1953, more than three years after the initial act of aggression in June 1950.

The dragging out and winding up of the war can be briefly recorded. Fresh Chinese attacks in April 1951 were soon held and both sides began to feel their way towards a truce. A broadcast in the United States at the end of June by the Russian member of the Security Council, J. A. Malik, led to truce negotiations which were begun at Kaesong in July and later transferred to Panmunjon. These negotiations were tedious, long, fruitless and punctuated by fears of a renewal of full-scale operations and by accusations against the Americans of recourse to bacteriological warfare. The most intractable issue was the fate of prisoners of war, many of whom in southern hands were alleged to be unwilling to return to the north, but an exchange agreement was eventually signed in June 1953 (shortly after the death of Stalin, although no connection between the events can be definitely proved). The agreement was then wrecked by Syngman Rhee who released prisoners rather than turn them over to the North Koreans, whereupon the Chinese launched a major offensive. Notwithstanding these turbulent episodes an armistice agreement was signed in July.

The Geneva conference which opened in April 1954 failed to produce a final settlement and Syngman Rhee then went to Washington to try to persuade the United States to sanction a joint invasion of China by South Koreans and Jiang Kaishek's forces. He argued that the régime in China was on the verge of collapse but he failed to win over Congress or Eisenhower or Dulles to his view. In the following year American and Chinese troops were gradually withdrawn. Korea remained bisected but it was clear that the war was over.

The year 1954 was something of a landmark in Asia's postwar history. The Geneva conference, although it failed to produce agreement on Korea, demonstrated that the country would revert to the position that ruled in 1949, bisected and freed from foreign occupation. In the same year the United States decided not to intervene at Dien Bien Phu. But also in the same year the United States concluded treaties with Pakistan and Japan and created Seato. The acceptance of the *status quo ante* in Korea and the refusal to engage in war in Indo–China did not betoken an American withdrawal from Asia. For the next eleven years – until the beginning in 1965 of the American attack on North Vietnam – the United States tried to play a major role in eastern and south-eastern Asia by displaying but not using military power. The principal object of American policy was to halt the territorial progress of communism by conquest or subversion. In Korea aggression had failed to annex southern Korea to a communist northern half, but in the American view communism was making dangerous strides elsewhere in Asia by means of subversion. In fact the opposite was the case in Malaya where the tide was running against the communist insurgents, but the growth of Chinese power, still supported by Russian aid at this date, made Washington tremble for the successor states in Indo–China and for Indonesia. American policy was thus anti-Chinese because China had become the fount of a new wave of communism, and by the same token it was ideological, claiming virtue for the stand against the evils of communism and imputing wickedness to those who refused to fight the good fight or at least applaud it.

The events of the early fifties strengthened and prolonged American links with the remnants of the Kuomintang. On the outbreak of the Korean War Truman gave Jiang Kaishek an undertaking to keep the new Chinese régime away from Taiwan and the Pescadores. In view of China's total naval incapacity, this commitment was easy to honour but it involved Washington in courses not approved by its principal European allies and it contained an awkward ambiguity. When Jiang was evicted from the mainland he had retained control of some small islands off the coast. Did the American umbrella cover these islands as well as Taiwan itself? The question was partly a question of the extent of Washington's unwritten commitments to Jiang, became to some extent a question of asserting American steadfastness after the vacillations over Dien Bien Phu, and was often discussed in terms of whether these islands were necessary for the defence of Taiwan or not.

The offshore islands were the Tachens, Quemoy and the Matsus, situated off Amoy and Foochow and forming an offshore screen similar to the advance guard which the Pescadores provided for Taiwan on the other side of the Taiwan Strait. In 1954 resolutions in favour of the liberation of Taiwan started to be manufactured and emitted by Beijing and provoked retorts from Washington showing that any attempt to attack Taiwan would have to reckon with the American fleet. In September the Chinese began to bombard Quemoy as a retort, it seemed, to the creation of Seato by the Manila Pact. The Kuomintang fired back and for several weeks this fire and counterfire looked like the beginning of a more serious encounter. In November thirteen American airmen, captured during the winter of 1952–53 when their aircraft came down in Manchuria, were sentenced in Beijing to terms varying between life and four years for espionage, and in December the United States and the Kuomintang concluded a new treaty which declared the defence of Taiwan and the Pescadores to be a common interest. Whether the retention of Quemoy and the Matsus was essential to the defence of Taiwan and the Pescadores was left unmentioned. In 1955 Jiang abandoned the Tachens under fire from the mainland.

The Chinese agreed to receive a visit from Dag Hammarskjöld who invited himself to Beijing to talk about the American airmen, but the Geneva summit conference in the summer of 1955 caused the Chinese to reflate the crisis. In July they started another major bombardment of Quemoy. The Americans had meanwhile apparently decided – whether on strategic or general political grounds – that no more territory should be ceded. The new bombardment served to make this resolve clear and after it had died away like its predecessor there followed a period of easier Sino–American relations marked by exchanges at Geneva, ambassadorial conferences in Warsaw and the release of the American prisoners. By the middle of 1958 there was even talk of American recognition of Beijing, but a statement from Washington in August showed that the Eisenhower–Dulles administration contemplated no such step.

This statement was immediately followed by a fresh bombardment of Quemoy. During the 1955–58 lull Jiang had moved troops into Quemoy until about one-third of all his forces was stationed just offshore from the mainland. In September 1958 Beijing demanded the surrender of the islands and was met by a declaration by Dulles to the effect that the Americans would fight to protect Taiwan and another by Eisenhower defining Quemoy and the Matsus as necessary for its defence. American escorts for Jiang's troops sailed within a few miles of the coast. War was feared. Washington's allies and sections of American opinion too became alarmed, and after a few days the crisis was deflated by the resumption of the Sino–American ambassadorial talks in Warsaw. Unpopular and hazardous though Dulles's policy of brink-manship (that is, using military power to make political threats) had been, it had achieved during these years the object of showing that the American decision not to intervene in Indo–China in 1954 did not betoken a general American failure of will. This determination was to be further sharpened and displayed in South Vietnam where the Americans first gave the anti-communist régime economic and military aid and then engaged themselves directly in war on the Asian mainland. But this engagement changed the nature of American power and policies in the Far East. The defeat of Japan in 1945 had given the United States total dominance in the Pacific. The conflict between Truman and MacArthur and its outcome showed that Pacific dominance was still the basis of policy, buttressed as it was by garrisons in the Japanese and Philippine islands and by alliance with Australia and New Zealand (concluded in 1951 as the price of these countries' consent to the peace treaty with Japan). But the collapse of the French attempt to resume empire in Indo–China, coming as it did after the triumph of communists in China, led the United States towards a new policy of Asian rather than Pacific dominance.

Communist China's conflicts with the United States coincided nearly with a sharp decline in its relations with the USSR in the course of quarrels which developed in the late fifties and were public news by 1960. One of the most startling consequences of the death of Stalin was the clash between the incompatible temperaments of Khrushchev and Mao which was superimposed upon the sometimes divergent interests of the Russian and Chinese empires and exacerbated by doctrinal dispute.

When Mao visited Stalin in 1949 there was an element of obeisance about this encounter between the Chinese leader and the man who, hyphenated with Marx-Engels-Lenin, was much more than just a Russian leader. Stalin's power had endured for a quarter of a century, his prestige had been enormously increased by the Second World War, he was a legendary figure, a little more than mortal man, a little like a long-lived and successful Chinese emperor. There was no doubt about the relationship between the two men and Mao, so far as we know, never questioned it. A Chinese leader might, in the nature of things, be a greater man than a Yugoslav or a Polish leader, or even a purely Russian leader, but in Stalin, Mao recognized a universal figure.

When Stalin died in March 1953, there was at first no agreement in the USSR about his successor and even a short-lived view that he had no single successor. A composite Stalin – Bulganin/Khrushchev – quickly replaced the committee rule of the Malenkov interlude and visited Beijing in 1954. Then Khrushchev emerged as the new Russian autocrat and was assumed by many to be *ipso facto* the chief of world communism as well. To Mao, however, this proposition was not self-evident; there was no rule which said that the world's leading communist had to be a Russian nor any disposition in Mao's scholarly mind to accept a rumbustious political boss in that role. During his visit to Beijing in 1954 Khrushchev had failed to establish with Mao either a hierarchical or a personal relationship.

For a while relations remained equable. China still needed the economic and technical help of the USSR and remained alive to the need for military support which the outbreak of the Korean War had dramatized. The Russians continued to help the Chinese to modernize their army; the Chinese Fourth Field Army which had entered Korea in 1950 was part of the force which had defeated the Kuomintang and which the Chinese were anxious to transform into a more modern instrument. Resentments, such as the feeling that the Russians had done very little to help the Chinese communists before they won power, were kept in the background. In 1954, with the Korean War clearly over, the Russians left Port Arthur and handed over its installations to China – two years later than the date set in the Russo–China treaty of 1950. They also transferred to China their half share in the joint companies formed in 1945 to exploit oil, non-ferrous metals and civil aviation in Jinjiang and to operate ship building and repair in Dairen. Finally, they entered into new agreements to give economic and technical aid in the shape of financial credits and the provision of skilled technicians and know-how.

The deterioration in Sino–Russian relations set in about 1956 and acquired a concrete edge in the two following years. At the twentieth congress of the Soviet Communist Party in February 1956 Mikoyan, followed by Khrushchev, set about the demolition of Stalin's memory. De-Stalinization involved points of doctrine on which Mao could fairly claim to be heard, but he was not consulted and was perhaps offended by the Russians' evident assumption that such matters could be settled by Russians alone. Khrushchev was still a new man, or at any rate unconfirmed in his new apogee, and it would have been at least becoming for him to consult an elder like Mao. In external affairs too Khrushchev was showing a dangerous unsureness. One of his first initiatives had been to try to repair the breach with Yugoslavia. Chinese attitudes to Yugoslavia were unsettled in the late fifties. On the one hand Yugoslavia's independence of Moscow appealed to the Chinese; on the other hand they harboured heretical notions. It would seem that the independence prevailed at first over the heresies, but that from about 1957 the heresies seemed to the Chinese more serious, especially when the independence became less pronounced and Moscow gravitated towards a Yugoslav policy of coexistence, of supping with the devil when needs must, a policy which the committedly anti-American Chinese considered reprehensible, inexpedient and silly. Furthermore, in 1955 Bulganin and Khrushchev demonstrated support for non-communists, notably Asian non-communists, by their visits to India, Burma and Afghanistan. Chinese doubts were next reinforced towards the end of 1956 when revolt occurred first in Poland and then in Hungary. In the Chinese view the Russians mishandled, or nearly mishandled, both emergencies. In the Polish case the Chinese intervened in support of the more independent communist Gomulka and cautioned the Russians against the use of military force; in the case of the anti-communist Hungarian rising they urged the Russians not to withdraw their troops prematurely. But these disagreements were not lethal, and in the next year the Chinese were advising the Poles to be more amenable to the Russians.

In 1957 in a new agreement on technical aid, Khrushchev (according to the Chinese at a later date) promised China samples of nuclear material and information about the construction of nuclear weapons. This, moreover, was the year in which the Russians perfected the first intercontinental missile and launched the first sputnik. The whole world drew exaggerated conclusions from this achievement. The Russians were thought to be overhauling the Americans, perhaps even to have done so, and the Chinese expected Khrushchev to exploit this marvellous advantage. The communists had long possessed superiority in sheer numbers; now they were ahead in technology as well. The east wind, in Mao's phrase, was prevailing over the west. The Russian nuclear armoury could be used to pin the Americans to the wall, while the communist states helped their friends to power throughout the underprivileged world; in Asia, Africa and Latin America there were revolutionary movements eager to discard the yoke of capitalist imperialism with the help especially of the Chinese, whose own experiences between 1922 and 1949 had taught them more than anybody else knew about the strategy of revolution in poor, backward, agricultural countries. The Chinese, preparing for the Great Leap Forward and their second five-year plan, felt that they could also make a fresh bid to take Quemoy and make themselves felt in communist and Asian affairs.

There were several points in the Chinese analysis with which Khrushchev and at least some of his senior colleagues disagreed. They may well have been the only persons in the world who knew at this time that the Russian sputnik had not put the USSR ahead of the United States, and therefore they did not believe that they could immobilize the United States by the threat of nuclear annihilation. To some extent they were caught in the toils of their own jubilation, for the more they magnified their technical successes, the more it was supposed that they had won for themselves a much freer hand in international affairs than was really the case. While the Chinese thought them capable of preventing nuclear war, they feared it. The Chinese concluded from the Russian achievements that nuclear war had become much less likely and that therefore the communist powers could afford to try more adventurous policies. They also maintained the orthodox Marxist position that war in some form at some day was inevitable because imperialism made it so.

The Russian view of war had changed, more because the Russians approached the topic from a different angle than because of any radical revision of doctrine. They had diluted the basic doctrine of the inevitability of war not so much for reasons of pure logic but rather because their fear and awareness of the frightful consequences of the use of nuclear weapons had led them to discard so baleful a belief; they were thinking specifically of nuclear war and not of war in general. The nuclear danger also caused them to differ from the Chinese in their approach to non-nuclear wars: both Moscow and Beijing endorsed wars of national liberation, but Moscow was more worried than Beijing about the risks of escalation to nuclear war and therefore more cautious in any particular case. These divergences were a further consequence of the death of Stalin which, in this as in other subjects, released a stifled debate inside the USSR. In March 1954 Malenkov had pronounced that a world war would be likely to destroy all civilization; during his term of office as prime minister he stressed the imbecility of war and coupled it with his policy of increasing the supply of consumer goods. Khrushchev, while still in competition with Malenkov, attacked the latter for defeatism and for advocating coexistence with capitalists and put forward a hard policy of building up the strength of the USSR. When, however, he himself became prime minister he set out to assuage the asperities of the Cold War because the USSR was technically behind the United States and because he found the Russian forces ill organized. At the twentieth congress of the Communist Party in February 1956 he said that war was not inevitable and might not be essential to the worldwide triumph of socialism. This view was repeated in the declaration issued in November 1957 at the end of the Moscow conference of communist parties (the Chinese included), and discussion seemed from this point to be shifting to the question whether all war, and not only nuclear war, had become inexpedient. In 1958, however, the Chinese view that the east wind was prevailing over the west turned a theoretical debate into a live tactical issue with the Chinese expecting the Russians to take positive action incompatible with the general trend of the debate since 1953.

At the same time a further cause of dispute emerged. In general the Russians and the Chinese were in accord on the need to turn Asia, Africa and Latin America away from the capitalist camp, but they differed over the means. The Chinese, intent upon multiplying the number of states under communist rule, wanted to help only communists, whereas the Russians, taking the more pragmatic attitude that any anti-western régime was an advantage, were willing to help bourgeois revolutionary movements where communists were non-existent or unlikely to succeed. At the conference of communist parties in Moscow in December 1960 this disagreement was temporarily smothered by the adoption of a compromise formula: national democracies were to be helped if they were evolving in a social direction.

The Russo–Chinese alliance, already ruffled by suspicion and friction in 1956–57, was completely unhinged in the next two years, during which the USSR showed itself indifferent to vital Chinese interests, or even hostile to them. Jiang's immunity on Taiwan under the protection of the American Seventh Fleet was an affront about which Beijing could in fact do nothing since it possessed no fleet of its own, but his possession of Quemoy and the Matsu islands just off the Chinese coast was an even less supportable and also a less irremediable taunt. Beijing resolved to make a bid for Quemoy and the Matsus by a policy of bang and bluff. A first attempt in 1955 failed and now a second also failed because Dulles refused to be rattled, and part of this failure was ascribed by Beijing to the luke-warmness of Russian support. The Russians, while sympathizing with Beijing's feelings about irredeemed Chinese territory, were wary of Pacific entanglements and determined not to be drawn into a war for the reconquest of Taiwan. They refused to set up a joint command for the Far East and made demands which amounted in Chinese eyes to impermissible infringements of Chinese sovereignty. Khrushchev seems to have been willing to establish nuclear bases in China but only on the basis that they would be Russian and that there would be no Chinese finger on the trigger. Some Chinese leaders, including the minister of defence, Marshal Peng Dehuai, apparently considered the price worth paying, but an opposite view prevailed. Marshal Peng was dismissed and the Russian attempt (if such it was) to create in eastern Asia the same sort of strategic position as the American position in western Europe failed. To make matters worse the Russians poured cold water on the Great Leap Forward at a time when their co-operation was essential to its success, adopted a neutral attitude in China's disputes with India in 1959, continued to give large amounts of aid to Indonesia even though Beijing was being driven to protest against the Indonesian government's behaviour to its Chinese popu-lation, and set out to improve relations with the United States. The Chinese were being forced to reassess the attitudes of the USSR and the balance of the major forces in the world.

Events in the Middle East may have contributed to this rethinking. In July 1958 the Iraqi monarchy was overthrown and the king, his uncle, his prime minister Nuri es-Said and other notabilities murdered. For a time it seemed to some observers that the Americans and the British would take up arms against this revolution and that a war of major or minor dimensions would begin. The Chinese were certainly interested in these events. At a later stage they demanded to be included in any conference assembled to deal with the situation, and their renewed bombardment of Quemoy began shortly after the Iraqi coup. They may have calculated that the Russians could be induced to use the nuclear threat against the Americans or even to become involved in fighting. If they were thinking in these euphoric terms, their disillusionment was sharp and they were forced to the profoundly melancholy view that, on the contrary, the Russians were engaging in a conspiracy with the Americans to dominate the world and prevent China from becoming a nuclear power.

When the world learned on 3 August 1959 that Khrushchev was going to the United States and would confer with Eisenhower at Camp David, the Chinese concluded that Khrushchev had rejected Beijing's thesis that the USSR should put forth its strength rather than negotiate from it. Although there had been some signs of Chinese endorsement for the Khrushchev policy, a change of mind in Beijing, coincident with changes in the top ranks of the Chinese Communist Party, had produced an unequivocally tough tone towards the United States and warnings against the naïve amateurishness of those who imagined that it was possible to lie down with imperialist lions. And not only was the Camp David spirit not shared by the Chinese leaders; the Camp David negotiations appeared to leave out Chinese interests as though China were nothing more than an impediment to a Russo–American *rapprochement*. In October, shortly after his return from the United States, Khrushchev went to Beijing, a visit which had the almost unparalleled consequence of producing no communiqué. If his hosts asked him what he had said to Eisenhower about Taiwan, it is unlikely that he had a palatable reply, and in the new year both the foreign minister and the prime minister of China made statements which amounted to declarations of no confidence in Khrushchev's foreign policy and proceedings. At a meeting of the presidium of the World Peace Council (a communist front organization) in Rome in January 1960 the Russian delegation attacked China, and at a communist conference in Warsaw in February the Chinese were observers only, although Outer Mongolia and North Korea were full participants. In April the ninetieth anniversary of Lenin's birth provided both sides with an occasion to expound their views at intemperate length, and a powerful Chinese propaganda campaign brought the quarrelling into the open. Mao, emerging from semi-retirement, made five separate statements explaining the Chinese attitude and pouring scorn on the folly of trusting the Americans.

It was no doubt the Chinese hope to convert or unseat Khrushchev, and the Russian leader, preparing for the Paris summit conference with the United States in mid-May, may have been in some danger. The Supreme Soviet met on 5 May, there was a reshuffle in the party secretariat, and there were rumours of splits and cabals. But Khrushchev went to Paris and, despite the U-2 incident and the failure of the conference, repeated his belief in peaceful coexistence on and after his return home. At a communist conclave in Bucharest in June, Khrushchev personally attacked the Chinese in the course of a meeting which was supposed to restore harmony and in August Russian technicians in China, to the number of about 12,000, were ordered to pack up and return home, bringing with them the plans on which they had been working. This bitterly unfriendly act, coinciding with the domestic setbacks of the great famine years, seemed to the Chinese tantamount to an invitation to the Americans to invade China and to the Kuomintang to incite a rising against the communist régime.

Correspondence and propaganda continued with increasing acerbity and in November 1960 eighty-one communist parties attended another general conference held in secret in Moscow to assuage the discord.

After vituperative debate this meeting produced a communiqué which too thinly papered a too large crack. The Russians had the better of the argument when it came to counting heads. By this date the Russo–Chinese alliance was non-existent and doctrinal solidarity a farce. The withdrawal of the Russian technicians was a cancellation of the economic co-operation initiated immediately after the establishment of the Chinese People's Republic, and Khrushchev's approaches to Eisenhower had revealed the strict limits of Russian support for China in external affairs. The attempt to operate a Russo–Chinese alliance in world affairs had run onto the rocks of Khrushchev's American policy.

But at the end of 1964 Khrushchev was overthrown and the second triumvirate which took over power *ad interim* (like the earlier collective leadership after Stalin's death) attempted a reconciliation. Kosygin went twice to Beijing. The Chinese, however, refused to attend a conference of communist parties in Moscow in May 1965 and subsequently frustrated Moscow's plans for a world communist conference. The Russian embassy in Beijing was attacked in 1967 and the next year Beijing condemned the Russian invasion of Czechoslovakia and Brezhnev's doctrine on the right and duty of the USSR to act outside its borders for the defence of socialism and the socialist bloc as a whole. In 1969 there were incidents on the Ussuri River, where the possession of a few islands had long been a matter for (not very heated) dispute. Men were killed and there was talk about the possibility of a Russian pre-emptive strike against China before its nuclear capacity assumed deterrent proportions. Russian forces in the east were increased in the seventies and eighties from 33 to 56 divisions, and from 1979 the Russian threat to China was magnified by the establishment of Russian naval and air bases in Vietnam. Negotiations in Beijing in 1969–70, to which the USSR sent one of its most senior and able diplomats, were lengthy but unproductive, and renewed talks in 1979 were wrecked by the Russian invasion of Afghanistan (with which China has a border).

Some compensation for the collapse of a grand communist alliance was provided for China by its readmission to the comity of nations and an unexpected relaxation of its relations with the United States. Canada and Italy established diplomatic relations in 1970. In the same year a majority in the General Assembly of the UN – but not the requisite two-thirds – voted in favour of China's membership and at the end of the year Mao's régime was admitted to be the rightful incumbent of China's permanent seat in the Security Council. China came into the UN on its own terms which included the rejection of an American–Japanese proposal to retain Taiwan as a separate member alongside China.

In Washington Nixon had decided to jettison the two Chinas policy if that were necessary in order to restore relations with Beijing, thus reversing a basic tenet of American policy. At the Geneva conference of

1954, Zhou had proposed discussions for a reduction of tensions. A first meeting took place in Geneva in August 1955 after China had released the eleven captured American airmen, but American recognition of Taiwan as a separate state proved an insuperable obstacle and the talks were broken off by the United States at the end of 1957. They were resumed in Warsaw the next year and the United States began to give visas to American newsmen who wanted to go to China, but the three months' crisis over Quemoy and the Matsu islands intervened to freeze attitudes on both sides. In 1960 Zhou proposed a Pacific non-aggression pact. For several years there was a stalemate, although contacts were maintained. In 1966 the American secretary of state Dean Rusk said that the United States would not try to overthrow the government in Beijing by force but however Beijing might interpret this disavowal of Jiang's persistent hope, the war in Vietnam put an end to even the mildest sign of normal relations between Beijing and Washington until the American withdrawal from South-east Asia revived the situation created in the fifties by the truce in Korea. The Americans were acknowledging the defeat of their efforts to be a continental Asian power. In 1971 an American ping-pong team which had been playing in various Asian countries was invited to China, the first recorded appearance of this sport in high politics. This move was followed by a further relaxation of the American trade embargo (there had been some relaxation in 1969). In July Nixon's adviser on national security, Henry Kissinger, went secretly to Beijing and it was then revealed that Nixon himself would follow the next year. This was a sensational piece of news and the Nixon visit, duly accomplished with the secretary of state William Rogers in attendance, heralded a stream of other highly placed visitors anxious to make their peace with China and recognize and trade with it.

The Mao–Nixon détente was a political demonstration made possible by the ending of the Vietnam War and valuable to both countries as a means of addressing a warning to the USSR – by the Americans, not to take Russo–American détente for granted; by the Chinese, not to make trouble on the Sino–Soviet frontiers. The demonstration had no precise content (and a visit by President Ford to Beijing at the end of 1975 gave it none) but it jolted thinking about international affairs at the great power level. There was now another piece on the board and it served to confuse a game which, by all the rules of a bipolar world, allowed for two players only. In military terms, however, China was still well below superpower standards. It could not touch the United States or greatly harm the USSR. (The Sino–Russian front had been quiet since incidents on the Ussuri in 1969 but the Russian armies in Mongolia had been built up from fifteen divisions to forty-four.) By 1975 China had set off some twenty nuclear explosions and possessed a stock of nuclear weapons estimated at 300. Some of these were intermediate range missiles but most could be delivered only by aircraft whose range was 2,400 km. By the end of the decade, however, there were good grounds for the belief that China possessed not only the missiles but also the delivery systems needed to attack targets in the European areas of the USSR.

China set out to become both an independent nuclear power and also the world leader of a new international of the underprivileged. Zhou Enlai, who had steadily built up China's diplomatic position in Asia from the Bandung conference in 1955 onwards, made a tour of African countries in 1963–64. China's exclusion from the United Nations, where the seat specifically allotted to China continued to be occupied by the Kuomintang's rump, may have contributed to its wish to assert its claim to a leading world role outside the UN and in defiance of the UN's principal members, even though its comparatively modest defence expenditure and its industrial growth pains made China a power of the future rather than a power to be reckoned with in the present. What China achieved in these years of travail was to project so menacing an image of its future power as to make the world take it very seriously in the present and even to be more afraid of China than of any other country in the world. This fear was not merely a consequence of adept Chinese diplomacy; it was also a product of the mysteriousness with which China was cloaked by the outside world's own determination to treat it as not just different but out of this world. It was a product in particular of confusion about Chinese attitudes towards nuclear war and a belief that China's leaders regarded such a war with equanimity on the grounds that China's vast size and few large cities would enable it to survive nuclear attack. The Chinese were in fact well aware that a nuclear war would be a universal disaster and that China and the Chinese Communist Party would be among the victims, and although they clung to the not implausible thesis that wars were inevitable they did not apparently regard nuclear war as inevitable. Like others they hoped to prevent a nuclear war by a policy of deterrence but, unlike others, they could not in the fifties and sixties do the deterring themselves. China in this period was exposed to nuclear threats or preventive war in the same way as the USSR had been exposed between 1945 and 1949.

In this situation the Chinese, like the Russians before them and regardless of whether their ultimate intentions were malevolent or peaceable, had to resort to minor non-nuclear deterrents while being careful to avoid any disastrous provocation of a nuclear power. They challenged and exposed Asia's largest non-nuclear state, India, and came to terms with lesser countries which might have been tempted into an enemy camp. Having taken Tibet because they could and postponed the conquest of Taiwan because they must, they pursued a policy of limited activity which fitted their limited capacities. The decision of North Vietnam to take an active part in war in the south was, it may be presumed, approved by the Moscow conference of eighty-one communist parties and by the government of the USSR, which could not resist appeals to communist solidarity and could have no objection to endorsing and even assisting a modest guerrilla war likely to prove embarrassing to the United States. When in 1963 the United States decided to take a leading part in the war and to raise the level of warfare in order to preserve an independent South Vietnamese state, they in effect served a no-aggression notice on China. The Chinese, faced with a conflict between two principles – the principle that a nuclear power must not be provoked, and the principle that a national liberation movement must be helped – opted for the former.

This dominant principle was further exemplified in Europe. Albania, one of China's few friends, received little more than the rhetorical support which the Russians could be expected to put up with. In any case the Chinese were only marginally interested in Europe. They were more interested in Africa, which presented in their view excellent prospects for revolution. More broadcasting time was devoted to African listeners than even to southern Asians, but the results were disappointing for by the time that China was ready to play a full part in world affairs, most of the nationalist movements in Africa had won power and independence and, being intent on retaining their power, were anything but insurrectionary and were suspicious of Chinese intervention in their affairs. The fall of Ben Bella in Algeria 1965 was a special setback, similar to the rout and slaughter of the Indonesian communists in the same year.

China was on the way to becoming a regional nuclear power but also was searching in vain for a more than regional role. Its emergence as a future giant power gave notice that the bipolar world of the Cold War was destined to be short-lived. China's first nuclear explosion in October 1964 was followed by a second in May 1965. A year later a first thermonuclear weapon, probably one capable of use in submarines (of which China had thirty, received from the USSR), was exploded. China's first guided missile test occurred in October 1966 and its first hydrogen bomb was exploded in June 1967. It would soon be formidable for a thousand miles around; it could be expected to have a wide range, if limited stocks, of nuclear weapons some time in the seventies; and it might spring a surprise by developing ahead of expectations a submarine nuclear armoury to threaten the United States and Latin America from the Pacific Ocean. But unlike the United States and the USSR it was not becoming the centre of a group. It had failed to detach more than a few, comparatively insignificant communist parties from the main body of international communism which, if faced with a choice, persisted in choosing Moscow rather than Beijing, even while reducing the intensity of Muscovite control; only the distant and ineffective Albanians and New Zealanders stuck staunchly at Beijing's side. Elsewhere China caught the fancy of sundry malcontents in France or Egypt or Zanzibar, but these were countries with nationalist rather than internationalist preoccupations and with discontents which were peculiar to each of them and provided no basis for common politics.

There is always a certain grandeur about isolation. Britain, Japan and the United States had all at various times dallied with its lures. Communist China made a virtue of its isolation and discounted the dangers by dwelling on a more distant future in which it would ultimately circumvent and discomfit the major powers whose hostility it had to bear in the present. China was used to having powerful enemies. Britain and Germany had been succeeded in this role by Japan, and Japan in 1945 by the United States – especially after the outbreak of the Korean War. The USSR, superficially a natural ally, had turned out within a decade to be an enemy, a foreign power upon whose goodwill China had mistakenly, if for a short space, allowed itself to become over-dependent. In this situation China's leaders seemed to veer towards a nationalism even more intense than might have been expected from a half century of impotence and revolution, and to seek reassurance in their country's vast size and splendid history, their faith in the revolution which they had made and an optimistic view of world politics. In their eyes Asia, Africa and Latin America were revolutionary, anti-colonial domains where their major enemies – the United States, the USSR and the principal western European states – would get into trouble because of their archaic political attitudes and economic contradictions. Western Europe and northern America would also develop similar revolutionary movements in which the bourgeoisie would be threatened and would finally be supplanted by the proletariat. Meanwhile China must assemble and develop its resources and – in the view of Mao himself and some of his associates – preserve the ardour of its revolution.

MODERNIZATION

Mao's government was pledged to end corruption in the public services, reverse the economic slide which had overwhelmed the Kuomintang, make China a modern industrial power and introduce sweeping reforms in land-holding and agriculture. These were huge tasks requiring money, authority and peace, and it was difficult to say which was the most pressing. Corruption, waste and bureaucracy were attacked in the Three-Anti campaign begun in Manchuria in August 1951 and extended to the whole of China two months later. A Five-Anti campaign followed, directed against bribery, tax evasion, fraud, the theft of state property and the betrayal of economic secrets. These campaigns seem to betoken, on the part of the government, a real concern to secure the approbation of the Chinese people and, conversely, an equal concern to ensure that the people should not only behave correctly but think correctly. The campaigns were pursued by means of public meetings, confessions and purges. They were indiscriminate and were used for attacks on unpopular or richer classes such as missionaries, merchants and private entrepreneurs. Landlords and kulaks were also singled out, partly as an acknowledgement of the debt owed to the poorer peasants who had ensured the survival and eventual success of the communists. The dispossession of landlords and kulaks, which began in 1950, was accelerated and made horrible by the panic which spread in China during the first months of the Korean War and claimed 2 million victims or more: the newly installed rulers, like the leaders of the French Revolution facing the armies of *émigrés* and hostile powers, lived in expectation of a counter-revolutionary uprising which would be supported and exploited by the United States.

Collectivization began slowly in 1951. The example of the USSR in the thirties, and the inadvisability of disillusioning and antagonizing the peasants who had just become proprietors in place of the vanished landlords, dictated caution. In 1953–54 Mao was ill and Gao Gang – the semi-autonomous lord of Manchuria, pro-Moscow, pro-heavy industry – was temporarily in charge. (He committed suicide soon afterwards.) On his return Mao decided to step up the pace of change, particularly in agriculture. After two poor years the 1955 harvest promised well; he did not want to leave the new peasant proprietors undisturbed for long for fear that a new class of kulaks might emerge from their ranks; the first five-year plan, covering the years 1952–57 (but not published until about half its course was run) was inadequately primed by the Russian pump and needed a further boost that could come only from brigading and driving the peasants into more efficient methods and greater productivity. The basic aim was to sap the peasant's resistance to the state; so long as he owned his land he would keep the will to fight, but as soon as he lost it the spirit would go out of him.

In the earlier years the approach to communal ownership had been cautiously prepared through a series of staging points beginning with co-operation on specified tasks at certain seasons; proceeding thence to a distribution of rewards partly on the basis of the size of a man's holding and partly on the amount of work done by him; and so leading to a final phase in which the ownership of the land would be transferred to the communal group (not the state), rewards would be calculated entirely on the basis of work done, and the group's affairs would be regulated by general meetings and elected committees. From the latter part of 1955 this progression was enormously accelerated and in something like two or two and a half years it was all but completed.

The speed of this vast economic and social revolution was characteristic of the methods and outlook of China's new leaders but it also sharpened the discomforts and resentments (especially among the better-off peasants) which such a programme would have evoked in any case.

During these years Mao, whose rapid collectivization was bound to offend the more conservative, also ran the risk of disgruntling the more radical faction by wooing the intellectuals who, though suspect because of their western training and thinking, were very useful to the régime. Mao, perhaps influenced by events in Hungary, wanted to initiate a genuine debate which would engender a genuine conviction of the correctness of his policies. The intellectuals, however, were extremely chary of beginning, even after Mao, by coining the slogan of the Hundred Flowers, virtually pressed them to believe that the régime wanted them to think for themselves and express their views with more freedom and less regard for conformity than they had hitherto dared to use. When criticism was evoked, it proved to be too exuberant. The inevitable disillusion which was eroding the high hopes and self-reliant optimism of the morrow of victory had been sharpened by inflation, labour troubles, and shortages of food and consumer goods, and in this atmosphere the hoped-for discussion about how to progress along the communist path extended to more radical questioning of basic communist tenets. A few months after the first mention of the Hundred Flowers the debate released by that slogan was abruptly closed.

It was succeeded early in 1958, at the commencement of the second five-year plan, by the Great Leap Forward and the vigorous introduction of the commune system in country and town. The Great Leap Forward (preceded by an earlier and unsuccessful Little Leap during 1956–57) was an incitement to greater exertions associated particularly with Liu Shaoqi, a leader of the more impetuous school who succeeded at the end of 1958 to the highest position in the state upon the unexpected retirement of Mao from the presidency. The Great Leap Forward was a short cut to greater production. After some experimentation it was ordained for the whole country in the autumn of 1958. The principal objects were to mobilize labour, set women free for industrial jobs, establish local industries as an adjunct to the larger units of production, and provide country people with an elementary introduction to industrial processes. One of the most publicized items in the programme was the making of steel in back yards (a system which produced much but poor steel), but the most important feature was the communes. These began to be formed at the beginning of 1958, were announced and explained in April, and were rapidly established throughout rural areas to the accompaniment of a propaganda barrage designed to drown criticism in a wave of enthusiasm. Property was brought into commercial ownership and individuals were told to look to the community for free food, services and entertainment. In many places results went ludicrously and tragically far; even cottages, trees, fowls and small tools were turned into communal property. The vast size of China made radical reform almost impossibly difficult since the central government had only faulty machinery for ensuring that its wishes were carried out sensibly. It operated in fact through cadres, a non-communist device added by the communists to the system of government in China. These cadres were the links between the central government and the people. They were responsible for much of the inefficiency, crudity and brutality with which new policies were implemented, but without them government would have broken down and, in reverse, government would have been without any means of discovering the mood of the people.

By bad luck the inefficiencies of the Great Leap Forward were magnified by natural disasters which produced great hardships and famines, and the whole experiment, in so far as it was meant to rationalize and boost agriculture production, was abandoned. It was a piece of wilfulness on Mao's part which lacked both the necessary labour and the necessary enthusiasm on the ground, a vast flop which was for a time concealed by false claims. Although the communes survived as new elements in society and in government, by 1960 the small team was once more the basis of the rural economy. The revolution moreover lost face seriously during the great famine years. It had exacerbated an inevitable crisis by grave overestimates of crop production and it had experimented unsuccessfully with a new communal pattern which the Russians had explicitly and correctly derided.

In the sixties the revolution began to devour its children. China's ruling group was disrupted with a violence more familiar in the USSR than in China, where the only major communist figures to have been purged had been Gao Gang in 1954 and Peng Dehuai in 1959, both suspected of being too Russophile. Mao, approaching the end of his life, became obsessed by the fear that his life's work was being eroded by bourgeois backsliding and compromise. He determined to displace all those leaders whose steadfastness and fervour were in doubt and to revitalize party and populace by turning to youth. After some years of reflection and preparation he revealed in 1965 to his principal colleagues plans for a cultural revolution and appointed the mayor of Beijing, Peng Zhen, to direct it. Peng Zhen, however, was soon at cross purposes with Jiang Qing, Mao's third wife, and sometime in the first half of 1966 he was dismissed. In May 1966 Mao reappeared in public after an effacement of six months and a few weeks later the Cultural Revolution got publicly under way with a series of rallies, demonstrations and denunciations and a much publicized swim by Mao in the Yangtse near the provincial capital of Wuhan. It so happened that at this time there was a major breakdown in the educational system which had forced the authorities to postpone for a year all entries into universities and similar institutions and so discharged millions of young people into temporary purposelessness. They were turned into Red Guards who were to replace the communist youth organization (which had supposedly gone flabby) and go to work to boost production in field and factory. From these useful, if unacademic, pursuits they were diverted to an ideological crusade and, in an exuberance of anti-revisionist spirits, demonstrated against revolutionary insufficiencies and pre-revolutionary attitudes and symbols, assaulting individuals and destroying property in a movement which spread so extensively that it disrupted communications and brought factories to a halt. Some 20 million young people were said to be involved, most of them in their teens.

'Cultural Revolution' was the misleading name for a reign of terror accompanied by the most revolting cruelty. It had its sources in internal and external problems – economic planning, devolution, consolidation versus forcing the pace of progress, attitudes to the Russians – which had troubled the party in the fifties and disrupted it in the sixties. The revolution split the party at all levels. Hundreds or thousands of leaders, from President Liu Shaoqi to much humbler officials, lost their posts. Inevitably the army advanced in power. Lin Biao, who had succeeded Peng Dehuai in 1959 and had invented and distributed the famous little red book, sided with Mao, thus ensuring Mao's victory and confirming the defeat of the pro-Russian faction once represented by Peng. Lin Biao was proclaimed Mao's eventual heir. But in 1971 he disappeared. Rumour had it that he fled to the USSR in an aircraft that crashed in Mongolia, killing him. Two years later at the tenth congress of the Chinese Communist Party he was openly attacked. He was accused of plotting to assassinate Mao and cement an alliance with the USSR. These charges were repeated at the joint trial in 1980 of the leaders of the Cultural Revolution and Lin's one-time closest military associates.

Mao Zedong died in 1976. Zhou Enlai died earlier in the same year. These two events released a struggle for power between three main groups. The first beneficiary was Hua Guofeng who was Mao's choice for the leadership and succeeded Zhou as (acting) prime minister. This was a setback for Zhou's 72-year old deputy and presumed heir Deng Xiaoping. Deng, general secretary of the Communist Party in 1956, had been purged during the Cultural Revolution but reappeared in 1974 and in the next year was appointed deputy chairman of the party, first deputy prime minister and chief of staff of the army. Demonstrations in Beijing in Deng's favour led to his disgrace and the further promotion of Hua to be first deputy chairman of the party (next to Mao) and prime minister. When Mao himself died Hua, temporarily free from attack from the right, moved swiftly against the radical left. The so-called Gang of Four, led by Jiang Qing, were arrested a few weeks later and Hua became chairman of the party. But in the following year Deng made a comeback and for the next three years Hua and Deng shared the principal posts and the limelight, until in 1980 Deng ousted Hua after a campaign in which Hua's position as Mao's successor was undermined in the name of democratic freedom and Mao himself was criticized for having acted autocratically by nominating his successor. At the same time the Gang of Four were brought to trial and linked with Lin Biao's abortive coup of 1971. The effect of the trial, and presumably its purpose, was to represent the Gang of Four as a conspiratorial group in the tradition of China's secret societies; to discredit the armed forces as treasonable and incompetent; and indirectly to implicate Mao himself in the economic and social disasters of the Cultural Revolution.

In Chinese communist terms Deng was a conservative pragmatist, even a reactionary. His victory meant a return to traditional types of competitive examination, the rehabilitation of the intelligentsia and other victims of the radical years, the restoration of the profit motive, higher prices for peasants and higher wages in industry and commerce, and wider openings to the west and Japan and even to the USSR. But although a revisionist and modernizer, Deng was no liberal or any sort of democrat. He wanted to modernize the Chinese economy without relaxing the political grip of the Communist Party. The Cultural Revolution had set back modernization and in his declining years Mao had failed in his primary task of bringing China back to its rightful place as the greatest power in the world. Deng and his colleagues elaborated programmes for the modernization of industry, the armed forces, agriculture and science and technology. Large sums were borrowed and spent but programmes were cut back when the financial establishment (bankers returning to posts which they had held before the Cultural Revolution or even before Mao's triumph over Jiang Kaishek) discovered that foreign funding was outrunning foreign revenues (exports, remittances from overseas Chinese, tourism). Growth was strong – with some poor spots in energy production from all sources and grains – but so too was demand. Inflation rose therefore to 20–30 per cent a year and corruption was magnified as the gap grew between official prices, unchanged for years, and prices on black markets. Price reform was urgent but anticipation of it further accentuated the gap, caused runs on banks as depositors rushed to change their money into goods, and so forced the government to postpone price reform. As in the USSR the problem of grafting market mechanisms into a command economy generated economic breakdown and bitter disputes between political leaders.

Deng was himself caught in these dilemmas. He both saw the need for liberal measures and feared them. He was alive to his dependence on the army and its ageing and conservative chiefs who had thrown him out in 1966 and restored him in 1975; he much enlarged the armed police force. He oscillated between an innate authoritarianism and a readiness to loosen the reins in order to foster economic progress – and an equal readiness to tighten the reins when relaxation encouraged political protest. His policies engendered therefore their own reversal. He tolerated and seemed to encourage the efflorescence of protest which in 1978–79 took the form of affixing popular complaints and demands on Democracy Wall in Beijing and he was able to combine for several years substantial economic expansion with tolerable political freedoms. But about 1985–86 economic advance faltered while popular demands became on the contrary more pressing. The price of economic progress was rising prices, rising inflation (to around 10 per cent), breakdowns and bottlenecks in communications, shortages of capital and energy, and corruption. Economic growth, instead of relieving want, was making it worse and fuelling indignation. Deng imposed import controls and devalued the currency in an attempt to restrain the economy and, in the face of rising student clamour for more and quicker changes, he relaxed censorship and permitted more open political debate. But in 1987, scared by the outcome of this liberalizing trend, he briefly changed course, muzzled liberal academics and compelled the Communist Party's comparatively liberal and comparatively young general secretary, Hu Yaobang, to resign (as he himself had been compelled by Mao to resign in 1966). After a few months Deng again changed course and reverted to a relatively liberal stance. At the end of the year he fulfilled his frequently announced intention to retire, taking with him into retirement a clutch of old conservatives and leaving at the head of affairs two younger men – Hu's successor Zhao Ziyang and a new prime minister, Li Peng. Deng's retirement was more apparent than real and not very apparent.

In 1989 Hu died. His funeral was made the occasion for massive demonstrations in which students from Beijing's universities were specially prominent, voicing protests against the slow pace of change, economic failure and persistent corruption. They were joined by discontented intellectuals and by workers, and suddenly they were making a big impact not only in the capital but also in some eighty other cities all over China. They posed a threat, not necessarily to the Communist Party, but to its elderly ruling clique. To the octogenarian Deng, however, and to others of his generation these two threats were indistinguishable and amounted also to a threat to China itself. Deng equated the party with the revolution which it had made, and the revolution with China. Anybody who opposed the party was therefore a traitor to his country. At this critical moment Zhao, who shared Hu's belief that economic reforms required some political reforms too, happened to be away in Korea. On his return to Beijing he took a conciliatory, even sympathetic and apologetic, line but behind the scenes his more conservative adversaries persuaded the mutable Deng to their side. The students were attacked and maligned in official publications. Over-optimistically they for their part refused to be intimidated. The resulting confrontation was briefly frozen because of the impending arrival of Gorbachev in Beijing. In Tiananmen Square, which was permanently occupied by huge but well-ordered crowds, the mood turned to hostility against Deng personally. Deng resolved to use force to dispel the crowds. The first moves by troops were blocked by unarmed civilians, the temper of the soldiers appeared uncertain or even friendly to the demonstrators, and two operations were called off; but eventually the drama which had riveted the attention of much of the world from the end of April to the first days of June was brought to its close by massacre. Governments all over the world expressed outrage, loudly but briefly.

These events checked Deng's external policies. A decade earlier Deng had visited Tokyo and Washington and some years later he had received Thatcher in Beijing and sent his foreign minister to Moscow. An eight-year commercial agreement with Japan, concluded in 1978, was followed by a full peace treaty. With the United States full diplomatic relations were established in 1978: Washington agreed to shift formal recognition from Taiwan to Beijing and remove its troops from Taiwan, while China watered down its demand for the complete abrogation of Washington's treaty relations with Taiwan. Reagan angered China shortly after his election by trying to square the new Sino–American concord with a revival of sales of arms to Taiwan but he was quickly forced to abandon this impossible stance. Bush pursued the Nixon–Reagan policy of making friends and contracts in China, overlooking brutal Chinese repression of risings in Tibet in 1987 and 1989 and a personal rebuff when the Chinese government prevented the outspoken critic Fang Lizhi from accepting an invitation to meet Bush at the American embassy in Beijing. At the same time Deng cautiously improved relations with the USSR. Whereas in the seventies he had advertised his discontent with Moscow by despatching Hua on visits to Romania and Yugoslavia and by publicly advocating a Sino–Japanese–American alliance against the USSR, he responded amicably to Gorbachev's first indications in 1986 that the USSR was prepared to make concessions on border disputes, withdraw troops from Mongolia and Afghanistan and end support for the Vietnamese occupation of Kampuchea. The Chinese foreign minister visited Moscow – the first such visit for over thirty years – and Gorbachev was invited to Beijing. Before going there in 1989 he announced the withdrawal of 500,000 troops from China's borders and a reduction by two-thirds of the USSR's 50,000 troops in Mongolia.

Over Hong Kong Deng made the most of a strong bargaining

position. The New Territories, which comprised 89 per cent of the territory under British rule, were occupied under a lease due to expire in 1997. Thatcher went to Beijing in 1982, seeking better relations and business deals with China and agreement therefore over Hong Kong. She tried unsuccessfully to get China to accept continuing British administration under Chinese sovereignty (the solution once mooted but discarded for the Falkland Islands). Unlike the people of Gibraltar – another offshore island – the people of Hong Kong were allowed no determining voice in their future when an agreement covering the cession of the colony as well as the leased New Territories was formalized in 1984. This agreement was an attempt to secure for Hong Kong after 1997 a greater degree of freedom than it had under British rule, but details were left vague and to the Chinese. The Basic Law which was to give Hong Kong a special status for fifty years after 1997, preserve its capitalist economy, guarantee free movement for its residents and maintain the existing legal system and civil rights (but with no appeal to London), was to be drafted by the Chinese. The agreement was therefore a surrender qualified by hopes for the best and in Hong Kong, particularly after the events of 1989 in China, hopes were minimal. The Basic Law approved by the National People's Congress in Beijing in 1990 provided that one-third of the sixty seats in the legislative council should be elective in 1997 and no more than half by 2003. It required the British not to allow elections beyond these limits in the intervening years 1990–97. This grudging, but hardly surprising, enactment, coupled with fear magnified by the massacre in Tiananmen Square, spread dismay in Hong Kong and presented Britain with the problem of preventing massive emigration and economic collapse. It resorted to measures which were both dubiously proper and dubiously effective. It proposed to give 50,000 Hong Kongers the right of entry to Britain with their dependants. The select few would be picked on a complicated points system which, however, could not conceal the fact that Britain was fulfilling its obligations not to the people of Hong Kong but to an elite of successful businessmen and colonial servants.

4 WORLD ORDER

So long as the state remained the basic element in international society the preservation of world order and the prevention of war could only be secured by the more powerful of these states. They had a choice of methods. Each major power might assume primary or exclusive responsibility in a given region, or all the major powers might together supervise and police the whole globe, or these same powers might equip and finance an association of other states to do the job vicariously on their behalf. After the Second World War international organization and international co-operation were theoretically based on the second of these methods after the first had been unsuccessfully advocated in some quarters; but the circumstances necessary for the success of the second method did not materialize, so that practice approximated rather to an adaptation of the third, imperfectly acknowledged and precariously pursued.

The forms of international organization were discussed during the war by the principal victors-to-be. Churchill and Roosevelt both inclined to a regional pattern, and Churchill elaborated a scheme for a number of local federations to be grouped in three regions under a supreme global council. Power would be concentrated in the three regions – European, American, Pacific – rather than above or below. This pattern did not appeal to Stalin whose suspicions of Churchill, based on his mistrust of the British governing class and on disputes over the timing of the opening of a second front in western Europe, were sharpened by proposals which included the creation of Balkan and Danubian federations in an area of special concern to the USSR: Stalin wanted untrammelled sovereignty and, so far as the two were not incompatible, a continuing association with his allies in order to avoid a return of the USSR's prewar isolation. On the western side too there was opposition to regionalism, especially among professional politicians like Cordell Hull and Eden who feared that it would produce autarkic blocs each dominated by a particular major power and would in particular revive American isolationism. At Moscow, in October 1943, the foreign ministers of the three allies adopted the principle of a global organization based on the sovereign equality of all states and, with a minimum of incompatibility, laid the foundations for a new world organization which was to perpetuate the alliance of democracy and communism against fascism and give to the principal representatives of the former the charge for keeping the peace by the joint exercise of their allied power, this joint charge being coupled with a guarantee for each of them of immunity from any substantive interference by lesser states which were to recognize their superior power and undiluted sovereignty.

The United Nations was, in form, a revised version of the League of Nations. The principal organs of the two bodies were very similar. The authors of the UN Charter aimed, not to devise a new kind of organization, but to retain a familiar framework and insert into it more effective machinery for the prevention of war. The Covenant of the League had not proscribed war. It had bound its signatories to pause before resorting to war and to attempt to resolve their differences by one of three recommended processes. If this interposition of reason failed, there was no covenanted ban on the resort to war, and international sanctions were only applicable in the event of a resort to war in defiance of the preconditions laid down by the Covenant. In 1928 a much more radical attempt to prevent war was made by the signatories of the Kellogg–Briand Pact, who engaged themselves to dispense with war altogether except for certain limited purposes, namely the defence of the Pact itself and of the Covenant and of existing treaties, and in the exercise of the right of self-defence (the justification for the exercise of this right being left to the state claiming it): the United States and Britain also attached conditions relating respectively to the Monroe Doctrine and the defence of the British empire. The UN Charter fell somewhere between the conceptions of war as permissible subject to a pause for taking counsel and war as impermissible subject to defined exceptions. The Charter went far towards banning war except in defence of the Charter, or in pursuance of the obligations contained in it, or in self-defence but it did not totally proscribe war. It explicitly sanctioned not only the use of international force but also the use of national force, by one state or an alliance, in self-defence. The Charter vested considerable authority in the Security Council which was empowered to determine whether a given situation contained a threat to international peace or a breach of the peace or an act of aggression and, if it so determined, to require all UN members to take action against the delinquent (except to use force, a sanction which remained voluntary to each member). On the other hand this collective authority was offset by the procedural obstacles to reaching in the first place a collective decision in the Council, namely, a majority of the Council and the assent of all its five permanent members. In the absence of such a decision it was improper for any UN member to reach an opposite decision or take measures of the kind envisaged in the Charter;

whereas an affirmative decision of the Council automatically placed all members under obligation, a failure to reach a decision precluded all action under the Charter. Consequently, although the Council was in this field sovereign over the members, each of the permanent members was sovereign over the Council.

Like the League, the UN was designed as an association of sovereign states (notwithstanding that its ban on interference in the internal affairs of a member – article 2(7) – did not extend to measures for peace enforcement under chapter VII), and like the League it attempted to assert a degree of collective judgment and a field for collective action against its constituent sovereign members in a period when these members had been massively strengthened by the growth of modern technology and of modern ways of influencing people. The state had turned the industrial and the democratic revolutions of the nineteenth century to its own advantage by annexing modern armaments and popular chauvinism to its purposes. Neither the League nor the UN was able to steal the control of armaments from sovereign states nor to create in the peoples of the world an attachment to international organizations which exceeded their purely national patriotism. Besides these general handicaps the UN saw its peace-keeping machinery rendered inoperative at an early stage of its existence. The efficacy of this machinery depended upon the unanimity of the major powers in the Security Council and the provision by all members of forces adequate for the execution of the Council's decisions. The unanimity of the major powers faded in the first breath of peace, so that the veto became a common tactical instrument instead of a weapon of last resort and the Charter's prescription for raising international forces – a series of bilateral agreements between the Security Council and members – was never implemented because the body appointed to negotiate these agreements, the Military Staff Committee, never agreed even the general nature and size of the forces required.

The veto given to the permanent members of the Security Council was a special feature of the UN. In the Council of the League every member had a veto. The authors of the UN Charter had to decide how far to depart from this unanimity rule. They decided to introduce majority voting as a general practice but subject to limited exceptions: in the Security Council, but not in other organs, special power was accorded special privileges with the result that major powers were able to prevent action against themselves or their friends, although they were not entitled to prevent discussion and criticism. No permanent member of the Council has ever objected to this principle, although particular permanent members have objected to the use of the privilege by other permanent members. During the late forties and fifties the USSR, being in a semi-permanent minority in the Council, used the veto to such an extent that other members complained of a breach of the spirit, if not the provisions, of the Charter. Russians argued in return that the UN had become a tool of American policies and that these policies were basically anti-Russian – as evidenced by Truman's use of his nuclear monopoly for political purposes, by speeches of prominent western leaders beginning with Churchill at Fulton and Byrnes at Stuttgart in February and September 1946. The USSR, after an initial attempt to use the UN for its own political purposes by raising or supporting complaints about the Dutch in Indonesia, the British and French in Syria and Lebanon, the British in Egypt and Greece and western tolerance of Franco's fascism in Spain, fell back upon the veto to meet western counter-charges and then in January 1950 ceased to attend meetings of the Security Council. This retreat from the UN was, however, reversed partly because it enabled the Security Council to initiate action in Korea in June 1950 and partly because the expansion of the UN – notably in 1955 and 1960, the years respectively of a package deal admitting an assortment of sixteen blocked candidates and of the major African afflux – altered the character of the organization and offered the Russians political opportunities outweighing its fundamentally minority position in the Security Council. (It was in this period that the Russians ceased to attack the leaders of new states as bourgeois stooges and began instead to make friends with them.)

American hostility to the frequent Russian use of the veto led to two attempts to circumvent it by transferring to the General Assembly some part of the Security Council's authority. In 1948 an *ad hoc* committee of the Assembly, popularly called the Little Assembly, was established as a means of keeping the Assembly in permanent session, but the Little Assembly's powers were circumscribed and it never became an organ of any importance. The Russians were not alone in regarding it as a contravention of the Charter and it faded away. More important was the adoption in 1950 of the Uniting for Peace resolution. This resolution was sponsored by the United States which saw that the UN operations in Korea had been made possible only by the absence of the Russian member and his veto from the Security Council and which sought to ensure that their presence on a future occasion would not fatally obstruct similar action. The resolution, which was adopted by the Assembly by fifty votes to five with two abstentions, introduced machinery for calling an emergency session of the Assembly at short notice; asserted the right of the Assembly to pass judgment on threats to peace, breaches of the peace and acts of aggression when the Security Council was prevented from doing so; created a Peace Observation Committee of fourteen, available for missions of exploration and elucidation in trouble spots; also created a (stillborn) Collective Measures Committee of fourteen to study international peace-keeping machinery; and asked members to earmark forces for service at short notice in UN peace-keeping operations. The Assembly twice stig-matized China as an aggressor in Korea under this procedure and again used it in 1956 to denounce the Anglo–Franco–Israeli attack on Egypt and raise an international force to supplant these aggressors. But the legality of the Uniting for Peace resolution was always in dispute. The USSR and other members attacked it and refused to pay for operations set in motion by the Assembly within its terms of reference. In 1962 the International Court was asked to advise on this issue and declared by nine votes to five that the Security Council's responsibility for peace-keeping was primary but not exclusive.

Thus disputes of a legal nature, reflecting fundamental political disagreements, threatened to thwart the hopes of those who had sought in 1945 to produce a document and an organization which would secure peace and order. Disharmony among the permanent members made a mockery of the Security Council's name and turned the Council itself into an arena for the public display of wrangling and propaganda charges. Open diplomacy became as discredited as secret diplomacy had once been suspect. Likewise the General Assembly became noted for the marshalling of block votes and the trading of unattached ones, especially after the afflux of new members had increased the number of those who were likely to have no direct interest in a particular issue and who would therefore vote either for ulterior reasons or not at all. Recourse to the UN became in consequence something of a gamble owing to the unpredictability of the attitudes of many members.

Disappointment with the functioning of the central organs of the UN led to a recrudescence of interest in regionalism. Although the authors of the Charter had come down on the side of centralism as opposed to regionalism, they had not totally excluded the latter from their design. The Charter recognized regional organizations in two ways. It affirmed by article 51 the right of regional self-defence and in effect sanctioned a regional collective system for defence which was an alternative to the machinery of the Security Council. This article covered regional alliances such as Nato, whose primary purpose was not the main-tenance of peace and order within their area but the defence of it from outside threats. Secondly, the Charter made provision in article 52 for regional organizations intended to police the region and resolve disputes arising within it. The Organization of American States was, however, the only organization of this kind to achieve any significant claim to effectiveness in the first thirty years of the UN's existence, with the result that regionalism did not in this period offer any substantial alternative to the UN's central organs as a means of keeping the peace within a region.

But although the Security Council failed to function as anticipated by its authors and although regional organizations failed to step into the gap, the UN became continuously active in security operations, developed a variety of experimental techniques and even engaged – in the Congo – in a major operation in which it deployed a total of nearly 100,000 men over four years. UN intervention in dangerous situations ranged from comparatively modest missions to establish facts, lower tension and gain time, through more complex mediatory operations involving military units but not the use of military force, to military expeditions prepared not only to defend themselves but also to attack others. The line between one type of operation and another cannot be precisely drawn. Thus UN intervention in Kashmir, Palestine and the Suez War could be classified as mediatory and in Korea and the Congo as military, whereas intervention in Cyprus could arguably be placed in either category, or in one category to begin with and in another at a later stage. But classification is no index of activity and the UN's activity in peace-keeping is not to be denied. Where the League had been criticized for passivity, the UN came to be criticized for doing too much.

In the first or pre-Korean phase of this activity the Security Council was faced with situations arising out of the war: the lingering of the Russians in Iran beyond the term set by wartime agreements, and the slowness of British and French troops to leave Syria and Lebanon. These matters were debated in the Council and resolved outside it without further ado. Precedents of recourse to the Council were quickly set. The Council declined to act on a Russian complaint of British interference in Greek affairs through British troops in Greece, but it later investigated Greek complaints of foreign aid to Greek rebels by Yugoslavia, Bulgaria and Albania. It despatched teams of observers who, after being denied access to the non-Greek sides of the frontiers in question, issued a report condemning Greece's enemies. The Council did not put an end to the fighting in progress (which was only stopped when American aid had re-equipped the Greek army and restored its morale and when Yugoslavia, after the breach with the USSR and its communist neighbours in 1948, stopped helping the rebels), but the UN had set a precedent for on-the-spot investigations and could claim that it had contributed to elucidating and holding a potentially dangerous situation until it was eliminated by other means. This function was further exemplified in Indonesia and Kashmir. In Indonesia the Council succeeded in establishing a cease-fire which temporarily halted the first Dutch police action against the Indonesian nationalists and secured a temporary agreement between the two sides through a conciliation committee. Although these achievements were at first transitory, the eventual transfer of sovereignty from the Netherlands to the Indonesian republic at the end of 1949 was mediated by international intervention. In Kashmir too the UN negotiated a cease-fire and succeeded in putting a stop to fighting, even though it failed to secure a withdrawal of Pakistani or Indian troops which had entered

Kashmir or to resolve the underlying political dispute between Pakistan and India. Kashmir was the first clear example of a paradox which was later to become explicit and teasing: the fact that a cease-fire and the immobilization of hostilities could obstruct the solution of basic disputes by relieving the contestants of the urgency to come to terms in order to save lives and money. UN observers, sent to Kashmir in 1949, were still there over thirty years later.

In Palestine, the final pre-Korean illustration of UN security operations, UN emissaries negotiated a cease-fire, repaired it when it was broken and helped to secure armistice agreements. The Arabs and Israel did not, however, make peace and a UN Truce Supervisory Organization found itself established in the Middle East for more years than its originators had contemplated, subjecting both sides to the hazards of having their infractions of the truce exposed by an impartial body of observers.

The Korean War which, like other events referred to in this summary of UN activities, is described in more detail elsewhere in this book, was a test of a different kind since it arose out of an act of aggression to which there could be no effective response except the use of force. Chapter VII of the Charter was invoked and the Security Council, in the absence of the USSR, in effect endorsed American action and commissioned the United States, which had forces available in Japan and the surrounding waters, to meet force with force. The Korean War became therefore a war conducted by an American general responsible to the American president acting as the agent of the UN. Fifteen other states, mostly allied with the United States for other reasons, sent units to the battlefield but half the ground forces engaged, 93 per cent of air forces and 86 per cent of naval forces were American, and when the Chinese invaded Korea and the war gradually evolved into a trial of strength between the United States and China (with the possibility of an even larger clash between the United States and the USSR whose aid for the communist side was not far in the background) many UN members began to feel that the UN's motives in going to war had been lost sight of and that no future UN operation ought to be conducted in the same way. After the Korean War it was an axiom that major powers should not be invited to make a fighting contribution to UN operations – an axiom only attenuated in Cyprus by the obvious advantage of using the British forces already present in the island. Korea became therefore an exception. But its part in typing the UN as an organization prepared to take action, as opposed to the League's failure to take action in Manchuria twenty years earlier, is not to be underestimated.

The next important operation – the UN intervention at Suez in 1956 – was a combined operation by medium powers set in motion by the General Assembly and placed under the executive control of the

NORTH ATLANTIC
OCEAN

SOUTH ATLAN
OCEAN

KEY

1	UNSCOB	UN Special Committee on the Balkans (1947)
2	UNSCOP	UN Special Committee on Palestine (1947)
3	UNCIP	UN Commission for India and Pakistan (1948)
4	UNMOGIP	UN Military Observation Group in India and Pakistan – Kashmir (1949)
5	UNCI	UN Commission for Indonesia (1949)
6	UNTSO	UN Truce Supervision Organization in Palestine (1949)
7	UNCOK	UN Commission on Korea (1950–53)
8	UNEF	UN emergency Force for the Middle East – Egypt (1956)
9	UNOGIL	UN Observer Group in Lebanon (1958)
10	ONUC	UN Force in the Congo (1960)
11	UNTEA	UN Temporary Executive Authority for West Irian (1962)
12	UNYOM	UN Observation Mission in Yemen (1963)
13	UNFICYP	UN Peace-keeping Force in Cyprus (1964)
14	UNIPOM	UN India-Pakistan Observation Mission – Kashmir (1965)

4.1   Scenes of United Nations Interventions since 1945

KOREA (7)

NS (1)

LEBANON
(9, 15)
PRUS (13)
PAKISTAN (3)
PALESTINE
(2, 6)
PT (8)

KASHMIR (4, 14)

THAILAND-
KAMPUCHEA
(16)

INDIA (3)

PACIFIC OCEAN

YEMEN (12)

CONGO (ZAIRE) (10)

INDIAN OCEAN

INDONESIA (5, 11)

NAMIBIA
(17)

5	UNIFIL	UN Interim Force in Lebanon (1977)
6	UNBOG	UN Border Observation Group – Thailand – Kampuchea (1980)
7	UNTAG	UN Observer Group to Namibian Elections (1989)

secretary-general. The force, which was recruited and despatched with astonishing speed, was equipped for self-defence but not for attack: ten nations contributed troops. Its arrival and deployment was secured in advance by agreement with Egypt (necessary, since the operation fell within chapter VI of the Charter on peaceful settlement of disputes and was not an enforcement action under chapter VII) and by the knowledge that the British and French governments would not use the power which they had to oppose it. The Anglo–French attack on Egypt having been halted by the United States, the UN was used to lever the Anglo–French forces out, to patrol the troubled areas along the Suez Canal and incidentally to clear the canal which the Egyptians had blocked when they were attacked. Peace was restored through the agency of the UN after the United States had displayed a determination, which neither Britain, France nor Israel could gainsay, to stop the fighting. The role of the UN in this crisis was performed within the framework of collective security but was in fact something different. The proponents of collective security, whether in the League or the UN, envisaged the mustering, under pre-existing commitments, of overwhelming force to deter or stop a transgressor. At Suez in 1956 the transgressors were not stopped by such a collective show of force but by the United States. The collective force sent to the area could not have fought the Anglo–French or Israeli aggressors, nor was it meant to. It was intended not to push the intruders out but to keep the major powers out, and the name found for this type of activity has been 'preventive diplomacy'. Hammarskjöld's aim was to forestall by a UN presence the incursion into the conflict zone of the Americans and Russians, and his experiences at Suez fashioned his policy in the Congo four years later. Some of the limitations on action of this kind were demonstrated when, in 1967, the UN force was removed on Egypt's abrupt demand. Others were demonstrated simultaneously with the war of 1956 when the USSR refused to allow even a personal visit to Budapest by Hammarskjöld.

Between Suez and the Congo, a period of less than four years, the UN was again invoked in the Middle East and was required to use its techniques as observer and mediator. In 1958 the Lebanese government complained of interference in its internal affairs by the United Arab Republic and called in American troops. The UN despatched a few groups of mobile observers to check and report on what was happening along Lebanon's borders and subsequently enlarged this mission to enable it to replace the American units, whose presence had become an embarrassment to all concerned, including the Americans. The UN thereby shed light on a confused situation, deflated it and finally smoothed the way for a return to normality. This was an adaptation of previous experiences. It was followed, more or less, in Laos in 1959; in West Irian in 1962–63 when a UN presence eased the transfer from the

Netherlands to Indonesia; in North Borneo and Sarawak in 1963 when UN investigators reported that the inhabitants of these territories were not, as Indonesia alleged, opposed to the creation of Malaysia; in Yemen in 1963–64 when a situation as obscure as it was contentious was to some extent clarified by UN observers; and in discovering the wishes of the inhabitants of the trust territories of Togoland and the Cameroons when the administering powers were about to withdraw between 1956 and 1960.

The involvement of the UN in the Congo was a consequence of the precipitate Belgian withdrawal and the mutiny a few days later of the Congolese army, upon which the Belgians returned to protect their nationals, Katanga purported to secede and the Congolese government turned to the UN for help in keeping order, securing essential services, getting foreign forces out and holding the new state together. This involvement had therefore from the start a mixture of international and internal aspects. It was international in so far as it aimed at removing the Belgians and pre-empting the Americans and the Russians – a further instance of preventive diplomacy. But it was also internal in so far as the UN forces were filling the gap created by the mutiny or inadequacy of the Congolese government's own forces and, besides securing law and order, became involved in maintaining the integrity of the new state by preventing the secession of part of it. Hammarskjöld used his right under article 99 of the Charter to bring the matter to the attention of the Security Council. In the four years in which the UN then operated in the Congo a force which reached a strength of 20,000 and averaged 15,000 was used (at a total cost of over $400 million, of which 42 per cent was paid by the United States and none by the USSR) to keep order, prevent civil war and, more contentiously, to force Katanga to acknowledge the authority of the Congolese state. Its operations were based on chapter VI of the Charter. Chapter VII was never explicitly invoked, although shifting circumstances produced a situation very like enforcement action under chapter VII. These operations were initiated by the Security Council, but they were conducted by the secretary-general and medium powers.

Once again only medium states were asked to supply combat units and the secretary-general was given executive control. He created an *ad hoc* advisory committee of representatives of the states with troops engaged, in order to help him to interpret the general directives given by the Security Council and apply them to the circumstances of the moment. Acting in this way the UN became the prime factor in preserving the unity and integrity of the new state and in preventing foreign intervention and perhaps a clash between major powers; it also alleviated human distress by containing civil war, minimizing bloodshed, helping refugees and providing a range of basic medical, administrative and other services; but in the short run it strained itself by incurring the hostility of major powers who distrusted the growth of the secretary-general's authority, sometimes disapproved of his objects and actions, and jibbed at the price which they were asked to pay towards keeping the peace. But if the major powers were not to allow and enable the UN to act in defence of international security, they would have to assume the role of policemen themselves, whether jointly or severally – or permit degrees of disorder in the world beyond the bounds of prudence. They were in fact placed in a dilemma, afraid on the one hand to tolerate too much international disorder and reluctant on the other to sanction the growth of an international peace-keeping authority with an independent competence of its own; and the only escape from this dilemma was to use the machinery of the UN which they had themselves constructed in the first place and which enabled them to act vicariously instead of directly and to keep a curb on any particular operation. The solution to their dilemma was to have a UN capable of acting reasonably effectively, but not too effectively, in keeping the peace; to have a competent but subordinate police force whose wish to become more competent would not be gratified if it entailed a serious move away from subordination.

The limitations were strikingly demonstrated in 1982 when two states, Argentina and Britain, went to war to assert their irreconcilable sovereign claims to islands of minimal value to either of them (see Chapter 27). Argentina's action was certainly, Britain's arguably, a breach of the Charter. Although only one among some 150 wars with which the world has been plagued since 1945, the Falklands War had a special standing as the only war deliberately waged by aggressive action by two members of the UN. It was also the first war waged by a European state other than the USSR since France abandoned its imperial pretensions in Algeria a generation earlier. The Argentinian seizure of the Falklands was a blatant breach of the obligations accepted by every state which is a member of the UN. Britain claimed that this act of aggression brought into play article 51 of the Charter which – by way of exception to article 2 – sanctions an act of war by a member state in self-defence. This claim is not without blemish. Neither in the Charter nor anywhere else is self-defence defined, so that there exists a grey area between self-defence and retaliation. The British government declared promptly its intention to recover the islands, if necessary by force, and wasted no time in assembling the means to do so. On the other hand, if self-defence is to be strictly interpreted, it could be held to mean no more than hitting back at the time of attack with the forces available at the point of attack. The question is a moot one, less clear than statements from the British side chose to portray it. But whatever the true legal judgment on this matter, it can more confidently be asserted that political considerations were uppermost and that, whatever the advice of any number of competent lawyers might have been (if sought), the British government would not have acted otherwise than it did.

The war for the Falklands was a setback for the UN as an organization and for those aspirations to world order which it embodied. For this setback the initial aggressors were overwhelmingly to blame, but the British government did not wholly escape the embarrassment of demonstrating that in a crisis a powerful state will not welcome UN diplomacy and will subordinate the rule of law and its treaty obligations under the Charter to its own assessment of national advantage and prestige. This was in 1982 no great surprise but it was not what the generation of 1945 had hoped for.

A more serious blow to the rule of law in international affairs followed when, in 1986, the United States delivered a heavy naval and air attack on Libya. The occasion for the attack was the explosion ten days earlier of a bomb in a night club in West Berlin. Two persons were killed. The perpetrators were Palestinians. Messages sent by the Libyan People's Bureau (embassy) in East Germany were intercepted and deciphered and disclosed official Libyan involvement. The precise nature of this involvement was uncertain since published English versions of these messages appeared to be not so much translations as paraphrases. Nevertheless Libyan support for Palestinian groups prepared to use violence was uncontestable. The American administration sought agreement for the use of aircraft based in Britain and the right for them to fly over France: the first was granted, the second not. The attack was at first described as reprisal or retaliation but later as self-defence within article 51 of the UN Charter. It was an act of war in clear violation of the treaty obligations accepted by all signatories of the Charter (the appeal to article 51 was so vapid as merely to add hypocrisy to illegality) and also in contravention of the laws of war which, for a thousand years before the Charter, had prescribed that the force used in a punitive venture must be not disproportionate to the offence which gave rise to it. The action was very widely applauded by the American people who, like their president, felt outraged and frustrated by such crimes as the Berlin bombing, the hijacking of the *Achille Lauro* (see p. 343) and more. Unable to get at the small gangs responsible for these crimes the US administration decided to label certain states (Libya, Syria) as 'terrorist' organizations and so claim the right to attack them. The attack was a political act undertaken in defiance of international rules and obligations but in the belief, or hope, that its political expediency would muffle and condone its illegality. This it was not well calculated to do. It had no logical or obvious effect on those small but fervent groups which, needing few arms and little money, could remain in business whether Libyan cities were bombed or not. Qadafi himself was neither killed nor overthrown and did not appear to be intimidated; domestic rivals who had been encouraged to intrigue against him by Libya's economic problems dropped their opposition at least for a time. Other Arab leaders, including those who disliked Qadafi as an upstart and a nuisance, rallied to him; an American attempt to enlist President Mubarak in the raid seriously, perhaps permanently, weakened his position (as Carter had unintentionally but fatally undermined Sadat at Camp David); Arab public opinion gave Qadafi undeserved sympathy as a victim of brute force. Washington's European allies, with the notable exception of the British Prime Minister and some of her colleagues, were aghast at what they regarded as political folly but muted in their public criticism of Reagan because of their own feebleness in response to Qadafi's lethal meddlings; they were reluctant to apply (alternative and legitimate) economic measures since economic sanctions against Libya would undermine their refusal to use such sanctions against South Africa. In Britain the prime minister's willingness to allow the use of British bases provoked questions about the secret Anglo–American agreement governing their use, particularly for operations which were in nobody's mind when the agreement was made and which had nothing to do with Nato. Although, like many acts of violence, the American attack changed little it accentuated some trends of which the more important were, first, the declining ability of the United States to solve rather than aggravate the turmoils of the Middle East and, secondly, the declining ability of Britain to stave off a choice between a junior – even humiliating and now unpopular – role in an Anglo–American partnership and a more wholehearted partnership with the European Community. In the last resort the American action was a massive political miscalculation. On the one hand was a widespread hankering, to which the American administration responded, to find a way to police international and cross-national affairs – even some readiness to put order before law. But in assuming the police role Reagan flew in the face of the fact that, not only the communist bloc, but neither the Arab world nor Asia nor Africa nor – most strikingly – western Europe were prepared to entrust this role to the United States. After the attack they were the less willing. So the action lacked not only legitimacy but also *post hoc* endorsement and defenders. American action in Nicaragua and Panama (see Chapter 27) underlined the difficulty of finding a policeman willing to undertake rough work and at the same time stay within the law.

The revolution in the USSR effected by Gorbachev changed this situation by smothering the Cold War, inducing the superpowers to cooperate in international affairs instead of opposing one another as a matter of principle, and by introducing therefore for the first time since 1945 the prospect of making the Charter work as it had been intended to work in the business of keeping the peace and upholding the law. The test came with Iraq's invasion and annexation of Kuwait in 1990.

This was a blatant act of aggression and it raised the question which had been raised on a number of earlier occasions, including Argentina's occupation of the Falkland Islands and Iraq's own attack on Iran ten years earlier: whether counter-action would be taken through or outside the UN. President Bush decided to do both. He despatched large armed forces to Saudi Arabia and he resorted to the UN to impose sanctions against Iraq. Both these undertakings were international in the sense that numerous states participated in both, but only the latter was action by the United Nations. The former was action initiated and led by the United States independently of the Charter. It did not conflict with the terms of the Charter but would do so if these forces were used to make war otherwise than in support of UN resolutions, at UN request and under a system of command established by the UN.

The Security Council took action under chapter VII of the Charter. This chapter comes into operation when the Council itself determines the existence of a threat to peace, a breach of the peace or an act of aggression. If the Council does so, it may prescribe action of two kinds: measures not involving the use of armed force (article 41) and action by air, sea or land forces (article 42 – blockade being specified under this article). In the case of measures under article 41 the Council may call on members of the UN to apply these measures and (by article 25) they are obliged to comply. There is no such compulsion in the case of measures under article 42.

In a series of resolutions adopted during August the Security Council, unanimously, demanded Iraq's immediate withdrawal from Kuwait and a negotiated settlement; imposed, by thirteen votes to two, a commercial, financial and military embargo (medical supplies specifically excepted and rules permitting the supply of food on humanitarian grounds to be worked out by a committee of the Council); declared, unanimously, that the annexation of Kuwait was null and void; demanded, unanimously, that Iraq allow and facilitate the immediate departure from Kuwait and Iraq of all nationals of third states; and authorized, by thirteen votes to two, the use of force to make the embargo effective by, if necessary, stopping and inspecting merchant ships. These first resolutions established sanctions against Iraq and the use of force to monitor them, but not the use of force for any other purpose. Further resolutions defined and regulated UN actions, culminating in a twelfth resolution on 29 November which, by authorizing the use after 15 January 1991 of all measures necessary to achieve the aims set out in the earlier resolutions, sanctioned recourse to war.

The governments of the United States and Britain maintained that, these resolutions apart, they were entitled under article 51 of the Charter to use military force against Iraq but this contention was almost certainly false. Article 51 is one of the least satisfactory articles of the

Charter. It expressly safeguards the state's inherent right to defend itself but it makes no attempt to define the line between self-defence and retaliation and, by using the phrase 'individual and collective self-defence', it perpetrates an ambiguity. There are two distinct issues to be met before article 51 may legitimately be invoked: first, the question whether the action proposed or undertaken is defence or retaliation (which was the question posed in the Falklands case) and, secondly, the meaning and scope of the term 'collective' in article 51. Collective self-defence, besides being a contradiction in terms, implies that an attack on one UN member may be resisted by forces other than those of the state attacked. They are presumably the forces of allies, but it is open to question whether the alliance needs to be in existence at the time of the attack or may be concluded after it. In considering this conundrum it is necessary to revert to the circumstances in which article 51 was drafted and adopted at San Francisco in 1945. It was a late addition to the draft Charter and was designed to meet the worries of members of existing regional alliances (the Organization of American States and the Arab League) who feared that by signing the Charter they would invalidate the arrangements in their regions for mutual help against aggression. It is evident that an attack on a UN member may be opposed by the victim's regional partners in accordance with the provisions of the regional alliance, but it is not evident – nor is it easy to argue – that states outside the relevant regional partnership at that time may intervene by force. The broader interpretation would permit any state to throw itself into a dispute simply by declaring itself an ally of the victim of aggression, with the result that every threat to or breach of the peace would become an invitation to military action by self-appointed white knights – or red knights or black knights – on the single condition that the victim of aggression was prepared to welcome that action.

In terms of world order and the usefulness of the UN Iraq's attack on Kuwait served to reanimate the mechanisms of the UN, testing its strengths and exposing its weaknesses. The use of the Charter by the United States was made possible by broad accord between the permanent members of the Security Council and particularly between the United States and the USSR, but few in Washington believed that action under chapter VII would by itself restore the independence of Kuwait or forestall further possible aggression by Iraq – against, for example, Saudi Arabia. The United States therefore established in Saudi Arabia a powerful force which, while it might by its presence in the area reinforce the coercion applied by the UN, was evidently capable of attacking Iraq and not unlikely to be used in order to overthrow the Iraqi régime as well as to restore the Kuwaiti. This display of American purpose and power was a unilateral act which was given international support by securing the participation of the host country and of numerous other states in and beyond the Middle East. It was also an expression of no confidence in the efficacy of the mechanisms and procedures of the UN.

The attempt made in 1945 by the United Nations to shift the making of war from the unsafe hands of the nation state to the safer hands of the community of nations had been obstructed by two things: the Cold War and the developing nature of war. The Cold War undermined the very existence of a community of nations and negated the Charter's provisions for assembling and using international force. The development of nuclear, chemical and other new weapons superposed on the question who should be authorized to use armed force the question whether the use of such force was acceptable or justifiable or even efficient in relation to specific political or military purposes. The crisis over Kuwait was prolonged in a way barely imaginable in the previous century by perplexity over the uses of armed force and a rising undercurrent of opinion against the resort to what war had become. There were, as there ever had been, three main ways of overcoming an enemy: starve him, scare him or beat him. Chapter VII of the Charter is the modern version of the siege, using deprivation to secure surrender but keeping in reserve, as did besiegers, direct force to back it and clinch it. But an embargo in accordance with chapter VII is, like siege warfare, likely to be slow and even ultimately ineffective: besiegers sometimes marched away. The American host assembled in Saudi Arabia was an alternative, a second string. It was intended to scare Saddam Hussein or, if he were not scared, to beat him. It represented the view that if measures under chapter VII failed or did not work quickly enough, the United States and those of like mind would resort to force rather than accept rebuff.

As the crisis developed month by month so did the dilemma between the two aims of chastising the law-breaker and resolving the crisis: between recourse to war and recourse to diplomacy. Saddam Hussein's violation of the Charter created the crisis. The first of the Security Council's resolutions required him to purge his offence by retreating from Kuwait. It required also discussion of matters in dispute between Iraq and Kuwait. It said nothing about the relative timing of these two requirements. Saddam Hussein proclaimed repeatedly that he would not budge from Kuwait, although he expressed willingness to participate in a general conference on Middle Eastern affairs with an agenda from which Kuwait would not be excluded. The United States and some of its associates refused to consider any matters before a total and unconditional Iraqi withdrawal. This was tantamount to the rejection of diplomacy in parallel with retreat. It was a high-risk policy which gave to surrender an absolute priority over negotiation, risking a war which – although caused in a primary sense by Iraq's aggression – would be caused in a second sense by the equal obduracy of the protagonists. In such a contest Bush suffered a double disadvantage. As chief in a democracy and chief of an *ad hoc* alliance he was constrained to a far greater extent than his autocratic adversary who could take much less heed, or none at all, of popular opinion or the misgivings of associates. The overwhelming power of the United States rendered the use of that power obnoxious to much public opinion and barely reconcilable with the well-established rule of law which, for well over a thousand years, had decreed that the use of force must be proportional to the object to be achieved. The tilt towards war was accentuated by the American tactics of reinforcing a policy of sanctions with a deployment of vast armed forces whose cost was unsustainable over a long run and which could not be brought back home without a commensurately unequivocal victory: Bush adopted measures which were economically and politically unsustainable.

That the United States should play the leading part in the UN's undertakings was proper and desirable. But Bush did both more and less. He conducted simultaneously an American operation which overshadowed the UN undertaking almost to the point of obliterating it; and in the American operation he relied on force and the threat of force to the exclusion of diplomacy, even insisting that the direct bilateral talks in Washington and Baghdad which he proposed in December must stop short of anything that might be labelled negotiation. He arrived therefore at a position in which he was demanding unconditional observance of UN resolutions which themselves demanded no such thing. During the Cold War the UN's role in keeping world order and upholding international law had been effaced, but the Cold War had provided the UN with an alibi for its ineffectiveness. The Kuwait crisis, the first serious crisis after the end of the Cold War, reanimated the UN – the United States was among the first to hail this change – but it showed also that the UN's new freedom to perform its central role in world affairs might still be cramped by its more powerful members and would have to be performed without benefit of the excuses for failure provided by the Cold War. Freedom of manoeuvre for the UN could turn out to be useless or – worse – catastrophic if it were to mean freedom only to demand unconditional surrender. By pressing UN resolutions beyond the objectives explicitly envisaged in them, and by conducting supposedly UN operations without reference to the UN, the United States abused the UN and weakened it while nevertheless fulfilling some of its aims. American aims – the overthrow of a barbarous regime which had among other things violated the Charter and the laws of nations – were widely approved but the methods used demonstrated something different: the power and will of a single national government in the context of a threat to its own national interests. International action and order were subordinated to a national purpose with consequences for the UN which were at best ambivalent. (For a fuller account of the Kuwait war see chapter 11.)

5 A THIRD WORLD – AND A FOURTH

One of the biggest changes that can occur in a world divided politically into sovereign states is the multiplication of these states. This happened in Europe with the dissolution of the Ottoman and Habsburg empires. A generation later it happened worldwide upon the dissolution of European empires outside Europe. This process was protracted but much the greater part of it was consummated during the twenty to twenty-five years after the end of the Second World War. This period was dominated by the Cold War in Europe and that conflict gave the nations emerging into statehood one of their initial basic characteristics.

Both the protagonists in the Cold War – the United States hardly less than the USSR – were uninhibited in their hostility to European colonialism, but as the Cold War created the Euro–American alliance embodied in Nato American hostility to the British, French and other European presences in Asia and Africa was transformed. While commercially it was frequently intensified by competition in areas hitherto dominated by the colonialists, governmentally it became muted as a result of the priority given to the need for European allies and bases. To nationalists in Asia and Africa this change of mood amounted to something between evasiveness and betrayal. It placed the United States alongside, if not actually in, the ranks of the imperialists, and it was the beginning of a decline in the high standing of the United States in the minds of what was coming to be called the Third World.

It was a Third World because it rejected the notion of a world divided into two, a world in which only the United States and the USSR counted and everybody else had to declare for the one or the other. It feared the power of the superpowers, exemplified and magnified by nuclear weapons. It distrusted their intentions, envied (particularly in the American case) their superior wealth and rejected their insistence that, in the one case in democratic capitalism and in the other in communism, they had discovered a way of life which others need do no more than copy. Nationalist leaders, although anti-European in the nature of things, had at least one characteristic in common with their retreating masters: their temper was pragmatic. Moscow's rigid communist dogmatism, and Washington's increasingly rigid anti-communism, offended them. Above all they felt beholden neither to the United States nor to the USSR for their independence from European rule, which they attained with unexpected speed and ease.

The decision of the newly emerging states of Asia and Africa, with few exceptions, to throw in their lot with neither superpower was much influenced by one man, Jawaharlal Nehru. Nehru was a world figure before becoming in 1947 prime minister of the most populous of the new states, and he held that office uninterruptedly for seventeen years. He was a pragmatic and eclectic patrician who had imbibed western liberal and democratic values and was also attracted by the USSR's record in auto-industrialization. He was repelled by Stalin's tyranny and police rule, but also by the crudities and stupidities of McCarthyism in the United States and by the arrogant and moralistic division of the world into communists and anti-communists. (Parenthetically, and with hindsight, it is worth emphasizing the worldwide impact of McCarthyism, a domestic upheaval in the United States which seemed to betoken a sharp swing to the right in American politics, coupled with a myopically over-simplified view of world politics. McCarthy's indiscriminate charges of treason and conspiracy flourished on the shocks of the Korean War. In the United States the mood and the methods induced by these shocks were mastered when the peak of the war passed but the damage to the American image abroad persisted for much longer.)

Nehru was the principal creator of the post-imperial Commonwealth as an association of monarchies and republics of all races whose links were not ideological but historical and accidental. When he decided that India should remain in the British Commonwealth (as it was still called at this date) he did so upon the conditions that India should become a republic and that it should have the right to conduct without cavil a foreign policy distinct from, conceivably even at odds with, the foreign policies of Britain and its other Commonwealth associates. Thus he stressed the political independence which all new states needed to assert, while retaining links which had economic, cultural and sentimental value. His example was widely followed. Although Burma severed these links with Britain in 1948, no other British possession did so and by 1990 the Commonwealth had fifty sovereign members (including Pakistan which resigned in 1972 but rejoined in 1989).

Nehru's insistence that each member of the Commonwealth should be free to devise and pursue its own foreign policy was crucial, for it meant that neither the Commonwealth as a whole nor its several members need follow Britain's example in taking the American side in the Cold War. This was the beginning of the Third World's neutralism or non-alignment, to which France's former colonies also adhered in the sixties. In western Europe there had been at the close of the Second

World War a hankering after a similarly independent – and mediatory – stance between the United States and the USSR (a so-called Third Force, championed for example by Georges Bidault), but it quickly shrivelled under the impact of heavy-handed Russian measures such as the Prague coup of 1948. Europe became the seat of the Cold War. But the rest of the world believed that it lay outside the arena.

Its attitudes passed through a number of phases. They were rooted in the concept of neutrality. Neutrality was a general declaration of intent to remain out of any war which might occur, but it had not proved very useful to its various adherents during the Second World War and in any case the new states were not thinking of a shooting war and how to keep out of it, but of the Cold War and how to behave in regard to it. Neutralism and non-alignment, therefore, as distinct from neutrality, were the expression of an attitude towards a particular and present conflict: they entailed, first, equivalent relations with both sides and, secondly – in the phase called positive neutralism – attempts to mediate and abate the dangerous quarrels of the great. In its more negative phase non-alignment involved a reprobation of the Cold War, an assertion that there were more important matters in the world, an acknowledgement of the powerlessness of new states, and a refusal to judge between the two giant powers.

The positive phase of neutralism represented the desires of new states to evade the Cold War but not to be left out of world politics. If at first sight the postwar bipolar world seemed to leave as little scope for small powers as in the days of the great struggles between the Roman and Persian empires, on second thoughts it seemed that the neutralists might nevertheless play a gratifyingly honourable and sensible part. When Africa as well as Asia became independent the number of neutralists and the space they occupied round the globe became considerable. They might at the very least prevent the Cold War from spreading to these areas; by merely setting limits to bipolar commitment they could reduce the occasions and areas of conflict. They could too, by virtue of their combined importance, cause the great powers to woo them, thus becoming a kind of lightning conductor in world politics. More positively still, they might exert influence by the time-honoured method of holding conferences to publicize their views or by the newer method of arguing and voting in the General Assembly of the United Nations. In this last respect the Indian voice was again decisive. The new states had hesitated at first in their attitudes towards the UN, not knowing whether it might turn out to be dominated by its European members, as the League of Nations had been, or by the west or by the great powers. They feared that the new organization might be used to buttress colonialism or to subserve the purposes of the Cold War, in either of which events they would have had little use for it, but after a little experience they decided otherwise and India in particular became prominent in its discussions and its field commissions and supplied for emergency operations units without which those operations could hardly have been contemplated (especially after Hammarskjöld developed the principle that major powers must not contribute fighting units to UN forces).

It is impossible to assess the precise effects of anti-colonialism, the Cold War and neutralism upon one another, but it is possible to show that the policies and actions of the neutralists had some effect on states outside their ranks. In the first few years after the end of the Second World War American attitudes to Asians were deeply, and adversely, affected by two things: the need to rescue western Europe and the call to fight against an aggressor in Korea. The European Recovery Programme absorbed a great deal of American talent and American attention as well as American money and it may have made Americans less critical of Europeans and particularly of the European colonialism which they had in the past so unequivocally decried. To Asians emerged or emerging from colonialism the American voice seemed to have become muted by concern for war-wrecked Europe and also by the need to find sure and strong allies against a Russian communist threat: in other words the Cold War was perverting the American attitude on colonialism and even carrying the United States, spiritually and physically, into the imperialist camp. To the Americans the war in Korea was a major event in the conflict between communism and anti-communism, in which too few people gave too little help (no more than 10 per cent of the combat effort) and some, notably Asians, indulged in ill-timed and ill-considered criticism. The American attitude to Asian neutralism was one of righteous indignation. Thus the events of these years made Asians dub Americans imperialists and Americans dub Asians traitors. Yet the American mood changed after a few years and it did so partly because the neutralists' behaviour and activities at the UN and elsewhere showed the inadequacy of judging them by a simple criterion of communism and anti-communism.

The Russians too were made to revise their opinions. As anti-imperialists they had been equivocal, supporting communist movements but doubtful about others. What struck them most about the leaders of new states was their bourgeois character, and they attacked them accordingly as western stooges. Men like Nehru and Nasser seemed to the Russians at first no better than any western European politician who joined Nato. But the arrival of such leaders at the UN in increasing numbers converted the Russians to the idea that they constituted, and must therefore be treated as, a separate group midway between the communist bloc and the USSR's enemies. This transition was easier for the Russians than the Americans because the adherence of strange and distant countries to the communist bloc was in any case an unreal and unsatisfactory way of extending Russian influence (perhaps, as a short experience with Iraq showed, even a way of making things more difficult for Moscow), whereas the Americans were used to picking up allies all over the world and holding them together by their easy familiarity with air and sea power. In any event the neutrals succeeded in getting both the Russians and the Americans to accept them in world politics in the role which they had chosen for themselves.

To be effective non-alignment, negative or positive, presupposed solidarity among the non-aligned. The new states were weak and aware of their weakness which – no less than their repudiation of the Cold War – was their hallmark. The two characteristics reinforced each other. Their weakness made them wary of too close an association with a single major power and so obliged them to seek strength by unity among themselves. Many of them were far from being nations, and such political unity as they possessed had been a function of xenophobia. Their governments were metamorphosed liberation movements which had to create the broadest possible consensus in order to prevent the new state from disintegrating or becoming ungovernable. In so far as this problem impinged on external policies it suggested the advisability of the broadest range of contacts and friendships among foreign states and the need to eschew any one precise and discriminatory alignment. Economic needs pointed the same way: no new state was so important to the world's rich powers as to be able to command from one rich power all the aid it needed; better therefore not to contract an alliance with one power which would rule out the possibility of getting aid from others. (This argument was not conclusive. Many of the small states which emerged from French rule in Africa were so weak that they had no choice but to take what they could get from France.) Similarly in the field of defence, while there was a superficial argument in favour of attachment to a particular strong protector, it was also observable that major powers wanted to keep out of the sort of local disputes in which new states wanted help – as opposed to local aspects of global conflict, in which new states did not want to get involved.

The search for solidarity preceded independence among both Asians and Africans. The first notable postwar Asian conference – the Asian Relations Conference held in New Delhi in March 1947 – assembled twenty-eight delegations of which only eight came from sovereign states. Its motive force was a desire to ensure that the United Nations should not become an organization dominated by European or white states and viewpoints, such as the League of Nations had been, but the tone of the discussions was not markedly anti-colonial. The conference was a gathering of Asians to discuss Asian problems including land reform, industrialization, Asian socialism and the application of non-violence in international affairs. The conference established a permanent organization which existed for eight years but did not do much else. Very soon afterwards India, Pakistan, Burma and Ceylon became independent. They did so in a world which had expected peace but not got it. There were guerilla wars and insurrections in Burma, Malaya and the Philippines, and open fighting in Indonesia, Indo–China and Palestine. The Cold War too was beginning. In domestic politics violence claimed notable victims in Burma in June 1947 with the assassination of Aung San and six colleagues, and an even more notable victim in January 1948 when Gandhi was killed.

In January 1949 another Asian conference assembled in New Delhi. The Soviet Asian republics, which had attended the 1947 meeting, were not this time asked, and Turkey refused an invitation. Otherwise Asia, including the Middle East, was very fully represented and Australia and New Zealand sent observers. The immediate occasion for the conference was Indonesia where an Asian liberation movement was being threatened with extinction by the Dutch and where to Asian eyes the UN seemed bent on facilitating the re-imposition of white colonial rule. In the previous December the Dutch had resorted to their second police action and had captured and imprisoned a number of Indonesian leaders. The conference demanded their release and also the immediate establishment of an interim government and independence for Indonesia by 1950 (the Security Council shortly afterwards chose 1960 as a suitable date). Like its predecessor this conference created a permanent organization which proved ineffective, partly because a number of Asian states were becoming jealous of India's predominance and did not wish to see it institutionalized. Owing to the Indonesian issue the conference had a clear anti-colonial note, but it was divided between friends of the west and neutralists. This division was accentuated in the following months when different Asian leaders took up different attitudes towards the two outstanding Asian events of the year, the victory of Mao Zedong and communism in China and the war in Korea. Asian solidarity was proving difficult to achieve, even on an anti-colonialist programme; the British and French campaigns in Malaya and Indo–China did not evoke the same united protest as the Dutch proceedings in Indonesia, partly because of the strong communist flavour in the Malayan and Vietnamese anti-colonialist movements.

In the fifties Asian solidarity and neutralism waxed and then wore thin. Some Asian states, putting their economic and strategic needs before their neutralism, signed not only commercial but even defence treaties with the United States or the USSR. India, by its treaty of 1954 with China embodying the Panch Shila, maintained its principles but in the same year Pakistan, Thailand and the Philippines concluded military agreements with the United States, while Afghanistan became the first non-communist country to receive Russian aid and the USSR, which already had a trade agreement with India and was about to conclude another with Burma, intensified the diplomatic and economic wooing of Indonesia which was to lead Sukarno to visit Moscow in 1956. The great powers were taking a gratifying interest in Asian affairs but one consequence of this interest was to make it more difficult for Asians to maintain a common attitude towards the great powers or to keep their distance as pure neutralism required.

During 1954 preparations were made for a conference, originally suggested by Ceylon and taken up by Sukarno and Nehru. This conference assembled at Bandung in April 1955. It was a grand assembly to stimulate co-operation among Asians and put Asia on the map. The background to it comprised the treaty between the United States and Taiwan (a consequence of recent crises in the Formosa Strait and offshore islands), and the creation of Seato and the Baghdad Pact. The USSR and China welcomed what looked at first like an anti-western conference, while Washington's friends – Thailand and the Philippines – were half inclined not to go. Israel was excluded on account of Arab opinion. The twenty-nine participants included six from Africa (Egypt, Libya, Sudan, Ethiopia, Liberia, Ghana), so that Bandung became the prototype of Afro-Asian as opposed to purely Asian solidarity. It was an assembly of the needy and the indignant, not a concentration of power. Its members were divided among themselves even on the issue of non-alignment, but the timing was propitious. The Cold War in Europe had, since the Berlin blockade of 1948–49 and the growth of Russian nuclear power to match the American, lapsed into a quiescent stalemate but not into a thaw. Both sides were looking elsewhere and were competing for the allegiance of states in other continents with the vague intention of building up a new preponderance by additional alliances, or of turning the enemy's flank by carrying influence and bases into new terrain. The Russians and the Chinese hoped to advance communism by exploiting anti-western nationalisms, while the Americans hoped to exploit fears of communism and of China and so create new, and if necessary heavily subsidized, military groups. American policy, freshly illustrated by the signing of the Manila Pact, ran counter to the spirit of Bandung. Zhou Enlai, on the other hand, who put in a personal appearance at Bandung, went some way towards showing that Chinese communism was reconcilable with other Asian nationalisms and that at least one Chinese leader was more sensible and amenable than some current pictures of the new China suggested. The Russians had already, by accident or astuteness, taken a number of steps which brought them into closer accord with the Asian mood. The proposal to neutralize Austria was welcome to Asian neutralists, and gestures like the return of Port Arthur to China and of Porkkala to Finland heartened those who hoped that Stalin's death had changed the face of world politics. In 1955

Bulganin and Khrushchev visited Asia with tremendous acclaim (Khrushchev paid a second visit early in 1960) and the Russian campaign to win over the neutralists was so well launched that even the suppression of the Hungarian revolt of 1956 only dented it (the Anglo–French attack on Suez being invaluable to the Russians in saving their new reputation at this juncture).

For the neutralists themselves the principal achievements of the Bandung conference were that they had met and got to know one another (most of them were new to international politics); that they had laid the foundations for joint action at the UN and, through solidarity, increased their security, their status and their diplomatic weight in the world; that they had attracted new men like Nasser to the group and made it bigger; that they were making the giant powers take them seriously and treat their policies as respectable (a trend which was fortified by the admission of sixteen new members to the UN by the package deal of 1955 and still further by the big increase in African membership in 1960); and finally that they had seen one of the leaders of the new, formidable China, had found him not at all frightening and had perhaps inducted China into their pacific circle. In the summer of 1956 Nehru and Nasser visited Tito at Brioni in Yugoslavia. This event was a sign of the development of Asia neutralism into a worldwide association. With an Asian, an African and a European leading them the neutralists became more ambitious in international affairs and hoped to be able to bring pressure to bear on the giant powers in Cold War matters, but this association was already passing the peak of its influence, partly because of the activities of those who wanted to turn it into an alliance of communists and black men against non-communist whites by emphasizing anti-colonialism in place of neutralism. Non-alignment became in practice anti-western non-alignment, particularly with the Afro–Asian People's Solidarity Movement which sponsored a variety of conferences in the late fifties.

In September 1961 a conference of the unaligned was held in Belgrade. Whereas Bandung had been an exploratory conference, Belgrade had about it an atmosphere of crisis. The background to it included French nuclear tests in the Sahara and the resumption of Russian tests, the Bay of Pigs and the Berlin wall, the Franco–Tunisian clash over Bizerta and the grinding crisis in the Congo. A new conflict between India and China seemed to be emerging, a conflict between the USSR and China certainly was. Bandung's twenty-nine participants had been overwhelmingly Asian and not overwhelmingly anti-western. The only serious conflict over admissibility had been the Arab veto on Israel. At Belgrade the African representation reflected the division of African states between radicals and moderates, Latin American participants were selected with a similar bias and the Europeans included Yugoslavia and Cyprus but not the traditional neutrals, Sweden and Switzerland. An attempt by Nehru to concentrate on peace rather than anti-colonialism and to get Russo–American talks going met with little success, and a number of delegations displayed a partisan indifference to the nuclear explosion which the Russians set off on the eve of the conference. A proposal to fix a terminal date for colonial rule throughout the world at two to six years was enlarged during the debates to a demand for its immediate and total abolition.

After a pause plans for another conference led to a meeting in Cairo, more African than Asian, in October 1964 and to a project for a conference in Algiers in 1965. This plan was, however, vitiated by the fall of Ben Bella a few days before a preliminary meeting in June and by increasing embarrassment among the likely participants at the prospect of a local Sino–Soviet conflict. The Chinese wished to exclude the USSR and assume the leadership of the underprivileged but at a second preliminary meeting in October the invitation to the USSR was approved, whereupon the Chinese threatened to stay away. In these circumstances a majority thought it better to have no conference at all and the plans were allowed to expire. The movement seemed to be wilting but it was re-animated during 1967 by visits by Tito to Asian and African countries and in 1969 a conference in Belgrade gave it fresh impetus. At Havana ten years later ninety-two full members attended (there were two absentees). Whereas the original members had been non-aligned in their policies and their sympathies, the much wider flock of the seventies contained a number of states which, although non-aligned by policy, had definite pro-western or pro-communist sympathies.

African solidarity and non-alignment, which began to join forces with the Asian current at Bandung in 1955, had its own remoter origins. Pan-Africanism began as an assertion of the distinctiveness and value of an explicitly African or (by extension to those lands to which the slaves had been consigned) Negro culture. As such it was primarily Caribbean and West African, but it became also part of the wider movement for colonial emancipation in which nationalists from all parts of Africa could consort with and seek strength from one another. Thirdly, there were those (Nkrumah, for example) who saw that political freedom was not the whole of freedom, that economic dependence would persist after the winning of sovereign statehood, and that Africa might stand on its own feet economically only by developing its continental resources in common. This third aspect of Pan-Africanism pointed logically to a political union or at least a federation and it was therefore in conflict with the creation of new sovereign states committed to the preservation of their integrity as well as their independence.

Six pan-African conferences had been held between 1900 and 1945.

The first of them and the four which followed in the twenties were predominantly Caribbean and North American but the last was dominated by African leaders from Africa itself. All of them were meetings of personalities. With the beginnings of independence came meetings of African parties and African governments. The former created an All African People's Organization which, at conferences in Accra in 1958, Tunis in 1960 and Cairo in 1961, discussed schemes for African unity or an African commonwealth on the basis that co-operation between governments was not enough. But the third meeting was the last. As the tally of independent states grew, the states' system took hold. Nkrumah continued to beat the drum for a union government until his fall in 1966 but this theme, although a standard item at conferences of the OAU (Organization for African Unity) for some years, attracted declining support both because it was regarded as unpractical and because it became increasingly identified with a left-wing radical minority.

At the date of the first meeting of independent African states, held in Accra in 1958, there were nine independent states in the continent. One of them, South Africa, declined the invitation to Accra. The others were Ethiopia, Liberia, Egypt, Morocco, Tunisia, Libya, Ghana and Guinea. They were chiefly concerned with anti-colonialism, the racial and nationalist struggles in South Africa and Algeria, and the problem of achieving some sort of African unity while at the same time respecting the independence and integrity of African states. This conference was followed in May 1959 by the Declaration of Conakry whereby Ghana and Guinea formed a union which was declared to be the starting point of a wider African union. This step was an unpremeditated retort to the ostracizing of Guinea by France, a practical demonstration of Nkrumah's pan-African principles and a lifeline for Guinea. It was followed in July of the same year by the Declaration of Saniquellie which, primarily on Liberian insistence, emphasized the independence and integrity of existing states.

By 1960, when the second conference of independent African states assembled in Addis Ababa, their number had almost doubled and their unity was about to be tested by the special strains of the Congo as well as by inherited border disputes. Fifteen states were represented. Active border disputes involved Ethiopia and Somalia, Ghana and Togo, Guinea and the Cameroons. The first of these disputes led to fighting on a not inconsiderable scale, but the others did not. More serious for the prospects of African unity was a contest between Ghana and Nigeria in which Ghana urged the case for immediate steps to unity and Nigeria argued in favour of a slow approach to something like a federation. This dispute was spiced with some bitterness between the protagonists since the Nigerians resented Nkrumah's assumption of leadership and distrusted his aims, while Nkrumah feared that Nigeria intended to throw the influence of its vast size on to the side of conservatism versus socialism and of Nigerian nationalism versus pan-Africanism. In the Congo the independent African states tried, both at the UN and in a conference at Leopoldville in August 1960, to present a united front and play a constructive and pacificatory role, but they were not successful.

From this point the independent African states began to form separate groups which were later reassembled in one organization by the founding of the Organization for African Unity. The largest of these was the Brazzaville group consisting of all the former French colonies except Guinea, with the addition of Mauritania (whose claim to be independent and not a part of Morocco was accepted by the group). The Brazzaville group began as an *ad hoc* meeting at Abidjan in October 1960 when the principal topic for discussion was Algeria, but at Brazzaville in December and at further meetings during 1961 at Dakar, Yaoundé and Tananarive it developed into a permanent association, discussed ways of perpetuating the co-operation and common services which had existed in the colonial period, set up an organization for economic co-operation, and considered joint institutions and defence arrangements. This group was neither pan-African nor regional, but an expression of common needs and a common outlook.

A second group took shape at a conference at Casablanca in January 1961. This group consisted of six independent African states plus the Algerian revolutionaries and Ceylon. The six African states were Morocco, Egypt and Libya (which soon afterwards transferred to the Brazzaville group) and Ghana, Guinea and Mali (which had joined the Ghana–Guinea union in the previous year). The Casablanca group opposed the independence of Mauritania and was pro-Lumumbist in the Congo, although at its second conference in May in Cairo Nkrumah strongly opposed proposals to withdraw troops from the UN force and switch them to Gizenga and prevailed upon his associates. This group too established permanent organs, including political, economic and cultural committees, a supreme command, and a headquarters at Bamako in Mali.

In August 1961 no fewer than twenty states assembled in conference at Monrovia. They included the whole of the Brazzaville group, Libya and a majority of former British territories. The Monrovia group thus subsumed the Brazzaville group and, owing to the prominence of Nigeria, acquired a specifically anti-Ghanaian and anti-Nkrumah flavour. The movement for African unity seemed to have been blocked by current problems (the Congo and, to a lesser extent, Mauritania) and by personalities. Nevertheless the idea remained alive. Even if Nkrumah's vision of a union extending into every part of the continent was unacceptable or impracticable, lesser unions might be attempted.

The Ghana–Guinea union, with or without Mali, had proved of little practical consequence, but it had been a political demonstration rather than a true regional association. In the north-west Morocco, Tunisia and Algeria espoused federation prematurely, at a meeting in Tangier in April 1958. In east and central Africa there was talk of a federation between Kenya, Uganda, Tanganyika, Zanzibar, Malawi, Zambia and Rhodesia – with possible extensions in some barely visible future to Rwanda, Burundi, Mozambique and even South Africa. A Pan-African Freedom Movement of East and Central Africa (Pafmeca) came into existence in 1958, was enlarged four years later by adding 's' for South as its penultimate letter and was dissolved in 1963; these were associations for self-help in the struggle for liberation.

The French connection was at the base of a number of interstate organizations: the Entente Council (Ivory Coast, Niger, Upper Volta, Toga and Dahomey; see Chapter 20); the Senegal River Association (Senegal, Mali, Guinea, Mauritania; *ibid.*); a West African and a Central African Customs Union. More important than any of these was the African and Malagasy Economic Union (UAMCE) founded in 1965 by thirteen formerly French and Belgian territories and converted into the African and Malagasy Common Organization (OCAM) whose charter, signed at Tananarive in 1966, declared it to be open to all African states – provided existing members all accepted each newcomer. OCAM created a number of useful agencies which were sometimes more effective than those of the OAU, but politically its members were often divided. In the sixties it was seen as a weapon for Houphouet-Boigny of the Ivory Coast against Nkrumah and in support of Tshombe; in the Nigerian civil war, in which it tried in vain to mediate, Ivory Coast and Gabon recognized Biafra while the remainder were strongly anti-separatist; some members had diplomatic relations with China, others with Taiwan. As the colonial period receded the common French inheritance became a weaker link. There were a number of absentees from the eighth congress held at Lomé in 1972 and Zaïre, feeling that it was not getting enough out of membership, resigned from the organization.

Although the Congo had demonstrated the difficulty of preserving unity among independent African states, it had no less demonstrated the advantages of doing so if at all possible, and a conference at Lagos in 1962 produced a draft charter for an organization of African states. At a further conference in Addis Ababa in 1963 the Organization for African Unity was born with an initial membership of thirty-two. The OAU was not a collective security organization as envisaged and endorsed by article 51 of the charter of the UN but an organization for the promotion of Africa unity and collaboration and for the eradication of colonialism. It consisted of an annual assembly of heads of state, a council of ministers and a secretariat. A projected commission of mediation, conciliation and arbitration did not materialize, although these functions were in fact performed: in border disputes between Morocco and Algeria, between Somalia and Ethiopia and Somalia and Kenya, and between Ghana and Upper Volta. In the last case, which rose out of the construction by Ghana of a school on territory claimed by Upper Volta, Ghana conceded the claim at a meeting of the OAU's council of ministers. In the other cases the OAU provided mediators and commissions of inquiry which helped to appease the disputes.

The establishment of this organization epitomized two processes which had been going on for a generation or more and had gathered force in the twenty years after the end of the Second World War. Africans ceased to be cut off from each other and they ceased to be cut off from world affairs. Their emancipation had a great variety of causes: the essential liberalism (reinforced by weariness) of the principal colonial powers, the growth of the movement for human rights, American and Russian attacks on colonialism, the Gandhian example, the development of roads and of international airways. While this process was taking place a new class of African, the politician, the lawyer, the intellectual, the *évolué*, was taking the place of the chief and was at the same time rejecting the models prepared for his country by the French and the British. The French had assumed that their colonies would grow into worthy pieces of France, but they had hardly noticed that their doctrine worked neither in terms of government, which was paternalistic and white, nor in terms of society, where low wages and even forced labour were too long tolerated and the favoured few tended not to become leaders in their society but to be extracted from it. The British, who had based themselves originally on paternalism and chiefs, realized the limitations of this model but planned to substitute for it an inapplicable British parliamentary system to be worked by an élite. Consequently the new states – albeit that many of their first leaders, themselves a western-educated and relatively affluent élite, had originally insisted on western democratic institutions as the best available and had expected them to work without essential modification – found that they had to innovate in theory as well as in practice. They had to find administrators, public servants, economists, teachers, doctors, accountants and trade-union leaders and at the same time construct institutions and develop conventions which would reconcile the Africans' traditions with their thirst for modernity and enable them to enjoy the fruits of efficiency, liberty and justice. They looked at the outside world with a mixture of admiration and suspicion, ready to take the best of what could be learned but convinced that however much they adopted they would evolve a distinct African way of doing things and a separate African culture. This community of aim gave the new states of Africa points of contact with one another which were implicit rather than advertised and which gave their organization a kind of initial cohesion which was not to be found in the Organization of American States or the Arab League or even the European Economic Community. But for all this the OAU was an association of sovereign states in a continent which, in the wake of decolonization, was becoming more fragmented than it had been under foreign rule. The OAU established particularism in Africa in the same way as the UN accepted it in the world at large.

The creation of the OAU represented not only a negation of federal ideas but also an emphasis on specifically African issues. The Charter of the OAU and its founding conference stressed the sacrosanctity of existing frontiers and the role of the new organization in the peaceful settlement of disputes between African states. To some extent therefore it derogated from the concept of Afro–Asian solidarity. The two continents were becoming increasingly concerned each with its own affairs; some of their common concerns faded as the anti-colonial struggle passed into history. Even within each continent solidarity came under strain. In Asia China's attack on India destroyed what was left of the Panch Shila, while India's unpreparedness compelled it to approach the giant powers from which, as leaders of the non-aligned, it had tried to keep at arm's length. India lost a degree of its detachment. After the Chinese invasion in 1962 Ceylon, Burma, Cambodia and Indonesia, in company with Egypt and Ghana, tried to use their good offices to effect a Sino–Indian reconciliation but their efforts were of little effect and were welcomed neither in New Delhi nor Beijing.

Yet there remained a powerful bond – poverty, and the realization that political independence and sovereignty did not remove economic dependence. In the same year as the Chinese invasion of India, and midway through the Congo crisis which threatened to split African opinion, the first UN Conference on Trade and Development (UNCTAD) was held in Geneva. This was not an Afro–Asian affair but something larger. It was a point of junction between the Afro–Asians on the one hand and a posse of other states, mostly Latin American, which were not only poor in comparison with the developed industrial world but also found themselves obliged to live in an economic system devised by and in the interests of the rich.

Before the Second World War ended the world's two major trading countries, the United States and Britain, agreed, at Bretton Woods, to apply to the international economy the principles of free trade, non-discrimination and stable rates of exchange. They created for these purposes two new organizations: an International Trading Organization and the International Monetary Fund, the one to clear the channels of trade of physical obstacles (tariffs and quotas), the other to provide the finance for international trade and its expansion. The latter came out of the Bretton Woods conference in an American rather than a British form: in particular Britain wanted but failed to get an international currency, a variable volume of credit geared to the expansion of trade, and much larger initial reserves than the $25,000 million with which the Fund actually started. The former never came into existence but was replaced by the General Agreement on Tariffs and Trade (GATT) which, if it lacked the institutional performance of the projected ITO, was nevertheless pledged to the same objectives, which it pursued by a series of meshed bilateral bargainings to reduce tariffs, abolish quotas, rule out new or extended preferences and assure to all every preference available to any.

The prime object of the GATT was the reduction of obstacles to trade in manufactured goods, particularly the reduction of tariffs. The average industrial tariff when the GATT came into force was over 40 per cent, but by 1980 this average had been reduced to not much more than 4 per cent and the volume of world trade had quintupled in twenty-five years. In the so-called Uruguay Round which opened in 1986 – the eighth in a sequence begun in Geneva in 1947 – the members of the GATT turned their attention to other areas of trade: agricultural produce, services and intellectual properties (royalties, patents). Fifteen areas were chosen for the Round, and among these agricultural produce was the most important, the most politically sensitive, the most intractable. By this date the patterns of world trade had changed considerably from those prevailing forty years earlier. In place of a multitude of states the commercial world was congealing into blocs. The United States, losing its imposing universal dominance, was creating a powerful regional position with a free trade treaty with Canada which came into force in 1989, the prospect of a similar treaty with Mexico and the reconnoitring of further extensions in South America. Japan was developing an East Asian and Pacific commercial zone with Australia, New Zealand and again parts of South America within its horizons. The European Community was developing another similar sphere with an ambit, in commercial matters, reaching beyond the EC itself to embrace members of the European Free Trade Association (EFTA) and other European states outside the Community. In this situation agricultural subsidies were a prominent bone of contention and the United States, supported by the Cairns Group of fourteen food exporters, demanded that the EC reduce its support prices by 75 per cent and its export subsidies by 90 per cent, but the members of the EC could agree on nothing more forthcoming than a cut of 30 per cent in support prices and an unspecified cut in export subsidies over ten years and departing from the high levels prevailing in 1986. France and Germany, overwhelmingly for electoral reasons, were the principal opponents of larger cuts. The progressive freeing of trade engineered by the GATT in relation mainly to manufactured goods was therefore endangered by the attempt to extend it into other fields.

In addition to the IMF and the GATT the Bretton Woods conference created the International Bank for Reconstruction and Development, later known as the World Bank. The World Bank was founded to assist in the postwar reconstruction of Europe. When this task was largely taken over by the Marshall Plan the Bank gradually turned its attention to development and to the rest of the world. Like the IMF, with which the Bank was allied by their common location in Washington and by the requirement that the Bank must be a member of the Fund, the Bank was governed by a professional board where the larger contributors to its capital funds carried commensurate weight. Besides these funds the Bank raised money by floating its own bonds on international stock exchanges. It made loans to creditworthy states at commercial rates of interest, for limited periods (at the end of which the funds could be lent again elsewhere) and principally for economic infrastructure. Its strictly conservative policies were necessary in order to enable it to borrow in money markets at the best available rates but these policies restricted its initial activities to financing the rich rather than aiding the poor. For the latter purpose it established the International Finance Corporation which was designed to help the poorer states to get finance from the private banking sector and, in 1960, the International Development Association which made fifty-year interest-free loans to poorer states. These IDA loans were financed mainly by western governments, were used mainly for economic infrastructure and were expected to produce a reasonable, if belated, return. In development therefore the Bank's principal function was that of mediator or procurer. Until the seventies its activities were restrained but in that decade the scale of its operations was magnified by a factor of ten or more and this expansion was accompanied by a new doctrine which, in order to justify lending to less conventionally creditworthy recipients, emphasized the potential economic value of poor societies, once they were developed or developing.

The parallel function of the International Monetary Fund (IMF) was to facilitate commerce by ensuring stable exchange rates, thus avoiding the financial anarchy of the thirties when competitive devaluations engendered worldwide recession by halting trade. The Fund was created as the guardian of the Bretton Woods system of fixed exchange rates – fixed in relation to a dollar which was itself convertible into gold. The Fund, like the Bank, was originally funded by members' contributions which both measured those members' voting weight and their drawing rights. It made short-term loans, principally to cushion balance of payments difficulties and principally to developed states, and it provided a monitoring and forecasting service on national and international economic affairs. Its basis was called in question by the almost simultaneous abrogation in 1971 of the dollar's convertibility into gold and the pegging of other currencies to the dollar. The context in which it operated was then transformed by the drastic oil price rises of 1973 and 1979 which created massive imbalances (particularly for states which were oil importers and relatively underdeveloped), while the consequent flood of petrodollars made floating currencies float more wildly. The Fund was all but swamped, lost prestige and influence, and was forced to reconsider its ambit and its methods. Ostensibly worldwide in its purposes, the Fund – like the Bank – had operated as an adjunct of an economic system created by and largely for the developed capitalist world, but from the seventies it was impelled to take a wider view as the developing (and now independent) Third World clamoured to be treated as part of the world's economic problems and the richer countries began to realize the extent of their economic involvement with the poorer.

The trading system designed at Bretton Woods presupposed a certain community of interests between all trading nations and it also supposed that tariffs and quotas were the principal barriers to commerce between states. But neither assumption was true of the economically weaker states. Although they needed to enter the international economy, they needed also to be protected in it; freedom worked against them. Further, their main problems were not tariffs or quotas but the instability of world prices for their products and the difficulty of getting into foreign markets to sell them. They were for the most part not only very poor – with an average annual income per head of $100–150, compared with over $1,000 in the Nato countries, even with Greece and Turkey included – but also ill equipped for international economic competition. Many of them had inelastic one-crop economies. Their products were primary products, for which the demand (except in the case of oil) was rising less quickly than world income. Their customers were making synthetic or substitute products and, especially in the case of agriculture, were susceptible to domestic protectionist lobbies anxious to close the market to imports from overseas. Although the Korean and Vietnam wars produced booms in commodity prices from which a number of these countries benefited, they did so only temporarily. Another palliative was aid, that is to say, cash, credits, goods or skills given free or transmitted at less than the ruling market price. Considerable benefits were transferred in this way and the donors, totting up the yearly sacrifices, congratulated themselves on their generosity.

The recipients, however, thought otherwise. They came to the conclusion that aid was the wrong answer to their problems. Apart from the fact that there was too little of it, and apart too from the realization that most of this aid was given for political purposes in the Cold War, aid was condemned for a variety of reasons: because the burden of interest payments and capital repayments became a sizeable charge on export earnings; because aid was frequently tied so that the recipient, instead of using it to buy what he wanted where it could be had most cheaply, was obliged to accept schemes not at the top of his list of priorities or buy goods from the donor instead of more cheaply elsewhere; because aid perpetuated an economic pattern created in colonial times, when colonies were kept to the business of producing raw materials for their owners' needs; because, therefore, aid impeded the essential business of diversifying the post-colonial economy and making a start with industrialization in order to enable the new state to create capital. For all these reasons the weaker countries quickly found that aid was no substitute for what they really wanted – a change in the rules governing the international economy and particularly guaranteed prices for their products and ease of access to the world's more affluent markets where, if at all, these products must be sold. The UN, which first set aside special funds for developing Third World countries (SUNFED) in 1960, asked the richer countries to contribute 0.7 per cent of their GNP to help the poor to grow at the rate of 5 per cent a year and convened a special conference, planned in 1962 and held in Geneva in 1964. This conference was intended to be a single event but turned into a permanent institution whose main thrust was for higher and more stable commodity prices. In 1967 the poorer states of Asia, Africa and Latin America established the Group of 77 which held its first meeting in Algiers in 1967 and chose Raul Prebisch of Argentina as its director. These proceedings transformed the international scene by demanding for economic relations between states as much attention as their political relations. The Group of 77 stressed the unfairness of an economic order dominated by purchasers and consumers of raw materials and by the volatility of the world prices of these materials and argued in favour of commercial preferences as opposed to the GATT's rules of equal treatment for the economically weak and strong, for transfers of technology at bargain prices and for cheap borrowing. But although the Group of 77 changed the way in which people thought about international affairs it had much less success in altering the way they behaved. It became divided between so-called moderates and radicals and was further divided when the oil price rises of the seventies served the oil producers well but impoverished the Group's oil importers. The emergence of OPEC as a distinct group illustrated this cleavage. OPEC maintained a general Third World stance while at the same time gravitating into the western economic order as an operator rather than a rebel. When in 1974 the UN proclaimed the need for a New International Economic Order the declaration testified to the number of votes commanded by the Third World in the General Assembly but the sequel testified to the limited effectiveness of national votes in economic affairs. With its overwhelming economic power the west was able to fend off the complaints and campaigns of the Third World and keep western economic relief at levels of charity to be set by the west itself.

The European Community took note of these problems with benevolent but measured intent. When the treaty of Rome was being negotiated France insisted on the insertion of special provisions for an associate status. It had in mind its own African territories, then all still colonies. Part IV of the treaty therefore provided that the Community might enter into arrangements with non-European states, by which these would be accorded the benefit of tariff reductions and quota extensions while being entitled at the same time to impose tariffs of their own to protect their infant industries (provided that these tariffs did not discriminate between members of the Community). The Community also established a Development Fund which disbursed $581 million in a first quinquennium and $730 million in a second. In 1964, by the first Convention of Yaoundé, eighteen former French colonies took advantage of these provisions and in 1969 three former British territories – Kenya, Uganda, Tanzania – were granted the same privileges for one year (until, that is, a revised Yaoundé Convention should come into operation in 1971). Nigeria too negotiated an agreement with the Community. Although at first suspicious of these arrangements as a form of neo-colonialism Nigeria could not afford to see its neighbours trading on better terms than itself with the Community, to which two-thirds of its exports were despatched. Again, the relations between the Community and its African associates could be attacked on the grounds that, despite their tangible advantages, they tended to perpetuate the colonial pattern instead of modernizing and diversifying the post-colonial economy. Further, some embarrassment was caused by the fact that a minority of the members of the UNCTAD lobby had, by securing a special position for themselves, broken the solidarity of the weaker nations. In 1974 a new convention for five years was signed at Lomé, this time between the EC and forty-six African, Caribbean and Pacific (ACP) states. It made provision for non-reciprocal tariff reductions, created an aid fund of $1,600 million and a scheme for stabilizing export prices, and promised the Commonwealth sugar producers access to the EEC for all their sugar at the prices assured by the Commonwealth Sugar Agreement. By Lomé II, which followed in 1979, the European Community undertook to take exports from the ACP countries to the value of $15,000 million a year and to provide annually aid rising from an initial base of $850 million, most of it designed for roads, education, hospitals, water and electricity. Lomé III and IV followed at quinquennial intervals but by 1990 aid flowing from the conventions, while certainly helpful, was equivalent to no more than half of the aggregate given by members of the Community separately and bilaterally. Recipients were irked by the concomitant dependence and also by the costs and bureaucratic formalities of operating the conventions. Under Lomé IV, concluded in 1990, recipients numbered

Key

////// member of OPEC

Figures in brackets are 1987 estimated oil
production figures in million tonnes

5.1 The world's major oil producers

USSR (625.01)

Iraq (101.2)

Kuwait (61.0)

Iran (112.5)

India (30.5)

Saudi Arabia (209.5)

Qatar (15.0)

Egypt (45)

United Arab Emirates (72.0)

Malaysia (23.5)

Nigeria (64.0)

Indonesia (64.1)

Gabon (7.9)

INDIAN OCEAN

Angola (16.5)

Australia (27)

sixty-eight, most of them worse off than they had been when Lomé I was launched.

While money and other benefits flowed to the poorer countries from a variety of sources, their debts grew and, most depressingly, so too did the cost of borrowing. From the seventies debtor states became more pressingly concerned to reschedule their debts than to attract new money on crippling terms. At UNCTAD IV in Nairobi in 1976 the Third World presented a comprehensive plan for the rescheduling of its debts, technical aid, the promotion of manufacturing industries and the diversification of one-crop economies. The plan was severely mangled by the richer countries who – particularly the former colonial powers among them – were irked by the view that they were not so much commercial creditors as moral debtors. Largely in vain they pointed to the fact that the expansion in the fifties and sixties of the world market had been halted and reversed. The effects of world recession on the attitudes and capabilities of the rich were even more in evidence at UNCTAD's fifth conference in Manila in 1979. The desperate poverty, in some areas famine, in the Third World; the prognosis of a world population doubled by the end of the century, with cities under siege and the outbreak of wars for raw materials; a Third World external debt of $300 billion or more; and western aid in decline and western protectionism rising – all these pointers produced a sense of gloomy despair which the conference could find no way of alleviating. By this date the concept of a Third World was becoming obsolete. A new group of countries had come into being whose wealth distinguished them dramatically from the world's poor and whose solidarity enabled them to play a forceful role in international affairs. This was the Fourth World of OPEC (Organization of Petroleum Exporting Countries) whose members owed their wealth to oil and their political and economic clout to the fact that, although very different in geographical extent and population, they were few enough and united enough to subordinate their differences to common action. In the seventies they raised the price of oil so steeply as to make all their customers, rich and poor, tremble for their economic future. They were able to do this because oil had been gravely under-priced in relation to demand and because its ownership – and therewith the power to fix prices in a sellers' market – had shifted from western companies to producer governments. The OPEC countries were peculiar because, in a world accustomed to regard all developing countries as poor, they were developing countries which were rich in cash. But they were rich in a special way, rich from selling a finite resource, not rich from the infinitely repeatable process of manufacture. They foresaw a fixed term to their years of affluence. Their motives in forcing up the price of their commodity were economic (to coin money for development, affluence and ostentation); strategic (to amass armaments); and political (to put anti-Israeli pressure on customers, a majority of OPEC's thirteen members being Arab). The effects of these price rises were the more disturbing because they coincided with and intensified other unsettling economic factors: a decline in the value of the dollar (already under strain from excessive overseas spending, culminating in the Vietnam War), the collapse of the Bretton Woods system, and international inflation. Many OPEC members made more money than they knew what to do with in their relatively underdeveloped and underpopulated countries. By investing their huge surpluses (over $100,000 million a year by the end of the seventies) in an unstable industrialized world they found themselves acquiring property which, partly as a result of their own actions, was being steadily devalued; while their price increases were squeezing their customers to the point where these must cut their purchases. Furthermore the massive transfer of capital from countries which could use it productively to countries which could not – from the industrial world to the members of OPEC – mothballed resources and so caused a shrinkage of the world economy.

The Third World was doubly hit. It could no longer pay for an essential commodity and it could no longer expect the financial assistance which it had been getting from the governments and private banks of the industrialized countries. The oil-importing developing countries had incurred foreign debts totalling $300,000 million; the combined deficit on their balance of payments was edging up to $100,000 million a year and increasing by $25,000 million a year on account of oil alone. At this rate not only they themselves but their creditors too were facing bankruptcy. Their exports were in decline because of the squeeze on their own production and because their principal markets (the developed countries) were also being squeezed. The OPEC countries accepted some responsibility for alleviating these burdens. They did so by the established practice of giving aid to the poor. In the late seventies this aid was flowing at rates between 1 and 3 per cent of their GNP and three OPEC members touched 10 per cent. Such rates compared favourably with an OECD target of 0.7 per cent (achieved in practice by no OECD member except Norway, Sweden, Denmark and the Netherlands). On the other hand the OPEC total was achieved partly by stopping OPEC contributions to the World Bank (on political grounds) and much the greater part of it was given to the more impecunious Arab countries in the Middle East and northern Africa – Egypt excepted after Sadat's agreements with Carter and Begin at Camp David.

From the point of view of the Third World OPEC's munificence had its limitations. In terms of a proportion of GNP, OPEC aid was comparatively generous. But OPEC's GNP was very much smaller than the OECD's (by a factor of about sixteen), so that the volume of OECD aid remained much larger than OPEC's. Furthermore OPEC's aid programme was no more than one more palliative; and alms-giving, on whatever scale, was no substitute for the reform of a fundamentally unbalanced world economic system which was itself contracting. Givers and receivers – OPEC, the EEC or the OECD on the one hand, the UNCTAD majority on the other – assumed a tussle, an adjustment of conflicting interests and divergent fortunes. Theorists had been talking for decades about the interdependence and mutual interests of rich and poor without getting much of a hearing but in 1980 an unofficial group of public personalities under the chairmanship of Willy Brandt produced a report which attempted to restate the problems and propound practical remedies.

The Brandt Report attempted to persuade its readers that the so-called north–south conflict between rich and poor was as dangerous for the whole world as the more obvious east–west conflict between the armed camps of the superpowers. Given the catastrophic properties of nuclear weapons this was an exceedingly difficult point to make. It was common knowledge (of the kind that most people prefer to forget) that millions of poor people were dying because of the world's extreme economic imbalance: some 800 million were living below the harshest poverty line. But it was not at all evident that this constituted a danger as well as a disgrace. The Brandt Report did not set out to repeat familiar humanitarian pleas; it set out to give them an urgent practical turn, to add scare to shame. In the course of doing this it made implicitly a central assertion of great moment by arguing that the common interests of rich and poor were more potent than what divided them. It abandoned UNCTAD's essentially adversary stance. It did not speak for the poor against the rich but for everybody, on the assumption that everybody was sliding down the same slippery slope. It alleged a community of interest running through the entire roll-call of sovereign states.

The report then set about squaring a circle with a tri-cycle. In brief it said: let OPEC's plutocrats lend their surpluses to the poor; let these and other funds be used to end famine in the Third World and develop its agriculture and industry; help the Third World, rescued from stagnation, to buy the manufacture of the industrial world; and help the industrial world, reaffirming its faith in free trade, to expand its business with the Third World (the source of much of its profits in colonial days) and so find the money to pay OPEC for its oil.

At the core of the Brandt proposals was a massive transfer of resources to the poorer countries by the new rich and the old rich of the order of $50,000 million a year by 1985 (at 1980 prices) – an increase in official aid of $8,000 million a year so that this aid would be equivalent to 0.7 per cent of the GNP of the contributing countries by 1985 and 1 per cent by the end of the century. There were two major obstacles to the acceptance of this statistically modest recipe. In so far as it maintained that it would pay the rich to help the poor it seemed to affront common sense. Secondly, it presupposed something like world government, of which there was not the faintest sign, for it was virtually inconceivable that a programme of this nature could be initiated and pursued by a committee or conference of representatives of sovereign states lacking the executive authority to take decisions, to decree action and to tax. The Brandt Report required a politically fragmented world to tackle universal economic problems, for which it did not appear to have the requisite institutions. It was an exercise in persuasion, unbacked by authority or power.

The problem nevertheless persisted much in the terms of the analysis made in the Brandt Report and every improvement in the world's economy enticed the poor into more hopeless positions. Thus a short boom in the rich world in the early seventies stimulated, as had the Korean War, demand for primary products but when the demand petered out with the boom the producers of these products in the poor world found that they had been seduced into putting more eggs into leaky baskets. The oil price rises of the seventies, which did not cause but did aggravate the collapse of the boom, forced the poor to borrow, not for investment, but simply to keep afloat. The rich lent money openhandedly as banks, flush with money from oil producers and encouraged (notably in the case of United States loans to Latin America) to lend and so foster the private capitalist sector, searched for borrowers – to whom they might lend at rates far higher than they were paying to their own depositors. So long as this pattern persisted rich banks and other financial institutions got richer still but by the eighties the debts of the poor to the rich had become so obviously unpayable that one or two statesmen said so openly: President Nyerere in so many words and President Garcia of Peru by unilaterally limiting repayment of Peruvian debt to a fixed percentage of national income. The rescheduling of debts became a pretence, obscuring the fact that these were bad debts of such magnitude that the risk of insolvency was threatening creditors as well as debtors.

Insolvency – particularly the insolvency of states which were halfway between poverty and riches and had borrowed vast sums in order to accelerate the transition and in the expectation of being able to finance these loans out of oil revenues which disappeared with the slump in oil prices – enforced new measures. In 1982 Mexico defaulted on its interest payments. Such a default, and such an example, threatened disaster for many major banks. The IMF lacked the resources to cope with a crisis on this scale but it took the lead in co-ordinating a relief operation with funds contributed by the threatened banks, and it went on to deal with dozens of other indebted states, funnelling fresh funds to them from commercial banks in return for the adoption of rigorous economic reforms. The IMF thereby tided over a crisis. Besides lending sums of its own it extracted five or six times as much money from banks. But the debtors, who discovered that even states forced to beg cannot choose, were obliged to impose domestic economic programmes which, by raising prices and restricting social services, bore heavily on their poorer citizens and which purchased respite rather than lasting relief. During the eighties African debt (excluding South Africa and the northern fringe) increased by more than $7,000 million a year and passed $200,000 million; in a number of years payments to the IMF exceeded receipts. A plan to convert debt into long-term IOU's found favour with creditors who knew that they would never get their money back but preferred to postpone payment indefinitely rather than write the debts out of their balance sheets. Latin American debt was twice as large as this African debt, with Brazil and Mexico each owing (in round figures) $100,000 million and Argentina $70,000 million. The Third World as a whole, in spite of receiving $50,000 million (net) a year from the World Bank, was piling up $30,000 million of new debt every year: the total exceeded $1,300,000 million. So far from developing, its economies were growing by 1 per cent and its population by 2 per cent.

In 1985 the Secretary of the US Treasury, James Baker, proposed that creditor banks should advance a further $20,000 million and that international institutions should make similar new loans – that is to say, lend money to enable debtors to meet the interest on old loans. This idea was elaborated by his successor, Nicholas Brady, who devised a scheme whereby creditor banks might choose between three ways of relieving their debtors: by exchanging existing bonds for new ones at 65 per cent of their face value, redeemable after thirty years and paying the original rate of interest; exchanging existing bonds for new thirty-year bonds with the face value unchanged but interest reduced and fixed at 6.25 per cent throughout the thirty years; and fresh loans payable in annual instalments over three years. A prototype agreement under the Brady plan was signed with Mexico in 1990.

NOTES

A. *Very small states*

There were in the world by 1985 over 40 independent states with a population below 2 million and another 30 territories of similar dimensions which were geographically distinct but not fully independent. Virtually all the latter were islands or groups of islands. So were most of the former, which included 9 separate states in the Caribbean and 8 in Oceania. Within this category the states and self-governing territories differed widely among themselves in extent, population and wealth, but with comparatively few exceptions they were too weak to defend themselves against predators attracted by their strategic value or by some exploitable asset – the beauty that appeals to tour operators or the remoteness that appeals to crooks. They can be to all intents and purposes bought by foreign mafias in league with local politicians, since a little money suffices to buy the few votes needed to win elections and power. Against the displeasure or apprehensions of bigger states they have no defence, as the invasion of Grenada by the United States in 1983 showed. In the sixties proposals were canvassed for the invention of a new status for very small territories about to be released from colonial empires into a nominal independence which they lacked the resources, human and material, to defend; but these discussions came to nothing, largely from fear of giving offence to nascent nations. Association with a great power, or regional associations, offered some protection and hope of betterment. A number of islands, most of them in the Pacific, made association agreements with the United States or France (as Overseas Territories); others became associates of the Commonwealth. The South Pacific Forum, created in 1971, embraced by 1990 11 independent states and non-independent but self-governing territories; established links with other international associations such as ASEAN and the EC and with the Specialized Agencies of the UN; and combined with larger states in the much older (1947) and wider South Pacific Commission which included the United States, Australia, New Zealand, Britain and France. By a treaty of 1985 10 Pacific island states, with Australia, New Zealand and Papua–New Guinea, proclaimed a South Pacific Nuclear-Free Zone; ancillary protocols were signed by the USSR and China, rejected by France and 'not accepted' by the United States and Britain. The treaty imposed a ban on the manufacture, testing and deployment of nuclear weapons in the zone; called on the five principal nuclear powers not to test or locate nuclear weapons in it; but refrained from attempting to prevent warships or aircraft from using international waters or airspace.

The principal island states which achieved independence in the south Pacific were: Western Samoa, independent in 1962 after German and then New Zealand rule; Tonga or the Friendly Islands, a nineteenth-century monarchy which became fully independent in 1970 (and did not sign the 1985 treaty); Fiji, independent in 1970 (see below); the Gilbert and Ellice islands which were separated in 1975 and became independent in 1979 and 1978 as Kiribati and Tuvalu; Solomon Islands, independent in 1978; and the Anglo–French condominium of New Hebrides, independent in 1980 as Vanuatu after considerable internal dissension and some fighting. In New Caledonia, a French Overseas Territory from 1958, conflict between indigenous kanaks and white immigrants who had become the majority was at least temporarily resolved by the Matignon agreement of 1988 which provided for direct French rule for one year, the division of the territory into three regions (two of them with a kanak majority), considerable economic aid from France and a referendum on independence in 1998. For accepting these agreements the kanak leader Jean-Marie Tjibaou was assassinated by his more militant compatriots.

Fiji had a similar racial problem. Fiji, consisting of some 300 islands with a population around 750,000, made unsuccessful approaches in the nineteenth century to Germany and the United States for protection before finally yielding itself in 1874 to Britain. Under British rule Indians were encouraged to migrate

5.2 The South Pacific

to Fiji where they became the mainstay of the sugar industry and, by the time of independence in 1970, a majority of the population. Tensions between the races were supplemented by tensions between the western and eastern islands and between the generations. In elections in 1987 the ruling Fiji party, which rested upon chiefly paternalism, was defeated by a coalition under Sir Timothy Bavadra who assembled a cabinet with a bare Indian majority. With a considerable part of its small army away in the Middle East in UN service Colonel Siliveni Rabuka was able to stage a coup with a handful of men who invaded the parliament and seized the new prime minister. Bavadra appealed unsuccessfully to the British government and crown (Fiji was a member of the Commonwealth), but Rabuka had covert support from the CIA which looked askance at Bavadra as a neutralist. Rabuka had the support of the Tsakei movement for Fiji-for-the-Fijians, but he progressively lost ground, particularly in the eastern islands, and the beginnings of an Indian emigration exposed the dangers of scaring Indians away from the sugar industry which was Fiji's principal economic resource. Fiji was a member of the South Pacific Forum. Bavadra died in 1989.

The Bismarck archipelago, annexed by Germany in 1874 and administered by Australia first under mandate from the League of Nations and, after 1947, as part of the UN Trust Territory of New Guinea, became in 1975 part of the new state of Papua–New Guinea.

Further north, in equatorial waters, the Caroline, Marshall and Mariana groups of islands, acquired by Germany in the nineteenth century, occupied by Japan in the First World War and retained under mandate after that war, were occupied by the United States in the Second World War and then brigaded together as the UN Trust Territory of the Pacific Islands from 1947 to 1986. The Marshalls, including Bikini and Enewetok atolls which were used for nuclear tests until 1958, became the Republic of the Marshall Islands with a treaty or 'compact' of Free Association with the United States (1982). The Carolines became the Federated States of Micronesia with a similar treaty. The purpose of these 'compacts' was to allow the United States to acquire special rights after the end of the period of trusteeship. This device caused trouble in the westernmost district of Micronesia – the Pelau archipelago. In 1979 the Pelauans voted overwhelmingly to ban nuclear weapons from their islands. When attempts to reverse this decision (which included attempts to change the constitution) failed, the United States propounded a 'compact' whereby a third of the Pelau archipelago would become available to the United States for military exercises and experiments. The compact was repeatedly rejected by the Pelauans in campaigns which included bribery and murders. Finally, the Marianas – originally and opprobriously called by Magellan the Ladrones – comprised Guam and the Northern Marianas. Guam was taken by the United States from Spain in 1898 and has remained part of the United States. The Northern Marianas became in 1986 a commonwealth within the United States.

B. *Antarctica*

The Antarctic continent is rich in fish and minerals, including oil. Modern technology has given it possible military significance and has drawn attention to the damage which may be done there to the global environment. Seven states

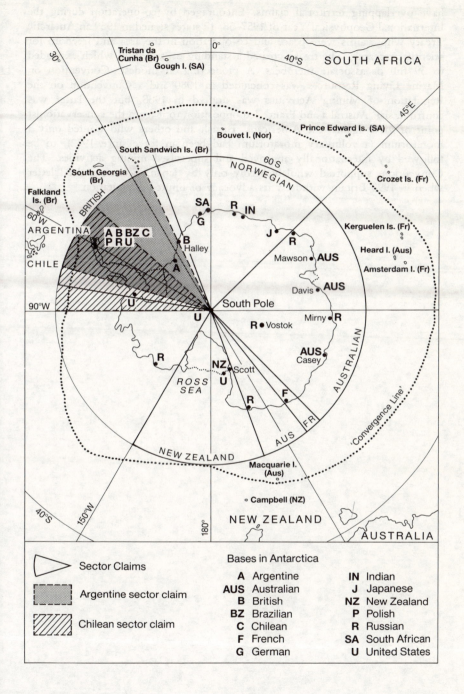

5.3 Antarctica (Source: *An Atlas of World Affairs*, William Boyd)

have overlapping territorial claims. Encouraged by co-operation during the International Geophysical Year of 1957–58, 12 states signed in 1959 an Antarctic Treaty whose aims were peace and co-operation in the area and freedom for scientific research. The treaty created a standing organization which expanded to 39 full or associate members. A pioneering, if modest, Convention on Marine Living Resources was concluded in 1980 and a Convention on the Regulation of Mining Activities was drafted in 1988, but the latter was controversial. Australia and France led opposition to it from the conservationist point of view against the Americans, British and others who wanted only a moratorium (a voluntary moratorium had been in force since 1972), to be followed by internationally approved and supervised mining activities. The Convention, supported wholeheartedly only by Japan, became a dead letter when in 1990 Britain withdrew its advocacy of limited exploitation.

PART TWO

EUROPE

6 WESTERN EUROPE

RECOVERY

Western Europe's recovery after 1945 was unexpectedly robust. Economic recovery, which required the restoration of severely damaged but essentially sound and skilled economies, was powerfully engendered through American financial aid which was itself impelled both by generosity and by fears of the collapse of countries of vital concern to the United States in the Cold War. The Marshall Plan (1947) was, with the North Atlantic Treaty (1949), a crucial factor in the tempo of western Europe's material repair and spiritual reassurance.

When the war ended the countries of western Europe were in a state of physical and economic collapse, to which was added the fear of Russian dominance by frontal attack or subversion. During the war plans had been made for the relief of immediate needs in Europe. The UN Relief and Rehabilitation Agency (UNRRA) was created in 1943 and functioned until 1947: a European Central Inland Transport Organization, a European Coal Organization and an Emergency Committee for Europe were established and merged in 1947 in the UN's Economic Commission for Europe (ECE). These organizations assumed that Europe's ills could be treated on a continental basis, but the Cold War destroyed this assumption and, although the ECE continued to exist and issued valuable *Economic Surveys* from 1948 onwards, Europe became bisected for economic as well as political purposes.

The immediate precursors of American economic aid were the failure of the conference of foreign ministers in Moscow in March and April 1947 and the Truman Doctrine whereby, in March, the United States took over Britain's role of supporting Greece and Turkey and rationalized it in anti-communist terms. In June General Marshall, then secretary of state, propounded at Harvard the plan which bears his name and which offered to all Europe (including the USSR) economic aid up to 1951 on the basis that the European governments would accept responsibility for administering the programme and would themselves contribute to European recovery by some degree of united effort. This American offer required the creation of a European organization; the Russian refusal of the offer, for the USSR and its dependants, turned the organization into a western European one. Sixteen countries established a Committee for European Economic Co-operation which assessed their requirements in goods and foreign exchange for the years 1948–52 and was converted in April 1948 into the more permanent Organization for European Economic Co-operation (OEEC). Western Germany was represented through the three western commanders-in-chief of occupation forces until October 1949 when German representatives were admitted. The United States and Canada became observer members of the organization in 1950 and subsequently co-operation was developed with Yugoslavia and Spain. At the American end the Foreign Assistance Act of 1948 created the Economic Co-operation Administration (ECA) to supervise the European Recovery Programme (ERP). In the following years the OEEC, using American funds, became the principal instrument in western Europe's transition from war to peace. It revived European production and trade by reducing quotas, creating credit and providing a mechanism for the settlement of accounts between countries. While it was a government-to-government and not a supra-national organization, it nevertheless inculcated international attitudes and fostered habits of economic co-operation which survived the ending of the ERP. (It was replaced in 1960 by the Organization for Economic Co-operation and Development (OECD) in which the United States, Canada and Japan were full members and which extended the work of the OEEC into the developing areas of the world.)

The establishment of the OEEC coincided with the signing in March 1948 of the treaty of Brussels by Britain, France, Belgium, the Netherlands and Luxembourg (the last three compendiously referred to as Benelux from the time when they formed a customs union in 1947). This treaty, like the Anglo–French treaty of Dunkirk of 1947, was a military alliance ostensibly directed against a revival of the German threat. It contained in addition provisions for political, economic and cultural co-operation through standing committees and a central organization, and it was also seen by at least some of its promoters as a first step towards a yet broader military alliance with the United States. President Truman, speaking of the need for universal military training and selective military service in the United States, so interpreted it and the leader of the Republicans in the Senate, Arthur H. Vandenberg, proposed and carried a motion in favour of American aid to regional military organizations which served the purposes of American policy: the senator was in essence advocating a military pact between the United States and western Europe, a military counterpart to General Marshall's economic plan. The North Atlantic Treaty, signed in April 1949, by the United States, Canada and ten European countries, gave the latter for at least twenty years a guarantee of their continuing independence and integrity against Russian attack by formalizing and institutionalizing the American intention to remain in Europe and play the role of a European power. At this date the Russians, like the Chinese fifteen years later, had large and frightening land forces which weighed heavily on all those within their reach but lacked a diversified, modern armament capable of engaging the United States. The North Atlantic Treaty was therefore a way of bringing American air power, including nuclear weapons, to bear in order to inhibit the use of Russian land forces in the area designated by the treaty.

The European members of this new alliance were at first comparatively passive beneficiaries who, in spite of the fact that they provided 80 per cent of its forces in Europe, were dependent on the far more significant American contribution, without which their own contribution was irrelevant to their main needs and fears. Although in terms the treaty was a collective security arrangement, in fact it was, to begin with, more like the protectorate treaties of an earlier age whereby a major power had taken weaker territories under its wing. The treaty created a permanent organization (Nato – the North Atlantic Treaty Organization) for political discussion and military planning and some of its makers and later devotees envisaged the growth of something more than a military alliance – an entente or community or union. But nothing of the kind emerged for a variety of reasons: the enormous disparity between the power of the United States and any other member, the failure of the European members to coalesce into a political unit commensurate with the United States, the breadth of the Atlantic Ocean, the unquestioning addiction of Americans to the sovereignty which seemed to them old-fashioned in others, the revival of European power and confidence, and the waning of the Russian threat halfway through the life of the treaty.

For almost half a century Nato was a principal instrument in the Cold War (which has been discussed in an earlier chapter). Western Europe, with the Atlantic and Mediterranean seas, was its theatre of operations. The European members of the alliance provided the bulk of its forces, the Americans the bulk of the equipment and most of the money. The Europeans were careful to avoid any form of military association among themselves which might seem to weaken the Euro–American link. They were also considerably more reluctant than the Americans to acknowledge that an anti-Soviet alliance entailed an end to hostility with Germans and the integration of West Germany into the alliance. This step – the most portentous in Nato's history and one which was to cause some confusion when the Soviet menace all but disappeared in the eighties – was precipitated by events thousands of miles away in Asia: the Korean War. Within little more than a year after the signing of the North Atlantic Treaty the outbreak of this war created fresh and substantial calls on the United States' resources and the fear of similar hostilities in Germany. Washington became therefore anxious to convert its allies from passive protégés into junior partners and to build up in Europe itself a counterforce to the Russian armies, distinct from the long-range American air power which, although based in Europe, was under exclusive American command and remained so even when a joint Nato command was created. The allies, however, were still weak. Britain and France, with much of their forces committed outside Europe, could give little help immediately and they were therefore the more easily constrained to accept an American emergency decision to rearm the Germans. The anti-Russian alliance feared by Moscow between two world wars now took shape and at the end of 1950 General Eisenhower returned to Europe as supreme commander of another grand alliance. In the same year Greece and Turkey were invited to co-operate with the allies in the defence of the Mediterranean, although they did not become full allies until early in 1952: their co-operation helped to establish an eastern flank to protect the allied central sector and to threaten the USSR from the south. Early in 1951 a new headquarters came into operation (Supreme Head-quarters, Allied Powers in Europe – SHAPE) and a year later, at Lisbon, the Nato council approved a plan to endow this command by 1954 with ninety-six active and reserve divisions, including fifty in the central sector, and 9,000 aircraft. Although these targets were never attained, the Lisbon decisions gave the alliance the shape which it ever afterwards retained, later debate focusing on strategic doctrine, new weapons and their deployment.

With one exception. In 1952 the German problem – that is to say, the status of West Germany as a political entity and its role in Nato's planning and operations – was still unresolved. With the Korean War American pressure to accelerate West Germany's sovereignty and therewith West German rearmament became irresistible, but France in particular was anxious to find a way to prevent the resurgence of autonomous German military power. René Pleven, the French minister of defence, proposed that German units be raised and incorporated in multinational divisions but that western Germany be allowed no separate army, general staff or defence ministry. Adopting the pattern of the European Coal and Steel Community, which had been launched on French initiative and was about to come into existence, Pleven devised a European Defence Community (EDC) with a council of ministers, an assembly and a European minister of defence. The French aim was to minimize the German military unit and at the same time to integrate the German military contribution, both operationally and politically, in an international organization. British participation was all but essential since without it the proposed international organization would consist only of France and Germany with some comparatively trivial makeweights. For France a British commitment was the only way adequately to offset the risks inherent in the rearmament of Germany and the reappearance of a sovereign German state, but no British commitment satisfactory to France was forthcoming during the four years in which the EDC was under debate.

In May 1952 agreements signed in Bonn and Paris created a complex new structure: six continental European states signed a treaty creating the EDC, the three western occupiers of Germany agreed to end the occupation upon ratification of the EDC treaty, and both Britain and the remaining Nato powers entered into separate ancillary treaties promising military aid in the event of an attack upon any of the EDC partners. But the French remained uneasy and undecided. They wanted British membership of the EDC and not a pledge to help it, and they disliked the provision in the EDC treaty permitting the raising of whole German divisions in place of the smaller units proposed by Pleven's plan for incorporation in international divisions. The United States and Britain brought pressure to bear on France, the former by threatening an 'agonizing reappraisal' of American policies if the EDC treaty were not ratified (which was taken to mean the cutting off of American aid to France) and the latter by giving in 1954 a further pledge of military and political co-operation with the EDC (a pledge echoed by President Eisenhower within the limits of his constitutional competence). In August of that year the French parliament finally came to a vote and refused, by 319 votes to 264 on a procedural motion, to debate the ratification of the treaty.

With this vote the EDC and all the Bonn and Paris agreements of 1952 collapsed. There was anger in Bonn, where Adenauer insisted that western Germany must have sovereignty none the less, and in Washington, where Dulles decided ostentatiously to cut Paris out of a tour of European capitals. In London, more constructively if belatedly, Eden set to work to put the pieces together again by diplomatic labours and a more specific pledge than Britain had so far been willing to vouchsafe. By the end of the year the Brussels treaty of 1948 had been expanded to take in the German and Italian ex-enemies and renamed Western European Union (WEU); this WEU took over the non-military functions of the Brussels treaty organization and became militarily an ingredient in Nato; Britain declared that it would maintain on the Continent forces equivalent to those already committed to the Supreme Allied Commander in Europe (Saceur), that is, four divisions and a tactical air force; the occupation of western Germany was ended; Adenauer undertook not to produce atomic, bacteriological or chemical weapons, long-range or guided missiles, bomber aircraft or warships, except upon the recommendation of Saceur and with the assent of two-thirds of the council of WEU; West Germany was to become a full member of Nato, and did so formally the following year. One other loose European end was clutched. France and western Germany agreed that the Saar, which France had hoped ever since 1945 to annex in one form or another, should constitute a special autonomous territory embedded in WEU, but the Saarlanders rejected this arrangement by plebiscite in October 1955 and the Saar became a part of western Germany at the beginning of 1957. Thus the first postwar decade closed with Nato in existence to extend American protection over western Europe, Britain as the firmest and most effective of the European members of the alliance, and a nascent German state back in the comity of western Europe.

The weak point appeared to be France. Whereas Britain had made an energetic recovery from the war and West Germany was on the verge of its economic miracle, France was relapsing into the political instability which had characterized it between the wars, accompanied by economic ineptitude and colonial overstrain. But France too was on the verge of economic reform and advance; was about to shed intolerable imperial burdens; and, with a radical political somersault, to find in Franco–German partnership a new base for French activity in Europe and beyond.

France had been a major European land power and a major imperial power but had failed in the contest with England for sea power. In the nineteenth century the decline of France's position in Europe had been matched by the acquisition of a second overseas empire to replace the territories lost to Britain in the wars of the eighteenth century, but by the beginning of the twentieth century France, slipping back in the demographic and the industrial race and spiritually still divided between the heirs of the Enlightenment and the Revolution and those who accepted neither, was becoming discouraged and unnerved and unresponsive to central government. The awful sacrifices of the First World War and the hardly less awful humiliation of the Second, separated by incapacity to face up to the problems of the economic crisis or to Hitler's challenge to basic values, brought France low in its own eyes until the exploits of the Resistance and the leadership of de Gaulle revived and personified the French spirit: de Gaulle's identification of himself with France and his constant use of the first person singular were precisely what was needed after the physical and spiritual lesions of a century.

When the war ended the French tried to strike out into a new world with some of the trappings of the old until they found that this would not work. They adopted a constitution and political methods unhappily reminiscent of the defunct Third Republic, made great efforts to retain or recover their empire in Asia and Africa, tried the old game of weakening Germany permanently, and made treaties with their traditional British and Russian allies. But they also revolutionized their foreign policies by joining the anti-Russian western alliance even though it entailed the rearming of Germany, took the lead in devising new political structures suitable to Europe's altered place in the world, accepted the end of empire and – most important – adopted under the lead of Jean Monnet a successful form of central economic planning for the modernization of industry and agriculture. During the war national production had fallen by 65 per cent but within two years of liberation in 1944 and before the inception of the Marshall Plan, 90 per cent of this loss had been recovered. From 1947 the series of Monnet Plans, elaborated and applied by a modest central government department and using Marshall funds mainly for the reconditioning or transforming of industries, allocated resources, determined priorities and master-minded the restoration of the economy sector by sector in association with state-owned enterprises and private businesses. From the date of the second plan (1952–57) socio-economic sectors such as education, research and training were included and led at the next stage to central direction of social policies and a welfare state financed by employers and employed.

The renunciation of empire brought France, over Algeria, to the brink of civil war, from which it was saved in 1958 by the return to power of de Gaulle and the thwarting thereby of a right-wing military plan to seize control of the capital and the state. De Gaulle tamed the generals and colonels, disposed of the politicians and the remaining colonies and, profiting from a rapidly improving economic situation, raised France from a position of pity and scorn to one of independence and attention.

De Gaulle inherited two recent decisions of his predecessors – the decision to become a nuclear power and the decision to join an economic community with avowed political implications (the EEC – see the next section). The first of these decisions was congenial to him. He believed that France could be a major power and he believed that power must be modern. Just as he had been an expert in tank warfare when many of his colleagues were still in favour of the horse, so now a generation later he held that there was a choice between nuclear power and no power, and he held too that beyond a certain point there was little difference between one nuclear power and another: a nuclear power which reached that point became a member of the first league even if it possessed fewer or less sophisticated weapons than other members of the league. The second decision may have been less congenial to him, not so much because he eschewed all unions or harboured antiquated notions about the ability of a country like France to go it alone, but rather because his ideas on the nature of useful unions were different from those of the authors of the treaty of Rome. While aware that the independent states of Europe were no longer what they had been (even if, by becoming nuclear powers, one or two of them could stand up for themselves in the exceptional circumstances when the nuclear argument is brought into play), he did not believe that the minds of Europeans had become supra-national. In his view the vast majority of Europeans still responded to the idea of the nation and he therefore based his European policies on the nation state and on associations of nation states with, however, the reservation that the base was a starting point and not a permanently limiting factor. De Gaulle's *patrie* was not identical with the state (*état*) and might be fitted into a partnership or association which recognized and protected national identities. Further, de Gaulle's pragmatic temper led him to insist on the differences between more and less powerful states and held that any association should be governed or guided by a directorate composed of the former – in this case either France, western Germany and Italy, or France and western Germany. Equality between states, with its corollary of one-state-one-vote, he regarded as a vicious pretence, whether portended in the EEC or practised in the UN General Assembly. (The directorate of the five permanent members of the Security Council, however, fitted his theory, subject to putting the right Chinese delegate in the Chinese seat.)

De Gaulle also inherited a position which he found intolerable in a Nato which he found anachronistic. Following his doctrine of directorates, Nato should be directed by the United States, Britain and France, but it was in his view dominated by the United States with a touch of special British influence achieved by British subservience to American policies. Shortly after his return to office in 1958 de Gaulle tried to establish with the United States and Britain a triumvirate within Nato, but his ideas were rejected on the grounds that the formation of an alliance within an alliance would lead to the loss of the other allies. Washington and London, moreover, underrated France at this stage: they derided French nuclear ambitions, did not see how France was to dispose of its Algerian incubus, and failed to see that the status of France was changing and would change more rapidly in the near future.

De Gaulle not only desired the revival of France: he rightly saw that it was happening. He also saw that Europe was changing. The Cold War was over. It might be renewed one day, but for the present the fear of Russian aggression which had prompted the creation of Nato was fading fast. It followed that the Americans could not be expected to stay in Europe indefinitely. Perhaps they would be gone by 1980. Again de Gaulle, taking a long view and a clear view, was probably right, since the development of weapons technology was converting the American presence in Europe from a strategic disposition into a political gesture, and a political gesture is more easily abandoned than a strategic position, especially if, as began to happen after 1960, difficulties with their balance of payments should cause the Americans to ask what their forces were really doing in Europe. Europeans were coming to doubt the automatic immediacy of an American response to a Russian attack since American cities first came under direct threat from Russian intercontinental missiles: either the Russians would not attack or they would do so in a way calculated to avoid an American response.

Immediately after de Gaulle's return Dulles offered France nuclear weapons in return for the right to put launching sites in France. De Gaulle refused and in 1959 withdrew the French contingent from Nato's Mediterranean fleet. He refused to be ruffled by the Berlin or the Cuban crises and was strengthened by both in his view that there was no pressing Russian danger. In 1962 when Kennedy offered France as well as Britain nuclear weapons he again refused and in 1966 he withdrew French forces from all Nato commands. This policy struck some responsive chords in the rest of Europe. The waning of the Russian threat and of the fear of economic collapse, the achievement of the prime purposes of Nato and the Marshall Plan, gave Europeans a new confidence which they translated into a desire to run their own affairs (notwithstanding that for the most part they already did so). Since western Europe had been saved by the Americans from having its affairs run by the Russians, the new mood was anti-American, for it was the Americans and not the Russians whose presence affronted a new nationalism which was further sharpened in the sixties by resentment and alarm at American economic penetration, the debit side of the American investment which gave Americans control over European enterprises and so over the hiring and firing of labour. De Gaulle's anti-Americanism, rooted in Roosevelt's partiality for Vichy and right-wing French generals and admirals during the war, was not out of tune with Europe's mood – until he gave the impression that he wanted to put an end to the American alliance altogether. For this western Europe was not prepared. The Cold War might be waning but it was not over, it might recur, and so long as there was a doubt there had better be an alliance. De Gaulle himself affirmed the need for an alliance more than once, but his desire to see the Americans at a distance from Europe created the impression that the alliance was itself in the Gaullist view expendable.

France in the sixties was ready to relinquish, or at any rate relax, an alliance which it had adopted in the forties out of economic necessity. The change in France's economic circumstances was at least as important as its change of ruler in 1958 in producing a change in policy. De Gaulle was not untypical of Frenchmen and many other Europeans in wishing to diminish political and strategic dependence on the United States as soon as economic dependence was no longer a fact. At the end of the war de Gaulle and other leading French politicians had wanted France to adopt an intermediate position between the United States and the USSR, but the onset of the Cold War and French military and economic weaknesses forced the French government in 1947 to make a choice and to choose the American side. The need for money and for food determined French policy. The Marshall Plan offered salvation and France took it. But – like the Americans themselves – they saw the programme as a short-term rescue operation and – unlike the Americans – assumed that the consequential alignment would also be reviewed at the end of the short term.

This postwar drift from an intermediate to an aligned policy was facilitated by, and also to some extent a cause of, the dropping of the communists from the government. From their role as national heroes and active partners in the resistance to the Germans the communists had reverted to a suspect, sectarian position in which the interests of Moscow counted for more than national unity and regeneration. Even before the Marshall Plan and its rejection by the USSR their continuance in the government had become next to impossible on account of the Truman Doctrine on aid to Greece and Turkey for the defeat of communism, the decision to abandon discussions with the Viet Minh and fight it, the stern suppression of revolt in Madagascar and of strikes in the nationalized Renault works, and a wage freeze; communists had already been dropped from the Belgian and Italian governments earlier in 1947. At the end of that year the French communists tried to exploit politically serious strikes which had genuine economic sources in the financial policies of the government of Paul Ramadier, but they failed, their representatives were dismissed from the government and the party lapsed into a long period of opposition. Political power shifted to the right and even when it swung back leftward in the mid-fifties it did not re-embrace the communists and France remained for a decade an acquiescent member of the western alliance. By the sixties France was ready to reconsider its role, and it so happened that, owing to the coup of 1958, its gradual disengagements from the American alliance took place not at the instigation of communists (who remained outside the pale of government) but under the guidance of de Gaulle.

A fourth principal element in de Gaulle's heritage in 1958 – along with France's nuclear programme, the treaty of Rome and membership of Nato – was the *rapprochement* with Germany. The principal architects of this *rapprochement* were Robert Schuman and Jean Monnet on the French side and Adenauer on the German. Adenauer proposed in 1950 a Franco–German union, to which Italy and the Benelux states and possibly Britain too might adhere. De Gaulle, then in retirement, welcomed the idea, and ten years later he turned it to good account by concluding a Franco–German treaty at a time when his relations with the EEC and Nato groups were strained. De Gaulle's return had coincided with a weakening of German–American relations. Adenauer's political attitudes were markedly personalist and the death of Dulles had removed the principal bond between him and Washington. He was moreover suspicious of the Camp David spirit and Eisenhower's attempts to find points of agreement with Khrushchev. Towards Britain Adenauer's feelings had been cold since, after the war, a British officer had found him unfit to be mayor of Cologne in spite of the fact that he had held that office continuously from 1917 to 1933. He did not like Macmillan, was caustic about his attempt to play the role of mediator between Washington and Moscow, and was angered by his visit to Moscow in 1959 to discuss a European settlement – affecting above all Berlin – without prior notice to Britain's German allies who were more closely affected by such a topic than anybody else. Adenauer also resented Britain's aloofness from the EEC and its attempt to block progress by forming EFTA. He was ready to turn to France and, after some initial hesitation, to find a new personal friend in de Gaulle.

In 1959 Adenauer, after ten years as chancellor and now 83 years old, toyed with the idea of accepting the West German presidency. For a man who was Stresemann's senior and had been considered for the chancellorship of the Weimar Republic in 1921 and 1926 the end was approaching and his colleagues considered that the time had come for him to retire to a less active post. But for Adenauer the transfer was only palatable if it were to be accompanied by a transformation of the presidency from an ornamental into an executive office. He was willing to be a president like Eisenhower or de Gaulle but not a president like his own predecessors or his Italian neighbour. When it became apparent that his compatriots did not relish a presidential democracy he decided to remain chancellor. In elections in 1961 his party, the Christian Democratic Union, lost its absolute parliamentary majority and in the ensuing inter-party negotiations for a new government Adenauer was forced to accept a conditional fourth term of office as chancellor, the condition being that he would retire in 1965 at the latest. During meetings with de Gaulle at Rambouillet in July 1960 and in Paris in July 1962 – the latter was followed in September by a triumphant tour of western Germany by de Gaulle – Adenauer opted for a continuing Franco–German understanding in spite of misgivings about de Gaulle's version of European integration and de Gaulle's opposition to a European political union and the inclusion of Britain in the EEC. By 1962 he was further disillusioned with the United States under the new Kennedy administration and with Macmillan's devious approaches to the EEC, and in January 1963 he signed with de Gaulle a treaty which formalized the Franco–German entente and sought to make it the core of European politics, a working alternative to or brake upon Nato, the EEC, the Anglo–American partnership, an American–Russian *rapprochement*, or the American–German entente of the fifties. This treaty was a peak in de Gaulle's diplomacy but he did not remain on it, for the accord was mistimed. Adenauer himself was on his way out and his immediate successors were unenthusiastic about this, among others, of his personal achievements. The Franco–German treaty became almost at once a dead letter, or at best a pointer of uncertain direction and import. De Gaulle failed to achieve the changes which he desired in the way Nato functioned at the top. He was credited with the belief that Britain was Washington's Trojan horse within Europe's walls, but he would have been more correct to see Bonn in this role, for whereas Britain in its chronic ill health was dependent on the United States economically, West Germany remained dependent on the United States for its defence.

By the late fifties problems over the distribution of power and weapons within the alliance were acknowledged and produced some bizarre schemes. De Gaulle's own proposals in 1958 for a Nato directorate comprising the three powers with extra-continental interests had been made in response to an American request for ideas about this problem, but they found no favour in Washington or London where they were regarded as no more than a French claim to equality with the United States and Britain. A year later, after the installation in Europe of IRBM (Intermediate Range Ballistic Missiles) under a dual control or 'two keys' system, the Supreme Commander, General Lauris Norstad, stressed the need for a multinational nuclear authority, and in 1960 the United States proposed to install in Europe 300 mobile Polaris missiles on road, rail and river under American control. De Gaulle, asked to accept fifty of these, said he would do so only if France produced its own warheads, thus making French control a condition of acceptance, whereupon the Americans dropped the plan. The Russians objected that it entailed the provision of nuclear weapons for Germany.

These discussions, abortive though they were, showed that Nato could not go on for ever on the basis of an American nuclear monopoly. Either the Europeans would themselves produce a deterrent force roughly equivalent to the American nuclear contribution to the alliance and so turn it into a more equal partnership, or some way must be found of creating an American–European nuclear force. The first solution – a distinct European force – presupposed a European political authority to control it, and although Europeans might have liked to have such a force, they showed no signs of evolving the necessary political authority. The solution must therefore lie on American–European lines, and there were two schools of thought, the multinationalist and the multilateralist. The multinationalists accepted national sovereign control and aimed at no more than the retractable commitment of national forces to a Nato commander, together with increased participation by all the allies in strategic planning and political consultation. The multilateralists devised a scheme for mixed forces in which nuclear weapons would be operated by units whose personnel would be drawn from different states. The American administration adopted multilateralism in 1962 not long before the British and French governments demonstrated their continuing addiction to, in the British case, multinationalism as the Americans understood it and, in the French case, a multinationalism which excluded the Americans. Since, however, the Americans hoped that multilateralism would provide the answer to the German question – how to give the Germans a satisfactory share in nuclear operations without alarming the Russians – they persisted with it despite the opposition of their other principal allies. They proposed in March 1963 a multilateral force (MLF) of twenty-five mixed-manned surface vessels, each carrying eight Polaris missiles, three-quarters of the cost to be paid by the United States and West Germany.

Western Germans welcomed the scheme as a means to restore the close relations with the United States which had characterized the fifties; alarmed by the American–Russian *rapprochement* which produced the test ban treaty of 1963, they saw in the MLF a way of securing a special position equivalent to the possession by Britain and France of the independent nuclear deterrent which was denied them. The Russians, for the same reasons, objected stoutly to the MLF and insisted on regarding it as a case of nuclear proliferation. The French ignored it and the British were scornful of its military value but agreed, for political reasons and after strong American pressure, to participate in it. The Italians, Greeks and Turks also agreed to join. At the end of 1964 the new British Labour government produced an alternative scheme without obvious appeal or virtue. Thereafter the MLF wilted because the Americans found that they no longer needed to entice West Germany away from France and because they came to believe that Russian objections were genuine and fatal to the progress of agreements to control further nuclear proliferation. So far as concerned harmony in the alliance they fell back on proposals to give the allies a bigger share in planning committees, and in 1966 such questions were temporarily submerged by a French decision to withdraw from all Nato's military organs and to expel such organs from France. France remained a member of the alliance and continued to insist on the need for it, but would have no part in its operations so long as it remained unreformed.

Restored sufficiently to semi-withdraw from the alliance, France was shaken in May 1968 by an outbreak of revolutionary violence in Paris. The causes were not peculiar to France. All over western Europe there were deep sources of discontent which overlapped and fused: urban squalor, revulsion against the horrors of the war in Vietnam, overcrowded universities and schools, the fight for higher wages in a period of inflating prices. In France de Gaulle's government irritated the young by its tone of paternalism and the liberals by its attempts to direct radio and television and to control the press: the progressive element in Gaullism had grown dimmer during the ten years since de Gaulle had returned to save France from fascism and military rule. The position in French universities and schools was far from being the worst in Europe (in some parts of Italy schoolchildren had to attend on a rota system because there was no room for them all at once), but it was bad enough to inflame a generation which had been attuned to political activism by the Algerian War and was politically better organized than anywhere else in Europe. Since the war the number of university entrants had been quadrupled by the rise in the birthrate and because no government had dared to change the rule that any boy or girl achieving the *baccalauréat* was entitled to go to a university. New universities were being built in Paris and out of it, but they were started too late. The resulting chaos was increased by bureaucratic centralization, the discontent by outdated syllabuses and outdated rules about personal conduct (sometimes enforced by the police). The new university at Nanterre on the edge of Paris became notorious for clashes between students and staff but it was typical rather than unique, and it was trouble at the Sorbonne in the heart of Paris which eventually converted such clashes into something like a revolution. After an occupation of university buildings by students the university authorities called in the police and the police behaved with such brutality that opinion in the capital, not normally on the side of students, swung massively in their favour. The troubles culminated in a night of battle in which the police (this time on government instructions) and the students fought one another for control of the Left Bank while the scenes of violence were relayed to France and beyond by radio reporters roaming the streets. The police won the battle but students continued for a time to occupy parts of the university. At the same time workers in Paris and other cities went on strike, occupied factories and set up action committees which began to look like a new government in embryo. The authority of the legitimate government was badly shaken. The prime minister, Georges Pompidou, was so alarmed that he advised de Gaulle to resign. There was talk of a new French Revolution. But a month later de Gaulle went to the polls and won a sweeping victory.

There were several reasons for this. Although a nucleus among the students had revolutionary political aims, many of them wanted no more than university reform and the strikers were not revolutionary at all. They were not trying to overthrow the government but to get better wages out of it and less unemployment. The leaders of the Communist Party were too much part of the system to want to risk its disruption, were afraid of the more left-wing groups and had no sympathy with students. Above all de Gaulle's nerve held. Although he had to hurry back from a state visit to Romania, he did not let himself be hustled when he got back. Having assured himself by a secret expedition to military headquarters that he had nothing to fear from the army, he correctly weighed up the situation, waited for the university authorities and the trade unions to begin to recover their control in their respective spheres and then, disdaining François Mitterrand's bid to replace him in the presidency, won a sweeping victory by the votes of frightened Frenchmen at the end of June and dismissed Pompidou. He then backed his minister of education, Edgar Faure, who made a radical attack on the problem of higher education in spite of some of his colleagues and of much conservative opinion. Faure introduced joint teacher–student management; abolished the centralized system under which France had in effect a single university and substituted for it sixty-five universities (thirteen in Paris), none of which was to have more than 20,000 students; and further decentralized control within each university by creating joint councils for each nucleus of 2,500 students.

But de Gaulle's days were numbered. One of his aversions was the French senate. One of his preoccupations at this point was the reform of the machinery of government by the creation of regional assemblies. He proposed to link this reform with the abolition of the senate and put the two issues together to the electorate by referendum. But the senate was not unpopular and de Gaulle's use of the referendum, coupled as it was with the implication that the rejection of what was proposed entailed his own resignation, was widely regarded as unfair tactics. A majority voted no. De Gaulle at once resigned. (He died the next year.) The president of the senate, Alain Poher, assumed the functions of the presidency in accordance with the constitution, a presidential election was held, and the Gaullist candidate Georges Pompidou won comfortably in the second round. This change at the top in Paris coincided with a similar change in Bonn.

Konrad Adenauer's long rule in western Germany (1952–63) established in Europe a new state which was resuming Germany's economic dominance on the continent. It was built on the economic policies of the western countries (currency reform and Marshall aid) and the division of Germany. Territories lost in the east were less valuable than those retained in the west; refugee labour from the east was opportune for reconstruction and peculiarly mobile. Investment boosted growth without inflation. Growth restored morale. High standards in education, industrial training and discipline, and efficient administration added their quotas. In the four years preceding sovereignty the combined western zones trebled industrial output and raised GNP by two-thirds. The population recovered its prewar numbers and was stabilized in the sixties at 60 million (eastern Germany's was 17 million). As output rose and unemployment did not, generous provision for public services and a welfare state attracted minimal opposition. Material success was matched by political success on two fronts: internally, a democracy which worked and (unlike Weimar) was respected and popular, and, externally, acceptance in the world's strongest alliance.

In the Adenauer years the west meant, overwhelmingly, the United States. Yet Adenauer himself edged in his later years towards a more precisely European stance, particularly in his relations with de Gaulle, and his successors began to probe Germany's traditional associations in central Europe. Adenauer's departure was followed by a short postlude to the Adenauer era with Ludwig Erhard as chancellor until, in 1966, he was forced out of office by his own party. From 1966 to 1969 the Christian Democrats and the Social Democrats governed in coalition with Kurt Kiesinger as chancellor and Willy Brandt as vice-chancellor and foreign minister. These three years constituted a bridge between the Adenauer era and the almost equally long socialist era to come. The grand coalition abandoned Adenauer's attitude of regarding half Europe as virtually non-existent. The sources of this evolution were détente in Europe and Washington's increasing preoccupation with establishing better relations with Moscow without as much regard for German susceptibilities as had been evinced in the past; the abandonment of the pretence that European security and the German problem were inseparable and that no European system could usefully be studied in the absence of German reunification; the growth of eastern European economies leading not only to restiveness against satellite status but also to a desire for the products of the new technology (computers, for example) which western Germany could provide; and to popular appreciation among West Germans of the barrenness of the promise of reunification via a western alliance, the realization that the road to reunification did not run through Washington. Bonn therefore entered into discussion with eastern European states and established in 1967 diplomatic relations with Romania. This eastern policy quickened after 1969 when Brandt became chancellor. Brandt and his foreign minister, Walter Scheel, opened discussions with east Germany, Poland and the USSR.

Progress was slow because of interlocking complexities. Besides renewing normal relations with wartime enemies (the USSR, Poland, Hungary and Bulgaria) Bonn had to negotiate agreements with Czechoslovakia which was demanding the abrogation of the Munich agreement of 1938 and with East Germany which was demanding recognition as an independent sovereign state. This last issue was complicated by the problems of Berlin, a city divided politically and physically and in which Germany's four principal conquerors still had special rights. Treaties with the USSR and Poland, which included the recognition of the Oder–Neisse line, were concluded in 1970 and ratified in 1972 after other agreements had been concluded. These included: a new four-power agreement on Berlin providing, among other things, for easier rail, road and water communication between West Germany and west Berlin and freer access for west Berliners to East Germany for a wide variety of purposes; a General Relations

Treaty between the two German states, a bundle of documents whereby both signatories recognized each other's sovereignty and frontiers and promised to be good neighbours and settle disputes peaceably; and an agreement establishing diplomatic relations between Bonn and Prague and a declaration that the Munich agreement was invalid. Bonn also established diplomatic relations with Hungary and Bulgaria. Both Germanies became members of the UN (1973). A quirky postlude to these transactions was the claim in 1975 by East Germany for the return to Berlin of works of art removed during the Second World War to safer places further west – some 600 paintings by major artists including 21 by Rembrandt, over 200 drawings by Dürer and Rembrandt, Queen Nefertiti and 3,000 other Egyptiaca, and more. But that the Hague Convention of 1954 could be held to apply to these circumstances was a hardly tenable proposition in law.

These various agreements, concluded in 1970–73, resolved much but not all of the business which a peace conference in 1945 might have been expected to settle. Berlin in particular was not purged of its anomalies. The four powers maintained their rights in the city, which remained two cities; the movement of west Berliners to the east became easier but not normal; West Berlin remained constitutionally attached to West Germany but physically contiguous only to East Germany. The reunification of Germany was not ruled out, although its attainment by force was. Brandt's *Ostpolitik* was much criticized by his countrymen and women and although he had strengthened his parliamentary position at elections in 1971, he lost ground in the ensuing years. In 1974 he was forced to resign the chancellorship by the discovery of a spy at work in his private office. His successor, Helmut Schmidt, inherited a situation in eastern Europe which had been thoroughly transformed in the five years of Brandt's chancellorship. A seal was set on this area of détente when Brezhnev visited Bonn in 1973.

Again by coincidence Brandt's departure was closely followed by change in France. In 1974 Pompidou died. In the first round in the ensuing election the socialist François Mitterrand, backed by the communists, came first but without the necessary margin for election. In the second round between himself and the runner-up, Valéry Giscard d'Estaing, the latter won by the narrow margin of 50.8 per cent to 49.2. The Gaullist candidate came third in the first ballot and so was eliminated together with nine other candidates who received only derisory support. In West Germany Schmidt remained chancellor until 1982 when his government was defeated in the Bundestag and his FDP partners switched their allegiance to give the conservative Helmut Kohl the chancellorship; at elections in 1983 the swing of the electoral pendulum confirmed Kohl in office. In the same year and with the pendulum swinging the other way Mitterrand became president in France.

Mitterrand was a politician with intelligence, cunning and patience. Domestically his main task was to reassert the socialists' predominance on the left and as far into the centre as possible. To do so he needed to recover votes which the working classes had given to de Gaulle but were not so ready to give to the general's successors on the right; and he needed also to make inroads into communist areas and make the socialists independent of communist support. After Pompidou's death Giscard d'Estaing challenged and defeated the Gaullist heir apparent, Jacques Chaban-Delmas, thus fragmenting the right. The united left was badly beaten in 1978 and the alliance of socialists and communists dissolved, but in the course of this defeat Mitterrand and the socialists overtook the communists in all but a few communist strongholds. Mitterrand then won the presidency in 1981. He briefly admitted communists to government for the first time since 1947 and initiated expansionist policies which, however, he was forced to abandon by an influx of German goods. He adopted left-of-centre policies not very different from the right-of-centre policies of his predecessors and moved to closer relations with West Germany within a European partnership (the policy spurned by Thatcher). The French economy, although it had by this date a GNP higher than Britain's, had weathered the rough economic climate of the seventies less well than the West German. Older industries which were in transition had to withstand depression as well as the strains of change; newer industries which France had successfully fostered wavered. After Helmut Kohl's re-election as chancellor in 1987 Mitterrand welcomed a German proposal for closer Franco–German military co-operation and the formation of a joint Franco–German brigade; the two leaders created a Franco–German defence council. Mitterrand was forced by electoral results in 1986 to collaborate with the right, appointed Chaban-Delmas prime minister but outwitted him and was re-elected to the presidency in 1988.

Britain's recovery from the war was strong, swift but not sustained. Morale at home and prestige abroad were very high. War losses had been severe but the financial management of the war had been prudent. Half the costs had been met out of taxation, the other half by selling foreign assets and borrowing. The abrupt end of American Lend-Lease in August 1945, followed by an American loan which was disappointingly low and accompanied by impossible conditions (the convertibility of sterling within one year), presented the new government with a daunting task which was mastered by a combination of wise management and American aid. Marshall funds, although available for four years, were dispensed with after two. They were used mainly to reinvigorate industry. Taxes remained high but interest rates low; unemployment was low and wages were under control; economic growth averaged 4 per cent a year. Prewar production, the prewar value of foreign assets and the prewar level of personal incomes were all recovered by the end of the decade. Simultaneously education was expanded and a comprehensive social security system was introduced.

But Britain's longer-term industrial decline was not mastered and the country remained therefore the more vulnerable to external vicissitudes and domestic mismanagement. Of the former the most damaging were rises in the cost of imported industrial materials such as were occasioned by the Korean and Vietnam wars and the huge rises in the price of oil stemming from war in the Middle East in the seventies. The relaxation of controls and trade liberalization, by removing protection from renascent industries, created from the fifties onwards serious imbalances on external account and distracted attention – and resources – from a more radical renewal of the British industrial base. This base had always been comparatively narrow – coal and a few prime industries such as textiles and engineering – and responded only sluggishly to the development of new methods, new competitors and altogether new industries. Adaptation there was, but not enough to preserve the economy from the buffets inescapable from a world economy no longer controlled from Britain. In addition Britain was losing its primacy in the provision of financial services and other invisible exports. Only rarely throughout the nineteenth century and the twentieth did Britain achieve a surplus on trade in manufactured goods, but the gap was consistently and comfortably covered by surpluses on invisibles. In the Thatcherite eighties, however, the collapse of manufacturing and manufactured exports induced by government policies widened the gap extravagantly and at the end of the decade the surplus on invisibles itself disappeared for the first time in recorded British history.

Politically as well as economically Britain was slow to shake off a long past whose characteristic feature was aloofness. Having lost their Continental possessions towards the end of the Middle Ages, the English people extolled their island status and fortified it with the Protestant secession and their seafaring gusto. Thereafter the British fought other Europeans rather less than they fought each other, but this amiable trait was more dismissive than pacific and the sense of distance – not always distinguishable from a sense of superiority – was far from extinct in the twentieth century. In 1945 the view from the island focused more easily on the Commonwealth and the United States than on Europe.

The Commonwealth, originally the British Commonwealth but renamed in the light of postwar decolonization, was a descendant of the British empire and a happy historical accident which eventually comprised fifty independent sovereign members. The dissolution of British rule in Asia, Africa and the Caribbean began with the retreat from India and Burma in 1947–48, a step long envisaged but not precisely programmed until the end of the war. This dramatic move had unexpectedly precipitate consequences throughout the colonial empire which (with the notable exception of Rhodesia) was abandoned with good grace and little fuss in the ensuing twenty years. But the emerging Commonwealth was not a power centre, still less an instrument for the exercise of British power. Its headquarters were in London but meetings of its political chiefs sometimes left Britain in a minority – in Thatcher's time in a minority of one – and although the Commonwealth provided Britain with special contacts and opportunities it did not reinforce British power in the world.

Nor did the special relationship with the United States which, like the links with the Commonwealth, was a reality but not a reality which gave Britain what it thought it was getting. (Washington's only special relationship was with Israel.) Before the war Anglo–American relations were poor to bad. During the war they were excellent, but the excellence was due to crisis and to personalities: what was special about the wartime relationship was the unusually close friendship and collaboration between Churchill and Roosevelt. After the war many wartime friendships and channels persisted, facilitated by a common language and by shared experiences and ideals, but old divergences – commercial, imperial – reappeared and attempts by British prime ministers on visits to the White House or in reaching for the telephone to play the part of Churchill degenerated into backscratching, not without a suggestion on the British side of subservience. The special relationship not only deflected British attention from political developments on the Continent but also gave Continentals – France in particular – grounds for barring Britain from the European Community.

Britain's ambiguous position in relation to Continental Europe was accentuated in the eighties by Margaret Thatcher's distaste for the European Community and by Britain's economic tribulations under her rule, two factors which called in question the depth of British attachment to the Community and Britain's value to it. From the mid-seventies all western European countries were afflicted by inflation stemming principally from steep rises in the cost of imported raw materials, notably but not exclusively oil, while in the same period exchange rates became embarrassingly unstable following the breakdown of the Bretton Woods system from 1973 onwards. By the date of Thatcher's first electoral victory in 1979 Britain, unlike its neighbours, was shielded from the worst consequences of the oil price rise because North Sea oil made it a seller as well as a buyer of oil. In addition the British Treasury reaped the benefit of sales of nationalized assets to the private sector, the proceeds of which averaged £5 billion a year during the eighties. Nevertheless Britain fared markedly worse than its neighbours. Thatcher's determination to master inflation by monetary measures, abjuring fiscal measures, severely damaged industrial production, exports and employment without producing any lasting control over prices which started to rise again after a few years. A second bout of monetary rigour drove interest rates up to new levels, which again crippled industry and retail trade, produced record trade deficits and failed to reduce inflation to comparable European levels or to stabilize the exchange rate of the pound. Thatcher's belief in the supposed, now mythical, sovereignty of a British government over the British economy made her eschew the haven of the European Monetary System which other members of the Community created in order to give their currencies some of the stability lost by the abrogation of the Bretton Woods system. By 1990 Britain was a country economically and politically adrift, a country which had lost its outstanding independent power but was reluctant – unlike France or Germany – to maximise its still considerable power by wholehearted co-operation with others.

THE EUROPEAN COMMUNITY

The European Community was created with two main purposes: to find a solution to Europe's German problem and to make its members richer and more influential in the world as partners than they could be as separate states.

From Bismarck's time to Hitler's Germany was, with only brief intervals, the state which most Europeans most feared. In a European states system Germany was inescapably the most powerful state, for although it was twice defeated in war and might be curbed in the immediate aftermath of defeat, its resources and skills ensured its resurgence. Its neighbours moreover, although they might fear it, depended on a prosperous Germany for their own prosperity. Even before the end of the Second World War a few Europeans, notably Dutch and Belgian, confronting this dilemma of reconciling their economic dependence on German recovery with their fear of German military might, envisaged a new European order in which the sovereign nation state would no longer be paramount. Whereas a states system by its very nature encouraged national aggressiveness, in a partnership each nation – including the German – might develop its resources and preserve its identity and cultivate its pride in a context more conducive to co-operation than aggression. Opinion in the more powerful states – France, Britain – was unsympathetic to anything so radically restrictive of their formal sovereignty and independence, but within a few years of the war's end French leaders became converted to ideas for a western European association which, in economic affairs, would maximize commerce and output and, politically, would circumscribe Germany's predominant power and redirect its ambitions. France abandoned the policy, entertained both in 1945 and 1919, of weakening Germany by partition and disarmament in favour of a policy of supporting and sharing in German recovery. Britain, on the other hand, although – or because – its own economic recovery from the war was at first more emphatic than France's failed to perceive either the economic advantage or the political calculation behind the movement towards a partnership which would make the sovereign state avowedly less than sovereign. British attitudes were partially reversed in the sixties and seventies when governments of both the right and the left came to fear the consequences of exclusion from a western European economic association, but in the eighties Thatcher personified and inflated British atavistic aversion to political association with the result that Britain was cast in the role of a disgruntled, even subversive, member of the Community whose development was bedevilled rather than strengthened by Britain's adherence to it.

On the Continent the prestige of the nation state suffered during the war. National governments failed to prevent nation states from being battered or their citizens from being killed, tortured and enslaved. In Britain, however, the institutions of the state were not diminished; they remained intact and functioned with remarkable efficiency and fairness. In British eyes the separation from the Continent by the English Channel remained axiomatic. The British were uninterested in giving the lead towards that strong and more permanent association which many Continentals desired and which Britain, uniquely in 1945, had the strength and prestige to offer. The British still thought of themselves as a maritime power and a world power, only peripherally European, unthinkably less than sovereign. For two and a half centuries Britain had had no land frontiers, since even its troubles in Ireland lay beyond the sea. Its principal preoccupations were the freedom of the seas, the movements of commerce, and peace. The first two of these objects it pursued by maintaining a naval lead over the combined strength of other substantial naval powers and by ensuring so far as possible that the European nations which dominated the world should include a number of land powers of the first rank but only one such naval power. In this context the Continent of Europe was a place to which negative principles applied: it must not be allowed to distract or threaten Britain, it must not fall under the dominance of one among its principal land powers. British diplomacy was directed to maintaining a balance and preventing a hegemony in Europe; if British diplomacy failed, then British arms had to shoulder the task which, though in a sense negative, was also vital to British interests as they had evolved since the Tudors had laid the foundations for a kind of British power altogether different from the Continental imperialism of the Plantagenets. The British

6.1   Growth of the European Community

therefore developed a state of mind which drew no distinction between the near and the far. Geographers might talk of the 'Far' East and measure the distance to India in thousands of miles, but to many an Englishman Delhi and Singapore and Hong Kong were psychologically no further away than Calais; they were often more familiar, and they were of course more British.

In 1945 Britain's innate inattention to European affairs was enhanced by the fortunes of war and the prospect of peace. During the war every Continental European combatant, including the USSR, had been overrun and at some point defeated or almost defeated. Britain had been terribly hard pressed and had been bombarded from the air, but it had not been invaded or occupied or defeated. Its victory vindicated its right to go on as before, since it is the prerogative of a victor to retain its past; whereas its shattered and disillusioned European neighbours were looking for a new start and not for a restoration of the old order of things which had failed. The British and Continental attitudes to the past were therefore completely different, and Continentals who expected British sympathy for radical political experiment in Europe were overlooking not only Britain's separate historical development but also its postwar psychology, the intent to repair and improve the structure of British life but not fundamentally to alter or find fault with it.

The advent of a Labour government in Britain in 1945 should have revealed the difference, for the Labour Party, although a reforming and not a conservative party, was no less traditionalist than the Conservatives. It consisted of pragmatic radicals and socialists who wanted to make life happier for the lower classes by continuing the gradual and non-revolutionary adaptation of Britain's social structure to modern notions of social justice. It had no intention of overturning the British apple-cart and not much interest in other people's apple-carts. It was a hard-working middle-of-the-road administration which was trying, in exceptionally difficult economic circumstances (aggravated by the end of lend-lease and American insistence on the premature convertibility of sterling), to restore the British economy and reform British society and it did not wish to be diverted from these tasks by unprofitable foreign entanglements. The Continent was chaotic and impoverished and, as the transfer of Britain's commitments in Greece and Turkey to the United States showed, could better struggle out of its troubles with American rather than British aid. Moreover, the new leaders in Europe were (quite apart from being foreigners) mostly conservatives and Roman Catholics; opponents it was wrongly thought of planned economies, uncomfortable partners for British socialists. In so far as they were attracted by federal ideas, these leaders were regarded as unpractical visionaries. For the British the nation state was one of those bits of the past which practically nobody questioned.

Winston Churchill had told the British during the war that they operated in three circles – the Anglo–American, the British imperial and the European – and that this triangularity gave Britain special opportunities and a unique position in the world. Until Harold Macmillan applied in 1961 to join the European Economic Community the European circle was the one which seemed to offer Britain the least. The most important was the Anglo–American. Britain – or at any rate Ernest Bevin, who became foreign secretary in 1945 – saw that the consolidation of Europe under the aegis of a single power could no longer be prevented by British diplomacy or British arms alone, and that if this bugbear of British foreign policy was to be avoided the Americans must be made a European power. Nato was the outward and visible sign of his success, but his endeavours to create an Anglo–American thrust in European affairs, in the place of the expired British power to intervene and rectify, made him suspicious of Continental federalists who might hanker after an independent

European power to the exclusion of the Americans. Their policies were at best irrelevant, possibly damaging, to his aim of bringing in the New World to create a balance in Europe. Furthermore, those in Britain who were hostile to the United States or wary of its preponderance were not for the most part European federalists. In so far as there was a party in Britain which was thinking in terms of a 'third force' in world affairs, it conceived at this period a third force provided by the Commonwealth rather than by a united Europe.

Britain's change of heart did not begin to occur until some ten to fifteen years after the end of the war and even then it manifested itself much more fitfully and slowly than the comparable revolution in Continental thinking which had been imposed by wartime defeats. Britain continued to think of itself as a worldwide, even if no longer an imperial, power – a somewhat uncritical adjectival substitution. One of the most striking consequences of the war was the British departure from India in 1947 (followed more rapidly than was expected by departure from Africa), but this abnegation of empire took place in such an atmosphere of self-congratulation that the attendant loss of power was overlooked. The loss of India was regarded as a victory for British commonsense, which it was, but not as a curtailment of British power, which it was too. For generations Britain had been a world power because it possessed in Asia an area where it could keep, train and acclimatize armies for use in distant parts of the globe, and this reserve of power was at least as important as the command of the seas in making Britain what it was in the world. The departure from India, coupled with the loss of wealth and strength during the war, sapped Britain's staying power in the Middle East and made Australia and New Zealand turn to the United States for their security. (The tripartite Anzus Pact of 1951, to which Britain was not a party, confirmed this lesson of the Second World War. It was one of the world's most equable alliances until the 1980s when the return of anti-nuclear Labour governments in both Australia and New Zealand created difficulties over naval exercises and visits. In 1984 New Zealand banned from its ports all nuclear-powered or nuclear-armed vessels.)

Britain did not, however, draw the conclusion that the end of empire and of defence commitments in Asia, Africa and Australasia had converted Britain into a primarily European state. The empire had been replaced by the Commonwealth, a more elevating concept perhaps but one of less substance since it lacked the empire's bonds of allegiance to the British Crown, government by a ruling class which regarded itself as all one kin, mutual comprehension through a prodigal exchange of secret telegrams, and a British commitment to the defence of all its territories. The Commonwealth became an association of monarchies and republics of widely differing traditions and inclinations, requiring above all development capital which Britain could not provide, and pursuing independent and even contradictory foreign policies on the basis that this permissive latitude was a necessary price to pay for a continuing association which was still worthwhile. And so perhaps it was, since the Commonwealth proved to be an international organization which worked up to a point. But it contained within itself racial conflicts which posed tests of statesmanship which the British governments of this period failed to pass. In Rhodesia Britain was credibly accused of dealing softly with rebels because they were white and at home the same government exposed itself to even more serious charges. In 1963 Britain had given Asians in Kenya the right to opt for British citizenship, which many of them took. In 1968 the most important element in this right – the right to enter Britain – was summarily removed from them by a government which, in its ignorance of the true facts and figures about coloured immigration and integration, allowed itself to be panicked into slamming the door against some of its own fellow citizens. This unprecedented act, grounded in colour prejudice in a section of British society and in racial discrimination by the government, made nonsense of the Commonwealth ideal – and was later challenged and condemned in the Council of Europe. Even if Britain had in the past thought of the Commonwealth as a source of political strength, Britain's rulers in the sixties were finding it more an embarrassment than a support. Community with Europeans seemed all the more real and manageable.

Unofficial pressure groups in favour of a European union had been encouraged, not least by Churchill who spoke more than once during the war of the need for European unity and advocated in a famous speech at Zürich in September 1945 a Council of Europe. These groups organized a convention at The Hague in May 1948 which was held under the sponsorship of many of Europe's leading figures, including Churchill, and which succeeded in persuading the five Brussels powers to set up a Council of Europe consisting in the first place of themselves and Norway, Sweden, Denmark, Ireland and Italy – to which were shortly afterwards added Iceland, Greece, Turkey, West Germany and Austria. The members, besides being European, were required to respect the rule of law and fundamental human rights. The constitution was a hybrid, an assembly without legislative powers yoked to a committee of ministers; the members of the assembly were appointed by national parliaments, in practice in accordance with the party representation in each parliament; the committee of ministers, which was included in the constitution on British and Scandinavian insistence against the more federalist wishes of other members, ensured that any authority which the Council of Europe might exercise should be subject to the control of national ministers responsible to their several national parliaments. In these circumstances the assembly never acquired any real authority and at the end of 1951 its president, Henri Spaak, resigned in despair.

But another and more substantial initiative was under way. In May 1950 the French foreign minister Robert Schuman proposed a European Coal and Steel Community (ECSC). Although multinational in scope, this was an essentially Franco–German venture with political as well as economic aims. It marked the conversion of France to a partnership with Germany which became one of the principal features of postwar Europe. Coal and steel were at the heart of Franco–German economic and military competition and by proposing to place these industries under joint international control France was, openly, burying the hatchet and, privately, acknowledging the foolishness of trying to compete: to this degree it accepted, consciously or not, that in the new Europe it would be a junior partner with Germany and also that being a junior partner was more sensible than trying to be an independent actor. Britain was sceptical on principle and mildly hostile because it hoped that British steel would undersell European steel. There has been argument whether Britain refused to join the ECSC or France made it impossible for Britain to do so; the one view does not exclude the other. In April 1951 six states signed a treaty establishing the ECSC which came into existence in the following year. It consisted of a High Authority of nine individuals acting by majority vote with power to take decisions, make recommendations, make levies on enterprises, impose fines and generally control production and investment in the six countries; a court of justice empowered to pronounce upon the validity of the High Authority's decisions and recommendations; a council of ministers; and an assembly entitled to censure the High Authority and by a two-thirds majority to enforce the resignation of the council of ministers. In the late fifties, when the demand for coal declined, differences arose between the High Authority and the council of ministers, and the High Authority suffered some attenuation in practice of its supra-national competence.

By the early fifties the Council of Europe had been joined on the European stage by the Coal and Steel Community and by an incipient Defence Community, and in 1952 Eden proposed the amalgamation of these three bodies and their parallel institutions. The Council of Europe appointed an *ad hoc* assembly to work out a scheme on these lines, to include provision for a directly elected assembly and a European cabinet. This was an attempt to build a political association, tentatively called the European Political Community, on the twin bases of economic and military co-operation and it was to embrace most of the non-communist countries of Europe. The prospective membership was large, even though Sweden's empirical neutralism, Switzerland's doctrinaire neutralism and the unpalatable autocracies of Spain and Portugal might exclude these countries in the shorter or the longer run. But the scheme was stillborn. The demise of the EDC in 1954 killed it and even without this blow it is difficult to believe that the rudimentary institutional economic association so far achieved sufficed to support so ambitious a parliamentary structure. As the nation states of Europe recovered from their postwar blues they became less disposed to abandon their essential legislative and executive identities, even though they might be prepared for permanent international co-operation in the less obtrusive bureaucratic field.

The Coal and Steel Community was from the outset a first step rather than an end in itself. For devotees of European union it was one move in a process of creating a series of functional associations which could later be agglomerated. Coal and steel were no longer the prime sources of energy in a world powered by oil and expecting to be powered by nuclear energy. By 1955 the six members of the ECSC had progressed far enough to be ready to convene a formal meeting at Messina where they resolved to form a European Economic Community (EEC) and a European Atomic Community (Euratom). The British attended the conference as observers and then withdrew, partly because they thought the new venture would be a failure, partly because they were opposed to a common external tariff which would be inconsistent with what was left of Commonwealth preferences, and partly because they wanted to limit co-operation to forming a free trade area – which they proceeded to form and which, unlike the EEC, was a failure. (Britain proposed a free trade area in which the EEC would be one member. It would remove internal barriers to trade and industry but not agriculture; have no common external tariff and permit each member to maintain existing preferences; have no obligation to permit free movement of labour or capital, align general economic or social policies, or to create common political institutions. Discussions began at the end of 1957 and collapsed a year later.)

The treaties establishing the EEC and Euratom were signed at Rome in March 1957 and both bodies came into existence at the beginning of 1958 and began to function a year later. In 1967 they were merged with the ECSC. The Treaty of Rome created a constitution in four parts: a Council of Ministers, a Commission, a Parliament and a Court. The Court of seven was the guardian and interpreter of Community law. The single-chamber Parliament – its members were elected from 1979 onwards (but later in Britain) – was primarily a debating body. Created at a stroke by treaty between states, it had only embryonic powers of the kind which national parliaments had accumulated through time in their attempts to constrain the executive power. It might reject but not amend the Community's budget and dismiss the Commission in its entirety but not in part; it possessed a limited share in framing legislation but no control over the Council of Ministers. The Commissioners, at first two per member state but after the Community's enlargement only one from each of the lesser members, were fully and exclusively occupied with Community affairs at the

Commission's headquarters in Brussels. Most of them had had ministerial experience in their own countries but performed in Brussels functions closer to those of departmental chiefs in a national civil service. (The Brussels bureaucracy was, however, small by comparison with national bureaucracies.) Finally, the Council of Ministers, representing the Community's several member states, was within the terms of the Treaty of Rome the Community's dominant organ. It was a replica of the similar Council which had been incorporated at a late stage in the plans for the Coal and Steel Community in order to ensure that that Community should be less a supra-national entity than a national collective, and the EEC's Council was even more clearly superior to the Commission in Brussels than the ECSC's Council was to the High Authority of the Coal and Steel Community. Consequently the most significant debates and decisions on the EEC's development took place in the Council and revolved not round the distribution of power among the Community's main bodies but round the exercise of power within the Council – which matters might be settled by a majority and which required unanimity. (There were some matters which might be decided by a 'qualified' majority. This was a prescribed majority reached after ascribing to each member's vote a weight commensurate with its economic power.)

The first stage in economic integration, which was to be completed in twelve years (and was), was commercial – a customs union with a common external tariff and, internally, the removal of all tariffs and the elimination of quotas. A second and overlapping stage envisaged a broader economic union with, in particular, a common agricultural policy (CAP); free movement of labour and capital; the homogenizing of social policies, laws (specially company law), and health and safety and other standards; and monetary union with a common currency and a single central bank. Political integration, so far as it might be necessary to secure the Community's economic aims, was an inevitable corollary but the Treaty of Rome was silent on this aspect. For some, political integration was an end in itself and a necessary means to strengthen the Community's influence not only in Europe but also in further areas of special concern to Europeans, notably colonial empires on the verge of independence and the Middle East whose oil was western Europe's most crucial import. The parallel aims of Euratom, embodied in the separate treaty creating that community, were to conduct nuclear research, construct nuclear installations, work out a safety code and set up a body to own and secure pre-emptive rights over nuclear raw materials.

The first six members were joined in 1973 by Britain, Ireland and Denmark, in 1981 by Greece and in 1987 by Spain and Portugal. Norway's adherence, negotiated alongside Britain, Ireland and Denmark, was rejected by plebiscite, and Greenland, which joined with its

Danish parent, seceded in 1986. Of all these additions Britain's was the most important and the most contentious, delayed and later soured by Britain's own ambivalence but also vetoed for a number of years by France.

Britain's scepticism about the EEC and its unwillingness to entertain so broad an association led it to form in 1959 a European Free Trade Association (EFTA) together with the three Scandinavian states, Switzerland, Austria and Portugal. EFTA was a rival to the EEC. Its aim was to abolish tariffs between its members over ten years but without any attempt to establish a common external tariff or any form of political union. The British believed that de Gaulle – who returned to power in France at this time – would kill off the EEC, but this was a misinterpretation since de Gaulle intended not to undermine the EEC but merely to delay its development while France's economic recovery gathered pace and France's political weight in Europe increased commensurately. De Gaulle's proclaimed objection to British member-ship on the grounds that it was a stalking horse for American interests had enough plausibility to carry conviction with other members of the EEC in spite of their anxiety to have Britain as a member to offset German and French dominance. By 1960, however, de Gaulle was ready to consider British membership and publicly proposed it. Harold Macmillan, who had repaired Britain's relations with the United States and the Commonwealth after the Suez débâcle of 1956–57, was also anxious to give Britain a stronger European role. His visit to Moscow in 1959 had shown him to be an honest broker in international affairs but not a necessary one; the cancellation of the British Bluestreak missile in 1960 had exposed the difficulties of maintaining an independent nuclear force with a sporadically uneven economy; and in 1961 he responded to de Gaulle's overture and negotiations for Britain's adherence to the treaty of Rome began that year. These negotiations, although laborious, were proceeding to a successful conclusion when they were overborne by a serious Anglo–French misunderstanding. In June 1962 Macmillan visited de Gaulle at the Château de Champs. What passed between them is uncertain and each may well have mistaken the intentions of the other: an interview between a devious man and a silent one can leave much unclear. It would appear, however, that Macmillan, who had made admission to the EEC a centrepiece of his foreign and economic policies, not only played down current difficulties over Commonwealth preferences and agricultural policy but also left de Gaulle with the impression that Britain was prepared to integrate with its Continental neighbours in the military sphere. This integration was a matter of the first importance to de Gaulle, who was looking for ways of making Europe independent of the United States but was unlikely to be able to create a credible European defence establishment without British participation.

In France opinion was divided about the admission of Britain to the EEC. Tangled discussions in Brussels over food prices disturbed many Frenchmen and during 1962 the *patronat* became increasingly hostile to British admission. But for de Gaulle these were minor matters if he could get Britain into an association which would be strategic as well as economic. After June 1962 he seems to have felt confident that he could do this. The French elections of November 1962 confirmed his authority by giving him a majority in parliament and a welcome success after a setback in October when his vote in a constitutional referendum had gone down. He was aware of Macmillan's domestic difficulties when the Labour Party came out in October against joining the EEC but he probably saw little reason to suppose that the British government would be defeated. (He may have been wrong. Macmillan might have felt constrained to go to the country before so momentous a step as joining the EEC, and it is not inconceivable that he would have lost an election fought on this issue. The main arguments against the EEC, other than the national distrust of over-association with foreigners, were: that the EEC was a bureaucracy and not a democracy, constitutionally speaking an irresponsible form of government; that the EEC was devoted to free competition as opposed to planning and that entry into it meant abandoning national planning, not for international planning but for *laissez-faire*; that Parliament would have to renounce its control over vital aspects of British public business; that the EEC was an inward-looking, Eurocentric organization with un-British traditions such as multiparty government and Roman–Dutch law in which British civil servants would be at a disadvantage; and that the process of government by qualified majority – that is, by giving a power of veto to a combination of one major and one minor partner – was a sure way to create disgruntled factions.)

Towards the end of 1962, when the British and French leaders both seemed intent on getting Britain into the EEC and the American administration was blessing the union, a decision in the Pentagon started a chain of events which led to the rupture of the negotiations. This was the decision to cancel the manufacture of the air-to-ground nuclear missile Skybolt, which the British had contracted to buy from the United States. The decision, taken in November on the grounds of cost, deprived Britain of the instrument with which it had hoped, after the cancellation of Bluestreak, to maintain an independent nuclear force up to 1970. By paying half the development costs Britain might have saved Skybolt and its own nuclear programme, but the price was too big and in December Macmillan went to Nassau in the Bahamas to meet Kennedy and find an alternative. He did not, to de Gaulle's disgust and perhaps surprise, turn instead to France and make the failure of Skybolt the occasion for switching from an Anglo–American to an Anglo–French or Anglo–European nuclear association. This demonstration of where Britain's first allegiance lay led de Gaulle to pronounce, at a gathering of the press on 14 January 1963, the exclusion of Britain from the EEC.

At Nassau Kennedy offered Macmillan the Polaris submarine missile in place of Skybolt. Macmillan accepted. Kennedy made the same offer to de Gaulle. This was a reversal of a decision in the previous year not to offer France nuclear weapons. This decision had been reached after a division between the proponents of such a deal who hoped thereby to improve Franco–American relations (a course initiated by Kennedy at a successful meeting with de Gaulle in June 1961) and its opponents who argued that it would change nothing but give a fillip to nuclear proliferation. De Gaulle refused the offer. Both Macmillan and de Gaulle were insisting on their nuclear sovereignty. De Gaulle refused to accept Polaris; Macmillan, while accepting Polaris and proposing to commit Britain's bomber and tactical air forces and Polaris units to Nato, insisted on ultimate British command and the right of withdrawal. The one attitude was not very different from the other, and both were essentially nationalist. The Americans, however, were looking for a supra-national solution to the problem of nuclear sharing in Nato and they may have believed at Nassau that Macmillan, as opposed to de Gaulle, had agreed to fall in with their plans in return for Polaris.

Macmillan and de Gaulle disappointed each other and the British approach to the Community lapsed. In 1964 the Labour Party returned to power with Harold Wilson as prime minister. Wilson renewed the British application. His approach was markedly different. Macmillan had given the impression that the main purpose of joining was to pull British economic chestnuts out of the fire, and that for Britain the economic benefits of joining would be considerable and would outweigh both the loss of sovereignty and the inconveniences of closer contacts with non-British folk. This prospectus was not an appealing one either in Britain or in the Community, and the procedure adopted to implement it was the bizarre one of sending a senior minister to Brussels to conduct protracted negotiations over details (unkindly dubbed the kangaroo tail syndrome) and without a firm policy decision on the main issue of whether Britain would in the end want to join or not. By contrast Harold Wilson told the British public that the economic disadvantages of joining would be considerable; he argued only that the advantages were in the long term more considerable. He also stated the aim unequivocally: to join the Community, accepting all its rules in advance. He himself, a convert to British membership of the Community, was much influenced by the conflict between the Community and the United States over the Kennedy Round which revealed the vulnerability of an economically isolated Britain in the event of a trade war between Continental western Europe and North

America. From the British point of view de Gaulle's stand against the Commission had made joining more attractive, since it had removed to the distant future, perhaps to a never-never land, the federal trappings and aspirations which scared Britain as much as they irritated the French president. The future form of a European entity had become even vaguer than before and the British liked it that way. But the chief obstacle remained. Although five of the six were ready and even eager for Britain to join, de Gaulle could still prevent it. Britain's links with the United States and its economic dependence, its recurring debits on external account, and its continuing commitments in other continents than Europe provided arguments, if arguments were needed, for classing Britain as a thing apart.

The question was whether France would continue to insist on these arguments. They had always, even in de Gaulle's mind, been counterbalanced by others, notably by France's uneasiness about a European Community in which two states – France itself and West Germany – outranked the rest and might one day confront each other on a major issue. Britain therefore had two faces. While on the one hand it was as an American appendage unacceptable, it was simultaneously as a counterweight to Germany very desirable. During 1967–69 the latter aspect began to overhaul the former, partly because of developments within the Community and partly because de Gaulle's resignation in 1969 facilitated a change of emphasis in Paris.

In 1969 de Gaulle once more dropped a hint that the time might be ripe for British membership. He invited the newly appointed British ambassador, Christopher Soames, who happened to be Churchill's son-in-law, for a general discussion of Franco–British relations in which he talked about closer four-power co-operation in Europe (France, Britain, West Germany and Italy) and an adaptation of the EEC to fit Britain in. These were basic Gaullist ideas of long standing but as a result of a chapter of ineptitudes the interview produced a public diplomatic row when the British divulged the tenor of the talks to other governments and allowed the impression to gain ground that France was offering Britain a place in a European directory of major states in return for the suppression of the EEC and perhaps Nato too. Britain's chances of getting into the Community either by the front door or the back seemed therefore to have receded. But not for long. That year de Gaulle resigned the presidency and was succeeded by a man of different temper and outlook, Georges Pompidou. Within a few months a change of government in Britain made Edward Heath prime minister in Britain. Heath had been the protagonist of British membership of the EEC at the time of the first application in 1961. In December 1969 the heads of government of the six, at a meeting at The Hague, had committed themselves to British membership and Heath lost no time in confirming that France, also under new leadership, would back a second application. Heath visited Pompidou in Paris in May 1971 and the negotiations for the treaty were completed within a few months. By treaties signed in January 1972 Britain, Denmark and Ireland became members of the EEC on the first day of 1973. The Norwegian government, which negotiated with the EEC in company with these three countries, also agreed to join but its act was disavowed on referendum. In Denmark and Ireland a referendum held in accordance with the constitution endorsed the treaty of accession.

The British case was peculiar. The treaty-making power of a British government requires no popular endorsement. Nevertheless a referendum was held, although not until two and a half years after the date fixed for Britain's accession. This unusual procedure arose out of the equivocations of the Labour Party. The Labour Party was more seriously divided than the Conservatives over the EEC and Harold Wilson, his natural ambivalence sharpened by fears of splitting his party and ruining its electoral prospects, declared that the terms secured by the Conservatives should and could be bettered. He said that when Labour returned to office these terms would be renegotiated. This was in effect a threat to denounce the treaty unless its other signatories agreed to alter its terms. Wilson also promised that revised terms would be submitted to the country as well as the cabinet. Early in 1974 Heath, having narrowly miscalculated his electoral advantage, called an election and lost it, whereupon Wilson's new administration (a minority government until strengthened by a second election in October) opened discussions with the EEC in which the main British effort, successfully accomplished, was to get new terms sufficiently different from those in the treaty to show that the Conservatives should have done better, while the main aim of the EEC negotiators was to concede as much as was necessary to retain Britain as a member but no more. The main issue was the size of the British contribution to the Community's budget, on which the foreign secretary James Callaghan obtained sizeable concessions. The British cabinet approved the new terms with few dissentients. The electorate, certainly confused by elaborate and conflicting economic arguments, probably somewhat bored by this long-drawn-out affair, and not a little impressed by the plea that it would be wrong to undo what a previous government had with all due form and propriety done, said yes to membership in June 1975 by precisely two to one. Thus, twenty-five years after it could have joined a European community on virtually any terms of its own choosing, Britain haggled its way into the Community which had been constructed without it.

At the core of the Community was the Franco–German entente, tentatively but enduringly established by the Coal and Steel Community. Britain's entry into the Community was expected to broaden and strengthen this core but did not do so. If the initiative in creating the entente was French, its affirmation was German. Adenauer's first concern after the formation of the West German state in 1952 was to anchor it to the west by unquestioning association with the United States and membership of Nato, but in his later years – and particularly after de Gaulle's return to power in France in 1958 – the Chancellor gave increasing attention to Germany's place in Europe. France was becoming, in Bismarck's phrase, more *Bündnisfähig* – a more worthwhile ally – and at the same time disenchanted with Britain and freed from postwar wrangles with Germany. The plebiscite in the Saar in 1955 removed the last serious Franco–German difference from the political agenda. Britain's unilateral abandonment under American pressure of the ill-designed and ill-executed Anglo–French attack on Egypt at Suez soured Franco–British relations. France was overcoming its reputation for political and economic instability and the firm handling of the Algerian crisis in May 1958 was followed by two meetings between Adenauer and de Gaulle at Colombey-les-Deux-Eglises and Bad Kreuznach which put Franco–German relations on a new footing. Between these meetings a French statement bluntly rejected British proposals (supported by Adenauer's finance minister Ludwig Erhard but not by himself) for a loose free trade area.

There were nevertheless serious divergences between French and German attitudes to the EEC's development. France, with Italian support, proposed in 1959 regular meetings of the six foreign ministers, backed by a secretariat to be established in Paris. The treaty of Rome was silent on political integration and it seemed to the Germans and to the Benelux members of the Community that the French were trying to create in Paris a political organization of an international character distinct from the institutions in Brussels and designed to bypass, throttle or even take over the supra-national economic activities which were proceeding there. These suspicions were sharpened in the next year when the French elaborated their plan and proposed a council of heads of government with a secretariat in Paris. Such a 'union of states', successfully pressed by de Gaulle on Adenauer at Rambouillet in July, was clearly incompatible with federalist ambitions. The whole subject was referred by the six to a special committee (the Fouchet, later Cattani, committee) which discussed two successive plans of French origin and the objections to them. These objections amounted in sum to the contention that the plans left out all the principal features of the EEC's own constitution, since they contained no provision for a parliamentary element or for an independent executive or for eventual decision by majority vote. The subject was allowed to fizzle out. Since it had been raised by France this outcome was a rebuff to France but also evidence that France was willing to accept some rebuffs rather than demolish the Community.

The next dispute arose over the elaboration of a common agricultural policy (CAP). The CAP was one of the Community's most pressing concerns. Its terms were not settled until 1967 (the travails of the CAP are examined later in this chapter). The principal bone of contention in the negotiating stage was the level of uniform prices to be set for cereals. In 1963 Dr Sicco Mansholt, one of the Commission's two vice-presidents and specially charged with agricultural matters, produced a plan for fixing a common price at one fell sweep instead of by instalments. The price was to be lower than the price ruling in Germany (and Italy and Luxembourg), so that French eagerness collided with reservations in Bonn which were all the more stubborn because the direction of affairs passed in 1963 to Erhard who had his eyes on the general election due towards the end of 1965. De Gaulle played on the fact that Erhard, while reluctant to accelerate the CAP, was anxious to establish an agreed EEC position in relation to the coming negotiations under the GATT (General Agreement on Tariffs and Trade). These negotiations, dubbed the Kennedy Round, were part of the series of periodic swapping of tariff cuts between members of the GATT, and the six were proposing to bargain as a single team with their most important trading partners, the United States and EFTA. The American president had been empowered by the Trade Expansion Act of 1962 reciprocally to cut tariffs by as much as half but his powers to do so were to expire on 1 July 1967. The tariffs imposed by the six were mostly bunched in a band ranging from 6 to 20 per cent, whereas American and British tariffs were either much higher or zero. Consequently the EEC Commission and also the French government pressed for the lopping of the higher tariffs (*écrêtement*) rather than general cuts (in which they were eventually forced to yield when the Americans proved adamant). Some Americans and British had expected and hoped that the six would split among themselves over a common approach to the Kennedy Round but at the end of 1963 compromises were accepted in order to permit both the Kennedy Round and the CAP to proceed.

During 1964, however, differences between France and Germany, instead of evaporating, became worse with France still holding up agreement on essential preliminaries to the Kennedy Round to extract Bonn's acceptance of a uniform cereal price but also to prevent it from joining the MLF and so swinging between the European and Atlantic groupings – an attempt to get the best of two worlds which de Gaulle was determined to block. The year ended with another of the compromises for which the Community was becoming noted. The American administration having tacitly abandoned the MLF, Bonn agreed to the uniform cereal price in return for special subsidies (also payable to Italy and Luxembourg) and the postponement of the Common Agricultural Policy from 1966 to July 1967. This was a victory for de Gaulle, but it left Bonn resentful and ready to give a lead against France in the new crisis which de Gaulle's policies evoked in the next year.

The crisis arose out of proposals by Dr Hallstein, the Commission's president, to extend the authority, within the Community, of the Commission and the Assembly at the expense of the Council of Ministers by, first, expediting the switch in the Council from unanimity to majority voting and, secondly, by channelling agricultural levies directly to the Commission instead of to national governments for transmission to the Commission. These proposals were a challenge to de Gaulle's views or at least to his timetable, and some of Hallstein's colleagues warned him that he was going imprudently fast. Moreover, by presenting his proposals first to the Assembly instead of to the Council as the rules provided, Hallstein gave de Gaulle an opportunity to put his foot down with some show of justification. The French ambassador to the Community was withdrawn and France attended no Council meetings for six months. These tactics succeeded. The crisis of the 'Empty Chair' was resolved at the beginning of 1966 in a series of meetings in Luxembourg (not Brussels) which were in effect a governmental negotiation between France and its five partners. By the Luxembourg Compromise the members of the Community accepted informally that any member might insist that a particular proposal which it considered of special interest should remain under discussion until unanimity was reached. France thus secured a veto in circumstances to be judged and defined on each occasion by itself. By accepting this compromise France's partners, although giving little away on paper, acknowledged implicitly that French membership and full co-operation were of the essence of the Community. Thereafter the Luxembourg Compromise receded into the background. It was not invoked by Britain when, in the eighties, Britain succeeded France in the role of reluctant or recalcitrant partner: by that date a Community which had existed without Britain for decades did not feel its very existence threatened by threats such as those posed by France in the sixties.

These were constitutional disputes. There were also financial troubles, particularly in connection with the CAP which by the eighties was absorbing 70 per cent of the Community's budget and dispensing more on buying up surpluses for re-sale at a loss than on subsidies to farmers. The Community needed an agricultural policy because so many of its inhabitants were engaged in agriculture and because the Community was not self-sufficient in many foodstuffs, but the policy ran away with itself and instead of turning under-production into sufficiency turned it into embarrassingly large surpluses. In addition, the Community was propelled into competition with the United States where also subsidies to farmers were producing surpluses which had to be sold or dumped in the same markets as Community surpluses.

Financially, the Community's problem was aggravated by fluctuations in exchange rates among its members. In order to reduce the impact of these ups and downs the Community created a special 'green' currency, which was, however, abused by currency dealers.

The main mechanism of the CAP was an annual fixing of prices by the Commission. These prices were set somewhat above world prices in order to give farmers and farm workers an attractive standard of living. The Commission undertook to buy surpluses at fixed prices and it levied import duties on foreign foodstuffs whenever prices fell below prescribed levels. When this system turned production into surplus the Community was faced with the logical need to reduce its agricultural acreage. In 1974 Dr Mansholt proposed a ten-year programme to this end but it was rejected by the Council of Ministers who, individually, were afraid of losing votes at their next national elections if they endorsed the plan. There was also a second and more respectable objection to the plan. Cutting agricultural production meant putting out of business smaller farmers who not only commanded emotional and sentimental admiration but were often the economic core of whole communities: an end to farming in a given district could impoverish and depopulate the whole district. Whereas an older industrial revolution had involved a switch from one kind of manufacture to another, agricultural revolution threatened to extinguish one economic activity without replacing it by another.

To finance the CAP the Commission had at its disposal the proceeds of agricultural levies and import duties and also 1 per cent of each member's GNP, but these sources of revenue were intended to cover all the Commission's expenditure, not only the CAP. From 1979 the Commission might cover a year's deficit by requisitioning from members a further contribution not exceeding 1 per cent of its receipts from VAT. In the eighties this further source ceased to bridge the gap, and since the main cause of the imbalance was the CAP members, had strong grounds for challenging the scope of the CAP and demanding a radical review of its subsidies to farmers as a condition for increasing the share of VAT to be transferred to the Commission. But in this respectable endeavour they – particularly Thatcher's Britain – so overdid the rhetoric and underplayed the genuine social obstacles to radical change that little was achieved and in 1984 the VAT ceiling was raised without any serious inroads into the CAP's excesses. Renewed attempts to grasp these nettles at the end of the decade were equally fraught. Coincidentally with the latest round of GATT negotiations (the Uruguay Round, 1986–90) the Commission produced proposals for cutting subsidies by 30 per cent over ten years. A number of members, including Germany, objected that this scale was too harmful to their farmers. The United States on the other hand, which had been demanding cuts in EC subsidies of 70 per cent or more, threatened to abandon the Uruguay negotiations and bring the entire GATT process to a halt.

Thatcher retarded the development of economic union, although her objections to it were not the only obstacle. The worsening of the general economic climate in the seventies, contemporaneous with Britain's entry into the Community, introduced serious currency instability, stunted the Community's economic growth and raised unemployment to 10 per cent or more of the workforce. The initial aims of the customs' union had been achieved ahead of schedule and the complementary integration of standards and other internal economic policies was proceeding at an acceptable pace, but monetary union was set back both by recession and by Thatcher. A series of programmes for assimilating currencies and credit policy – two from Raymond Barre and a third from Gustav Werner – were set aside. The last proposed a ten-year period during which fluctuations in currencies would be progressively restricted, movements of capital would become un-restricted, and national economic and budgetary policies would become subject to communal consultation with, at the end of the period, full monetary union with a single currency and a central Community bank. This plan was revived during Roy Jenkins's presidency of the Commission and particularly through a fresh Franco–German impulse from Valéry Giscard d'Estaing and Helmut Schmidt. The latter formulated a European Monetary System (EMS) with strict limits to currency fluctuations, a reserve currency and a central reserve of $50,000 million in gold and foreign exchange.

The EMS, which came into existence in 1979, was created by all twelve Community members but four of them – Britain, Greece, Spain and Portugal – stayed outside the mechanism (the Exchange Rate Mechanism – ERM) devised to operate the system. The function of the system was to keep currencies fixed in terms of one another, subject to variations not exceeding 4.5 per cent (with greater latitude for Italy) and subject also to annual review and, if necessary, readjustment of the fixed values. The system had two main purposes. Managed exchange rates were a compromise between floating and fixed rates, a way of controlling currency fluctuations whose volatility not only discouraged trade by making future prices peculiarly uncertain but also allowed trading rivals to engage one another in competitive inflation for short-term advantage. Secondly, the system was a step towards a monetary union (EMU) with a single currency. This currency was already taking shape as the ecu (European Currency Unit – ECU). Within a year of the EMS agreement loans were being negotiated and bonds issued in ecus; and within ten years ecu loans exceeded in value loans in currencies other than the dollar, yen, Deutschmark or Swiss franc, and the Council of Ministers had instructed the Commission to prepare the next steps towards monetary union. This last decision followed the signing in 1985 of the Single European Act designed to complete commercial union by the end of 1992.

In the ten years after the creation of the EMS EC members were occupied in seeking a compromise between the aims of, on the one hand, the Commission and most of the Community's members and, on the other, the reluctance of Britain with some support from some members some of the time to proceed towards broader economic and political integration. Jacques Delors, Jenkins's successor as president of the Commission, was an enthusiast for progress but aware also of the value of British membership and the need for British co-operation when progress should entail revision of the treaty of Rome. By 1989, however, the majority of members approved and Britain accepted a plan in three stages and without a time limit at any stage: the extension of the EMS with its ERM to all members (which Thatcher continued nevertheless to reject against the judgment of leading members of her cabinet and of bankers and other financiers in the City of London); the establishment of a central bank in tandem with national banks; consultation between members on some aspects of national economic policy, including the size of budget deficits; and ultimately a single currency and the vesting of control over budget deficits in the Community's central bank. So long as the veto prevailed in the Council of Ministers Britain held the power to block advances which, although accepted in principle, had no time tag attached to them. Concretely the Community's development was limited to its resolve, formally adopted by all members, to complete the single internal market by the beginning of 1993. Beyond that, plans were devised but indefinitely delayed. In 1990 the logic of events obliged Britain to join the ERM with varying degrees of distaste and without the prior satisfaction of conditions imposed by Thatcher, who continued none the less to oppose further steps along the road to economic and political integration. She, however, fell from power abruptly at the end of the year when half her party in the House of Commons revolted against both the style of her government and the failures of her policies: against her autocratic disdain of her colleagues and of the principles of cabinet government, against the discords within her government over the Community, and against gathering economic stringencies, the onset of recession and the prospect of electoral defeat.

The dissolution of the Stalinist empire in central and eastern Europe, and the precipitate reunification of Germany, created distractions for the Community. To meet the immediate need for aid to Europe's other half the Community created a European Reconstruction and Development Bank to be located in London. The question of admitting these states to the Community was raised by, on the one hand, those in the east who regarded membership as a short cut to economic repair and, on the other hand, those in the west who saw the enlargement of the

Community as a means to dilute its integration and (as had been the aim of EFTA) to confine it to little more than an association of allied sovereign states for limited commercial and economic co-operation.

The increase in the Community's membership by 50 per cent in 1973 had not seriously impaired its homogeneity or its efficiency. The accession of Greece (1981) and Spain and Portugal (1986) and the implication that the door was open to yet more postulants (Malta, for instance, or Cyprus or Turkey) threatened not only to transform the nature of the Community but also to make it dangerously cumbrous. Turkey's application was fended off on the pretext that the Community was unable to consider it while preoccupied with the completion of the single market by 1993; less publicly, the Community was loath to admit a state whose regard for civil rights and decencies was substandard. In economic terms the Community had been conceived as a self-help organization of advanced industrial states in north-western Europe with, by political accident, the addition of Italy which had been closely associated with western Europe since the fall of Mussolini in 1943. In the eighties the Community became an association of twelve states, four of which were Mediterranean or Atlantic and more or less economically weaker brethren. This expansion created administrative problems, economic strains (particularly on the funds established to help poorer regions) and political complexity. By weakening the Community's cohesion it called in question the basic political purpose of framing in Europe a new order in which Germany, the Continent's strongest single state by the eighties whether reunited or not, might choose to co-operate rather than bully. The events of 1989 in central and eastern Europe were, from this point of view, inopportune since they supervened at a time when the Community was, if no longer embryonic, yet still immature and lacking strong concentrated leadership. In these circumstances Germany chose to put its weight behind purposeful integration and, once more in concert with France, to champion progress towards economic and monetary union, closer co-operation in external affairs and constitutional changes requiring amendments to the treaty of Rome. At the end of 1990 two conferences assembled in that city to debate these advances. In the same year the five central members of the Community agreed, following a five-year experiment, to abolish their reciprocal border controls.

THE SOUTHERN FLANK

Command of the Mediterranean, although disputed during the Second World War, was not in doubt after it and all the European riparian states (and Portugal) joined over the years both Nato and the European

Community. Turkey joined Nato and became an associate member of the Community. Malta and Cyprus became members of the Commonwealth in 1964 and 1961 and associates of the Community.

Historical accident – its shift into the Anglo–American alliance against Germany in 1943 – and the uninterrupted predominance of the Christian Democrat Party after the war made Italy an original and unquestioned member of Nato and of the Community. Italy's retreat from fascism converted it into a parliamentary democracy but did not make it prosperous. Post-fascist governments inherited a situation in which 2 million out of a working population of 20 million were unemployed and nearly half of Italy's workers were employed (or unemployed) in agriculture. By 1970 this proportion had been reduced to 20 per cent but the fundamental problems of economic over-population remained, for which the classic remedy was emigration (not new, since Julius Caesar had founded Narbonne in Gaul for this purpose). The chief haven, the United States, had been progressively closed by quotas and literacy tests. Some 150,000 Italians left home every year for Australia, Canada and elsewhere, but there was still not enough work for those who remained (and who, since the leavers were the younger, became a senescent population). Schemes for helping the impoverished south failed to check the widening gap between the two halves of the country, and the twin problems of surplus manpower and depressed areas became two of the mainsprings of Italy's postwar European policies. Court Sforza persuaded de Gasperi that the only cure was participation in a European confederation and so Italy joined the European Coal and Steel Community as a founder member in 1951 even though it had no coal and, outside Elba, no ironstone. Instead of growing oranges and lemons for the delectation of richer Europeans beyond the Alps Italy would emulate them, even if it had to import iron all the way from Venezuela to feed the modern steelworks being constructed at Taranto; and twenty years later Italy was exporting 20 million tons of steel a year. In the fifties GNP was doubled by modernizing industry, investing in training and making good use of surplus labour; industrial output rose from a quarter to nearly a half of total output. The discovery of natural gas in the Po valley gave an unexpected boost from 1958 although supplies proved unhappily limited and this uncovenanted benefit lasted only a few years.

Throughout the whole of the post-fascist period up to and including the elections of 1987 the Christian Democrat Party was the largest in parliament. Unrelieved by respites in opposition and unwilling or unable to produce a new generation of political leaders, it evinced a declining sense of purpose, an incapacity to master economic problems and a laxness in regard to standards of public morality which would have ensured its defeat if its main opponent had not been the Communist Party. The socialist left was riddled by fissures but the communists, like the Christian Democrats, maintained their unity – in spite of the shocks of 1956 and 1968 which lost them some middle-class and intellectual support but did not erode their popular following. During the brief pontificate of John XXIII (1958–63) there was a lessening of papal interference in Italian affairs but no abrogation of the Vatican's special right to intervene under the Lateran Treaty of 1929. Pius XII's excommunication of communists was lifted, there was no repetition of the abuse levelled at President Gronchi for visiting Moscow, and although the debate on civil divorce in Italy in 1969–70 led to a recrudescence of clerical intervention, the church-and-state question did not rise above the level of an accustomed, if sometimes exasperating, family dispute. Italian democracy succumbed neither to communism nor clericalism. Nor did it suffer the fate of Greek democracy although a fascist plot contrived by Prince Valerio Borghese was detected in December 1970. Nevertheless by the seventies Italy was in poor health politically as well as economically. The government inspired little faith, public services were regularly breaking down, corruption was an open and even popular topic of conversation, inflation rose and in 1974, the year of the oil crisis, the deficit on the balance of payments reached an appalling $825 million (of which $500 million was for oil). West Germany and the IMF came to the rescue but Italy looked like being a permanent drain on the EEC and, particularly after the regional elections of June 1975, a political risk as the communist share of the poll edged up towards that of the Christian Democrats and Italy's allies asked themselves what they would do if the communists came into the government (they had last shared in government in 1947) or if communist successes in elections provoked the right into a coup. The problem was evaded, and thereby prolonged, when in the general election of 1976 the Christian Democrats managed to maintain a small lead over the communists but were forced to form a single-party government without a parliamentary majority and dependent on communist abstentions. The fall of this government two years later revived the arguments for and against a coalition of the two main parties, the Christian Democrat and the communist. Opponents included the United States and the Vatican on the one hand and also the extreme left which regarded communist participation in such an alliance as treason. Aldo Moro, chairman of the Christian Democrats, was kidnapped and murdered by extremists intent on making this point.

The Italian Communist Party (PCI) was exceptional among its associates. It was the largest outside the USSR; it played a leading part in Italian national and local politics, whether in power or not; and it had a strong native intellectual tradition which made it much less foreign than other communist parties appeared to be. It was at the centre of the Eurocommunism which became a talking point in the seventies and attracted in particular the Spanish and French parties (PCE and PCF).

Eurocommunism was an assertion that communist parties need not be blindly subservient to an international movement and particularly not to the Communist Party of the Soviet Union (CPSU); it was an attempt to deny the Stalinist past. It was also an attempt to bolster the central communist tradition against the New Left which, in many instances still further to the left, was representing communist parties as fossilized anachronisms. The Italian party was reverting to the nineteenth-century view that socialism could win substantial victories by democratic means – that fair elections fought between a plurality of parties could be turned to good account. This view was submerged in the twentieth century by Lenin's disciplined democratic centralism, by the sight of democrats taking the side of the whites in Russia after 1917, and later by western democrats' evident preference for fascism over communism. But the older view was never quite lost in Italy.

Palmiro Togliatti was an outspoken critic of the USSR even in the fifties, and at the conference of communist parties in Moscow in 1969 he alone opposed the Brezhnev theses which sought to justify the Russian invasion of Czechoslovakia and which were accepted even by the Spanish and French parties – the latter without reservations. He found an ally for his more nationalist outlook in the Spanish leader Santiago Carrillo who, after opposing Eurocommunism, was converted and wrote its basic text *Eurocommunism and the State*. The PCI supported the so-called historic compromise in Italy, the alliance of all anti-fascist parties. It approved Italy's membership of the EEC by contrast with the ambivalent PCF, which boycotted the European parliament until 1975 and opposed direct elections to it until 1977. (The first such elections were held in 1979.) The PCI also declared in 1974 that it did not require Italy to leave Nato.

The Italian example carried the Spanish and, more hesitantly and temporarily, the French parties into a loose Eurocommunist entente but there was little positive substance to it beyond disengagement from the taint of Russian tutelage. Communists in north-western Europe, including France, had next to no prospect of winning power through the ballot box, mainly because of the existence of sizeable socialist parties. In southern Europe they might hope to do better but if they did they would almost certainly be prevented from taking office by inflexibly anti-communist armies.

At the eastern end of the Mediterranean the western alliance secured a lodgement in Greece and Turkey which was strategically important but also embarrassing on account of the weaknesses and the mutual hostility of these two countries.

Modern Turkey was created out of the ashes of the Ottoman empire by Mustafa Kemal, called Atatürk, a secular and modernizing parvenu not unlike his contemporary Reza Shah in Iran. Atatürk ruled Turkey from 1923 to his death in 1938. His concept of the state was western, national and parliamentary and he believed that the right place for religious leaders was the mosque and not the government. His friend and comrade-in-arms Ismet Inönü (president 1938–50 and prime minister 1961–65) maintained this tradition, but after the Second World War Atatürk's revolution was increasingly called in question and enfeebled. The neutrality espoused until almost the end of that war was abandoned, partially upon the acceptance in 1947 of aid under the Truman Doctrine in the Cold War, and wholly in 1952 with adherence to Nato. At home the economy faltered and then collapsed, while disorder turned into persistent factional and lethal violence beyond government control. Underlying these failures was the alienation of the political parties from popular currents which were largely pre-revolutionary. The two principal parties opposed each other on the parliamentary stage, but that stage was shrinking. It no longer embraced more than a fraction of the national scene, and the parties, while regarding each other as adversaries, were seen as twin legatees of a system which half the country was rejecting. Consequently they became increasingly unrepresentative and incapable of winning decisive electoral majorities. Their lack of authority in parliament and in the country obliged the army to interfere sporadically and reluctantly, and assume the responsibilities of government. Turkey after Atatürk was a country as deeply riven as Russia in the century after Peter the Great, the westernizing Tsar.

Throughout the fifties Adnan Menderes, the pro-western leader of the Democrat Party, was prime minister. Under his guidance Turkey joined Nato and experienced an economic surge which, however, brought retributive inflation. After an army coup in 1960 Menderes and some of his colleagues were put on trial and executed, and Inönü became prime minister with Generals Cemal Gürsel and Cevdet Sunay as successive presidents. But in 1965 Inönü's Republican People's Party (RPP) was defeated and replaced by the new Justice Party created by Suleyman Demirel out of the ruins of Menderes's Democrat Party. Demirel and Inönü's successor as leader of the RPP, Bülent Ecevit, moved in and out of office while the country plummeted and public order evaporated. After 1977 neither leader had a parliamentary majority. Demirel formed a coalition with the nationalist and pan-Türanian Alpaslan Türkes but defections from his own party forced him to resign before the end of the year. Ecevit was obliged to introduce martial law in 1978 and to resign in his turn in the next year. In 1980 the army did what it had been threatening to do and took over the government once more. Although no less baffled than the civilians by Turkey's economic problems, the army thought that it knew how to restore order but seemed in no hurry to eliminate torture from the standard apparatus of government. Civilian rule was restored in 1983 with Turgat Özal as prime minister and Turkey was readmitted to the Council of Europe, from which it had been expelled when its democratic constitution was abrogated. A fresh defence and economic agreement with the United States was concluded in 1987 after laborious negotiations. In 1989 Özal was promoted to president. Turkey was becoming a lucrative family business at one level and a harsh place for Kurds and other second-class citizens at a lower.

In Greece politics had been transformed by the communist attempt to take power in Athens at the end of 1944. This attempt was foiled by British troops and the communists in retreat committed atrocities (to some extent reciprocated by their antagonists) which seared the Greek consciousness for a whole generation. These atrocities also set Greek politics in a cold war mould before the Cold War began. In place of the old strife between royalists and republicans a new pattern of communists and anti-communists was created; it not only preceded but also survived similar patterns in other parts of Europe. The government which fought the communists in 1944 was presided over by a liberal republican, George Papandreou, who had suffered at the hands of the pre-war right-wing dictatorship of General Metaxas, which had been supported by King George II. After the rising this same king returned and after his death in 1947 his brother Paul was widely accepted as a symbol of anti-communist unity. This pattern was reinforced by the renewal in 1946–49 of the communist rebellion, which was only defeated after Yugoslavia seceded from the Stalinist bloc and the Americans had equipped and trained a large Greek army. The officers in this army were carefully selected and rigorously right-wing. The continuing conflict of the late forties was an economic and social disaster for Greece, partly alleviated by American aid. Greece joined Nato in 1952. Already dissociated from its nearest European neighbours by the ideological right, it became also a cog in the formal alliance of western against eastern Europe. Yet it lay in eastern Europe and its alliance with western countries could comfortably continue only so long as it was democratic.

During the fifties and most of the sixties it was democratic. There was some oppression of communists and, particularly towards the end of the period, some political gerrymandering, but the conservative governments of Field Marshal Papagos and Constantine Karamanlis had solid popular support. The latter, in the course of an unprecedented eight-year period of office, stabilized the currency and achieved some economic development (especially in tourism). A scarcely disguised Communist Party re-entered the political arena but never got more than 15 per cent of the vote, except in the special circumstances of 1958 when its 25 per cent included a big protest vote against the government's handling of the Cyprus crisis. The centre was fragmented by personal jealousies and out of office until, in 1963 and under Papandreou's leadership, it won more seats in parliament than any other party. During the next few years Papandreou initiated a programme of social improvement, notably in education and health, but he soon got into trouble with the palace, where on Paul's death his young, inexperienced and badly advised son Constantine now reigned, and he roused the hostility of the class of persons who equate all social reform with communism. This hostility was accentuated by the activities of the prime minister's son Andreas, an economist who had been induced by Karamanlis to exchange an American professorship for a non-party professional post in Athens. Andreas Papandreou was a social democrat of the type found in Scandinavia or the left wing of the American Democratic Party (he had been an active campaigner for Hubert Humphrey); his incursion into Greek politics irritated other leaders more particularly because the Centre Union led by his father was not a left-wing party like the British Labour Party so much as a centre or right-centre party like the French Radical Socialists. He became a useful bogey for the right which began to raise the cry that the country was in danger from communism, and in 1965 he was alleged to have become implicated with a left-wing secret society in the army called Aspida – a society which can hardly have been very left-wing if it existed in the Greek army, and a charge which was probably a put-up job(after the coup expected revelations failed to materialize.

So long as king and prime minister worked in harmony there was little chance of a coup, but after an initial amicability these two fell out over the control of the armed forces. The king regarded this control as part of his royal prerogative, to be exercised through a minister of defence acceptable to him. Papandreou, while retaining the palace's man in the post, believed on the contrary that the armed forces should be subordinate to civil control exercised through the prime minister and cabinet. The clash came when Papandreou sought to change the chief of staff and the minister of defence refused to dismiss him or to accept his own dismissal from the government. Papandreou decided to solve the tangle by becoming his own minister of defence but the king refused to appoint him and dismissed him from the premiership. The king had meanwhile been intriguing with some of Papandreou's party colleagues who were induced to abandon him and so bring the government down in parliament. There followed a period of squalid manoeuvres accompanied by minor demonstrations in the streets and a few strikes, until the moderate elements of both the right and the centre came together to put an end to an unedifying spectacle which had been started by the king's unconstitutional behaviour and to hold office pending fresh elections. But the extremists on the right, assuming as did most people, that the Centre Union would win the election, resolved that it should not take place.

This was the immediate cause of the coup of April 1967 by a small group of army officers, a grade below the top ranks and outside the upper-class crust which had normally monopolized these upper grades. They owed their advancement to the expansion of the army after the Second World War and inasmuch as this expansion had been a riposte to a communist threat they were in some sort its product. They were also fanatical, if unintelligent, anti-communist salvationists who, no less than Hitler, saw politics in black and white terms, a simple and fierce contest between good and evil. Their coup was therefore not a conservative one but a radical one, although it had at the start the acquiescence and even the support of traditional conservatives (as the Nazis had been supported by aristocrats like von Papen and by conservative industrialists). Whether the coup had also American support is doubtful. American interference in Greek affairs was undoubted and so was American suspiciousness of the centre politicians who were ousted by the coup, but of the variety of possible coups under more or less open discussion at the time the Americans may be presumed to have preferred something more traditional than the one which in fact occurred. Colonels Papadopoulos and Makarezos and Brigadier Pattakos were neither particularly eminent in the service nor particularly appealing to the public. What is certain, however, is that the Americans were widely assumed to have had a hand in the plot and behaved afterwards as though they had. Their support of the régime was, in its turn, conditioned by the balance of American and Russian forces in the eastern Mediterranean and by the continuing war in the Middle East.

After the coup little was heard of the communist threat which was supposed to justify it, and the seizure of the papers of the left-wing party failed to produce any evidence in support. The coup was a simple seizure of power by a handful of military bigots. At the end of the year the king attempted a counter-coup which was as incompetent as the first coup was efficient; after a few hours he fled to Rome. The new régime dismantled the apparatus of the state, purged the armed forces and the Church, annulled Papandreou's social reforms, browbeat the judiciary and established strict control over the press and broadcasting. In addition it resorted to torture and brutality on a big scale and, as an international commission of lawyers subsequently found, as a deliberate instrument of policy. Torture by the police was not unknown in Greece but the extent to which it was practised and approved by the régime appalled the outside world when the facts became inescapable. As a result charges brought against Greece in the Council of Europe by the Dutch and Scandinavian governments for breaches of democratic safeguards were amended to more serious charges under the European Convention of Human Rights and Greece was forced to leave the Council in order to escape suspension from it. The American government, however, viewed these proceedings with no more than embarrassment and after a brief period of indecision gave the régime its accolade in the shape of arms supplies. Greece as a *place d'armes* for Nato seemed more important than Greece as a conforming member of the society of free and democratic nations which Nato was proclaimed to be.

The Greek dictatorship, which began as a triumvirate of colonels (George Papadopoulos, Stylianos Pattakos and Nikolaos Makarezos) was modified in 1971 when the last two were eliminated by the first; in 1973 when, following a mutiny in the navy, the monarchy was abolished; and later in that year when the army transferred effective power from Papadopoulos to Brigadier Dimitrios Ioannides, the chief of the military police. The funeral of George Papandreou earlier in the year had provided the occasion for a portentously large demonstration in Athens against the régime and students in particular continued to harass it with an indignant boldness which cost them dear. The régime collapsed in 1974 under the weight of its bungling in Cyprus where it tried to get rid of Makarios and annex the island in the belief that the Americans would prevent Turkey from interfering with this plan. The Americans had twice before blocked a Turkish invasion but this time they did not. Makarios escaped, the Turks invaded and the Greek government, having brought upon itself a confrontation with Turkey, ordered a general mobilization for which no preparations had been made. Karamanlis, who had been living in exile in Paris, returned to form a democratic coalition government and consolidated his position by winning for his party a clear majority over all others in elections held at the end of the year. The electorate also voted by two to one to abolish the monarchy.

Karamanlis knew that Greece needed friends: he renewed the campaign to join the EEC and visited Balkan and other communist capitals. He was also anxious to defuse conflicts with Turkey which had become many and acute. He had exceptionally wide popular support and a rare overall majority in parliament. Elections in 1977 reduced but did not destroy this majority and when he ascended to the presidency in 1980 his colleague George Rallis moved smoothly into the premiership.

The most pressing of the Greco–Turkish quarrels lay in Cyprus (see Note C at the end of this Part) but it was not the only one. There was also a complex of disputes over the Aegean. At the time of the Turkish invasion of Cyprus Greece fortified islands in the eastern Aegean which had been demilitarized by the treaties of Lausanne (1923) and Paris (1947). There were also disputes over territorial waters, the continental shelf and air traffic control.

Territorial waters – that is to say, the reach of sovereignty beyond the water's edge – created no troubles so long as both sides observed, as they did, the traditional six-mile limit. On this basis Greece held sovereignty over 35 per cent of the Aegean, Turkey over less than 10 per cent. If, however, the limit were stretched to twelve miles, the area of Greek sovereignty would be almost doubled, the Turkish would be affected only slightly; the points of direct contact between international and Turkish waters would be drastically reduced; and Turkish vessels would be obliged to take passage through Greek waters or stay at home. The international community had not endorsed a twelve-mile limit for territorial waters but it did move in that direction when the first international conference on the law of the sea (1958) recommended that for certain defined purposes (customs, immigration and health control) national jurisdiction be extended from six to twelve miles. Neither Greece nor Turkey signed the convention drafted by the conference, but the trend was one calculated to disturb the Turks.

The continental shelf, a postwar concept introduced into international law by the United States, caused more friction. The question here was the right to exploit, and the proprietorship of, the seabed beyond the limits of territorial waters. Rights in the shelf carried with them no rights in the waters or the air space above it. A convention, called the Geneva Convention, elaborated by the 1958 conference, was signed by Greece but not Turkey. It defined the debatable area as the seabed beyond territorial waters if no deeper than 200 metres or capable of being exploited for the extraction of minerals. It provided that islands should confer on their sovereign owners the same rights – and Greece has over 2,000 islands in the Aegean. Exploitation of rights in the shelf was, however, to be subject to freedom of navigation, fishing and scientific research. Where two sovereign states confronted each other in such a way as to create overlapping shelves, the median line should normally constitute their submarine frontier. In the disputes over the Aegean Greece maintained that this convention, being declaratory of international law, was legally unalterable and so not politically negotiable. Greece had some support for this contention in decisions of the International Court of Justice and also for the even more highly contested assertion that islands had continental shelves of their own. All these contentions were opposed by Turkey.

The issue became acute at the end of 1973 when Turkey published a provocative map of the Aegean continental shelf and granted submarine exploration licences to a parastatal corporation. A few months later it despatched the survey ship *Candarli* into the Aegean with a massive escort of warships. This move was quickly, although coincidentally, followed by the invasion of Cyprus and a consequent exacerbation of the conflict over air traffic control.

From 1952 air traffic control over the Aegean had been exercised by Greece; Turkish flights had to be notified to Athens and Turkish pilots in the area had to take instructions from Athens. But during the first stage of the Cyprus crisis Turkey claimed the right to take control over the eastern half of the sea. Greece rejected the claim and declared the Aegean airspace unsafe as a consequence of the conflict. Turkey later extended its claim to cover international as well as Greek and Turkish flights and, in the Greek case, military as well as civilian flights.

The years 1974–75 were a tense period, sporadically lightened by bouts of discussion between Greek and Turkish ministers or lawyers. On both sides the parliamentary opposition was more bellicose than the governments. In February 1976 another Turkish ship, *Sizmik I*, carried out a series of surveys accompanied this time by a single warship only. Nerves began to tingle again, particularly when the Turkish government, under pressure from its own opposition, rejected a Greek proposal formally to renounce force as a way of settling the two countries' disputes. Greek approaches to the Security Council and the International Court provided no alleviation. The Court refused to grant an interim protective order or to accept jurisdiction, while the Security Council passed the buck back to the protagonists with only platitudinous exhortations to settle their problems themselves. This was marginally a victory for the Turks, who preferred bilateral political discussions to international intervention, juridical or political. Karamanlis and Ecevit met in 1978 and instituted regular meetings at lower levels at the rate of three or four a year. They served to prevent the situation from getting worse but there was not substantial lifting of the clouds until the military takeover in Turkey in 1980, at which point the new Turkish government made a concession on another front.

In protest against its allies' inactivity at the time of the Turkish invasion of Cyprus in 1974 Greece had withdrawn from co-operation with Nato. Karamanlis wanted to return to full partnership but Turkey under civilian rule tried to set conditions, in particular by securing in advance a redefinition of Greek and Turkish responsibilities in the Aegean. These pre-conditions were dropped by the new Turkish government in return for a Greek promise to exclude no Greco–Turkish issue from future discussions. Greece therefore returned to Nato with all these issues open and undecided but avowedly negotiable.

The foremost aim of Karamanlis's foreign policy was to join the EEC. His reasons were political and economic. On the political side nearly all Greeks in 1974 found dependence on the United States obnoxious because they believed that the Americans had not only supported the colonels' dictatorship but had helped it to power in the first place. There was no thought, except among communists who had done badly in the elections, of switching to the Russian camp. But in the EEC Karamanlis hoped to find friends against Turkey (the United States always found it difficult to choose between the two) and a barrier against another lapse into dictatorship in Greece. Economically too Greece needed the EEC. The dictatorship had reversed the favourable economic performance of the sixties when prices in Greece had been remarkably stable and the booming economy of Germany had provided some relief for Greece's chronic state of economic overpopulation. The dictators, anxious to win support at home, had distributed favours to various classes. In order to do this they had inflated the money supply with the result that the lucky favourites had stimulated an import boom which had seriously upset the balance of payments and produced heavy and largely short-term foreign debts. Inflation reached an acknowledged 35 per cent and was certainly higher.

Furthermore Greece, as a predominantly agricultural country, faced a basic problem which was politically insoluble without the goad of foreign pressures such as an organization like the EEC might provide. Greek agriculture employed 40 per cent of the working population but contributed only 16 per cent of GNP. (By the date of entry to the EEC these figures had changed little: agriculture still provided work for 32 per cent of workers and contributed 14 per cent to GNP.) Greek agriculture, like agriculture in other Mediterranean countries, was as much a way of life as an economic activity. The land was owned in small and often separate parcels (the national average was about 12 acres, most holdings much smaller), Greek convention and testamentary law promoted fragmentation, and the consequent inefficiency drove peasant proprietors into the towns whence they neglected their holdings either through absenteeism or because of the family feuds which were a common consequence of the division of property enforced by law. The produce of the land went primarily to the rich foreign markets of western Europe; the domestic market got what was left over and since demand exceeded supply the Greek consumer had to pay high prices. The trade, foreign and domestic, was in the hands of middlemen who made their profits not only in exports but also at home since they bought the whole of a farmer's crop early in the year before domestic prices had begun to rise and sold it (after satisfying export markets) on a rising market. In order to appease the farmers, who were a substantial proportion of the electorate and also commanded more sympathy than middlemen, governments disbursed subsidies which condoned the structural shortcomings of the industry and paid for them out of the public purse. While economists believed this mismanagement, politicians could see no alternative – unless membership of the EEC were to enforce changes in practices which were incompatible with the EEC's own rules. Whether this was what the EEC was for had not been discussed among its members when in 1975 Greece formally applied for full membership.

By a treaty of accession signed in 1979 Greece was to become a full member at the beginning of 1981. Papandreou's socialist PASOK and the communists boycotted the parliamentary debate on the ratification of the treaty and opposed membership of the EEC, mainly on the grounds that it would inhibit the development of Greek industry and intensify the parasitic relationship of the Greek on the European economy.

Both Karamanlis and his defence minister Evanghelos Averof cultivated Greece's traditional friendship with Yugoslavia. Although no formal pact eventuated continuous comings and goings created close relations. Karamanlis also tried to promote some form of Balkan entente. He received Zhivkov in Corfu in 1979 and later in the same year Greece, Yugoslavia, Bulgaria and Romania all attended a conference on communications in the Turkish capital. Karamanlis became the first Greek prime minister to visit Moscow since 1917 and the first ever to go to Beijing. In 1980 he assumed the presidency. In 1981 the Socialist Party of Andreas Papandreou (PASOK) scored a decisive victory, confirmed (in spite of losses) in a further election in 1985. Papandreou's dislike of Americans in general and their military presence in Greece in particular, and his leanings towards non-alignment, made him an awkward partner in Nato and the EEC but he agreed to an extension of the bases, secured American aid at a fixed percentage of American aid to Turkey, and preferred to argue in the EEC rather than leave it. He improved relations with Albania but not with Greece's far more important neighbour, Turkey, with whom animosity over oil exploration in the Aegean rose in 1987 to near boiling point. More temperate relations were restored the next year and the Turkish prime minister made an unprecedented visit to Athens. The Papandreou government collapsed in 1988 under the weight of financial scandals, the prime minister's increasingly authoritarian handling of a mediocre cabinet and economic failure – one-third of government expenditure was absorbed in the servicing of an unmanageable foreign debt. Since, however, the right-wing New Democracy led by Constantine Mitsotakis failed to win a decisive victory the country was subjected to repeated elections and government by coalitions composed of incompatible partners united only by their hostility to PASOK. Mitsotakis finally prevailed by a narrow margin in 1990.

At the other end of the Mediterranean it had been axiomatic to suppose that in Spain nothing much would happen so long as Franco lived, although the discontents of liberals, separatists and others were plain and sometimes violent, as when the prime minister, Admiral Carrero Blanco, was assassinated in Madrid in 1973. Two years later, in November 1975, Franco died in his bed. His death made Spain a kingdom in fact as well as name. Franco had pronounced Spain a kingdom in 1947 but he had no liking for the last king's son Don Juan and had no intention of relinquishing his own monarchical control. He therefore ignored Alfonso XIII's act of abdication in favour of Don Juan and gradually prepared the latter's son, Don Juan Carlos, for the succession. Juan Carlos played an equivocal role in an equivocal position, so that on Franco's death his character and political ideas were something of a mystery. His first government was a mixture of Francoists and democrats but within a year he appointed as prime minister the 47-year-old Adolfo Suarez, an able and single-minded politician who fitted no precise faction. This was a skilful move which alarmed conservatives and the army without giving them distinct cause for revolt and pleased moderate groups on the right and the left which believed that Spain needed change. The appointment of Suarez signified the king's intention to accelerate change and also to be seen as a monarch capable of picking his own man. He was fortified by the approval of the Cortes and a referendum in favour of substantial constitutional changes. Within two years of Franco's death the king and Suarez were strong enough to face parliamentary elections with confidence.

Franco's Spain, although politically fossilized, had not been immune to all change. Franco's autarkic economic policies had begun to crack in the fifties under the weight of their own irrationality and of increasing American intervention in Spanish affairs induced by Washington's policy of diversifying its anti-Russian deployment in Europe. But his modernization was ill regulated and careless of the poorer classes and the new régime inherited a distorted economy. It also inherited the perennial problem of regional discontent, particularly in Catalonia and among the Basques. The Socialist and Communist Parties were legalized, the latter in spite of American and military pressures to the contrary. The socialists, led by Felipe Gonzalez, proved the stronger of the two. The right was torn between those who wanted a new clean Christian Democratic Party and those who wanted a broader party including as many old Francoists as possible. In the first popular test in 1977 the communists and the right fared badly and Suarez's right-centre triumphed. In further elections in 1979 the right was routed, the communists staged a small recovery and the voters opted for two broad centre groups, giving Suarez a slight advantage over Gonzales. But Suarez's handling of economic affairs was tentative and of the Basque separatists insensitive and indecisive: in the Basque country (Euskadi) violence became serious and Basque extremists carried their violent protest into other parts of Spain.

In 1981 the constitutional and democratic monarchy sponsored by the king was challenged by an army coup. The army, which had no properly military function, was dominated by officers whose ideas were archaic and anti-democratic. They engaged in sporadic plots which, although ludicrous, were also dangerous until an overt but incompetent attempt to overthrow the régime, which included a spectacular assault on the Cortes, forced the king to disavow its leaders and confront the army as a whole with a choice between himself and their Francoist past and predilections. Suarez, however, did not survive nor did his right-centre bloc. He resigned and was succeeded by Leopoldo Calvo Sotelo, but at the end of 1982 fresh elections brought Gonzalez to power. His supporters included many who wanted Spain to leave Nato (which it had just joined) and he promised to hold a referendum on the question: he subsequently declared himself in favour of continued membership and carried the day in a referendum, although Spain then insisted on the removal of American aircraft by 1992 (Italy agreed to receive them). Having only narrowly retained power in elections in 1986 Gonzalez lost his parliamentary majority after bye-elections in 1990 (unless four Basque members could be debarred, in which case Gonzalez's socialist majority would be restored). The conflict with Britain over Gibraltar was unfrozen to the extent that the frontier was reopened and the British government, while repeating its commitment to honour the wishes of the Gibraltarians, agreed that sovereignty be an item in future discussions. Talks in 1987 preserved goodwill without altering either party's stance.

Unexpectedly change in Spain was preceded by change in Portugal when, in April 1974, a group of middling and junior army officers overthrew the dictatorship and installed a junta of seven under the presidency of General Antonio de Spinola, a returned and critical African governor. A tussle for power followed within the dominant Armed Forces Movement and between the political parties which took shape after the coup. General Spinola resigned in September and fled the country in the following March after becoming involved in an unsuccessful anti-communist coup. A communist bid for sole or predominant power failed. Elections in April 1975 gave the socialists led by Dr Mario Soares 38 per cent of the vote and relegated the communists with 12.5 per cent to third place behind the right-centre Popular Democrats (26 per cent). Portugal seemed many times on the brink of civil war. The Armed Forces Movement and the army itself were split, but a coup in favour of the extreme left misfired and senior officers, alarmed by the prospect of anarchy, combined to support a minority socialist government and the installation of the relatively uncommitted General Antonio Ramalho Eanes as chief of staff.

Elections in 1976 gave no party a clear majority, the most successful being the Socialist Party which won 107 of the 263 seats. In the presidential election which followed General Eanes won 61.5 per cent of the votes distributed among four contenders. Soares formed a minority socialist government which was attacked both from the communist left and by the right representing not only the old régime but also the poor, anti-communist and conservative farmers of the north. Soares resigned at the end of 1977, formed a new coalition but was dismissed in 1978 by the president who appointed a government of technicians and, when this faltered for lack of a parliamentary base, another under Portugal's first female prime minister, Maria de Lurdes Pintassilgo. The president was trying to find a parliamentary coalition or a non-parliamentary alternative which would stem the country's post-revolutionary swing back towards the right, but this swing became more manifest at the end of 1979 when Francisco Sá Carneiro won nearly half the seats in parliament. He became prime minister but found himself at odds with the president who, using his constitutional right to interpret the constitution, blocked a number of measures whereby Sá Carneiro intended to steer the economy back into the paths of free enterprise. President Eanes won a further term of office in 1980. Portuguese politics continued to oscillate between centre-right and centre-left. In 1983 Soares, having failed to win an overall majority, formed a government with the social democrats to his right but this alliance collapsed in 1985 and Soares resigned. He became Portugal's first civilian president for over sixty years with the conservative Anibal Cavaco Silva as prime minister. Minor changes were made to the constitution in order to expedite the denationalization of industries and decollectivization of agriculture. With Spain, Portugal joined the Western European Union in 1988.

7 COMMUNIST EUROPE

STALIN'S EMPIRE

The partition of Europe after the Second World War was the consequence of a trend and an accident. The trend was the decline, accentuated by war, of the European nation states. Europe was a continent which had functioned in the form of comparatively small and comparatively strong entities, capable of maintaining separate existences because of the industrial sophistication of some and the addiction of all to the principle of self-determination. Thus the stronger European states existed because they were strong, while the weaker ones existed because it seemed right to the stronger that they should. But with the waning of the strength of the strong the basic element in the pattern of Europe disappeared and Europeans ceased to be able, for the time being, to maintain truly independent states. The question was what new forms would be imposed by dependence.

The answer to this question was determined by accident, by the fact that the precipitating cause of the war had lain in the centre of the continent – in Germany – so that the course of war meant a convergence of anti-German forces on the centre from the sides. Despite some plans to the contrary, the Anglo–American and the Russian advances into Germany were in substance separate operations which created separate American and Russian dominances to the west and to the east of Germany. Anglo–American sea power modified this pattern by decreeing that Mediterranean Europe as far as the Aegean should fall into the American and not the Russian sphere. This new distribution of power was recognized by Stalin's abandonment of Greece to Churchill, his refusal to pay attention to the Greek communist revolt or help it, and by the subsequent attachment of Greece and Turkey to Nato. At the other end of Europe Finland fell into the Russian sphere not only because of its strategic importance for the defence of Leningrad but because Anglo–American sea power did not overlap Europe round the north as far as it did in the south. Only Germany and Austria were designated common ground and, as we

UNION OF SOVIET
SOCIALIST REPUBLICS

Gdansk

Berlin

EAST
GERMANY
(to 1990)

Warsaw

POLAND

Prague

CZECHOSLOVAKIA

Vienna ●

AUSTRIA

● Budapest

HUNGARY

ROMANIA

Belgrade ●

YUGOSLAVIA

Bucharest ◆

BLACK
SEA

Sofia ●

BULGARIA

ADRIATIC SEA

ALBANIA

0   500 km

▨ Countries belonging to Warsaw Pact.
(Albania formally withdrew from the
pact in 1968)

7.1   Eastern Europe

have already seen, even here the new principle of Russo–American partition prevailed and created in Germany a partition within a partition which assumed crucial and critical significance in world affairs as the focus of the Cold War. In the rest of Europe the Americans and the Russians let each other be, but in Germany they could not – partly because Germany was the cause and prize of war, partly because of its central position and potential power, and partly because the old notion of the nation state remained strong enough to make the division of a state seem much more unnatural than the allocation of whole states to great power spheres of influence.

It has been argued that the division of Europe and the resulting Russian overlordship in eastern Europe were the consequence not of historical accident but of agreement, notably agreement at Yalta by Roosevelt and Churchill to give Stalin a position of power which otherwise he could not have achieved. This argument cannot be sustained. Roosevelt and Churchill conceded at Yalta nothing that it was in their power to withhold. The Russian armies were already in occupation of positions in Europe from which they could not be expelled and Stalin's postwar dominance in eastern Europe derived from his victories and not from any bargain with his allies. The most that Roosevelt and Churchill could do was to try to get Stalin to accept certain rules governing the exercise of the power that was his. This they succeeded in doing by persuading him to endorse a Declaration on Liberated Countries which promised free elections and other demo-cratic practices and liberties. When, later, Stalin ignored the engage-ments contained in this declaration western governments could do no more than protest. Action in eastern Europe was impossible. Only in western Europe could they do anything and steps such as the formation of a West German state were their riposte and also a further manifestation of a division of the continent which preceded, and was not determined by, Yalta.

Within the Russian sphere Stalin's problem was the nature of Russian control and its mechanisms. He created a satellite empire in which the component states retained their separate juristic identities – separate from each other and from the USSR – but were subjected to Russian purposes by the realities of Russian military power and the modalities of Communist Party and police rule and unequal economic treaties. There was soon little difference between former foes like Hungary, Romania and Bulgaria, and wartime allies like Poland, Czechoslovakia and Yugoslavia. This indifference was manifested at an early stage: in Poland the Lublin Committee, a communist-dominated group of leaders formed in July 1944 from among the Polish resistance and then groomed in Moscow, was established in Warsaw as the government of Poland in order to frustrate the London Poles who had conducted the fight against the Germans from exile; in Romania the king was compelled in March 1945 to appoint a government controlled by communists and to cede to the USSR its Moldavian province (which had been part of Russia from 1812 to 1917). In form the defeated enemies were equated with the allies by the conclusion of peace treaties in February 1947 and of further treaties between each of them and the USSR during 1948 (with the allies the USSR already had treaties dating from the war years). The peace treaties cost Hungary Transylvania which (as in 1920) went to Romania, and a smaller piece of territory awarded to Czechoslovakia; confirmed Romania's loss of Bessarabia and northern Bukovina to the USSR, and southern Bukovina to Bulgaria; and gave the USSR the Petsamo area of Finland and a fifty-year lease of the naval base at Porkkala with an access corridor. The treaties of 1948 provided for mutual assistance against Germany and proscribed any alliance by the one signatory which might be construed as directed against the other.

But Stalin aimed at more than formal arrangements and by the end of the forties he had, except in Yugoslavia and Finland, transferred the machinery of government into the hands of obedient communists who were not merely conscious of the realities of Russian power but determined puppet-like to serve it. This transfer involved the suppression or emasculation of non-communist parties and the elimination from the communist ranks of communists who were more national than Muscovite. This process was successfully achieved in the short run, unsuccessful in the longer run in that it failed to secure for Moscow a trouble-free zone of influence round the USSR's European borders. Yugoslavia rejected Russian dominance in 1948, Poland and Hungary kicked against it in 1956 and Romania led a campaign against it in the mid-sixties. By the seventies it was in evident decay but still sustainable, even though the use of force – which was its ultimate guarantee – was becoming more a memory and a bluff than a plausible practicability. The advent of Gorbachev triggered the collapse in 1989 which had long been impending.

In 1946 Yugoslavia, Czechoslovakia, Bulgaria and Albania had communist prime ministers: Tito, Klement Gottwald, G. M. Dimitrov and Enver Hoxha. In Hungary and Romania the post was occupied by Peasant Party leaders, in Poland and Finland by socialists. All these countries had coalition governments, although only the governments in Prague and Helsinki gave the appearance of a real distribution of power. In Finland the communists were left out of a new government formed after elections in July 1948, in which they fared badly. Elsewhere communist control was intensified during 1947–48, although in Yugoslavia the communist monopoly of power worked against and not for the Russian interest and culminated in June 1948 in the eviction of Yugoslavia from the fraternity of communist states.

Poland's history is a struggle against neighbours, not least against

Russia. Polish communism has also had its anti-Russian side: Rosa Luxemburg disputed Lenin's peasant policy, and the Polish Communist Party later deprecated Stalin's campaign against Trotsky. The leadership of the Polish party was wiped out in 1937–38 and the party itself was dissolved by the Comintern when Stalin was laying his plans for his pact with the Nazis. It was resuscitated in 1942 and nourished by the hideous behaviour of the Germans in Poland, which caused some revulsion of feeling towards Russians and communists. The discovery in April 1943 of the Katyn massacre (only implausibly ascribed by the Russians to the Germans) reminded the Poles that, for them, the choice between Russians and Germans was a hopeless one, but the Germans were at that time the present pest from which the Russians were future liberators. At the beginning of 1944 the Russians entered Poland in pursuit of the Germans and in July of the same year they accepted the Curzon Line as Poland's frontier in the east and sanctioned the Lublin Committee, which shortly afterwards became the country's provisional government. In August the people of Warsaw rose against the Germans in the expectation of swift help from the advancing Russians, which however failed to materialize; the victims included many leaders of the resistance, national communists as well as non-communists. The rising, besides being directed against the Germans, was an attempt by the London Poles and their secret army in Poland to establish their authority in Warsaw before the arrival of the Russians.

The looming Polish problem was twofold: what were to be Poland's boundaries and who was to rule? The Russians wished to shift Poland to the west in order to gain territory for themselves in the east and, perhaps, to perpetuate a pro-Russian and anti-German slant by adding German lands in the west to the Polish state; the Russians were also determined to insist on a government which was wholly or preponderantly communist. At the Yalta conference in February 1945 the Americans and the British disputed the Russian plans at length but irresolutely; they recognized the force of Stalin's arguments about the importance of a reliable Poland between the USSR and Germany, they did not regard the Polish question as the most important on the agenda, and they believed that no great harm would come from leaving the composition of the future Polish government vague since they had Stalin's agreement to the broadening of the provisional government and to fair and early elections after the end of the war. Before the Potsdam conference in July the Poles had been put by the Russians in possession of German lands beyond their old western borders and at that conference Churchill's forebodings and remonstrances were uttered in vain. The British and the Americans accepted the accomplished fact provided it were called an interim measure which would be reopened upon the negotiation of a peace treaty with Germany.

Stanislaw Mikolayczyk, chief of the Polish government in exile in

London and leader of the Polish Peasant Party, had been added to the provisional government in Warsaw as a deputy prime minister. The other principal figures in the government came from the Lublin group: the communist Boleslaw Bierut as president, the socialist Edward Osobka-Morawski as prime minister and the communist Wladyslaw Gomulka as a deputy prime minister. The promised elections were held in January 1947 to the accompaniment of every conceivable electoral abuse, which failed however to conceal the underlying popular strength of the Peasant Party. This party was said to have won 10 per cent of the vote and 28 of the 444 seats in the parliament but Mikolayczyk felt obliged to seek safety in flight, as did many others. The rump of the Peasant Party was absorbed into the newly created Democratic Bloc, which took the place of the Communist Party. In the following year the Social Democrat Party was led by Josef Cyrankiewicz, who had taken the place of Osobka-Morawski, into a merger with the Democratic Bloc which thereupon became the United Workers Party. The Americans and the British protested in vain over proceedings which they had no power to rectify. But within the communist leadership the old division between Polish and Muscovite communism, already visible in the days of Rosa Luxemburg, reappeared with Gomulka, now secretary-general of the single party, as leader of a faction which wanted to make communism more Polish, more popular and less subservient to Moscow. The quarrel between Stalin and Tito gave him an occasion to express support for Titoism, as a result of which he was gradually denuded of all his posts and disappeared into the background for the next eight years.

These events coincided with the transformation of the political scene in Czechoslovakia. Eduard Beneš, who resumed the presidency after the defeat of Germany, was the principal symbol in central Europe of the wish to conduct a state in accordance with western values and in friendship with the USSR. His government, in which the communist Klement Gottwald was prime minister, was a balanced coalition of several parties, and it is not impossible to suppose that the Russians might have found such a régime acceptable had they not been faced, early in 1948, with a menace of civil war in Czechoslovakia at the time when the quarrel with Yugoslavia was about to lead to a public breach. In February 1948 the minister of the interior, Vaclac Nosek, dismissed eight police inspectors in Prague. The cabinet voted to reverse this step but the prime minister supported Nosek, and the arrival in Prague of a deputy foreign minister of the USSR, Valerian Zorin, suggested outside interest of an unusual kind. Nosek declined to reinstate the policemen and eleven ministers tendered their resignations. They were the non-communist ministers, minus however the socialists who, although they had voted with the majority of the cabinet against Nosek, were reluctant to break their association with the communists in government – despite the fact that three months earlier they had selected a new leader to replace the fellow-travelling Zdenek Fierlinger. Anti-communist demonstrations, chiefly by students, occurred in Prague. Police were brought into the capital from outside. Amid fears of increasing tumult Beneš tried to restore calm by accepting the eleven resignations. Two ministers were killed by falling from windows, one of them – Jan Masaryk – having perhaps been pushed out. In June Beneš resigned. He was succeeded by Gottwald. The mopping up operations consisted of amalgamating all Czech parties or remains of Czech parties with the Czech Communist Party, and likewise in Slovakia, whereupon the single Slovak party was amalgamated with the single Czech party to make the National Front. A similar attempt to extend Russian control in Finland in 1948 was dropped when it ran into difficulties.

Concurrently in Hungary, the monarchy having been abolished in January 1946 – nearly thirty years after it had ceased to function – a coalition government was formed with the Smallholders and Socialist parties. The leaders of the former, Zoltan Tildy and Ferenc Nagy, became president and prime minister and it won 56 per cent of the vote in the first postwar election. In the winter of 1946–47 rumours of a plot against the state were put about, trials were staged and the secretary-general of the Smallholders Party, Bela Kovacs, was abducted by the Russians. The Americans and British, who were partners with the Russians in the Control Commission for Hungary, protested but were helpless. In May 1947 the prime minister went to Switzerland to see a doctor and, while he was away, was asked to stay away and resign. A new plot was discovered. Elections in August were patently rigged. Members of non-communist parties fled or were put on trial, their parties were split and partially absorbed, as elsewhere, into a single National Independence Front. Tildy resigned the presidency in July and was succeeded by a complaisant social democrat, Arpad Szakasits.

In Romania the Peasant leader Ion Maniu was accused in 1947 of plotting against the state with American and British agents. He and others were tried and condemned, and the Peasant Party was dissolved. In December the king abdicated. In the following February the Social Democrat Party was merged with the Communist Party, and in March this party won 405 of the 414 seats in parliament. But before this election dissension had struck the Communist Party too and one of its veteran leaders, Lucretsiu Patrasceanu, was dismissed from the government, arrested, expelled from the party and, according to rumour, lodged in the Lubianka prison in Moscow. In Bulgaria the leader of the Agrarian Party, Nicola Petkov, was arrested with others in June 1947 and executed. The Fatherland Front, product of the usual socialist–communist merger, appeared in the next year.

During this period of regimentation Moscow's central purpose was to refashion each satellite in accordance with a single general pattern and to attach each of them to the USSR by all means short of incorporation. But there was to be no incorporation. The newly fashioned states were to be People's Democracies; they were not to become Soviet Republics. Talk of incorporation was dowsed by Moscow, which made it clear that a People's Democracy was something short of a fully communist state and something different from a Soviet Republic. Communist enthusiasts with visions of admission to an extended Soviet commonwealth were disabused. The reasons for his policy may be found in Stalin's essentially cautious nature; or in his realization that these areas would, if fully absorbed, cease to be a buffer zone; or in the inability of the war-ravaged USSR to make radical changes in its structure in the mid-forties; or in the knowledge that some of the satellites had enjoyed and expected a higher standard of living and of public administration than the USSR could provide; or in Stalin's desire to avoid unnecessary provocation of the western powers and to hoodwink them by getting the substance of empire without making constitutional changes which they would not stomach.

At the same time Stalin prevented the satellites from making new political associations among themselves. Everybody visited everybody and piled up bilateral treaties of friendship and mutual assistance until almost all the possible permutations had been employed, but schemes of a more radical kind withered quickly. Various such schemes were in the air immediately after the end of the war. Czechoslovak minds reverted to the Little Entente with Yugoslavia and Romania; and Hungary, whose relations with Czechoslovakia were marred by problems of exchanges of population, riposted in some alarm with a plan for a Danubian confederation. (A Danubian conference at Belgrade in July 1948 left the Russians in effective control of half the river. The Americans, British and French, outvoted at every turn, protested that the convention of 1921 remained in force in the absence of a universally accepted substitute. The riparian states were no counterpoise to the USSR so long as they remained separate.) Downstream the notion of a south Slav federation flourished for a while and produced some talk of a Romanian–Hungarian counterweight. The south Slav federation was the least unlikely of these federative ideas, if only because it was sponsored by two leaders of the first eminence, Tito and Dimitrov. But their plans became too grandiose for Moscow's liking and a Yugoslav–Bulgarian union looked uncommonly like a take-over of Bulgaria by Yugoslavia: the chief city of such a union would be Belgrade not Sofia. In June 1947 Tito told the Bulgarians publicly that he looked forward to a monolithic entity of free Balkan peoples. In August Dimitrov, visiting Yugoslavia to sign four pacts, secretly ceded Pirin Macedonia to the Yugoslav Macedonian Republic. In December

Traicho Kostov, deputy prime minister of Bulgaria, spoke of a union of all south Slavs in the near future, and a month later Dimitrov spoke in the Romanian capital of a customs union leading to a federation or confederation which would include not only the south Slavs but also the north Slavs (other than those in the USSR) and Hungary, Romania, Albania and Greece. At this point Moscow intervened, summoned Yugoslav and Bulgarian leaders to Moscow and told them that Romania must be left out of their plans, although Albania might later be added to a Yugoslav–Bulgarian state. The Yugoslavs were also told to drop plans for sending troops into Albania. No union of any kind was effected. Dimitrov died in Moscow in July 1949, a year after Yugoslavia was expelled from the communist bloc.

The dispute between the Russian and Yugoslav leaders was conducted by correspondence in the months of March, April and May 1948. The heart of the matter was the refusal of Tito to accept direction from Moscow and his insistence on the right to think out Yugoslavia's own problems in their own context and apply its own solutions in preference to Russian principles and Russian programmes. Tito maintained that Yugoslavia was not only separate from the USSR but different, and that communist doctrine and practice were not so rigid as to be unable to take account of the differences. On his side Stalin wished to secure in Yugoslavia a régime as obedient as any other in eastern Europe. If Tito were recalcitrant there were other Yugoslavs prepared to toe the Stalinist line. Stalin was intent not on casting off Yugoslavia but on casting out Tito, and the harsh retribution inflicted by Tito on these Stalinists (particularly in Serbia) after the breach suggests that the struggle within the Yugoslav party was acute and Tito's victory a narrow one. The dispute ranged over such topics as the proper organization of a communist state, the role of the Communist Party, agrarian policies, Yugoslavia's laxity in liquidating capitalism and the person of the Yugoslav foreign minister, Vladimir Velebit, whom the Russians accused of being a British agent. Friction was increased by the presence in Yugoslavia of Russian civilian and military advisers who seemed to the Yugoslavs to represent a Russian claim to superiority and to be paid too much; Russian attempts to put pressure on the Yugoslavs included threats to withdraw these experts. Throughout the correspondence the Yugoslavs were evidently anxious to avoid a breach, an attitude which may have strengthened the Russian resolve to exact admissions of error on the points in dispute. But the outcome was a Yugoslav refusal to accept the status of pupil and in June the breach was made public by the eviction of Yugoslavia from the Cominform, the international association of communist parties which had been formed in the previous September to ensure ideological unity and conformity.

Tito was a convinced communist but not an obsequious one. He had envisaged the adherence of a Yugoslav communist republic to the Soviet Union but he had also in his younger days been disturbed by the Russian purges of the thirties, had been shaken by the Russo–German pact of 1939 and had had experience of Stalin's attitude to lesser communist leaders. In 1948 he abandoned the Stalinist mode of international communism out of national and personal pride; his genuinely national roots distinguished him from communist leaders who had lived longer in the USSR than in their native countries, and his position as a successful communist chief against the Germans had given him self-confidence and a popular following. He was fortunate in the fact that Yugoslavia had no frontier with the USSR and that western aid enabled him to parry communist economic blockade. Yugoslavia became an international anomaly, a communist state dependent on American and other western aid, an ally of Greece and Turkey in the Balkan pact of 1953 and then a protagonist with Nehru and Nasser of neutralism and non-alignment. The Yugoslav secession entailed the end of schemes for a Balkan union round a Yugo-slav–Bulgarian core, diplomatic and economic breaches with the remaining satellites, and shifts in Yugoslavia's relations with its non-communist neighbours. It contributed to the defeat of the communist rebellion in Greece and the settlement by partition in 1954 of the problems of Trieste (Italy finally renounced its claim to the whole Free Territory in 1975). It dispelled the myth that a communist government not subservient to Moscow was a contradiction in terms. It promoted a series of witch-hunts in the satellite bloc where the Russians proceeded to eliminate communists who might be sympathetic to Tito or tempted to follow in his footsteps.

The most spectacular consequence of the breach was the trial of Laszlo Rajk in Hungary. The secretary-general of the Hungarian party, Matyas Rakosi, had fallen under suspicion but, having confessed to errors, survived. Then in September 1949 Rajk and other Hungarian communists were brought to trial on a compendium of charges to which they confessed and which included spying for the pre-war Horthy régime, for the Nazi Gestapo, for the United States and Britain and, more significantly, for Tito. The trial was an anti-Tito demonstration, all the more forceful in that it ended with the execution of the accused. It was repeated elsewhere. In Bulgaria the veteran communist Traicho Kostov was expelled from the party in March 1949, arrested in June and, along with others, tried and executed in December. The charges ranged from Trotskyism to Titoism; their essence was conspiracy against the state. In Albania Koci Xoxe, who had favoured a union with Yugoslavia, was eliminated by his anti-Yugoslav rival, Enver Hoxha (who survived an inept Anglo–American attempt to unseat him in 1949 and a Russian coup after a quarrel with Khrushchev in 1960, evicted his erstwhile Chinese friends in 1978 and died in 1985). In Poland Gomulka lost his remaining badge of respectability by being expelled, with others, from the central committee of the party after accusations of collaboration with the Pilsudski dictatorship and the Gestapo and of nationalism and deviationism. He was not, however, put on trial. Moscow preferred to strengthen its position in the most important of the satellites by sending the Soviet marshal Konstanty Rokossovsky to Warsaw where he became a Polish citizen and minister of defence. In Czechoslovakia Tito's secession and the Rajk trial were followed by a purge of suspected pro-Titoists and of communists who had spent the war years in London. The victims included the foreign minister, Vladimir Clementis, who resigned in March 1950 but was not made to stand trial. At the end of 1951 communists of the wartime Moscow group, including the party secretary Rudolf Slansky, were put on trial in proceedings which had a distinct anti-Jewish tinge and seemed intended to use Jews as scapegoats for the unpopularities of the régime.

These years were critical for Stalin's hold on the satellites – or, judging by Russian actions, were deemed by him to be critical. The rejection of the Marshall Plan in 1947 had been followed by the Russian blockade of Berlin and by more militant action by communists in western Europe (particularly in France and Italy), but these ventures had failed and their failure coincided with a challenge to Russian rule in eastern Europe which succeeded in Yugoslavia and looked like becoming contagious. Stalin's first response was harsh and practical: he stamped, where he could, on threats to Russian interests. In addition, he added to the apparatus of communist integration in two ways – by creating in Comecon an institution for economic assimilation and by creating the beginnings of military co-ordination as well. These measures, although primarily conceived as retorts to western measures and although not developed during the remainder of Stalin's lifetime, ultimately affected the nature of the relations between the USSR and its satellite neighbours.

Comecon – the Council for Mutual Economic Assistance – was founded in January 1949 as a counter to the Marshall Plan. Its founding members were the USSR, Poland, Czechoslovakia, Hungary, Romania and Bulgaria, which were joined almost at once by Albania and a year later by eastern Germany. It was in form an association of sovereign states: communist propaganda was at this time attacking the Marshall Plan as an American device for overriding European sovereignties. But in Comecon there was for many years no question of any insistence on sovereign rights to dissent, and the dominance of the USSR was underlined by the exclusion of Yugoslavia. For ten years Comecon had no constitution, meagre quarters and a tiny staff in Moscow, and few activities. In so far as it was anything more than an anti-American gesture, it was an adjunct of the Russian policy, chiefly pursued by other means, of using planning to annex the satellite economies to Russian needs and not to develop the area as a whole in the interests of all its parts. The satellite governments were themselves in the process of adopting the rigid communist system of planning by setting national targets and instructing each separate enterprise how much it must contribute to the aggregate (a system which the head of the State Planning Commission in Moscow, Nikolai Voznesensky, was trying to reform until his dismissal by Stalin in March 1949). Until the crises of the mid-fifties Comecon occupied itself modestly with statistical research, technical exchanges and the promotion of bilateral and triangular trade treaties, but from 1956 considerable changes were introduced. Twelve standing commissions were established in different capitals, Yugoslavia and China were admitted as observers, a constitution was worked out and came into effect in 1960, an international executive was inaugurated in 1962, and meetings of these various organs became regular and frequent. Comecon organized aid for Hungary in materials and credits after the revolution of 1956, promoted joint planning and investment, and expanded satellite co-operation on a broad multilateral basis; for example, for the distribution of electric power and in the construction of oil pipelines.

In military matters Moscow exercised control and supervision through officers in the satellite forces who had been trained in the USSR and were regarded as dependable. The despatch of Marshal Rokossovsky to Warsaw was a uniquely overt and elevated gesture but one which had numerous parallels at lower levels. In 1952 this tentacle policy was supplemented by the creation of a military co-ordinating committee with Marshal Bulganin as chairman, and at a conference in Warsaw at the end of that year a combined general staff was instituted with headquarters in Cracow under a Russian general. Military facilities, involving considerable displacements of population, were developed along the Baltic coast, in Poland and eastern Germany and round the Black Sea. The satellites were at this stage contributing something like 1.5 million men to military and security forces, were incurring a commensurate financial burden, and were being obliged to adjust their industries, their industrial revolutions and their economic planning to the military requirements of the bloc as assessed by the USSR. There was, however, no formal multilateral defence treaty until, after Stalin's death, the admission of western Germany to Nato prompted the inauguration in May 1955 of the Warsaw Pact. This treaty, to which the USSR and all its satellites were parties, was expressed as a regional arrangement for self-defence within the meaning of article 52 of the Charter of the United Nations: it was renewed in 1975 and 1985. It created joint organizations with headquarters in Moscow under the command of Marshal Koniev. It incidentally regularized the presence of Russian troops in Romania and Hungary where they would otherwise have had no legal standing after the termination of occupation rights in Austria by the treaty which restored Austrian sovereignty in that year. In general the Warsaw Pact was a formalization of existing dispositions and added little of substance to them. Membership of the alliance became, however, a touchstone of the reliability of Moscow's associates in the Cold War.

AFTER STALIN

Stalin's death in March 1953 stimulated unrest. His death did not initiate unrest: there were strikes in Czechoslovakia, for example, the previous year. But in June 1953 serious disorders occurred in East Germany which the government was unable to bring under control without the help of Russian tanks. In Hungary tens of thousands were confined in camps in a campaign directed in particular against the peasants, the majority of the population. In June 1954 Moscow gave evidence of new thinking about relations with the satellites when it sold to the satellite governments the Russian share in joint companies created after the war for the control of key industrial and commercial enterprises, and at about the same time the liquidation of Beria in the USSR was copied further afield: in Hungary the chief of the security police, Gabor Peter, was sentenced to life imprisonment, and the first secretary of the ruling party, Istvan Kovacs, was forced to confess to unjust arrests and false witness. In 1956 Hungary and Poland gave much sharper testimony to the insecurity of Russian rule.

In June 1956 there were strikes and riots in the Polish city of Poznan. They were directed chiefly against low wages for long hours. Industrial unrest coincided with intellectual ferment and with Roman Catholic demonstrations in August at Czestochowa, the home of a specially venerated shrine of the Virgin Mary. A meeting of the central committee of the party in July was attended by Gomulka, and when Bulganin and Zhukov arrived from Moscow in the hope of taking part, they were not allowed in. The first secretary of the party, Edward Ochab, became at some point persuaded that Gomulka must be readmitted to grace and power. During visits to the USSR and China Ochab seems to have convinced the Chinese, but not the Russians, of the need for this reversal. In October the politburo resolved to reconstitute itself, admitting Gomulka and excluding Rokossovsky. On 18 October a powerful Russian delegation arrived consisting of Khrushchev, Molotov, Mikoyan and Kaganovich, and Russian troops in Poland and eastern Germany began to move. Gomulka was included in the Polish team chosen to confront the visitors. These were not allowed to attend a meeting of the Polish central committee and after twenty-four hours they left. Hot words were spoken but rough action was stayed. Gomulka was appointed first secretary on 21 October. On 29 October Rokossovsky left for Moscow. He was followed within a few days by Gomulka. The upshot of these events was that the Russians, who had presumably gone to Warsaw with the intention of checking Gomulka and his party, decided after a quick look to accept them. The alternative, a direct use of Russian forces in Poland, was too risky because Russian forces might well have been resisted by the Polish army and a fight in Poland could have led to serious trouble in other countries. Gomulka was a communist and had no illusions about Poland's need to keep on reasonably good terms with the USSR. He did not propose to take Poland out of the Warsaw Pact or to share power in Poland with non-communists. He could be lived with. If the Russians had initially feared that a new Polish government would go too far in jeopardizing essential Russian interests, they concluded on second thoughts that Gomulka would not exceed the bounds of the tolerable. In December a new treaty gave the Russians the right to retain troops in Poland.

In Hungary the revolution which immediately followed the settlement in Poland did exceed those bounds. After the death of Stalin Imre Nagy was wafted into the premiership on a wave of general relaxation and of reaction against old-school hard-liners. In April 1955, however, he was ousted by Rakosi who took over the post himself and held it until July 1956. But Rakosi was unable to stem the rising tide of opposition emanating from the Petöfi circle (the centre of intellectual debate and dissatisfaction) and from the keen dislike of Tito, his neighbour to the south. When even the party newspaper *Szabad Nep* turned against him, the Russians realized that he had become a handicap and put their money on Erno Gerö. But Gerö too was disliked by the malcontents and by Tito, and in October Nagy regained power. He was in fact, if not reinstated, at least confirmed by the Russians, who had been forced to the conclusion that Rakosi, Gerö and communists of that ilk must be expended. Military operations by the Russians against Budapest had been begun on 24 October but the next day Mikoyan and Suslov arrived in Budapest and signified their acceptance of a Nagy régime – but without knowing, perhaps, what kind of government Nagy intended to form. Everything depended on whether Nagy could shape a policy acceptable both to the Russians and to the upsurge of Hungarian nationalism. He announced his government on 27 October and included in it two leaders of the suppressed Smallholders Party, Zoltan Tildy and Bela Kovacs. On the next day a cease-fire was arranged and the day after that the Russian troops began to withdraw from Budapest. Nagy then announced the end of one-party rule and the complete evacuation of Russian troops from Hungary. Nagy had now gone much further than Gomulka and it is probable, though not certain, that he had exceeded the limits of what the Russians deemed tolerable. By 30 October it seemed that the withdrawing Russian troops were preparing to return, or at least were being redeployed with a view to a possible return. The die was cast either on 31 October when Mikoyan and Suslov were told that Hungary intended to leave the Warsaw Pact, or at the latest on the following day when Nagy made a public statement to this effect and declared that Hungary would become a neutral. On that day an alternative government was set up by the Russians under Janos Kádár and when, two days later, General Pal Maleter, Nagy's minister of defence, went to negotiate with the Russians over the withdrawal of their troops, he was kidnapped. Budapest was attacked on 4 November (the day on which Gomulka went to Moscow) and thereafter the revolution was quickly suppressed. Thousands of Hungarians were deported to the USSR or executed. Kádár applied himself to running Hungary within the limits imposed by Moscow: no elections and no quitting the Warsaw Pact. He ruled for thirty-two years. He was on friendly terms with Khrushchev. He proclaimed a general amnesty in 1963, cultivated a comparatively unautocratic style, abated the use of torture and imprisonment, and permitted the discussion and introduction of economic reforms. Under Gerö, a poor economist, Hungary's manufacturing output had at first been increased but the productivity of a greatly enlarged industrial workforce did not improve, there was only pitiful investment in plant or technology, and when the workforce ceased to grow manufacturing growth subsided to zero. Investment in roads, housing, education and research was negligible. By the mid-seventies economists were advocating a drastic abandonment of central economic planning and direction, the unleashing of market forces of supply and demand, and schemes for allocating the profits of particular enterprises between workers, the state and reinvestment. These discussions were open and even broadcast on television. But intellectual barriers were coming down faster than the political. Actual reforms were unheroic and the ruling party unadventurous and, unlike its counterparts in Poland and Czechoslovakia, small.

The suppression of the Hungarian revolution of 1956 was one of those brutal acts of policy which do grave damage to the perpetrator but are undertaken none the less upon the calculation that graver damage would otherwise result. Communist parties lost members on a considerable scale and even communist governments which reckoned that Nagy had gone imprudently far shuddered at the display of Russian might and determination. Before long they found new cause for unease in the Russo–Chinese split. The Chinese were judged to have given Moscow the right advice on Poland and Hungary – that is, to acquiesce in changes and, in Hungary, to use force only after Nagy had given the revolution an anti-communist course – and Zhou Enlai visited Poland and Hungary early in 1957 to consolidate this advantage and stress the need for good Russo–Chinese relations. Khrushchev's subsequent handling of the quarrel with Beijing disturbed satellite leaders who disliked the way in which Khrushchev insisted on bringing it into the open and making communists take sides. In June 1960 Khrushchev used a congress of the Romanian party to stage a demonstration against the Chinese, and although in November 1961 eighty-one communist parties (Yugoslavia alone abstaining) signed in Moscow a declaration intended to lessen strife and paper over cracks, Khrushchev continued until his fall in 1964 to conduct a public campaign against the Chinese. On this issue Romania took the lead first in persisting with attempts to resolve the disputes and then in refusing to take sides. Gheorghe Gheorghiu-Dej, the virtual ruler of the country since the end of the war (and undisputed ruler after the fall in 1952 of Ana Pauker, Vasile Luca and other Muscovite leaders), also challenged the Russians in Comecon where, in 1962, Khrushchev proposed to create a supra-national planning organ with powers to direct investment throughout the bloc and prescribe what should or should not be done in each member state. The Romanians, who wanted a steel mill but were cast for the role of producers of raw materials, invoked the principle of national sovereignty which the Russians themselves had made much of when Comecon was founded. They displayed their dissatisfaction by entering into a separate agreement with Yugoslavia for a hydroelectric scheme at the Iron Gates on the Danube, by proposing that China be a full member of Comecon and by threatening to leave it. Romanian leaders visited Paris, London, Ankara and other non-communist capitals. After Gheorghiu-Dej's death in 1965 his successor as party secretary, Nicolae Ceausescu, also talked of the dissolution of the Warsaw Pact and of the loss of Bessarabia to the USSR twenty-five years earlier. After a tactful visit by Brezhnev to Bucharest in July 1965 the more implausible Romanian proposals abated as the realities of the situation reasserted themselves: the satellites might have more room for diplomatic manoeuvre but Russian predominance remained. Romania continued to assert its idiosyncracy by establishing diplomatic relations with western Germany in 1967.

The year 1968 brought a fresh challenge from a different quarter: Czechoslovakia. Before the Second World War, the Communist Party of Czechoslovakia was, unlike its neighbours, neither illegal nor underground. It was the second largest political party in the country. It escaped being compromised by the general communist alliance with Hitler in 1939–41 because Czechoslovakia was already occupied by the Germans and its parties banned. It played a patriotic role during the war and emerged after it as the biggest party owing to the proscribing of the collaborationist Agrarian Party. Its leader, Klement Gottwald, was therefore the natural prime minister. He and his colleagues had operated before the war in a democratic system and they now co-operated with other parties in what was at first a genuine coalition of all anti-fascist groups. The first postwar elections endorsed Gottwald's position by giving the communists 39 per cent of the vote in a free election, the highest percentage. Moreover, when in 1948 the non-communist parties tried to undermine communist authority (a legitimate aim) by resigning *en bloc* from the government and forcing President Beneš to install a government of officials (a dubiously democratic procedure), Beneš backed Gottwald and the scheme collapsed. But so too did genuine coalition government. The communists began to make a mockery of it and to govern increasingly through tyranny and terror. Czechoslovakia became a police state. The Yugoslav secession gave Gottwald a motive and an excuse for tightening his control (there were more executions in Czechoslovakia than anywhere else) and the bleak years of the Cold War with their talk of American action to liberate eastern Europe put a clamp on all meaningful criticism of the government. Although the government was distrusted, it was not seriously opposed; fear of the police stifled talk and prevented organization. Within the governing party itself debate was atrophied. Even the events of 1956 in Poland and Hungary struck no visible spark in Czechoslovakia, which came to be rated as the most docile of the satellites.

Presiding over this inertia was Antonin Novotny, first secretary of the Czechoslovak Communist Party from 1953 and president of the republic from 1957. Novotny was a Czech who despised Slovaks and did not conceal the fact. This became one item in a movement against his leadership which led to his removal from his party post in January 1968, from the presidency in March and from the party in May. Ditched by Moscow he was succeeded in the first office by the first secretary of the Slovak Communist Party, Alexander Dubček, and in the second by General Jan Svoboda. The first and more important of these changes was effected by a special meeting of the central committee of the party called to resolve a deadlock in the presidium. It amounted to a reversal of power within the party, largely instigated by Slovaks.

Dubček, besides being a Slovak nationalist, was an economic reformer, in government relatively humane and in economics relatively liberal: the sort of communist who makes other communists look peculiarly tyrannical and incompetent. He presented Moscow with a conundrum and for several months Moscow could not make up its collective mind what to think or what to do about him. The new government's first measures were vague and without explicit threat to the communists' monopoly of power or to the Warsaw Pact, but its Action Programme published in April and a promise of elections in

May put Moscow in a dilemma which it resolved at the end of August by invasion.

Czechoslovakia was an industrial state which was specially hampered by the drawing of the Iron Curtain where it was drawn. Economically its western half belonged with the western world, even if Slovakia did not. The country's economy made a decent recovery from the war but was slack and even stagnant in the sixties. Its prewar strength in the manufacture and export of consumer goods was undermined by Russia insistence on expanding heavy industries whose products were required by the USSR but had no markets outside the satellite bloc – since in western terms their technology was outdated. Its methods were (like Poland's) dangerously polluting. It produced twice as much steel as it could sell. It became isolated from the rest of the world. The standard pattern of central communist direction and control engendered ossification, and a return to consumer goods was obstructed by new vested interests in heavy industry (which would however be specially vulnerable if disarmament took hold). Czechoslovakia avoided excessive indebtedness to the west on the Polish or Hungarian scale but could not readjust or repair its economy without western capital.

Economists were alive to these dangers. Some mainly ineffective reforms were initiated in 1958 and a more far-reaching programme for decentralizing industrial management, elaborated by Professor Ota Sik, was approved by the Central Committee of the ruling party in 1965. Similar ideas had been discussed in neighbouring countries, including the USSR itself, and more radical measures than Sik's had been adopted in Hungary. There was in 1968 no compelling reason to suppose that Moscow would veto the kind of economic policy which the Dubček government wished to implement.

But pressure for such changes was accompanied by a second kind of ferment. Decentralization of economic management was equated with liberalization of controls and worker participation (or industrial democracy) and these trends overlapped naturally with demands for more freedom generally, notably freedom of expression in the press and on the radio and the democratization of party politics and the parliament – all of which posed more serious problems for the Russian guardians of the established order. Whereas in January 1968 the Russians had apparently decided that Novotny had lost his grip and was expendable, and that Dubček was acceptable in his place (Dubček proclaimed the solidarity of Czechoslovakia with the USSR and visited Moscow immediately after his appointment), a couple of months later Brezhnev and his colleagues were becoming worried by Dubček's programme and perhaps also by the likelihood of Dubček being forced further in a liberal direction by the enthusiasm released by the change of government in Prague. This change had been followed by a considerable relaxation of the censorship, by a number of ministerial changes and by the prospect of political democratization as well as economic liberalization. There was popular pressure on Dubček to make such radical internal reforms that these would be bound to raise questions about Czechoslovakia's external relations. Dubček had taken care to make personal contacts with Russian, Polish and Hungarian leaders before meeting the suspect Romanians and for a couple of months his neighbours evinced no distrust of him or his new course, but from the end of March criticisms began to appear in east Germany and Poland and the Russians had to ask themselves whether the changes in Czechoslovakia were not more portentous than they had at first seemed. The reformers were growing in confidence and were exciting ever greater popular expectations. Their Action Programme, produced at the beginning of April, made radical proposals concerning the reorganization of the respective functions of party and the government, the rehabilitation of victims of the purges of 1949, the position of Slovakia, the revival of the parliament and some freedom for minor parties (within the National Front which the communists would continue to control).

To the Russians the Action Programme was objectionable in itself and doubly objectionable in the wider context of central and eastern Europe. It brought personal and political freedom to the centre of a debate which could hardly be confined to Czechoslovakia. The first major upheaval in the postwar communist bloc had been caused by the example of Yugoslavia in 1948, the second by the examples of Poland and Hungary in 1956. Both had required, and in Moscow's eyes justified, recourse to violent measures including judicial assassination and force of arms. It was vital to prevent Dubček from setting a third bad example. Romania, particularly since Ceausescu's accession to power in 1965, had been making itself awkward in Comecon and the Warsaw Treaty Organization; it had ceased attending meetings of the latter. Tito was still alive and vibrant. (Both these leaders were to visit Prague in August within a few days of each other and to rapturous acclaim.) Czechoslovakia under Gottwald and Novotny had been a key element in the western sector of the USSR's European dominions, aligned with Poland and eastern Germany. The prospect of Dubček's Czechoslovakia sliding out of this sub-bloc and into alliance with Yugoslavia and Romania was both strategically alarming and an unacceptable display of political independence. Political changes in Prague, themselves a sequel to economic and managerial changes, might in their turn have dangerous strategic consequences. And some in Moscow were becoming alarmed by signs of declining communist authority in the government of Czechoslovakia and even in its police.

If the Russians were becoming uneasy about Czechoslovak actions, so were the Czechoslovaks about possible Russian reactions, particularly in view of the fact that popular pressures had induced Dubček to accelerate to early September the party congress which would presumably acclaim and endorse the reform programme. At the beginning of May Dubček and other leaders of the new course went to Moscow. Two weeks later Kosygin paid a prolonged visit to Prague and so too – at the same time but separately – did Marshal Grechko, accompanied by Marshal Epishev, the chief of the Soviet army's political intelligence. These visits pointed in opposite directions. Kosygin seemed to be seeking an accommodation, the generals to be preparing for action if there were none. In June the forces of the Warsaw Pact held manoeuvres in Czechoslovakia. These had been arranged a long time earlier, but they were considerably enlarged and the Russian tanks which came with them seemed in no hurry to leave. This hint or demonstration by the Russians coincided with the publication of a new liberal manifesto – the Two Thousand Words – which put further reformist pressure on Dubček and sharpened the tension between democratic and counter-reformist elements in Prague. The situation was now so dangerously charged that the French and Italian communist parties tried to mediate and the West Germans, equally alarmed by the turn of events, withdrew their forces from the Czechoslovak border in order to belie rumours that they and their allies were instigating a secession from the Warsaw bloc or were proposing to take advantage of the rifts within it.

Intervention in the affairs of a neighbour was neither new nor ideologically entirely unjustifiable, but the extreme form of military invasion was to be avoided if possible – perhaps to be eschewed altogether on some estimates of the damage that such strong-arm methods might do to international communism and the USSR's place in it. The debate on how and how far seems to have engaged the Russian leaders throughout July and half of August. A first meeting at Warsaw, not attended by the Czechs (or the Romanians) produced a letter warning them that their proposed reforms were tantamount to allowing power to escape from the Communist Party. They were asked to explain their doings. This meeting was followed by a Russo–Czechoslovak meeting held, on the latter's insistence, in Czechoslovakia – at Cierna-nad-Tisou on the Slovak border. It began on 29 July and lasted four days and was immediately followed by yet another meeting, at Bratislava of all members of the Warsaw Pact except Romania. Before Cierna the Russians issued a threatening statement saying that a cache of American arms had been found on Czech soil and it is difficult to judge whether Cierna was anything more than window-dressing. Bratislava reasserted the military threat. Russian troops moved out of Czechoslovakia. Moscow's propaganda against Prague stopped. But on 20 August the Russians, accompanied by East German, Polish, Hungarian and Bulgarian units, invaded.

It is not possible to say whether the decision to do so had been taken in principle before the July meetings or whether it was taken at short notice after them. If there was a change of plan during August, then the event most likely to have caused it was the publication on 10 August of the new statutes of the Czechoslovak Communist Party which amounted to the ending of democratic centralism and the granting of substantial rights to minor parties. These statutes were to be considered at the party congress a month later and would certainly be adopted unless drastic steps were taken to change the party leadership once more and prevent the holding of the congress. That the Russians invaded at short notice rather than after long and concealed premeditation is suggested by the fact that this political programme was only partially fulfilled. Although the invasion was militarily precise and efficient (the Czechoslovak armed forces offered no resistance and the Dubček government had said they would not do so), its political tactics were palpably confused and its political aims only partially achieved. Dubček was not overthrown. He was seized, flown to Moscow under arrest, possibly maltreated, but then reinstated. If, as there are many reasons to suppose, the Russians expected the presidium in Prague to displace Dubček and his associates, install a new government and issue an invitation to the Russians to validate the invasion, they were ill informed and their disposition insufficient. They came as blatant conquerors and although their power was irresistible they had to negotiate with Dubček and Svoboda.

But if Dubček remained in office, the Russians had to remain in the country. In October the Czechs signed a treaty permitting Russian troops to be stationed in Czechoslovakia, in undefined numbers. Thereafter the Russians and their allies in the Czechoslovak party worked slowly to demote Dubček, who was first sent to Turkey as ambassador and then recalled to be expelled from the party. The reformers and their reforms were progressively eliminated, but the Russians shrank from installing their extreme supporters in power and preferred instead a relatively neutral government under the Slovak Dr Gustav Hušak. Whether impressed by the spirit and discipline of the Czechs and Slovaks, or by the damaging comments of the world at large, or by the hostility within the communist world to Brezhnev's doctrine that the USSR had the right to intervene in a communist state to safeguard communism generally, the Kremlin used its victory with more circumspection than might have been expected once the initial step had been taken – but without foregoing its major aim of putting Czechoslovakia back under the sort of communist system which Dubček's followers in the party had tried to reform. Hušak remained president until 1987 when, two months after a visit to Prague by Gorbachev, he resigned; the prime minister Lubomir Strougal, a pallid reformer, also resigned later in the same year.

The invasion of Czechoslovakia was from the Russian point of view a regrettable necessity and a well-calculated action. Some western tremors notwithstanding, it created no threat to international peace and it did not halt the course of Russo–American détente: there was no more than a brief interruption in the talks that led to the opening of SALT in 1969 and the agreement with Bonn in 1970. As a crisis manager Brezhnev proved to have many of the qualities which had served Kennedy well in the Cuban crisis of 1962. But the invasion forced Moscow to proclaim an extreme doctrine about the limits of sovereign independence within the communist bloc and to make plain that Russo–American détente implied no loosening of the reins of power therein. The invasion and the doctrine unsettled eastern Europe by the violence of the action and the implications of the doctrine, and the use of the ostensibly anti-western Warsaw Pact against one of its own members emphasized the strains prevailing within the bloc twenty years after its consolidation.

These strains had two main sources: nationalism and conflicts of economic interest. Nationalism was endemic throughout the bloc, although weaker in some places than others. Bulgaria, at one end of the scale, endorsed the Brezhnev doctrine in a new constitution in 1971 and so elevated socialist internationalism above traditional nationalism and states' rights. This was an echo of Dimitrov's old-style international communism coupled with Bulgaria's perennial leanings towards Moscow to offset its perennially uneasy relations with its neighbours. (But in the seventies Bulgaria sought to improve its relations with Romania and Yugoslavia and even with Greece and Turkey too.) Most eastern Europeans, however, were as loath as western Europeans – or, for that matter, Arabs – to subordinate their national identity to supra-national organizations or causes. To some extent the USSR had contributed to this particularism not merely by its heavy-handedness in moments of crisis but also by obstructing regional associations within its sphere (Balkan, Danubian or other). Any association had to be all-embracing and it must of course include the USSR itself.

Of the two principal organs of eastern European integration the Warsaw Pact was little more than an expression and deployment of Russian power. Its forces were commanded by a Russian commander-in-chief and its headquarters were a departmental office of the USSR's high command. It had been created in opposition to Nato and its principal function was to face Nato's forces in Europe. But whatever their avowed purpose, the Pact's forces had other potentialities of which the invasion of Czechoslovakia was an uncomfortable reminder. The defence of eastern Europe included, according to the Brezhnev doctrine, firing shots in anger against enemies within the gates. The doctrine raised questions not about power but about sovereignty. All eastern European countries knew that they had to live with Russian power and observe the limitations which it imposed on their own freedom of action, but they wished at the same time to maintain, even if they might not always exercise, their sovereign rights. This was for the most part a vain aspiration, a kicking against the pricks exemplified by Romania's continued refusal (maintained in spite of a visit to Bucharest by Marshal Grechko in 1973) to take part in Warsaw Pact activities and by Ceausescu's symbolic visit to Beijing in 1971 and his reception in Bucharest in 1972 of the presidents of the United States and western Germany.

In Comecon, the second quasi-international body, strains were more concrete. Having come to life in the late fifties after a somnolent start, Comecon was endowed in 1962 with a Basic Plan of International Socialist Division of Labour. This title proclaimed the intention. In 1971 a second basic document was adopted: the Complex Programme for the Development of Socialist Economic Integration, incorporating a long-range programme reaching fifteen to twenty years ahead. (In this year Albania rejoined the organization after a gap of nine years.) Comecon's practical problems were fundamentally no different from those of any international organization trying to reconcile the good of each with the good of all. Its members had divergent views of their interests and the harmonization of these was further complicated by the immense preponderance of power of one member – a complication absent from the similar problems of the EEC. In eastern Europe the division of labour meant two things in particular: that each non-Russian member should concentrate on one or two economic activities prescribed for it by the organization as a whole, and that the resulting exchanges within the group should largely take the form of trading these prescribed manufactures for Russian primary products – notably oil: Russian exports of oil to other members of Comecon rose from 8.3 million tons in 1965 to a projected 50 million tons in 1975. Such a division of effort within a state would seem natural enough but when applied in advance of political unification it entailed a supra-nationalism which members – Romania in particular – distrusted because it removed decisions from national control (the same objections were heard in western Europe) and threatened to reduce particular members to dependence on a single industry or crop, with consequent further loss of political independence. There was also the question of payments, the fear that the terms and benefits of trade with Comecon would be manipulated to the disadvantage of the weaker brethren by arbitrary fixing of unfavourable currency parities. The 1971 Complex Programme acknowledged these fears to the extent of envisaging a common currency or convertible rouble by 1980 after a period in which separate currencies would be equitably and permanently adjusted in terms of one another.

Members of Comecon had a common interest in raising their economic performance and their trade with one another, but particular members also had an interest in trading with, and therefore producing for, countries outside the bloc: some of their needs could be satisfied only by buying from western countries, their trade would expand faster if they dealt with western as well as eastern countries, and there were political advantages in a commercial diversification which would reduce economic dependence on one or two neighbours. The USSR itself set an example which it could hardly denounce in others by concluding with the United States in 1972 an agreement designed to treble Russo–American trade by 1975. (This agreement was terminated by the USSR at the beginning of 1975 after the US Congress had inserted into the Trade Reform Act 1974 an amendment linking the expansion of Russo–American trade with the relaxation of the USSR's emigration policies. The author of the amendment, Senator Henry Jackson, hoped to facilitate Jewish emigration from the USSR but succeeded only in checking trade between the two countries.) From 1973 Comecon engaged in talks with the EEC about agreements between EEC and particular Comecon members embodying quota reductions and most favoured-nation clauses. Western countries were particularly attracted by the possibility of increasing their purchases of non-Middle Eastern oil.

But these horizons were not all fair. Increased east–west trade coincided with increased world commodity prices and increased inflation in the west. Eastern Europe, experiencing inflation in its own economies for domestic reasons including higher wages, was faced with the alternatives of importing a further measure of inflation with western goods and raw materials or of cutting back its trade. When Romania, which had redirected half of its foreign trade to countries outside Comecon, was preparing a new five-year plan in 1975, it altered its first intentions by reducing the share of its trade which it proposed to do with the west; but, loath to retreat into the closed circle of Comecon, it began to explore the prospects for more trade with the Third World and for this purpose applied for and was given membership of the conference of non-aligned states convoked in Lima in that year (but held in Colombo the next year). Even Czechoslovakia, consistently the strongest economy and a creditor country within the bloc, was caught in this dilemma, partly because of the vigour of its trade and industry. Its trade with the west, facilitated in some measure by the establishment of diplomatic relations with western Germany in 1973, brought in the world's goods but at the world's inflated prices, and since Czechoslovakia could not abandon incomplete projects which depended on foreign contracts it found itself having to increase the value of its exports to the west by more than 20 per cent if it was to pay for its imports by trade.

In Hungary decentralization in economic affairs troubled the Russians and the more conservative wing of the Hungarian communist establishment, but a visit by Brezhnev to Budapest in 1972 was taken to carry with it continuing Russian support for Kádár and cautious liberalization. Nevertheless Kádár remained harassed. Hungary's import bill rose vastly, with Russian as well as world prices increasing so much that the government, unable to bridge the gap by greater productivity and exports, was obliged to pass price increases on to the consumer. At the eleventh party congress in 1975 Kádár himself survived criticism but his prime minister, Jenö Fock, and other senior personages had to resign and new policies of austerity and recentralization were adopted primarily in order to cope with an unmanageable deficit in the balance of payments.

Much more serious from the Russian point of view was Poland, where economic difficulties led to the overthrow of the government by workers' demonstrations, a phenomenon rare in any quarter of the globe and least expected in an authoritarian communist state. Increases in food prices provoked at the end of 1970 strikes and riots which the government tried but failed to control by force. Forty-five people were killed and over a thousand injured. Gomulka, who had been brought back to power in the midst of the troubles of 1956, resigned. A new government under Edward Gierek cancelled the price increases, raised wages and social security payments, imported foreign consumer goods (at considerable cost) and purged party and administration by dismissing officials at all levels and placing new men and women in half of the top positions at the centre and beyond. The press was given greater freedom (but was restricted again in 1974) and in 1972 wages and benefits were raised again – the government demanding in return harder and more punctual work – and a new parliament was elected with many new faces but also the standard 99 per-cent vote for the communist candidates. By 1973 many economic indicators were so propitious that it was permissible to speak of a boom: industrial and agricultural production up, real wages up, investment up, prices stable. But the cost was a large increase in the import bill and foreign debt, as the government satisfied consumer demand and the needs of industrial modernization by buying abroad and financing its purchases by foreign borrowing and encouraging foreign investment. By 1974 Poland, like Romania, was doing half its trade with the west. Huge price increases, specially for food, led in 1976 to strikes, riots, deaths and heavy prison sentences. A Committee for the Defence of the Workers (KOR) came into existence to help the families of the dead and imprisoned and to protest against the heavy-handed brutality of the police. The price rises were rescinded, wages in industry and prices to farmers were raised, and Gierek persuaded Moscow to send substantial quantities of food and industrial machinery to Poland. This was a policy of repression tempered by concession. It did not work. The wage increases accentuated the demand for imported consumer goods and so increased inflation and the already unmanageable debt to western trading partners. The deaths of 1970 and 1976 were not forgotten; further demonstrations and hunger strikes forced the government to grant in 1977 an amnesty to those prosecuted for the previous year's disturbances; and Gierek, who held his first meeting with Cardinal Wysczynski, was seen to be appealing to the Roman Catholic Church for help. The election of Cardinal Wojtyla to the papacy – the first Polish pope since Poland was Christianized 1,000 years earlier – had an unmeasurable but far from insignificant effect in a country which regarded itself as the jewel of the Counter-Reformation. Pope John Paul II paid an emotional visit to Poland in 1979, which was another year of bad harvests and mounting foreign debt. Gierek's task was becoming beyond his powers and the industrial workers were moving, albeit cautiously, towards another confrontation with the government.

In 1980 they struck again, bringing the shipyards along the Baltic to a halt against a background of unmanageable foreign debts, soaring prices and severe shortages. Earnings on exports were almost wholly absorbed by the charges on a massive foreign debt of over $20,000 million, increasing by $2,000 million a year. Meat was alternatively unobtainable and prohibitively expensive. Wage increases of 10–20 per cent, granted by the government in the summer, threatened to aggravate inflation without making life tolerable for the recipients. There was nobody to blame except the government, but equally there was no constitutional way of blaming the government or seeking redress, even explanation, from it. Consequently the ensuing strikes in August were inevitably and immediately political. Not only could they not be settled by collective bargaining between the workers and their employers; but such bargaining was itself impossible because the workers were permitted no lawful organizations to do the bargaining. The system could solve nothing. If the strikers stayed out the government would have to choose between using force and bypassing the system.

But the government itself was not free to choose. It had to consult the USSR. Gierek flew to see Brezhnev to discover how much rope he was allowed. Neither he nor Moscow wanted a showdown with the strikers (which would rapidly become a showdown with a far wider segment of the population), but the use of force by the USSR could not be ruled out. Gierek had to find out what he might in no circumstances concede, and the agreement ultimately reached with the strikers in the Gdansk yards in August showed what these limits were. In that agreement, signed on behalf of the strikers by Lech Walesa and subsequently copied in similar terms in the Silesian coalfields and other areas, the strikers accepted the leading role of the Communist Party, Poland's socialist system and its membership of the Russian bloc. In return for recognizing these limits Poland's remarkably mature and disciplined opposition leaders won, on paper, astonishing victories: the right to strike, the right to form trade unions independent of the state, wider discussion of the government's economic policies, an abatement of censorship, appointments and promotions on merit and irrespective of party membership, increased wages and pensions, promises on working conditions, housing accommodation and maternity leave, a second day off in the week, and regular broadcasts of Roman Catholic church services. Some of the clauses were vague; others could hardly be implemented without an economic miracle which nobody expected. Nevertheless nobody doubted that something extraordinary had happened. An officially non-existent opposition, using non-violent industrial muscle, had forced a totalitarian government to meet many of its demands, to change the country's constitution and to reintroduce political dialogue where there had been none for a generation. The immediate and most potent cause of the government's defeat was its economic failures, but the workers' demands showed how far discontent spread beyond the purely material sphere to questions of human freedom and dignity such as the right of industrial groups to manage (some of) their affairs for themselves and to express and publish their own views.

Communist control was preserved in diluted form when General Jaruzelski, prime minister from February 1981, was appointed head of the party later in that year. To make assurance doubly sure he then proclaimed martial law. Walesa's control over Solidarity, by contrast, faltered as the government's measures and the arrest of some of its leading members produced divided counsels. When martial law was lifted after a year the main focus of opposition had shifted from Solidarity to the more tractable hands of the Roman Catholic Church, traditionally accustomed and disposed to deal with lay power. An uneasy accommodation was tacitly sealed by a visit by the Pope in 1983, followed by an amnesty for (most) political prisoners which emphasized the army's confidence. But tensions persisted. There were no economic answers and the problems were accentuated when President Reagan applied economic sanctions. The drain in membership of the Communist Party continued and the murder in October 1984 of Father Jerzy Popieluszko, one of a number of outspoken priests whose sermons praised Solidarity in patriotic terms, revealed the fires beneath the surface. It revealed also the inadequacy of the government's control over its own agencies: Father Popieluszko was kidnapped and tortured to death by the police.

The extraordinary significance of the Polish protest lay in its source – the industrial workers. In the USSR protest against bad government had been endemic for over a hundred years, back to the days of Alexander Herzen; but this was intellectual protest, as ineffectual as it was honourable and admirable. It reappeared in the postwar USSR and elsewhere, for example Hungary and Czechoslovakia. But only in Poland – and East Germany (1953) – were there, before the late eighties, any industrial protests on a politically significant scale. Stanislaw Kania, who replaced Edward Gierek as secretary general of the Polish Workers Party, faced a situation unique in the bloc. For externally little had changed. In spite of the domestic convulsions which brought him to the top Kania had to reckon with the fact that Moscow was still the master. This mastery was moreover intensified by Poland's economic plight. Poland could either pay its debts or feed itself but not both: the meat which had been at the centre of the summer's discontents could either be exported for foreign currency or released into the home market where, as a result of the wage increases granted before and after the strikes, it was more in demand than ever. Coincidentally a bad harvest was adding to import bills for grains and feeding stuffs, and although Poland's principal western trading partners – the United States and West Germany in the lead – were willing to extend fresh loans (within limits), only in Moscow could Poland's new government get credits commensurate with its difficulties. Poland in 1980 was a portent of trouble within the bloc but not, like Yugoslavia when Tito confronted Stalin thirty-two years earlier, a detachable part of the bloc. As the Poles themselves saw, geography ruled out anything like the Yugoslav secession and, by the same token, the massive financial and political aid from the west which sustained Tito from 1948. The degree to which Kania might succeed where Gierek had failed would therefore be settled in Moscow whence alone Kania might get the economic aid or concessions needed to maintain the treaty with the strikers – a compromise which Kania could not honour if Moscow chose not to let him do so. The USSR permitted the August settlement as the least of a number of evils but there was no guarantee of its continuing endorsement, still less of approval for further tinkering with the constitution or with the dominance of the Communist Party.

That the USSR was capable of reoccupying Poland was never in doubt and the examples of Czechoslovakia and Afghanistan showed that the Kremlin did not lack the nerve to use force. There were nevertheless strong reasons for supposing that it was extremely averse to doing so. These reasons derived neither from Poland's fighting spirit, which could be presumed to be as splendid and as ineffectual as it had been in 1939; nor from any American deterrent, for an American military threat was not credible and economic sanctions – as the recent Afghan crisis underlined – were slow to operate and fairly easy to circumvent. What made the USSR recoil from an invasion of Poland was the prospect of finding there nobody to govern the country – no Kádár as in Hungary in 1956, no Hušak as in Czechoslovakia in 1968. Poland's communists, already identified with economic catastrophe and internal repression, could not affront Polish nationalism by playing a

similar role, and so a Russian invasion would entail direct Russian rule
– as in tsarist times. But this was a policy which had been rejected both
by Stalin in 1945 when he poured cold water on the idea that the
countries of eastern Europe should join the USSR as Soviet Republics
(the three Baltic states alone excepted), and by Brezhnev when he
rejected in 1970 Gomulka's plea to use Russian forces to save his falling
régime. Therefore Moscow adopted a minimal policy. It wrote off the
Polish Communist Party and fell back on the Polish army in the hope
that Jaruzelski could, by martial law if necessary, keep Poland a one-
party state and in the Warsaw Pact. Failing such an outcome Stalin's
recipe for the control of central Europe was – in Poland's case at least –
in ruins. In 1944–45 Stalin had occupied this area as a prelude to
establishing in it governments which would be both subservient to
Moscow and wield adequate authority each in its own zone. That done,
Stalin could withdraw all or some of his armed forces. But if the
authority of these governments were to collapse the system collapsed.
The USSR would then have to choose between tolerating a multiparty
system and reimposing direct Russian military rule. The appointment
of General Jaruzelski as prime minister was a makeshift response to a
hopeless dilemma. Polish military rule might avoid the extremes of
overt Russian dictation and party political competition, but it could
solve neither Poland's main problems nor those of the USSR in Poland.
Martial law from 1981 to 1983 delayed an inevitable dialogue with
Solidarity while further damaging the economy by angering western
countries which, venting on Poland their displeasure with the USSR,
refused to renew their loans or to extend their trade.

ANNUS MIRABILIS 1989

In 1985 Gorbachev came to power in Moscow prepared to abandon the
Stalinist empire. In 1989 it vanished. Everywhere except in Romania it
vanished almost bloodlessly. The sources of these revolutions in central
and eastern Europe were similar, their outcomes less so. The East
German state disappeared; in central Europe communist rule was
decisively rejected and centre-right governments were installed; further
east, in Bulgaria and Romania, the old régime with a new face was not
so clearly removed.

In Poland Jaruzelski's government tried to stave off economic
collapse by imposing painful reforms, but since his government lacked
popular legitimacy its programme was rejected in a popular referendum
in 1987. Two years later, in April 1989, Jaruzelski, overriding
opposition from the military and the communists, legalized Solidarity.

He agreed to introduce a multiparty system, remove censorship of the press and broadcasting, and hold elections for the Senate and the Seym (the lower chamber), reserving however for communists and their minor allies two-thirds of the seats in the Seym. Two months later elections were held and the communists routed. After the second round of voting Solidarity had won 99 of the 100 seats in the Senate and the maximum open to it in the Seym (162 out of 460). In the reserved seats many official communist candidates failed to win the 50 per cent of votes required for election on the first ballot. This outcome produced consternation in ruling circles and astonishment practically everywhere. Jaruzelski, having resigned his party post, was elected unanimously to the state presidency by the two chambers of the parliament but the communists failed to form a government acceptable to parliament and their minor allies switched to the side of Solidarity which found itself propelled inexorably, but not wholly willingly, into government. After tortuous negotiations one of its leaders, Tadeus Mazowiecki, was made prime minister, most of the communists in the Seym voting for him. His appointment was welcomed by Gorbachev. But the economy continued to plummet so disastrously that the European Community established a special emergency fund to buy food for Poland and provide three-year subventions from the EC itself, its principal member states, the United States and Japan. During the decade wages lost a fifth of their purchasing power, inflation came near to 200 per cent a year, and Poland's debt to the west of $35,500 million was much the largest of the satellites'. (Hungary's at $13,700 million at the beginning of 1989 was higher per head of population. Others were: East Germany $7,600 million; Bulgaria $5,400 million; Czechoslovakia $4,000 million; Romania $3,900 million but then paid off almost entirely at Ceaucescu's quirky resolve. Yugoslavia owed the west $17,600 million.) In 1990 Jaruzelski extricated himself from a hopeless position by prematurely resigning the presidency which was thereupon contested between Lech Walesa with demands for speedier but unspecified action and, on the other hand, the more prosaic but more reflective Mazowiecki: the man of destiny who had challenged the communist order, against the man who seemed to many better equipped to pick up the pieces. The contest between them was bizarrely bewildered by the incursion of a third candidate, Stanislaw Tyminski, who had spent the previous twenty years in Canada and Peru making himself (so he said) a millionaire and promised to do the same for countless Poles. He beat Mazowiecki into third place on the first round and although overwhelmed on the second by Walesa secured a quarter of the votes cast.

In the same month as the Polish elections of 1989 the body of the murdered Imre Nagy was brought to Budapest and given a reburial which turned into a vast popular demonstration against the régime. Kádár's thirty-two-year rule had been brought to an end the year before (he died in 1989). He had advocated economic reforms before the advent of Gorbachev in the USSR but after that event his concept of reform was made to seem too lame and was overtaken by a new momentum. His successor as general secretary of the ruling party, Karolyi Grosz, came into collision with his colleagues over the scope and pace of change – notably with Miklos Nemeth, the prime minister, and Imre Poszgay, the régime's economic expert, who wanted not only to accelerate economic reform but also to introduce radical political changes such as the abandonment of the communist monopoly of political power. Elections in a multiparty system were promised for early in 1990 and the party set about salvaging some of its power by changing its name and putting on a new public face: the Hungarian Socialist Workers' Party became the Hungarian Socialist Party. Two main opposition parties emerged: the Hungarian Democratic Forum, a centre-right party akin to the Christian Democrats of western Europe, and the Alliance of Free Democrats, the vehicle primarily of urban intellectuals. Fifty other parties appeared too. The non-communists defeated the communists (who were reduced to 10 per cent of the vote) and formed a coalition which, however, proved uneasy and remained intact for only a few months.

Hungary played an eliptical role in the next act of the year's drama. In May East Germans began to desert their state in a mass emigration when Hungary, in a gesture with no special reference to German affairs, removed restrictions on its frontiers with Austria. East Germans on holiday in Hungary found that they had an open road through Austria to West Germany where they had automatic rights of access and citizenship. They took the road at a rate initially of 5,000 a day. This exodus was swollen a few months later when Hungary abrogated an agreement with East Germany and virtually constituted itself a transit area for mass emigration of the discontented and the desperate. Others in East Germany staged huge anti-government demonstrations in Leipzig, Berlin and other cities and under these pressures – and with the example of events elsewhere in central Europe derived from West German television – new escape routes to the west were fashioned through Czechoslovakia, from Poland through East Germany in special trains, and eventually direct from East to West Germany. By the end of the year about half a million had left and they were still leaving at the rate of 2,000 a day.

At the beginning of the year Erich Honecker's inclination had been to hold on to power, if necessary by force, and to treat his people as Deng had treated the Chinese in Tiananmen Square. Honecker's position, however, was in one crucial respect the weakest among communist leaders since the state which he ruled was a Russian creation without a national identity of its own. The USSR was the ultimate source of the ruling party's power (as it was throughout the satellite empire) but also, and uniquely in the German case, the USSR was the source of the state's legitimacy and *raison d'être*. When therefore Gorbachev arrived on a visit to Berlin in October 1989 his appearance in the midst of a crisis not only recalled his appearance in Beijing in similar circumstances six months earlier but also underlined the essential difference that, whereas in Beijing he had been an accidental observer, in Berlin he held a key to future developments. In terms which were at once guarded and unmistakable he warned Honecker against the dangers of not moving with the times and privately made it clear that the East German régime must expect no help from the USSR in suppressing violent demonstrations. He may have gone even further, thwarting Honecker's assumed willingness to use East German forces in the manner of Deng and encouraging Honecker's removal from power. In a flurry of unforeseen events Honecker was replaced as general secretary of the Socialist Unity Party by Egon Krenz, a younger but not much less tarnished member of the inner core of the communist élite; and Krenz, who barely outlasted the year, was himself replaced by Gregor Gysi, under whose guidance the party renounced its monopoly of political power, changed its name and prepared for multiparty elections early in 1990. Hans Modrow, mayor of Dresden and a comparatively respectable communist, became prime minister in an interim administration formed to conduct negotiations with non-communist groups which were pupating into political parties. These parties, campaigning under the management of their West German counterparts, submerged but did not obliterate the communists in elections in which nearly half the votes were cast for the right, fewer than a quarter for socialists and 16 per cent for communists. The Berlin wall was demolished and the city united as men and women from east and west were once more free to pass from one side to the other. Germany itself was reunited in fact while German and foreign politicians argued about the terms and timing of reunification. The West German government, desperate to stem the wholesale migration of East Germans to the west, promised to convert the East German currency into Deutschmarks at a basic rate (there were exceptions) of one-for-one – a measure which entailed an increase in the money supply in West Germany by 14 per cent and corresponding inflation over an indefinable period – but nothing could prevent the collapse of east German industries. Kohl promised to drag East Germany up to the levels of prosperity enjoyed by West Germans. The means to this end were to be investment in the East by the West and by non-Germans. The immediate reality was the halving of industrial production in a single year, a persistent migration of East Germans fleeing not a police state but economic disaster, and unemployment among those who remained at between a third and a quarter of the workforce.

The dissolution of the East German state catapulted the unification of

Germany on to the international agenda. Gorbachev briefly tried and predictably failed to secure the neutrality of the newly enlarged state. At a meeting with Kohl in July in the Caucasus he acquiesced in the new Germany's membership of Nato but he secured much in return: the presence of Russian troops in what had been East Germany until the end of 1994, a substantial German contribution to their costs, and an undertaking that no German units committed to Nato nor any Nato units stationed in Germany should be deployed in the former German Democratic Republic. In October the unification of the two Germanies was formally completed and the East German state was converted into five Länder of the German Federal Republic. This republic was not prewar Germany. East Prussia remained part of the USSR, the lost lands beyond the Oder–Neisse line remained part of Poland. On the first anniversary of the piercing of the Berlin wall Germany signed treaties formally affirming these frontiers.

In central Europe revolution in Czechoslovakia came last but fast. President Hušak's dour successor Milos Jakes and his prime minister Ladislas Adamec were replaced by Karel Urbanek and Marian Calfa, but the first of these changes was only a marginal manipulation as a tide of popular demonstrations rising to a climax in November destroyed the old régime. Vaclav Havel, who had served more prison terms than any triumphant national hero since Mahatma Gandhi, was chosen to be chairman of Civic Forum, a co-ordinating committee of various groups which had come into being to demand the end of the communist monopoly of power, the release of political prisoners and the removal of censorship and other restraints on freedom. Before the end of the year Havel was president by popular acclaim and the unanimous vote of the parliament. His position was confirmed by elections in 1990, although it was less solid in Slovakia, traditionally the more reactionary half of the country, than in the 'historic lands' of Bohemia and Moravia. Alexander Dubček reappeared and was rewarded for his past endeavours and sufferings with the post of chairman of the parliament. Uniquely in Stalinist Europe the Czech and Slovak communists decided not to change the name of their party. By agreement with Moscow the 70,000 Russian troops in Czechoslovakia were to be withdrawn by 1991 (Gorbachev having already agreed to withdraw his 50,000 troops in Hungary by that date).

In Bulgaria Todor Zhivkov had ruled for even longer than Kádár in Hungary. In 1988 he tried to fortify his position and breast the tide of dissension within and beyond his party by dismissing his more liberal deputy Chudomir Alexandrov, but to no avail. His fall a year later was preceded by an episode peculiar to Bulgaria: the persecution and flight of its Turkish inhabitants. These people, called Pomaks, had increased from about half a million in 1945 to twice that number forty years later. This rate of increase was not in itself startling but it was higher than the increase among ethnic Bulgarians and the Pomaks, being Muslims, were at a disadvantage whenever the government wanted to curry favour with Bulgarian Christians by diverting attention to people who could be stigmatized as undesirable aliens. In 1950 Bulgaria had asked Turkey to grant visas to 250,000 Turks in Bulgaria, and under an agreement of that year 154,000 left Bulgaria for Turkey without their relatives, who were however allowed to emigrate under a second agreement of 1968. At that point the Bulgarian government declared that there were no Turks left in Bulgaria and that all remaining Muslims were the descendants of Bulgarians who had been forcibly converted in the past to Islam. In 1985 these Muslims were required, for the purposes of the census, to adopt Bulgarian names. This decree revealed massive discontent and even panic, and in the face of Bulgarian obduracy Turkey opened its frontier to all would-be migrants without requiring visas. The result was an exodus. Although Bulgaria refused to allow males of military age to leave, at least 300,000 persons did so, whereupon Turkey reversed its earlier decision and reintroduced visas. (Bulgaria evicted some 2,000 Turks into Romania and Yugoslavia, whence most of them proceeded to Turkey. After the revolution of 1989 the remaining Turks in Bulgaria were given the right to choose their own names but ethnic hostility persisted.) But the final blow to the Zhivkov régime was delivered not by the Pomaks but on the occasion of a conference of environmentalists in Sofia which was turned into the setting for demands for *glasnost*. These were met by police brutality of a kind which had served its purpose in the past but led now to the ousting of Zhivkov by his rattled colleagues. Like Honecker, Zhivkov was arrested and charged with crimes against the state. Under his successor Petar Mladenov the Bulgarian Communist Party changed its name to Socialist, renounced its political monopoly and began negotiations with other parties – the Agrarian People's Party and the Union of Democratic Forces, the latter an assemblage of anti-communist groups – to form a traditional government. These talks having led nowhere, the communists remained in office and contrived to win what appeared to be reasonably conducted elections, but the ensuing popular clamour forced Mladenov to resign the presidency to Zhelu Zhelev, the leader of the UDF. A split in the Communist–Socialist Party deprived the prime minister Andrei Lukanov of his majority and, with inflation bounding upward and the state obliged to default on its external debts, more popular demonstrations forced Lukanov too out of office.

By contrast the fall of the dictatorship of Nicolae Ceausescu in Romania was accomplished only with sickening bloodshed. The Romanian Communist Party, never large, had been used by Ceausescu as a base for converting Communist Party rule into a personal or family tyranny of intense malignity, supported by extensive and efficient delation, a well-equipped private army, a peculiarly ruthless police and driving megalomania. Like Stalin, whom he admired, Ceausescu was obsessed with getting things done and damning the human cost. He aimed to modernize and aggrandize Romania by the force, not so much of communist doctrine, as of his own authority and personality, but like many a dictator he failed increasingly to draw the distinction between Romania and himself, with the consequence that he embarked on spectacular enterprises reminiscent of those of the madder Roman emperors. Both at home and abroad he won for a time a measure of approval through anti-Russian policies and gestures, including his refusal to co-operate in the Warsaw Pact or allow foreign troops on Romanian soil. He was rewarded with lavish praise from, among others, George Bush and with a British knighthood and was received effusively in countries as diverse as China, India and Israel. At home, however, he proceeded to denude the economy and even to order the destruction of 7,000 villages whose inhabitants were compelled to migrate in search of a livelihood and were employed in building ostentatious palaces in the capital on starvation wages. Serious riots were first recorded from Brasov in 1987, and at Timisoara in Transylvania at the end of 1989 the army refused to fire on large popular demonstrations which turned out to protest at the persecution of a fearlessly outspoken Protestant cleric, Laszlo Tokes. This spark lit a fire which Ceausescu, returning from a visit to Teheran, was unable to quench. His security police or private army was opposed by the regular army as well as by large unarmed crowds, and thousands were killed before Ceausescu and his wife took to flight. They were captured and executed after the merest formality of a trial. Paradoxically Ceausescu, the least satellite-minded communist leader, paid the grimmest price in the débâcle of the Stalinist empire. Paradoxically again, his removal allowed other communists to make a bid to keep power. Ceausescu's communist opponents had formed a National Salvation front which had been ineffective so long as the dictator lived but which after his death declared itself a transitional government, emerged victorious from internationally supervised elections and thrust its chairman Ion Iliescu into the presidency.

The year 1989 witnessed revolutions in the grand tradition – the assertion of civic rights and human values – but, like the French Revolution of two hundred years earlier, they were grounded in economic collapse and sustainable only through economic improvement. They were revolutions against tyranny, corruption and incompetence. Since communist parties had been responsible for these evils, the revolutions were also revolutions against these parties and against communism itself. The parties were demoted from their privileged positions and removed from power in most places for (probably) a long time, but they were not eliminated and might be expected to find some place in the spectrum of multiparty politics. The principal features in the overthrow of the Stalinist empire in Europe were economic disaster, Gorbachev, persistent intellectual and popular protest over decades, and the rulers' lack of a plausible claim to legitimacy. The principal consequence was articulation in both senses of the word: the expression of opinion triumphing over suppression, and the re-emergence of the half-buried pattern of sovereign nation states. Gorbachev saw that the Stalinist system did not work. It was an expensive millstone round Moscow's neck and had lost the strategic rationale which had been its prime justification after 1945. Forty years later an American attack on the USSR, which was in any case far less probable than Stalin might himself have imagined, would bypass the satellites by passing miles over their heads instead of moving across their territory. Gorbachev's disenchantment with Stalin's system was not concealed from the regional satraps whose business it was to operate it. They could see that they were no longer wanted. They had become proconsuls in a defunct empire and they could not look to their fellow citizens for support since they had grossly abused their power and, besides destroying basic freedoms, had allowed whole economies to moulder. Although in the fifties economic growth had reached 10 per cent in the more favoured parts of the zone, by the eighties it was zero or nearly zero practically everywhere. Hence hardship, indignation, tensions, demonstrations, repression (often extremely brutal) and so to revolution. All the revolutions were swift and thorough: second-rank communists who were thrust into leading positions disappeared almost as soon as they appeared. Most portentous was the standing of Gorbachev, the president of the USSR which had imposed the régimes which were being discarded. Instead of being reviled he was acclaimed by crowds which chanted his name with grateful enthusiasm and seemed to regard the United States and other western democracies as peripheral. Yet Gorbachev, however crucial his role in the transformation of European affairs, was not the only begetter of the revolutions in central and eastern Europe. These were not as sudden as many bewildered observers imagined. They were part of a sequence (to which they owed much) of abortive risings reaching back to the first postwar decade: 1953, 1956, 1968, 1980. All these commotions, including the formation and early achievements of Solidarity in Poland, ante-dated the elevation of Gorbachev and were made by people – some of them out of the ordinary, but many of them people commonly dubbed ordinary – who won attention for their indignation and their values and eventually triumphed on the streets in the tradition of the barricades. Solidarity, for example, ignited a jet of popular pressures which could not be capped. The destruction of the imperial superstructure by the fires of revolution uncovered the perennial alternative: a *Mitteleurope* articulated into separate states, conceived as nation states but in reality conglomerates of greater or less coherence. In the eyes of the new men and women these states were real and legitimate. Only the old rulers had lacked legitimacy – except in East Germany where the state itself did so too. Revolution had therefore strong nationalist ingredients. Its leaders shared a common plight and common aims and were in that sense linked internationally, but revolution was in no sense supra-national even to the limited extent that supra-nationalism was taking hold in western Europe.

The revolutions did not solve economic problems. By the standards of western Europe the material state of these countries was pitiable. Yet most people in central and eastern Europe were materially better off than most people in Asia or Africa. Their economies suffered from distortion, not from sterility. They possessed agricultural and mineral resources and experienced growth in output, reaching in some places 10 per cent a year – albeit growth from a low postwar base and increasingly in the wrong directions. In Poland's large agricultural sector, four-fifths of it in private hands, output rose throughout the postwar decades but investment was inadequate and the agricultural workforce failed to contribute to GNP commensurately with its numbers or to feed the population. Investment in Polish industry increased output but not productivity; exports declined and foreign debt accumulated. Czechoslovakia, with a lengthy history of good education, good administration and technical skills, with the highest income per head in central Europe, with a flourishing export business and enviable natural resources, was converted under communist rule from the things it did best (notably medium industries such as making shoes) to serving the satellite bloc's appetite for heavy industrial goods and armaments. It lost old skills and concentrated on products which, with the end of the Cold War, were wanted neither at home nor abroad. Hungary, the smallest of this central European trio, possessed rich and well-watered agricultural land and significant mineral re-sources, although these were not – with the exception of its bauxite – of the first quality. Postwar modernization boosted output and industrial exports, but the economy was neither adequately capitalized nor efficiently managed, returns on investment were low, foreign debt high. In all three states much effort brought little reward. Food and consumer goods became dearer and scarcer. Industrial pollution was the worst in the world. Eastern Europe fared no better. Romania embarked on an ambitious, even ruthless, attempt to modernize its economy on the basis of its coal, oil and other minerals, its chemical, hydroelectric and metallurgical industries, and its underpaid and overworked labour force. Ceausescu's megalomania turned failure into catastrophe. In Bulgaria a similar, if less ruthless, expansion of industry increased output, much of which was however unsaleable because of its poor quality. In sum, considerable efforts to catch up with western Europe left central and eastern Europe further behind, impoverished, polluted and verging on hopelessness.

YUGOSLAVIA AFTER TITO

Tito lived for thirty-two years after his rift with Stalin. After Stalin's death Khrushchev paid two conciliatory visits to Yugoslavia. The first, in 1955, was tantamount to a confession of error and an apology for the Russian stand in 1948. The second, in June 1956, followed the twentieth congress of the Communist Party of the USSR at which, earlier in the year, Khrushchev had indicated that relations with the satellites needed to be put on a new basis; it followed also the dissolution in April of the Comintern, the body which had pronounced Tito's excommunication. But Russo–Yugoslav relations remained distant and distrustful, if less bitter. Internally Tito, having won the right to tackle his problems in his own way did so only tentatively, although the introduction of workers' management in industry in 1950 and the abandonment of collectivization in the countryside in 1953 attested a willingness to moderate doctrinal rigidity. The constitution of 1945 had nationalized all industrial, commercial and financial enterprises, limited individual landholdings to 60 acres, and organized the surplus agricultural land into collective farms. The first Five Year Plan was an immensely detailed, voluminous and bureaucratic blueprint for a Russian–style command economy. It was gradually dismantled in the 1950s, mainly because it was hopelessly cumbersome. In 1950 and again in 1961 industrial control was devolved on to workers' councils with wide powers of management, including the right to allocate investment funds and to decide what to do with profits. In the early 1960s new lines of credit were made available through local banks (as opposed to the central bank) and the system of fixing prices centrally was relaxed. Although these measures failed to give industry the expected stimulus and were succeeded by a brief reaction, the liberalizing and decentralizing strands were – also briefly – resumed round 1965, partly because the economy still remained stagnant and partly to attract funds from the IMF and the United States. So in fits and starts the economic sector was fragmented into tens of thousands of autonomous units. Whether the psychological stimuli of decontrol and self-management outweighted losses in efficiency and productivity was inconclusively debated both inside Yugoslavia and out. More certainly, these industrial changes created a new base for political power by opening careers for talents in industry besides the traditional ladders of the Communist Party and the armed forces.

7.2 Yugoslavia and its republics

Besides the economy Tito's second main concern was the cohesion of
the state and the creation of a Yugoslav identity over and above the
Serb, Croat and other nationalisms within the Yugoslav federation.
Tito, half Croat and half Slovene by birth, was determined to preserve
the Yugoslav state which had emerged from the destruction of the
Habsburg and Ottoman empires in the First World War. He was aided
by the camaraderie of the partisan warfare of the Second World War,
during which he had been careful to assemble an ethnically diverse
leadership in the Communist Party and army. The integrity of
Yugoslavia was not seriously threatened so long as this generation
remained in sole charge. By the 1970s, however, a new generation had
grown up, which was more nationalist and separatist, partly because
the wartime magic was receding and partly because peacetime
competition for goods and investment fostered far from forgotten
sores. In Croatia agitation for more autonomy went to the length of
demands for sovereign independence (but within a Yugoslav confederation) and a separate seat in the UN such as had been granted to Ukraine
and Byelorussia. A time of troubles loomed – with Tito close on
eighty. In 1971 Tito decided to stamp on his aberrant younger

colleagues. He made it plain that he was the judge of when enough was enough, and that in his judgment Croat separatism was unpardonably threatening the integrity and welfare of the Yugoslav state. Once he resolved to intervene he carried the day. Significantly the Croat elder statesman Vladimir Bakarić stood by him. The younger leaders resigned. Tito then repeated this performance in Serbia where the younger politicians were no less nationalist; and in Slovenia and Macedonia (but here dissent was not purely nationalist).

Separatism was an extreme form of the continuing problem of decentralism which called in question the powers of the central government and – an even more sensitive matter – the central organs of the Communist Party. In the 1950s and 1960s both centralism and permanent communist rule were questioned. Centralism was attacked on grounds of efficiency and offended local patriotism. Criticism was open and lively. It raised the question how political authority could be dispersed without denting communist control. The decentralisers argued as technocrats, managers and grassroots politicians. Their arguments either skated round the consequences for communist control or, as in the case of Djilas, accepted the conclusion that the Communist Party had no automatic right to permanent power. They became a double source of offence to the centralizers who, pre-eminently Ranković, not only preferred central to dispersed authority for its own sake but also saw in decentralization a menace to the communist monopoly of power. Tito allowed the debate to flourish until it seemed to become dangerously disruptive. He was not an enemy of limited debate, but he did not intend that either side should win. In the liberalizing atmosphere of the 1950s the first need was to curb the liberalizers. Djilas was persecuted and imprisoned. Ranković remained in office – and was even promoted – until his anti-liberal campaign overstepped the bounds and he was found to be spying on Tito himself, whereupon he was dismissed. At the end of this phase Tito devised a new constitution which created an Executive Bureau of Presidential Commission consisting of two representatives of each federal republic and one from each autonomous district with Tito as permanent federal president. (After his death the presidency was to revolve.) This arrangement was intended to signal a compromise but it left the realities untouched and conflict no more than deadened.

The outcome of the separatist and decentralizing currents of the 1950s and 1960s was to block secession but at the same time to allow a federation with a strong centre to evolve towards something approaching a looser confederation of sovereign entities on the model of Switzerland. And the state remained a communist one. In 1958 the Communist Party had been renamed the League of Communists. This change was taken to indicate that the party might not always be the right organ for running local government bodies or industrial plants.

But the party, or League, remained unique. Such was the reality which Tito did not intend to change, however he might permit its face to be modified.

When Tito died in 1980 Yugoslavia was unique. It was the only communist neutral in the world. But it was also fragmenting and indigent. It was no more cohesive as a communist federation than it had been as a triune kingdom. The task of the tail end of the Karageorgević dynasty had been to compound Serbs, Croats and Slovenes into a Yugoslav state and nation, but this task was no more than half achieved before the Second World War reopened old divisions, particularly between the Serbs and Croats, whose grisly wartime leader Ante Pavelić tried to create a separate Croat state, buying Italian support by ceding marginal Croat lands to fascist Italy (which was looking across the Adriatic for its version of *Lebensraum* – *spazio vitale* – in Albania and Dalmatia). On the other hand, the communist resistance to Italians and Germans produced an aura of Yugoslav confraternity which, after the war, Tito sought to enhance by giving ethnic minorities – Montenegrins, Macedonians, Albanians (in Kosovo), Hungarians – equal or approximately equal status with the three original constituents of the Yugoslav state. But Tito could not give these different groups anything approaching economic equality. Their national and religious differences – within Christianity and, for Muslims, beyond it – were not offset by any economic fruits of federation. Aid from the west which followed the rift with Moscow was used mainly to develop industries. The consequent drift from the countryside to towns was at first a welcome relief for a problem of rural overpopulation insufficiently tempered by emigration, but in the longer run it weakened agriculture without commensurate benefit from industry which faltered when reforms in management and financing were applied too slowly and without turning the right to manage into competent management. Western helpers lost interest when they lost money and when aid to Yugoslavia lost its political edge with the cooling of the Cold War. Foreign debt piled up, so that paying the interest on it became a burden on the Yugoslav economy bigger than the benefits conferred by the loans in the first place. The economic balance spread over a generation showed a net loss. In 1989 the federal prime minister, Ante Marković, adopted desperate measures, instituting a convertible currency, commercial banks, a stock exchange and other apparatus of a capitalist market economy. Inflation was reduced from 2000 per cent to zero in a matter of months and exports and the reserve rose, but at the price of catastrophic unemployment and bankruptcies and dire want. Endemic tensions between the several republics were accentuated. In the largest, Serbia, which contained 40 per cent of the population, nationalists led by the flamboyant Slovodan Milosević – who made up in Serb nationalism what he was in danger of losing as a communist – were intent, first, on annexing the autonomous districts of Kosovo and Vojvodina; second on restructuring the federation in its original tripartite form; and thirdly, in absorbing all the newer republics and dominating the federation itself. The issue in Kosovo went back to the Second World War and to the Middle Ages. During the war promises of autonomy had been used to enlist the co-operation of Albanians against Italians and Germans. But Kosovo, although now inhabited by ten Albanians for every Serb, was the historic heartland of Serb nationalism and the symbol of Serb resistance to the Turks in the fourteenth century – the six hundredth anniversary of the fateful battle of Kosovo which extinguished Serbia for seventy years fell in 1989. In 1990 the Albanian majority in Kosovo declared the district to be a full republic and the Serbs retaliated by adopting a new constitution which extinguished the autonomy of both Kosovo and Vojvodina. Milosevic's rhetoric and a sweeping victory in multiparty elections in 1990 accentuated Croat and Slovene tendencies to secede from what in their eyes was becoming Greater Serbia. Croat disputes with Serbia extended into Bosnia since Croatia claimed a strip of it and the more militant Serbs claimed the whole of it. There were a million Croats in Bosnia and half a million Serbs in Croatia, many of them agitating for the transfer of their districts – for example, the (Dalmatian) district of Knin – to Serbia. In multiparty elections in 1990 Franjo Tudjman, ex-communist turned chauvinist, won over 40 per cent of the vote and 70 per cent of the seats in the Croat parliament. Similar elections in Slovenia installed a communist president but an anti-communist majority in parliament which organized a referendum which demanded independence for Slovenia. The Slovene Communist Party changed its name and seceded from the Yugoslav Party. The Yugoslav federation and its dominant party seemed to be no less fissiparous than those of the USSR, the federation likely to fall to pieces unless the army, in which Serbs dominated the officer ranks, were to intervene to hold it together. Alternatively, with independence possibly meaning less than the sovereign independence of classical political theory, Yugoslavia might evolve into an association of states linked with one another more closely than with any other state, but in a federation more skeletal than any classical federal structure. Yugoslavia, like the USSR, might be arriving centrifugally at something like the political form which western Europe was approaching from the opposite direction.

Albania, which broke off relations with the USSR in 1961, maintained a Stalinist dictatorship of its own under Enver Hoxha until his death in 1985. His successor Ramiz Alia did not seem minded to change this situation until changes in the world round Albania turned him, like others in eastern Europe, into a reverse-Kerensky trying to find a way back from the extremes of communist rule while at the same time preserving his own position in a country where multiplicity entailed not only many parties but also the rivalries of many peoples and religions.

NOTES

A   *Northern Ireland*

Northern Ireland, frequently but wrongly called Ulster, was that part of Ireland which remained part of the United Kingdom when in 1922 the rest of Ireland broke away from the union created in 1800. During the winter of 1921–22 there were two principal issues in debate between the English and the Irish. The partition of Ireland was only the second of these since it was widely regarded as inevitable and the more heated debates, in London and among the Irish leaders themselves, were about the status of the Irish state which, the English insisted and a narrow majority of the provisional Irish parliament agreed, should be a Free State within the British Commonwealth and Empire, owing allegiance to the British Crown and presided over by a British governor-general. In Ireland a republican minority pressed its case to the point of civil war but lost, and Ireland, although a separate member of the League of Nations from 1923, did not become a fully independent republic until 1937.

In the north-east a border was eventually agreed in 1925. The province of Northern Ireland inherited from the Act of Union of 1800 the right to elect members to the parliament at Westminster. It had also, under the Government of Ireland Act 1920, a bicameral legislature and an executive of its own with a considerable degree of internal autonomy (extended in 1948). The province was governed from its inception until 1972 by a Protestant oligarchy dominated by landowners but embracing in later years representatives of the more prosperous urban and professional classes, one of whom, Brian Faulkner, became its last prime minister. The power of this oligarchy rested fairly and squarely on the electorate in which Protestants outnumbered Roman Catholics by two to one. The people of Northern Ireland were divided three ways. There was, first, the most striking and emotive religious division, a relic of the antiquated politics of seventeenth-century Europe. There was the division between those who wanted the unification of Ireland, those who opposed it and those who felt no urgent concern about it; and finally there was the division between bosses and workers, rich and poor. These divisions overlapped and the overlapping made the province's politics. The bosses were all Protestants but not all the Protestants were bosses. The partisans of a united Ireland were all Roman Catholics but not all Roman Catholics wanted Ireland united; or not immediately; or not by force. The aim of the dominant class – part of a majority in religious terms but a minority in socio-economic terms – was to remain in control, making such reformist concessions as calculation might enjoin (as to which opinions would differ). The aims of the opposition, and so their tactics, varied and in 1969 the IRA (descendants of the Irish Republican Army formed to evict the English from Ireland) split. The larger group, adopting a Marxist interpretation of the situation, aimed to enlarge its base among the deprived Roman Catholic minority by enlisting the support of the poorer Protestants; this group put socialism first and abandoned violence in favour of propaganda. The other group, called the Provisional IRA, maintained the traditional policy of achieving a united Ireland by the eviction of the English (who had conveniently returned) by the traditional weapon of violence. Their interpretation of the situation was not class conflict but national war. English aims, finally, were negative. The English had lost all will to remain in any part of Ireland and regarded a united Ireland as a natural but probably remote eventuality. They felt an obligation to stand by the established order in Northern Ireland but both Conservative and Labour governments saw the need to push the provincial oligarchy into civil and political reforms, as a matter of expediency and as a matter of justice. Both believed, or acted as though they believed, that no more than this was necessary, a delusion from which they should have been disabused by the events of 1969–72.

These were the last years of the old order and in them the province had three prime ministers. Disorders, particularly on historic or religious festivals, were a normal feature of political life but not normally lethal. In 1966 disorder had been aggravated by a spate of killings by the newly formed (Protestant) Ulster Volunteer Force, but the authorities regained control until in 1969 political murder reappeared. In that and the next year the number of victims was small (thirteen and twenty respectively) but they sufficed to induce the British government to send troops. This seemingly extreme reaction was an aspect of the peculiar dilemma of the province. The local forces of law and order – the Royal Ulster Constabulary supplemented by the B-Special Constables – were composed of Protestants and were regarded by Roman Catholics as instruments of the Protestant sectarian supremacy. Their use to suppress disorders, even their continued existence, were incompatible with a policy of recognizing and rectifying Roman Catholic grievances. Consequently some other force had to be imported. Conversely the dissolution of the B-Specials and the disarming of the RUC, on which the British government insisted in 1970, intensified Protestant apprehensions for their own fate and reinforced their intransigence.

Having intervened thus far the English, anxious to retire again as soon as possible, pressed the provincial executive to introduce reforms to satisfy those among the Roman Catholics who were agitating for civil rights. Successive prime ministers, Terence O'Neill and James Chichester-Clark, were willing in principle but inhibited by their own supporters who regarded reforms as a prelude to further concessions leading to the unification of Ireland with dire consequences for the plight of Protestants and the economy of the northern counties. The hold of such leaders over the Protestant majority was further weakened by the emergence of new leaders whether, like Ian Paisley, eloquent anti-papalists of a kind no longer found outside Northern Ireland or, like William Craig, protagonists of the right of the majority to have its way and fight for it. Nevertheless a number of reforms were enacted. Unhappily they were years too late. They divided Protestants and no longer satisfied Roman Catholics whose attention was being diverted from civil rights to sectarianism by the Paisleyites on the one hand and the Provisionals on the other. Killings multiplied (173 in 1971) and in August a new prime minister, Brian Faulkner, resorted to detention and internment without trial. In one night 342 persons were arrested. A number of them were clearly the wrong persons. More important, not one of them was a Protestant. This was not surprising since the object of the operation was to break the IRA.

But the operation had the opposite effect. It strengthened the Provisionals. It swung Roman Catholic opinion, which had at first welcomed British troops as protection against Protestant militants, over to the IRA and forced the official IRA to join the Provisionals in denouncing the British government, without whose endorsement Faulkner could not have acted. Stories of brutality and torture by the English, subsequently endorsed by the European Commission on Human Rights, added fuel to the flames. The Protestants were both emboldened and alarmed, a fateful combination: emboldened because Faulkner had not ventured to intern even the most militant UVF leaders and alarmed because they felt denuded in the face of increasing IRA violence and the emasculation of their own means of securing law and order. A new Protestant self-help force appeared, the Ulster Defence Association, as a counterpart to the Provisionals. The provincial executive became ineffective and in March 1972 it was suspended. The British government assumed direct responsibility.

Direct rule from Westminster involved Britain in direct confrontation with the opposition and the opposition now was not the Roman Catholic parties or civil rights movement but the Provisional IRA. Nevertheless the Heath government set to work to find a constitutional answer to Northern Ireland's problems. The policy had two pillars and they were incompatible. The one was power-sharing, that is to say an insistence on Roman Catholic participation in government at all levels including a restored provincial executive which was to be permanently a coalition and, secondly, democratic endorsement by the province's electors. By 1972 the Protestant majority of the electorate was prepared to endorse no such thing. Protestants as a whole were justly enraged by the murderous activities of the Provisionals, and Protestant militants took to killing twice as many civilians as the Provisionals (who directed their fire more particularly at the British troops). Thus the British government's policy, enshrined in a White Paper of March 1973 and apparently triumphant at a conference at Sunningdale in December, was for a second time foredoomed by unreality, and the addition at Sunningdale of a gesture towards unification by the creation of a Council of Ireland (north and south) only made its rejection doubly certain. The British general election, unexpectedly called by Heath in February 1974, gave the electors in Northern Ireland a chance to show their mind and they decisively rejected the Sunningdale scheme and made it unworkable. The restored executive survived for a while but was brought down in May by Protestant demonstrations and a general strike against power-sharing, leading to the declaration of a state of emergency. London's answers were to fly in more troops and resume in May direct rule: the two things it least wanted to do.

From the winter of 1972–73 both sides within the province had produced groups which were trying to reach out to one another but they were too tentative and submerged to be much heard amid the clash of arms and rhetoric. Truces were arranged but were imperfect and short. Horrors multiplied but produced for the time being more horrors rather than revulsion. The English put a brave face on their helplessness and justified their presence by predicting, with some superficial plausibility, a blood bath if they were to leave. That they would leave one day was obvious to all but themselves: a repetition of the blindness of the French to the realities of their tenure of Algeria. That they should do so sooner rather than later was an argument which the larger part of them was emotionally unprepared to entertain. In 1980 two new prime ministers, Margaret Thatcher and Charles Haughey, were trying to devise a way round the blockage created by the claim of the Protestants of Northern Ireland – and accepted by all British governments – that, being a demographic majority within the province, they had a democratic right to veto constitutional change and, to that extent, to regulate the relationship between Britain and Ireland. Discussions continued after a switch in Dublin from Haughey to Garret Fitzgerald but the two governments were far apart, not because of divergent attitudes to violence but because of their presuppositions. Dublin saw no end to the troubles without significant political change; it did not seek immediate or even early change but the various changes which it advocated at one time or another all pointed in that direction. Thatcher, on the other hand, believed that the first task was the conquest of violence by force and her readiness to consider change, even in the long term, was strictly circumscribed by her view – familiar from the Falklands, although less inflexible in Gibraltar and discarded in Hong Kong – that British policies must be subordinated to the wishes of the majority of the people of the territory concerned. When in 1984 the New Ireland Forum, an association of Irish republic parties, proffered a series of possible formulas for political manœuvre pointing towards unification or a condominium in the north, Thatcher dismissed them with marked asperity. Nevertheless in 1985 she and Fitzgerald agreed by the Hillsborough or Anglo–Irish agreement to establish a standing joint body or 'ministerial conference'. The immediate practical purpose of this agreement was to improve police co-operation and border control. Its larger purpose was to marginalize the IRA. The British government, looking to Dublin for help on the first count, was willing to allow the Republic to become associated with the affairs of the province. Irish governments felt constrained to co-operate with the British to some degree since the *status quo* was, from the Republic's point of view, less hazardous than the alternatives: either, on the one hand, war in the north leading to victory for the Protestants or the extreme right; or, on the other hand, a union which would saddle the Republic with a million Protestant dissidents and bankrupt it. The agreement carried, however, a price for both parties. Revelations of serious miscarriage of justice in British courts, which neither Fitzgerald nor Haughey (who returned to power in 1987) could easily overlook, made the agreement peculiarly and unexpectedly uneasy for the Irish. On the British side the agreement entailed political stagnation in the province and an end to attempts to return it to parliamentary rule so long as the Unionist (Protestant) parties made discussions on devolution conditional on the abrogation of the agreement. The Unionist leaders, James Molyneux and Ian Paisley, profoundly hostile to Dublin's involvement in the province's affairs in any shape or to any degree, believed that they might nullify the agreement by non-cooperation with the British Secretary of State. The British government, although it was as much determined as the Unionists to keep the province in the United Kingdom, never affirmed this resolution convincingly, and although the agreement provided that the 'status of Northern Ireland' would not be altered without the assent of a majority in the province, the Unionists retorted by pointing to the article in the Irish constitution which described the whole island as the territory of a single nation – a provision which had been interpreted by the Supreme Court in Dublin as laying upon the Irish government a duty to re-integrate Ireland. To Unionists the British government had been hypocritical when it signed the Anglo–Irish agreement without securing, or even asking for, the abrogation of this article in the Irish constitution. One effect therefore of the agreement was to marginalize not the IRA but the Unionist parties. These, however, were mistaken in their belief that they could wreck the agreement, since the British refused even temporarily to suspend its more obnoxious manifestations (joint conferences of ministers and officials). The agreement achieved little by way of policing the border which could not have been achieved without the agreement. It failed to stop or reduce the murderous activities of the IRA in Ireland or in England, and it froze – at least for a number of years – attempts to bring direct rule to an end. The IRA's campaign to evict the English by force – a campaign which included an attempt to kill Thatcher and other ministers at Brighton in 1984 and intensified violence with imported weapons and explosives from 1988, and which was met by British attempts to pick off and kill leading IRA activists – kept the conflict alive but with scant prospect of the success sought by the IRA. Despite its name the IRA was not an army and it could not dislodge the British army which needed to send to Ireland no more than 15–20,000 troops (briefly increased to some 30,000 for a special operation in 1972).

B   The Basques

The Basques are a people of sharp self-consciousness and obscure origins. They have preserved a cultural identity based on an unaffiliated language and romantic historical claims. Straddling the occidental Pyrenees they have been acquiescent in France but effervescent in Spain. Prosperity in Spain's Basque provinces in the 1960s led, as it did in the 1890s, to an influx of non-Basque workers which split local discontent between nationalist separatism and a workers' movement. After violence in the late sixties, sixteen persons, mostly from the middle class and some of them priests, were put on trial in 1970 before a military court in Burgos charged with murder, bombings, illegal possession of arms and illicit propaganda. The trial lasted several years and gave a boost to the Basque separatist movement, ETA, which in 1973 carried its war into the Spanish capital and there assassinated Franco's prime minister, Admiral Carrero Blanco. After Franco's death the new régime in Madrid offered the Basques as much autonomy as it dared and so divided ETA between acceptors and rejectors. But in spite of some police successes against ETA leaders and police brutality in what amounted to civil war in the eighties both ETA tendencies survived.

C   Cyprus

In 1878 Disraeli, prompted by British military opinion, contemplated the seizure of Cyprus but contrived to secure it by diplomacy. On the eve of the Congress of Berlin he entered into an agreement with the Turks to defend their empire against Russia upon being permitted to occupy Cyprus which, however much the Turks might regard it as an anti-Russian base, was for the British of those days the key to western Asia. Britain, contemplating the collapse of the Ottoman empire or alternatively the substitution of German for British influence at the Sublime Porte, was on the look-out for vantage points in the eastern Mediterranean. The occupation of Cyprus in 1878 was followed a few years later by the occupation of Egypt. The British remained in both for the best part of three generations.

Cyprus was annexed by Britain in 1914 on the declaration of war between Britain and Turkey, and British sovereignty was recognized by Turkey by the treaty of Lausanne in 1923. Between the wars British rule was challenged by the partisans of *enosis* or union with Greece but was never seriously threatened. For the British Cyprus was a colony which could gradually be granted the degree of self-government compatible with its usefulness as a staging-post and a base in the British imperial scheme of things. For the Greek section of the population, however, the British themselves and their programme of limited democratic development were simply obstacles to a more natural scheme of things in which all Greeks were being brought together in the single nation state which had been inaugurated by the Greek revolt against the Turks in 1821. The Turkish minority was a spectator of Anglo–Greek conflict, sometimes worried and sometimes not. At the end of the Second World War the British estimate of the value of Cyprus rose as a result of the retreat from Palestine and the weakening of the British position in Egypt. The British assumed therefore that they would and should stay in Cyprus. The Greek Cypriots assumed the opposite. They expected a reward for their loyalty to Britain during the war and they regarded the British withdrawal from Egypt as a step which should logically entail a withdrawal from Cyprus and not a reinforcement of British rule there. Discussions for a constitutional advance towards limited self-government were abortive. To the Greeks they were irrelevant.

In 1946 the exiled bishop of Kyrenia returned to the island and in 1950, at the age of 37, he was elected to the archiepiscopal throne of the autocephalous church of Cyprus, which had been vacant during the years 1937–47. He took the regnal name of Makarios III, and he became at the same time the ethnarch or national leader of the Greek community. Makarios was therefore both the head of one of the most venerable of the churches within the Orthodox communion (it had been founded by the Cypriot apostle Barnabas) and also the leader of a modern nationalist movement which had fought the Turks for a century and a half and was now to fight both Turks and British on this last remaining battlefield. He and his fellow enotists considered that the kingdom of Greece had a sacred duty to support them, a belief shared by very many – probably most – Greeks outside Cyprus but embarrassing nevertheless to Greek governments which were reluctant to impair their good relations with Britain and even had reasons for co-operation with the traditional Turkish enemy after the admission of both Greece and Turkey to Nato. In 1950 a plebiscite organized by the church returned the inevitable (but not, as the British deludedly imagined, faked) response in favour of *enosis*; the Greek prime minister, General Plastiras, equally inevitably responded to it in a tone of mixed encouragement and moderation. About the Greekness of Cyprus no Greek bothered to think twice. Four Cypriots in five were Greek by race, tongue and religion, and called themselves Greeks. Whether they supported the left-wing party AKEL or the right-wing KEK they shared a common nationalism, for which they were soon to fight together in the insurrectionary movement of EOKA.

The Turkish section of the population (18 per cent) was no less alive to the Greekness of the island but it naturally drew opposite conclusions from the same facts. Although the government had passed from Turks to British, the Turks knew that they remained the principal and hereditary enemies of the Greeks, and they feared Greek rule. These fears may not have been great in the first postwar years, since the Greek record in relation to Turkish minorities was no bad one, but they were latent fears which could easily be inflamed. The Turkish state, as opposed to the Turks of Cyprus, also feared *enosis* because Cyprus was only 64 km from the Turkish coast, because post-war Greece seemed for a short while to be exposed to communism, and because Greece might still cherish the ambition to conquer Constantinople and the coasts of Asia Minor (which it had tried unsuccessfully to do immediately after the end of the First World War). Turkish governments showed, however, little inclination to intervene in Cypriot affairs until encouraged to do so by Britain.

In 1951 the Greek government sought a way of satisfying its Cypriot compatriots and its British allies by offering Britain bases in Cyprus – and also in Greece itself – in return for *enosis*, but Eden was not interested in a solution which would have been more attractive to Britain than the eventual settlement of 1959 and could have saved much bloodshed. In 1953 Eden gravely exacerbated the situation by declaring that there was no question of a British withdrawal. This statement forced Greeks to decide between an indefinite acceptance of the existing position and a resort to violence to change it. At first Makarios tried an intermediate course. In 1954 he went to Athens to try to get the Greek government to raise the Cypriot question at the UN. Eden repeated that no discussion was possible; a junior British minister with a lamentable sense of history and a notable lack of caution declared that Cyprus would 'never' be fully independent; and the colonial secretary affronted the Greek government by advancing as an extra reason for the maintenance of British rule the argument that Greece was too unstable to be allowed safely to extend its sway to Cyprus. The Greek government then raised the question of self-determination for Cyprus at the UN but half-heartedly and without pressing the case, which was shelved. The enotists, disappointed by this effort, reverted to the local scene and organized demonstrations which evoked an excessive British counter-reaction (including measures against schoolchildren). The British in Nicosia and London believed that the *enosis* movement was a bubble blown in their faces by a small and unrepresentative group of irresponsible agitators who had succeeded in cowing the bulk of a law-abiding and pro-British population. This was, at the very least, a serious exaggeration, just as the British appreciation of the value of Cyprus as a base was also seriously mistaken: Cyprus, though valuable as a command headquarters (HQ Middle East Land and Air Forces was transferred there in 1954)˙ and as an air staging point, was a poor country with meagre resources, a hostile population, no adequate naval base (Famagusta being too shallow) and a manifest vulnerability to Russian nuclear attack. The Suez War of 1956 proved that it had some value for the Royal Air Force but no other.

In 1955 Eden and his foreign secretary Harold Macmillan decided to fortify the British position in Cyprus by bringing the Turkish government officially into the matter. The Greek and Turkish governments were invited to a conference in London. The result was the collapse of the Greco–Turkish alliance. In Turkey hideous atrocities were perpetrated against Greek residents, and Greece boycotted Balkan Pact meetings and Nato exercises.

In Cyprus the governor and the archbishop met for the first time, and a British colonial secretary appeared in the island also for the first time. At the end of the year the governor was replaced by Sir John Harding, a field-marshal and former Chief of the Imperial General Staff. The policy entrusted to him was to separate the ethnarch-archbishop from the insurrectionary movement which had come into the open in 1954, to negotiate with the one and to extirpate the other. This policy, which was pursued until the end of 1957, was a total failure because it was based on false premises and poor information and because, at one decisive point, it was abandoned by the British government. The Harding–Makarios negotiations were proceeding early in 1956 towards a promising conclusion when the British government intervened and decreed the deportation of the archbishop to the Seychelles. Eden appeared to have been swayed at this juncture by pressure from the right wing of the Conservative Party, by the dismissal of General Glubb by the king of Jordan (which Eden interpreted as a deliberate slight to his government), and by the failure to manoeuvre Jordan into his prized creation, the Baghdad Pact. These rubs roused in him the assertiveness of a weak man and he resolved to teach his enemies a lesson, foremost among them Makarios and Nasser. But Makarios was released in the following year, much to the annoyance of the Turks and without any compensating advantage since the archbishop refused to return to Cyprus and took up residence in Athens.

The British attempt to quell the insurrection was equally unsuccessful. This revolt was led by Colonal Grivas, an officer of the Greek army and a Cypriot by birth who set himself to evict the British by a combination of military skill, faith and ruthlessness. Grivas had fought on the same side as the British in two wars and was outraged to discover at the end of the second that, despite the UN Charter and frequent British promises in the past, Britain had no intention of allowing the Cypriots to choose how and by whom they should be governed. Like Cavour after the Crimean War Grivas took the view that his compatriots had paid for self-determination with their blood, and when he saw that the British view was different, he set about shedding more blood. He decided, according to his own account, to resort to violence in 1951 but he laid his plans with considerable professional care, carried out an extensive and open reconnaissance of the terrain and waited until 1954 before making his first purchase of arms and setting up a headquarters in a suburb of Nicosia inhabited chiefly by British families. He launched his revolt in April 1955, survived a drive against him at the time of Makarios's deportation in March 1956 and immediately struck back. His main weapons were bushcraft, discipline and terrorism, his victims frequently Greek civilians, his armoury and front-line manpower always small. He provoked the British into retaliatory measures which failed – collective fines on villages, high but ineffective bribes, hangings and torture. He defeated the policy which Harding had been sent to implement.

In the course of the year in which Makarios was in the Seychelles and the

Harding–Grivas duel was taking place, the first Greco–Turkish riots also occurred and the British government began, although unintentionally, to transfer the initiative from London to Ankara and Athens. During 1956 Eden produced a plan by which Cyprus would be allowed self-determination after ten years of self-government, but instead of applying his scheme he submitted it for approval to the Turkish and Greek governments and accompanied it with a proposal for a tripartite treaty. The Turkish government rejected the plan and this rejection both killed it and gave Turkey a new commanding position. Later in the same year new constitutional proposals, elaborated by an eminent British judge, Lord Radcliffe, were in the same way submitted to the Turkish and Greek governments. The Radcliffe plan rejected self-determination and mentioned partition. It was accordingly rejected by the Greeks, while Turkey was emboldened to suggest that either half of Cyprus or the whole of it should be annexed to Turkey. The Greeks, thoroughly alarmed, threatened to leave the western camp. In 1957 General Ismay, the secretary-general of Nato, offered to mediate, but although the Turks were willing the Greeks were not. The Turks believed that a majority of the members of Nato were sympathetic to Turkey; the Greeks believed that their cause would prevail in the UN but not in Nato. There was deadlock internationally and continuing disorder and murder locally. The government of Harold Macmillan reviewed Eden's Cyprus policy and, faced with the threat to Nato's eastern flank which had been created by it, decided that Britain no longer needed to be sovereign in the whole of Cyprus. Sovereign bases would do and the Greek and Turkish governments must be brought to accept independence for the rest of the island. For Turkey independence was acceptable, since it automatically excluded enosis. Upon Greece independence might be forced, since Greece abominated partition and was afraid that in the absence of a settlement Greeks in Istanbul and other parts of Turkey would be stripped of their property and either killed or expelled.

In December 1957 Harding was replaced by Sir Hugh Foot who produced a new plan: self-government as a colony for a period followed by self-determination, with the proviso that *enosis* would need Turkish approval. The mention of *enosis* was too much for the Turks and demonstrations were organized in Ankara when Selwyn Lloyd (now foreign secretary) and Foot visited that capital. The Foot plan disappeared. It was succeeded by the Macmillan plan which was a further step away from undiluted British rule. Macmillan proposed to introduce representatives of the Greek and Turkish governments alongside the British governor and to create a mixed cabinet and separate Greek Cypriot and Turkish Cypriot local administrations. The last provision was unacceptable both to Makarios and to the Greek prime minister, Constantine Karamanlis. Their rejection of it led to fresh riots in Cyprus in which the Turks seemed to be applying pressure in order to enforce acceptance of the Macmillan plan. The revolution in Baghdad in July 1958 may have inclined the British government, threatened with the loss of its Iraqi ally and the collapse of the Baghdad Pact, to lean further to the Turkish side in Cyprus, and Macmillan set out on a tour in the course of which he slightly modified his plan, failed to reconcile Makarios or Karamanlis to it, but resolved to apply it nonetheless. Violence increased horribly.

The spreading communal hatred shocked and alarmed the Greek and Turkish governments into an accord. After exploratory contacts at the UN and Nato between their foreign ministers they conferred together in Zürich in February 1959 and announced that they had agreed that Cyprus should be independent. Britain would be accorded sovereign rights in certain areas which would be British military bases. The new state would have a Greek president, a Turkish vice-president with a veto in certain matters, and a cabinet of seven Greeks and three Turks; this 7–3 proportion would be repeated right down the administrative ladder. The Greek and Turkish states would station small armies of 950 and 600 men respectively in Cyprus. This scheme was accepted with the greatest reluctance by Makarios, who declared it unworkable. He was, however, threatened with abandonment by the Greek government and on 1 March 1959 he returned at last to Cyprus. Grivas, infuriated by the politicians' betrayal of the cause of *enosis*, was fêted, promoted and sent back to Athens. Instead of driving the British out and making Cyprus part of Greece, his campaign had ended with the British still in possession of sovereign bases and Cyprus still not part of the Greek kingdom. Cyprus became independent in August 1960, a member of the UN the following month and a somewhat strange member of the Commonwealth in 1961.

The Zürich settlement was an attempt by frightened men to prevent the situation from getting completely out of control. That was its one merit. But Makarios was right in regarding the constitution as unworkable. The Turkish Cypriots were entitled to 30 per cent of the posts in the administration, although they did not have the men to fill so many posts. Each of the five principal towns was to have two separate municipal bodies, though this concession to communal distrust produced such absurdities in practice that it was never implemented. Discussions for an improved system broke down and when the Turkish leaders in the island proposed the extension of the existing arrangements for a year, the Greek majority in parliament rejected the proposal. The constitutional court, upon being appealed to, pronounced both the Greek and Turkish cases to be wrong, and in December 1963 Makarios made proposals which were meant to force the Turks into further discussions but were taken by them to be a breach of the constitution and an attack on their safeguards. Serious fighting developed and attempts by leaders on both sides to arrange and enforce cease-fires broke down. Moreover the progenitors of the Zürich agreement had by now passed from the scene. Both the Karamanlis government in Athens and the Menderes government in Ankara had fallen. The former had been replaced by a government under George Papandreou which began its existence without a parliamentary majority, while in Turkey a military coup had overthrown the parliamentary system in May 1960, indicted over 400 people and executed fifteen of them including Menderes himself. General Gürsel, who was successively provisional head of state and then in October 1961 president, installed a coalition government, but the new military régime was assailed by an abortive coup from within its own ranks in May 1963 and by the recrudescence of Menderes's Democratic Party under the new name of the Justice Party. In December 1963, when fighting broke out again in Cyprus, the veteran Ismet Inönü had just resigned the premiership and been persuaded to retain it, albeit with a majority in parliament of only four.

Some 200 Turks were killed in this new bout. Turkish jet aircraft flew menacingly over Nicosia, a Turkish naval invasion was thwarted by the American Sixth Fleet prowling in the vicinity, the Greek and Turkish forces in

Cyprus took up hostile battle positions, and the British colonial secretary, Duncan Sandys, abandoned his Christmas holiday to fly overnight to Cyprus. After four years of independence Cyprus had brought Greece and Turkey to the verge of war.

Britain tried at first to transfer the Cyprus problem to Nato. The Greek and Turkish governments were willing to accept Nato intervention but Makarios was not; nor were other members of Nato anxious to become embroiled. In February a second Turkish invasion threat was unostentatiously foiled by the American fleet and Britain accepted the need to invoke the UN. The raising of a UN force coincided with a third invasion scare, but by mid-March the Canadian advance party of a UN force reached Cyprus. It was followed by units from Eire, Sweden, Denmark and Finland which, together with British units transferred to UN command, constituted a force of 7,000 under the Indian General Gyani and subsequently under his compatriot General Thimayya and, after his death in 1966, the Finnish General A. E. Martola. This force gradually asserted control, although occasional outbursts continued to occur – and led to occasional reprisals against the Greeks in Istanbul.

In addition to the peace force the UN secretary-general appointed a mediator to seek a political solution, but neither of two incumbents of this office was able to find a solution acceptable to both sides. The United States, alarmed by the consequences of a Greco–Turkish conflict, also took a hand through the former secretary of state Dean Acheson who produced a scheme for *enosis*, excluding an area in north-eastern Cyprus which would go to Turkey. The Turks thereupon asked for a larger area and so converted the plan into partition in a new form. Acheson then revised his plan and proposed that the north-eastern area should merely be leased to Turkey for twenty to twenty-five years. At this point the plan became unacceptable to everybody and the Turks, already disappointed in their hopes of Nato and frustrated by the American fleet, turned tentatively towards the Russians (who may at this time have sensed a possibility of undermining the entire Baghdad Pact since Pakistan was also disappointed by the United States and Iran was internally unstable and internationally plastic). Early in 1965 the UN mediator proposed a demilitarized independent Cyprus, debarred from *enosis*, in which the Turkish minority would be protected by a UN guarantee and a resident UN commissioner. A new government in Ankara rejected the idea.

With the UN force preventing a resumption of civil war, the basic political fact reasserted itself: namely that Turkey, Cyprus's nearest neighbour and a country with three times the population of Greece, was capable of preventing *enosis* but was not capable of achieving the reconquest of the island. Hence the independent status of Cyprus, an independence resulting from a balance of external forces which was countered by an opposite balance of internal forces. Externally power lay with the Turkish state and not with the Greek state; internally power lay with the Greek community and not with the Turkish community. The power of the Greek community was limited by the power of the Turkish state, and the power of the Turkish state was limited by forces which were not native to the area itself. Cyprus therefore was an international problem-child destined, so long as these circumstances prevailed, to independence tempered by ungovernability. The UN stopped the killing but could not resolve the underlying dispute. Two UN mediators tried but failed, whereupon the Turkish and Greek governments insisted on assuming the role but did very little about it.

Year after year, and twice in each year, the mandate of the peacekeeping force was renewed by the UN who feared the consequences of saving money by removing it. Talks between the two communities were started and stopped more than once. Any whiff of *enosis* from the Greek side was met with Turkish talk of double *enosis*, a new name for partition and the attachment of northern Cyprus to the Turkish state. In 1971 Grivas was back in Nicosia. The only new element in the situation was the worsening relations between Makarios and the military junta which had seized control of Greece in 1967. The junta supported Grivas's heirs, now called EOKA B, against Makarios whom they regarded as a troublesome red priest. They tried to force him to change his government (and did succeed in making him remove his foreign minister) and they incited his fellow bishops to bring charges of simony against him for combining the presidential and archiepiscopal offices. They were more and more anxious to score a popular victory by forcing the pace in Cyprus in order to be able to pose as Greek patriots who had united Cyprus with the Greek heartlands. But Makarios was re-elected president in 1973 without opposition, routed the bishops and had them unfrocked for good measure, and struck back at Athens in 1974 by demanding the recall from Cyprus of the officers of the Cypriot National Guard who were doing the junta's bidding and subverting rather than protecting the Cypriot state. At this point, 15 July, the junta acted. Makarios, who had already survived at least one attempt on his life, was attacked in his palace by the National Guard. He escaped in a helicopter with British help and was flown to England. The insurgents proclaimed Nikos Samson president in his place, a choice as unwise as it was unsuitable, as Samson had been a notorious EOKA gunman and had to resign at the end of a week.

The independence and integrity of Cyprus had been guaranteed by Greece, Turkey and Britain. Greece was in the process of destroying both. Turkey saw in Greece's foolhardy action an opportunity to intervene and occupy at least a part of the island. Britain was unwilling to do anything, partly because of the difficulty of finding reinforcements for its units in the British bases but more emphatically because intervening meant intervening against Turkey and so on the side of the Athens junta and the equally unattractive Samson. Consequently Turkey invaded Cyprus five days after the coup against Makarios. A cease-fire was imposed two days later and the next day the junta in Athens collapsed.

The three guarantors met at Geneva. Turkey's attitude was threatening but realistic: either there must be a new constitution acceptable to Turkey or Cyprus would remain *de facto* partitioned. The constitution proposed was a loose confederation not far short of independence for the components, and the proposal was accompanied by an ultimatum. The talks were broken off. The Turks attacked again, occupied 40 per cent of the island in two days and turned 200,000 Greeks into homeless refugees. The American ambassador in Nicosia was murdered by Greeks who took American inaction to betoken sympathy for or even complicity with Turkey. The British too were criticized violently in Cyprus and in Greece for not doing more, as a guarantor, to help Cyprus escape the plight brought upon it by a Greek government. Makarios returned at the end of the year. Cyprus was in effect partitioned but nobody was prepared to say so and its affairs were therefore back to inter-community talks, hampered by the emotions of war, charges and counter-charges of atrocities, the plight of refugees, economic disruption and the unreality of any attempt to restore the integrity and independence of Cyprus with a Turkish army in control of a large part of it. Makarios, who died in 1977, was succeeded by Spyros Kiprianou.

Both the UN, which tried to mediate from 1977, and the Greeks had tacitly to accept federalism as the basis for any possible settlement. In discussions between the leaders of the two communities within Cyprus, and between the Greek and Turkish governments, the Greeks were intent on securing a strong federal centre together with a substantial Turkish withdrawal from the territories which they had conquered. At the end of 1983, however, the Turks forced the pace by declaring the northern part of the island independent – partition in all but name. The UN secretary-general, Javier Perez de Cueller, who had considerable personal knowledge of Cypriot affairs, contrived to persuade leaders from both sides to discuss a loose federation: the Turks, in possession of 37 per cent of the territory, seemed willing to reduce their share to 29 per cent and to accept a Greek, not a rotating, presidency; the Greeks seemed willing to allot to the Turks 30 per cent of the seats in a lower and 50 per cent in a second chamber. Progress was, however, imperceptible. In 1986 the Turkish régime accepted a UN plan for reunification but the Greeks, hoping for better terms, countered with a different plan. Talks continued, punctuated in 1987 by the election of a new president of Cyprus, George Vassiliou, who promised progress towards agreement but could not make any.

PART THREE

THE MIDDLE EAST

In the seventh century A.D. the Arabs, united by a single tongue and a single faith, surged out of the Arabian peninsula and created an empire which stretched at its zenith from the Pyrenees, along North Africa, through what was later called the Middle East and deep into central Asia. The successors of Mahomet, or caliphs, failed to preserve the unity of this vast and increasingly polyglot realm but they imposed their religion on non-Arab peoples, so that in the twentieth century there were Muslims under Russian rule after there had ceased to be Arabs under the rule of other Europeans. This Arab empire lost first its unity and then its independence, and for something like 1,000 years Arabs were subject to Kurds, Turks, British and French. But they never lost the enormously powerful links of a common language and a common faith, and when they began to recover their independence these links served to revive and give substance to visions of a renewed unity. The collapse of the Ottoman empire in Asia in 1918 offered to its Arab subjects a prospect altogether different from that offered, by the more gradual withdrawal of the same empire in Europe, to the racially and linguistically divided Christians of the Balkans.

But in 1919 the Arabs were disappointed. The Ottoman empire was virtually partitioned between the British (who already held Egypt and Cyprus) and the French, and one effect of this Balkanization of the Middle East was to foster separate Arab particularisms (Syrian, Iraqi, Jordanian and so on) and dynastic feuds at the expense of Arab unity: the Arab world was more united under the Turks than without them. The new rulers from the west, lured by international politics and by oil back to the scene of their crusading adventures, became obstacles both to Arab unity and to Arab independence, not least because of the deadening effects of their overwhelming power on the Arab will to struggle for these aspirations; a second world war was needed to get the westerners out. French rule was eliminated by the British when the French authorities in Syria and Lebanon declared for Vichy; British rule on the other hand was maintained and even temporarily strengthened in spite of powerful anti-British currents in Egypt and an attempted pro-German coup in Iraq in 1941 by Rashid Ali el-Gailani. The veiled occupation established in neighbouring Iran by Britain and the USSR did not immediately affront the Arabs, and when the war ended the British were therefore the sole surviving target of Arab nationalism, whose temper was sharpened not only by this concentration of one enemy but also by Britain's administration of the mandate over Palestine where, in consequence of Britain's endorsement in 1917 of the Zionist aim of a Jewish National Home (the Balfour Declaration), a new non-Arab and non-Muslim community had gradually taken hold and was claiming the right to be not a home but a state.

Faced with this powerful and stubborn remnant of the imperialist centuries, and with the vigorous new threat of Zionism, the Arabs were exceptionally divided among themselves.

At the level of power monarchs, Saudi and Hashemite were divided by inherited rivalries; more important, there was a rift between an old order, largely monarchical and traditionalist in its views on society and religion, and a new order which, with its beginnings in Arab intellectual movements of the nineteenth century, aspired to modernize religious and political thought and forms and to reduce the huge differences between the style of living of the very rich and the very poor. This revaluation inevitably produced within the Arab world internal conflicts and strains which enfeebled the Arab capacity to remove the British or defeat the Jews. The British were able to leave in their own time, which was slow; and the Jews established their state of Israel.

The British had struggled for a generation to reconcile their pledges to the Jews and to the Arabs (the latter reinforced by Britain's desire to be on good terms with the oil-producing Arab states and to retain bases in the Arab world), but the two were irreconcilable and the attempt to find an accommodation passed imperceptibly into a hand-to-mouth evasion of the most urgent current complications until the whole responsibility of the mandate was abandoned in 1948. At one point Britain tried partition. The Peel Commission proposed (1937) a tripartite division into an Arab and a Jewish state, leaving Britain with a mandate over a reduced area which would include the holy places of Jerusalem and Bethlehem with access to the Mediterranean. But upon closer inspection this scheme proved impracticable and Britain, forced by the approach of war in Europe to choose between the two sides, chose the Arabs and undertook, in the White Paper of 1939, to keep the Jewish element in the population of Palestine to one-third of the whole (it had risen since 1919 from 10 to nearly 30 per cent) and so to stop Jewish immigration after a further 75,000 Jews had been admitted. Thus Hitler cast upon Britain the odium of refusing asylum to Germany's persecuted Jewry because the imminence of a war against Germany made Britain even more sensitive to the need for Arab friendships: grand strategy, as well as oil strategy, dictated the terms of the White Paper.

8.1 The Middle East

After the 1939 White Paper Zionists had switched their main effort from Britain to the United States, abandoning their hope of achieving their aims by persuasion in London in favour of an actively anti-British policy to be financed (after the war) with American money. During the war the political effectiveness of Zionism was greatly enhanced in the United States and the Zionist cause was embraced by the two most

8.2   Israel and its neighbours

powerful Americans of the forties, Franklin D. Roosevelt and Harry S
Truman. At the same time other Americans were beginning to
experience the old lures of oil and strategy, with the result that the
United States slid, half unsuspectingly and more than half unwillingly,
into the same sort of position as Britain. Initially, and because of
Zionism, this American involvement set the United States and Britain
in opposition to each other. The prime American concern was to
persuade Britain to admit Jews to Palestine as generously and quickly as
possible. On the assumption, roughly verifiable, that some 100,000
Jews had survived the Nazi abomination the United States adopted

David Ben-Gurion's plea, made in August 1945, for the issue of that number of entry permits. Both Churchill and Attlee, themselves men of generous disposition and proven sympathies for the Zionist cause, wished to do something for the unhappy survivors and hoped, not incompatibly, to secure at the same time American support for British policies in the Middle East as a whole. But this co-operation was not to be had. The Americans wanted to help the Jews without becoming entangled in British positions of a suspiciously imperialist nature (the British only became respectable allies in these parts in American eyes in terms of a Cold War threat from the USSR); they failed to appreciate the full extent of Britain's difficulties in Palestine in terms of the surrender of power in India in 1947 and the challenge to the western position in Berlin in 1948; and they accepted uncritically the charges of anti-Semitism which were thrown at the new British foreign secretary, Ernest Bevin, and which that statesman did not a little himself to promote.

The campaign to get Britain to issue the 100,000 entry permits was regarded in London as an extravaganza based on irresponsibility and ignorance and inspired by ulterior motives. American support for the campaign was resented, especially when the Jews took to terrorism in Palestine, as a section of them did immediately after the end of the war. Nevertheless the British government opted for a joint Anglo–American approach to the problem, and in October 1945 a committee of six Britons and six Americans set off to take soundings in Palestine, five Arab states and the European camps where the survivors of Nazism were waiting. Its report, published in April 1946, endorsed the estimate of 100,000 homeless Jews in Europe and the plea for their immediate admission to Palestine; it also rejected partition, recommended the continuance of the British mandate and – besides urging massive Jewish immigration – proposed the abolition of existing limitations on the purchase of land by Jews. The committee had hoped to produce an acceptable package deal, but Truman endorsed only the plea for 100,000 entry permits and the Arabs and the British government rejected the proposals as a whole. The appearance of the committee's report coincided with a Jewish terrorist attack in Tel Aviv which seemed to have no other purpose but murder and which succeeded in killing seven persons. This attack provoked counter-terrorism from the British side, which indicated that the British nerve in Palestine, no less than British tempers in Whitehall, were beginning to break. While it was still widely supposed that Jewish atrocities were the independent work of special units (the Stern gang and Irgun Zvai Leumi) undertaken without the approval of the main Jewish defence force (Haganah) or established political bodies (the Jewish Agency and Zionist organizations), there was already evidence that the case was otherwise and that the British authorities were faced with a concerted nationalist attempt to coerce or remove them. The extent of the violence to be used was demonstrated in June 1946 when a part of the King David Hotel in Jerusalem was blown up and ninety-one persons were indiscriminately killed.

After the rejection by Britain of the report of the Anglo–American committee the idea of partition was revived. Ambassador Henry Grady for the United States and the British home secretary, Herbert Morrison, produced in July a plan for two autonomous but not sovereign provinces, and the issue of 100,000 permits a year after the establishment of this hybrid state. Truman rejected the plan and the British government next tried the expedient of a round table conference, but the Jews refused to engage in anything except bilateral discussions with the British. There was this time no American participation, and the repetition by Truman of his support for the 100,000 permits during his campaign for the presidency was not a help. Discussions nevertheless continued sporadically between September 1946 and February 1947. They were abortive. The realities of the situation were reflected by increasing terrorism and the execution by hanging of the young Jew, Dov Grüner, the first victim of British exasperation.

In February 1947 Britain announced that the problem, and possibly the territory too (though this was not clear), was to be transferred to the United Nations. In May a special session of the General Assembly created Unscop (United Nations Special Committee on Palestine) and its eleven members set off for Jerusalem. While they were there, and possibly because they were there, 4,554 refugees aboard the *Exodus 1947* arrived at Haifa after having been collected by the Jewish Agency at Sète in the south of France and furnished with travel documents for Colombia. These pawns in the Zionist game were refused permission to land by the British authorities and were shipped back to Sète whence, again refused permission to land, they were directed with a horrible insensitivity to a German port. In July the toll of innocent suffering was dramatically increased when two British sergeants were hanged by an Irgun band. Unable to solve their problem, or to keep order, or even to defend themselves, the British were now more than ready to go. When Unscop produced, by a majority, a new partition plan of ridiculous complexity (three Arab and three Jewish segments linked in a sort of economic union with Jerusalem under international trusteeship), they said they would do so.

The Unscop plan was adopted with modifications by the UN in November. It was accepted with misgiving by the Jews and rejected by the Arabs. Jewish acceptance was superficial and misleading: the Jews were willing to accept publicly the promise of a Jewish state whatever their reservations about its size and shape, but they did not accept the corollary of a Palestinian Arab state and entered into secret talks for the annexation of the designated Arab sections by the emir Abdullah of Transjordan. The prevention of a Palestinian state was a cornerstone of Israeli policy for a generation and more, beginning with the creation of the Israeli state. The UN plan, whatever its validity (the UN had no authority to make states), was quickly made irrelevant and the Jews won their state by conquest. Fighting began before the end of 1947 with attempts by the Jews to get control of the segments allotted to them. There were also disorders in Arab towns. The British were impotent and lost even the reputation for fairness which they regarded as one of their special contributions to public morality. On 11 December they declared that they would surrender the mandate on 15 May 1948. Fighting increased. The Jews managed to procure arms in substantial quantities, with which to meet the expected invasion by the regular armies of neighbouring Arab states. In April 1948 they contrived at Deir Yasin a massacre which set in train an exodus of refugees who were to constitute, with their as yet unborn progeny, one of the bitterest bones of contention between Arabs and Jews and one of the sorriest human spectacles of the times. By the end of the month 150,000 had fled, over half a million by the end of the year. Then and later Arab propaganda made the most of this story, while a telegram of regrets from Ben-Gurion to King Abdullah of Jordan passed and remained almost unnoticed.

The last British official left Palestine on 14 May 1948. The state of Israel was movingly proclaimed by Ben-Gurion who became its prime minister, embodiment and inspiration; Chaim Weizmann, the veteran leader of Zionism who enjoyed worldwide respect, became the first president despite the fact that, in the previous December, the twenty-second Zionist Congress at Basle had marked the passing of his influence and had even exposed him to some ruderies. Truman immediately recognized the new state and Stalin was not far behind. In its fledgling years Israel was more beholden to the USSR than the United States for practical help, but it quickly observed that the United States had more to offer in money and arms and from about 1950 alliance with the United States had become the sheet anchor of the new state. In these same years Israel formed a similarly enduring, if less crucial, alliance with Iran which provided asylum for Jews fleeing from Iraq in the late forties and recognized Israel in 1950. This alliance was strengthened in the ensuing decades by commercial ties and exchange of military intelligence and, surviving the fall of the shah, contributed to Khomeini's successful resistance to the Iraqi attack on Iran in 1980. Its cement was hostility to the Arabs which had been a persistent theme in Iran's history and became the determining factor in Israel's fight for survival. In 1948 five Arab states marched against Israel, but the promptness of their reaction was no index of their keenness for a fight or their effectiveness in it. The Syrians did little and the Lebanese less;

the Iraqis retired early and the Egyptians arrived late; the Jewish defence of Jerusalem, which thwarted the Jordanians, combined with the Arabs' incoherence to give Israel the victory. The UN intervened by appointing the Swedish Count Folke Bernadotte to mediate. He effected a truce which lasted from 11 June to 9 July and was followed by more fighting in which the Israelis were decisively victorious. Bernadotte was murdered on 17 September by the Stern gang; he was succeeded by a UN official, the American Ralph Bunche. The Israelis gained further successes in renewed fighting in October but by the end of the year the war was virtually over, Palestine and Jerusalem itself had been partitioned by the verdict of arms, and during the first half of 1949 armistices were effected between Israel and four of its assailants (Iraq being the absent fifth). In the second phase of the fighting the Israelis had secured their sovereign state by defeating the regular forces of Arab states as well as the Palestinian Arabs and they were ready to consolidate their gains. They wanted peace. But they could not get it. The Arabs, out of their deep humiliation and their just concern for the Arab refugees from Palestine, refused to recognize Israel's existence or make peace with it and continued the war by economic means – notably by closing the Suez Canal to Israeli shipping and to goods going to or from Israel. This action was condemned, fruitlessly, by the Security Council which also, equally fruitlessly, asserted that Israel should either readmit the refugees or compensate them. Since these refugees outnumbered the Jews in Palestine the Israelis argued with much plausibility that they could not be expected to readmit them so long as the Arab nations as a whole continued to proclaim their intention to eliminate the state of Israel. The Arabs themselves did little to integrate the refugees in their places of refuge since, politically, the most important point about a refugee was his refugee status and plight. From 700,000 in 1949 their numbers swelled by natural causes to over a million and a quarter.

The creation of the state of Israel was a most extraordinary political phenomenon. Israel came into existence as a result of the tenacious memories of a persecuted people whose misfortunes in various parts of the world had given them an intense addiction to the words of their holy books; as a result of atrocious crimes perpetrated against European Jewry in sight of Europe and the world; and as a result of the exertions of leading Jews who worked with vigour and intelligence to capture a piece of territory not their own, and who would probably have failed to do so if they had not believed that their end was one of those which justifies every means and had not enjoyed the advantages of working under a British umbrella. The state which they founded was as exceptional as its origins. By adopting the principle that the door to it must be open to all Jews everywhere, it became a mixture of tongues and cultures and unequal skills, held together by the unifying power of a Hebrew revival and by a community of race and of hope (though not of religion, since the Jewish religion meant little to many Israeli citizens). The Law of Return of 1950 gave all Jews the right to come to Israel. The Law of Citizenship of 1952, however, conferred on them Jewish, not Israeli, citizenship and Arabs in Israel were designated persons of Arab nationality, not Israeli citizens. These Arabs suffered certain disadvantages – for example, in the acquisition and holding of land. Israel was dependent on external aid, which it received liberally from American and other Jews and, by way of reparation, from the German Federal Republic; and its life was conditioned by external hostility, since the Arabs refused to accept its existence and insisted that, as an imperialist subterfuge for the maintenance of Anglo–American power in the Middle East, it must be dismantled. It adopted, in spite of its economic and military stringencies, a democratic form of government, and it presented to the world the unaccustomed sight of a state ruled by a governing class characterized above all by a progressive intelligence successfully applied to the diverse and taxing problems of everyday public life.

To the Arabs none of this was admirable. That the Jews had suffered at the hands of Christian Europeans through the ages seemed a poor reason for allowing them to expropriate a part of the Arab world and drive a million Muslims out of it. The failure of the armies of five Arab states to prevent the establishment of Israel was a humiliation which could only be met by rounding on the leaders who had so conspicuously failed and by declaring that the verdict of 1948 was only an interim one which would be reversed later. Those – mainly outsiders – who thought that time would heal or at any rate soften the acerbities of this conflict had to retreat to a more pessimistic view as officially sponsored Arab propaganda maintained a vicious anti-Zionism and as the new generation in the refugee camps was consciously nourished on visions of a return to Palestine after a gloriously successful war which would erase Israel from the map. Zionist nationalism and Zionist extremism were matched by Arab nationalism and Arab extremism. Although the situation remained frozen by external factors – in particular by the Tripartite Declaration of 1950 by which the United States, Britain and France undertook to maintain a balance of armaments between Arabs and Jews and to consult together over any infraction of frontiers – basic attitudes within the area of conflict changed little, if at all. What did change as a result of the war of 1948 was power in the Arab states immediately concerned. The defeat of 1948 accelerated the demise of some ancient régimes. In Syria Husni Zaim seized power in March 1949, held it for a few months before being ousted by Sami al-Hinnawi who was in turn ousted after a few months by Adib Shishakli who ruled until February 1954. In July 1951 Abdullah, having transformed his emirate of Transjordan into the kingdom of Jordan, was murdered as he entered the Al Aqsa mosque in Jerusalem; neither then nor later could Palestinians easily forgive him for collaborating with the Jews to enlarge his own principality at the expense of the Palestinians who, in the UN plan accepted by the Jews, were to have a state of their own. More significantly, in the following July the Egyptian monarchy was overthrown by officers who had bitterly resented the unpreparedness and ineptitude of their country's operations in 1948 and now despatched the last representative of Mohamed Ali's line into exile.

The titular leader of the Egyptian revolution of 1952 was General Mohamed Neguib but the real leader was Colonel Gamal Abdel Nasser, who became prime minister in April 1954 and supplanted Neguib as president of the new republic a few months later. Nasser was a young man of 36 who had made a career in the army from origins in what might be called the lower middle class. He had the necessary impetuousness and indignation to make a nationalist revolutionary, but he had also the qualities of coolness, shrewdness and humour which keep the revolutionary sane and afloat after success. He was also sufficiently quick-witted to keep more or less abreast of the problems which assailed him when he found himself required, as head of the most important of the Arab countries, to elaborate and execute policies in world affairs. The first of these problems was the unfinished business of getting rid of the British. In addition he had to find his place in the Arab world, African as well as Asian, and take a stand in the Cold War for or against the west or the Russians or neither.

The British occupation of Egypt began in 1881 with a debt-collecting expedition but its real motive was and remained strategic – to secure control of the eastern Mediterranean (threatened when British influence over the sultan's government in Constantinople was challenged by German influence), of the route to India and the east, and of the Nile valley. Egypt remained formally a province of the Ottoman empire under the hereditary rule of the heirs of Mohamed Ali, but it became in effect semi-independent under the British instead of semi-independent under the Turks. When Britain and the Ottoman empire went to war in 1914 Britain proclaimed a protectorate over Egypt which was converted in 1922, under nationalist pressure, into a treaty relationship. Britain secured in 1936 the right to station 10,000 men in the Suez Canal zone for twenty years, an arrangement which was rendered acceptable to the Egyptians because this base could serve to protect Egypt against the ambitions of Mussolini who was engaged at this very time in conquering Ethiopia. During the Second World War Churchill resolved to maintain and strengthen Britain's Middle Eastern position. The Arabs had shown certain pro-German proclivities which threatened to give Germany dominion in the Middle East after the German conquest of the Balkans and Crete in 1941. The British therefore occupied Syria, Lebanon and Iran and wooed Turkey (unsuccessfully until 1944 when Turkey severed relations with the Axis – it entered the war the following February); they also forced the pro-British Nahas Pasha on King Farouk as prime minister. Nahas hoped that in return the British would give Egypt after the war the unshackled independence which they had promised over sixty times since 1881, but the king, preferring a tougher to a waiting game, dismissed Nahas in October 1944.

At about this time Eden was preparing a post-war British position in the Middle East, based on an association of pro-British Arab states. Eden encouraged the hardened pro-British Nuri es-Said, Iraq's prime minister, to revive the concept of the Fertile Crescent as a political unit with Baghdad as its capital and embracing autonomous Zionist and (Christian) Maronite communities. Eden also promoted a pro-British Arab League, but in September 1944 at Alexandria, Egypt, as well as Iraq, Syria, Lebanon and Transjordan, concluded the Protocol of Alexandria which preceded the treaty of March 1945 whereby these five states plus Saudi Arabia and Yemen constituted the Arab League: this larger issue was not the league designed by Britain. From the beginning Egypt was much the most important member of the League by virtue of its greater population and sophistication and the influence which radiated from Cairo's universities, printing presses and radio. But the British and Egyptian interests in the Arab League were fatally crossed. For Britain the League was to be an ally and a pillar of support; Egypt, however, obsessed with the continuing British occupation not only of the Canal Zone but also of the points in Cairo and Alexandria where the Union Jack had been hoisted during the war, saw the League as an anti-British lever and not as a symbol of partnership. Britain's plight in Palestine helped to draw Arabs together in an anti-British attitude which suited Egypt and belied Eden's hopes. (Palestine, or rather Israel when it came into being, also affected the Arab League by converting it from a regional organization which, in its members' opinion, concerned nobody but themselves into an alliance with wider objectives and therefore international significance.)

After the war Britain appreciated the need for a revision of its treaty relations with Egypt – and also with Iraq and Transjordan – but had no thought of an early departure from the Middle East. British forces were withdrawn from the Nile delta to the Canal Zone, but only tardily; it still seemed axiomatic that Britain, victorious in a war in which British exertions and tenacity in the Middle East had played a major role, was and should be a Middle Eastern power. In addition, the withdrawal from India in 1947 would have made it difficult for the new British Labour government, accused by the opposition of 'a policy of scuttle' in India, to propose further substantial abdications in the Middle East. But the British position had been gravely weakened. Britain owed Egypt

£400 million and Iraq £70 million; and these debts were only a part of the economic strains which were intensified by the abrupt ending of American Lend-Lease and were soon to force Britain to ask the United States to take over British responsibilities in Greece and Turkey. In 1948 the strain would be further increased by the Palestine finale and by the need to defend the western position in Berlin by the airlift. Such were the circumstances in which Bevin set about negotiating fresh treaties with Egypt, Iraq and Transjordan. He quickly succeeded in the last case (1946), but King Abdullah was much criticized for allowing British troops another twenty-five years' lease of Jordanian soil. With the Egyptian and Iraqi governments Bevin also succeeded in reaching agreement, but the draft treaties accepted by Sidky Pasha for Egypt and Salih Jabr for Iraq (the Treaty of Portsmouth, 1948) were rejected by their parliaments and people because they did not provide for complete British evacuation.

There followed an uneasy and unproductive period which was broken in 1951 by a clash between two rival concepts. By this time the Korean War had begun and the western allies were anxious to create in the Middle East an anti-Russian alliance similar to Nato. With this end in view the American, British, French and Turkish governments produced plans for a Middle East Defence Organization (Medo) which would include Egypt and the Suez Canal base; the British would evacuate the base but the allies, adapting an idea once produced by Bevin, would have the right to return in certain eventualities. This scheme with its roots in the world situation ran foul of Egypt's conception of a foreign garrison on the Canal as a symbol of indignity, and since Egypt was not moved by the fear of the USSR which animated the west, Egypt rejected Medo. At the same time and for good measure Egypt denounced in October 1951 the Anglo–Egyptian Treaty of 1936, which had five years to run, and began guerrilla attacks on the Canal Zone. In January 1952 anti-British riots in Cairo caused extensive damage.

When therefore Neguib and Nasser seized power a few months later they were confronted not only with the traditional problem of the British, whose occupation of Egyptian soil was a standing national affront, but also with the new problem created by the desire of the west as a whole to enlist Egypt in the Cold War and make the Canal Zone an anti-Russian arsenal and base. Provided they could secure total British evacuation, the new Egyptian leaders were anxious to come to terms with Britain, but they had less positive ideas about an association with the west.

In the two years after the revolution Egypt and Britain settled their outstanding differences. They began not with the Canal Zone but with the Sudan, which had been an Anglo–Egyptian condominium since its recapture from the Mahdists in 1899. Egypt wished to restore the union of Egypt with the Sudan because of the vital importance of the Nile waters and because of ancient pharaonic vistas of the unity of the Nile valley. The British, who had been effective rulers of the Sudan for half a century, insisted that the Sudanese must decide their future for themselves and the Egyptians, wrongly believing that the Sudan would opt for unity with Egypt, so agreed in February 1953. In the event the Sudan chose independence in spite (or because) of Egyptian propaganda and pressure, and became a sovereign state in 1956. Nasser accepted this first reverse in the foreign field with a pragmatic acquiescence which he was to have to display again on future occasions.

Agreement on the Canal Zone was reached in July 1954 (and a treaty signed in October) on the basis that the British would depart in twenty months but would have the right to return if any member of the Arab League or Turkey were attacked by any outside foe except Israel. Iran was not included in the reverter clause in spite of British attempts to put it there. This treaty represented considerable, if sensible, concessions by Britain which were unpalatable to a section of the ruling Conservative Party but were accepted by the government partly on the grounds that the existence of nuclear bombs had turned the base into a death trap and partly – if less so – in response to pressure from the United States where continuing bad relations between Britain and Egypt were regarded as a serious impediment to the Middle Eastern segment of American world policies. But for Egypt the agreement of 1954 with Britain was not a preliminary to alignment with the West. The West on the other hand believed during 1952–54 that better relations with Egypt implied such an alignment. Consequently the better relations soon took a turn for the worse.

In 1955, the year of the Bandung conference of neutralists, Egypt became wedded to non-alignment. The issue did not arise in the first postwar years because alignment meant alignment against the Russians and there was as yet no Russian presence in the Arab world to be aligned against. The traditional Russian spheres of activity in the Middle East were the non-Arab states of Turkey and Iran, and in both the USSR had experienced and apparently accepted rebuffs at the end of the war; claims for the return of Kars and Ardahan (lost to Turkey in 1921) and for the revision of the Montreux Convention governing passage through the Straits of Constantinople were ineffective, while the attempt to subvert the régime in Iran by sponsoring the Azerbaijani republic and a Kurdish bid for independence was defeated by the unexpected astuteness of Qavam es-Sultaneh and the unexpectedly firm reactions of the United States and Britain. The prompt Russian recognition of Israel was not followed up and seemed to have been regarded by Moscow as a blind alley.

When therefore the Medo plan was first presented to Egypt, it seemed foreign and irrelevant to Egyptian interests. It was also vaguely repugnant. The Korean War, which lay behind it, was regarded by most Arabs as no concern of theirs, so much so that all the Arab members of the United Nations except Iraq refrained from voting on it in the General Assembly. Nasser himself came under the influence of Nehru, especially after the latter's visit to Cairo in August 1953 and during K. M. Pannikkar's embassy there in 1953–54. But the principal factor in Nasser's route to neutralism and the 1955 Bandung spirit was provided by the western powers themselves.

In 1954 the Americans were arming Turkey and Pakistan. They decided to help Iraq in the same way and to brigade these countries and Iran in a new anti-Russian organization which would stretch from the Bosphorus to the Indus. The inclusion of Iraq was enthusiastically welcomed by the British who saw a way of getting a new treaty with Iraq in place of their existing treaty which was due to expire in 1957 and which Bevin's negotiations with Britain's Iraqi friends had failed to prolong. But the inclusion of Iraq was a cardinal mistake. In 1953 Dulles had decided that it was no good trying to get the Arabs to join a Cold War front (the Medo policy) and that the west should therefore construct instead a non-Arab group of friends along the so-called northern tier of countries bordering on the USSR. Iraq was not a necessary member of this group, since it had no frontier with the USSR and was in any case an Arab state. Moreover, the attraction of Iraq into this northern orbit roused the deepest suspicions in Cairo both on account of existing tensions between Egypt and Iraq and as a manoeuvre by outsiders to disrupt the unity of the Arab world. The Americans were proposing to arm Iraq (and Pakistan) against the USSR, but Egypt interpreted the agreements as a strengthening of the Iraqi side in Arab politics (just as India regarded the arming of Pakistan as a threat to itself in Kashmir).

Egypt and Iraq stood for different brands of Arab unity long before the Egyptian revolution of 1952 made Egypt a socialist republic by contrast with the traditionalist monarchy which lasted in Iraq until 1958. Both before and after 1952 Egypt's leaders wished to be the leaders in the Arab world and planned to use the Arab League for this purpose; they were conscious of Egypt's natural claim to leadership and they sensed the advantages which would accrue to them in their dealings with the outside world if Egypt were the acknowledged head of an Arab commonwealth as well as an independent sovereign state. Their approach to Arab politics was Egyptian first and Arab second, and their plans stopped a long way short of Arab unity in any organic or institutional sense. The Iraqis on the other hand inherited other ideas, notably the vision of a vast Arab kingdom which had been nurtured by the British and French during the First World War and then thwarted by them. Although the sons of the sherif of Mecca – the Hashemites – came to rule in Baghdad and Amman and briefly in

Damascus, they had been evicted from Saudi Arabia by the rise of Ibn Saud and had been foiled further north by the mandates system (which did not bother the Egyptians). Nevertheless the vision persisted, embracing in its changing forms – whether Greater Syria or the Fertile Crescent – Iraq, Syria, Lebanon and Palestine. But any union between Iraq and Syria would deprive Egypt of hegemony in the Arab world.

The Hashemite regent of Iraq, Abd ul–Ilah (who never forgot that he ought to have succeeded his father and grandfather as king of the Hejaz) aimed to be king in Syria when he ceased to be regent in Iraq. Had he succeeded, the Hashemites would have formed a powerful bloc, for Abd ul–Ilah's young cousin Feisal became king in Baghdad and his uncle Abdullah was emir, later king, in Amman. After the first Syrian postwar revolution Husni Zaim turned to Iraq, although later in his short period of power he veered towards Egypt and Saudi Arabia; his successor, Sami al–Hinnawi, favoured an Iraqi–Syrian union but by so doing he precipitated his own fall, and his supplanter, Adib Shishakli (1949–54), the strong man of the Arab world before the advent of Nasser, rejected any close association with Iraq because it was monarchical and pro-British. The overthrow of Shishakli in February 1954 by the Syrian army, helped by Iraqi gold and by British well-wishing at the least, revived for Nasser the danger of an Iraqi–Syrian union at the moment when its other principal opponent, Ibn Saud, had just died and the western powers were preparing their new treaty with Iraq. In the event opposition among Syrians to the Iraqi royal family and its British connections, manifested at elections in 1954, prevented the consummation of the union.

The first formal step towards the Baghdad Pact complex was the treaty of 4 April 1954 between Turkey and Pakistan. It was followed by American military aid agreements with Iraq (21 April) and Pakistan (10 May). Turkey and Iraq signed a mutual assistance pact on 24 February 1955. This was the Baghdad Pact itself and it was declared to be open to all members of the Arab League and other states interested in the peace and security of the Middle East. Britain joined on 5 April 1955, and Pakistan and Iran in September and October. But no other Arab state followed Nuri's lead into the western camp. The Arabs rejected Nuri's belief that salvation lay in alliance with old friends in the west – partly because, to a younger generation, Britain did not appear a friend. Syria, by rejecting the pact, swung the bulk of the Arab world to Cairo and away from Baghdad, and in March 1955 a counter-alliance was formed between Egypt, Syria and Saudi Arabia. This was a victory for Nasser over Nuri and the British. It also marked the end of the period of improving relations between Egypt and the west and the beginning of violent polemics within the Arab world. Shortly after signing the treaty of March 1955 Nasser set out for Bandung where, in obedience to the prevailing anti-colonialist and neutralist wind, Iraq was censured for joining the Baghdad Pact and Pakistan for joining its eastern equivalent, Seato (South East Asian Treaty Organization).

Whatever the relative merits of British and American approaches to Middle Eastern problems at this time, the failure of London and Washington to find a common policy was manifest and significant. Britain may have been wise or unwise to use the Baghdad Pact for special purposes of its own in Iraq, and the United States may have been wise or unwise to join only the pact's economic and anti-subversion committees, but the most obvious consequence in Arab eyes was the discrepancy between the two western powers and the attempt of the Americans to look un-British by not signing the pact or joining its central organs. A more forthright American policy might have persuaded the Jordanian and Saudi monarchies to join a pro-western alliance in 1954, but at that date American anti-imperialism (not yet killed in Vietnam) and Anglo–American oil rivalries were still making Washington wary of entanglements with Britain in the Middle East with the result that there was a time lag between the adoption of essentially identical policies first in London and later in Washington.

Besides the division within the Arab world Nasser was concerned with the enduring feud between the Arabs and Israel and with the fact that Israeli retaliation against Arab propaganda and provocative raids was being turned against Egypt. Shortly before the signature of the treaty of March 1955 Egypt experienced an exceptionally sharp Israeli attack in the Gaza area. The threat from Israel, where Ben-Gurion returned to office (first as defence minister and then as prime minister once more) alarmed Nasser who had become aware that Israel was seeking arms from France. This Franco–Israeli association, although never enshrined in a formal alliance, became an additional prime factor in Middle Eastern politics and one of the principal ingredients in the Suez War of 1956. The tripartite declaration of 1950, which was supposed to prevent an arms race in the Middle East, was circumvented by Israel which found in France sympathizers ready to help Israel in secret. French motives were various: there was a feeling of obligation to the Jews as a people who had suffered too much; a feeling of admiration for what they had achieved in Israel: a feeling of socialist solidarity between men like Guy Mollet and Ben-Gurion. These affinities were played upon by skilful Israel lobbyists who found their task much facilitated when the Algerian revolt of 1954 and Nasser's help for the rebels led many Frenchmen to conclude that a blow at Nasser was the right way to solve their troubles in Algeria – or at any rate a necessary pre-condition. In addition some Frenchmen shared Eden's view that Nasser was a menace like Hitler and must be put down before it was too late. French policy, traditionally pro-Arab, was therefore pulled in a new direction. France agreed in 1954 to supply Israel with fighter aircraft.

On his return from Bandung Nasser too began seriously to look for arms. The three signatories of the tripartite declaration refused to supply Egypt or Syria with all they requested. Syria turned successfully to the Russians who had become interested in the possibility of playing a more active role in the Middle East since the Gaza raid had exposed Egypt's weakness. But Nasser was reluctant to buy Russian. After trying Beijing (where he got a hint to try Moscow) and then Washington and London once more, he finally took the Russian plunge and announced in September 1955 that he was to receive Czech arms without strings. It was now Israel's turn to be alarmed. By the Czech deal Egypt was to get a wide range of weapons including 80 MiG 15s (the fighters used in Korea), 45 Ilyushin 28 bombers and 115 heavy tanks equal to the best in the Russian army and superior to anything which Israel had. Israel pressed France to revise the agreement of 1954 by supplying Mystère 4 jet fighters instead of Mystère 2s. France complied and Israel received in April 1956 a contingent of the best fighter aircraft in Europe. (Their arrival just after the French foreign minister, Christian Pineau, had paid a successful visit to Cairo evoked an indignant anti-French outburst from Nasser and destroyed what chance there was of the Arab wind prevailing over the Israeli in the French cabinet.)

Like most countries Egypt wanted both guns and butter. Nasser had hoped to get both from the west but had been forced to buy communist arms or go without the guarantee which he was seeking. He then faced the question whether he could get economic aid from the west after accepting military aid from the communist bloc. The answer proved eventually to be no, but it was in doubt for some months. The test was the Aswan High Dam, and it proved that not only France but also Britain and the United States were turning against Nasser.

The high dam was designed to transform Egypt's economy and society by adding 860,000 hectares to the area of cultivable land, making the Nile navigable as far south as the Sudanese frontier and generating electricity to service industrial plants which would provide some of the growing population with a living. It was to cost $1,400 million, including £400 million in hard currency, of which the World Bank would advance $200 million and the United States and Britain $56 million and $14 million respectively at once and the remaining $130 million between them later. During 1955 negotiations to this end seemed to be proceeding without more than normal hitches. During the first half of 1956, however, they petered out. Britain and the United States decided not to help. Nasser's credit, in both senses of the word, was running down, especially as a result of his purchases of communist arms.

During 1956 he strengthened his enemies by recognizing the communist régime in Beijing – a step which caused special irritation in

Congress in Washington, even though the real reason may have been Nasser's fear that the new Russian leaders might, on their visit to London, be persuaded to join the western powers in a new Middle Eastern arms embargo. The Czech arms deal had broken the 1950 embargo, to the general delight of the Arab world which resented the embargo as a clog on their sovereignty, but that embargo could be reimposed if the Russians were looking for inexpensive ways of showing goodwill towards the west, and in that event Beijing would be the only alternative source of supply. In addition the cotton lobby in the American Congress disliked laying out American money to help Egypt to grow more cotton to compete with American cotton. Egypt was blamed for not coming to terms with the other riparian states along the Nile (Sudan, Ethiopia and Uganda) and for pledging for arms purchases money which would be needed to service its foreign loans. In the United States it was argued that it was imprudent to allocate so much American money to a single project since the United States would then have to refuse all other requests for aid to Egypt for many years, leaving the Russians to step in and say yes. But behind all these reasonings lay the plain fact that Washington and London did not like Nasser and thought (like the French for a different and more specific reason) that it would be salutary to administer a snub to him and cut him down to size. This attitude was strongest in Britain where it found vent in the obsessive misinterpretations and miscalculations of the prime minister, Eden, who mistook Nasser for a fascist dictator and thought he could be easily replaced. (Eden's animosity had been sharpened in March by the dismissal of General Sir John Glubb and other British officers from Jordan's Arab Legion, of which Glubb was the commanding officer. Fortuitously this anti-British move by King Hussein coincided with a visit to Cairo by the British foreign secretary, Selwyn Lloyd, and it was therefore erroneously regarded by Eden as a deliberate affront to Britain contrived by Nasser.)

On 19 July 1956 Dulles informed the Egyptian ambassador in Washington that the Anglo–American offer to finance the dam was revoked. The French ambassador in Washington, Couve de Murville, had predicted that in this event Nasser would retaliate by seizing the revenues from the Suez Canal. On 26 July, in a speech in Alexandria, he did just that.

The Suez Canal was indubitably a part of the Egyptian state but it was also the subject of two, very different, instruments – a concession agreement and an international treaty. The former, granted to Ferdinand de Lesseps by the khedive or viceroy of Egypt, Said Pasha, and confirmed by the Ottoman sultan, conceded the right to operate the canal for ninety-nine years from its opening, which took place in 1869. The concession had passed from de Lesseps to the Universal Maritime Suez Canal Company, which was an Egyptian corporation with headquarters in Cairo and Paris and with a diversity of shareholders including the British government and a host of ordinary French *rentiers*. The concession, which was a valuable one, had twelve years to run in 1956. Thereafter the operating rights would revert to the Egyptian state. Nasser's action amounted to the nationalization of the company's rights, but since he promised compensation it was difficult to maintain that he had done anything illegal or, in the twentieth century, particularly unusual – although the company might well ask where the compensation money was to come from. Nasser would, however, be on the wrong side of the law if he broke the terms of the second relevant instrument. This was the convention made in 1888 between nine powers including the Ottoman empire, which was at that date suzerain over Egypt. The parties engaged themselves to keep the canal open to all ships of commerce or war, in times of war as well as peace, and never to blockade it. Should Nasser fail to keep the canal open he would be in breach of the convention and the signatories would be entitled to take measures to reopen it. There was some ill-judged expectation that if the canal pilots were withdrawn, the canal would cease to function and the right to intervene could be said to have arisen, but in the event the canal continued to function smoothly until bombarded by the British and French, even though the company's pilots were nearly all withdrawn as a result of pressure by outside powers.

The nationalization of the canal company gave Britain and France an excuse for the forcible action which they wished to take against Egypt. The British cabinet allocated £5 million (imperialism on a pittance) and resolved to use force within a week, only to discover that Britain's military preparedness was such that nothing could be ventured before the middle of September or without calling up the reserves. This delay enabled the United States to intervene. Eisenhower and Dulles agreed with the British and French governments in wishing to put the canal under international control but, although they had little love for Nasser, they were opposed to the use of force until all methods had been tried and had been seen to have been tried. Eisenhower, who made his position clear in letters to Eden and in public statements, was temperamentally averse to force and was also convinced that force was inexpedient because it would lead to sabotage of pipelines, would encourage other leaders (for example, Jiang Kaishek and Syngman Rhee) to claim American support for the use of force in their quarrels too, and would turn the uncommitted world against the west. Eisenhower sent a special emissary to London who reported on 31 July 1956 that the British were intent on using force, and thereafter a duel developed between Eden and Dulles, enemies since the crisis of 1954 in Indo–China, with Eden manoeuvring to get American sanction for a forward policy and Dulles side-stepping and playing for time.

First the British and French, with American support, convened in London a conference of the canal's principal users and presented to it a plan for a new operating board to ensure international control of the canal. The conference did not approve this plan unanimously; it was criticized as an unjustifiable infringement of Egyptian sovereignty. Nevertheless the Australian prime minister, Robert Menzies, and four other members, representing the majority view, went to Cairo to present the plan to Nasser, who turned it down and pointed out that the canal was functioning normally. Next Dulles, perhaps merely in order to keep talking and avoid shooting, propounded a Suez Canal Users' Association with the right to organize convoys and take tolls from the vessels in them. This plan appealed to the British who saw a chance of running a convoy through the canal against Egyptian opposition and so putting Egypt in the wrong in American eyes. Dulles, who was consistently pragmatic throughout this phase, then killed the scheme upon becoming suspicious that Britain and France might use it to start shooting; he pointed out that the American government had no power to force the masters of American vessels to pay tolls to the association and not to the Egyptian government. Britain and France then referred the dispute to the Security Council while explicitly stating that they reserved the right to use force. When the Council met on 5 October Egypt proposed negotiations, while Britain and France produced a plan for international control of the canal. Unofficial negotiations outside the Council made substantial progress but Egypt persisted in its refusal to accept international control and the Anglo–French plan was defeated by a Russian veto.

During these months the French became increasingly exasperated with the British. Joint Anglo–French commands had been set up at the beginning of August but the prospects of action by the slowly assembling hosts diminished as the British wavered between their desire to keep in step with the French and their anxiety not to get out of the Americans' good books. By the end of September or early October the French were reverting to their old line of co-operating with Israel, from which they had been distracted by the lure of a joint Anglo–French operation in response to the nationalization of the canal company.

Israel had powerful reasons for wishing to make war on Egypt. Raids into Israel by *fedayeen* based in the Sinai peninsula had become more audacious and more frequent. Land near the frontier was becoming too dangerous to farm and the Israeli government feared outrages even in the centres of its cities. Only a spectacular gesture could end this murderous nuisance. Further, Israel wished to break the Arab blockade of the gulf of Aqaba and so win a sure outlet to the countries of Asia and Africa from the port of Eilat which was languishing at the head of the gulf; even Israel's air links with Africa were insecure. The opening of the straits of Tiran at the entrance of the gulf would compensate

Israel for the Egyptian refusal to allow ships bound to or from Israel to use the Suez Canal. But Israel's capacities were not the equal of its intentions. Egypt's new Russian bombers were in a position to bomb Israel's cities and cause panic among the newer immigrants who had not yet become tempered to life in a besieged state. Israel's air force was barely able to defend these cities even with its new French fighters, or to protect Israeli land forces operating in the open desert, and it was quite unable to bomb Egyptian airfields and so prevent the Egyptian air force from taking off. When therefore the French bethought themselves once more of the Israeli attack on Egypt for which they had been suppling arms, they found that the Israelis wanted more than arms. They wanted active French co-belligerence in the form of units of the French air force to be stationed on Israeli airfields for the defence of Israeli cities, and they also wanted British co-belligerence and the bombing of Egyptian airfields by the only locally based bombers capable of the task – which were British bombers using British bases in Cyprus.

The French set about engineering this combined tripartite operation and succeeded. During October French ministers divulged Israel's plans to British ministers; a meeting in Paris on 16 October between Mollet and Pineau, Eden and Lloyd, with nobody else present was particularly important. The British ministers, however, were reluctant to embark on any but the most furtive co-operation with Israel because of the repercussions in the Arab world. But Ben-Gurion insisted on a formal commitment from the British, whom he did not trust, and this he secured at a secret meeting at Sèvres where, on 23 or 24 October, the British foreign secretary joined French and Israeli ministers, subsequently authorizing the signature of a secret tripartite treaty. At this point the Israeli commander-in-chief altered his battle orders, which had envisaged an Israeli raid in force similar to earlier raids but bigger, and proposed instead to commit his forces to open desert upon the assumption that British attacks on Egyptian airfields would give the Israeli troops immunity from air attack.

Israel attacked on 29 October and duly received the anticipated support of Britain and France (the French also prevented the Egyptian fleet from attacking the Israeli coast), but the Egyptian air force was in any event incapacitated since the Russians, who were still in operational control of the Ilyushin 28s, ordered their pilots out of the battle area. Britain and France also issued an ultimatum to Israel and Egypt requiring both sides to withdraw 16 km from the canal. This was a ruse intended to preserve the fiction that Britain had not colluded with Israel. Neither side paid attention to the ultimatum, Egypt because the canal was 160 km within its own frontiers and Israel because its forces were some way from the canal and were not intended to go there. The Israeli campaign was virtually over on 2 November when its principal objectives – the clearing out of the *fedayeen* bases, the opening of the straits of Tiran and a resounding victory against Egypt – were assured.

A few hours after the initial Israeli attack the Security Council met to consider an American resolution requiring the Israelis to return to their borders. Britain and France vetoed this resolution but the General Assembly, convoked under the Uniting for Peace resolution (a procedure adopted in 1950 on western initiative to enable the Assembly to consider and make recommendations on matters on which the Security Council was stultified by a veto), adopted in the early hours of 2 November an appeal for a cease-fire. At the UN a small group which included the secretary-general, Dag Hammarskjöld, and the Canadian minister for external affairs, Lester Pearson, worked to stop the approaching Anglo–French sea and land attack on Egypt (which, unlike the Israeli, had not yet been launched) and to recover control over an alarming situation by imposing a cease-fire and despatching an international peace force to the area. The Anglo–French attack began with a parachute drop on 5 November. On the next day a seaborne armada from Malta landed troops but on the same day Britain cried halt and France after some hesitation desisted too.

The British decision was the result of an accumulation of pressures, of which one was decisive. Britain, unlike France, was split. The parliamentary opposition, much of the press and a substantial part of the public were opposed to the government's policy. Eden's own party and a majority of the country as a whole supported him consistently except on the use of force, for which there was never a popular majority. The existence of doubts within the government itself was common knowledge. The independent members of the Common-wealth were also split; Australia and, less enthusiastically, New Zealand supported Eden, but Canada and the newer dominions did not (there were as yet no independent African members). This opposition had, however, been foreseen and discounted and for that reason the usual processes of Commonwealth consultation were omitted and Common-wealth governments, like senior advisers in Whitehall and all the pertinent British ambassadors abroad, were kept in the dark. But the decisive reason for calling off the operation was the failure to secure American endorsement and the failure to see what American opposition entailed.

The attack on Egypt caused the biggest financial crisis in Britain since 1945. Britain lost on balance $400 million during the last quarter of 1956; withdrawals were probably half as much again but were partly offset by one or two exceptional influxes which were credited during the quarter. Sterling was healthy and the reserves more than adequate for ordinary purposes, but losses of this order could only be borne for a number of weeks without external aid to preserve the exchange value of the pound. It became clear that Britain would have to borrow to save the pound (which, apart from the war, was not threatened) and that neither the United States nor the IMF would lend the necessary sums until the fighting was called off. Britain could not support an international currency and at the same time conduct independently an aggressive foreign policy.

There was in these calculations one other subsidiary element which may have had some effect on some people. This was the entry of the Russians upon the scene. Until 5 November the Russians were too much preoccupied with the suppression of the Hungarian rebellion to take a hand in Middle Eastern affairs, but on that day they proposed to Washington joint action to force Britain and France to desist and threatened vaguely to use rockets against Britain and France. They also indicated that they might allow volunteers to go to the Middle East but statements to this effect were made only after the fighting was over, except in one case when Khrushchev made, at a diplomatic party in Moscow, remarks about volunteers which were not reported in the Russian press. The Russian threat to use rockets was countered by an American threat to retaliate, whereafter no more was heard on this subject. By their intervention the Russians gained a sizeable propaganda victory in the Arab world; it is very improbable that they ever intended anything else.

9 FROM SUEZ TO THE DEATH OF NASSER

The Suez War raised Nasser's prestige high. He had secured the leadership in Egypt only in 1954. Suez confirmed him in it and made him a popular leader as well as a military ruler. He had kept his head and his dignity, had emerged intact from an imperialist onslaught and an Israeli invasion, and had demonstrated his power in the Arab world when even Nuri's Iraq had felt obliged to condemn Britain's action and propose Britain's eviction from the Baghdad Pact. Jordan too rejected its traditional British links and the subsidies which went with them, denounced its treaty with Britain and joined instead the Egyptian–Syrian alliance of 1955 (to which Saudi Arabia and Yemen also now belonged). Nasser kept the Canal and showed he could work it and got the Dam too. The Americans, who might be said to have precipitated the whole affair by abandoning the Dam project, had had to come to the support of a régime which they had notoriously ceased to admire and were left in the aftermath without a policy. The Russians were jubilantly claiming all the credit and getting much of it, and they undertook to finance the Aswan Dam in place of the Americans and British.

While the debris was still flying the United States tried to make a fresh start with what came to be called the Eisenhower Doctrine. This venture proceeded from the assumptions that, with the defeat of Britain, it had become necessary for the United States to take some sort of initiative and that the decline of British power had created a vacuum which must be filled by the United States if it were not to be filled by the USSR. Between $400 and $500 million were to be disbursed in two years in the form of economic and military aid to willing recipients who would enter into agreements with the United States authorizing and inviting the use of American arms to protect the integrity and independence of the signatory if threatened with overt aggression from any nation controlled by international communism. Neither Egypt nor Syria was expected to conclude an agreement with the United States on these lines, but a special emissary was sent by President Eisenhower to tour the Middle East and get as many takers as possible. His only success was in Lebanon where, more out of courtesy than enthusiasm, a Christian leader entered into the requisite agreement – and was later to suffer for this decision. King Saud of Saudi Arabia was also polite and paid a visit to Washington but evaded signing any agreement. In Jordan there were anti-American riots. The Eisenhower Doctrine was a new version of the old plan of constructing an anti-Russian front in the Middle East, and its failure was due to the spread of neutralism among Arabs who realized, especially after the lessons of the Suez War, that they were no longer helpless against major outside powers and that the decline of Britain might be followed not by a fresh foreign domination but by none.

During the late fifties both the Americans and the Russians absorbed this lesson. For the Russians the test came in Syria and then more decisively in Iraq where events seemed to offer opportunities for intervention in a classical mode but brought instead disillusionment. Upheavals in both these countries opened for Moscow the possibility of alliances and even bases in the Middle East from which power could be exercised in imperial fashion. Syria, whence came reports of spreading communism in 1957, entered into economic and military agreements with the USSR, expelled three American diplomats and carried out a purge of the army. Turkey, disturbed by these pointers, concentrated forces on its southern borders. Egypt sent troops which were received in Damascus with acclaim. The tension was temporarily eased but in January 1958 some Syrian officers went to Egypt and asked Nasser to declare a union between the two countries in order to avert a communist takeover in Damascus. The pan-Arab nationalists of the Syrian Ba'ath Party had become alarmed at the growing influence of the Russians and of Syria's principal, and somewhat lonely, communist Khaled Bakdash. Preferring Egyptians to communists they instigated a political move which Nasser, though embarrassed and hesitant, felt unable to reject upon being faced with the argument that an Egyptian refusal would leave no alternative to communism. The creation of a United Arab Republic, consisting of Egypt and Syria, was proclaimed on 1 February 1958. Yemen became loosely attached to it in March.

The Hashemite monarchs in Iraq and Jordan retaliated with an Arab Federation. This union was, however, insubstantial and shortlived, for on 14 July in the same year King Feisal II, the former regent and other members of the royal family, and Nuri es-Said were murdered in a military uprising led by Generals Aref and Kassim. The revolutionaries included communists whose presence at the centres of power alarmed the west and enticed the Russians. The Americans and the British, dismayed by this revolution in the centre of the Baghdad Pact, at once moved forces into Lebanon and Jordan in order to prevent the trouble from spreading, President Camille Chamoun of Lebanon invoking the Eisenhower Doctrine and King Hussein of Jordan the Anglo–Jordanian treaty. (Jordan's request to Britain to intervene was drafted in London.) In Jordan British force saved the monarchy at a time when its fall would have produced turmoil, laying it open to attack from Israel. In Lebanon there was already a civil war in progress which was threatening the religious equilibrium on which the life and prosperity of the country had been based for decades. The Lebanese government had invoked the United Nations in May but by the time of the revolution in Iraq in July the dangers of increasing civil and religious strife had become so great that the marines sent in by President Eisenhower were welcomed by a large majority. In both countries therefore foreign intervention was a stabilizing factor and was not held against the intervenors, especially as they contrived to get themselves out again rapidly with the help of Hammarskjöld. In Lebanon a new president, General Fuad Shehab, a member of an old Maronite family, was able to re-establish the country's traditional equilibrium.

The Baghdad revolution looked at first sight like another link in the lengthening chain of Russian opportunities which included Arab hostility to the Baghdad Pact, the Czech arms deal, the Suez War, the financing of the Aswan Dam, Russian attendance at the Afro-Asian conference in Cairo in December 1957, and a visit by Nasser to the USSR in April–May 1958. Iraq left the Baghdad Pact (which was renamed the Central Treaty Organization – Cento – and moved its headquarters to Ankara). But Kassim was himself no communist and his rule, which lasted until he was assassinated in February 1963, was hampered by general inefficiency and because it provoked a Kurdish revolt in the north. He was partly dependent on the communists but much less successful than Sukarno in similar circumstances in manoeuvring between the mutually hostile communist and nationalist forces which had brought him to power, and after much chaotic in-play the communists failed to consolidate or improve upon their advantages and Iraq too became more or less a neutralist state where the Russians were as unwelcome as any other major power. The Russians, who had been careful not to offend the nationalists by committing themselves to the communists, swallowed their disappointment and adapted them-selves to the temper of the Arab world. They also reverted to more familiar ground. They tried (unsuccessfully) in 1959 to inveigle the shah of Iran away from the western camp, and they began to show an interest in better relations with Turkey after the fall of Menderes in 1960, in which attempt they were later assisted by Turkish disappoint-ment over the American refusal to permit a Turkish invasion of Cyprus. The USSR recognized Kuwait in 1963 and Jordan in 1964, and the presence of Khrushchev at the opening of the Aswan Dam in 1964 reasserted the usefulness of the Russian presence in the Arab world.

The Iraqi revolution also occasioned intervention by China in the affairs of the Middle East or, in Chinese terminology, west Asia. Until this time American and Russian interests in the Middle East had been openly antagonistic. Russian policies in Iran in 1945 on the one hand,

and on the other the Truman Doctrine, the Baghdad Pact, American bases at Dhahran in Saudi Arabia and Wheelus Field in Libya and the US Sixth Fleet in the Mediterranean, made the Middle East look like an annexe of the Cold War. In 1956, however, the Americans and the Russians had found themselves in agreement on the need to thwart the British and the French at Suez, and the Russians had even proposed joint Russo–American action; and in the aftermath of the Iraqi revolution of 1958 there appeared some prospect of an open or tacit accord between the two giant powers, an acknowledgement that both had legitimate interests in the Middle East and that some of these interests might be the same. This accord was not to the liking of the Chinese and when an international conference on Middle Eastern affairs was mooted Beijing objected to the holding of such a conference without Chinese participation. The conference never took place. Although Chinese effectiveness in the Middle East was minimal, China began in 1958 to venture there. It gave exclusive support to the Iraqi communists, while the Russians were advocating a front policy; it championed Egypt's gaoled communists, to whom the Russians were turning a deaf ear; it gave some aid to the Yemeni republicans; and, more anti-Israeli than the Russians, it received the Palestinian Arab leader, Ahmed Shuqeiri, in Beijing almost as a head of state and promised him military aid. Zhou Enlai visited Cairo in December 1963 and April 1965. But the Chinese, besides being remote, proved little more popular than other outsiders.

Within the Arab world itself the Iraqi revolution, which was wrongly expected to entail the early disappearance of the monarchy in Jordan, created a new pattern by shifting Iraq from the traditionalist monarchist category into the revolutionary republican one. But Iraq, under whatever régime, was traditionally a rival of Egypt and Kassim himself disliked Nasser. Kassim was murdered in 1963 and succeeded by the Aref brothers – Abdul Salam, killed in an air crash in 1966, and Abdul Rahman, ousted in 1968. The Arefs were hostile to the Ba'ath and so to Syria. The new Iraq was more nationalist than pan-Arab or pro-Nasser and too much preoccupied with internal affairs to play a substantial role in external affairs for the first decade and a half after the revolution.

During the early sixties Nasser's prestige began to decline from its post-Suez peak. The fall of the senior branch of the Hashemite line had brought no gain to Egypt. The union with Syria was not a success: Egypt and Syria had no common frontier; Nasser and the Ba'ath had too little in common beyond a superficial socialism; and the influx of Egyptians into Syria and Nasser's policies of land reform and of forcing all political parties to merge in a single movement or front strained a union which had been a shot-gun marriage from the start; Syrians swung back to the idea that a union with Iraq would suit them better (especially after the Iraqi Ba'ath helped to oust Kassim). In 1961 a shortlived right-wing revolution in Syria brought about the dissolution of the union.

In Yemen, loosely attached to the United Arab Republic from the start, an attempt to overthrow the imamate and install a republic led to a civil war in which Nasser backed the republican leader Brigadier Sallal without realizing that he was thereby entangling himself in Yemen for several years and to the tune ultimately of 50–60,000 troops. The imam on the other hand was supported by Saudi Arabia, so that the Yemeni civil war developed into a contest between two of the principal Arab states. After two years both sides found the effort unrewarding and in 1965 Nasser travelled to the Saudi capital of Riyadh to meet King Feisal (a relatively progressive member of his house who had displaced his brother Saud the year before), put an end to the civil war and even effect a *rapprochement* between Egypt and Saudi Arabia, the protagonists of the opposing socialist and traditionalist tendencies in the Arab world. Earlier in the same year he had initiated a *rapprochement* with Jordan.

This re-emergence of the theme of Arab unity probably owed at least as much to apprehension about Israel's plans for diverting the Jordan's waters as to war-weariness in Yemen. An American plan in 1955 for an equitable apportionment of these valuable waters had been rejected by the Arabs on political grounds, whereupon Israel had started to construct engineering works which would take water from the Galilee region in the north to the Negev desert in the south. Israel maintained that the quantities to be pumped out of the Jordan's main stream would neither exceed the Israeli quota in the 1955 plan nor leave the lower reaches of the river unduly salty. The Arabs denied both these propositions. They also saw that the Israeli engineering works would come into operation in 1964 and in January of that year they convened a conference in Cairo, attended by traditionalist monarchies and progressive republics alike, in order to concert counter-measures. These measures included the diversion of two of the Jordan's tributaries, the Hasbani in Lebanon and the Banias in Syria – the latter at points within sight and within range from the Israeli frontier; they also included the creation of a unified Arab High Command which, with a useful ambivalence, could be construed either as a means of preventing Israeli attacks on the work on the Banias or as a covert way of keeping the Syrians, the most unpredictable and volatile of the Arab allies, from starting anything on their own. And thirdly, Arab counter-measures included the promotion of the Palestinian Arabs to something approaching sovereign status with a Liberation Organization, an army and a headquarters at Gaza.

This unity was, however, imperfect. To King Hussein the pretensions of the Palestinians amounted to a threat to disrupt the Jordanian state forged by annexing parts of Palestine and to end the monarchy. Syria, Lebanon and Jordan all jibbed at the idea of having Egyptian troops stationed on their soil. Feisal turned out to be a dubious ally. Not only did the agreement of 1965 on Yemen come to nothing, but Feisal began to create a traditionalist or Islamic bloc within the Muslim world. He paid visits to the shah of Iran and to Hussein and ordered arms from the west in alarming quantities. Thus despite pan-Arab conferences at Alexandria in 1964 and Casablanca in 1965 Arab unity and Nasser's role as its leader were in decline in these years.

In the decade after the war of 1956 Israel enjoyed its gains without confirming them. The tranquillity on the Egyptian border achieved by the extirpation of the *fedayeen* was maintained and was for a while repeated on Israel's other borders. Eilat flourished, growing from a small town of fewer than 1,000 inhabitants to a flourishing port of over 13,000, trading over a large part of the world and rendering the continuing blockade in the Suez Canal harmless. Israel's warlike spirit was also kept up and, allied with its technical skills, placed Israel in a position to become a nuclear power, should it so choose. Although Arab talk of eliminating Israel went on unabated, it was believed by some to have become a mask, hiding the secret conviction that Israel had come to stay. Israel's reliance on its own might and the divisions of its enemies was reinforced, at second remove, by continuing the alliance with France which had preceded the war of 1956 and by new undertakings from the United States and Britain, as well as France, which followed it. These states declared in March 1957 that they regarded the straits of Tiran as an international waterway and would take action to ensure free passage through them into the Gulf of Aqaba. (The straits were indubitably territorial waters but international law required riparian powers to permit innocent passage for all vessels through such straits if they led to non-territorial waters or to the territory of another state.)

Until 1967 therefore there was some hope that the third round in the Arab–Israeli contest might be postponed *sine die* but by that year growing threats from Syria and from the terrorist organization Al Fatah supported by Syria had changed the climate. An Israeli attack on Syria, leading possibly to a war with both Syria and Egypt, became a matter for practical speculation. The Israeli response to Al Fatah's raids, which began in 1956, was to retaliate in force and by daylight with regular army units against villages in Jordan and Lebanon from which these raids originated. Forays across the Syrian border presented more difficult problems because the lie of the land favoured the Syrians and also because there were no specific limited objectives for the Israeli forces; an expedition into Syria would have been an open-ended *promenade militaire* with no precise stopping place short of Damascus. The brunt of Israel's counter-measures fell therefore on Jordan, notably in a raid on the village of Es Samu in November 1966 in which eighteen Jordanians were killed and much of the village destroyed.

The Egyptian moves which initiated the third round were to a large degree prompted by the state of Syrian politics. The Ba'ath Party, founded in Syria in the early forties as a pan-Arab party of secular socialism and mild reform – not anti-religious but opposed to the interference of mullahs in politics and to fanaticism of all kinds – had merged in 1950 with the left-wing Arab Socialist Party. It was dissolved (in Syria) in 1958 after the union with Egypt but was in alliance with a group in the army led by General Salah Jedid, an Alawi. The Alawis, a Shi'ite offshoot, one of the principal communities in Syria, strong in the western parts of the country, distrusted by the orthodox Sunnis, by the Druzes and by the Christians, had been favoured by the French during the period of the mandate. The dominant Alawi group in the army established a working partnership with the civilians of the Ba'ath; this partnership was rendered uneasy by the Marxist and atheistic elements on the left wing of the Ba'ath, but on the other hand the military leaders found the left wing's anti-parliamentary leanings congenial and contrived in any case to secure control of much of the Ba'ath's provincial organization. Between 1963 and 1966 the military leadership split between General Jedid and his adherents and General Hafiz Assad (another Alawi) and his. When Jedid carried out a coup against Assad in 1966 the Ba'ath leaders sided with Jedid but became increasingly prisoners of the army at risk if Assad should ever turn the tables on Jedid. The latter's position was inherently precarious and within a year of his coup clashes with Israel laid bare Syria's vulnerability and also its isolation (Algeria was its only friend). At the same time Jedid found himself threatened by a scandal caused by the publication of an atheistic article which provoked demonstrations against his government. Anxious to deflect these attacks the government tried to lay the blame on Zionists and Americans, whom it accused of fabricating lies in order to destroy it. The Russians, alarmed that Jedid's fall might entail a conservative reaction, abetted the story of an external threat to Syria. So too for similar reasons did the Palestinians. The cry was taken up throughout the Arab world and even kings Feisal and Hussein were moved to expostulate and promise aid. Israel was said to have moved troops to the Syrian border, a report which was first thought to have reached Syria from Lebanon but may have been given to the Syrians by the Russians. In Israel the Russian ambassador refused an invitation to go and see for himself that there had been no such troop movements.

Nasser had been anything but in the lead during this clamour. He did not like the Syrian government but he could not stand against the tide of Arab feeling and, as in 1958, he was ill informed about the true state of affairs inside Syria and afraid that its government might indeed be about to fall and be replaced by another that he would like even less. His standing in the Arab world had been diminished over the past years, notably by his unsuccessful Yemeni venture; he was being taunted by Jordanians and Saudis for his inactivity; gradually he became convinced that he had to do something. So he took the field. On 16 May he presented a demand for the withdrawal of the UN Emergency Force (UNEF) which had been in Sinai since 1957 and despatched troops to harass UN positions. Two days later, his demand having been rejected by the UN commander who said he had no authority to entertain it, Nasser repeated it to U Thant. After consulting his advisory committee on UNEF, U Thant complied and on the 23rd UN forces pulled out of Sharm es-Sheikh, leaving Egypt in control of the straits of Tiran. On the previous day Nasser had declared that the straits would be closed to vessels flying the Israeli flag and to contraband of war on whatever vessel (but not to Israeli commerce in non-Israeli ships).

The moves of these days created a clear danger of war between Egypt and Israel. Syria's troubles were overtaken. In 1957 Israel had withdrawn from Sharm es-Sheikh in reliance on western promises to guarantee free passage through the straits, the opening of which had been one of Israel's prime objectives in making war on Egypt in October 1956. Israel had stated that the closing of the straits would constitute a *casus belli* and on the day when the UN troops departed the Israeli prime minister, Levi Eshkol, publicly called on the western powers to implement their guarantee. Washington and London issued statements about international waterways and the British foreign secretary, George Brown, propounded a maritime declaration whose bearing on the crisis appeared, however, remote. De Gaulle proposed four-power talks but the Russians refused. In the early hours of the morning of the 26th the Russian ambassador in Cairo got Nasser out of bed to tell him to go carefully, but the Egyptian moves had caused a wave of enthusiasm and foolish optimism in the Arab world which carried Nasser even further forward. King Hussein arrived in Cairo to make friends with Nasser, a defence pact was signed and a joint command established, Iraq joined the pact a few days later, Egyptian troops moved to Jordan. Israel, which had viewed Egypt's first moves with equanimity, concluded that the danger of war was real, and a few hours after Iraq acceded to the Egypt–Jordanian pact, Israel – after delaying, partly under American pressure, for longer than some members of the cabinet thought prudent – struck the first blow. Victory was swift and total. Although the war has since been designated the Six Day War, Israel defeated both Egypt and Jordan within two days, annexing Jerusalem and occupying all Jordan west of the Jordan River and the whole of the Sinai peninsula. Syria was dealt with later but no less summarily. Nasser, who had moved back to the centre of the stage only to collapse even more humiliatingly than

Farouk twenty years earlier, resigned but other scapegoats were found (and executed) and Nasser survived to fall in a later war.

There was much debate over the legal correctness and political consequences of U Thant's decision to withdraw UNEF and to do so speedily. UNEF had been deployed with Egypt's agreement, which was required because the operation was launched under chapter VI and not chapter VII of the UN Charter. But Hammarskjöld had made an agreement with Nasser and the question arose whether, by this agreement, Nasser had abrogated to any degree Egypt's sovereign right to require the removal of the force. On the one hand it has been argued that the effect of the Nasser–Hammarskjöld correspondence was to make the stationing of UNEF on Egyptian soil terminable only by mutual consent. On the other hand it was said that this limitation, if and so far as any had been intended, applied only so long as UNEF was fulfilling its original role of bringing the hostilities of 1956–57 to an end, which role had undoubtedly been completed long before 1967. (It was never part of UNEF's role to keep the straits of Tiran open. This was an obligation of the western powers, if anybody's.) But whatever the true construction of the relevant documents, U Thant had to consider practical matters as well. His Advisory Council was divided, the UN's forces in the field were being forced out of their positions, two of the governments supplying forces indicated that they would withdraw whatever U Thant decided. In these circumstances it is difficult to see how U Thant had any choice. Even if he had prevaricated and delayed, as some of his critics maintained, he would probably have done no more than get some of his own forces killed.

Israel's new conquests made it safer. Although its territory was much larger, its frontiers were shorter and easier to defend. Its troops stood beside the Suez Canal and the straits of Tiran, while in the north the commanding Golan heights had passed from Syrian to Israeli possession. For many Israelis at this time (but fewer and fewer as time went by) this new territory was not for keeping but for bargaining with. Israel hoped that it now had the power and the counters to force its neighbours to make peace and to recognize a state of Israel with defined frontiers not very different from those existing before the war. Strategic details apart, the one gain to which Israel intended to cling with non-negotiable tenacity was the emotion-sodden old city of Jerusalem. For some months this mood prevailed but it was backed by no effective moves, even though Egypt and Jordan were thought by many observers to have signalled a readiness to negotiate. In August Arab leaders met in Khartoum. Saudi Arabia and Kuwait agreed to make good to Egypt its losses from the closing of the Canal and to Jordan its losses from the capture of all its lands west of the Jordan River, which included the revenues provided by tourists and pilgrims visiting Jerusalem. In return Egypt agreed to quit Yemen and to make no fuss about the ending of the ineffective and burdensome boycott which the oil-producing countries had applied against western customers. Unofficial sanction was given for separate and secret discussions by Jordan with Israel. Various peace terms were mooted, including free passage for the Israeli flag through the straits of Tiran and the Suez Canal and eventual Egyptian recognition of Israel. But this piecemeal approach did not satisfy Israel which remained inflexibly intent on a formal peace conference and direct Arab–Israeli negotiations without intermediaries (as opposed to the so-called Rhodes formula by which each side would communicate with the other through a UN or other mediator). Fighting began again. The USSR, which had lost prestige as well as, vicariously, materials of war, decided to rearm Egypt. In October an Israeli destroyer was sunk by Egyptians using Russian weapons. As the exchanges of fire across the Canal increased Israel resolved to force Egypt to revert to a cease-fire by massive and deep retaliation but Egypt, instead of complying, called for and got more Russian help. The Russian position in Egypt was fortified; the Americans were correspondingly alarmed.

On the Jordanian front the principal changes effected by the war of 1967 were, in addition to the shifting of the frontier, the influx of a further 250,000 Palestinian refugees into Jordan, a more effective organization of Palestinian guerrilla forces and the conversion therefore of Jordan into a primary target for Israeli attacks. The humiliating collapse of the regular armies of Arab states had intensified the Palestinian belief that it was futile to rely on these states for the recovery of the lands and rights which they had lost in Palestine. They resolved to fend for themselves and, because their cause had a compulsive emotional appeal throughout the Arab world, they had a degree of political influence on Arab capitals out of proportion to their military effectiveness and felt themselves to be in a position to block proposals for an accommodation with Israel which fell short of their irredentist demands. Their principal weapon was the threat to disrupt the kingdom of Jordan where, besides constituting more than half the population, they now also had armed forces. Militarily they were no serious threat to Israel – a further reason why they had to pursue their aims by threatening Jordan – but their guerrilla tactics provoked Israel to retaliations which fell upon the countries which harboured them. In 1968 a section of them took to hijacking aircraft. In July an aircraft of the Israeli line El Al was forced to land at Algiers where its Israeli passengers were held until released through Italian mediation, and in December the Israeli air force destroyed thirteen aircraft on the ground at Beirut in response to an attack by Palestinians on another El Al aircraft at Athens.

In November 1967 Britain had succeeded in getting the support of the United States, the USSR and France for a resolution in the Security

Council which condemned the acquisition of territory by force, required Israel to withdraw from its recent conquests and advocated a settlement which would include recognition of Israel and a fair deal for the Palestinian refugees. This resolution (242/67) was endorsed by the Arabs (other than Syria) after some hesitations; it was rejected by Israel. This unaccustomed solidarity among the major powers – long but unsuccessfully sought by France – was facilitated by the fright of Washington and Moscow at finding themselves on opposite sides in a shooting war which, fortunately for them, lasted only six days. Both the superpowers wanted stability in the Middle East. So long as the state of war lasted the Americans were committed, if in uncertain degree, to Israel and therefore debarred from improving their relations with Arab states. By the same token the Russians were able greatly to improve their standing as a Middle East power and their military facilities in the Middle East.

The cessation of American aid to Egypt in 1966 (including free food under Public Law 480) had cast Egypt into the arms of the USSR even before the disasters of the 1967 campaign and so enabled Moscow to bring to a culminating point the capture of vantage points which it had begun after Eden, by adhering to the Baghdad Pact, and Ben-Gurion, by the Gaza raid of 1955, had initiated the Russo–Egyptian alliance. Their gains in this short period gave the Russians an interest in the stability of the Middle East where they had become something of a status quo power; and the emergence of an independent Palestinian power, hostile to Arab governments which were friendly to the USSR, and partly nourished by China, threatened to complicate Moscow's diplomatic problems if peace were not made. Moscow also wanted to see the Canal reopened for the passage of supplies to North Vietnam and for the flotilla established as a permanent symbol of its expanding reach and pretensions in the Indian Ocean. France, no longer dependent on Middle Eastern oil after the opening of the Algerian and Libyan oilfields, had extricated itself from the Israeli alignment into which the Mollet government had led it and, alarmed by the growth of Russian naval power in the eastern and (prospectively) western Mediterranean, tried to break the Russian monopoly in the Arab world and give Arabs some freedom of diplomatic and commercial manoeuvre by offering to sell arms to Iraq and Libya. As in 1956, so in 1967, France's main concern in the Middle East was the implications of events there upon the balance of power in the western Mediterranean. Britain, still dependent on Middle East oil and still enmeshed in the Persian Gulf, wanted peace on general grounds and particularly for the commercial convenience of reopening the Canal. But resolution 242 of November 1967 did not bear fruit.

In 1968–69 a war of attrition was waged on the Suez front to which Israel resolved, early in 1970, to put a stop by making air raids into

Egypt to within a few miles of Cairo itself. This tactic failed because it led the USSR to bolster Egypt's defences with Russian missiles and Russian pilots and rocket crews: by the end of the year the USSR had stationed 200 pilots and about 15,000 men in missile crews in Egypt and were manning eighty missile sites in addition to earlier sites manned by Egyptians but also equipped with Russian missiles. Israel was forced to desist. Fighting was once more confined to the Canal and its environs. The United States and the USSR pressed their clients to start talking instead of fighting. Israel agreed to talk upon the basis of a withdrawal to pre-1967 limits and Nasser said that Egypt would recognize Israel. Israel agreed that talks might be indirect (through a UN negotiator, the Swedish Ambassador Gunnar Jarring) or direct. In June therefore the American secretary of state William Rogers produced a plan for a cease-fire as a preliminary to indirect negotiations having as their goal an Israeli withdrawal and Egyptian recognition of Israel. Israel disliked this plan, as did the Palestinians; Nasser rejected it. But in July Nasser spent two weeks in Moscow, and Egypt and Israel both accepted the idea of a cease-fire. In August a ninety-day cease-fire and standstill agreement was concluded: within an area of 50 km. on each side of the Canal fighting would cease and no fresh units would be introduced, and talks would begin under Jarring's aegis. This agreement was renewed in November and again in February 1971, but it was immediately infringed by Egypt which moved missiles into the stand-still zone. Israel responded by quitting the Jarring talks and demanding massive American aid. It got only part of its demands, waxed indignant with Washington and was forced back to the talks before the year ended.

These talks greatly alarmed the Palestinians who foresaw an Israeli–Egyptian deal, followed perhaps by an Israeli–Jordanian deal, which would leave them out in the cold. They decided to wreck the proceedings. George Habash's Popular Front for the Liberation of Palestine, a small but specially militant group among the dozen or so separate Palestinian organizations, hijacked four American and British airliners, held the passengers and crews hostage and burned the aircraft. In Amman King Hussein, yielding to pressure from his extremist anti-Palestinian advisers, decided on a trial of strength with the Palestinians who were turning his country and his capital into an armed camp and exposing it to enemy attacks. He proved the power of his army which inflicted heavy casualties on the Palestinians but shocked the Arab world by the spectacle of fratricidal war and suffered a political rebuff when peace was restored by the intervention of other Arab states (notably Syria which invaded Jordan) and he had to sign, in the embassy of a foreign state, what was in effect a treaty of peace with the Palestinian leader Yassir Arafat, who was thus accorded the status of a head of state without the inconveniences of having territory to defend and control. The king committed himself to support the Palestinians' aims, though he soon afterwards entered into secret discussions with Israel which were unlikely to produce terms of peace acceptable both to Israel and to the Palestinians.

During the fighting in Jordan Iraqi troops stationed in that country made no move to help the Palestinians. Syria on the other hand sent a small detachment of tanks across the border but withdrew it, probably under Russian pressure induced in its turn by the prospect of Israeli or American intervention against this intervention. General Jedid's ill-fated gesture recalled his failure in 1967 to defend the Golan heights against Israel and contributed to the overthrow of the Syrian government later in the year by his rival and defence minister, General Hafiz as-Assad, a leader no less anti-Israel than Jedid but more solicitous about good relations with Egypt and other Arab countries. More important by far, among the consequences of Jordan's internal war, was the sudden death of Nasser from a heart attack caused by his exertions in restoring peace in Jordan. He was succeeded with constitutional smoothness by vice-president Anwar as-Sadat.

The death of Nasser removed from the scene the first Egyptian to rule in Egypt since before the days of Alexander the Great. The movement which brought him to power had had complex sources. It sought national emancipation, a spiritual (Islamic) revival, social reform and economic modernization. Nasser wanted to rid Egypt of a parasitic monarchy and upper class, to extinguish British domination over Egypt and the Sudan, and to raise the miserable standard of living of the Egyptian people by a more equitable distribution of land, the extension of the cultivable area and the promotion of industries. He acquired the further aims of leading all Arabs against Israel and against Arab régimes deemed reactionary.

The revolutionary movement, in which he was at first only one among a number of leaders, was predominantly but not exclusively a military collectivity in which Nasser soon came to be the leading figure by force of personality and by the elimination of possible rivals. The enemies of the old régime had included elements – the Muslim Brotherhood on the right and the communists on the left – which constituted distinct centres of power. They were suppressed almost as quickly as the pashas of the old order. Political parties were banned. Nasser out-manoeuvred the nominal leader of the coup, Neguib, who was suspected of being insufficiently implacable against some pre-revolutionary élites. By 1954 Nasser's position had been secured. In the same year he secured Egypt's national aims by negotiating with Britain the removal of British forces from the Canal Zone and British rule from the Sudan. The stage seemed set for the economic reforms which would convert the coup of 1952 into a genuine revolution.

Egypt's economy was weak at home and abroad. Egypt had too little cultivable land, a one-crop economy (cotton), a stagnant agriculture, no mineral wealth, a very small share of international trade, little industry, little capital with which to develop industries and a population growing at the rate of 3 per cent a year. The relatively small sector of modernized industry was in foreign ownership. There was, however, a native bourgeoisie with some capital resources and Nasser aimed at first to get its co-operation in the development and diversification of the Egyptian economy. But this class had no faith in the new régime and preferred to put its money into unproductive savings at home or abroad rather than venture it in industry. By the end of the fifties massive unemployment and crushing poverty had been scarcely affected and Nasser turned to other ways. The western refusal to finance the Aswan Dam and the Anglo–French attack on Egypt in 1956 had given him cause to seize the assets of foreign companies, and in the early sixties he went further and established state control over the greater part of the economy (other than retail trade). He also extended land reform from the modest and largely ineffective first steps of 1952 (when a limit of 200 feddan had been set on individual holdings, a reform which was evaded by various devices such as transferring parts of estates to relations: this reform did not apply to state or religious lands). A five-year plan for the years 1960–65 aimed to increase the gross national product by 7 per cent a year and did in fact increase it by 5.5 per cent, but this improvement was hardly felt by the working population whose numbers increased in the same years by 4 per cent.

Nasser's economic problem was never an easy one and it was made impossible by his foreign policy. He may well have intended in 1954 to devote more of his attention and resources to domestic affairs, but the resolution in that year of his differences with Britain was almost immediately followed by a more aggressive Israeli policy and by Britain's adherence to the Baghdad Pact, which Nasser interpreted as British intervention in Arab politics on the side of adversaries intent on stifling Egypt's revolution. So Nasser found himself increasingly concerned with foreign affairs instead of the reverse. The authors of the revolution had always intended to create a stronger, more efficient and better equipped army than Farouk's. This aim was intensified by the seeming need to defend the country against Israel and the revolution against Nuri's Iraq and its British friends. Nasser's consequent search for arms – and for the means to pay for them – first pushed Egypt's defence spending up beyond all normal percentages of national income and then forced Nasser into borrowing sums which Egypt had little prospect of repaying. Aid and other resources which might have gone into development were appropriated to finance a deficit on external account which increased alarmingly from 1961 onwards. The war in Yemen made matters worse. The continuing war with Israel deprived Egypt of American aid and free food. At the time of Nasser's death Egyptians were materially hardly better off than they had been eighteen years earlier (though there had been some improvement in living conditions in towns); and Egypt itself was in pawn to the USSR.

When Nasser died in 1970 the politics of the Middle East (excluding Iran) were dominated by a bipolar pattern: Israel–United States versus Egypt–USSR. Within a few years they looked very different. The Russian alliance with Egypt was broken. The United States, while not abandoning Israel, was increasingly embarrassed in its role of protector which was barely compatible with the role of peace-maker which it also cherished. The Palestinians acquired a new strength, only to see it gravely jeopardized. The Arab oil exporters gave a startling demonstration of the efficiency of economic sanctions. The Lebanese state was all but destroyed.

Sadat, like Nasser, found himself under pressure from Moscow to reach some accord with Israel on the assumption that Israel was under equivalent pressure from Washington. In fact both the United States and the USSR were oscillating between putting pressure on their clients and acceding at least in part to their demands for aid and arms: by the end of 1971 American aid to Israel, after being reined back for political reasons, was again substantial. After the fighting in Jordan in 1970 and the death of Nasser, Egypt, Syria, Libya and Sudan had agreed to form a new federation of Arab republics, but Sadat's diplomacy was multifaceted. He wished to improve Egypt's relations with the Saudi and Jordanian monarchies and also to effect a reconciliation between Syria and Jordan, which had been within an ace of fighting each other over the Palestinians. He was well equipped for these exercises since he scared the heads of other states less than Nasser had done, and although he made the mistake of assuming and saying that he would bring the Arab–Israeli matter to the point of decision within a year, he contrived not only to establish himself at home but also to consolidate much of the Arab world while at the same time pursuing the policy of edging towards a bilateral agreement with Israel. Having inherited the cease-fire and stand-still of August 1970 and the consequent talks, he offered in February 1971 to open the Canal to Israeli cargoes in return for a partial Israeli withdrawal or the convoking of a conference to be attended by the four major outside powers, but neither in this wise nor in the Jarring talks (which Israel again cold-shouldered) was any progress made during the year. In the next year Sadat twice went to

Moscow, found he could not get the help he wanted, concluded that Brezhnev had betrayed Egypt by promising Nixon to keep Egypt on short commons, and with wholly unexpected boldness told the Russian specialists and advisers in Egypt to leave. They did so in a matter of weeks, leaving Moscow – which had lost an earlier foothold in Israel – looking for new centres of influence in the Middle East.

In 1973 Sadat waxed even bolder. His Arab fence-mending complete and his hopes for a bilateral agreement soured by increased American aid to Israel and increased Israeli settlement in the occupied areas contrary to international law, he decided to take the offensive, and on 6 October Israel and the rest of the world were taken by surprise by an Arab attack on two fronts. The Egyptian army attacked across the Canal and pierced Israeli positions, but these successes were nullified when the Egyptians ventured to operate beyond air cover and the Americans rushed aid to Israel by every available military and civil aircraft. The Russians, determined not to be left out, sent aid to Syria, Iraq and Egypt. Nine days after the first shots Israel counter-attacked, found a gap in the middle of the Egyptian front and, crossing the Canal westward, surrounded an Egyptian corps. The Egyptian stroke had been stymied and the next day Kosygin arrived in Cairo. In effect the war was over, although there was still some fighting to come. In the north it was even shorter. The Syrians, with the help of Jordanian, Iraqi, Saudi and Moroccan units, attacked the Golan heights but were held and pushed back after two days.

Stalemate suited the United States and the USSR, the latter as soon as it became clear that the Arabs were not going to win and the former because, once Israel had been saved, the principal American concern was to prevent an Israeli counter-attack which would provoke a more forceful Russian riposte. Kissinger accordingly was invited to Moscow whence he proceeded to Jerusalem, and the United States and the USSR jointly presented to the Security Council a resolution requiring a ceasefire, implementation of UN resolution 242/67 and peace talks under 'appropriate' auspices. Egypt and Israel accepted this resolution and it was adopted by the Council on 22 October. The Russians had privately proposed to the Americans that American and Russian troops be sent to the Middle East but Washington rejected this idea emphatically. It was, however, reintroduced by Egypt either spontaneously or at Russian instigation, and the USSR then publicly supported it. The American reaction was extreme. All American forces throughout the world were brought to the most advanced state of alert, whereupon the USSR retracted. Washington had demonstrated implacable opposition to the arrival of Russian units in the Middle East; but some European allies were disturbed by what they deemed American over-reaction, provoking in return from Kissinger some acid comments on their nerve and reliability.

There were two ways of winding up the war – a conference or diplomatic exchanges. A conference was convened at Geneva at the end of 1973 and was dignified by the presence of Kissinger, Gromyko and the Secretary General of the UN, Kurt Waldheim, but the ensuing year was devoted primarily to personal diplomacy by Kissinger while the conference was held in abeyance like a net under an acrobat. A first Israeli–Egyptian disengagement agreement was reached in January 1974; both sides withdrew and a UN force took station between them. On the northern front negotiations were slower because Israel insisted on proper notification of the numbers, names and fates of Israelis captured by the Syrians, which the Syrians either would not or could not give, and because it was impossible for Israel to withdraw more than a mile or two without endangering its entire strategic position and its settlements within range of the Golan heights. Nevertheless Kissinger, by persistent shuttling between capitals, succeeded in getting a first agreement here too. (Both agreements were extended in November for six months and then again for another six months.) At the next stage the main crux was the status of the Palestine Liberation Organization (PLO) and its demands. Israel refused to recognize the PLO as anything but a terrorist organization or the Palestinians as anything but refugees. Israel also refused to consider territorial retreat except in the context of a general peace agreement. The PLO's proclaimed position was that it did not accept the existence of the state of Israel, but it was supposed that it might be brought to negotiate on the basis of the borders obtaining before the war of 1967. It insisted on being a principal party in negotiations as opposed to having the Palestinians represented by some Arab government. Israel wanted a series of bilateral arrangements beginning with Egypt (and side-tracking the Palestinians). Sadat was disposed to seek such an agreement provided it was quickly followed by similar agreements between Israel and its other neighbours, so that Egypt might not be accused of breaking Arab ranks or leaving the Palestinians in the lurch. Kissinger wanted an Israeli–Egyptian agreement as quickly as possible; he wanted the United States and not an international conference to be the peace-maker of the Middle East; and he wanted to fortify the American–Egyptian link without too greatly offending Israel or American Jewry: everything else could wait. Kissinger saw an Israeli–Egyptian peace as a stage towards peace in the Middle East and he did not believe that peace in the Middle East could be attained except by stages. Peace moreover was increasingly important for the United States, whose attempts to get away from a policy focused on support for Israel had been encouraged by Sadat's break with the USSR and then made urgent by the Arabs' use of oil sanctions during the war. The weakness of Kissinger's tactics was his emphasis and his dependence on Egypt which he was pressing into a bilateralism offensive to Egypt's Arab allies and into a disregard of the Palestinians whose claims remained none the less more central to the Arab–Israeli conflict than such purely Egyptian–Israeli questions as their common frontiers or the passage of Israeli cargoes and vessels through the Suez Canal. In order to succeed Kissinger had to divorce, and get Sadat to divorce, Egyptian–Israeli issues from wider Arab–Israeli issues and above all from the Palestinian cause. He risked therefore damaging his new Egyptian friend throughout the Arab world.

The Arabs were in no mood to abandon the Palestinians, however much they might wish that the Palestinians had never been heard of. The Palestinians brought trouble and danger, but at an Arab conference in Rabat in October 1974 even their most ruthless enemy, King Hussein, who had been firing on them four years earlier and had forced 15,000 of them to flee from Jordan to Syria, joined with everybody else in acknowledging that the PLO represented Arab Palestine; and from Rabat Yassir Arafat, chairman of the PLO's executive council, proceeded to the UN General Assembly which received him and listened to him as though he were a head of state and adopted a strongly pro-Palestinian resolution affirming the rights of the Palestinians to sovereignty inside Palestine and to be principals at a peace conference. In the winter 1974–75 it seemed likely that the PLO would declare itself a government in exile and be recognized by a majority of the United Nations, despite the lesions which weakened its claim to represent all Palestinians and despite the extremism of splinter groups whose indiscriminate kidnapping and killing shocked most people. (The PLO was formed in 1964. Its strongest component, created in the fifties, was Al Fatah which came to prominence from 1965 onwards by staging commando operations. The more militant PFLP of George Habash crystallized out of earlier groups in 1967. From it later broke away the PDFLP – People's Democratic Front for the Liberation of Palestine – and the PFLP High Command. Al-Saiqa, the organization of the Palestinians in Syria, was created in 1966 with the support of the Syrian Ba'ath. And there were other groups.)

If the war of 1973 gave the Palestinians a boost and a chance to recover from their drubbing in Jordan in 1970, it also boosted Arab morale and hopes in other ways. Quite apart from showing that the Egyptian army had become a match for the Israelis (at least for a week), it demonstrated Arab power against greater states. The Arab oil producers, banded together in the Organization of Arab Petroleum Exporting Countries (OAPEC, a division of OPEC), shocked the whole of the developed world by cutting off oil and raising its price. These measures were very effective and there was every reason to believe that in another emergency the oil weapon would be used yet more effectively.

For the oil-producing states oil was not merely, or even primarily, a weapon. It was above all a source of revenue and for some states the only or overwhelming source. All of them were concerned to safeguard and increase their oil revenues and in 1971 they had made, at Teheran and Tripoli, agreements to secure these ends for the next five years. They also insisted through OPEC in 1972 that purchasing countries which devalued their currencies should revise the terms of these agreements so that the producers should not lose by the devaluation. They also changed their attitudes towards the way in which they would take their profit. Whereas hitherto they had done so mainly by fiscal measures, by taxes on offtake at the wellhead, they now moved towards participation or part ownership of operating companies and resolved to appropriate 25 per cent of the share capital of major companies, rising to 51 per cent by 1982. They felt moreover that what they set out to get they would get because – even before the war of 1973 – the developed world was worrying about an energy shortage amounting to an energy crisis. This crisis began to push up prices alarmingly in 1970–71 and made the producers more conscious of the advantages of restricting production: restrictions on output would prolong the life of reserves of an irreplaceable asset, put the screws on customers, and yet maintain producers' revenues if prices were raised – as they easily could be in a seller's market – to compensate for a lower volume of sales. Importing countries were vulnerable either way. Restrictions, let alone a stoppage, would jeopardize their industry and their daily life; price increases would disfigure their balance of payments. (The companies, however, were not in the same position as the importing countries. They suffered only one way. Restrictions and stoppages harmed their profits, higher prices did not.)

When the war began the Gulf producers raised their prices by 70 per cent. OAPEC threatened to cut deliveries by 5 per cent a month until Israel undertook to evacuate Arab territory and accede to the legitimate rights of the Palestinians. Saudi Arabia cut deliveries by 10 per cent; to the United States and the Netherlands, Israel's main champions, totally. Iraq nationalized parts of certain foreign companies and Libya talked of total expropriation. As a result of this multifarious, if ill-coordinated, Arab action oil prices in Iran, Nigeria and elsewhere shot up. Also as a result the EEC expressed its sympathy for the Palestinians, Britain stopped supplies of arms to Israel and Japan reversed its pro-Israeli proclivities. Arab threats did not fully materialize – it was, for example, not possible to boycott the Netherlands when oil despatched to other countries could be transshipped to Rotterdam – and within the Arab world there were some who feared the effects on themselves of harming western economies which were their principal customers. But the point had been made and taken. A long-standing major factor in international affairs had been shaken. Primary producers were no longer the exploited but, where there was co-operation and shortage, could call the tune and use economic leverage for political ends. The change was so startling to public opinion in the industrial world that it was greeted with cries of blackmail. For the Middle East it meant that so long as there was an energy crisis Arabs could not be trifled with.

Thus the Kissinger–Sadat axis was a brittle one, and although Kissinger's stage-by-stage diplomacy was admirably motivated, it was less well grounded in practical terms. The arguments which Kissinger could bring to bear on Sadat without discountenancing him in his own country were limited by the availability of so efficacious a new weapon and by the enhanced prominence of the Palestinians. Nor were the Israelis on their side to be pressured so easily. They had not been defeated. They had on the contrary satisfied themselves that in spite of initial reverses they had been on the way to another victory. But they had been severely shaken by the failure of intelligence services which, in so small a country, were vital to prevent instant obliteration. In elections at the end of 1973 the government parties lost six seats; the gains were on the right but there was increased support too for doves critical of Israel's Arab policies. The chief of staff and other senior officers resigned. Moshe Dayan, ultimately responsible for national security as minister of defence, lost some of his hero's image and was left out of the new government formed in April 1974 when General Yitzhak Rabin succeeded Mrs Golda Meir as prime minister. The spectacle of an American president touring Arab capitals in June was a disturbing one, even though Nixon came to Jerusalem too. The speed with which the USSR more than made up Syria's and Iraq's losses in arms was more disturbing, even though the United States did the same for Israel. At the end of 1974 Syria, by proposing a new joint military command with Egypt, Jordan and the PLO, emphasized the underlying unity among Israel's neighbours and their commitment to the Palestinians. Perhaps Israel had never been so unsettled. This was not a situation in which an American secretary of state could wield too big a stick, certainly not in public view.

Kissinger renewed his shuttle diplomacy early in 1975 with the aim of getting a further Israeli–Egyptian disengagement agreement. At first he was unsuccessful, owing mainly to Israeli obduracy. Sadat, after a meeting in May with President Ford at Salzburg, announced the reopening of the Suez Canal and in September a new agreement was reached. Fresh front lines and force levels were accepted; the keeping of the agreement was to be monitored by a string of early warning stations, some of them manned by American civilians; Israel abandoned the Mitla and Giddi passes and Egypt's oilfields in Sinai, in return for which it was promised massive American aid and the passage of Israeli cargoes (but not vessels) through the Canal. This was the crown of Kissinger's exertions and by comparison it seemed to matter little that on the northern front the greater acerbity of the adversaries and Israel's persistence in planting new settlements in occupied territory prevented any equivalent relaxation. Yet it was in this area that the next crisis was about to occur.

One of the recurrent features of Middle Eastern politics from 1919 onwards was the attempt to forget about the Palestinians. From the time when Emir Faisal and Chaim Weizmann talked at the Paris peace conference without troubling about them the Palestinians had been overlooked or worse, but they refused to disappear or lose their identity. By 1975 there were rather more than 3 million of them, of whom close on half lived in Israel, or under Israeli occupation. Of the remainder 750,000 were in Jordan, 400,000 in Lebanon, 200,000 in Syria. Through half a century they had persistently posed political problems, tugged at consciences (non-Arab as well as Arab) and resorted to violent means – including in the seventies guerrilla operations, kidnapping, murder and hijacking – in order to draw attention to themselves and their grievances. After their pounding in Jordan in 1970 the centre of these activities was Lebanon.

Lebanon has been called the Switzerland of the Middle East. This meant two things: first, that the Lebanese were highly successful merchants and bankers, good at making money, richer than their neighbours and rich because of the services they rendered rather than from domestic natural resources; and secondly, that the country was a patchwork of communities held together by political skill and tolerance in the service of material self-interest. The patchwork was imposed by geography as much as history, and the cohesion of the patchwork was a condition of the survival of the state. Two parallel ranges of mountains, one close to the sea and the two separated by a narrow valley, cut the country into vertical strips which are again divided by transverse barriers, and within this grid separate communities had preserved their individualities and mutual hostilities. These had been sharpened by religions – Muslim and Christian – and by further divisions within religions: Sunni, Shia and Druze; Maronite, Greek Orthodox and Greek Catholic. They had also been sharpened by varieties of economic experience, for not all Lebanese were rich. The richest group were the Maronite Christians who held in addition the presidency, given to them by the constitution and at a time when Christians as a whole outnumbered Muslims. (A decline in the Christian proportion of the population was one of the ground factors in Lebanese tensions.) The other Christian communities were neither so rich nor so powerful, but so long as Lebanon presented the appearance of a prosperous mercantile community in the guise of a state, by so much was it Christian rather than Muslim.

The largest of the Muslim communities were the Shia, but the Sunni, who monopolized the post of prime minister by constitutional right, were more influential politically. The Shia, many of whom had drifted from being poor countrymen to becoming poor townspeople, felt themselves to be equally neglected by Maronite Christians and Sunni Muslims. They were most exposed to Israeli incursions. The Druzes on the other hand, who still preserved much of the fierce exclusiveness which had marked their origins in the eleventh century, were confident and assertive because, though for the most part poor and frequently indignant, they formed a compact and well-knit society in an hereditary mountain homeland and under a hereditary leader, Kamal Jumblatt, who commanded their loyalties and expressed an appropriate left-wing have-not philosophy.

Into this delicate cat's cradle of criss-crossing confessional and economic tensions had come in 1948 refugees from Palestine who, by 1975, numbered about 400,000, mostly housed (an ironic word) in dreadful camps. They included some five or six thousand active gunmen whose aim was the recovery of lost lands in Palestine by any effective means and the extinction – if that were necessary, as it was assumed to be – of the Israeli state. Since such an aim could never be attained by a few thousand armed men it had to be prosecuted through Arab states which had to be induced to make war on Israel. Since these states were only half willing to do so, and since when they ventured they got beaten, the Palestinians had a survival problem which led them to look even further afield for aid and sympathy, notably to the leading left-wing powers, China and the USSR (although the latter preferred to put its money on governments rather than on movements which were attacking governments), and to universal left-wing opinion which would rally to dispossession and destitution and not be too gravely offended by the use of terror as a weapon justified by desperation. Within Lebanon Palestinians could count on support, not from the political and mercantile élite which regarded them as a nuisance, but from other sections of the population which had to recognize them as fellow Arabs and fellow underdogs. By the seventies the Palestinians were more than a nuisance. Their militant organizations, encamped on Lebanese soil, regarded themselves as being at war with Israel, which was Lebanon's neighbour, and did not hesitate to strike back when attacked from Lebanon. The Maronites in particular, as conservative Christians, disliked and feared the Palestinian organizations because they were left-wing, militant, Muslim and a threat to the stability of the state which gave the Maronites their wealth and their influence. It was an important coincidence that the Maronite position in Lebanon was already under some threat from the country's changing demographic balance and from the nemesis which (cf. Northern Ireland) haunts a too prosperous exclusivity.

In 1975 a group of Muslim fishermen who felt aggrieved by a concession granted to a group of Christian fishermen staged a demonstration which turned into an affray. Some Palestinians took sides with the Muslims. Christians saw in this episode a writing on the wall: the Palestinians, already a standing incitement to Israeli aggression against Lebanon, were now interfering too in the balance of internal Lebanese politics. Anti-Palestinian incidents followed, caused by the Phalange, a right-wing Christian faction. Violence escalated; the government, always weak in a crisis because of conflicting loyalties implanted in it by the constitution, fell; the army, small and itself divided, failed to keep order. The disorder, which had begun as faction fights, turned into a battle for territory. The Palestinians, who had arms in plenty, became more and more involved (against the wishes of some of their leaders) and their opponents more and more provocative. There were innumerable truces of insignificant duration. Battle having been joined, opportunity beckoned to both sides. A left-wing alliance of Druzes and Palestinians seemed set to take over the country, the Druzes in order to supplant the existing ruling groups and the Palestinians in order to make Lebanon safe for Palestinians and a base against Israel. On the other side the Maronites and their allies sensed the chance to do to the Palestinians in Lebanon what King Hussein had done to them in Jordan: expel as many as possible, kill some leaders and perhaps even, as tempers became uncontrollably bitter, exterminate them with Israel's help.

As the civil war threatened to entail the destruction of the state Syria had to consider what to do. Lebanon had been a part of Syria (as had Palestine) under Ottoman dominion and before, but Syria hesitated to intervene for a number of reasons. If the Syrian army were to go into Lebanon the Israeli army would most probably do so too and a new conflict would be staged, unwelcome to Syria and to Syria's Russian patrons. Nor would Jordan, with which President Assad had been improving relations for some years, take kindly to any move which looked like a step towards recreating Greater Syria. The same argument applied at least as strongly to Iraq. Syria therefore, though inclined as a Muslim and left-wing state to favour the Druze–Palestinian side, was more concerned to end the fighting and put the Lebanese state back on its feet; and Assad concentrated on finding a way of restoring the constitutional proprieties under a Maronite president (though a new one), even if this entailed attacking the Palestinians. Syrian intervention took therefore an anti-Palestinian and pro-Maronite flavour which outraged other Arab states which, suspicious of Syrian designs, tried to substitute pan-Arab for Syrian management of the crisis by introducing a mixed Arab force and an Arab League mediator. But these moves had little substance. Assad chose his moment to put his own troops in and imposed a provisional settlement whereby the Maronites would retain the presidency *de jure* but the president would no longer choose the prime minister and the Muslims would have equal representation with Christians in the parliament. This was a restoration which amounted to a defeat for the leftish Shi'ites and Druzes (Kamal Jumblatt was killed, probably murdered) who had scented power only to be denied it by foreign intervention; and it was a defeat for the Palestinians, who had made common cause with the Druzes and other anti-Maronite elements and in doing so had backed the losing side and been battered first by the Maronites and then by the Syrians. It was also a defeat for the Russians who, having perforce shifted their pivot in the Middle East from Cairo to Damascus, saw Syria acting with a degree of independence and in a direction which were both unpalatable to Moscow. Yet Moscow gave no help to Jumblatt or Arafat; its influence in the crisis was minimal. Assad, not Arafat, had become the dominant force in the state. Lebanon itself was in ruins and in tutelage. It could eject Syria from its system only at the price of letting loose new conflicts between the private armies of Maronites, Druzes and others, which no purely Lebanese army could control. The Maronites, although rescued by Syria, were no less hostile to it and remained prone to flirt with Israel in spite of the fact that this flirting fatally divided them. The Palestinians, having been attacked by Jordan and by Syria, having lost their stronghold in Lebanon, and conscious that Sadat's sympathy for them was offset by Egypt's contrary interest in peace with Israel, had once more nobody to rely on but themselves. Arafat had looked for support in the wrong quarter. Disillusioned with Arab governments and nervous about leftish breakaways from his own movement, he had formed an alliance with the Arab left and so become a target for Arab governments determined to annihilate the left.

The civil war in Lebanon, which lasted from April 1975 to November 1976, cost 40,000 lives and huge material and commercial damage. The new president, Elias Hrawi, less committed to the Maronite ascendancy in its old form than his predecessor Suleiman Franjieh, lacked the authority and the armed power to make his government's writ run. The fighting was brought to a stop by the Syrians but Assad's position in Lebanon was both taxing and embarrassing. Syria was reviled by the rest of the Arab world; Iraq cut off oil (but Saudi Arabia provided credits to fill the gap). Assad had neither the means nor probably the wish to take the whole responsibility for Lebanon's affairs. He reverted to negotiation. At Shtoura in July 1977 Syria, Lebanon and the PLO reaffirmed a Lebanese–PLO agreement made in Cairo in 1969 whereby the PLO would withdraw its armed units from Beirut and the frontier zone in the south. This disarming of the Palestinians was put in train in Beirut but not in the south where fighting started again between Palestinians and Lebanese Christians. The Israelis invaded and with their help Major Saad Haddad established (in a largely Muslim area) a semi-independent Christian state of Free Lebanon. Neither the Lebanese army, always helpless in the face of communal strife, nor the UN Interim Force in

Lebanon (UNIFIL) could do anything to counter this creation of an Israeli puppet state, while in the rest of the country private armies resumed their battles and assassinations. There were about forty armies or armed bands in this small state. In 1980 battles between the two principal Maronite forces resulted in victory for the Phalange and the Gemayel family over the National Liberal Party of the Chamoun and other prominent Maronite clans. The victors were the more determined to remove from Lebanon all Palestinians, civilian refugees as well as armed units, and they had Israel's armour to help them. A new no-go area, like Major Haddad's and beyond the reach of the Sarkis government, was created in and around Beirut, a Phalangist autonomous canton.

This disintegration of Lebanon was consciously promoted by Israel. South Lebanon was part of the lands claimed for Israel by Zionist irridentism, but this claim might have remained muted if the area had not become during the seventies a refuge of Palestinian revanchism. Israel was determined to eradicate the militant arm of the Palestinians by force, and most Israelis regarded any aggressive action for this purpose as a legitimate exercise of the right of self-defence. In its earliest days the threat to Israel's existence came from Arab states. Israel believed that, by its superior efficiency and American aid, it could always defeat enemies who would be perpetually at odds with each other. At this stage the Palestinians were no more than a minor instrument of the Arab states, useful mainly for propaganda purposes. But they became the central issue, evolving a fighting force of their own, attracting international sympathy and commanding the support of Arab states – a reversal of roles which turned them into a more persistent danger to Israel than any Arab government.

Israel's increasingly aggressive response was a recognition of this change. Whereas Arab states could not be destroyed, the political power of the Palestinians might be if enough Palestinians could be killed or dispersed. A change of government in Israel helped to put this reasoning into practice. During 1976 the Labour-dominated coalition struggled in vain with economic problems and disorders on the West Bank. Splits developed within the coalition and within the Labour Party itself. At the UN the United States was increasingly alone in vetoing anti-Israeli resolutions in the Security Council and eventually joined the majority in condemning Israel's ruthless and illegal behaviour in the West Bank. The prime minister Yitzhak Rabin resigned when his wife was accused of a currency offence but his successor Shimon Peres did not survive a general election and in 1977 Menachem Begin, veteran fighter against the British and biblical fundamentalist, formed Israel's first government without the Labour Party. He declared that Israel must keep the West Bank and should accelerate the creation of new settlements there. President Carter, among others, called these settlements illegal. He proposed that the Geneva conference be reconvened (with Russian participation) and that the PLO be invited to attend it on condition that it recognize Israel's right to exist. Begin was willing to see Palestinians at a conference but adamant that he would never at any point negotiate with the PLO, thus allowing Arafat to avoid giving a straight answer to Carter's question. In November Begin, to general amazement, invited Sadat to Jerusalem and Sadat, who was thought to have contrived the invitation, possibly through Ceausescu, at once accepted. He badly needed peace. He had fought a four-day war with Libya on his other flank; the Egyptian economy was in tatters; and domestic disaffection had turned into riots.

Addressing the Knesset with a directness and modesty which attracted worldwide praise Sadat deplored delays in reconvening the Geneva conference and appealed for peace between Egypt and Israel, Israel's withdrawal to its 1967 frontiers and the right of self-determination and statehood for the Palestinians; he did not mention the PLO by name. Before the year ended talks between Egypt and Israel began in Cairo and Begin visited Ismailia where he spoke of an autonomous Palestinian entity with an Israeli military presence for twenty years. His formal proposals for the West Bank, published at the very end of the year, envisaged continuing Israeli control of security and public order, a choice for the inhabitants between Israeli and Jordanian (but not Palestinian) citizenship, Arab immigration in 'reasonable numbers' to be agreed between Israel, Jordan and the new authority of the autonomous territory, and freedom for Israelis to buy land. Carter approved this response, thus opposing the creation of a Palestinian state.

This was the beginning of the process which ended the war between Egypt and Israel but, contrary to the expectations roused on many sides, did nothing for the Palestinians. Begin, while prepared to abandon valuable forward positions and defences in Sinai (which was demilitarized), had no intention of abandoning control over the West Bank; he proposed on the contrary to accelerate its demographic transformation by encouraging settlements regardless of their strictly military justification; the Jewish population of the occupied West Bank quintupled in three years of his government. Egypt secured a much needed peace and the return of the territory and oilfields in Sinai which it had lost in 1973. But Sadat was violently attacked by almost the whole of the Arab world for failing to make this peace settlement with Israel contingent upon an equitable deal for the Palestinians. He lost his Saudi subsidies and became dependent on American charity.

Carter, having failed to reactivate the Geneva conference, became an eager champion of this strange Israeli–Egyptian concord which he saw as the forerunner in a series of agreements between Israel and all its circumambient enemies. The United States assumed the role of a principal negotiator with Israel and Egypt and at a tripartite conference at Camp David in September 1978 got both Begin and Sadat to subscribe, alongside the bilateral peace terms, what was described as a framework for a Middle East settlement: Israel was gradually to leave the West Bank (and Gaza), creating an autonomous Palestinian entity with a temporary Israeli presence, all other problems to be deferred for five years. Begin and Sadat – like Kissinger and Le Duc Tho some years earlier – were awarded the Nobel Prize for Peace, thus repeating the curious deviation by which the prize was bestowed on warriors who mended their ways rather than on more exemplary men of peace.

The euphoria generated by Sadat's appearance in Jerusalem in 1977 lasted about a year. American pressure on Jordan and Saudi Arabia to applaud what had been done and to further it failed completely. The Arabs were divided into the hostile and the very hostile. Israel continued its economic decline (its rate of inflation became one of the highest in the world) and pursued its tough policies on its northern borders and the West Bank. Begin's cabinet lost its more eminent members and its popular support; General Dayan, who had crossed the floor when Begin won the election of 1977, deserted him over his government's insistence on promoting settlements which had a political but no strategic purpose, and General Ezer Weizmann did so too on similar grounds. But although Begin's abrasive and unyielding manner lost him friends, there were few signs that his basic objectives had become unpopular. The election of the outspokenly pro-Israeli Ronald Reagan to be President of the United States was a relief for Israelis who had begun to ponder the future policies of an American administration forced to choose between its devotion to Israel and its material and strategic interests in Saudi Arabia and the Gulf. And the war launched by Iraq against Iran in 1980 re-advertised the fissures among Israel's enemies as some Arab governments supported Iraq and others did not.

At Camp David Begin had bought off Egypt, a rare diplomatic feat in Israel's history of military triumphs. But he secured his southern flank as part of an expansionist policy in other directions. Israel kept its hold on the occupied West Bank with little difficulty. Although it was obliged to use harsh measures which did it no good in the outside world, internally there was minimal Israeli criticism of either the occupation or its seamier side, and Begin used his freedom of manoeuvre to the south and east to launch a war northward into Lebanon. A narrow electoral victory in 1981 left him dependent in the Knesset on small and myopic religious parties whose impact on policy was both hard and adventurous. Israel's creeping colonization of the West Bank became more brutal and precipitate – the Jewish population was to be increased from 20,000 to 120,000 by 1985 – and the Israeli air force displayed its muscle by destroying a nuclear installation near Baghdad in June and raiding Beirut in July: a left and right against Iraq on the one hand and Syria on the other. The former exploit, designed to pre-empt or delay the emergence of Iraq as an offensive nuclear power, was condemned at the UN even by the United States which delayed, by a few token weeks, the delivery to Israel of new military aircraft. The attack on Beirut was prompted by discord within Lebanon over the presence of Syrian forces – the so-called Arab Defence Force (ADF), created to keep Lebanon in one piece and independent, but a force which was Syrian in all but name. The ADF was challenged by the Christian Phalange which was hostile to Syria and alarmed about the gradual decline of (mainly Maronite) Christian *vis-à-vis* Muslim power in Lebanon. When at the end of 1980 the Syrians evacuated Zahle to the east of Beirut the Phalange forestalled the regular Lebanese army and occupied it. The Syrians supported the army's attempts to oust the Phalange. Fighting spread. Israel saw its opportunity. Besides raids into southern Lebanon it flew demonstrative sorties over Beirut and when Syria then introduced ground-to-air missiles it attacked them. Israel hoped to propel President Bashir Gemayel, who was not only a Maronite Christian but also the son of the founder of the Phalange, to take sides with that militant body and so entrench a Christian and anti-Syrian statelet in parts of Beirut and its surroundings. But President Gemayel was persuaded by Syria and other Arabs to denounce an Israeli–Phalange alliance. Torn between Syria and Israel, the Maronites were on the slippery slope to the loss of their once dominant role in Lebanon.

At the end of 1981 the Saudi prime minister, Prince Fahd, presented a plan for peace which required the withdrawal of Israel to its 1967 borders and implied the recognition of the Israeli state within those limits. This plan was anathema to Israel but was aborted by the Arabs themselves when President Assad refused to go to a conference at Fez to discuss it. King Hussein strongly supported the Saudi initiative, patched up his quarrel with Morocco by his first visit to that country for five years, but displeased President Reagan by his insistence on including the PLO in any peace process notwithstanding that the Palestine National Council refused formally to abate its demand for the elimination of the Israeli state.

Reagan was still clinging to the view that peace could be achieved without the concurrence of the PLO but his commitment to Israel and to his predecessor's Camp David programme received two knocks at the end of 1981. In October President Sadat was assassinated. More of a hero outside his country than in it, Sadat offended many Egyptians by his style as well as his policies. A notable feature of his death was the peaceful transfer of power to Hosni Mubarak, demonstrating the comparative stability of Egypt's political system. The new president, although too cautious to make any abrupt changes of policy, was concerned to garner the full fruits of the Camp David agreement so far as they related to Israel's retreat from Egyptian soil (which was completed in April 1982) but also to mend Egypt's relations with the rest of the Arab world which had been wrecked by Sadat's incautious acceptance of the agreement's vague reference to Palestinian claims. By 1984 Mubarak was strong enough to legalize a revived, if fairly tame, Wafd and allow it to take part in a general election. Secondly, President Reagan was obliged to recognize some linkage between different parts of the Middle East and so implicitly to modify his belief that the Palestinian issue could be kept in a tight compartment. Concerned by the extension of the Iraqi–Iranian war to the Gulf he agreed, and narrowly persuaded the Senate to agree, to the sale of AWACS intelligence aircraft to Saudi Arabia (for delivery in 1986) but at the cost of giving Israel still more military aid, an agreement for 'strategic co-operation' and an enhanced capacity for independent adventures. By the same token the American room for manoeuvre in the Middle East was becoming more inhibited even before Israel marginalized all peace plans by launching on 6 June 1982 a full-scale invasion of Lebanon.

The ostensible and limited object of this operation was to root out the Palestinians from south Lebanon who were harassing Israel, but there were deeper causes and wider ambitions. For Menachem Begin and Zionists of his kind parts of Lebanon belonged to Israel by divine and biblical right and all Israel's governments since the creation of the state had mooted the destruction of Lebanon by arraying its Christian against its Muslim communities. The spark for the invasion was provided by the attempted assassination of the Israeli ambassador in London. Its scope was immediately made clear as the Israeli forces advanced rapidly from southern Lebanon to the outskirts of Beirut. It was a military success but a political disaster. In the first stage Israel failed to secure the eviction of the PLO from Beirut since the Israeli government shrank from an assault on the capital which would entail heavy Israeli casualties and American displeasure, but in July east Beirut was taken with Christian help and the Palestinian fighters were evacuated by sea. In September President Gemayel was assassinated, probably with Syrian connivance or at Syria's instigation. He was succeeded by his brother Amin. Israel attacked west Beirut. At this point and in revenge for Bashir Gemayel's death, appalling massacres of defenceless Palestinian refugees were perpetrated in two camps at Sabra and Chatila. The perpetrators were Phalangists but Israelis were present at Phalangist headquarters throughout the three days and nights of atrocities which continued ceaselessly with the help of lighting provided by Israelis. Subsequently an official Israeli inquiry, forced upon a reluctant Israeli government by international outcry and internal disquiet, censured a number of highly placed Israelis for their responsibility in these doings.

By invading Lebanon Israel put at stake the virtually unconditional support which successive American governments conceded to it. Whether the invasion alone would have permanently eroded that support is questionable but the massacre made a deep mark on an American view of Israel which, ever since the foundation of the state in the wake of the Nazi holocaust, had permitted a double standard to be applied to the more dubious Israeli actions. In Israel itself the shock was profound and, coupled with continuing complications and deaths in the occupation of southern Lebanon over the next few years, created at least the beginnings of a revulsion against the more unacceptable features of Israeli aggressiveness, a suspicion that Israel's policies were in the long run hopeless, and some disinclination to accept the majority view that only the Palestinians were blameworthy. Above all the invasion's declared aim of peace for Galilee was not attained.

A multinational peacekeeping force of French, Italian and American units, later joined by a minute British contingent, had arrived in Lebanon before the massacre in order to oversee the evacuation of the PLO and Syrians from west Beirut. Casualties at this stage were around 12,000, including Lebanese civilians (and 350 Israelis). At the same time President Reagan produced another peace plan. Since it included a ban on Israeli annexations, an end to Israeli settlements on the West Bank and an autonomous West Bank state in association with Jordan, it was immediately rejected by Begin. Reagan's simultaneous plea for the mutual withdrawal of Israeli and Syrian forces was ignored by both and was a dead letter from the start. The Arabs produced their own plan which again implicitly recognized an Israeli state (within the 1967 frontiers) but also demanded a Palestinian state with Jerusalem as its capital: this was a refurbishment of the Fahd plan of the previous year (Fahd had become king in June on the death of his brother Khaled). Lebanon's faction fighting continued and the Syrians and Israelis remained in the country. The Palestinian fighters (about 7,500) were dispersed in ten different directions, half of them to Syria, but Syria failed to promote an effective alternative to Arafat as the Palestinians' outstanding leader.

The Syrian position was initially precarious but was gradually consolidated, mainly because neither the Israeli–American front nor Syria's Arab enemies had anything viable to offer. The Israelis were overstretched and unhappy, the Lebanese army impotent, the multinational force decamped when it got caught in the crossfire of Lebanese politics: 239 US marines were killed in a single suicide raid in October 1983 after the US navy bombarded Shi'ite and Druze positions from off-shore. Begin resigned in 1983 from a combination of personal domestic grief on his wife's death and political frustration, leaving Israel militarily, politically and morally weakened. President Assad on the other hand, having survived two rounds of risings against him in the first months of 1982 (although only at the cost of massacring his domestic enemies to the number of perhaps 10–20,000) was left locally in control. In Lebanon Amin Gemayel had nobody but Assad to turn to and when in 1983 Gemayel tried to secure an Israeli withdrawal by direct negotiation with Israel his partners in the Lebanese government denounced his efforts and Assad forced him to cancel the deal which he had made. Gemayel's task of piecing together a coalition from his country's warring forces was repeatedly frustrated by one or another of them and Gemayel himself was reduced to insignificance.

The Israeli withdrawal was completed in 1985. The Israelis took with them 1,000 Lebanese captives. To get them back a group called al-Jihad hijacked an American B-727 on its way from Athens to Rome and brought it to Beirut. The American and Israeli governments, emphasizing their refusal to deal with terrorists, refused to negotiate for the release of its passengers and crew but the Shi'ite leader Nabih Berri did so and secured their freedom in return for the release of Israel's 1,000 captives. The Americans contented themselves with threats of retaliation which did not materialize.

Syria failed to find a way to pacify or unite Lebanon. The PLO, buffeted but not eradicated, rebuilt its positions in the camps round Beirut and Sidon and so presented Syria with the possibility of another Israeli invasion to destroy them. This time Syria, abandoning its policy of restoring the Maronite–Sunni ascendancy, promoted an alliance of the Shi'ite Amal Party of Nabih Berri with the Druzes led by Kemal Jumblatt's son Walid, but the Palestinians offered stiff resistance to attempts to dislodge them from the camps and re-established their armed presence in them. The Shi'ite–Druze alliance evicted the Maronites from west Beirut but not the Palestinians. Syria's vexations were compounded by the surreptitious activities of its supposed ally, Iran, which split the Shi'ites between the pro-Syrian Amal and the pro-Iranian Hizbollah whose purpose was to create an Islamic state in Lebanon and use it as a springboard for war with Israel and the recapture of Jerusalem – policies regarded by Syria as impractical and suicidal. Amal and Hizbollah came to blows in west Beirut and the latter attacked the South Lebanese Army which was under Israeli protection. In addition Iran supported fundamentalist Sunnis (Tawhid al-Islam) who raised their own army and used it to fight Syrian units in Lebanon. Among the Maronites Gemayel was from the Syrian point of view a broken reed; by attaching himself to Syria he antagonized half his own community, half the Phalange and half the (Christian) Lebanese army – all bodies where Syria was as much disliked as Israel. The Phalangist Samir Geagea, commander of the Lebanese Forces, challenged Gemayel's authority but the Maronites, fearful of these divisions among themselves, created a Salvation Council as a means of getting rid of Geagea and retaining their hold on east Beirut. Another leading Maronite, Elie Hobeika – a former commander of the Lebanese

Forces, displaced by Geagea in 1986 – threw in his lot with Syria, went to Damascus and agreed to a truce with the Shi'ites and Druzes and to Syria's political programme: parity between Christians and Muslims, a reduction in the powers of the Maronite president, and a special relationship between Lebanon and Syria. But these moves failed to restore unity in Lebanon or to stop the fighting. President Gemayel, who had not been consulted, repudiated the agreement with Berri and Jumblatt, and the Maronites disowned Hobeika in favour of Geagea. In 1987 Maronites murdered the Sunni prime minister Rashid Karawi and developed in east Beirut a single-minded and militant hostility to the Syrians, who returned in force.

Lebanon was divided three ways and then four ways. In the south Israel supported its puppet régime under Christian military control. The rest of the country had rival governments headed by Karami's successor Selim al-Hoss (a Sunni) and Michel Aoun (Christian commander of the Lebanese army). Aoun's main aim was the eviction of Syria's 30,000 troops, in which he had help from Syria's perennial foe, Iraq. Fighting increased. In 1989 a rump of the Lebanese parliament elected in 1972 was assembled at Taif in Saudi Arabia, reformulated the Fahd programme and chose a new Christian president – René Mouawad – to replace Gemayel. Mouawad re-appointed al-Hoss as prime minister but was then killed. His successor, Elias Hrawi, purported to dismiss Aoun from his command of the Lebanese army but the army remained loyal to him. Geagea's Lebanese forces opposed and were attacked by Aoun – two Christian leaders at war with each other until Aoun was bombarded by Syrian projectiles into surrender in 1990. Geagea then withdrew his forces from Beirut, leaving Hrawi's government ostensibly, Syria effectively, in control of the whole capital and hoping to reunite not only the capital but also the country along the lines adumbrated by the Taif agreement and with a new prime minister.

In the wake of the Israeli invasion of Lebanon King Hussein resumed his efforts to find a settlement between Israel and its neighbours. The rebuff to Israel in Lebanon and the worsting of the PLO by Syria revived the king's hopes of an agreement whereby Israel would cede some territory in exchange for peace. These hopes had long been shared by Shimon Peres, leader of Israel's Labour Party and joint head of the coalition formed in 1984 with Likud, led after Begin's resignation by Yitzhak Shamir; under a power-sharing agreement Peres was prime minister from 1984 to 1986 when he switched posts with Shamir and became foreign minister. These hopes were, however, unreal. Among the terms of such an agreement each side had a non-negotiable item which was unacceptable by the other. Likud, while outwardly ready to discuss some form of autonomy for Palestinians, insisted on keeping control over all territory conquered in and since 1967 and on negotiating only with Jordan. From its earliest days Israel had refused to countenance a distinct Palestinian state and it refused to enter into talks with the PLO or with a mixed Jordanian–PLO team. Hussein on the other hand believed that no peace was possible or sustainable without the participation of the Palestinians and that the PLO was their natural and proper representative. In this view he was supported by western European governments while the United States, obedient to Israeli insistence, interpreted direct talks to mean talks between Israel and Jordan only with no wider international conference. Since one main element in any peace talks must be the cession (or other disposition) of territory occupied by Israel, not to Jordan but to Palestinians, the pattern was lop-sided unless Jordan were to abandon its plea to include the PLO and the PLO were to give Hussein an open mandate to negotiate the fate of the Palestinians independently of themselves. Hussein's task in these circumstances was to reach the conference room by some dexterous fudging and not surprisingly he failed.

He began by reaching agreement with the PLO on the principle of territory-for-peace and on convoking an international conference which would include all five permanent members of the UN Security Council, Israel and a joint Jordan–PLO delegation. This formula buried the PLO in a large assembly but it implicitly rejected Israel's form of direct negotiation and, by making no reference to the Security Council's resolution 242, affronted Israel's demand for prior recognition of Israel's right to exist as a state. Hussein's manoeuvre got no support from other Arab states apart from Egypt (still an outcast because of Sadat's evasion of the Palestinian crux in the Camp David agreement) and it split the PLO. In 1985 Hussein made one of his repeated visits to Washington in order to assure the United States that the PLO would endorse resolution 242. He also asked for American arms. Reagan refused to modify the American–Israeli formula for direct negotiations but alarmed Israel by agreeing to supply Jordan with missiles and aircraft. His rejection of Hussein's plans for a peace conference was the penultimate nail in their coffin and later in the year they foundered completely when even the moderate Arabs such as King Fahd refused to attend an Arab meeting to discuss them.

Hussein blamed the PLO for this setback. Encouraged by their partial recovery in Lebanon the more militant PLO leaders were keen to draw attention to themselves and their cause by startling and violent acts. In one incident in Cyprus they killed three Israelis. Later in 1985 four Palestinians boarded at Genoa the Italian *Achille Lauro* as it set out for a cruise in the eastern Mediterranean. They intended (so they later said) to leave the ship at Ashdod in Israel and there execute some spectacular destruction of Israeli property and lives. They were, however, discovered on board before reaching Ashdod and thereupon – and apparently on the spur of the moment – seized the liner and issued a demand for the release of a number of Palestinians held captive in Israel. One of the hijackers murdered an American passenger. Alarmed by this turn of events Palestinian leaders – notably Abu Abbas, an associate of Arafat, if not always in total accord with him – ordered the hijackers to return the liner to its captain and come ashore in Egypt on being assured that they would thence be conveyed to a safe place (presumably Tunisia). This resolution of the incident was made possible by President Mubarak who provided the means of getting the hijackers off the *Achille Lauro* and out of Egypt. But the Americans, incensed by the murder of the hapless passenger, intercepted the Egyptian aircraft carrying the hijackers and Abu Abbas to Tunisia and, by threatening to shoot it down, forced it to land in Sicily where armed Americans from a Nato unit tried to seize its passengers. This last part of the exploit was foiled by the Italians who arrested and charged the hijackers but allowed Abu Abbas to escape to Yugoslavia. The consequences of these adventures included the fall of the Italian government (subsequently reinstated); the weakening of President Mubarak whose mediation brought him the humiliation of having one of his aircraft brought down by the Americans; the raising of illegal violence to higher levels, not only by the PLO but also by Israel which bombed the PLO's offices on Tunisian soil; the final abrogation of Hussein's peace plans and of his co-operation with the PLO; and a new hiatus in which no party was offering any viable proposals for an approach to peace in the Middle East.

In the next year (1986) the United States tried to reflate the peace process by offering to accept the PLO at a broad international conference if it would accept resolution 242 and forswear violence – a belated conversion to the defunct Hussein plan. But Hussein, increasingly occupied with the war in the Gulf between Iraq and Iran, washed his hands of the PLO; Peres came to the end of his term as prime minister; and the PLO retorted to the American initiative by demanding that the United States publicly endorse the Palestinians' right to self-determination – that is, to a state of their own. In 1987 the Palestinian National Council abrogated the 1985 accord between Arafat and Hussein and affirmed its demand for an independent Palestinian state and separate representation at any peace talks.

As 1987 ended the Palestinians under Israeli occupation surprised everybody, including the Israelis, by staging a rising – *intifada* – on their own account. It began with a traffic accident in Gaza, where the Palestinians' living conditions were peculiarly disgraceful and Israeli police brutality peculiarly barbarous. Stones were thrown, mostly by children, and the Israelis retaliated by opening fire and killing people. The rising spread to the West Bank and Jerusalem and evoked from the startled Israelis a riposte so harsh that Israel's already tarnished repute was severely damaged throughout the world and even governments protested publicly. Israel failed to suppress the *intifada*. The *intifada* failed to achieve anything more concrete than the violent advertisement of Palestinian grievances. The arrival in the late eighties of thousands of Jews from the USSR hardened attitudes on both sides: 200,000 immigrants in 1990 and the tide still rising presented Israel with demands for housing and jobs which it could not satisfy. Israel was losing its grip on southern Lebanon and the crisis over Kuwait was to add to its worries by allowing Syria to come in from the cold and win some (limited and grudging) goodwill in Washington by contributing to the American assemblage of armed force in Saudi Arabia against Iraq. And Jordan, Israel's sometime interlocutor, was fading from the picture.

The *intifada* and Israel's handling of it caused King Hussein finally to disengage from the West Bank, leaving Israel with the entire responsibility for its affairs and accentuating the transformation of Jordan itself into an annexe of Palestinian hostility to Israel. Hussein turned to Iraq for support against an increasingly belligerent Israel. The United States, which was by this stage providing Israel with aid up to and beyond $2 billion a year (in despite of laws which forbade aid to governments which flouted human rights), was embarrassed by Israel's behaviour and by the foundering of the peace process and felt driven in 1989 to talk for the first time officially and directly to the PLO. But in Israel Shamir, under pressure from colleagues such as David Levy and Ariel Sharon, reverted to Begin's position at Camp David. The Likud declared that it would trade no land for peace, would continue to expedite Jewish settlement of the West Bank, would never give votes to Arabs in east Jerusalem and would attend no conference so long as the *intifada* lasted. In the next year Sharon increased the pressure for bold Zionist policies by resigning from the cabinet. The Likud–Labour coalition, looking for ways of preventing a peace conference without giving too much offence to the United States, broke up and after lengthy bargaining by both major parties with minor religious parties Shamir was able to form a new government but one uncomfortably dependent on the fanatic fringe. The Labour Party was openly divided between adherents of Peres and of Rabin. Arafat, under similar pressure from colleagues, also took refuge in a regression to extreme positions. The United States tried to use Mubarak as a mediator but with no success.

Iraq's invasion of Kuwait (see the next chapter) deflected attention to more urgent conflicts. It was also one more setback for the always tenuous prospect of Arab unity and peace among Arabs. Arabs were no more united, or more likely to unite, than other kindred. But since the waning of the Ottoman power, and more specifically since the creation of the Arab League in the 1940s, they had made a point of the search for unity and had been correspondingly downcast among themselves and mocked by others when it eluded them. The late seventies had been a bad time by these standards. Egypt, the most prestigious Arab state, was made an outcast by its Camp David policies and was not even invited to attend the Arab conference at the end of 1980. Syria was cast as another deviant on account of its intervention in Lebanon, supported only by Libya and Algeria in the remote west and by South Yemen in the remote south. In the first Gulf War Saudi Arabia, carrying with it all the Gulf states, supported Iraq against Iran, whereas Syria supported Iran; Jordan took Iraq's side with unexpected directedness. When the war ended King Hussein embarked on an attempt to refashion the politics of the Arab world. His aims were pacification in the Middle East and the preservation of his own kingdom: they were interrelated. To the north and west the king faced enemies in Syria and Israel; to the south was the Saudi monarchy, hereditary enemy of the Hashemites; to the east was Iraq, waxing strong under a leader as ambitious as he was unpredictable but a man for whom the king had feelings of friendship and misplaced trust; and further off was Egypt which was re-admitted to the Arab League in 1989. During his arduous but fruitless efforts to inaugurate peace talks between Palestinians and Israel the king had become disenchanted with the United States and, if to a lesser degree, with Britain and the more convinced that the Arabs themselves must take a concerted and purely Arab initiative. At his invitation the presidents of Iraq and Egypt – and of the newly reunited Yemen at Saudi Arabia's back door – met in Amman early in 1990. But a few months later both his main guests torpedoed his plans and endangered his throne, Saddam Hussein by invading Kuwait and Hosni Mubarak by precipitately joining the forces being assembled by the United States in Saudi Arabia. The king denounced the Iraqi invasion and taking of hostages, insisted on an Iraqi retreat and the restoration of Kuwait's independence, and supported UN sanctions; but he continued to import Iraqi oil out of necessity and advocated the continued supply of necessary food and medicines to Iraq. He also continued to champion an exclusively pan-Arab resolution of the crisis. His attitudes were popular in Jordan but hardly anywhere else, and even in Jordan his own position was weakened by the addition of new to old economic strains. In attempting once more to play the role of honest broker he found himself snubbed by President Bush and received by Thatcher with the barest courtesy. The Kuwait crisis cruelly demonstrated that he was the most well intentioned but the least effective statesman in the Middle East.

Iran is in traditional parlance a part of the Middle East but it is emphatically not part of the Arab world. It remembers the Arab conquest of the seventh century more resentfully than the Mongol which is more recent by 600 years. It is the unique stronghold of Shia Islam, the tense and highpitched deviant from Sunni orthodoxy: unique because the Shia, although a majority in Bahrain, Iraq and perhaps Oman too, are everywhere except in Iran subject to a Sunni dynasty or ruling class. Iran is rich in oil but, unlike the Arab world, not only in oil. Its dominant Iranians rule over a heterogeneous variety of races and religions. It has never been subject to western imperialisms although it has been obliged on occasions to humble itself before them, particularly the British and Russian. The world's thirst for oil has given it the means to turn itself into an industrial and military power without equal in its surrounding region.

If history and geography made Iran wary of both the British and the Russians, oil made it particularly suspicious of the former. In the Second World War both powers occupied Iran on the plea of strategic necessity (the Iranians resisting for three days), and enforced the abdication of the founder of Iran's new dynasty, Reza Shah Pahlavi, who was exiled to Mauritius and later died in South Africa in 1944. His son and successor, Muhammad Reza Pahlavi, had had neither the time nor the opportunity to make a mark among his people by the time that the war and the occupation ended. The treaty of 1942 which had sanctioned foreign occupation provided for the withdrawal of the British and the Russians six months after the end of hostilities. The Russians made an attempt to retain influence in the province of Azerbaijan, comparatively rich, traditionally hostile to the central government and situated on the borders of the USSR. They also lent support to Kurdish separatism and may have entertained hopes of establishing a Russian sphere of influence stretching southwards from the Kurdish republic of Mahabad through other Kurdish territories to the Persian Gulf. They were assisted by the Tudeh Party, an amalgam of Marxist communists with an older liberal tradition which had infused the Constitutional Movement earlier in the century.

11.1 Major oil pipelines of the Gulf (Source: Dilip Hiro, *The Iran-Iraq Military Conflict*)

British troops left Iran punctually in March 1946 but Russian troops had to be manoeuvred out by the Iranian government. The astute elder statesman Qavam es-Sultaneh, who became prime minister in January 1946, visited Moscow in February on the heels of an Iranian complaint to the newly established Security Council and contrived to persuade Stalin that Russian aims in Iran could better be attained through good relations with the Iranian government than by the continued presence of Russian troops in north-western Iran. The Russians, who were at least as keen on an oil agreement with the central government as on fostering separatist movements against it, withdrew their troops only a few weeks late. Qavam entered into discussions about an oil agreement but evaded any conclusive step on the plea that, constitutionally, the ultimate decision lay with the parliament which was about to be elected; he also delayed the elections. Qavam simultaneously played a double game with the Tudeh Party. Having taken some of its members into his cabinet in order to mollify the Russians, he then welcomed (to put it no higher) a revolt by powerful southern tribes which demanded the dismissal of Tudeh ministers and other Tudeh members in prominent positions. The new Majlis (the lower house of the Iranian parliament) duly censured Qavam for engaging in discussion with the Russians for an oil agreement and declared it null and void. In spite of these oblique achievements Qavam was defeated and resigned at the end of the year. Having outwitted the Russians and seen the British depart too, he was embarking on a policy of co-operation with the United States, whence he hoped to get financial aid and diplomatic support in Iran's traditional search for means of keeping both the Russians and the British at arm's length.

Qavam's successors were nevertheless to be sharply engaged with the British in a quarrel in which the United States, after some hesitation, gave Britain firm support. Although the British had left Iran in strict accordance with the terms of the 1942 treaty, Anglo–Iranian relations were soured by the existence of the Anglo–Iranian Oil Company which had a monopoly of Iran's proven oil fields and in which the British government itself held a substantial number of shares. This unusual connection gave the company a political tinge and involved the British government in commercial affairs, two developments which were, in Iranian eyes, neither natural nor welcome consequences of the grant of a concession to a private individual early in the century. Iranian discontent was further increased by the suspicion that this rich and foreign company sold oil to the British navy on unduly favourable terms, by its secretiveness about the extent of these sales and about its accounts generally, by its failure to publicize in the rest of Iran the good wages, working conditions and other benefits which it provided for its labour force. On the other hand the company's shortcomings were not all its own fault: its failure to advertise its own virtues was due to the fact that, since it was practically unique in complying with the labour laws, it could not claim credit where credit was due without casting aspersions on other employers.

The concession inherited by the company had been granted in 1901 to a certain W. K. D'Arcy and acquired by the company before the First World War. The Iranian government had bargained to receive a percentage of the company's net profits, but this bargain turned out badly for Iran since the Iranian share was rendered dependent on the level of taxation in Britain. It was further affected by the slump between the wars and in 1932 Iran purported to cancel the concession. As a result of negotiations between Reza Shah and the company a new agreement, duly ratified by the Iranian parliament, gave the company a new concession running for sixty years from 1933 (instead of sixty years from 1901) over a substantially diminished area, and gave Iran royalties to be calculated on the quantity of oil extracted. By 1950 this output was 32.5 million metric tons, three times the amount produced in 1938; Iran was the largest producer in the Middle East and contained at Abadan the largest refinery in the world.

The revenues from the oil were much needed. After the Second World War Iran embarked on economic expansion and a plan adopted by the Majlis in 1947 envisaged the expenditure of $651 million of which $242 million were to come from oil. But oil revenues in 1947 and 1948 were a disappointment in spite of huge increases in the company's profits and the company, sensing trouble, entered into discussions for a revision of the agreement of 1933. In 1949 a supplemental agreement was concluded: the royalty rate was raised by 50 per cent and the company agreed to pay £5.1 million at once out of its reserves and thereafter to make further payments out of reserves annually instead of waiting until 1993, as the 1933 agreement provided. This agreement was very favourable to Iran but it was also complicated to the point of incomprehensibility and was unacceptable to a group of nationalists who wanted to terminate the concession entirely and take the management and profits of the oil industry into purely Iranian hands. General Ali Razmara, who became prime minister in 1950, refrained for a while from pressing the supplemental agreement on the Majlis. When he recommended its adoption – largely on the grounds that Iran was short of qualified technicians – the Majlis special oil committee demanded the nationalization of the oilfields and refinery, and the prime minister withdrew the agreement. The company, unexpectedly made aware of terms being offered by the Arab American Oil Company (Aramco) to the Saudi Arabian government – terms which were more favourable (in good years) and above all easier to understand – prepared to reopen discussions and simplify the supplemental agreement. Razmara produced a series of reports by experts who opposed nationalization but he was assassinated in March 1951 by a fanatic nationalist belonging to the semi–religious Fidayan-i-Islam. On the next day the Majlis approved the oil committee's proposals and a few weeks later it nationalized the oil industry.

General Razmara was succeeded by Husain Ala, a friend and nominee of the shah who wanted to avoid appointing the chairman of the oil committee, Dr Muhammad Musaddiq, in which attempt the shah failed. Dr Musaddiq began at the end of 1951 a spell of power which lasted tumultuously until August 1953. Musaddiq was a rich and aristocratic hysteric and hypochondriac who appealed to a wide variety of emotions; he was supported by xenophobic chauvinists, by religious fanatics, by communist and non-communist radicals, by the old landowning aristocracy to which he belonged, and by all those who distrusted the shah's attempt to resurrect the authority of the dynasty which had been abased by his father's abdication and the foreign occupation during the war. His political stock-in-trade was a blinkered nationalism which, though it may have been intended as a screen, became the substance of his political actions. If, as seems probable, Musaddiq intended to combine the nationalization of the oil industry with the continued employment of foreign technicians and continuing foreign finance, he was soon defeated by his own extreme professions and supporters. Musaddiq became almost a figure of fun to the world at large, certainly to the western world, but in his own country he roused genuine popularity (quite apart from the bought support of the capital's mobs) and even his political opponents were to acknowledge his success in reducing corruption in public affairs. He failed, however, to retain control over the course of the oil dispute or to retain his own confidence in himself, he became the prisoner of his own rash attitudes, and he underrated the effectiveness of the economic sanctions which the British government was able to deploy against him.

The oil nationalization law expropriated the British company and created a new Iranian company to take its place. Throughout the ensuing controversies Dr Musaddiq insisted on British recognition of the validity of the nationalization decree as a prerequisite for any negotiations on compensation for the British company. The British on the other hand maintained that the decree was illegal and inoperative, that the company's title remained intact, and that the concession agreement of 1933 could not properly be revoked by unilateral act of one party to it even if that party was a sovereign state. Consequently Britain claimed not only compensation for the loss of the benefits secured to the company by the concession agreement but also a further sum representing damages for a wrongful breach of contract.

The controversy involved not only the British company but also the British government which was responsible for the safety of British citizens (who might be endangered by nationalist frenzy) and wished to safeguard its own financial stake in the British company; it was also concerned to stand firm in defence of British rights for fear that weakness in one part of the Middle East might provoke attacks on British interests elsewhere. During 1951 various attempts were made to negotiate with Dr Musaddiq – by the British company, by a special emissary of President Truman and by a British delegation led by a cabinet minister. The American administration chose the British side after some initial hesitation. Its sympathy for the British case was to some extent countered by its desire to attract Iran into the western camp; since the oil dispute threatened on the contrary to separate Iran from the west, there were some Americans who were anxious not merely to mediate but to secure a settlement without necessarily getting the full measure of what London thought fit and proper. But Dr Musaddiq's extravagant histrionics alienated American sympathy and a visit by him to New York (to address the Security Council) and to Washington in October 1951 did him no good and some harm. His flirtations with Moscow and his indebtedness to Iranian communists helped to persuade the Americans to make common cause with the British and to support his internal enemies' plans to overthrow him.

The dispute was not in the last resort ruled by the legal rights and wrongs but by the British government's unwillingness to use force (except to protect British citizens); by the Iranian company's inability to sell Iranian oil in face of obstacles interposed by the British company and the lack of solidarity among producers; and by the economic collapse of Musaddiq's régime which, deprived of its revenue from the British company, was unable to find alternative sources of cash. Having failed to raise loans from the United States or the World Bank, Musaddiq called in the renowned Dr Hjalmar Schacht who judged him, after a few days's acquaintance in September 1952, to be one of the wisest men of the age but was unable to help him. Meanwhile some of Musaddiq's allies were wavering. He was reappointed prime minister in July 1952 after a routine resignation upon the convening of a new Majlis, but the members showed some reluctance to grant him the full powers which he asked for. When the shah refused to give him the war ministry he resigned. But Qavam, who succeeded him, was only able to stay in office for four days and then had to take flight; the mob demonstrated in Musaddiq's favour, the Majlis voted him full powers, and the throne itself seemed to be in danger. Only the army had the capacity to unseat him, and a year later it did.

Musaddiq's triumph had exposed his political dependence on the mob without lessening his financial dependence on the British, which in turn was conditioned by his dependence on the extreme nationalist mullah Kashani who had become president of the Majlis and would countenance no approach to the British. By the end of 1952 Musaddiq and Kashani had fallen out. In the next year Musaddiq triumphed over Kashani and dismissed the Majlis but failed to prevail over the shah. In August the shah dismissed Musaddiq and appointed General Zahedi in his place. Three days later the shah and the general were both in flight, but whereas the shah fled to Rome the general withdrew only a little distance and within a week of his original appointment he returned to put an end to the Musaddiq régime once and for all with not inconsiderable help from the CIA and the British secret service. The shah returned too. The helping hand of the United States was barely concealed and was not forgotten when the shah was once more forced into flight a quarter of a century later.

Peace was soon made in the oil dispute. New agreements were worked out on the basis, ironically, of recognizing the validity of the Iranian nationalization decree. The Iranian oil company remained in being and in possession of the oil. A consortium of eight foreign companies – British, American and French – was created. The British company accepted, not without demur, a 40 per cent share in this consortium and received from its seven associates £214 million for the remaining 60 per cent which they bought between them. The British company was also to receive £25 million, spread over the years 1957–66, from the Iranian government in compensation for its losses since nationalization. The consortium was given effective control over the Abadan refinery and the principal oilfields for twenty-five years, with a series of options of renewal, and undertook to pay the Iranian government 50 per cent of profits. Thus nationalist doctrine was satisfied, the consumers were assured of their requirements and the producers of their revenues. Full diplomatic relations between Iran and Britain were restored early in 1954. Musaddiq spent the next two years in gaol.

The fall of Musaddiq was a victory for the shah. Musaddiq's left-wing supporters were persecuted with a thorough ferocity and the shah gradually asserted the paramountcy of the throne, first through military rule which lasted until 1957 and then through a series of prime ministers who were either submissive or turned out. The death of the shah's only brother late in 1954 jeopardized the dynasty and obliged the heirless shah to divorce his second wife and marry a third, who bore him a son a year later. Thus fortified the shah began to implement a policy of land distribution and reform which proved so unpopular with the landowning classes and the Majlis (in which they were well represented) that the shah dispensed with parliament for the two years 1961–63. In 1963 he felt strong enough to hold a plebiscite which confirmed his personal ascendancy and the decline of the power of the provincial notables. The world of the urban politician, the tribal chiefs and the educated young remained for diverse reasons disgruntled, but oil revenues increased and Iran's gross national product began to register annual increases of the order of 7 per cent.

In foreign affairs the shah had to decide whether to join the Baghdad Pact and to identify his country with the west. He did so in 1955, after becoming the first recipient of American Point Four aid, and in 1959 he paid a state visit to London and received President Eisenhower in Teheran. After a short period of frigidity, Russo–Iranian relations improved and in 1963 President Brezhnev too was officially received in the Iranian capital, a reminder that the traditional suspiciousness between the two countries had to take account of the fact that Iran had a long undefended frontier with the USSR and looked to northern trade routes for the export of the produce of its northern provinces. The shah undertook not to permit the installation of nuclear missiles in Iran and, without abandoning Cento (as the Baghdad Pact had become), or joining the unaligned group, he moved towards a more independent position in world politics. By 1969–70 he was able to play a decisive role in shaping the political future of the Persian Gulf after the departure of the British and, relishing the role of a crowned entrepreneur, to use mineral wealth and a bounding economy to turn Iran into a military and industrial power of considerable significance. The shah's policy and bent was growth at all costs and the key was oil, although oil was not the country's only resource. (It was rich too in natural gas, other minerals and agriculture and was establishing industry as fast as 50 per-cent illiteracy and a wretched educational system would allow.) When in 1973 war in the Middle East gave the oil producers the excuse to push up prices the shah insisted on maximum increases, successfully but against the wishes of more cautious Arabs who hesitated to damage western countries which were their best customers. In two years the Iranian government's revenue per barrel was multiplied by ten and its total annual oil revenues rose from $2.3 billion to $18.2 billion. In the year after the oil price rise of 1973 GNP rose by 42.5 per cent. Spending rose too, particularly defence spending which also multiplied by ten in the half decade and passed the $10 million mark; by 1975 Iran was spending on defence a larger proportion of GNP than any country in the world except Israel. The results of this explosion were not all happy: 1975 saw a deficit in the balance of payments of nearly $1 billion. Waste and corruption flourished commensurately; inflation took hold. Those hurt by inflation and least able to make a profession of corruption had to be compensated and wages were nearly doubled in 1974–75 with the usual cyclic nightmare: demand for goods, inadequate supply, rising prices and increased exports to fill the gaps, further price rises and further wage demands. The shah, who had dealt roughly with the landed aristocracy in the early sixties, showed signs of imperial displeasure with the new, ostentatious and corrupt rich, and toyed with schemes for handing over half the ownership and profits of industry to the workers. Yet wages remained derisory and Teheran became a shanty town of 5 million for whom housing was shamefully inadequate. His régime's weaknesses were the uncertainty surrounding an autocracy with an infant heir, the opposition of the conservative mullahs, the opposition of radical students and other protestors which even one of the world's most ferocious secret police apparatuses could not mute, and his own refusal to listen to others. He became dangerously ignorant of the state of his own country, where the savagery of his police SAVAK (trained by Americans and Israelis) and blatant inequality alongside ill-gotten wealth ensured that when the tocsin sounded thousands of civilians rushed unarmed into the streets, prepared to face his fearsome military machine. Between his return in 1953 and his second flight in 1979 the shah worked a revolution in Iran, using the country's wealth to create prosperity and strength; but the headlong pace and fearful inhumanity of this revolution united conservatives, radicals and liberals against it and so generated a counter-revolution. When in January 1979 the shah asked Dr Shahpur Bakhtiar to assume the premiership, Bakhtiar consented only upon condition that the shah leave the country.

If the shah was the chief engineer of his own destruction, the chief beneficiary was Ayatollah Ruhollah Khomeini, an aged and obdurate cleric incensed by the shah's material values and animated by personal hate born of the shah's refusal to allow him to attend the funeral of one of his sons. Khomeini was the principal spokesman for those who were opposed to secular government and believed that the modernization of Iran in the American mould was sinful. This movement was evident from the early sixties, broke into serious and harshly repressed riots in 1962–63, and led in 1964 to Khomeini's flight to Turkey and exile – at first at Najaf in Iraq and then in France – whence he continued to animate opposition to the shah. The personalization of this struggle culminated in the flight of the shah and Khomeini's return: the triumph of imam over shah. One month later Bakhtiar too fled the country.

Khomeini was all powerful. Other groups opposed to the shah judged it expedient to rally behind Khomeini or keep out of sight. He proclaimed an Islamic republic and instituted a régime even more intolerant than the shah's, although possibly less murderous and less corrupt. He appointed as prime minister Mehdi Bazargan, a devout layman with a scientific education, but there was in fact no central government. Bazargan was harassed from left to right, by Kurdish and Arab minorities, and by conflicting pronouncements from the ayatollah himself who retired to the holy city of Qum, dominated the scene by sporadic utterance and allowed a kind of religious hooliganism to prevail. Local Islamic committees spent their time rounding up and executing those whom the hazards of denunciation exposed to their indiscriminate wrath. In November radicals in Teheran invaded the American embassy and took fifty-three of its inmates hostage. This coup was partly directed at Bazargan, who finally succumbed, but more overtly against the United States. It incidentally, but portentously, alarmed the Russians who feared a retaliatory American *coup de main* in Iran at a time when their own hold over neighbouring Afghanistan was becoming insecure.

Restored to his throne in 1953 by the Americans, and thereafter showered with American aid of every kind, the shah was widely regarded as an American creature and the American government as accomplices in his misgovernment. Via Egypt and Mexico the shah reached the United States in search of the best medical treatment for the disease which would soon kill him, but many in Iran regarded his arrival in New York as the prelude to another American attempt to put him back on his throne. Moreover the younger militants were at one with the vindictive clerics in wanting to get the shah back to Iran and put him on trial for his alleged crimes against the state. The seizure of the hostages was a move towards this goal, and the anti-Americanism which it exemplified and fuelled was useful to Khomeini in rallying the splintered fragments of Iranian society behind himself. At every turn over the next twelve months the ayatollah supported the hostages' captors, whose urge to lay hands on the shah and to humble the United States overrode the milder counsels of those – Bazargan and, after him, Abolhassan Bani-Sadr, appointed president in January 1980 – who wished to restore normal relations with Washington, if only to unfreeze Iranian assets in American banks and, after Iraq's attack, to get spare parts for its weapons. Bani-Sadr was forced into flight by a fresh wave of terror in 1981 of which his successor was an early victim, one of many.

Imperial powers have been wont to accept with a certain equanimity the disasters which befall their servants in foreign lands. But not so the more responsible American public. There was no evidence that the hostages were ill-treated but the mere fact of their detention was regarded as a slur and disgrace not to be borne. Their fate became an obsession and the situation was further inflamed by the Russian invasion of Afghanistan a few weeks later. On the one hand the United States had an interest in preserving Khomeini's rule because he seemed to be the one man who could prevent Iran from falling to pieces; civil war in this sensitive area was not only to be feared on general grounds but also because it might provide the USSR with a legitimate excuse to intervene under its treaty with Iran of 1921. On the other hand the United States saw politicians like Bani-Sadr as its natural allies and wished to strengthen them against the coalition of extremes represented by the ayatollah and the radicals. Washington calculated that it would reinforce the moderates by imposing severe sanctions, for which however Washington needed European and Japanese collaboration. But this strategy was vitiated by a latent contradiction. Bani-Sadr was trying to negotiate goods-for-oil agreements with Europe and Japan, so that American attempts to get these countries to impose sanctions on Iran hampered Bani-Sadr whom the Americans were hoping to bolster and placate.

For their part Washington's allies had little faith in sanctions but were disposed to fall into line partly in order to show solidarity with Washington against a blatant breach of diplomatic practice and partly also to prevent Washington from resorting to force to free the hostages. Force, they reckoned, would not succeed and it might lead to the closing of the Gulf and the loss therefore of shipments of oil far more important than Iran's. Iran responded to this threat of sanctions by making economic agreements with the USSR, East Germany, Czechoslovakia and Bulgaria. These agreements were economically marginal but, for the west, politically disturbing.

Early in January 1980 President Carter told the US Congress that the use of force to rescue the hostages would almost certainly fail and might lead to their deaths. In April he made the attempt. It was a gamble and it failed. Eight Americans were killed and six helicopters and one troop carrier lost. The hostages were not killed but they were dispersed. American prestige suffered. The allies, in the course of preparing sanctions which were to be an alternative to force, were vexed at not being told that force was after all to be used. Moscow was pleased that the world should have another military incursion to talk about besides Afghanistan. Muslim countries felt obliged to rally round Khomeini, whose personal power was strengthened by this episode, and again at the end of the year when Iran was attacked by Iraq.

In Iraq the Aref regime had been overthrown in 1968 by a coup which put General Ahmad Hassan al-Bakr in the presidency. This was a victory for the Iraqi branch of the Ba'ath Party and more particularly for Saddam Hussein Takriti, the brutally strong man of the new régime. Saddam Hussein remained half in the background until 1979 when he took open control after a plot of obscure origins (probably by a disgruntled rival clan within the Sunni establishment). He looked south rather than west. His first ambition was to reassert Iraq's position in the Gulf. His chief adversaries therefore were not Syria, Egypt or even Israel but Iran and Saudi Arabia, and since both of these were supported by the United States he turned to the USSR and concluded in 1972 a treaty for, among other things, the supply of arms. But Saddam Hussein did not intend to get hitched to the Russian wagon and three years later he concluded an agreement with France for the supply of a nuclear reactor and set up a nuclear research establishment with a staff of 600 engineers. Iraq, which had signed the Nuclear Non-Proliferation Treaty, maintained that all the safeguards prescribed by the International Atomic Energy Agency were being observed, but Iraq's adversaries – particularly Israel – feared that it was preparing to produce nuclear weapons: the plant where the reactor was being built in France was sabotaged, material destined for Iraq was sabotaged at Toulon, an Egyptian nuclear physicist in Iraqi service was murdered in Paris. Iraq also turned to Italy for help in training naval and air officers and for the delivery of ten vessels of war. Given Iraq's geography these could be used only in the Gulf. Contacts outside the USSR and eastern Europe, particularly with West Germany and Japan, were intensified after the displays of Russian power in Aden and Ethiopia in the late seventies. In 1980 Iraqi nuclear installations were bombed by Israel.

Iraq's development was not purely military. The government embarked also on literacy and other educational programmes, technical training, industrial expansion and an agricultural plan designed to enable Iraq to produce all its food instead of a mere quarter. All these measures were based on oil. Oil provided 98 per cent of Iraq's export revenue and financed 90 per cent of the government's investment. Output reached 2 million barrels a day in 1973 and 2.5 million in 1977, and hit a brief peak of 3.7 million before the end of the decade. Iraq became the world's second exporter. (Exports to the USSR remained comparatively trivial: 220,000 barrels a day in 1973, declining to 70,000 in 1979.)

In 1980 Iraq attacked Iran. The causes of this war included the weakness of Iran after the fall of the shah – a temptation to score off Iran; Saddam Hussein's profound dislike of Ayatollah Khomeini, whom he regarded as a religious lunatic; unease about the consequences of Khomeini's Shia fanaticism and intrigues among the Iraqi Shia, an underprivileged majority who staged serious riots at the end of 1979; possibly a suspicion that Khomeini had been involved in the unsuccessful coup of that summer against his régime; and, finally, the perennial question of the Kurds, a sizeable minority in Iraq (18 per cent) with awkward claims in the oil-bearing region of Kirkuk and an even more awkward propensity for allowing themselves to be used by Iran against Iraq.

Saddam Hussein hoped that he had settled the Kurdish question in 1975 (for its antecedents see the note at the end of this Part). After admitting Kurds to the Iraqi cabinet in 1973 and granting autonomy to the Kirkuk region in 1974 Iraq bought from the shah in 1975 a promise to stop Iranian aid to Kurdish dissidents. But Saddam Hussein could not be sure that the shah's promise would be honoured by Khomeini and in any case he resented the price he had had to pay for it and wanted to go back on his own promise. This was the immediate cause of the war. It concerned the respective rights of Iraq and Iran in the Shatt al-Arab.

The Shatt al-Arab carries the waters of the Euphrates and Tigris to the Persian Gulf. These rivers are in Iraq but the Shatt itself marks the frontier between Iraq and Iran, and half-way along its course of 200 km it is joined by the Iranian River Karun. The Shatt is Iraq's only outlet to the sea and it carries also the traffic of the Iranian ports of Khorramshahr and Abadan in the province of Khuzistan, whose population consists of Iranian citizens of Arab race. The Gulf into which the Shatt debouches leads, not directly to the open sea, but to the Straits of Hormuz which are 800 km from Iraq but easily commanded by Iran. When in 1971 Iran had seized the small islands in the straits (the Tunbs and Abu Musa) which Britain had wished to transfer to two of the Arab emirates, Iraq was unable at that date to do more than break off diplomatic relations with Iran and expel Iranians from Iraq.

The first treaty concerning the frontier between the Iranian and

Ottoman empires along the Shatt al-Arab was signed in 1555. It has many successors. No treaty ever satisfied both parties to it and the complexities have been increased by shifts of the terrain, waterways and islands and (eventually) by the discovery of oil. At the beginning of the twentieth century the Ottoman empire had secured control over almost the whole of the Shatt and this position was inherited between the two world wars by the successor state of Iraq. It was, however, challenged by the resurgent power of Iran under the Pahlavi dynasty which claimed that the frontier should run down mid-channel. In 1937 a new treaty considerably improved the Iranian position, notably by making the Shatt freely usable by naval and merchant vessels of both states. After the Second World War, and particularly after the 1958 revolution in Iraq, Iran began to put pressures on Iraq. In 1969 Iran abrogated the 1937 treaty. Iraq riposted by declaring the whole of the Shatt to be Iraqi territorial water but Iran's support for Kurdish revolts against Baghdad forced Iraq in 1975 to accept a deal whereby the shah would abandon the Kurds in return for recognition of the mid-channel frontier. In 1978 the fall of the shah again transformed the situation. Iran lapsed into something like chaos and lost the American support which had been so conspicuous an element in the expansion of Iranian power. Iraq on the other hand had been gathering strength since the coup in 1968. In 1980 Saddam Hussein abrogated the 1975 agreement and invaded Iran.

He miscalculated. The war was not the walkover which he hoped for. Khomeini's Iran did not fall to pieces and Iraq became committed to wearing operations which exposed its weaknesses as well as its ambitions. The Iranians stemmed the Iraqi attack despite the disorganizations of their country and the reluctance of the clergy to give the army – a possible rival for power – a free hand. Saddam Hussein, like Ayub Khan in Kashmire in 1965, failed to get the quick victory which was the only kind of victory worth having. The war entered upon years of ding-dong slaughter. Iraq's gamble on a quick victory, inspired by the post-revolutionary chaos in Iran, a lull in Kurdish turbulence and a treasury filled by the oil-price rises of the seventies, failed and with it Iraq's vision of dominating the Gulf and the Arab world. Khomeini was able to throw thousands of conscripted Iranians into battle with revolutionary and religious ruthlessness, insisting that he would accept no terms for peace short of the overthrow of President Saddam Hussein.

Although it all but won the war in the first few weeks, Iraq then made a fateful pause in the false belief that it had done so. Iran held the main Iraqi offensive and an extension of the front northward to Desful; retaliated by attacking Basra from the sea and targets as far north as Mosul by air; achieved limited successes over the next two years; emboldened Syria to block the flow of Iraqi oil through Syria to the Mediterranean; and proclaimed in 1982 war aims which amounted to a demand for Iraq's surrender – the replacement of the Iraqi régime and substantial reparations for aggression. But Iran's military successes were too modest to match these aims. Year after year small gains were made at hideous cost in death, mutilation and destruction but without denting Iraq's resolve. Iraq, thwarted on land, developed a new twofold strategy: it attacked Iranian oil installations (oil exports were crucial in financing Iran's war effort) and internationalized the war by raising fears of an oil shortage as a consequence of damage to shipping in the Gulf and the closing by Iran of the Straits of Hormuz. Iran's export earnings were significantly curtailed but it reacted cautiously to this escalation of the war and refrained at first from interfering with foreign shipping. In 1985 Iraq launched a second major land offensive – the first since the beginning of the war – but this attack and an Iranian counter-offensive made small impact and confirmed the stalemate on land. Even when Iranian forces crossed the Shatt in the following year and subjected Baghdad to regular bombardment no military decision seemed to be in sight; and a further Iranian offensive against Basra in 1987 was equally inconclusive.

In the Gulf, however, Iraq had some success with its economic warfare and its policy of goading Iran into activities which would invite international intervention. Iran's economy was more susceptible than Iraq's to the loss of oil revenue, since Iran was financing the war largely by exporting oil in excess of the quotas prescribed by OPEC, whereas Iraq – although it had lost one of its main oil outlets at the outset of the war – was sustaining its war effort with subsidies from Kuwait and other Arab states: Kuwait, although traditionally hostile to Iraq which had territorial claims against it, was nervous about possible Iranian subversion among Kuwait's Shi'ites who numbered nearly a third of its population. Iraq's new strategy presented Iran with the problem of scaring Kuwait into desisting from aiding Iraq without at the same time scaring western states into active participation in the Gulf against Iran. This was a particularly delicate operation since the war presented President Reagan with an opportunity to settle old scores with Iran over the taking of American hostages in Teheran and new scores over the humiliating exposure of the arms-for-hostages traffic in which the United States (and Israel) had been engaging. Reagan, hoping to succeed where Carter had failed, hoped to get Iran to secure the release of American captives in Lebanon in return for the supply of American and Israeli weapons. This covert manoeuvre was contrary to the United States' principle of never negotiating with hostage-takers or terrorists. It was later justified on the grounds that its aim was to encourage so-called moderates in Iran, but these moderates were for the most part mythical and in so far as they existed their influence was diminished when the American proposals and furtive visits to Teheran were revealed.

By opening a second front at sea Iraq aimed to inveigle the United States into blockading Iran and even perhaps into hostilities against it. The initiative was taken by Kuwait which, economically dependent on the free flow of oil through the Gulf, asked the United States to protect Kuwaiti tankers by allowing them to fly the American flag (contrary to the Geneva Convention of 1959) and to send a substantial naval force to the Gulf where it was likely to become engaged in hostilities with Iran. This request followed an attack on the US frigate *Stark* which was hit by an Exocet missile (albeit launched by Iraq, not Iran) and it was reinforced by reports of the installation of Chinese ground-to-sea missiles at Hormuz and by a judiciously similar Kuwaiti appeal to the USSR for the use of the Soviet flag which raised American fears of an expanded Russian naval presence in or near the Gulf.

Simultaneously with these moves the Security Council unanimously approved a call for a cease-fire in terms which sidestepped Iran's demand that Iraq be labelled the aggressor in the war. Iran therefore prevaricated, while Iraq stalled in the hope of increased American action against Iran both in the Gulf and in the Security Council where the United States was believed to be contemplating the invocation of chapter VII of the Charter and military sanctions against Iran. In the Gulf the provision of armed escorts for shipping was only moderately successful but it succeeded in dragging reluctant European forces in too and in exposing Iranian mine-laying. But the United States shrank from outright war on Iran in support of the Iraqi aggressor and the war went on until a cease-fire was accepted by both sides in 1988. The next year Khomeini died. He had established a theocratic state and become the international symbol of active opposition to the seamier side of western civilization, but he had also imposed on his country a tyranny as savage as the shah's and a war which entailed vast slaughter and economic catastrophe (inflation at 30–40 per cent a year, plummeting production, negative investment at home and abroad, loss of oil revenues which constituted 90 per cent of Iran's foreign earnings). An armistice and proposals for an exchange of prisoners indicated the prevailing war-weariness. Neither side had defeated the other. The main issue of rights in the Shatt was resolved only when Saddam Hussein, having precipitated a different crisis, abruptly conceded to the new government of Ali Akbar Hashemi Rafsanjani all that he had fought for so ruthlessly and lethally against Khomeini.

On 2 August 1990 Iraq invaded and annexed Kuwait. The sheikhdom of Kuwait was something of an anomaly in the Gulf. Much smaller than Iran, Iraq or Saudi Arabia, it was however more populous and richer than the Gulf's other minor states and was a long way away from them: it was a solitary small state surrounded by larger ones. It had been part of the Ottoman empire under the autonomous rule of a family which established its local rule in the eighteenth century and was still ruling in the twentieth. Kuwait was also the subject of special treaties between the Ottoman and British empires. Unlike the rest of the Gulf Kuwait concerned Britain not because of the piracy which impeded British commerce and prompted British intervention, but because of fears of German or Russian expansion to the Gulf by means of railway concessions and Ottoman favours. To allay these fears treaties were concluded in 1899 and 1913, and after the First World War Kuwait became a British protectorate. In the 1930s the new state of Iraq claimed that Kuwait, as a former part of the Ottoman pashalik of Basra, belonged by right of succession to Iraq. More particularly Iraq laid claim to the islands of Bubijan and Warbah at the head of the Gulf and to the tip of the Rumeila oilfield which, mainly in Iraq, extended beneath the frontier into Kuwait. (These claims were not in themselves substantial. The islands were barren, without oil, partly submerged for part of the year, and no help or hindrance to Iraq's commerce to or from the Gulf. Kuwait's extraction of oil from the Rumeila field amounted to about 1 per cent of its yield. But the claims could be used to stalk bigger prizes in northern Kuwait.) In 1961 Britain left Kuwait, which became fully independent and a member of the United Nations. General Kassim repeated Iraq's traditional claims and the ruler of Kuwait, afraid of an Iraqi attack, appealed to Britain for help. A small British force was expeditiously landed, the Iraqis (who had remained a long way from the frontier) subsided, the British troops were quickly withdrawn and were replaced for a short time by contingents from other Arab states. Two years later Iraq recognized the independence and sovereignty of Kuwait, which became a member of the Arab League.

Upon the Iraqi invasion in 1990 the emir of Kuwait and his family fled, a puppet administration was installed and Kuwait was declared to be a province of Iraq. It was also despoiled. Saddam Hussein's motives were greed and need: Kuwait's wealth was fabulous, Iraq's postwar needs were urgent and Saddam Hussein may have believed that Kuwait was ripe for the taking. In 1986 the emir had disbanded the Kuwaiti parliament and in 1989 he rejected pleas to reinstate it; half the emirate's population were immigrants without citizenship or full civic rights; nomadic bedouin were denied rights because they could not prove fixed residence, as too were Palestinians and others, even if they had been born in Kuwait. But if Saddam Hussein was counting on some sort of a welcome he was greatly mistaken. He was no less mistaken about Arab and international reactions. The invasion was an incontestable act of aggression by one member of the UN against another and by one Arab state against another, and unlike the equally blatant act of aggression by Iraq against Iran a decade earlier the attack on Kuwait was also a threat to the interests of the United States and other countries. The appropriation of Kuwait's oilfields considerably increased Iraq's weight in OPEC and its influence over the pricing of oil worldwide and its flow in and from the Middle East. It might furthermore be a prelude to an attack on Saudi Arabia, which would place virtually all Arab oil under Iraq's control, cause widespread political chaos by unseating the Saudi monarchy and weakening other Arab régimes, and precipitate universal economic instability and recession if, with or without an attack on Saudi Arabia, oil prices doubled or trebled.

Saddam Hussein's action was therefore a miscalculation of massive proportions which created an impressively broad coalition against him and, given the gravity of its possible consequences on the one hand and his own stubbornness on the other, a confrontation not easily to be dispelled without war. Over previous decades Iraq had enjoyed western and Soviet help in creating powerful, partly modernized armed forces. To Iraq's aggression against Iran the United States, Britain and other countries had turned a blind eye; some had given significant direct or indirect aid to the Iraqi war effort, as had a variety of Arab states. Even more culpably leaders in most of these states had disregarded Saddam Hussein's slaughter of thousands of Kurds with chemical weapons; in the United States attempts to chastise Iraq through economic sanctions had been thwarted in Congress and the White House. To Saddam Hussein's delusions therefore about the international effects of his second major act of aggression foreign states had themselves contributed and one of Washington's principal concerns in the months after the invasion of Kuwait was to drive home the message that in American eyes this act was not to be condoned as had Iraq's earlier misdeeds. In addition the context in 1990 was changed as well as the stakes. Since the fall of the shah in Iran the United States had become determined to prevent a similar fate overtaking the Saudi monarchy. The Cold War had come to an end with both sides looking for occasions to display co-operation. Arab governments which had supported Iraq against Iran were angered by Saddam Hussein's attack on one of themselves. They feared his pretensions to leadership or dominion in the Arab world – pretensions partly based on his view of himself as successor to Michel Aflaq, the founder of the Ba'ath who died in 1989 in Paris after long years in exile in Iraq from his native Syria.

The American response was two-pronged: invocation of chapter VII of the UN Charter and a distinct and massive American military expedition into the Middle East. But although the American response was swift and vigorous its motives were confused. The occupation of Kuwait provided justification, even an obligation, to take international action to reverse the invasion by embargo, extending if necessary to blockade and the implementation of these measures by force, under articles 41 and 42 of the Charter (see Chapter 4). But the occupation of

Kuwait was not the prime cause of the distinct American action, and the reversal of the occupation not the United States' sole object. Since similar infractions of international law by Iraq (and others) had evoked no such response the despatch to the Middle East of a quarter of a million troops could not plausibly be attributed to Kuwait's fate alone. The cause of this vast effort was plainly something more than solicitude for international law or for the emir of Kuwait; the cause was fear of further aggression by Iraq with the possible consequences already noted and a general fear of the temper and intentions of the régime in Baghdad. Fears of an imminent Iraqi assault on Saudi Arabia were probably baseless, but in the absence of adequate political and military intelligence and appraisal they could not safely be discounted and President Bush – apparently taken by surprise in spite of some timely warnings – felt unable to pause to weigh the question whether such an attack was probable or merely possible. He committed himself therefore to a display and deployment of force which, while it relieved his immediate fears, hampered him in a variety of ways: it narrowed his room for future manoeuvre, cast doubt on the sincerity of the UN prong of his two-pronged strategy (which was the centrepiece of his appeal for international support), sowed seeds of uneasiness about his aims and methods, and created trouble for himself on the home front both by declaring that this obviously offensive capacity was strictly defensive and by committing the United States to huge expenditure and a humiliating need to tout for foreign contributions. The use of overriding force had weaknesses which, unlike the weaknesses of the UN embargo, were accentuated by the passage of time. The embargo, if it worked at all, would do so *accelerando* after an interval which might be longish: the Achilles' heel of the Iraqi economy was its need for grain and therefore for exports of oil to pay for the grain from the spring or early summer of 1991 to the tune of perhaps $2 billion. The American armed threat on the other hand was a threat with diminishing returns since, first, the supplementary 200,000 men and women despatched by Bush at the end of the year did not remotely double the threat posed by the 250,000 despatched at the beginning of the crisis and, secondly, the implied intention to abandon the strategy of embargo alienated the American public and churches and gave opportunistic allies – Syria, for example – a handle which Americans (and Israelis) much disliked.

Bush's initial and impressive success lay in his rallying of international support both at the UN and for his fighting forces in Saudi Arabia. His problem lay in keeping either coalition together when his purposes appeared to be different from theirs. The forces assembled in Saudi Arabia comprised, besides the essential co-operation of Saudi Arabia itself, units from Egypt, Syria, Morocco, Britain, France, Pakistan, Bangladesh and more (recalling in some instances Cavour's despatch of Sardinians to the Crimean War as part of his diplomatic effort to stand well where it mattered). But this heartening multiplicity created problems. Iraq's aggression meant different things in different places; the aims of the anti-Iraqi alliance were diverse. The common aim was the restoration of Kuwait's independence. Americans, however – and more exaggeratedly the Thatcher administration in Britain – wanted to take the opportunity to overthrow the régime in Iraq or at least Saddam Hussein himself, to exact reparations for the considerable destruction and suffering perpetrated in Kuwait, to initiate war crimes trials, and to secure the destruction of Iraqi weapons including weapons which, however horrible, were not prescribed under international law and were manufactured and held by a number of states. It was this proliferation of aims beyond the original aim of removing the Iraqis from Kuwait which dictated the doubling of the American forces in Saudi Arabia; it also delayed American preparedness to strike since the forces deemed adequate to defend Saudi Arabia remained for months inadequate to conquer Iraq; and it laid bare Washington's concerns over Saudi Arabia and Iraq rather than the liberation of Kuwait.

To Arabs on the other hand, from King Fahd of Saudi Arabia to President Hosni Mubarak of Egypt, Saddam Hussein's offence was above all his flouting of the principles, proclaimed by himself in 1980, that no Arab state should attack another and that all issues in the Arab world should be settled by the Arabs themselves without seeking or provoking non-Arab intervention. By flouting these principles Saddam Hussein put his fellow Arab leaders in the awkward position of having to choose between two unpalatable courses – acquiescing in an extension of Iraq's unprincipled abuse of power, and allying themselves with the Americans whose behaviour and very presence in force in the Middle East were offensive to many Arabs and Muslims. Even those Arabs who chose the latter course were having misgivings a few months later. In November the king of Morocco revived the notion of an Arab conference; by December Saudi Arabia was secretly discussing through Arab intermediaries a possible revision of the Iraqi–Kuwaiti frontiers; Kuwaities in exile revived an old proposal for a long lease of Bubijan and Warbah to Iraq; in January Mubarak was to be seen in the unlikely company of Qadafi whom he visited in Tripoli along with Assad; and no Arab was untouched by the prospect, floated by Saddam Hussein and cautiously approved by sundry Europeans and the USSR and China, of an international conference on the Middle East which would embrace Israel's occupation of the West Bank, Gaza and Jerusalem and be held in tandem with a settlement of the Kuwaiti crisis or soon thereafter. (The Arab League had at this date twenty-one members: twenty states and the PLO.)

The initial flurry of diplomatic and military activity was followed by an uneasy pause lasting several months, necessitated partly by the very nature of action under chapter VII of the UN Charter, partly by American determination to launch nothing less than an immediately crushing blow and partly by genuine, if tenuous, hopes of scaring Saddam Hussein out of Kuwait by demonstrations of military might but without bloodshed on an unpredictable scale. Between the Iraqi invasion on 2 August and the recourse on 29 November to article 42 of the Charter (supplementing measures not involving force under article 41) the United States held its disparate coalition together while at the same time accumulating more and more force in the Middle East in the hope of ensuring that, in the event of war, a first blow against Iraq (whether in Kuwait or in Iraq was understandably left uncertain) would achieve its purpose without unbearably long and costly operations. Publicly at least the United States sidestepped the uncomfortable question whether these purposes, whatever they might be, warranted a war whose cost in lives, money, general economic disruption and long-term influence in the Middle East might prove disastrous. It also played down, to the point of trying to expunge, that part of the first Security Council resolution which – besides requiring complete Iraqi evacuation of Kuwait – required also a negotiated settlement of the crisis: negotiation, for the United States (and Britain) meant negotiation after the end of the crisis and not in order to end it. For his part Saddam Hussein played a militarily weak hand with some dexterity but limited success. He seized foreigners in Kuwait (who numbered several thousands and came from two dozen countries) and transported some of them to Iraq where about 340 were dispersed to likely targets in and outside Baghdad as a shield against armed attack; he prevented foreigners in Iraq as well as those in Kuwait from leaving the country; he threatened to set Saudi oilfields and installations ablaze and to attack Israel if he were attacked by the United States; he tried with minimal success to sow discord among the United States' associates and to inflame anti-American Arab and Muslim emotions; he mended his fences with Iran in the hope of securing a sizeable gap in the UN's economic cordon. His refusal to allow foreigners to leave Iraq or Kuwait and his planting of them in and around sensitive installations (a clear violation of the Geneva Convention on the treatment of civilians) provided ammunition for extended denunciations of his law-breaking and barbarity, but the presence of these possible victims was an embarrassment to their governments which had to present themselves as undeterred as well as outraged and criticized unofficial rescue attempts by assorted emissaries – Kurt Waldheim, Jesse Jackson, Edward Heath, Yasuhiro Nakasone, former US Senator John Connally, British MP Tony Benn – whose motives governments tried obliquely to impugn. Women and children were permitted to leave from September, and in December, by which date the propaganda disadvantages of these violations of international law were outweighing their anticipated strategic advantages, Saddam Hussein declared that all who wished might be home for Christmas.

The period of waiting was, if not ended, given a prospective term when the Security Council approved on 29 November a resolution – the culmination of a sequence of twelve – authorizing the use after 15 January 1991 of any necessary measures to secure the removal of Iraq from Kuwait and the restoration of its former rulers. This explicit legitimization of the recourse to war was meant to frighten Saddam Hussein more than it might disturb the American public, whose vivid remembrance of war in Vietnam and its failures remained a prime ingredient in American policy-making. American diplomacy secured the passing of this resolution by twelve votes to two (Yemen, Cuba) with one abstention (China). The firmness of the Arab with the non-Arab members of the anti-Iraqi alliance was bolstered by American and British somersaults in their attitudes to Syria whose anti-Iraqi credentials were held to outweigh its earlier ostracism as a paymaster of international terrorism; and by subventions to Egypt which, while gravely damaged by truncated tourism and by loss of remittances from Egyptians forced to leave their jobs in Kuwait and Iraq, was compensated by substantial remission of its foreign debts and the provision of large new credits (mainly from the United States and Saudi Arabia). Saddam Hussein, although his hopes of dissolving the array against him were slimmer than he believed, continued to insist that his occupation of Kuwait was irreversible. Bush, refusing to believe this proposition, adopted increasingly exclusive eyeball-to-eyeball tactics, complaining repeatedly that the obstacle to a peaceful implementation of the UN's resolutions was Saddam Hussein's failure to understand the American position. In what he described as a last effort to save the peace Bush proposed talks in Washington and Baghdad on the basis however that such talks must be explanatory only and entail no negotiation. Saddam Hussein prevaricated over the timing and objected that there was no point in talks which amounted to no more than a restatement of known positions. The foreign ministers of the two states met, however, in Geneva. Neither side gave way, the Iraqis showing themselves to be as adamant as the Americans. The Secretary-General of the UN, Javier Perez de Cuellar, made a despairing attempt to fend off war, meeting Saddam Hussein in Baghdad two days before the date set by the Security Council for the permissible use of force to secure compliance with its resolutions. On the previous day the US Senate and House of Representatives authorized President Bush, albeit by narrow majorities, to go to war.

These last moves were undertaken under the shadow of the deadline which had been adopted by the Security Council on 29 November at American insistence. The United States had wished to set 1 January as the deadline but had accepted 15 January in response to criticism that sanctions were not being given time to work. Since, however, sanctions were never expected to have a serious effect before the spring or early summer the difference between 1 January and 15 January was inconsequential. The deadline was set not because sanctions were falling short of expectations but because Bush could not afford to keep vast forces inactive in the Middle East: their cost, although more than half underwritten by Saudi Arabia, was alarming and the alliance which sustained them was less than solid and in danger of being exposed as such. The crisis was caused by Saddam Hussein's invasion and purported annexation of Kuwait in violation of the UN Charter. It was made unmanageable by the American deployment of large forces whose primary objects were not the redress of this offence but the defence of Saudi Arabia and American interests there and, secondly, the destruction of the Iraqi régime and its warmaking capacities. These aims, whatever their virtues or legitimacy, were incompatible with a peaceful settlement, within the terms of the UN's resolutions, of the crisis provoked by the Iraqi aggression.

When 15 January was reached the United States wasted no time and opened hostilities during the night of 15–16 January. It did so without informing the Secretary-General of the UN in whose name the hostilities were launched. But for six weeks these hostilities were muted while the United States and its allies assembled ever larger forces and attempted to win the war by bombardment at long range and without recourse to the hazards of general land warfare. The Iraqi air forces were reduced to impotence and put to flight, seeking refuge in Iran where they were interned; the navy fared no better; Iraqi ground forces, armour and communications were severely pounded and Baghdad was subjected to destruction grater than anything which it had suffered for 700 years. Iraq countered with largely ineffective missiles aimed at Saudi and Israeli cities and by devastating Kuwait City and barbarously maltreating its inhabitants. As the contest's extreme inequality became obvious Saddam Hussein was driven to attempt negotiations but did so equivocally and obliquely. Bush responded by insisting on unconditional compliance with all pertinent UN resolutions, by inviting Iraqis to revolt against their government and by adding conditions of his own in order to maintain pressures for unconditional surrender. Attempts, notably by the USSR, to broker an Iraqi withdrawal from Kuwait on acceptable conditions were rejected by the United States which evaded their discussion by the Security Council and on 23 February, a date chosen ten days earlier, converted the six-week war into a general onslaught for the defeat of Iraq which would, it was hoped, involve the removal or death of Saddam Hussein but would not lead to Iraq's dismemberment, which Bush explicitly disavowed (but was nevertheless a likely sequel to defeat).

The final stage, lasting less than a week, was for the Americans and their allies little more than a *promenade militaire*, for the Iraqis a massacre of fugitives by unopposed air power, mitigated only by surrender. Victory, mainly by encirclement of the principal Iraqi formations, was swift and cost the allied forces extraordinarily few lives. Kuwait was liberated and an unsavoury regime in Baghdad was humiliated. Some 50,000 Iraqis were killed, perhaps 100,000. The infliction of comprehensive and undeniable defeat on a cruel dictator was very widely welcomed but since this American purpose was neither avowed by the United States nor licensed by the UN, the former stood accused of being two-faced and the latter, made used of rather than used, was weakened.

The financial and political costs of the war were heavy, although the latter were not easily assessable immediately. The US Secretary of State and the British Foreign Secretary toured the Middle East and other rich capitals soliciting contributions and succeeded in collecting sums equal to about four fifths of their costs. They demonstrated, however, that they had embarked on a war which they could hardly afford and, by side-lining the UN, had been obliged themselves to undertake the business of levying contributions which would otherwise have been performed by the Secretary-General. The political costs included evident strain on the Soviet-American detente, but the mutual interests of the Superpowers took the strain; also a pronounced accentuation of anti-Americanism from Morocco to Iran, but one possibly more clamourous than enduring. These rising costs were evident enough to the United States to persuade President Bush to launch his attack sooner rather than later in February and to terminate it promptly after Iraq's evident defeat even though at that point the overthrow of Saddam Hussein had not been accomplished. The war did not make the Middle East more stable. American intervention to protect Saudi Arabia exposed the inability of that country and others to defend themselves and introduced into the Middle East the spectacle of rules of behaviour – extending from democracy to irreverence to sexual tolerance – which Arab rulers must find hard to swallow and hard to resist. Extremist opposition to regimes in Egypt and the Maghrib received a fillip. Jordan's support for Iraq unified the country but bank-rupted it. Saudi-Yemeni hostility was sharpened. Kuwait itself was pushed into an uneasy experiment in tempering established absolutism with a degree of democracy. On the future of of Iraq, with or without Saddam Hussein, its neighbours had conflicting ideas and the Americans seemingly none. In the Gulf Iran moved closer to recovering its dominant position. To the north the use of Turkish air bases recalled Turkish claims on northern Iraq. The international arms trade, as lucrative as the oil business, was more stimulated than strangled. Israeli intransigeance was, if possible, further entrenched. In spite of missile attacks on its cities Israel, pressed and generously rewarded by the United States, refrained from entering the war and used this forbearance to extract large American subventions: the fact that much of this money was recouped by the United States from Saudi Arabia and Kuwait did not go unremarked in the Arab world. Israel improved its relations with the United States and saw its principal enemy battered and humiliated and the PLO – which had denounced Iraq's aggression against Kuwait but otherwise supported Iraq – discredited and weakened. Finally, most immediately disruptive and most appalling, Bush – having failed to secure the death or removal of Saddam Hussein – publicly opined that the Iraqis themselves would do so and in consequence Kurdish and Shi'ite groups revolted on the assumption that Saddam Hussein's military power had been destroyed. But it had not and it was used against them ruthlessly. The Kurds in particular suffered in battle and still more in flight, misery and death on a scale unusually bitter and devastating even for them. Iraq was attacked and defeated because it had invaded Kuwait and was supposed to be intent on invading Saudi Arabia too, but the latter threat (supposing it to have existed) was not to be removed by substituting one Iraqi regime for another. Iraq's aggressiveness, whatever its scale, raised one of the central issues in international politics in the second half of the twentieth century: how to ensure the supply of essential resources lying outside the territorial confines of powerful and avid consumers. The United States and other powerful states were dependent on Middle Eastern oil but unable to secure it by occupying or dominating the relevant areas in the manner of the Ottoman empire or the Anglo-French mandates system. (The Kuwait war was fought to assert the rule of law forbidding one state to appropriate the territory or resources of another). The alternative to this outmoded imperialism was to secure national interests through international peace and stability and the operation of market forces. When that order broke down, as it did upon Iraq's annexation of Kuwait, force had to be used and the UN Charter so provided. But the *casus belli* was the infringement of national sovereignty, not the interruption of trade or threats to trade. Consequently legitimate international action in defence of national supplies depended on a simultaneous breach of the law relating to sovereign independence. The United States showed that it could and would fight for its interests. The display of American will, no less than the display of immense technical competence, both logistical and operational, was a major event in international affairs but there was a proviso: that there had to be a legal loophole, which in this case was provided by the violation of Kuwait's sovereignty and independence. How the United States would act in the face of a threat to its interests arising from domestic upheaval and not from international aggression was not only dubious but also peculiarly germane to the Middle East where conflict (Israel apart) came from internal threats to governments rather than from hostilities between them. Until Iraq attacked Kuwait no Arab state had attacked another in 70 years and if the Kuwait war were to restore that pattern the occasions for American or other foreign intervention would be limited to aggression by or against Israel.

The Saudi kingdom is an historical alliance which has lighted on a crock of gold. In the eighteenth century the Saudi clan and the puritan sect of the Wahabis formed an alliance which was so far successful that it got possession, early in the nineteenth century, of the holy places of Mecca and Medina and pushed its tentacles as far afield as the areas now called Syria and Iraq. Success was temporary, for with the help of Egyptian arms the Ottoman sultan threw the Saudis back into the desert whence they had erupted and for the rest of the century they had to struggle with neighbouring clans to stay alive. They barely did, but fortune returned to them with the young Abdul Aziz ibn Saud (c. 1880–1953) whose sword created a new realm, called from 1932 the kingdom of Saudi Arabia. The crown of this kingdom belongs to the family of Saud, all the sons of a deceased monarch having claims over grandsons. Abdul Aziz was succeeded by four sons: Saud (1953–64), Feisal (1964–75), Khaled (1975–82) and Fadh; and in 1980 there were in existence some thirty more princes of this generation and 3,000 adult princes related to Abdul Aziz in different degrees. Territorially the kingdom was nearly coextensive with the Arabian peninsula, bounded by the strategic waterways of the Persian Gulf, Indian Ocean and Red Sea; but to the east and south a number of principalities and republics impaired the tidier pattern which seemed to have been designed by nature but was not yet accomplished by Saudi man. The departure of the British in 1971 from the Gulf and Aden removed one great power from the area without substituting another.

Saudi Arabia was a country of great size and, after the Second World War, vast wealth. But in human terms it was a small state. Its population in 1980 was no more than 6–7 million, but some estimates make it much smaller, and about a third of the inhabitants were not Saudis. The richer it grew the more tempting its riches (which lay in the north) to a predator. It was therefore driven by prudence to seek a powerful ally and to build powerful armed forces. The ally – and main supplier of the hardware for these forces – was the United States.

American penetration of the Middle East began in Saudi Arabia where the American oil company Aramco concluded in 1950 with the Saudi government a fifty–fifty deal which was considerably more

Shi'ite Muslim population

Note: Countries with significant Muslim populations but which are not members of the OIC include Nigeria, Soviet Union and India

12.1 The Islamic world showing member states of the Islamic Conference and distribution of Shi'ite Muslim population.

BANGLADESH

PACIFIC OCEAN

MALAYSIA

BRUNEI

INDONESIA

IAN OCEAN

generous than the terms traditionally vouchsafed by British and French companies and was designed to enable American companies to compete with and ultimately displace the British. From this commercial vantage point the United States developed a political relationship with the dependably anti-communist Saudi royal house. This alliance lacked the fervour of Washington's commitment to Israel or the thrust of its alliance with the shah of Iran, but it was the one abiding feature of its relations with the Arab world and had special strategic connotations which increased with the growth of Russian naval power. For much of the postwar period Americans contrived to shut their eyes to the fact that the Saudis were deeply opposed to both Israel and Iran, the two principal pillars of the Middle Eastern policies of the United States.

One legacy of the creation of the Saudi kingdom was its opposition to the Hashemite descendants of the sherif of Mecca whom Abdul Aziz had evicted from his temporalities and spiritualities alike. These descendants ruled in Jordan and (until 1958) Iraq. They were also the butt of Nasser's reformist drive and so provided a bond between the conservative Saudi monarchy and revolutionary Egypt. Abdul Aziz's successors were anxious to escape from an isolation which was no longer safe for a country so rich but so under-equipped in human and material terms; and they began in Cairo. The association was, however, half-hearted. Nasser was anti-American but King Saud was not. Egypt and Saudi Arabia took opposite sides in the civil war in Yemen. King Saud's conservative instincts proved stronger than his anti-Hashemite inheritance, so that in Jordan in 1957 he supported King Hussein against a Nasserist opposition. An ambitious ten-year pact between Saudi Arabia, Egypt, Jordan and Syria, concluded in 1957, faltered from the start and quickly went the way of the numerous inter-Arab pacts of these years when Arabs were finding it difficult to decide which of their kin were friends and which were not.

After Nasser's death in 1970 King Feisal, who had been the power behind the throne even before he came to occupy it in 1964, moved towards the leadership which had been slipping from the more exuberant Nasser – particularly after the war of 1967 with Israel and the failures of the Egyptian expeditionary force in Yemen. Feisal had already in the sixties strengthened Saudi links with the United States and improved relations with the shah; he visited Iran in 1965 and concluded an agreement on the ownership of the possible submarine wealth of the Gulf; and in 1968 the shah went to Mecca. Feisal's leadership in the Arab world was evident at the conference of Arab states at Rabat in 1969, where he succeeded in institutionalizing, by the creation of a standing Islamic Conference, an idea which he had cherished for some years. Egypt became a natural part of this scheme when Sadat evicted the Russians from Egypt in 1972 and, much more conservative than Nasser, stemmed at the centre of the Arab world the revolutionary current which had characterized it from the early fifties. (But Egypt, having forfeited its place in the Muslim family as a result of its separate peace with Israel at Camp David, was not invited to the Islamic assembly which, at Taif and Mecca itself early in 1981, brought together forty-two monarchs and other heads of states covering northern Africa and southern Asia from Morocco to Indonesia – an imposing advertisement of slowly maturing Saudi tactics.)

The war of 1973 further enhanced Saudi Arabia's international importance. For the first time an economic weapon – oil – was brandished almost as frighteningly as tanks and aircraft. Saudi Arabia cut its production by 30 per cent, more sharply than any other exporter. By this action it put its anti-Israeli before its pro-American policy. The price of oil shot up from $3 to nearly $12 a barrel in a few months. Saudi Arabia's GNP rose by 250 per cent in a year (and went on rising: oil revenues of $4 billion in that year passed $40 billion four years later). Saudi action had profound political effect as the rest of the world digested the implications of a cutback in oil exports, while at the same time Saudi Arabia's great wealth rose to legendary proportions. By 1980 one-third of the financial reserves of the whole world outside the USSR and its satellites belonged to Saudi Arabia. Nor was this a fleeting boom, for Saudi Arabia possessed also a quarter of the world's known reserves of oil, was producing 9.5 million barrels a day at comparatively low cost and could increase this production by about 70 per cent with little effort.

Saudi Arabia was therefore more of a prize than ever. But the world in which it lived was becoming progressively less tranquil and there were doubts about its own internal stability.

The rule of the royal family, however bizarre or anachronistic in western eyes, was reasonably well assured so long as the princes maintained the historic alliance with Wahabi Islam and established a fresh understanding with the classes, civilian and military, which worked the new institutions engendered by wealth and power. The princely house was on the whole successful in these tasks and in preserving its own discipline. The royal family was extensive, all powerful and very rich. Its stability was maintained by a strict hierarchy. Which prince would be the next king was well known, and which would follow after him. The thousands of lesser princes had their allotted places in what was in effect a *nomenklatura* of aristocrats. Rarely did any of them step out of line. The régime appeared to be impregnable so long as there were sons of Abdul Aziz to occupy the throne, but it was evident that the system would be more difficult to operate, the hierarchy more difficult to define, when the first generation of brothers and half-brothers was followed by the next generation of – far more numerous – cousins. Nevertheless the monarchy had a nasty shock when in 1979 250 Oteiba bedouin seized the Great Mosque at

Mecca and held it for two weeks in protest against the worldliness and corruption which were gaining ground in Saudi society – in spite of draconian enforcement of rigorous laws. This incident coincided with riots, stimulated by Khomeini's successes and precepts in Iran, among the Shia minority – a very small minority of 120,000 but a major component of the workforce in the oilfields. Saudi society was also vulnerable by reason of its backwardness and lack of professional and technical skills, a weakness which obliged it to employ large numbers of workers from other Arab countries and from east Asia (Korea, Thailand, the Philippines) and to devote to education as large a share (15 per cent) of government spending as it allotted to defence in the five-year plan for 1975–80.

In external affairs Saudi Arabia was embarrassed by the failure to resolve the Arab–Israeli dispute and the consequent divergence between itself and the United States. Saudi Arabia kept out of the more militant aspects of this dispute but it was in a sense more committed than any state. In politics most things can be compromised, even frontiers, but the Saudi claim against Israel was not political. It was religious: the demand by the custodian of holy places for the return of Jerusalem, another holy place, to Muslim hands (but not to Saudi Arabia itself). No Saudi prince was willing to abandon this claim, which the west consistently failed to take seriously enough, and it united the Saudis with King Hussein of Jordan, whose grandfather had been murdered in the Al Aqsa mosque in Jerusalem. At the conference in Baghdad summoned to protest against Camp David Saudi Arabia tried to moderate the more extreme Arab reactions to Sadat's separate peace with Israel and at the same time retain the leading role which Iraq might snatch out of the heat of general Arab indignation.

In the wider conflict between the superpowers the advent of the Russians to Aden and the Horn of Africa created a new war zone in the Indian Ocean with all eyes trained on the Straits of Hormuz, traversed by 140 ships a day, three-quarters of them oil tankers. Saudi Arabia's traditional border concerns acquired an added international dimension. These concerns were: first, to the south-west, Yemen; secondly, to the south, Oman and the ocean; and thirdly, to the east, the Gulf and all its riparian states.

Yemen, part of the Ottoman empire from 1872 to 1919, was ruled until 1962 by hereditary imams whose rule was one of the least amiable and admirable in the world. Yemen had a coast-line stretching northward from the Bab el Mandeb along the Red Sea but no access to southerly waters. By the treaty of Sana in 1934, made between Britain and the Imam Yahya (1918–48), Britain recognized the imam as sovereign and accepted an adjournment until 1974 of territorial disputes arising out of Yemeni claims against the protected sheikhs and the colony of Aden. The Imam Yahya's policy was to temporize but his son Ahmed revived Yemen's claims and argued that constitutional changes in the colony and in the protectorate were a breach of the treaty of Sana inasmuch as they prejudged matters which were to be settled in 1974 and created an anti-Yemeni group intended to disrupt the Yemen which Britain had recognized. Border affrays resulted and the imam concluded in 1956 the treaty of Jidda with Egypt and Saudi Arabia and in 1958 the federal association with the United Arab Republic.

In 1963 the Imam Ahmed died and was succeeded by his son, Muhammad al Badr, who in 1956 had visited Moscow and Beijing. A revolution broke out immediately and a republic was proclaimed by Brigadier Sallal who invoked Egyptian help under the treaty of Jidda. The imam invoked Saudi help under the same treaty, and there ensued a mixed civil and international war, not unlike the Spanish civil war of the 1930s. At Riyadh in August 1965 Nasser and Feisal agreed to discontinue their aid and withdraw their troops; the Yemenis were to install a coalition and hold a plebiscite at the end of 1966 to decide their country's form of government. But this agreement was abortive, troops were not withdrawn and Nasser later said that Egyptian forces might stay indefinitely. After the war with Israel in 1967 he had to change his mind again and withdraw them. The war ended in 1970 in compromise. The republic prevailed but royalists joined its government.

At precisely this time the adjacent Aden protectorates and colony were being vacated by Britain in the course of its retreat from global power, a retreat which affected the Persian Gulf as well as Aden and the command of the southern entrance to the Red Sea.

The port of Aden was in the possession of the East India Company and then of the government of India from 1839 to 1938, when it became a British colony. It was given a legislative council in 1947 and elected members were introduced in 1955; under a new constitution in 1958 the elected members became a majority of the council. During the period of Indian government (first as part of the Bombay presidency and finally for a few years as a separate province under the direct control of Delhi) Adenis complained that they were a neglected outpost of the Indian empire. After the transfer of their affairs to the British colonial office nationalist demands for independence appeared and waxed. Important as a port for 2,000 years. Aden also became in the middle of the twentieth century the site for a big new oil refinery and for the headquarters of Britain's Middle East Command. Conservative ministers therefore decided, and stated with incautious boldness, that nationalist aspirations could not be allowed to go to the lengths of independence. The nationalists, led by Abdullah al Asnag, the secretary-general of Aden's trade unions, proceeded to press their views by means of strikes which seriously threatened a base so dependent on native Adeni and immigrant Yemeni labour, and by boycotting the electoral processes with which Britain had hoped to satisfy local political aspirations.

The adjacent Aden protectorate consisted of twenty-three sheikh-doms divided for administrative convenience into a western protec-torate embracing eighteen sheikhdoms and an eastern protectorate containing the other five. All these principalities had entered into protection agreements of some kind with Britain between 1839 and 1914, and Britain had performed a useful pacificatory role in this part of the world. After the Second World War Britain negotiated new treaties under which British political officers were appointed to advise the sheikhs who agreed to accept the advice given them except in relation to Islamic law and customs. In the western principalities the appointment of a new sheikh had to be confirmed by the British governor of the colony. The sheikhdoms and the colony constituted a geographically compact, religiously homogeneous area, but the colony differed from its surroundings in being populous, comparatively rich and hostile to the monarchical principle. The nationalists in the colony envisaged a union with the protectorate territories, and ultimately with Yemen also, but not under their existing rulers.

Aden was a small and neglected world of its own until Britain's final departure from the Suez base in 1956. In that year a British minister told the colony's legislative council, in the course of a speech which was particularly patronizing and insensitive in its references to self-government, that the British government foresaw no possibility of changes in Aden's affairs and was confident that this immobilism would be welcomed by a vast majority of its inhabitants. Later in the year the blocking of the Suez Canal by Nasser as a result of the Suez War caused unemployment, strikes and unrest in Aden. At the same time the sheikhs became aware of the threat to their way of life. In 1958 the sultan of Lahej decided to take the road to Cairo, while in 1959 six of the western sheikhs, caught between the devil of Adeni nationalism and the deep seas of Yemeni subversion, formed the federation of Arab emirates which the British had been working for in vain since 1954. This group, renamed the Federation of South Arabia in 1962, was gradually enlarged but never embraced all the sheikhs in spite of British grants fifty times bigger than those provided theretofore.

Britain, intent above all on retaining the Aden base as other bases in Kenya, Egypt and Cyprus vanished or became unreliable, decided in 1963 to attach the colony to this new federation, uniting the sheikhs and the merchant class and circumventing the nationalists. Under the British scheme Britain retained its sovereignty in the colony; it undertook not to extract the whole colony from the federation, although it might withdraw parts; during the seventh year of this symbiosis, but not before or after, the colony might of its own volition secede but if it did it would have to revert to colonial status and could not become an independent state; whereas each normal member of the federation had six seats in the Federal Council, Aden was to have twenty-four. This bizarre concoction intensified nationalist agitation in the colony. The Adeni nationalists refused to co-operate with Britain or recognize the federation, turned to Egypt for help and took to terrorism to accelerate the British departure and ensure the collapse of the rest of the British plans. The federated sheikhs tried to get promises of continuing British military support which the British Labour government was unwilling to give since they would virtually negate the policy of withdrawal and retrenchment and would entangle Britain in Arab feuds: by accepting a military commitment while abandoning political power Britain would get the worst of two worlds. The British government preferred to accelerate departure. Aden and its hinterland became in 1967 the independent People's Democratic Republic of Yemen (PDRY). The departure of the British, who had provided most of the jobs, and the closing of the Suez Canal in the same year plunged the new state into economic distress which accentuated its inherent instability. It was also at odds with its northern neighbour, the Yemeni Arab Republic (YAR), whence it was invaded with Saudi help in 1972. A short war ended with talk – but no more – of amalgamating the two Yemeni states. The island of Socotra, south of Aden, a British colony from 1880 to 1967, became part of the PDRY.

From the Saudi point of view a union, or federation, of the PDRY and YAR would be an advantage only if the resulting entity were right-wing and not left. Saudi Arabia wished to exercise control over the YAR and to seduce the PDRY from Russian influence. In 1976, after the secret meetings in Cairo, Saudi Arabia established relations with the PDRY. This move, a logical step in Feisal's diplomacy but a surprise to those who overrated the role of ideology in international politics, was made possible by the termination in the previous year of the rebellion against the sultan of Oman in his Dhofar province, in which Saudi Arabia and the PDRY had been on opposite sides. Thereafter Saudi Arabia and the USSR vied with each other in offers of aid to the PDRY.

In the YAR the president, Colonel Ibrahim al-Hamdi, was assassinated in 1977 after three years of power and was succeeded by Colonel Ahmad al-Ghashni who was assassinated a year later. Although these murders seemed motivated in the main by tribal feuds there was also some reason to suspect al-Hamdi of trying to play a separate game of his own with the PDRY, and in 1979 the PDRY invaded the YAR in company with discontented refugees from the YAR. In the same year President Abdel Fattah Ismail of the PDRY concluded a twenty-year treaty with the USSR. He was succeeded in 1980 by his prime minister Ali Nasser Mohammed, who wanted to find a way of reconciling the Russian connection with better relations with the YAR and Oman. The two Yemeni states were united in 1990 under the presidency of the president of the YAR. The new state, whose capital was Sanaa, had burgeoning oil revenues and a population larger than Saudi Arabia's. The unification of Yemen was not to the liking of the rulers of Saudi Arabia.

In the sultanate of Muscat and Omam, where a coup brought a new sultan to power in 1970, the People's Front for the Liberation of Omam and the Arab Gulf (PFLOAG) sustained with Russian and Chinese help a civil war which the sultan, with British and Iranian help, overcame in 1975. Behind Britain and Iran stood the United States.

Between the powerful American fleets in the Mediterranean and the South Pacific lay a gap. For twenty-five years after the Second World War this gap was filled by the British who, up to the mid-sixties, insisted that they would go on filling it. The Defence White Paper of 1957, the first to appear after the fiasco of the Suez War contained a mixture of old and new ideas. It still envisaged local forces not only in Aden and Cyprus but also in Kenya (which, however, on becoming independent in 1963 granted Britain only limited facilities by an agreement of March 1964); but it also envisaged a carrier group in the Indian Ocean. The Kuwait operation of July 1961 (see below) reinforced arguments in favour of local garrisons for acclimatizing troops, since between a quarter and a half of the men flown to the scene of that action from temperate climes had been quickly prostrated by the heat. On the assumption that such operations remained an inescapable part of Britain's lot in the world, tropical bases seemed essential. The White Paper of 1962 reiterated the need for a British presence to assure stability and with it the need to maintain forces in Aden and Singapore.

But the arguments and assumptions of the framers of Defence White Papers were challenged by those who counted the cost of these establishments (especially after the Labour victory of 1964 in the middle of a financial crisis) and by those who believed that bases in Arab territory created political ill will out of proportion to their military usefulness.

Finally, the Persian Gulf. The Gulf became in the seventies what Berlin had been in earlier decades – a point so charged with tension that a dispute involving its navigation or installations might prove to be beyond the control of statecraft.

The Gulf is an arm of the Indian Ocean which here makes a long and narrow penetration into the Middle East, dividing Arabia on the one hand from Iran on the other. This arm of the sea is at its narrowest at the Strait of Hormuz. Southward lies the Gulf of Oman leading to the ocean, northward the Persian Gulf. The whole of the eastern shore of both gulfs is Iranian territory, but the opposite shore counts fourteen sovereigns. At the head of the Persian Gulf is Iraq and next to it Kuwait, separated by 560 km of Saudi coastline from the other principalities – the island of Bahrain, the promontory of Qatar, the Trucial States and lastly the corner state of Muscat and Oman. Kuwait's political and business affinities have been with its Arab neighbours to the north and its sons have gone to Cairo or Beirut for their education, whereas the links of the remaining Gulf states have been rather with Pakistan and India and their sons have gone to school in Karachi.

Britain's initial concern in these waters was to secure a monopoly or dominance over the routes to India and to protect British trade from the lawless depredations of the so-called piratical sheiks who, at the southern end of the Persian Gulf, lived off piracy and earned for this strip of land the name of the Pirate Coast. From 1820 onwards the British imposed a maritime peace by a series of treaties or truces with these Trucial sheikhs and in 1861 extended the system northwards to Bahrain by an agreement which pledged Britain to protect Bahrain in perpetuity. Later in the century Britain negotiated fresh agreements by which it assumed control over the external policies of the sheikhdoms and also of Kuwait and Qatar. Finally, as pearling and oil made the states in this area increasingly important for their own sake and not merely as pieces of territory adjoining an important trade route, a series of twentieth-century agreements gave Britain exclusive rights in the commercial exploitation of local riches but without any control over or responsibility for internal affairs.

Throughout most of this period of developing British control the landward frontiers of these states, lying vaguely in uninhabited and supposedly worthless country, were of no concern, and the obligations contracted by Britain as a part and consequence of the maritime truce remained for a long time unquestioned since Britain had additional reasons for remaining in the Persian Gulf and was undisturbed by commitments to local rulers in an area which it intended to go on policing by naval and air forces for complementary purposes. These purposes were the continuing need for communications with the east and the new traffic in oil.

In the endless traffic between Europe and Asia the Middle East must either be crossed or circumvented, and in this context the Arab nationalism of the twentieth century affected Europeans in exactly the same way as the Muslim conquests which posed the alternative ventures of the crusades and the voyages round Africa. In the heyday of British power in the Middle East the British travelled freely across it, but after the Second World War the direct central route was lost as one Arab government after another denied to Britain the special rights and facilities which it had previously enjoyed by treaty or by occupation. The withdrawal from Palestine and the Canal Zone, the revolution in Iraq in 1958 and the abrogation of the Anglo–Jordanian treaty at the time of Suez in 1956 eliminated this route and made it necessary to find a southern or a northern detour. The southern route lay through Libya and the Sudan to Aden, but in 1964 the Libyan government sought a revision of its 1952 treaty with Britain and in the same year the Sudan attached virtually prohibitive conditions to overflying rights. Going south meant flying across central Africa or even southern Africa, both routes being politically awkward as well as expensively long. The northern alternative, by Turkey and Iran and the Persian Gulf, remained therefore valuable, even though it could no longer be described as essential since technical developments were opening up a new, if arduous and expensive, route from Britain westward to Singapore.

Communications provided therefore an argument, effective though not conclusive, for staying in the Persian Gulf a little longer provided it was understood that the days of the British presence were already numbered. Oil provided only a weaker argument. The importance, even the growing importance, of Middle Eastern oil to Europe was undeniable, but the policy of ensuring supplies by a physical presence seemed increasingly dubious and anachronistic. Europe, unlike the other major consuming areas, the United States and the USSR, had become dependent on Middle Eastern oil. Britain for example, which before the Second World War imported more than half its oil from the American continent, was by 1950 importing half its needs from Kuwait alone, and it was estimated in 1965 that Europe's annual consumption of 300 million tons would rise in fifteen years to 750 million tons, despite the greater use of natural gas and nuclear power. Important discoveries of oil in the Sahara in 1956 and Libya in 1959 would decrease the proportion of Middle Eastern oil in Europe's consumption but not the total amount of Middle Eastern oil required. Oil was thought likely to remain cheaper than gas or nuclear power or submarine hydrocarbons, and Middle Eastern oil was cheaper than other oil, but this European dependence was not as frightening as it seemed to a number of European statesmen since Middle Eastern producers were on their side heavily dependent on their European customers. By the mid-sixties when a British retreat became a reality the oil revenues of the states concerned exceeded £2,000 million and provided between 70 and 95 per cent of the budgetary income of the several producers. Neither the increasing demand from Japan nor the prospect of China's entry into the market seemed likely to counter the need of the Middle Eastern producers to sell their oil to Europe, and if this were so military bases were as irrelevant to the flow of oil as to the supply of any other commodity.

There was, however, a further argument of a political rather than an economic nature. The British, it was said, had gone to the Persian Gulf to keep the peace and provide the stability without which commerce is endangered, and they had done so. A British withdrawal could be followed by disorders which would interrupt the flow of oil. These disorders might be the result of sabotage or of frontier disputes between the states of the region. Sabotage, however, is not a thing which regular military units are particularly suited to prevent, while one of the more usual causes of sabotage is nationalist resentment against the presence of foreign garrisons. Frontier disputes certainly existed: Iran claimed Bahrain; Iraq claimed Iran's province of Khuzistan and also Kuwait; Saudi Arabia had disputed frontiers with some of its smaller neighbours, many of whom were at feud with one another. So long as such disputes persisted Britain might claim to be rendering a service by remaining in the area and performing the policeman's task which it had once exercised over half the world.

In the Trucial States Britain tried but failed to promote a federation as a first step towards release from its perpetual obligations. Britain was not supposed to interfere in the internal affairs of these states but was often obliged to do so because of their mutual disputes, the shortcomings of some of their rulers and the aid which the pooer ones required. The rulers, though no longer in need of protection from the seaward, felt the need for protection against Saudi Arabia and against their own not very numerous subjects. The ruler of Qatar (which had loosely formed part of the trucial system in the early nineteenth century but had left it in the 1860s) asked for British help against internal troubles in 1963 but was refused it. The principal problem, however, was the relationship between the sheikhs and Saudi Arabia. Britain wished neither to let the sheikhs down nor to prop them up indefinitely.

Britain's relations with the Saudi royal house had been traditionally good, notably in the days of King Abdul Aziz ibn Saud, although less so after the accession of his son Saud in 1953 and the substitution of American for British influence in Saudi Arabia. Britain was also embarrassed by the apparently complete imperviousness of the Saudi régime to the slightest touch of modernity, except in the accumulation of oil royalties which were expended by the royal family with lavish uselessness. It did not seem right to abandon states once redeemed from piracy to the mercy of a big neighbour still noted for slavery. Moreover in 1955 a running dispute over the Buraimi oasis led to a minor military confrontation. This oasis, a collection of ten villages partly in the possession of the sheikh of Abu Dhabi and partly in that of the sultan of Muscat, was coveted by Saudi Arabia whose claims had been rejected by Britain for a generation. The dispute, which involved the two powerful forces of honour and oil, was referred to an arbitral tribunal at Geneva but the Saudis, having too little faith in their cause or in the tribunal, bribed witnesses on such a scale that Britain was moved to public protest. The Saudis also sent troops into the villages, whence they were forcibly expelled by the British. Yet Britain was loath to pursue the quarrel, which died down once more.

As in India, so too in the Middle East, the positions of power vacated by Britain were transmitted to no single successor. The post-British régime in the Gulf was the outcome of negotiations between Britain itself, Iran and Saudi Arabia. The shah renounced the Iranian claim to Bahrain which became in 1970 a fully independent member of the United Nations. Populous and wealthy enough to stand on its own feet, it was unwilling to become a member of the proposed new federation of Gulf states, unless it were accorded an equivalently overwhelming representation in the projected Union of Arab Emirates. This federation came into being at the beginning of 1972 but without Qatar and Ras al-Khaimar (one of the seven Trucial States), both of which chose independence. All existing treaties with Britain were abrogated. Iran, pleading strategic exigency, seized the islets of Abu Musa and the Tunbs in the narrows between the Persian Gulf and the Gulf of Oman, causing Iraq to break off diplomatic relations with Iran and expel Iranians from Iraq. The new order rested essentially on agreement between Iran and Saudi Arabia, on the latter's inability to secure at this stage full control over the western shores of the Gulf to match Iran's control on the other side, and on the fortuitous absence of Egyptian and Iraqi voices owing to the former's defeat in 1967 and the latter's continuing war with the Kurds and other internal weaknesses; but none of these factors was necessarily permanent. The assassination of Feisal in 1975 and the peaceful succession of his brother Khaled did not disturb the pattern, but in the same year Iraq began to recover its freedom of action.

Iraq is the link between the western and eastern sections of the Middle East. More than any other state in the Middle East Iraq looks both ways: westward over west Asia, eastward to Iran and therefore to the Gulf. In 1918 the Ottoman order in the Middle East was dismantled. It was succeeded by an Anglo–French order which was dismantled in its turn after a second World War. The main outcrops of the Anglo–French order were Palestine and Lebanon. They became the battlegrounds of the next phase. Further east, where the Ottoman Turks had confronted Iran, they had no single successor except in so far as Britain ruled the Persian Gulf. With the departure of the British Iraq and Saudi Arabia disputed the primacy in the area, the Iraqis as champions of Arabism and the Saudis as the guardians of Islam's holiest places: a new sultan and a new caliph. And both feared a modern Iran which rejoiced in their quarrels and profited from them.

NOTES

A *The Kurds*

The Kurdish peoples trace their tribal names further back in time than any other peoples in the world and their presence in western Asia for about 4,000 years. In recent centuries they have been divided between Turkey, Iraq and Syria. In the mid-twentieth century they numbered about 30 million, the greater part in Turkey (16 million), Iran (8 million) and Iraq (4 million). There were about 350,000 of them in Syria and perhaps 200,000 in the Armenian SSR and Soviet central Asia. Their fortunes had been in decline since the days of their twelfth-century sultan known to Europeans as Saladin.

Between the wars the Kurds in Turkey were among the opponents of Atatürk's rule. There were Kurdish risings in 1925, 1930 and 1937 but after the Second World War – and particularly during 1950–60 when the Democratic Party was in power – relations eased. There was some recrudescence of racial hostility in the sixties but the Kurds' worst enemy was the poverty of eastern Anatolia, an area of agricultural decrepitude. In Iran the Kurds were harried by Reza Shah between the wars and then led up the garden path by the Russians who paid diligent attention to Kurdish notables during the war, fostered Kurdish nationalism and supplied a separatist movement with arms. In January 1946 the Kurds proclaimed the independent republic of Mahabad, but for the Russians the Kurdish movement was meant to be no more than an appanage of the separatist Azerbaijani republic which they had contrived in Tabriz at the end of 1945. The Mahabad republic was an expression of genuine non-communist local feelings, whereas the Azerbaijani republic was a communist artefact. Attempts to ally the two were never more than superficially successful although the Kurds, dependent on Russian support, were half tied to the Azerbaijanis. After the withdrawal of Russian troops in May 1946 the Azerbaijanis negotiated, without reference to the Kurds, a favourable agreement with the Iranian government which restored Azerbaijan to the Iranian state as an autonomous province. At this time the Iranian government was a coalition including communists, but later in the year the prime minister, Quavam es-Saltaneh, evicted his communist colleagues in Teheran and sent his army against Tabriz where the communist provincial administration was immediately overthrown with the help of the local populace. The Mahabad republic was now at the mercy of the Iranian army. It was annihilated, its leaders fleeing or being hanged.

In Iraq the Kurds were at first encouraged after the First World War to hope that the British would reward them for their anti-Turkish activities by creating an autonomous Kurdish state. The Iraqis opposed this idea and the British, after a short period of divided counsels, abandoned it. The British were concerned in the first postwar years to prevent the new Turkish republic from recovering the

Kurdish area of Mosul which had been allotted by the peace treaties to Iraq, while the Iraqis were no less concerned to ensure that the Kurdish area of Kirkuk, south of Mosul and rich in oil, should not be alienated to the Kurds. After the British had failed to entrench Kurdish rights in the Anglo–Iraqi treaty of 1930, fighting broke out in which the Kurds were defeated by the Royal Air Force and temporarily dispersed. The Second World War, like the first, led the Kurds to hope for rewards from Britain for services rendered and to hope in vain. An anti-Iraqi rising under Mullah Mustafa Barzani in the last years of the war was defeated by the Iraqis and some 10,000 Kurds fled to Iran, whence Barzani himself proceeded to the USSR. The revolution of 1958 in Baghdad destroyed the alliance between the three anti-Kurdish states of Iraq, Turkey and Iran and substituted for the Iraqi monarchy a republic of 'Arabs and Kurds'. Barzani returned from Moscow and was honourably and even munificently received by President Kassim, who looked with favour on the Kurds because of the left-wing tendencies among them. In 1960 a Kurdish Democratic Party was allowed, but the Kurds were divided in their views on Kassim and even their left wing disliked the communist ideas and excesses which gained ground in Iraq after the revolution. After some internal dissension the Kurdish Democratic Party became definitely anti-communist, rapidly lost Kassim's favour, was persecuted and officially extinguished, even though the communists also fell from grace at this time.

In 1961 the Kurds rebelled. Kassim claimed that they were receiving military supplies from Britain and the United States. He turned for arms to the USSR, which found it opportune to forget its earlier support for the Kurds in the hope of finding a more useful ally in Kassim. The Iraqi army started a full-scale campaign against the Kurds with napalm bombs and rocket-carrying aircraft. In February 1963 Kassim was overthrown and killed and the pan-Arab nationalists of the Ba'ath party took control of the government under the presidency of General Aref who engaged in discussions with the Kurds and gave them to understand that they would get something like autonomy. Later in the year, however, the discussions were broken off by the seizure of the Kurdish negotiators and the Iraqi army, supported in the field by the Syrians where the Ba'ath had also come to power, embarked on an even more ferocious campaign against the Kurds than the operations of 1961–62. But the Ba'ath anti-communist nationalism had alienated the communist world which raised the cry of genocide. Early in 1964 a truce was negotiated. It proved fragile, but in 1970 President al-Bakr renewed it.

The Kurdish revolt put a strain on relations between Iraq and Iran, which were in any case none too good. The shah feared the newer type of Arab régime, especially Nasser's. The Iraqi revolt of 1958 was therefore unwelcome to him, and the succession of Aref to Kassim in 1963 more so. He wanted the Shia Muslims to have an established part in the government of Iraq, and if the Shia were to be so treated, the Kurds would have to be too. He refused to help Aref's anti-Kurdish operations even when Iraqi Kurds took refuge in Iran and he gave the Kurds in Iraq surreptitious and not so surreptitious help. His *rapprochement* with King Feisal in 1965 encouraged him to think in terms of a Persian Gulf regulated by a Saudi–Iranian compact without the need to include or accommodate Iraq. In 1980 Iraq turned the tables on Iran by supporting Kurdish separatists within Iran. In 1991 the Kurds in Iraq, believed that the United States had destroyed the Iraqi army and that President Bush was inviting them to overthrow Saddam Hussein, revolted and paid horribly for their mistake and Bush's reckless language (see Chapter 11).

B The Shi'ites

The Shi'ites, who separated from the main Muslim stock over 1,000 years ago, comprise about a tenth of Islam. They revere the Prophet's son-in-law Ali and his two sons Hassan and Hussein as the originators of the true line of divinely inspired imams (leaders). Most of them await the reappearance of the twelfth imam who disappeared in A.D. 880 but some of them await other reappearances. They are widespread in Islam but strongest east of the Euphrates. They dominate Iran where they have had the control of power for 500 years, outnumber other groups in Iraq and Lebanon, and constitute important minorities in Syria, Pakistan and elsewhere. Khomeini's successes boosted their standing wherever they were to be found but also scared non-Shi'ites, particularly Arabs who distrusted Iranians and Sunnis who disliked clerical intervention in government. Their faith is imbued with suffering and persecution, a bottled bitterness directed chiefly against Sunnis whose faithlessness to the true line has been further sullied by western – notably American – modernism and immorality; also against Jews and Baha'is. The legitimacy of violence is more obvious to Shi'ites than to Sunnis or most Europeans.

C The Muslim Brotherhood and sectarian violence

The Muslim Brotherhood was founded in Egypt in 1928 by Hassan al-Banna who died in 1949. Its main tenets were opposition to the separation of church and state and to foreign influence upon Islam. Hassan al-Banna preached patience but not all his followers achieved it. The Brotherhood murdered the Egyptian prime minister Nokrachi Pasha in 1948, was dispersed and dissolved, revived in the anti-British climate of the fifties, supported the movement which brought Neguib and Nasser to power but was discarded by them, tried to kill Nasser, suffered thousands of deaths in prisons but recovered after Nasser's death. Sadat, who was more partial to religious groups, tried to split the Brotherhood into violent and anti-violent wings, but his pro-western policies alienated both. It was saddled with responsibility for his murder and again suffered arrests on a large scale. The murder in 1990 of Rifaat al-Mahgoub, the chairman of the Egyptian parliament, provoked a similar operation against religious revolutionaries.

But although the Muslin Brotherhood, or parts of it, condoned and practised violence, fundamentalism was not the chief source (other than war) of violence in the Arab world. The chief source was disintegration and communal strife in Lebanon, whence it assumed the forms of kidnapping, hijacking and the murder of hostages and casual victims. Towards the end of 1983 pro-Iranian Shi'ites attacked public buildings and the American and French embassies in Lebanon. Twenty-one persons were arrested, most of them Iraqis but three of them Lebanese: seventeen were gaoled. Attempts to get these Lebanese captives released included the kidnapping in west Beirut of hostages (most of them American or French) to be offered in exchange for the Lebanese prisoners, and the hijacking at Teheran airport in December 1984 of a Kuwaiti aircraft on which two Americans were murdered. An American flight to Beirut was hijacked six months later and in the following year terrorists, probably based in Syria, made attacks at Rome and Vienna airports. In 1988 a Kuwaiti airliner was hijacked, flown to Mashad in Iran, thence to Beirut where it was refused permission to land, and ultimately to Cyprus where its passengers were released. From these and other episodes Iran, whose government was credited with compelling influence over the groups engaged in these activities, contrived to extract arms from the United States and France.

PART FOUR
ASIA

The half century preceding the departure of the British from India had seen a series of reforms, evolved by the British and leading logically and explicitly to Indian independence; the growth of divisions within India which led to the partition of 1947; and a growing awareness of world politics, in which nevertheless the new rulers were for the most part but imperfectly versed. In the nineteenth century India, though less closed to the outside world than China or Japan, had a view of the world which was vastly overshadowed by the British presence; and the principal episode of the century was the Sepoy Revolt or Mutiny of a part of Britain's subjects against British rule. This view was changing by the end of the century. The Russian advance towards Afghanistan; Curzon's preoccupation with the north-western frontier and Tibet; the extension of British Indian power into the Middle East; the alliance of Britain with Japan in 1902, followed by Japan's defeat of Russia in 1905; revolutions in Turkey, Iran and China – all these impinged on India and turned the Indian mind or part of it outward. Although in 1947 Jawaharlal Nehru was the only member of his cabinet with any claim to expert knowledge of foreign politics, his colleagues and many others among his compatriots had grown up with the feeling that, if India's special problem was the defeat of the British raj, there were also other problems and other powers to be reckoned with, notably Russia, China and Japan. Even though many Indians misjudged the nature of the problems, deceiving themselves with the belief that their cause was the British presence and their cure would be the British departure, this mistake was a matter of misinterpretation and not of cloistered ignorance. Within India nationalism, which was one of the by-products of the Hindu and Muslim intellectual revivals of the nineteenth century and took visible shape in the founding of the Indian National Congress in 1885, was inevitably anti-British. Like most nationalist movements it came to be divided into a more militant and a less militant faction (led in this case by B. G. Tilak on the one hand and by G. K. Gokhale and then by M. K. Gandhi on the other), but unlike others it was also divided in a more enduring way before the day of victory. As independence approached, the ability of Hindu and Muslim to work together diminished until it proved impossible to maintain a single successor state to the British raj and at independence the two great religious communities feared and hated each other more than they feared or hated the British.

Britain had long envisaged the surrender of empire in India but without formulating a timetable. The Second World War imposed the timetable. At the beginning of that war the viceroy made the ludicrously inept mistake of declaring war on India's behalf, as he was entitled to do, without consulting a single Indian. Congress ministries, in office under the constitution of 1935, thereupon resigned. In 1942, Sir Stafford Cripps was sent by the British cabinet to India to offer it dominion status with the right to secede from the empire, but the exercise of this option and all other internal advances were to be postponed until the end of the war. The Congress, which may have misjudged British intentions and certainly – if recruiting figures meant anything – misjudged Indian sentiment, decided to have no part in the war and to use it to wage a Quit India campaign against the British. In 1944 Britain, now sure of victory in all theatres, appointed a new viceroy, Lord Wavell, and released Indian leaders who had been put in prison. After the general election of 1945 the Labour government sent three cabinet ministers to India to try to get agreement between the Congress and the Muslim League as a preliminary to independence, but relations between these bodies had deteriorated during the war (the reverse of the experience of the First World War) and the British attempt failed. The League and its leader Mahommad Ali Jinnah were convinced that Britain was partial to the Congress; in August 1946 Jinnah inaugurated Direct Action by the League to secure a separate sovereign state for Muslims, and the winter of 1946–47 was marked by violent communal riots. Early in 1947 the viceroy came to the conclusion that no single Indian central authority could be constituted and he accordingly advised the British government either to retain power for at least a decade or to transfer it, fragmented, to the several provinces.

The British government rejected this advice, replaced Wavell by Mountbatten and announced that Britain would abdicate in June 1948. It proposed to resolve the dilemma by neither of the methods recommended by Wavell but to partition India and hand over power to two separate central governments. The 562 princely states, which were not part of British India, were to be cajoled into one or other of the new states. Their relationship with the British Crown was regulated by the doctrine of paramountcy. Britain did not propose to transfer its paramount rights to the new India or to Pakistan but declared that paramountcy would lapse, with the result that each ruler would be free in law to accede to India or Pakistan or neither – and free in practice to accede to India or Pakistan. Junagadh made the impractical choice of acceding to Pakistan with which it had no border; the ruler was forced to see his error, departed for Pakistan and left his state to become part of India. Three states toyed with independence: Travancore, Hyderabad and Kashmir. Travancore's ambitions were quickly seen to be illusory: Hyderabad had first to be blockaded and then (in 1949) invaded. Both became part of India. With Kashmir we shall be further concerned.

Britain's shock tactics were intensified when Mountbatten reported that even June 1948 was too late for the transfer of power. With earlier visits in mind he concluded that violence would become uncontrollable by then, and the British cabinet accepted his view. By advancing the date to August 1947 it left scant time for settling the biggest of all the issues raised, the lines of partition between India and Pakistan. It was apparent that Pakistan must consist of two widely separated areas, each containing large non-Muslim populations. A boundary commission was created, consisting of two Hindu and two Muslim judges with Sir Cyril (later Lord) Radcliffe as chairman. On most contentious points the two Hindu and the two Muslim voices cancelled each other out and Radcliffe was left to take, in two months, a series of detailed decisions on localities which he did not know and had no time to visit. One of the most important of these decisions was an award which gave India access to Kashmir. But the new borders did not serve to contain the peoples within them; probably no borders could have done so. Fear drove millions across them and in the course of this mass exodus millions were slaughtered. Sikhs, quitting the homes in the Punjab in which they no longer felt safe, attacked Muslims moving westward for the same reason; Muslims retaliated; atrocities were multiplied over a wide area reaching to Delhi itself. Probably two million men, women and children died, and this horrible feast of violence was capped in January 1948 by the assassination of Gandhi himself, Hindu apostle of non-violence killed by a Hindu fanatic.

In the new Indian state two men took control – first and foremost Jawaharlal Nehru and with him Vallabhai Patel. Nehru became Prime Minister and held that office until his death in 1964. Patel, to whom fell the task of consolidating the Indian federation of former British provinces and former princely states, died untimely in 1950. The Congress remained paramount, though divided. In 1950 it chose the right-wing Purshottandas Tandom to be its president but in the following year Nehru enforced Tandom's resignation by resigning from the Working Committee which was the Congress's power house. Nehru remained president of the Congress until 1955 when he handed the office over to a reliable subordinate. In general elections in 1952, 1957 and 1962 the Congress received a slightly rising share of the vote (45–48 per cent) and a consistently massive majority in the federal parliament, despite its internal divisions and despite growing criticisms from right and left. Its principal adversary, the Communist Party, won

13.1 Pakistan, northern India and Bangladesh

CHINA

NEPAL

Kathmandu

Lucknow

UTTAR PRADESH

MADHYA PRADESH

SIKKIM

ARUNACHEZ
PRADESH

BHUTAN

ASSAM

NAGALAND

MEGHALAYA

MANIPUR

BANGLADESH

Patna

BIHAR

WEST
BENGAL

Calcutta

Dacca

TRIPURA

MIZORAM

MYANMAR
(BURMA)

(EAST
PAKISTAN)

ORISSA

BAY OF BENGAL

3.3 per cent of the vote in 1952 and around 10 per cent in the two following elections, but this vote was so concentrated as to be more effective than mere arithmetic would suggest. In the province of Kerala the communists won power on a minority vote and formed a government, but it was dismissed by the central government in 1959 and an anti-communist alliance won elections in 1960 despite a rise in the local communist vote to 42.5 per cent. The Sino–Soviet quarrel produced a rift in the party; its secretary, A. K. Ghosh, attacked China in 1961, and the Chinese invasion of India in 1962 further discomfited the party in general and its Chinese wing in particular.

But Indian political life was less disrupted by party conflict than by other divisive forces, pre-eminent among which was the language question. India's sixty-odd languages included a great many derivatives of Sanskrit, predominant in the north; a group of non-Sanskrit languages, including four principal ones, in the south; and a kind of lingua franca in Urdu/Hindustani. Some of these languages generated in their speakers a devotion so ardent as to provoke bloodshed. In particular Hindi, one of the northern Sanskrit derivatives, had enthusiasts who wished to make it the single official language of the country, an ambition which was opposed not only by those who realized the value of English and did not want to discourage or demote it, but also by Bengalis proud of their own tongue and by southerns who were affronted by any implied denigration of Tamil, Malayalam, Kanada or Telugu. In the south the language question became an ingredient in a Tamil separatist movement which was sufficiently weighty to cause concern though not to cause any actual disintegration, and all over India pressures grew to redraw the map on linguistic lines. A new province, Andhra, was in fact created on this basis in 1953, and in Bombay a serious crisis ensued between Marathi-speakers (who were a majority in Bombay city) and Gujarati-speakers. Feeling ran so high that the central government deemed it necessary to choose between two possible solutions; an avowedly bilingual state or the promotion of Bombay city to be a state on its own. The government chose the former course and displeased everybody, until in 1960 the Marathi-speakers were able to insist on a partition and the transfer of Bombay city to the state of Maharashtra. In the Punjab, to cite a final example with religious as well as linguistic aspects, the Sikhs campaigned for a Punjabi-speaking Sikh state which would have entailed a division of the Punjab. Despite fasts by their leader, Master Tara Singh, they were not successful.

In external affairs Nehru was determined to remain in the Commonwealth (especially if Pakistan did) while adopting a republican constitution and conducting a foreign policy which might be not merely independent of Britain's but contrary to Britain's. He succeeded in persuading the other prime ministers of the Commonwealth (as the

British Commonwealth was significantly renamed at the period) that India might remain a member even though it became a republic. This was a revolutionary step. Without it the expanding postwar Commonwealth, with its strong republican tendencies, could not have taken shape. In 1949 a Commonwealth conference accepted an Indian plan to declare the British sovereign head of the Commonwealth and leave each member free to adopt a monarchical or republican form of constitution. India itself became a republic at the beginning of 1950, and within a few years there were many more republics than monarchies in the Commonwealth. The independence of each member of the British family of nations had been accepted for a generation but none had so far consistently pursued a foreign policy which ran counter to Britain's. This Nehru set out to do without impairing his good relations with London, and once more he was substantially successful. Although Britain was a committed protagonist in the Cold War was none of India's business and that the two camps were behaving with an equally deplorable folly. Having taken a conspicuous part in bringing the Korean War to an end he went on to elaborate a policy and posture of neutralism in the hope of keeping sizeable powers out of the Cold War, of limiting its evil effects and paving the way for its eventual termination. In 1955 he visited Moscow, and India received a return visit from Bulganin and Khrushchev (who made the mistake of making the anti-British speeches which Indians were capable of making themselves but did not countenance in others). In the following year the Anglo–French attack on Egypt and the Russian intervention in Hungary confirmed Indian belief in the wickedness of all major powers, even though Nehru himself was less censorious of the Hungarian episode than of Suez (perhaps because of the latter's implications for Commonwealth solidarity). Nehru's determination that Asia should give the rest of the world an example in sanity caused him to pursue the myth of Sino–Indian friendship with an unrealistic tenacity which, when China attacked India in 1962, gravely weakened his prestige, his policy and his country.

One source of the refusal of many Indians to give the Chinese menace sufficiently serious attention was the all-consuming quarrel with Pakistan. Even India's claims against western colonial powers like France and Portugal were emotionally trivial compared with the animosity against Pakistan. (These claims were admittedly small in territorial extent. France ceded Chandernagore – virtually part of Calcutta – in 1951 and its remaining possessions – Pondicherry, Karikal, Mahé and Yanan – in 1954. Portugal adopted in India, as in Africa, the device of converting its colonies into provinces of metropolitan Portugal, but this nominal metamorphosis was of short avail and in 1961 India took the Portuguese territories – Goa, Danan and Dia – by a show of force.) Unlike India, Pakistan lost its father

figure early. Jinnah, who had become governor-general on independence, died in September 1948. Moreover Liaqat Ali Khan, Pakistan's
first prime minister, was assassinated three years later. For several years
Pakistan wasted much of its tenuous substance on barren constitutional
disputes while public figures succeeded each other in high offices,
corruption became scandalous and the army wondered how long to let
it go on. Khwaja Nazimuddin succeeded Jinnah as governor-general
and then succeeded Liaqat Ali Khan as prime minister in 1951; in 1953
his own successor as governor-general, Ghulam Mohammad, dismissed
him and installed Muhammad Ali Bogra in his place.

These changes, which involved deliberate attempts to preserve a
balance between West and East Pakistan, were accompanied by a
gradual collapse of authority and by rioting. In 1954 the Muslim League
was severely defeated in provincial elections in East Pakistan and the
central government, humiliated and jeopardized by this reverse,
despatched General Iskander Mirza to East Pakistan as military
governor. This appointment was the beginning of the movement
towards military rule. In the next year General Mirza became governor-
general on the death of Ghulam Mohammad who had been ailing for
some time, and appointed Chaudri Mohammad Ali, an able and
honourable civil servant, to be prime minister. He, however, resigned
in 1956 and was succeeded in 1957 by Firoz Khan Noon, a
distinguished veteran. A constitution was finally adopted in 1956, but
in 1958 parliamentary democracy came to an end after the deputy
speaker of the East Pakistan parliament had been hit on the head with a
plank during a debate, so that he died. Martial law was proclaimed with
General Ayub Khan as administrator and subsequently as General
Mirza's successor as head of the state. Political parties were banned. A
new constitution was introduced in 1962 based on the American
presidential rather than the British parliamentary system.

Pakistan's instability gave India the excuse to justify its fears of its
neighbour on the grounds that there was no knowing what governments in such straits might do next. When unstable government was
succeeded by military government, Indian fears were merely transposed
into a different key and it was alleged that an efficient junta was
necessarily even more of a danger than an inefficient civilian régime.
The ill will between the two countries was concentrated on Kashmir,
but Kashmir was not its only cause. The massacres of 1947 had given a
spectacularly bad start to a relationship which was almost foredoomed
in that it arose out of the inability or refusal of India's two communities
to live on good terms with each other. The tendency in India to treat
partition as an ephemeral aberration was an additional source of
irritation in Pakistan. There were also disputes over the distribution of
the waters of the Indus and its tributaries, and over the property of
those (about 17 million of them) who had fled from one country into

the other and found themselves unable to sell the pieces of land which
they had left behind. Further, the division into two parts of what had
been a single economy produced economic tensions which developed
into a trade war and reached a high pitch of acrimony when India
devalued its currency in 1949 in step with Britain but Pakistan refused
to follow suit until 1955. But worst of all was Kashmir.

The state of Kashmir consisted of Kashmir proper; Jammu; an upper
tier running from the north-west to south-east and consisting of Gilgit,
Baltistan and Ladakh; and a western fringe which included the small
territory of Poonch. Kashmir had been under Afghan rule when it was
conquered by the Sikh prince Ranjit Singh in 1819. The same prince
shortly afterwards installed Gulab Singh as ruler over Jammu, and
Gulab Singh duly added Ladakh and Baltistan to his realm. In the 1840s
all these territories, Gilgit in the far north-west still excepted, became
part of British India as a result of the two wars between the British and
the Sikhs for the mastery of the Punjab. The Sikh princes remained in
power as maharajahs of Kashmir and Jammu, and in 1947 the British
were turning a blind eye to the notoriously unsatisfactory rule of the
rich and incompetent Hari Singh. This maharajah's Muslim subjects,
four-fifths of the total, were solidly opposed to his rule and so were
many of the Hindu minority. Muslim opposition was divided between
the Kashmir Muslim Conference, to which no Hindu could belong, and
a larger organization led by Sheikh Abdullah which, following the
example of the Indian National Congress, included members of both
creeds.

As independence approached in 1947 the maharajah delayed and
prevaricated, partly because he was toying with the notion of an
independent Kashmir and partly because his interests lay in directions
other than statecraft. In October the small territory of Poonch
purported to secede and was immediately invaded by tribesmen from
Pakistan. How far the Pakistani government had foreknowledge of
these events has remained obscure. The maharajah appealed to India
which refused to come to his help unless he formally acceded to India.
This he did just in time to enable Indian troops to be flown into
Kashmir to forestall the capture of its capital, Srinagar, by the
tribesmen. The maharajah was then removed and, in 1949, deposed,
and Nehru made in November the first of a number of promises to
hold a plebiscite. Early in 1948 India referred the situation to the
Security Council and Pakistan sent regular army units into Kashmir
which recovered some of the ground which the tribesmen had lost to
the Indian army. A UN mission proposed a cease-fire, which came into
effect on the first day of 1949, and a plebiscite, which was never held.
The cease-fire hardened into partition along an adventitious line. Parts
of Kashmir became integrated with Pakistan; these were the west
including Poonch, and also Baltistan and Gilgit. The rest of the

country, including Ladakh, was ruled by Sheikh Abdullah as prime minister under the nominal authority of a member of the princely house as head of state, until in 1953 the Indians, suspicious that Sheikh Abdullah too wanted an independent Kashmir, had him put in prison and replaced by Bakshi Ghulam Mahommad, with whom they proceeded to work out a new constitution for Kashmir in order to make it a fully integrated part of the Indian federation.

During the 1950s a number of abortive attempts were made to supplement the cease-fire by a political settlement. The first UN attempts were immediately unsuccessful. The American Admiral Chester Nimitz, who was appointed to supervise the plebiscite, never even went to Kashmir. A UN conciliation commission (UNCIP) abandoned its task at the end of 1949. An Australian judge, Sir Owen Dixon, was appointed UN mediator but was obliged to announce failure. Talks in 1951 between Nehru and Liaqat Ali Khan also failed. Dr Frank P. Graham took over Sir Owen Dixon's task with the same result. After the dismissal of Sheikh Abdullah in 1953 there was a new round of talks between Nehru and Mahommad Ali but again fruitlessly. Then in 1954, at the time when Kashmir's constitution and status were being altered, a decisive event occurred. The United States and Pakistan entered into an agreement which provided for American military aid to Pakistan. From the American point of view this was an anti-Russian move, part of the American policy of containment or encirclement, but from the Indian point of view it was a powerful reinforcement of India's principal enemy. India deeply resented this American move and Nehru made it the occasion finally and explicitly to go back on his promise to hold a plebiscite in Kashmir. During negotiations in 1954–55, during which the Pakistani governor-general Ghulam Muhammad went to Delhi, Nehru refused to entertain the idea of a plebiscite. At the beginning of 1957 Pakistan asked the Security Council to order the withdrawal of all troops from Kashmir, to send a UN force there, to organize a plebiscite and to require India to abandon the new constitution which was about to integrate Kashmir in India. India opposed UN intervention and the USSR vetoed the resolution endorsing Pakistan's plan. A year later Dr Graham made similar proposals to India, which rejected them.

During the Indo–Pakistani dispute over Kashmir in the fifties it was often forgotten that Kashmir also had a frontier with China and this frontier had, since 1948, been partly in Indian hands and partly in Pakistani. In the late fifties, however, Indians became suddenly aware of hitherto unsuspected Chinese activities in Ladakh. At the same time the flight of the Dalai Lama to India attracted popular attention, and especially Indian attention, to Chinese activities in Tibet; an incident in the far north-eastern corner of India revealed a Sino–Indian clash at this point; and politics in Nepal split openly into pro-Indian and pro-Chinese strands. China became a factor in the Kashmir dispute between India and Pakistan, and likewise Kashmir became a factor in the evolving Sino–Indian dispute which ran all the way along a frontier of more than a thousand miles and involved, besides Kashmir, the small Himalayan states of Nepal, Bhutan and Sikkim and the much larger and constitutionally anomalous country of Tibet.

Since India and China are the two largest Asian countries their attitudes towards each other are a major element in the politics of Asia. In 1954, in the context of a commercial treaty about Tibet, they proclaimed five principles for the regulation of their mutual and possibly conflicting affairs. These principles, often known as the Panch Shila, were: respect for each other's sovereignty and territorial integrity, non-aggression, non-interference in each other's internal affairs, equality and mutual benefit, and peaceful coexistence. On Nehru's side the Panch Shila reflected certain basic aims of his foreign policy: to eschew war, to create an Asian order resting on the mutual trust and respect of the two leading Asian powers, to obviate anything like a cold war in Asia, and to give the rest of the world an example in international behaviour. That the context should be Tibet was partly accidental but also fitting and prophetic, for it is along common frontiers that the resolutions of states are most frequently tested.

China's subjugation of Tibet, undertaken in 1950, was a logical implementation of the determination to reunite all China's 'five races' under the control of Beijing, and it brought China to the borders of India. Indians had various reasons for viewing this confrontation – a meeting, as it turned out, of ideologies as well as power – with surprising unconcern. There was first of all the determination to get on well with China, a determination which was heightened by the challenge of ideological differences and which therefore obfuscated the difficulties of doing so. Then there was a pervasive if vague belief that bad-neighbourliness was a mark of capitalist, power-minded states rather than a consequence of rubbing shoulders, coupled with a similar belief that many of the troubles of the past in India (including the troubles which the British had had along its frontiers) were part and parcel of an alien imperialism and had automatically been removed with the British. Finally, there was the obsession with Pakistan, so that the division of British India into two states proved not merely a weakness in the sense of a dissipation of material resources but also a weakening of the power to see things in proportion. Whether or not the Chinese were emboldened by this division, it certainly gave them opportunities, not least the opportunity to play for years a hazardous frontier game which many Indians preferred in their myopia not to notice.

The Sino–Indian border runs for about a thousand miles through some of the most daunting territory in the world. To the west Tibet marches with Ladakh, the south-eastern portion of Kashmir which, jutting eastward, thrusts a wedge between India and Tibet. The border then touches Indian territory and makes the turn to the eastward which carried it all the way to Burma by way of Nepal, Sikkim, Bhutan and the North-East Frontier Agency of India (Nefa).

The Chinese claim to regard Tibet as an integral part of China had not seriously been contested by other sovereign states, however uneasy they might have been about this extension of Chinese power. The Tibetans themselves, conscious of their wholly different culture, religion and language, took a different view, partly on the grounds that *de facto* independence since 1911 had ripened into full independence and partly by construing vague and ancient declarations of Chinese respect as formal grants of independence and not the mere courtesies which the Chinese said they were. The Mongol Khan Kublai, a grandson of Jenghiz, who became emperor of China in the thirteenth century and was converted to Buddhism, bestowed favours and rights on a lama who established in Tibet a local dynastic rule of uncertain radius. A hundred years later a schismatic line of so-called Yellow Hat Buddhists appeared and after a further two hundred years supplanted the line installed by Kublai as effective rulers of Tibet. The chief of this line was the Dalai Lama (he claimed spiritual descent from a contemporary of the Buddha in the fifth century BC), and in the seventeenth century he received from the first Manchu emperor in China marks of respect which may or may not have amounted to something approaching sovereignty. In the next century the Chinese entered Tibet to protect the country against Mongols and refused to go away again. They also defended it against a Gurkha invasion later in the same century and consolidated their position during the nineteenth century, aided by the tendency (sometimes described as mysterious) of the boy Dalai Lamas to die just before or soon after reaching the age to assume full powers.

The nineteenth century also witnessed the approach of the British and the Russians, and in 1903 Sir Francis Younghusband rapped on Tibet's southern door, proceeded to Lhasa and so served notice of Britain's unwillingness to leave China a free hand in Tibet. This was the period of Chinese disintegration but any British notion of taking China's place in Tibet was soon abandoned. The thirteenth Dalai Lama fled in 1903 to Mongolia and thence to China, where his reception was disappointing. He returned to Lhasa in 1909 but fled again in 1910, this time in fear of the Chinese and into India. The collapse of the Chinese empire in 1911 seemed to open the way to real independence but at the Simla conference of 1913–14 between Chinese, Tibetans and British the latter proposed a recognition of Chinese suzerainty in return for a Chinese promise of Tibetan autonomy. This proposal, repeated in 1921, was never bindingly adopted. The Simla conference also propounded a frontier between India to the south and Tibet and China to the north and north-east (the so-called McMahon line) in a document which was initialled by the Chinese but never ratified, not because China questioned the line but because its acceptance was linked with a division of Tibet into inner and outer zones and the exclusion of Chinese troops from the inner.

Upon the death of the Dalai Lama in 1933 the Chinese took the opportunity to return to Lhasa. A mission bearing condolences arrived and remained until 1949 when it was ejected as a result of the general collapse of the Kuomintang. Before this exodus China supported a revolt by the regent of Tibet against his ward, the fourteenth Dalai Lama, who was still a child. The Kuomintang patronized and recognized as Panchen Lama a boy who had been discovered in China in 1944 and was still there: the Panchen Lama, another Yellow Hat hierarch with at least temporal superiority over the Dalai Lama in eastern Tibet, was a spiritual and temporal rival of the Dalai Lama. (The previous Panchen Lama had fled to China in 1923 and died there in 1937.) This last throw by the Kuomintang proved useful to the communists, who took over the new Panchen Lama and set him at the head of provisional Tibetan government in exile. He lived in Beijing with a Chinese wife but in 1962 he disappeared after refusing to attack the Dalai Lama. He reappeared in 1979, having apparently been severely ill-treated in the interval, and died in 1989.

During 1950 there were attempts by the authorities in Lhasa to negotiate with Beijing in Hong Kong, Calcutta, Delhi or wherever contact could be made, but in October the Chinese invaded and soon secured control of the capital and much of the country. Tibet appealed unsuccessfully to the United Nations and the Dalai Lama fled in 1959 to India. The authorities remaining in Lhasa accepted Chinese suzerainty in return for a promise of a measure of autonomy as an Autonomous Region of China.

The Indian government protested to China and deplored the use of force but to the Chinese argument that Tibet was a part of China the Indian government had no reply. Nehru pursued his endeavour to reach amicable and rational solutions to current problems. After discussion in Beijing during 1953 a Sino–Indian agreement on trade and intercourse in Tibet was signed in April 1954. It dealt with the rights of traders and pilgrims, transferred to China postal and other services previously operated by India as Britain's successor, provided for the withdrawal of Indian military units from Yatung and Gyantse, and enunciated the Panch Shila. India also recognized Chinese sovereignty in Tibet. Two months later Nehru and Zhou Enlai met for the first time as the latter returned home to Beijing from the Geneva conference on Indo–China and Korea, and in October Nehru went to Beijing. The Dalai and Panchen Lamas were already in Beijing where they stayed from September to December 1954. Like the British before and after this period, and like the Americans after it, Nehru was more interested in his relations with China than in the status of Tibet or the fate of the Tibetans (who numbered only about six million, not all of them in Tibet, and were in the process of being swamped in their own country by politically inspired Chinese immigration). American and British governments periodically expressed sympathy with Tibet so long as they were on poor terms with China but both gave the Dalai Lama the brush-off when they became engaged in improving relations with Beijing – in the American case after Nixon's visit to China, in the British case when Thatcher was trying to get acceptable terms for the cession of Hong Kong.

In the late 1950s there were a number of incidents leading to Chinese complaints of Indian troops crossing into Tibet and Indian complaints of Chinese troops found south of the frontier. These aberrations could be accounted for by the difficulty of knowing exactly where one is in such country and the Indians in particular, anxious to prove that Indian and China could coexist peaceably in Asia, were not on the look-out for more serious or sinister explanations. The possibility that the two sides had radically different ideas of where the frontier ran on the map was evaded. Yet by the mid-fifties the Chinese had entered the Aksai Chin or Soda Plains in Ladakh. This area, between the two mountain ranges of the Kuen Lun and the Karakoram, had long been disputed ground because it had never been agreed which range marked the Sino–Indian border. To the Chinese the Aksai Chin was important because it lay in the path of a road which they wished to built to link the Tibetan capital with their western province of Jinjiang. This road they now proceeded to build. Their operations can hardly have been concealed from the Indians. What is conceivable, and indeed probable, is that knowledge of what was going on did not immediately reach Nehru himself and that both locally and at the centre there was a conspiracy of silence among Indians whose animosities against Pakistan blinded them to the significance and consequences of what China was doing in territory claimed by India.

The Chinese occupation of Tibet had thus become something more than a rounding-off of the traditional domains of the Chinese empire. It was also a step towards Chinese involvement in international affairs. The continued exclusion of China from the United Nations gave China an appearance of detachment which was later reinforced by its diplomatic isolation after the breach with the USSR, but during the fifties China was prosecuting active interests in central Asia which brought it into contact with the Himalayan states of Nepal, Sikkim and Bhutan and with Kashmir and so with the Indo–Pakistani dispute. The subjugation of Tibet was an extension of Beijing's authority throughout the Chinese empire in more senses than one. Tibet was reduced not only for its own sake but also as a step towards the more effective control of the great province of Jinjiang to the north and north-west of it. This was the purpose of the Tibet–Jinjiang highway and the chief cause of the flouting by China of the Panch Shila.

Jinjiang, conquered by the Manchu dynasty in the middle of the eighteenth century, had borders in the twentieth with Kashmir, Afghanistan, three Soviet Republics (the Kirghiz, the Kazakh and the Turkomen) and Outer Mongolia. It has in the past been one of those provinces where a governor exercises unusual powers by virtue of his very distance from the imperial centre. He was a semi-independent proconsul who had sometimes looked to the Russian rather than the Chinese empire for help in troubles which he could not cope with himself (as, for instance, during Muslim revolts in 1930–34 and 1937). With China in disarray he could expect little from the east and had to turn west; when, however, the Russians became fully occupied by the German invasion in the Second World War, he faced about and became the friend and ally of the Kuomintang, who were in law his suzerains. In 1944 the Russians helped to foment and sustain a revolt in the Ili district of Jinjiang where an Eastern Turkestan Autonomous Republic was proclaimed, but in the Stalin–Jiang treaty of August 1945 Moscow recognized Chinese sovereignty in Jinjiang and promised not to interfere there – a promise which seems to have been inadequately kept. During the last phase of the Kuomintang the Russians tried to extend their pre-war (1939) monopoly of civil aviation in JinJiang and to recreate a Russo–Chinese partnership in economic opportunities. At the time of the collapse of the Kuomintang the former object had been achieved on paper but not the latter, and after the governor of JinJiang had gone over to Mao, the Russians opened negotiations with the new régime. In March 1950 agreements were signed for the creation of joint (50/50) companies to exploit oil and non-ferrous metals for thirty years and to operate civil airways for ten. Mao was evidently in no position to hold out for complete Chinese control in the province, indubitably Chinese though it was in law, but he immediately set about improving its communications with the rest of China by rail and by road. In casting his eyes on the Aksai Chin he was, as in so many other things, following a line of policy which had occurred to his predecessors fifty years earlier. If in 1950 Mao had had to temporize over Jinjiang, in the same year he was successful in Tibet.

The later fifties were a period of mixed gains and disappointments for the Chinese in external affairs. On the credit side were Zhou Enlai's appearances at the Geneva and Bandung conferences and his visits to Asian capitals; commercial agreements (1957) with Nepal and Ceylon, a Sino–Burmese border settlement and a Sino–Cambodian treaty; the failure of western policies in Laos and South Vietnam, and the progressive abrogation of democracy in Pakistan, Burma, Ceylon and Indonesia. On the debit side were the failure to take Quemoy in 1958, the quarrel with the USSR, the strains of domestic revolution and economic misfortunes. Most surprising perhaps to Beijing was the uninterrupted construction of the Tibet–Jinjiang highway and its implied claim to 31,000 square km of territory claimed by India and without any protest from Delhi. But an incident involving the capture of an Indian patrol by the Chinese in Ladakh brought the issue into the open and in 1958 the Indian government formally expressed surprise and regret that Beijing had not seen fit to consult Delhi about the highway.

In 1959 Tibetan discontents mounted into a serious anti-Chinese revolt. The Dalai Lama again fled to India from Chinese retaliation. In March Nehru wrote privately to Zhou to express his concern but received no answer until six months later when a public Chinese reply laid claim for the first time to extensive stretches of Indian territory. In the interval Moscow had agreed to give India financial aid and Khrushchev, before setting out for the United States, had adopted a neutral instead of a pro-Chinese posture. India likewise was maintaining a neutral position as between China and the United States and refusing to take an anti-American line. The Chinese accused India of interfering and stirring up trouble in Tibet, and in the summer the border incidents which had been going on for several years without attracting wide attention produced casualties, publicity and bitterness. In August an Indian policeman was killed at Longju at the eastern end of the Sino–Indian frontier, and in October several Indians were killed in a skirmish in the Changchenmo valley which lies about midway along the north–south border between Tibet and Kashmir and on the Kashmiri side. It was no longer possible to conceal the fact that the dispute was not about who was where on the occasion of a particular clash, but about where the frontier itself was supposed to run. Up to 1960 Nehru refused to discuss the border problem with China. In 1960–61 a conference of officials met at Beijing but failed to produce agreement. Nehru neither pressed the matter nor prepared his armed forces to meet any attack in what had now become a dangerously contested area.

The eastern half of the frontier was of much less concern to the Chinese than the vital Aksai Chin, and Chinese pretensions in the east may well have been regarded by Beijing as a useful lever for the extraction of concessions in the west. To India the eastern areas were more sensitive than the western, for they provided easier access into India itself; included the Himalayan principalities which were under Indian protection but would, upon any reversal of alliances, provide a Chinese springboard into India off the southern ledge of the Himalayas; and included also Nefa where the Naga tribesmen were in revolt against Indian rule, were tying up Indian forces and were damaging India's moral standing and prestige as stories of vicious Indian tactics leaked out to the world. The unratified McMahon line, the rebellious Nagas and the weak Himalayan states (where alone frontiers were defined) gave the Chinese a small orchestra of opportunities.

Sikkim, the central and smallest of the three Himalayan states, received from India in 1950 a guarantee of internal autonomy and a subsidy in return for Indian control of its defence and foreign relations. India was allowed to station troops in Sikkim. Bhutan, the easternmost of the three, agreed in 1949 to accept Indian guidance in foreign affairs in return for an Indian promise of non-interference in its internal affairs. In both cases India was continuing the policy of the British. In the background was a Chinese claim to Bhutan rejected by Britain early in the century, and the uncomfortable fact that Sikkim, governed by a minority of Tibetan stock, had been virtually part of Tibet in the eighteenth century.

Of the Himalayan states much the largest, and the only fully independent, was Nepal, the home of the Gurkhas who had provided famous regiments for the armies of Britain and India. It had been a refuge for Hindus fleeing from the Moghul conquest and had become a separate unified state in the mid-eighteenth century. From the middle of the nineteenth century to the middle of the twentieth it was under the dual control of a royal family without power and the less than royal but more powerful family of the Ranas who ruled it much as the mayors of the palace ruled Merovingian France or the shoguns ruled Japan between the fourteenth century and the Meiji restoration of 1867. By the middle of the twentieth century the dominance of the Ranas was threatened by a recrudescence of the royal power and by Congresses on the model of the Indian National Congresses, of which there were two: the Nepali National Congress founded in 1947 in Calcutta and led by B. P. Koirala and his relatives, and the Nepali Democratic Congress, founded in Calcutta in 1949 by a member of the royal family. In 1950 King Tribhuvana provoked a constitutional change by fleeing first to the Indian embassy in Katmandu and then to India itself. The next year he returned, entered into an unofficial compact with the Ranas, introduced a parliamentary régime and installed a coalition government which included Ranas and Koiralas.

These dissensions were embarrassing to the Indian government whose object was to dominate Nepal politely and keep it out of the news. India recognized Nepal's sovereignty by a treaty of 1950. The Ranas had tended to look to China as a counter against India, and Nehru therefore wanted correct and amicable relations with the king. It was also important for Nehru that the king and the Koiralas should co-operate, since in any clash India's natural sympathies would be with the National Congress rather than the monarch and such a clash might induce it to turn to China.

King Tribhuvana was succeeded in 1955 by King Mahendra who proceeded to visit Moscow and Beijing and to receive in his own capital not only the Indian president and prime minister but also Zhou Enlai. Alive to the possibilities of exploiting his strategic position he sought economic aid from all quarters and concluded with China in 1961 a border agreement which gave Nepal the whole of Mount Everest. He also agreed to the construction of a road by the Chinese from Lhasa to Katmandu. (He died in 1972. His son King Birendra was regarded in India as more pro-Indian but not very intelligent, his queen and her family as grasping. A Nepali arms deal with China in 1988 alarmed India and when in the following year an Indian–Nepali trade agreement expired India closed thirteen of the fifteen border points between the two countries, thus imposing an embargo which caused much economic distress in Nepal and fuelled disgruntlement with the king's absolute rule. Riots in Katmandu in 1990 reminded the king of Nepal's dependence on India and also impelled him towards a measure of constitutional change which greatly reduced his status and his powers.)

In the same year as its border agreement with Nepal in 1961 China proposed to Pakistan negotiations for the settlement of border disputes in Gilgit and Baltistan. In the next year, 1962, it broached its Indian border questions in a very different way. In October it put troops across the McMahon line, skirting Bhutan to the west and entering a part of India which was peculiarly difficult to reach from the rest of India. (Nefa, bounded to the south by East Pakistan, has a panhandle stretching westward to Darjeeling, whence a thin corridor runs between Nepal and East Pakistan into the Indian province of Bihar.) Nehru, who had consistently admitted that the frontiers were ill defined and needed to be discussed, refused to begin talking unless the Chinese withdrew behind the line. The Indian army in the north-east had been reinforced during 1962 but its intelligence and logistical services were conspicuously bad and when the Chinese attacked in earnest India was humiliatingly defeated and was saved from greater disasters only by the intervention of the Americans or Russians or both – or alternatively because the Chinese had had limited aims and had attained them.

China's vigorous action against India was at variance with its approach to its frontier problems with Pakistan and Nepal, and surprising in the light of its domestic preoccupations. The antecedents of this operation are unclear but there are grounds for supposing that China acted as it did in response to a change of policy by India where counsels were divided. Nehru himself and his army chiefs had been opposed to a forward policy which would precipitate the issue of the disputed frontier by occupying disputed areas, but there was an opposing view which regarded forceful action as opportune and Chinese retaliation as unlikely. If, as may be supposed, Nehru became converted to this view he was quickly and bruisingly undeceived and the riddle of Chinese moderation in victory would be explained on the hypothesis that China wanted to do no more than stop Indian infiltration into the disputed areas (by pushing forward police posts) and put the frontier problem back on ice until India was prepared to negotiate about it. China in fact offered to negotiate but the humiliation of defeat prevented Nehru from accepting: the Indian army had lost 3,000 men killed and 4,000 captured. Following a cease-fire at the end of the year a group of India's fellow neutralists – Burma, Sri Lanka, Indonesia, Cambodia, the United Arab Republic and Ghana – offered to mediate, but they did so in so neutral a spirit that many Indians were indignant, hoping for greater sympathy and support. This attempted mediation produced no resolution and the crisis simply petered out.

The coincidence of this short war with the Cuban crisis prompted speculation about deeper Chinese calculations and more dramatic international pressures behind the scenes. While it is exceedingly unlikely that Moscow took Beijing into its confidence over Cuba, it is more than likely that the Chinese were kept informed by the Cubans. That being so, the Chinese could have seen in the possibility of war between the USSR and the United States an opportunity to press their claims against India and force out of Delhi a cession of the territory in Ladakh which they had occupied. Even larger motives could be imputed to them: to inflict severer defeats and losses on India, to bring Nehru's government down in chaos, to help Indian communists, to strike at India's economic planning. But for such grand designs there is no firm evidence, nor is there evidence for the surmise that China's advance was stopped by external threats. Once the Cuban crisis had been peacefully resolved the Americans were in a position to help India by bombing Chinese airfields and communications, but it is not known that they threatened to do so. The Russians, with obvious irritation against Chinese action, were willing to supply India with Russian aircraft, but whether they also threatened to cut off China's oil is another unknown.

Nehru's standing in his own country was both weakened and strengthened. He had been forced to seek military aid from the United States and Britain and his neutralism had led India into acute danger – because a neutralist, more perhaps than anybody else, needs to be prepared and strong – but he himself seemed more irreplaceable than ever and he was in no danger of losing office. The British government hoped to use this shock to India to bring about a settlement in Kashmir, but once the Chinese attack had been suspended, the shock to Indian security became less than the shock to Indian pride, so that India was in no mood to compound its differences with Pakistan, whose attitude towards India during the critical weeks had been the reverse of soothing. India moreover believed that Britain was on Pakistan's side. Conversations therefore, though initiated, produced nothing, and at the end of the year relations between the two countries were suddenly inflamed by the theft of a hair of the Prophet from its shrine at Hazratbal, in Kashmir. This incident produced riots in both countries and led Nehru, aware that his life was approaching its end, to make an endeavour to resolve the Kashmir problem. In April 1964 he released Sheikh Abdullah who had talks with both Nehru and Ayub Khan. These were fruitless. In May Nehru died and was succeeded by Lal Bahadur Shastri. By the end of 1964 Pakistan, convinced that nothing short of force would serve, was preparing for war. It feared that the time for success in war was running out. On the other side India was worried by Pakistan's American arms and its overtures to China: Ayub Khan visited Beijing early in 1965. Both governments were suspicious and weaker at home than they had been. Temporarily attention was diverted from Kashmir to a desolate and uninhabited mudflat called the Rann of Kutch. This unattractive area, under water for part of the year and above water for the rest, was regarded by India as part of the state of Kutch which was undeniably part of India, but Pakistan claimed that the border between Pakistan and India ran through the middle of the Rann on the principle that boundaries in water-courses lie in midstream. The dispute, in itself somewhat ridiculous, brought the two countries to the verge of fighting but abated after an offer of British mediation. In 1968 Pakistan got by arbitration one-tenth of its claim. More serious was the arrest of Sheikh Abdullah. Since his release the Kashmiri leader had visited Britain and a number of Muslim countries and he was about to go to Beijing. The Indian government, alarmed by his undiminished independence, took the view that he would be better back in prison.

On 28 August 1965 Pakistan troops crossed the cease-fire line in Kashmir which had been established and kept under UN observation since January 1949. A second attack was launched on 1 September. The Pakistani air force conducted some successful operations but the crucial land attacks were held by the Indian army and on 6 September India retaliated by invading Pakistan itself. Thereafter the fighting rapidly came to a stalemate. China delivered a threatening note to India but took no effective action in support of Pakistan. U Thant went in person to Asia and secured an (imperfectly observed) cease-fire. The USSR offered to mediate if Shastri and Ayub Khan would meet Kosygin in the Uzbek capital of Tashkent. Britain and the United States also urged both sides to stop fighting and there were at least implications that economic aid and military supplies would be stopped if they did not.

Pakistan had presumably hoped to score a quick and decisive military victory as a preliminary to negotiations from a position of strength. Its precise political aims were unknown but probably entailed the cession to Pakistan of considerable areas of Kashmir, including perhaps the central Vale of Kashmir with or without a plebiscite. These hopes were frustrated by the Indian army whose performance surprised all who were still judging it by its failures against the Chinese three years earlier. India's successes in the fighting were matched by stubbornness on the political front. Having agreed to a cease-fire India, which remained in occupation of a slice of Pakistani territory, showed no more inclination than it had after 1949 to proceed to a political settlement. Sentiment apart India had two substantive grounds for its continued refusal to treat with Pakistan. The first was strategic. The only serviceable road for the Indian army to use in order to reach Ladakh ran through the Vale with the result that the abandonment of the Vale would have crippled India in any further encounters with the Chinese in Ladakh. An alternative road skirting the Vale could be constructed but only at considerable cost and over a period of years. Secondly, Indians were genuinely averse to a settlement on a religious basis. A plebiscite in Kashmir meant counting Muslims and Hindus and determining the political future of a territory by reference to the religion of the majority of its inhabitants. India (unlike Pakistan) was a secular state, firmly committed to a non-confessional view of politics. It could hardly accept any procedure in Kashmir which was also acceptable to Pakistan without betraying this principle and also – a matter of practical urgency – endangering the 50 million Muslims in India whose property and lives could well be jeopardized if they were regarded as adherents of Islam rather than citizens of India.

The brief war in Kashmir enabled India to re-establish its military prestige and to score a modest diplomatic point against the feeble intervention of the Chinese. India was not obliged to cede anything to Pakistan. Pakistan on the other hand failed to secure its objectives and gave its larger neighbour an opportunity to demonstrate the strength of its negative position over Kashmir. China had felt compelled to do something in support of Pakistan and had chosen to do the least. The USSR was embarrassed by a possible renewal of the Sino–Indian conflict and also by the possibility of having to take sides between India and Pakistan. India, intrinsically the more important of the two countries if only because of its size, had been cast by the USSR as a useful adjunct in the Sino–Russian conflict, was in receipt of Russian aid and had been championing the USSR's claim (rejected by China) to be an Asian country and a proper member of Afro–Asian conferences. The USSR therefore had powerful reasons for not offending India, but on the other hand it wished also to have good and improving relations with Pakistan. It disliked Pakistan's recent tendency to look for aid and comfort to Beijing, from whose lukewarm cajolements Pakistan ought in Moscow's view to be weaned. Further, the Kashmir War had disenchanted Pakistan with the United States. Pakistan had accepted Seato and Washington's general alliance system but when the crunch came in Kashmir the Americans had failed to give Pakistan the support which it supposed itself to have bought and paid for. Consequently there was at least a possibility of detaching Pakistan from the American system as well as from the Chinese flirtation. More than that, the similar disenchantment of the Turks, whom the Americans had prevented from invading Cyprus, and the perennial fluidity of Iranian politics, where too the shah might be glad of a friend uncommitted to the Arabs, gave Moscow the exciting prospect of dissolving the Northern Tier. But since Russian diplomacy in Pakistan must not lose sight of more important Russian interests in India, it was essential for Moscow to reduce Indo–Pakistani animosities to the minimum. The Tashkent meeting, which took place at the beginning of 1966, was designed both to illumine the USSR in the role of peace-maker and to clear the complex channels of Russian diplomacy in Asia. The meeting stayed the expiring war and boosted Russian prestige but produced no answer to the basic problem in Kashmir. Shastri died suddenly at the end of the conference.

Britain's position during the Kashmir War was that of a friend who is so impartial that he has become useless to both sides and distrusted by both. India and Pakistan each believed Britain to be committed to the other side under a cloak of pious objectivity. In India Britain's position was made worse when Harold Wilson deplored India's invasion of Pakistan without having previously deplored Pakistan's original act of aggression. (Although Pakistan had attacked in Kashmir and not in other parts of India it transpired that there had been a slight incursion into other Indian territory by Pakistani forces.) The Americans were in a similar position: Pakistanis judged that they had failed to live up to their engagements, Indians that they had done as little as had been expected of them.

In India itself the war in Kashmir, coming the year after Nehru's death, intensified an inevitable debate about his foreign policy. Traditionally the central point of a country's foreign policy is its own security, elaborated in national defence forces and foreign alliances. The weakness of India's foreign policy in the age of Nehru was that it decried these traditional concerns and gave more attention to the exercise of influence upon the conflicts between major powers which affected Nehru's vision but did not directly affect India's independence or integrity. In order to play this role in world affairs India needed an exceptional prestige (to command the attention of the great and to collect a following of less great, without which India by itself would be of comparatively little account) and exceptional detachment. Nehru personally provided both and so succeeded in winning for himself and his country a position which, if not always popular with the great or the less great, was nevertheless gratefully used by the great on such occasions as the ending of the Korean War and the Indo-China settlement of 1954 when Indians were accepted as impartial chairmen or mediators. But Nehru's detachment, and also his refusal to allow his policy of non-alignment to be prejudiced by arms deals and alliances, was only compatible with India's own prime requirements upon the basis that its relations with its neighbours were good. And this was not the case. Both India's most powerful neighbours were hostile: China and Pakistan claimed territory under Indian control, and the attacks delivered first by the one and then by the other forced India to consider whether a policy of non-alignment between the United States and the USSR was not at least irrelevant, and possibly a hindrance, to the defence of its Himalayan borders and the retention of Kashmir. Could India be non-aligned and safe? Could it, as Nehru had believed, be safer non-aligned than dependent on one great power and forced into hostility to the other? Perhaps non-alignment remained the wisest attitude, but if so, must not India become a nuclear power as well as a neutral one?

Shastri's successor was Nehru's daughter, Mrs Indira Gandhi, and India entered a phase in which internal affairs increasingly over-shadowed the world role which had so engrossed and appealed to Nehru. The contradictions within the vast Congress Party led to dissensions and splits which foreshadowed a re-formation of Indian political patterns. After elections of 1967 a number of provinces were governed by unstable coalitions and within a year five of them had been replaced under president's rule. The central government faced threats to law and order from strikes, students and the continuing failure either to come to terms with the insurgent Nagas and Mizos in the north-east or to silence them. (The Mizos became India's twenty-third state in 1986.)

Pakistan too was suffering internal distractions. Ayub Khan's rule had gone on too long with too few results. In East Pakistan secessionist feeling grew and the leader of the Awami League, Sheikh Mujibur Rahman, was arrested. In West Pakistan as well as East there was resentment against Punjabi domination. Leaders appeared to crystallize political and social discontents which reached sufficient proportions to force Ayub Khan to step down in 1969. He was succeeded by General Yahya Khan who proposed to guide Pakistan along much the same lines but perhaps a little faster. Elections were held in 1970 for a constituent assembly to be charged to produce a constitution within 120 days. Ayub Khan's selective democracy – a form of indirect choice based on local elections and proceeding upwards by stages by the election at each stage of delegates to the next – was set aside and universal suffrage permitted. The result in East Pakistan was an overwhelming victory for Sheikh Mujibur, in West Pakistan a somewhat less decisive victory for Zulfikar Ali Bhutto, who had been Ayub Khan's foreign minister in the years 1963–66 and formed the Pakistan People's Party (PPP) in 1967. Sheikh Mujibur's victory had been predicted, though its proportions had not; they were probably inflated by a hideous cyclone which, among other things, demonstrated the incapacity of the central government to organize relief and so accentuated East Pakistan's conviction that the government in the west did not care about its problems. The success of the Awami League was primarily an expression of Bengali separatism. East Pakistan, the more populous of the two halves of the country, objected to its status (under Ayub and Yahya) as one of five provinces, the other four all being in the west; it wanted a generous measure of autonomy in a loose federation in which the central government's authority would be confined to defence, foreign affairs and some currency matters. The president and Bhutto envisaged a stronger centre. After the elections talks began between Bhutto and Mujibur. The latter was now able to point out that he was the leader of the largest party in parliament. In the background was the fact that the ultimate repository of power was the army and the army was largely western. But recourse to the army to coerce the east could mean the disruption of Pakistan.

The Bhutto–Mujibur talks got nowhere and in the east Mujibur began to act like the head of an independent administration. He was again arrested. The president gambled on stopping secession by jailing the seceders, but he provoked instead full-scale fighting. It lasted two weeks. India, moved as some thought by anti-Pakistan venom but more certainly by fears of an anti-Indian left wing coming to power in West Bengal, and by a flood of Hindu fugitives quoted at 10 million, intervened in arms and the Pakistani forces in the east were forced to surrender: 90,000 men were taken prisoner. American and Russian warships appeared briefly in the Bay of Bengal. India also overran the Rann of Kutch and a slice of Azad Kashmir. Pakistan suffered substantial losses in men and material on land, at sea and in the air. The president resigned and Bhutto took his place. Mujibur Rahman was released to become the prime minister of the new state of Bangladesh.

The outlook for the new state was bleak in the extreme. Mujibur was popular but weak and during 1972 he was away ill in England for two months. Postwar chaos was aggravated by a catastrophic wave of disease and death, and then by general disorder, crime and corruption on such a scale that a distracted government had to proclaim a state of emergency in 1974. A year later Mujibur lost the support of the army and was murdered in a coup which was followed by a struggle for power between sections of the army. The economic activity of the country was in ruins and foreign aid ($1 billion) was quickly swallowed up. China, acting in support of Pakistan, vetoed the admission of Bangladesh to the UN for three years. Relations with Pakistan, the unravelling of the foundered association of what had been West and East Pakistan, and the release of prisoners and return of fugitives were hampered at the outset by Bangladesh talk of war crimes trials (which never took place). After the assassination of a second president General

Hussein Mohammad Ershad became president in 1982. He possessed at the outset of his rule the reputation of being neither corrupt nor violently Islamic, but in 1985 he made Islam the state's religion (85 per cent of the population were Muslims) and hopes of honest government evaporated. He introduced a measure of stability but little hope of relief for a country crushed by war, poverty and frequently by nature: appalling floods in 1988, for example, put three-quarters of it under water. Opposition, divided between twenty groups of which the two most prominent were led by the widow and daughter of former presidents (whose mutual animosities were hardly less acute than their hatred of Ershad) was rendered the more ineffectual by its habit of boycotting such elections as the government ordained. After elections in 1986 Ershad lifted martial law but a year later he reimposed it and dissolved the parliament. He won fresh elections in 1988, but mounting popular disorder and waning support in the armed forces (which he failed to appreciate) undermined his position and he was obliged to resign in 1990. He was arrested and charged with corrupt practices.

For Mrs Gandhi the bisection of Pakistan was no bad thing. India's decisive intervention in Bangladesh was immensely popular in India. She crushed opposition to herself in the Congress Party at elections in 1971, getting 40 per cent of the vote and making her opponents look like clueless has-beens, but she produced no solutions to the prime needs of a huge population growing at the rate of 2.5 per cent a year or to those of India's industry whose rate of growth was in decline. The consequent stresses, together with an ill-conceived scheme for compulsory sterilizations, led to disturbances in different parts of the country and although elections in a number of states went well for her in 1972 food problems were becoming acute in the early seventies and were alleviated only when the USSR supplied 2 million tons of grain and the United States resumed aid; some basic goods and commodities disappeared altogether. In 1974 India brought Sikkim more closely under its control by turning the Chogyal into a figurehead (in the name of democracy) and making Sikkim an associate state of the Indian republic with representatives in both houses of the Indian parliament. China was upset and so was Nepal. The Chogyal committed suicide two years later.

In 1975 a judge of the High Court started a train of unexpected events by ruling that Mrs Gandhi had offended against the Corrupt Practices Act in the elections of 1971 and by imposing on her the statutory disqualification from political activities for five years. The Supreme Court granted a stay and suspended the disqualification pending appeal but two days later Mrs Gandhi declared a state of emergency, arrested hundreds of her political opponents and introduced a stiff censorship. Mrs Gandhi explained that a conspiracy against progress and democracy had been discovered but no convincing evidence of so serious a threat was provided. She was ousted in 1977 by the Janata, a coalition of four parties including seceders from the Congress who were outraged or simply disappointed by Mrs Gandhi's authoritative manner of governing; they were also disconcerted by the growing political influence of her favourite son Sanjay. Morarji Desai, aged 82, became prime minister but the Janata, having achieved the removal of Mrs Gandhi, achieved nothing else and collapsed in 1979. Mrs Gandhi won sweeping victories in elections early in 1980 and resumed her rule. Sanjay Gandhi was killed in an air accident a few months later. His elder brother Rajiv was adopted by their mother as heir apparent.

Mrs Gandhi was assassinated in 1984 by Sikhs with whom she had developed something of a personal feud. The Sikhs had long wanted and agitated for greater autonomy in Punjab, the incorporation into it of Chandigarh (shared with the neighbouring state of Haryana under central control) and a reallocation of river waters. These were political claims arising out of the Sikhs' religious identity. Mrs Gandhi's hostility was directed to the former which smacked of separatism, not to the latter which gave no offence in a secular and multireligious state. The Sikhs aggravated their offence in Mrs Gandhi's eyes when their party, the Akali Dal, made common cause with the Janata in 1977, and after her return to power she sought to discredit it by allowing extremists among the Sikhs latitude for their wilder ways. Under a militant leader, Sant Bindranwale, they occupied and stocked with arms nearly forty Sikh shrines, including the Golden Temple at Amritsar. Faced with this threat of insurrection, Mrs. Gandhi ordered the army to clear the shrines and in the course of the main operation at the Golden Temple 1,000 Sikhs were killed, including Bindranwale who was thus promoted to martyrdom. A group of 300 Sikhs later recovered possession of a part of the Golden Temple in defiance of their own leaders and the army again resorted to force to evict and arrest them. The army's operations, which included the use of tanks, appeared incompetently crass and unnecessarily destructive. In revenge two Sikhs of Mrs Gandhi's bodyguard killed her.

At the invitation of Congress leaders Rajiv Gandhi took over the premiership in a remarkably smooth transition. Known as a retiring man without political ambition or experience he was regarded as a convenient but temporary figurehead whose presence could forestall chaos. Within a year he had become a leader in his own right who impressed Indians and others by a quiet determination and obvious integrity but this unexpectedly auspicious start was not maintained. Although he held his ground at the centre he lost it in many provinces. He had some success in economic affairs; growth rose to 9 per cent a year and consumer goods became more plentiful. He was genuinely opposed to religious factionalism but alienated both Muslims and Hindus. He distanced himself from the crusty barons of the Congress Party but replaced them by personal cronies. He bewailed corruption but failed to deal forthrightly with scandals. His good sense did not suffice to solve the Sikh problem and although he improved India's relations with Pakistan and China his well-intentioned effort to prevent massacre and civil war in Sri Lanka was not rigorously thought out and at best brought a dubious respite.

His most urgent problem was Punjab. He sought and gained an accord with the Sikh leader Sant Harchand Singh Longoval, giving Punjab the city of Chandigarh in return for the cession of a number of villages to Haryana and an allocation of river waters vaguely favourable to Haryana. Although Sant Longoval was then assassinated by Sikh militants the agreement stood the test of provincial elections in Punjab which were won by the Akali Dal, campaigning for its endorsement. In Haryana on the other hand the proposed loss of Chandigarh gave great offence to the state's Hindus and led to a crushing defeat for the Congress (I) Party in 1987. Nor did the agreement itself survive. Disputes over its detailed application gave the more militant Sikhs the excuse to disavow their leaders, pull down parts of the Golden Temple on the grounds that it had been polluted by Hindus, and proclaim their separate state of Kalistan (1986). The Golden Temple was recovered from the militants but the underlying conflicts persisted, among Sikhs and between Sikhs and Hindus. Violent disorders occurred from time to time.

The setback to the Congress (I) Party in Haryana was preceded, if less dramatically, in other provinces – West Bengal, Kerala. Gandhi's personal standing was tainted by the resignation of his esteemed defence minister, V. P. Singh, in protest against the government's reluctance to explore financial scandals, particularly those relating to defence contracts with Bofors of Sweden, and continuing dissensions within the ruling party caused further electoral losses at by-elections in 1988. Huge trade deficits, as exports declined and imports rose, added to the feeling that the government was as precariously in control of the country's economy as of its cohesion. On the credit side Gandhi pacified Assam's discomfort over the influx of Muslim refugees from Bangladesh; a fence was built to stem the flood while plans were made to send refugees back. On balance, however, Gandhi's performance in domestic affairs began to look like honourable inadequacy. Abroad he improved relations with China but achieved no concrete settlement of the two countries' frontiers. He reaffirmed India's good relationship with the USSR and made some improvement in relations with the United States; he got credits from the one and technical aid from the other. He was a principal author of the South Asian Association of Regional Co-operation (SAARC), an association of seven states – India, Pakistan, Sri

Lanka, Bangladesh, Nepal, Bhutan and the Maldives – which, by deftly avoiding all contentious issues, engineered some useful co-operation in commercial and technical matters and transport: it established an headquarters in Katmandu. In the all-important direction of Pakistan Gandhi met both General Zia and Benazir Bhutto to demonstrate goodwill as a cautious prelude to reducing mutual fears and suspicions. But in 1989, his virtues having been overtaken by his shortcomings, he lost a general election to a motley association of opponents, led by V. P. Singh and stretching from the Bharatiya Janata (BJP) on the Hindu right to assorted communists on the left. The Congress (I) Party fared particularly badly in the northern states but it remained the largest party in the Lok Sabha and Gandhi was quickly re-elected chairman on the motion of the man tipped to supplant him in the event of electoral defeat. V. P. Singh commanded a majority in the Lok Sabha only so long as the extremists of right and left continued to support him. He jeopardized this majority with proposals for positive discrimination in the job market for the lower castes and he lost it in 1990 when he ordered the arrest of Lal Krishna Advani, leader of the BJP, who was conducting a long march across northern India with the aim of pulling down a mosque and building a Hindu temple in its place – a threat to communal peace and even to international peace in the sub-continent. Chandra Shekhar, who was Singh's colleague and adversary in his own party, Janata Dal, took the opportunity to split the party, destroy Singh's majority and succeed him as prime minister by winning from Gandhi a promise of parliamentary support. Gandhi thus steered clear of an immediate return to power and responsibility but his attempt to be recognized as leader in the Lok Sabha of the opposition to a government which he had promised to support failed amid some derision.

The abiding sore in the sub-continent was the bad relations between its two biggest states. Mrs Gandhi and Zulfikar Ali Bhutto had concluded in 1972 a comprehensive agreement in the course of direct talks in Simla and by the end of that year they had fixed provisional lines of demarcation in Kashmir and begun the business of repatriating prisoners taken in the war over Bangladesh. The Bangladesh crisis had shaken settled attitudes in both countries. It caused Mrs Gandhi to abandon India's traditional non-alignment and conclude a treaty with the USSR to offset the partiality of the United States and China for Pakistan. (Washington had gone so far as to stop aid to India and denounce it for aggression.) Bhutto's main problem was to build a new state. Pakistan had lost not only face and half its territory but also half its domestic market, a major part of its raw materials and manufactures, its overseas markets (which had been supplied by East Pakistan) and its foreign earnings; and the constitutional problem, unsolved since 1947, remained. This last problem was temporarily laid to rest in 1973 by the adoption of a presidential, federal constitution, but in the same year economic problems were exacerbated by disastrous floods.

Bhutto set Pakistan on the nuclear road. He sought French help which was initially promised but then revoked upon American remonstrance. Nevertheless Bhutto succeeded, at first secretly, in starting a programme under the charge of a Pakistani scientist who had acquired the requisite expertise in the Netherlands. Bhutto's expressed attitude was that, since Hindus, Jews and Christians had nuclear weapons, there ought to be an Islamic bomb too. (India achieved a nuclear explosion in 1974: Mrs Gandhi and the pacific Desai both forswore the ambition to develop a nuclear armoury.) Washington tried by pressures and cajolery to stop Pakistan's progress; it cut off economic aid as required by the Foreign Assistance Act 1976, refused to relax debt repayment terms and offered Pakistan modern fighter aircraft if it would apply international safeguards to its nuclear activities. Washington's dilemma was how to make Pakistan a secure ally but without fatal injury to its relations with India.

In 1977 the Pakistani army stepped in once more, installed General Zia ul-Haq as president, hanged Bhutto two years later and inaugurated a cruelly repressive régime. In external affairs Zia continued the programme initiated by Bhutto to give Pakistan the option of becoming a nuclear power; some Pakistanis professed to fear a combined Indian and Israeli operation against Pakistan's nuclear installations. Zia took Pakistan out of the moribund Cento alliance and made it a member of the non-aligned group but the Soviet invasion of Afghanistan in 1979 turned him back to the United States camp and consolidated his personal position. The army, which had put him in power and on which he was wholly dependent, had shown few signs of keeping him as president until the Soviet invasion made an early change inopportune: initially the extension of direct Soviet power to Afghanistan seemed to entail a possible threat to Pakistan also. That fear abated when it became apparent that the USSR was less interested in Pakistan than in Afghanistan itself and Iran and that the puppet régime in Kabul effectively controlled little more than a fifth of the country. Zia thereupon set himself successfully to use the invasion as a lever to recover American military aid and funds. The Soviet action, although a costly blunder, was interpreted in the United States as a dangerous increase in Soviet power which – the shah of Iran having been overthrown – could be checked only by arming Pakistan and using it as a channel for arming opposition to the USSR in Afghanistan. Zia lent himself to this policy with enthusiasm. He received American aid in profuse quantities, notwithstanding much American dislike of Pakistan's nuclear programme and its role in the drug trade and notwithstanding too the Symington Amendment which prohibited aid to states manufacturing nuclear weapons.

By 1983 the remission of fears of Russian aggression against Pakistan revived pressures within the country for an end to military rule, and in an attempt to preserve his position Zia surprisingly announced at the end of 1984 that he would hold a referendum to test popular approval of his policies in general and himself as head of state, with the corollary that, if approved, he would serve for another five years and intensify the Islamicization of the constitution and the application of the severest Koranic penalties for infringements of religious rules: penalties which delighted many Muslims and shocked others. The votes cast were almost all in his favour. Martial law was removed at the end of 1985 – a show of moderation which, however, was preceded by an act of indemnity for past actions and a substantial increase in the presidential powers, including the extension of Zia's own term of office to 1990.

Zia had done nothing to lessen tensions between Punjabis on the one hand and Sindis and Baluchis on the other and the return to Pakistan in 1988 of Bhutto's daughter and political heir Benazir increased bitterness and uncertainty. The persistent weakness of the Pakistani economy was aggravated by the profligacy of a military régime which allocated 40 per cent of the budget to the armed forces, ran huge deficits on the budget and external account, and allowed foreign debts to escalate ominously: defence costs and the service of the foreign debt together absorbed 85–90 per cent of the budget. Zia was constrained to seek a large loan from the IMF, for which he had to submit his country to severe austerity, higher prices, new taxes and collapsing social services and roads (the health budget was cut to less than one-fiftieth of the defence budget). Zia's problems were multiplied by declining remittances from Pakistanis in the Gulf and other foreign parts, by a sequence of crop failures, by the stream of refugees from Afghanistan, and by the private armies of drug syndicates which operated even in the capital where Pathan immigrants clashed with the non-Pathan inhabitants. Opposition to Zia therefore grew but it was not compact. After her return Benazir Bhutto pulled discordant groups together, but not seamlessly. The first local elections after her return disappointed her followers. She was handicapped as a woman and a Sindi, particularly in the dominant province of Punjab; by a personality in which intelligence was not unmixed with arrogance; and by an inauspicious marriage arranged by her mother. The government had some success in denigrating and marginalizing her PPP until two events in 1988 transformed her position: Zia abruptly dismissed his civilian prime minister Mohammad Khan Junejo and was himself killed in an air accident. Two other generals, several senior officers and the American ambassador died with him.

The elections which followed this catastrophe were fought between two consolidated groups: the Islamic Democratic Alliance which consisted of the Muslim League and minor associates, and the PPP and its associates. In a low poll the PPP won much the larger number of seats but not a majority and it failed to win in any province except Sind and the North West. Benazir Bhutto was installed as prime minister and the army made one of its periodic retreats into the background. But not for long. In varying degree the army, the president and a majority of the provincial governors were hostile to Bhutto and awaiting a chance to get rid of her. Her heritage of corruption, drug trafficking, Afghanistan, economic decline, inter-provincial squabbles and growing Islamic fundamentalism was too complex for a government which controlled only two provinces and was ultimately dependent on army officers whom she could neither conciliate nor subordinate. Her government was accused, not without reason, of incompetence, corruption and nepotism and in 1990 she was dismissed by the president, using the pretext of violence in Sind which she had failed to control. (Violence in Sind was endemic between Sindis and Muhajirs, post-1947 immigrants from India.) In fresh elections later in the year she lost to the accompaniment of far from implausible charges of ballot rigging. The victors were the Islamic Democratic Front, an amalgam of nine parties with a strong flavour of religious intolerance and extremism and the backing of the army. The Front came to power in Pakistan at the same time as the government of V. P. Singh in India was destroyed by the actions of intolerant Hindu militants.

During the eighties Pakistan's conflict with India had been over-shadowed by the war in Afghanistan but it was not obliterated and it was in two respects sharpened: by India's Sikh problems and by Kashmir once more. Indians accused Pakistan of inciting the more militant Sikhs in India's province of Punjab and moved troops to stop Sikhs from crossing into India from Pakistan. Pakistan concentrated its own forces on the same border. In 1985 fighting broke out between India and Pakistan over possession of a glacier north of Kashmir. India had the advantage; mediation was proposed in 1987; but more fighting followed and in 1989 the central Kashmiri issue was once more inflamed. Sheikh Abdullah having died in 1983, his mantle had fallen on his son Faruq Abdullah (a lightweight character too close to New Delhi for the taste of most Kashmiri Muslims) and his son-in-law Ghulam Muhammad Shah, and the family disagreements of these two compounded political feuds and led to disorders in 1989–90 in which a number of people were killed. India blamed Pakistan for the disorders. Pakistanis laid the blame on Indian neglect of the province. Outsiders increasingly wondered how much longer Hindu governors appointed by New Delhi could govern an overwhelmingly and self-consciously Muslim province. In an ominous development the Kashmir issue began

to be turned into an all–Muslim cause and Iran and Saudi Arabia to vie
with each other in protestations of support for Pakistan.

The identity of the modern state of Afghanistan began to be formed by Ahmed Shah in the eighteenth century after the assassination of Nadir Shah of Iran whose empire had extended over Pathans, Turkomen, Uzbek and Hazars (descendants of the Mongols) who lived between the deserts of eastern Iran and what was to become the north-west frontier of the British in India. In the nineteenth century the British, after defeating the Sikhs, extended their rule westward and came into collision with Amir Abdur Rahman of Afghanistan who, having consolidated his position after a time of troubles, was moving in the opposite direction. In 1893 the Durand line, named after the foreign minister of India and running through Pathan country, was drawn but the nature of this line was not precisely defined and successive Afghan governments denied that it was ever meant to be an international frontier.

Between eight and nine million Pushtu-speaking Pathans live on either side of the Afghan–Pakistani frontier. On the eve of Pakistan's independence in 1947 and after it Afghanistan tried to persuade first Britain and then Pakistan to agree to the creation of an independent Pathan or Pushtu state which would not, however, have included the Pathans living in Afghanistan (who were alleged to desire no change) but would stretch from Chitral in north-western Kashmir down to Sind and might embrace parts of Baluchistan and Sind and even Karachi. Pakistan rejected the notion. For some years there was border fighting – associated in particular with the faqir of Ipi, a persistent thorn in Pakistan's flesh – and a series of domestic protests and flurries. An offer by the shah of Iran to mediate in 1950 was accepted by Pakistan but never eventuated. Shortly afterwards the dispute died down, but it continued to affect relations between Afghanistan and Pakistan and, together with the former's tradition of friendly relations with the USSR, was a factor in keeping Afghanistan out of the negotiations for the Baghdad Pact, sponsored by the west. From 1953, when it became the first non-communist recipient of Russian aid, Afghanistan moved into the Russian sphere, but its dependence on the USSR remained discreet for twenty-five years. Afghanistan stayed off the international map.

Modern Afghanistan has been governed by the Pathans of the south-east with the reluctant acquiescence of other races, among whom the more important were the northerners who, although quick to stigmatize the Pathans as idlers, found in the comparative richness of their own lands and herds compensation for their disproportionately low political influence. Afghanistan was a country with few natural resources and a medieval fiscal system. Since the parliament refused to impose any but the lightest taxes on land, public revenue was derived from customs duties which were necessarily small. Smuggling was a major economic activity. Mahammad Zahir Shah, who came to the throne in 1935, was well disposed to modest progress but obstructed by a parliament which he, unlike his neighbour the shah of Iran, was not strong enough to dismiss or manipulate. He was deposed in 1973 while on a visit to Europe, the monarchy was abolished and a republic inaugurated under the presidency of one of his relations, Mohammad Daud Khan. During the sixties foreign aid (Russian, but also Chinese and French) was used mainly for road building. Some of this activity, notably the road and tunnels built by Russian engineers from Mazar-i-Sharif near the frontier with the USSR and over the Hindu Kush to Kabul, had obvious strategic significance, particularly alarming to Pakistan.

Mohammad Daud had been helped to power in 1973 by a section of the (more or less) communist People's Democratic Party (PDP) which came into existence in 1965 and almost immediately split into two parts. The one – the Khalq – led by Nur Mohammad Taraki and Halizullah Amin was broadly rural and Pathan. The other – Parcham – led by Babrak Karmal was predominantly urban and stronger among Tadjik and other non-Pushtu-speaking peoples. Parcham supported Mohammad Daud and was rewarded with places in his cabinet. But Mohammad Daud was trying to play off east against west and vice versa. He sought aid from the shah of Iran (and possibly the United States), persecuted both Parcham and the Khalq and in 1977 put their leaders in jail. Both factions, however, had made headway in the army and in 1978 the tables were turned and Mohammad Daud was ousted. This was a victory chiefly for the Khalq which, after a brief spell of co-operation with Parcham, despatched Karmal and other Parcham leaders into dignified exile as ambassadors. When later summoned to return home they preferred not to.

Taraki and Amin quickly came to grief. Their impulsive reforms enraged landowners and the clergy and precipitated rioting in which many were killed (including incidentally the American ambassador whose role behind the scenes, if any, has remained a mystery). In what may have been an abortive coup against the government some fifty Russian advisers in Herat, close to the Iranian frontier, were gruesomely murdered. Taraki's star waned and Amin tried to recover

14.1 Afghanistan

control by ordering ferocious razzias in the countryside and killing his enemies by the thousand. Alarmed by these disorders, by seething Islamic opposition provoked by Amin's persecution and the example of neighbouring Iran, and perhaps also by events in Iran which constituted both a temptation and an excuse for an American armed coup there, the Russians resolved to get rid of Amin and tighten their grip on Afghanistan. But as Taraki, with Russian encouragement, was about to remove and kill Amin, Amin removed and killed him. Amin, who was proving less subservient than Moscow required, lasted another three months at the end of which the Russians, having tricked him into asking for their help against the rebellion which he could not master, invaded the country in the closing days of 1979. Amin was executed, Karmal reappeared and was installed as president.

This act of aggression was interpreted in Washington as a calculated move in Russian global strategy rather than as a response to the dangerous flounderings of an incompetent puppet. From Moscow's point of view the rule of Taraki and Amin had created chaos in a frontier zone and, if Moscow's proclaimed interpretation of events was to be believed, was playing into the hands of Moscow's enemies in Iran, Pakistan and the United States. This troubled area had moreover a special characteristic. It was a Muslim and largely Turkic country which bordered on republics of the same texture within Soviet central Asia where, as every member of the Politburo could recall, *bashmak* or robber insurgency had been endemic for half the lifespan of the USSR. Here were sufficient grounds for the invasion which a majority of the Politburo endorsed at the prompting, as it seemed from outside, of its military members, influenced by the arguments of leading personalities in the central Asian republics.

But the consequences were wider than these motives. The Russian invasion coincided with the post-revolutionary disarray in Iran and with continuing uncertainty in Pakistan where, shortly before the invasion, General Zia ul-Haq had advertised his insecurity by cancelling elections and all party political activities. Moscow had been accusing both Iran and Pakistan of interfering in Afghan affairs and these charges, whether or not true, might herald further acts of aggression. The invasion brought first-class Russian armed forces to within an hour's flying time of the Persian Gulf and the Indian Ocean and to Baluchi country: the Baluchis had been fighting against their Iranian and Pakistani overlords from 1973 to 1976 and many had fled into Afghanistan and to the USSR. After the initial phase of the invasion two-thirds of the Russian invaders were seen to be in south-western Afghanistan where they could not fail to be seen in Washington as a threat to Iran and the Gulf. Movements of American vessels of war to the Gulf had in Moscow the same message in reverse.

The United States chose to react by playing up the invasion's frightening implications. This was not difficult since the invasion was a blatant act of aggression. It was also necessary from the American point of view because American prestige and influence had been severely dented by the continuing captivity of the hostages and also by the fall of the shah; the shah in person had been portrayed as a major bastion of American strength and Washington was accused – by, in the first place, dismayed Americans themselves – of having failed to stand by and salvage a powerful friend. The American position in and around the Gulf was weakened by this charge, even though Arabs secretly rejoiced over the discomfiture of a non-Arab monarch whom none of them loved. President Carter had also a legitimate interest in switching the international limelight from his own dilemma over the hostages to the enormity of Russian behaviour in Afghanistan and he was strongly supported by the Muslim world. The Islamic Conference, the institution created in 1969 by the Saudi monarchy, held an unprecedented emergency meeting at which Khomeini inveighed against the USSR as almost as satanic as the United States and all Arab members joined in condemning the invasion. The Gulf states were more emphatic than the anti-Israeli Confrontation Front (Syria, Algeria, Libya, South Yemen and the PLO), but even the latter could not forbear to curse.

In terms of action, however, President Carter's range was limited. Earlier in the year he had announced, with special reference to the Gulf, the formation of a Rapid Deployment Force of 100,000, but no such force yet existed. Nor was it clear what it would do if it did. The President was therefore thrown back on to long-term measures such as stopping the export of grain to the USSR (unpopular with American farmers who sold the grain to Argentinians whence it found its way to the USSR) or trying to orchestrate international displeasure by a boycott of the Olympic Games in Moscow, which annoyed the Russians but did them little harm and evoked a mixed response from the rest of the world. In geopolitical terms the principal immediate consequence of the invasion was that the USSR had to commit some 90,000 troops to pacify a country already in its sphere of influence and see this large force fail to regain convincing control over it.

From Moscow's point of view the invasion made the immediate situation both worse and better. The substitution of Karmal for Amin softened and improved the régime's domestic standing but the invasion boosted opposition by endowing it with American funds, which rose to something like $1 billion a year, and with modern American missiles and other weapons. Karmal's government reintroduced religious instruction in schools, allowed religious programmes on television and even built new mosques, thus winning the allegiance of younger mullahs. It also wooed tribal leaders. Its opponents, collectively known as the *mujaheddin*, controlled about two-thirds of the country but were seriously divided between seven groups based in Peshawar and a further eight based in Iran. The lion's share of American aid, channelled through Pakistan and allocated with Pakistan's advice, went to Muslim Sunni fundamentalists who were distrusted by Shi'ite groups operating in the western parts of the country with Iranian support, by more intellectual or secular leaders, and by partisans of the ex-king (who lived in Rome and showed no wish to leave it). A small number of individuals enriched themselves by trafficking in arms and drugs, while much larger numbers of brave men fought and died in frightful warfare which was kept going by the superpowers.

From 1982 the UN issued annual pleas for a cease-fire, for a timetable for the expeditious withdrawal of Russian forces, and for agreements between the Pakistani and Afghan governments to stop aid to the *mujaheddin* through Pakistan and to return the thousands of Afghan refugees who had fled to Pakistan. Pakistan and the United States were uncooperative so long as the *mujaheddin* appeared to have a good chance of overthrowing the communist régime in Kabul, and the Reagan administration was also reluctant to forgo the advantages of exploiting the discomfiture which Moscow had brought upon itself by invading.

The advent of Gorbachev to power in Moscow transformed the situation, if only slowly. Gorbachev was determined to get out of a venture which was disastrously costly in money and lives. He wished to preserve the communist régime in Kabul, but if he had to choose between saving it and evacuation he would choose the latter. In 1986 he offered an immediate token withdrawal and total withdrawal as soon as hostilities against Kabul were abandoned. A year later he dropped the condition and announced total withdrawal within ten months. In the interval he tried to strength the Afghan government by jettisoning Karmal in favour of Muhammad Najibullah, a tough Pushtu police chief, who became the general secretary of the ruling People's Democratic Party and later head of state. Najibullah had the dual task of controlling the factions which made up the PDP and of enticing the opposition (or some of it) into a broad coalition with a newly elected parliament and under a new constitution. But his conditions, which included the reservation of a leading role to the PDP and a special relationship with the USSR, were comprehensively unacceptable to the *mujaheddin* who were at this point given doubled American aid and more and bigger weapons. The Russian invaders departed on schedule but the anticipated collapse of the government which it left behind did not occur and the *mujaheddin* failed to take Jellalabad and other key points in the east. Najibullah contrived both to stay in power in the capital and in much of the country and gradually to come to terms with a sufficient number of the guerrilla groups to prepare the ground for peace under a broad-bottomed government.

15 SRI LANKA

Ceylon gained its independence from Britain in 1948 as a consequence of the British departure from India. In 1972 it became Sri Lanka and a republic.

It was governed alternatively by two main families and the parties which they formed: the United National Party led in turn by D. S. Senanayake, his son Dudley Senanayake and his nephew Sir John Kotelawala, and the Sri Lanka Freedom Party, founded by Solomon Bandaranaike, a defector from the UNP, and after his murder in 1959 by his widow. The UNP governed from 1948 to 1956, from 1965 to 1970 and from 1977 onwards; the SLFP the rest of the time. The most important election campaign was that of 1956 in which Bandaranaike defeated the UNP by running on a combined racial and religious ticket, pro-Sinhala and pro-Buddhist. His success was followed by persecution of the Tamil minority (a quarter of the population) and a permanent increase in the political influence of the Buddhist establishment which had subsequently to be courted by the UNP as well as the SLFP. Alongside the contest for power between these two parties opposition was provided by a variety of left-wing parties of which the most notable was the Lanka Sama Samaj Party, founded in 1935 as an expression of anti-colonialism and a member of the Trotskyist international until 1963 when it joined Mrs Bandaranaike's government (this alliance was dissolved in 1975). Mrs Bandaranaike also brought the pro-Russian Communist Party into government and since other left-wing groups had lost ground her coalition was expected to win the elections of 1965. That it did not was mainly due to an economic situation which neither main party had contrived to control but which had deteriorated alarmingly during the SLFP's years of office in the sixties.

After independence, as before, the economy of Sri Lanka was heavily dependent on the export earnings of tea, coconut and rubber estates owned by British companies. The revenue from these products fell steadily while at the same time the import bill rose, the largest single item being for food. This was a typical Third World situation in which the economy was dominated by increasingly less remunerative dealings with the former metropole and an increasing inability to feed a growing

15.1 Southern India and Sri Lanka

population without ruinous expenditure of foreign currency or, when
that failed, foreign borrowing. The population was rising fast. It
roughly doubled between independence and 1975. In the sixties alone
the external debt quadrupled. Unemployment rose from around 40,000
at independence to something near to 700,000 when, at the next turn of
the electoral wheel, Mrs Bandaranaike and her associates handsomely
won the elections of 1970 and reformed the coalition that had been
defeated five years earlier. In April 1971 it was severely shaken by a
carefully prepared, well-armed peasant rising.

This rising, which came as a surprise, was organized and directed by the Janatha Vinukhti Peramuna (JVP) or Popular Liberation Front, formed in 1965 as a splinter from the ailing Maoist Communist Party. It regarded the SFLP and UNP as two virtually indistinguishable aspects of a post-imperialist and neo-colonialist bourgeoisie which was prevented by self-interest from tackling the country's basic economic problems and social ills. The emphasis of its doctrine and its practice was on the peasants and it attempted to use the peasants to strike a direct blow at the government and the system. There was later the usual insoluble squabble about who struck the first blow, but there was no doubt about the outcome. After seven weeks the government had prevailed but the challenge to it was such that the number of people killed in the process of asserting its authority ran into tens of thousands. A most unusual constellation of states supported Mrs Bandaranaike materially or orally. They included the USA, USSR and China; India and Pakistan; Britain, Australia and Egypt. Mrs Bandaranaike maintained until 1977 the state of emergency proclaimed in 1971 but was then defeated by the UNP under Junius R. Jayawardene who became prime minister in that year and president the next. This swing to the right was marked by a dash for growth to emulate the fortunes of Singapore, Hong Kong and Taiwan, but economic ambitions were wrecked by acute racial and religious conflict in which the government became involved with the Tamil minority, once the country's rich ruling class and 18 per cent of its population.

The Tamils constituted a majority in the north and parts of the east. Distinct in race and religion they sought autonomy or independent statehood from the Sinhalese Buddhist majority which had established a powerful central government but had failed to use its power to allay Tamil fears and separatism. By the eighties time for an accommodation was running out. The more militant Tamils formed the Liberation Tigers of Tamil Eelam and civil war began. Both sides committed atrocities. India became involved because Rajiv Gandhi could not ignore the outrage felt by the Tamils of Tamil Nedu in southern India. In 1986 the governments of India and Sri Lanka agreed that the Tamils of Sri Lanka should be granted autonomy but they could not agree on the area of the autonomous province. Talks therefore collapsed and the next year Jayawardene decided to extirpate the Tigers. He failed, and Gandhi intervened to stop massacres of Tamils by the Sinhalese army. Jayawardene was obliged to let the Indian army into Sri Lanka to protect Tamils. But the Tigers, who were set on independence and therefore opposed and ignored the Indo–Sri Lankan agreement, refused to surrender their arms as envisaged by that agreement with the result that the Indian force, whose original complement of 15,000, was doubled within a few months, found itself trying to enforce the surrender of Tamil arms instead of protecting Tamils. To do so it had to abandon its peacekeeping role and use force whereupon India was accused of planning to detach northern Sri Lanka and annex it to India. In 1988 Gandhi declared that he would withdraw his force the next year. For his part Jayawardene was accused of opening the way to Indian imperialism and also for having made undue concessions to Tamil autonomy. His tribulations were aggravated by a revival of the JVP which had abandoned its communist character and turned into a right-wing Sinhalese nationalist movement. Massacres and political assassinations multiplied, in the south as well as the north. In 1988, Jayawardene's term in office being over, his prime minister Ramasinghe Premadasa was elected to succeed him in a three-cornered contest in which his principal rival was once more Mrs Bandaranaike whose civil rights had been restored in 1986 after several years' suspension.

As the Indian force prepared to depart – its last members left Sri Lanka early in 1990 – the government engaged in talks with the Tamil Tigers but these broke down and fighting was renewed. The Tigers had boycotted the 1988 elections with the result that seats in Tamil areas were won by the Eelam People's Revolutionary Liberation Party, backed by its Tamil National Army. The Indian intervention had strengthened the more intransigent and militant elements among the Tamils.

In wartime Burma the nationalists, a group of men without much knowledge of the outside world, pro-Japanese at the beginning of the war but later anti-Japanese and supplied with British arms, were associated together in the Anti-Fascist People's Freedom League (AFPFL). As the war came to an end there was doubt among the British whether to recognize and deal with the AFPFL. The government in London was opposed to recognition but the supreme commander, who was faced with the problems of installing a new administration without adequate resources of his own, favoured it. The Labour victory in the British general election of July 1945 and the precipitate surrender of the Japanese in August operated to produce a decision to recognize. The new British governor of Burma, who wanted to arrest the nationalist leader Aung San and nearly did, was replaced, the AFPFL was treated as an embryonic government of Burma, and although Aung San and other leaders were assassinated in July 1947 their surviving colleagues achieved their goal of independence from Britain on 4 January 1948. There was no fighting. The British, strongly influenced by their own pledge to leave India and also by the belief that it was not possible to use the Indian troops of South East Asia Command against the Burmese, retired, leaving the AFPFL to struggle with its own internal divisions and with the hill peoples round the central Burmese plain whose traditional distrust of Rangoon created a string of separatist problems. The AFPFL included communists who not only split off from the main association but also split among themselves and waged separate campaigns against government; assassination had robbed Burma of a number of coming leaders during 1947 and 1948; revolt in Arakan along the west coast, added to troubles in the east (from the Karens over against the border with Thailand, the Shans wedged between Thailand and China, and the Kachins in the far north) threatened independent Burma with disruption. The Shans and Kachins were mostly Christian. There were also Muslims in most parts of Burma, the majority of them in Arakan where, known as Rahingya, they had been since the seventh century AD.

In 1950 a new danger was introduced with 4,000 Kuomintang troops who crossed into Burma from China under General Li Mi and gave rise

Glossary

Current Name	Former Name
Myanmar	Burma
Yangon	Rangoon
Tanintharyi	Tenasserim
Bago	Pegu
Magway	Magwe
Ayeyarwady	Irrawaddy
Dawei	Tavoy
Pathein	Bassein
Bamar	Burman
Kayin	Karen
Mawlamyine	Moulmein
Hpa-an	Pa-an

Mountains

Name change: On 18 June 1989 the name of the country was changed to the Union of Myanmar. The English spelling of many towns, divisions, states, rivers and nationalities was changed.

0   500 km

16.1 Burma (Myanmar)

to fears that the new Chinese régime would follow its retreating enemies. But Beijing made a point of not blaming Rangoon and after a while General Li Mi and his followers were removed by air to Taiwan by the Americans. Nevertheless Burma felt it wise to edge politely and circumspectly away from its British and American connections. Although the Chinese in Burma numbered only about 300,000 Burma had a frontier with China and this frontier was straddled by the Kachins (300,000 in China, 200,000 in Burma and a small number in India). In 1953 the Burmese government intimated that it did not wish to renew the expiring Anglo–Burmese defence treaty or retain the British military mission which had been in the country since independence; it also informed Washington that it wanted no more American aid. Zhou Enlai visited Rangoon on his way back to Beijing from Geneva in 1954 and the Burmese prime minister, U Nu, returned the visit later in the year. Further meetings led to the initiation of frontier discussions which were completed when General Ne Win displaced U Nu (who returned to power in 1960 but was again displaced by Ne Win in 1962 and this time imprisoned for six years).

Ne Win was a general with a taste for philosophical and socialist discourse which he combined with the suppression of parliament and the imprisonment of his political opponents. His seizure of power was, in the first place, a response to the threat of disintegration posed by the country's dissident movements. The demands of the Shans in particular for a new federal and so looser constitution created a fear that the refugee Kuomintang forces in the north-east might, with American help, launch an invasion of China which would turn Burma into a battlefield (like Korea), while the existence in Burma of at least three different communist rebel movements made a Chinese invasion of Burma in support of communists against the government in Rangoon not improbable. The government's failure to remove these dangers of disintegration and foreign intervention were the chief causes of its removal by Ne Win and the army. The new régime, being overtly military, looked less feeble but it too failed to eradicate the various rebellions in spite of a policy of tough measures combined with declarations of willingness to talk with rebel leaders. It watered down U Nu's socialism but also watered away democracy: political parties were suppressed and universities closed in 1964. Burma's traditional fear of China (and of its friends in Burma, many of them of Chinese descent as well as communist ideas) persuaded Ne Win to visit the United States but the American war in Vietnam was all but universally regarded in Burma as unjustifiable and ominous interference in Asian affairs.

In economic matters Ne Win was even less successful than his predecessors in restoring Burma's economy. Under the Japanese occupation the acreage under rice had been halved and although this area was increased after the end of the war production was ruined by civil wars and general anarchy. Exports fell to one-tenth of their pre-war figure and by 1966 domestic consumption was rationed. Desperate measures, such as the remission of all agriculture rents, did little good. The overall decline of the country's economy left farmers with nothing to buy even when they were paid for their produce, so that they had no incentive to produce more than they could themselves eat. Rice, once the source of Burma's wealth, was no longer worth growing, let alone exporting. Inflation accompanied by static wages impoverished the bulk of the population.

In 1977 an attempt on Ne Win's life was followed by discrimination against Muslims, torture and killing. A massacre in Arakan caused flight into Bangladesh. Ne Win assumed nevertheless a new term of office in 1978. He had become autocratic, secretive and out of touch and in 1981 he made way for General Sam Yu who ruled in his shadow rather than in his place. The various peripheral wars continued in the north-east and south-east, with the Burmese communists joining in where they were welcome. The economy deteriorated to such an extent that Burma graduated downward to the status of a Least Developed Country (LDC – eligible for specially soft international loans) and in 1987 the state cancelled all notes below a certain face value, thus extinguishing the savings of countless people. Discontent spread from the poor to the middle classes and the army. Demonstrations were brutally repressed by the police, and General Sein Lwin, noted for his ferocity, was thrust into the presidency which Ne Win had resumed but now once more abandoned. After more demonstrations Sein Lwin resigned and was replaced by a civilian, Maung Maung, who was quickly evicted by General Saw Maung who dissolved parliament. When fresh elections were promised, some 200 parties appeared but only those acceptable to the government were licensed. Aung San's daughter, Aung San Kuu Kyi, returned from exile in England to lead a National League for Democracy but she was arrested. The League claimed a massive victory in elections in 1990 but the official results mirrored the government's wishes rather than the voters' and the government remained unmoved. Some opposition leaders fled the country. In 1989 the country's name was changed to Myanmar.

The most disputed postwar arena in South-east Asia was Indo-China. This area, put together by the French, contained the protectorates of Annam and Tongking and the colony of Cochin-China (Annamite by race, Chinese by culture, and together called the three Kys) and the protected kingdoms of Luang Prabang or Laos, and Cambodia (Thai by race, Hindu by culture). The Khmer forebears of the modern Cambodians ruled an empire which, at its peak in the twelfth century, reached from sea to sea and included the southern parts of Burma, Siam, Laos and Annam. In Laos invading Thais had established an ascendancy in the thirteenth century. By the nineteenth Cambodia and Laos were threatened by Annam but were saved by the French.

The French established themselves in Asia later than the other European powers. Their defeats in the Franco–Prussian War of 1870–71 on their own soil had deprived them of territory, valuable resources, population, prestige and self-respect, and although recovery was surprisingly rapid, the acquisition of a new colonial empire in the eighties was in some sense a compensation. It took the form of entering the competition for whatever might be made out of the disintegration of the Ottoman and Chinese empires. Tunisia was virtually annexed as an extension of French power in Algeria, Madagascar was occupied, and in Asia Annam, Tongking and Cochin-China were made the nucleus of an Indo-Chinese dominion which might provide a way into southern China and was extended by taking the kingdoms of Cambodia and Luang Prabang under the French wing. The acquisition of Annam and Tongking led to an unpopular war with China, while the western and Hindu-ward move brought France into competition with the British in Burma, where they were checked by the viceroy, Lord Dufferin (who feared – or perhaps invented – a French threat to India), and also into a more enduring hostility with the independent kingdom of Thailand. But French power remained substantially unshaken until 1940.

During the Japanese occupation in the Second World War the three Kys became the autonomous state of Vietnam and upon the Japanese withdrawal Ho Chi Minh, the leader of a communist-dominated nationalist coalition, proclaimed the independent republic of Vietminh.

17.1   Vietnam, Cambodia and Laos

Again, as in Indonesia and Korea, practical reasons of convenience dictated the course of events with more far-reaching effects than were contemplated at the time. The British took control south of the 16th parallel and the Chinese north of it; both withdrew during 1946 but the latter were not disposed, and the former not able, to do much to smooth the path for the returning French who arrived to find Ho Chi Minh in control of a sizeable area in the north and presiding over a government. The Annamite emperor Bao Dai, having abdicated in 1945, had accepted the post of chief counsellor to Ho.

The French began by recognizing Ho's government as autonomous within the French Union but refused to accept his demand for the union of the three Kys. Towards the end of 1946 French policy stiffened as a result of right-wing pressures. In November Haiphong was bombarded and in December the French in Hanoi were attacked by the Vietminh, convinced that France now intended to overthrow Ho: some forty Frenchmen were killed and 200 abducted. This was the beginning of a war which lasted seven and a half years. After some hesitation the French decided to give up further negotiation with Ho and to switch instead to Bao Dai, to whom they offered the union of the three Kys which they had refused to Ho. The so-called Bao Dai experiment was an attempt to separate communists from other nationalists and to preserve with Bao Dai's complaisance a general French overlordship throughout Indo-China. An agreement signed in Along Bay in June 1948 embodied this policy (which was to be reflected in the south in the next decade by the Americans with President Diem as the anti-communist nationalist) and a new state of Viet Nam was formally constituted in June 1949. Bao Dai, who had been in France during the negotiations, returned to his own country as head of state. Viet Nam was proclaimed an Associated State in the French Union in December, and Laos and Cambodia were given the same status. Among those who refused to co-operate with Bao Dai was the Roman Catholic leader and future president of South Vietnam, Ngo Dinh Diem.

But the Vietminh did not give up and the victory of the Chinese communists across the northern border transformed the situation. The attempt of the French to retain power by the device of the semi-independent Associated State led to protracted bickering between themselves and Bao Dai and failed in the end to achieve its aim. France had not been able to nerve itself to take the extreme but simple step taken by the Attlee government in India, and the history of the next few years suggested that nothing less was of any avail. In 1950 five months of conferring at Pau about constitutional advances exacerbated all parties, while in Indo-China the Vietminh took the field under its able general Vo Nguyen Giap. A Vietminh offensive in September was strikingly successful. Marshal Juin was sent to the scene. Bao Dai also returned. Pierre Mendès-France and others began to say that it was time for France to clear out of Asia. The French government, which had been resolutely opposed to admitting that the situation was in any sense international, relented to the extent of accepting American economic and military aid; to fight for French supremacy brought neither sympathy nor success, and the only way to continue the fight was to call it a fight against communism and invoke the aid of anti-communist friends. On this new basis General de Lattre de Tassigny was appointed high commissioner and commander-in-chief in December 1950. With a new general to raise morale (in which he was very successful), with American aid and with the negotiation of a political settlement of the status of the Indo-Chinese states within the French Union, the French made their final effort.

But the Vietminh struck first and showed that it was capable of waging open war as well as guerrilla operations. Its attack was renewed in October 1951 and a few weeks later the French lost de Lattre who was invalided home to France and died there in January. Bao Dai's Vietnamese army was coming into existence with extraordinary slowness, and the private armies which complicated the picture were not being reduced to his control. Chinese aid to the Vietminh was increasing, although the invasion which could have brought the Americans in never materialized. During 1952 French losses in men, material, morale and prestige were considerable, and in 1953 the Vietminh carried the war into Laos, threatened the royal capital of Luang Prabang and forced the French to divert forces from Vietnam to the Plain of Jars in Laos. In Cambodia King Norodom Sihanouk raised the political stakes by asking for a status in no way inferior to that of India and Pakistan in relation to Britain, and then put the French in great embarrassment by temporarily decamping to Thailand. Amid this scene of disintegration the French could do no more than offer to review the constitution of the French Union and begin yet another round of negotiations with Bao Dai as well as the Laotian and Cambodian monarchs. (Sihanouk had succeeded to the throne in 1940 at the age of 18. In 1955 he abdicated in favour of his father who reigned until 1960 with Sihanouk as prime minister. In 1956 Zhou and Sihanouk signed a non-intervention agreement. Sihanouk visited Beijing, Moscow, Prague and Belgrade; also Madrid and Lisbon. He adopted a policy – the reverse of Burma's – of the widest diplomatic contacts and aid from as many places as possible. He seemed, however, to have a preference for China, which he again visited in 1958 and 1960. In 1960 he resumed the top place in the state with the title of Head of State.)

There was by this time nothing left for the French in Indo-China except a need to salvage pride, but since the French have quite enough to be proud of without retaining distant satrapies, they became increasingly fed up. Moreover they were now preoccupied with the revival of German strength, beside which the strength of the Vietminh seemed both inconsiderable and irrelevant to France's position in the world. France had failed to brace itself to give its Indo-Chinese territories independence after 1945 and had entrusted their affairs to generals who, often unrealistic and at odds with one another and their civilian colleagues, had fought and lost an old-style colonial war. If the Vietminh mattered to anybody, it mattered to the Americans who were already paying for the war indirectly and saw it as a new-style anti-communist war. It required only a climactic event to make France acknowledge that what it really wanted in Indo-China was to get out. This event occurred at Dien Bien Phu.

Dien Bien Phu was a small garrison or camp in a bowl in the north-west. Its possession was important in relation to the Vietminh's threats to neighbouring Laos, which were themselves important inasmuch as they demonstrated French inability to protect a protectorate and at the same time diverted French forces from the defence of the strategically and politically central Red River delta and Hanoi. Dien Bien Phu had changed hands more than once during the war. It was taken by the French in November 1953 and after some hesitation they decided to stay there.

General Navarre, now in command of French and Vietnamese forces which considerably outnumbered the Veitminh, believed that if he could force the enemy to battle he could inflict upon them a major defeat and permanently reduce their operations to minor guerilla scale; he believed that the Achilles's heel of the Vietminh was in numbers and that the Chinese or Russians, though willing to supply arms and equipment, would not send fighting men across the borders for fear of American retaliation. Dien Bien Phu was therefore to provide the setting for the battle which would cripple the Vietminh.

Early in 1954 agreement had been reached among all the principal powers concerned to hold an international conference on Indo-China and Korea, and as the preparations went ahead it became increasingly clear that the outcome at Dien Bien Phu would have a powerful influence on the course of negotiations. It also became clear that the French, so far from delivering a knock-out blow, were being surrounded and pounded by an unexpectedly large force and were in danger of having to capitulate. What was not so clear in these circumstances was whether France's allies would be well advised to make a special effort and intervene. The Americans, who had been opposed to any such involvement, began to have second thoughts and to propound the view that the loss of Indo-China would be a fatal blow to the fortunes of all South-east Asia and even further afield. In a famous speech in January Dulles threatened 'massive retaliation' as a means of stopping communist expansion and aggression, and at the end of March he appealed for united international action to prevent the imposition of communism on South-east Asia. Congressional leaders and allies were sounded on joint intervention in Indo-China and retaliation against China itself in the event of a Chinese counter-strike. The response was unfavourable.

The Korean War had left Americans with little appetite for Asian adventures and the allies had not recovered from their distrust of MacArthurism which they detected reviving in the views of Admiral Radford, the naval chief of staff, who advocated American air strikes. Eisenhower was prepared to give his consent to Radford's policy if Congress were to agree and the United States were not the only intervenor, but General Ridgway, chairman of the chiefs of staff, opposed intervention on the grounds that it would force the Chinese to enter the war as they had done in Korea. Eisenhower, who had campaigned for the presidency on a promise to stop the war in Korea, may have known that his conditions for intervening were most unlikely to be met, but he allowed Dulles to pursue the question of allied co-operation. Dulles discussed intervention in London and Paris on 11–14 April and returned to Washington under the impression that he had secured agreement for a general conference to devise a plan but Eden, with whom his personal relations were bad, immediately denied this interpretation of their talks and refused to send a representative to a preliminary discussion. Dulles returned to Paris later in the month with a proposal for unilateral American air intervention and Eden, who was also in Paris on his way to Geneva, flew back to London where a Sunday meeting of the cabinet refused to give its endorsement. Eden communicated this decision to Georges Bidault, the French foreign minister, at Orly airport on his way to Geneva and so acquired the reputation of being the man who saved the world from being plunged into a new world war by American temerity at Dien Bien Phu. It seems, however, truer to judge that American intervention had already been dismissed because of the opposition of the American chiefs of staff (Admiral Radford alone excepted) and American congressional and public opinion. Within a very short time the view that Indo-China was essential to the free world had been temporarily dropped and the fate of Vietnam was once more being treated as a local affair.

The Geneva conference, convened to discuss Korea and secondarily Indo-China, opened on 26 April. Dien Bien Phu fell on 7 May. The French government also fell and Mendès-France took the place of Laniel (who resigned on 13 June) with a promise to reach a settlement in Indo-China by 20 July or resign. On 23 June Mendès-France and Zhou Enlai had a long private discussion in Berne before the latter set off for Beijing via India and Burma during a break in the conference. At the same time Churchill and Eden visited Washington to discuss a variety of topics and repair the damage to Anglo-American relations caused by the Dulles–Eden misunderstandings of April. Soon after the conference resumed three armistice agreements were signed. Vietnam was partitioned roughly along the 17th parallel (a compromise choice), the Vietminh agreed to withdraw from Laos and Cambodia, and three armistice commissions were constituted with Indian, Polish and Canadian members to supervise the implementation of the agreed terms. The conference marked above all the defeat of France and its withdrawal from all the states of Indo-China. It purported to proclaim the creation of three new independent states: Laos and Cambodia, which were to be safeguarded in this condition against their hereditary enemies in Vietnam and Thailand by guarantees by China, France, Britain and the USSR; and Vietnam which had won independence but not perhaps integration.

In Laos, although the Geneva settlement provided for the withdrawal of Vietminh forces, there were other forces to keep revolt going. The Pathet Lao, created in 1949 by Ho as an adjunct of the Viet Minh and led by a member of the Laotian royal family, Prince Souvannouvong, had established itself sufficiently to be able to retain control of the two northern provinces of the country. In 1956 this prince visited Beijing and Hanoi, and in the next year he entered a coalition with his half-brother Souvanna Phouma (already prime minister) on the basis that Laos would be neutralized. This experiment lasted less than a year. It was succeeded by an anti-communist phase during which Laos received an American military mission as well as the economic aid which was already flowing copiously. (American aid to Laos, totalling in the end $200 million, became a byword for waste and the promotion of corruption.)

This right-wing phase led to a two-year civil war, at the end of which Laos reverted to neutralism. The new government, making the most of North Vietnamese incursions, asked for a UN mission and a UN force. Hammarskjöld visited Laos in person and sent a special representative to observe and report and so gain time for temperatures to fall, but in December 1959 General Phoumi Nosavan staged a successful coup which had the opposite effect. It also evoked, a few months later, another coup led by Captain Kong Le, a rather naïve symbol of the irritation of ordinary men who were fed up with feuding and corruption. This coup acquired significance because Souvanna Phouma declared his support for Kong Le. The former was made prime minister once more and contrived briefly to reconcile the general and the captain, again on a neutralist ticket. But his solution did not last, largely because the Americans equated neutralism with pro-communist inclinations and were able to rebuild a right-wing front under General Nosavan and Prince Boun Oum, a distant relative of the reigning family and mediatrized ruler of Champassak (in the south). Souvanna Phouma fled to Cambodia, whence he was transported in a Russian aircraft to confer with his half-brother and Kong Le. He was also courted by Boun Oum and Nosavan but preferred to set off on a world tour. Meanwhile Kong Le had inflicted a defeat on Boun Oum and Nosavan. In 1961 the three princes met in Switzerland and agreed that Laos should become a neutralized state without military alliances. This agreement did not, however, have any immediate effect. Fighting went on until a further and more formal agreement was signed at Geneva in July 1962.

The war of 1960–62 led not only to increased American intervention in Laos (chiefly on account of the increasing involvement of North Vietnam in South Vietnam in the same years), but also to private American disenchantment with the anti-communists in Laos and so to a determination to support the anti-communist régime in Thailand, if necessary by a military presence. The war was brought to an end because the United States and China reached agreement behind the scenes on a neutralized Laos and the evacuation of foreign troops – that is, American troops which China feared and the United States felt to be engaged in a worthless cause. But Laos continued to be used by Ho for supplies into South Vietnam, the authority of the Pathet Lao spread and the American forces were replaced by an active communist army – part Laotian and part Vietnamese – which probably numbered 60,000 or more. In 1963 the Laotian coalition government dissolved and the country became virtually partitioned with the Pathet Lao ruling in the north-east and Souvanna Phouma the rest. From 1964 the United States reversed its policy of withdrawal, gradually built up very large ground forces and used its air forces in operations by the Laotian government against the Pathet Lao. Laos became an important American theatre of war, ancillary to the waging of the war in South Vietnam and to the protection of American forces of about 50,000 men in Thailand.

In Vietnam the 1954 Geneva settlement gave Ho Chi Minh half the country and the expectation of the rest in less than two years if the terms of the settlement were fully accepted and implemented. The formal agreement concluded at Geneva was an armistice agreement signed by generals on behalf of France and the Vietminh. It drew a line (roughly the 17th parallel), imposed a cease-fire, and made arrangements for the regroupment of military forces and the resettlement of civilians on either side of the line. The conference also produced a number of declarations, including a final declaration propounded but not signed. The United States and South Vietnam dissociated themselves in particular from this declaration's provision for elections throughout Vietnam by the middle of 1956; they believed that such elections were bound to transfer the whole of the country to communist rule since the part north of the armistice line contained a majority of the population – which was in addition likely to vote with that 90 per cent solidarity characteristic of authoritarian régimes. The government in South Vietnam, which had been established in Saigon by the authority of Bao Dai before the Geneva conference, considered itself bound by nothing that was settled there.

For the French the armistice agreement of 1954 was a means of escape. They were able to conclude a war which they were losing. Thereafter they watched with an excusable but irritating smugness as the Americans repeated in the next phase many of the mistakes which they had made between 1945 and 1954. For the Russians and the Chinese the settlement was a political arrangement which they pressed upon Ho, the Russians because they wanted France to stifle the nascent European Defence Community and the Chinese because they wanted to remove western forces and influence from a country on their borders; both may have supposed that Ho would soon rule as effectively in Saigon as in Hanoi and were faced with fresh problems when this did not happen.

For the Americans the Geneva settlement marked the end of a French presence in Asia which, however obnoxious at one time to Americans on general anti-colonialist principles, could have been rendered useful in anti-communist terms. Having decided in 1954 not to buttress French rule any longer, the United States sought an alternative anti-communist and anti-Chinese force. They disapproved of the Geneva settlement because it not only failed to constitute such a force but also threatened to accelerate Chinese communist expansion by giving Ho the whole of Vietnam in two bites – the north by the armistice agreement and the south through elections: they regarded Ho as a satellite and discounted his chances of becoming the Tito of Asia. They resolved therefore to maintain the independence of the anti-communist régime established by Bao Dai in the south, and also to create a new anti-communist alliance to check China in Asia as Nato had checked the USSR in Europe and to facilitate in future the united action which Dulles had tried and failed to organize for the relief of Dien Bien Phu. Accordingly the South-East Asia Collective Defence Treaty (the Manila Pact, establishing a South-East Asia Treaty Association – Seato) was signed in September by three Asian and five non-Asian states: the Philippines, Thailand, Pakistan, the United States, Australia, New Zealand, Britain and France. These signatories bound themselves to take joint action in the event of aggression against any one of them in a designated area, and to consult together in the event of threats from action other than armed action (namely, subversive activities). The designated area was the general area of South-east Asia including the territory of the signatories and the general area of the South-west Pacific to 20 degrees 30 minutes north; the area included therefore Vietnam, Cambodia and Laos but not Taiwan or Hong Kong.

Seato never became an impressive organization. No purely Asian state of substance joined it except Pakistan which, distant from China and not really concerned about Chinese expansion in South-east Asia or anywhere else, joined for ulterior reasons – to please the United States and get American support against India. France became an increasingly cynical member; Britain became an increasingly embarrassed one, balancing the obligations of a loyal ally (with a special interest in the area so long as it retained obligations to Malaysia) against the wish to keep out of Vietnam and the temptation to criticize American mistakes there. Seato was no more than the United States writ differently. Its purpose was to ensure the independence of South Vietnam but it could not save that ill-governed country from the dilemma of either collapsing or surviving as an American protectorate. It was dissolved in 1975.

Ho had accepted the Geneva armistice reluctantly and under Russian and Chinese pressure. It may be surmised that only the prospect of elections in 1956 persuaded him to come to terms with France when he was entitled to expect not only the surrender of Dien Bien Phu but the collapse of the entire French position in any event and in the same year. He soon saw that his hopes were to be falsified and that the 17th parallel was another armistice line destined to harden into a political frontier. It was moreover a line of graver consequence than the division between the two halves of Korea, for in Vietnam the south fed the north and the perpetuation of the division entailed economic problems as well as disappointment over the denial of reunification. In the period of uncertainty between the signing of the armistice and the date fixed for the elections which were never held Ho initiated a programme of agrarian reform and sought also to expand industry and exploit North Vietnam's mineral wealth, but the agrarian reform, modelled on Chinese collectivization, provoked a peasant rising which provoked a reign of terror which got out of hand and caused at least 50,000 deaths. Industrialization required help from advanced countries such as the USSR and Czechoslovakia rather than China, and after the Sino–Russian split in the fifties Ho had to balance between Moscow and Beijing. At first he allowed relations with the latter to deteriorate and in 1957 he received Voroshilov in Hanoi, but this partiality displeased some of his colleagues and may even have caused a threat to his own position. Ho himself had associations of a lifetime with the USSR and Muscovite communism, and General Giap, backed by the North Vietnamese army, expressed the traditional Vietnamese distrust of China, but other leaders were reputedly pro-Chinese, including Truong Chinh whose strength lay in the Lao Dong Party (founded in 1951 and essentially a communist party although it embraced a few non-communist notables). Ho spent two months in Moscow in 1959, returning to Hanoi via Beijing. By this time fighting had been resumed in the south and the problem of getting rid of the French was succeeded by the far bloodier problem of getting rid of the Americans. He lived just long enough to see it happen, dying in 1969.

South Vietnam started its independent career comparatively peace-fully and prosperously in spite of the arrival from the north of nearly a million refugees (two-thirds of whom were Roman Catholic Chris-tians). The prime minister, Ngo Dinh Diem, a northerner and a Roman Catholic, eliminated Bao Dai, who was declared deposed in 1955, and a year later inaugurated a republic with himself as president. Although the last French troops did not leave until April 1956, American aid was transferred from the French to the Diem government from the first day of 1955. To the Americans Diem was an anti-communist ally who would direct a new state described by them, with marvellous inexactitude, as a democracy. But they misjudged their man. Diem was an anti-French intellectual, not particularly pro-American and in no way a democrat. He treated South Vietnam as a personal or family demesne which he administered through a network of secret societies, nepotistically, intolerantly and unintelligently. He antagonized the Buddhists, the dominant religious group, and the hill peoples who, although only a small minority of the population, inhabited more than half of the countryside in which subversive movements might be sustained. In the cities too Diem and his relatives, who included five brothers, became increasingly unpopular. The cities became generators of inflation and vice while the countryside became an open field for the settlement of private grudges and for extortionate demands which drove the peasants into the arms of the communist opposition.

A first coup against the régime in November 1960 failed but three months later the opposition was strong enough to attack Diem's palace from the air. At about the same time Ho decided to give material aid to the forces gathering against Diem in the countryside. Despite American pressure Diem had refused to supply food to North Vietnam in the mistaken belief that the northern régime was about to collapse under the weight of peasant revolts. Thus Ho was given an economic as well as a political motive for reopening the war. At the time of the Geneva armistice the communists in the south, many of whom retreated to the north, had concealed their arms against a possible resumption of fighting. An active communist opposition to Diem had come into existence under the name of the Vietcong – originally a term of opprobrium, like Whig or Tory. In 1960 a National Liberation Front was formed and in 1962 the International Control Commission, an observer group established at Geneva eight years earlier, reported that North Vietnam was intervening in civil war in the south in support of the National Liberation Front.

In 1963 Buddhist hostility to the Diem régime reached a climax. Buddhist monks publicly burned themselves to death in gruesome protest against persecution. The authorities retaliated by looting and sacking pagodas and torturing monks. The Americans cut off aid to Diem and instigated a coup against him. In November Diem and his most markedly unpopular brother, Ngo Dinh Nhu, were killed, the régime collapsed and General Duong Van Minh ('Big Minh') became the head of the first of a series of transient military governments. In the next eighteen months half-a-dozen coups took place. General Minh was forced into the background within two months of Diem's end. General Nguyen Khanh, more militant in relation to North Vietnam but no more secure in Saigon, was opposed by Buddhists and students demanding an end to military rule. He survived a coup against him in September 1964 but was displaced early in 1965 by the yet more militant general Tran Van Minh ('Little Minh'). From the latter part of 1965, however, the rising men were General Nguyen Cao Ky, the most militant of the generals to gain power and the most determined to carry the war beyond the 17th parallel, and General Ngyuen Van Thieu.

The United States had two incompatible aims. It was determined to prevent communist government in Vietnam and it was determined – particularly in the case of Eisenhower – not to become directly involved on the Asian mainland. The failure of France's Bao Dai experiment, which the United States supported, and of Bao Dai's non-communist successors created a dilemma which the United States resolved by rating its first aim above its second, with disastrous results. During the early sixties the Americans became both alive to the weaknesses of their policy of supporting weak South Vietnamese régimes and more committed to it. One of Kennedy's early decisions on taking office in 1961 had been to increase American aid in men and material but without committing combat troops. He accepted the advice of General Maxwell Taylor, a former chairman of the US chiefs of staff, to build up American forces and by 1962 American aircraft were flying combat missions and the CIA was conducting more or less underground operations. The pretence that the Americans were in Vietnam as no more than advisers had worn desperately thin. During 1963 and 1964 the Vietcong, aided by the misrule of Diem, the confusion among his successors and by North Vietnam and China, extended its control, until the South Vietnamese and American forces were in danger of suffering the same fate as the French in Algeria and the British in Cyprus and of being driven into a few fortified footholds. The policy, copied from Malaya, of isolating villagers from guerrillas was unsuccessful because the differences between Vietnamese villagers and Vietnamese guerrillas were insignificant compared with the differences between Malay villagers and Chinese guerrillas in Malaya. The Americans, seeing that the Vietcong was winning, decided further to increase their military effort and their control over the direction of the war, and as a result the position of the Vietcong rapidly worsened. Thereupon the government of North Vietnam, seeing that the Vietcong was losing, began to send regular divisions to its rescue. The war became, with scant disguise, a war between the United States and North Vietnam. In the south the Americans aimed to subjugate the whole country. Ultimately they failed and, with hindsight, it could be said that they would have been wiser to have adopted General Salan's strategy of holding the centres of population from which no enemy could have dislodged them, and of securing and sealing off the rich, easily defensible and ethnically distinct Cochin-China. Instead American forces were multiplied year by year: from 23,000 at the end of 1964 to 390,000 two years later and 550,000 by the beginning of 1968. When American withdrawals began in July 1969 these forces had lost 36,000 dead. At their peak the combined American, South Vietnamese and allied forces numbered one and a quarter million, backed by a mighty air force. Against them General Giap proved himself a brilliant guerrilla commander who knew how far to follow and how far to deviate from the strategic teachings of Mao Zedong.

The war was extended to the north in 1964. In July of that year a US destroyer, operating with South Vietnamese sea and land forces against North Vietnam, was attacked by two North Vietnamese torpedo boats in the Bay of Tonkin. President Johnson used this episode, tendentiously explained, to obtain from Congress authority to use US forces in open naval combat. At the end of the same year Johnson became the elected instead of merely the accidental president of the United States. He was seduced by visions of a quick victory by the air bombardment of a fourth-rate foe. In February 1965 a successful attack on an American garrison at Pleiku near the armistice line was followed by sharp American bombing reprisals. American ground forces were also now committed to the battle against the north. But the quick victory was prevented by Russian aid to Ho, notably for the anti-aircraft defence of Hanoi, and as the American bombardment became fiercer, so did opposition to the war develop within the United States.

As the American war effort was intensified President Johnson also began to bid for peace. In April he offered to treat unconditionally with North Vietnam for a cessation of hostilities on the basis that South Vietnam would be an independent and neutral state; and he offered $16,000 million in aid to South-east Asia, including North as well as South Vietnam. But he was not willing to accept the Vietcong as a party to the negotiations. In reply Ho enunciated a set of conditions which were not irreconcilable with the American proposals and in July Johnson implicitly but not explicitly opened the door of the negotiating chamber to the Vietcong as well. He was, however, unwilling to stop all bombing immediately (a bombing pause in May lasted only a few days) or to agree to withdraw all American troops before negotiations began. At the beginning of 1966 Johnson conferred with Ky and Thieu in Honolulu. Bombing was interrupted for several weeks and negotiations seemed not improbable, but they remained in the event elusive and the war went on, increasing in weight and horror. Vietcong adherents and others were slaughtered by the most up-to-date weapons. They were hunted by and thrown out of helicopters, tortured, raped and murdered in cold blood. In a celebrated instance at My Lai in 1967, which later led to a criminal trial and conviction in the United States, 300 civilians were killed by a US army unit.

In 1967 Washington tried to enlist Russian aid to end the war and Johnson had a personal discussion with Kosygin at Glasboro in New Jersey. But no concrete results were forthcoming. The Ky-Thieu government split but was re-formed as a Thieu-Ky government (which lasted until 1971 when Thieu prevailed). Ky fell foul of the Buddhists, many of whom went over to the NLF. The conflict was increasingly polarized between the NLF and the Saigon régime to the advantage of the former. In a spectacular, if ultimately unsuccessful, offensive by Giap during the Tet festival at the beginning of 1968 all the main US bases in South Vietnam were simultaneously attacked, Saigon was in danger of falling to the NLF and Hue was captured and held by the NLF for two months. These events, and their presentation on television, strengthened opposition to the war in the United States and criticism of the way in which it was being conducted. Later in the year Johnson replaced his commander-in-chief. But domestic criticism was not merely directed to the competence of generals. The use of napalm, defoliants and poison gases caused a revulsion which became not only vociferous but violent. In May 1968, after a further bombing pause accompanied this time by an American offer to withdraw, talks between the United States and North Vietnam opened in Paris. Later in the year South Vietnam and the Vietcong joined the discussions. But they led nowhere. North Vietnam had discovered that it could survive the American onslaught and maintain the supply of men and material to the south by using routes and methods which, being comparatively primitive, were never wholly disrupted by aerial bombardment. North Vietnam had also discovered that the Americans really wanted to get out and either turn the war over once more to the South Vietnamese (whose army was brought up to a strength of over one million and given the most modern equipment) or end it. The war was making Johnson so unpopular at home that, fearing defeat in the coming presidential election, he announced that he would not run. He could neither win a victory, since he was not prepared to use nuclear weapons, nor negotiate a peace, since North Vietnam preferred waiting to negotiating. Johnson, who tried unsuccessfully to end the war, was pursuing incompatible aims – to get out and to secure the existence of a separate, non-communist South Vietnam. North Vietnam was not convinced that it need concede the latter in order to get the former, and when the Democrats went down to defeat in November the new president, Richard Nixon, found himself in the same dilemma.

Although he had pledged himself to end the war, he immediately sanctioned the extension of American bombing to Cambodia in another vain hope to find the quick victory. So Cambodia was brought into the field of war.

In March 1970 its ruler, the neutralist Prince Sihanouk, was unseated by a coup by his own prime minister, General Lon Nol. Sihanouk had ensured comparative peace and quiet from 1955 to 1965 but forfeited American friendship by his neutralism and his friendship with Zhou Enlai. Cambodia, like Laos, had been used by North Vietnam without much regard for its neutrality and Sihanouk had been reproached by some of his compatriots for putting up with too much infringement of the country's rights. The new Cambodian government asked for American arms to defend itself against intruders. It got instead American armies, accompanied by South Vietnamese forces (hereditary enemies) and by all the devastation of which the American military machine was capable. The American command in Vietnam was justifiably anxious to counter the use of Cambodia by the north Vietnamese and unjustifiably convinced that it would capture vast communist stores and major headquarters. The operation was militarily successful, though doubtfully necessary; politically it was at best irrelevant. It was stopped by the US Congress which refused to vote funds for troops or advisers in Cambodia and, in 1973, by the same means stopped Nixon's resumed bombing of the country. Lon Nol protested that he had never been told that American and Vietnamese forces were to enter Cambodia.

Although American bombing of North Vietnam was resumed in 1972 these operations were the last lashes of the frustrated American giant. The withdrawal proceeded steadily and only 25,000 Americans remained at the end of the year. Since 1970 the governments of the United States and North Vietnam had been secretly in contact through Henry Kissinger and Le Duc Tho and in January 1973 representatives of the United States, both Vietnams and the Vietcong met in Paris and agreed on a cease-fire, to be internationally supervised, and on the creation of a Council of National Conciliation in Vietnam to prepare elections. These agreements endorsed the American retreat but did not bring peace. There was heavy fighting in the latter part of 1973 and throughout 1974, with Thieu expressing confidence that his new army of a million men could win the war. He expected American aid but did not get it and proclaimed himself let down by his ally. His army and his power distintegrated in the face of 200,000 North Vietnamese and 100,000 Vietcong adversaries. In 1975 he resigned and Big Minh returned from the shadows to surrender what authority was left in Saigon. The war was over. About two million people had been killed. In Laos, which had been invaded in 1971 by South Vietnam with American air support, North Vietnam won decisive victories and fighting came to a stop in 1973 on the basis that yet another coalition would be constructed and all foreign troops withdrawn. The new government came laboriously into existence in 1975 and perished the same year. The monarchy perished too. Prince Souvannouvong, now president, and the Pathet Lao had won the internal battle. Laos became a dependency of Vietnam under the name of the Lao People's Republic. In spite of its name its first elections were not held for fourteen years.

For Cambodia the end of one war meant the beginning of another. The United States abandoned Lon Nol, Sihanouk entered into an alliance with the communist Khmer Rouge, and in 1975 the latter took Pnom Penh a few days before the North Vietnamese entered Saigon. Lon Nol fled and the Khmer Rouge, led by Pol Pot, inaugurated one of the more sickening reigns of terror. The Americans bombed Cambodia (now Kampuchea) once more in 1975 when the Khmer Rouge captured the US intelligence vessel *Mayaguez* but the war was now between Kampuchea and Vietnam. It was provoked by the Khmer Rouge which attacked Vietnam in debatable border lands and in indisputably Vietnamese territory. Vietnam retaliated with a successful invasion of Kampuchea at the end of 1978 and installed a subservient government with Heng Samrin as president and Hun Sen as foreign minister, later also prime minister; both of them were Khmer Rouge renegades with a heavy responsibility for past atrocities. Hun Sen introduced some beneficial reforms, including land distribution and encouragement for small businesses, and permitted wider freedom of speech and religion, but his rule was brutal and corrupt. The Khmer Rouge offered little resistance, retreating to the north-west where it was pursued by the Vietnamese invaders. Kampuchean troops and refugees crossed indiscriminately into Thailand, whence the troops were able to filter back and fight again.

The war between Vietnam and Kampuchea was of prime concern to China for reasons both ancient and modern. China's traditional enmity towards an independent Vietnam had been overlaid during the sixties and seventies when the Sino–Soviet split created competition between China and the USSR. China helped the Vietcong in order to pre-empt Russian aid and influence, but this amity did not last. The Cultural Revolution, derided by the Vietcong, severely curtailed Chinese external activity, and Nixon's visit to China and the subsequent Sino–American *rapprochement* were bitterly resented in Vietnam. North Vietnam's victory over the United States, the unification of north and south in 1975, this new state's large army, its alliance in 1978 with the USSR (when it became also a full member of Comecon), and its conquest of Kampuchea – all these factors ignited China's hostility. In particular, Vietnam's invasion of Kampuchea seemed to pose a threat to the hegemony in Indo-China which China had pursued for a thousand years, while Vietnam's links with the USSR betokened a dependence which, occasioned by the exhaustions of war, economic mismanagement and a sharply rising population, heralded a Russian dominance in Indo-China even more distasteful to China than Vietnamese or American dominance. There were also two other irritants: territorial conflict in the South China Sea and the treatment of Chinese in Vietnam.

There were about a million Chinese in Vietnam, most of them in the south. These Hoa, as they were called, were economically successful and commensurately unpopular. Their nationality was open to argument and their loyalties to doubt. In 1977 many Hoa, including some from the remote south, trekked into China in what the Vietnamese described as migration and the Chinese as expulsion. Whether or not incited in the first place by China, this trek acquired a momentum of its own and continued for two or three years, after which it subsided. Conflict in the South China Sea, however, was more enduring. Old disputes were fanned by the belief that there might be oil under the waters of the Gulf of Tongkin. This belief enhanced the value of contested groups of islands to which both China and Vietnam laid claim. In 1974 a Chinese evicted a Vietnamese force from the Paracel islands whereupon South Vietnam occupied the Spratly islands – small, numerous, uninhabited and further south. Both these groups were within the 200-mile offshore limit recognized by China and Vietnam. In 1988 the growing Chinese navy took possession of some of the Spratly islands.

China's manifold preoccupation with Vietnam gave Kampuchea a powerful friend. China strongly berated Vietnam's aggression and Deng Xiaoping, on a visit to the United States, threatened to teach Vietnam a lesson. The USSR came to the help of Vietnam by vetoing its condemnation by the Security Council and, when Chinese troops invaded northern Vietnam, sent a flotilla which included a missile carrier into Vietnamese waters. But China's demonstrative riposte across its frontiers with Vietnam, although it did much damage, did not stop Vietnamese forces from sweeping across Kampuchea as far as the Thai border. More persuasive in Hanoi was the burden of keeping 250,000 troops in Kampuchea, and by 1987 Vietnam had resolved to get out of a troublesome and very costly situation – Gorbachev's critical review of the USSR's foreign entanglements being a contributory element in the decision. Vietnam announced that its forces would begin to withdraw at once and would all be evacuated by 1990. They left in 1989.

Simultaneously discussions began for a replacement. Sihanouk and Hun Sen had a number of meetings in France and Indonesia, encouraged by China (to a limited degree, for China was not wholly averse to a war which was a drain on Vietnam's resources and on the popularity of its government at home). But neither Sihanouk nor Hun

Sen nor both of them together could construct an effective alternative régime without the Khmer Rouge which had substantial armed forces as well as Chinese – and some American – support: the United States, like China, was prepared to give at least one cheer to any enemy of Vietnam and had been urging Sihanouk since the early eighties to make common cause with the Khmer Rouge and with Son Sann, a former prime minister under Sihanouk and the leader of the third effective anti-Vietnamese force. (Sihanouk and Son Sann each commanded perhaps 10,000 armed men, the Khmer Rouge 30,000 at the very least. Hun Sen's army amounted to about 40,000, including a number of Vietnamese who remained in or returned to Kampuchea because they saw small prospect of a decent living in Vietnam.)

Partly at Australian prompting the idea of overthrowing Hun Sen was replaced by attempts to unite all the main factions in a Supreme National Council in which Hun Sen would have six seats and the three opposition groups two each. At a late stage Sihanouk, the chairman-designate, insisted on being the thirteenth member of this Council, thus raising his contingent to three. This obstacle was surmounted by proposing that Hun Sen be deputy chairman to Sihanouk with a seat of his own additional to his six nominees. The plan envisaged a gradual return to normal political activity after eighteen months of supervision and administration by the UN, but Hun Sen's distrust of Sihanouk and his Chinese backers, and his fear of Khmer Rouge preponderance, made him prevaricate in the hope of getting some international recognition for his own régime without being forced into a coalition. By so doing he risked an escalation of civil war and a new victory for the Khmer Rouge.

One persistent aspect of the travails of Vietnam after its victory over the United States was a stream of refugees trying to escape from the miseries of life in Vietnam under an incompetent and harsh régime. They went by sea, many of them being attacked, despoiled, raped and killed on the way. Most of them came from the north of the country but the tally of refugees from the south increased during the eighties. 57,000 of them reached Hong Kong where they were most unwelcome and were detained and confined in large pens in insanitary and degrading conditions. All but a fifth of them were adjudged by the colonial government of the already overcrowded island to be economic refugees (a new term) and not genuine political refugees whose return to Vietnam was precluded by international conventions. In 1989 the government of Hong Kong announced a scheme for the voluntary return of these refugees with one aircraft a month, but few were willing to go. At the end of the year fifty-one men, women and children were sent back against their will in a night-time operation which occasioned such an international outcry that the scheme had to be abandoned. In the next year the British and Vietnamese governments and the UN High Commissioner for Refugees concluded an agreement for the repatriation of refugees 'not opposed' to it. Britain, while it did not abjure its claim to be entitled to repatriate economic refugees by force, enlisted the help of the UNHCR in persuading them to go and hoped that many would do so after discovering that their treatment in Hong Kong was as bad or worse than anything which they might have to suffer in Vietnam.

18   SOUTH-EAST ASIA

The term 'South-east Asia' is used to describe the countries which lie between India, China, Australasia and the open expanses of the Pacific Ocean. Diverse by race, religion and wealth they had before the Second World War one nearly common feature: with the solitary exception of Thailand all were ruled by foreigners. The British, French, Dutch, Americans and Portuguese had spread over the area and appropriated varying amounts of it. This state of affairs was viewed with dissatisfaction within the region and also by the Japanese, whose New Order had been expanded into the Great East Asia Co-Prosperity Scheme under the direction of a special ministry in Tokyo. When war brought the Japanese to South-east Asia they came as anti-imperialist and pro-nationalist liberators, promising to remove European over- lords, an operation which proved in the circumstances astonishingly easy. Three days after the attack on Pearl Harbor the Japanese sank the British warships *Prince of Wales* and *Repulse* (10 December 1941); Singapore fell in February 1942 and Corregidor in May; western dominance finished.

It was succeeded by a very short Japanese phase in the course of which the new overlords, like Napoleon in Germany, found that nationalism is not a commodity that can be turned on or off at will. Some Japanese genuinely believed in the co-prosperity theme and wished to help the peoples of South-east Asia, but more were simply new imperialists who quickly alienated the local nationalists. As the fortunes of war turned against the Japanese, so did the nationalists, preparing to achieve their ends partly by services rendered to the former colonial powers and partly by a new strength that would not be overborne by war-weary Europeans. In Burma and the Philippines the end was easily achieved, in Indonesia less easily. In Malaya indepen- dence was delayed by an insurrection that was more communist than nationalist. Indo-China (see the previous chapter) was fated to suffer the long war which assumed international proportions and whose settle- ment posed further international problems in the successor states of Vietnam, Laos and Cambodia.

Throughout this region, the Philippines apart, the predominant power as the war ended was the British, represented until 1946 by the

18.1 South-east Asia

supreme commander in the South East Asia Command, Lord Mountbatten. The British expected to resume their former stations in Burma, Malaya, Singapore and smaller territories and to restore the French, Dutch and Portuguese in Indo-China, Indonesia and Timor and the white rajah of Sarawak. The intentions of the British, conditioned by the limitations set by circumstances to their actions, were, together with the ambitions of nationalist leaders backed by arms, the principal factors in a situation of considerable uncertainty.

In *Malaya*, a conglomeration of principalities plus small British colonial territories, even less of a unitary state than Burma, the British had no easy way out. The naval base on the adjacent island of Singapore (itself a British colony) created arguments for staying which did not exist in Burma, and the strength of the Chinese (in Malaya a substantial minority and in Singapore a majority) made many Malays less resentful of British rule than apprehensive of the local Chinese, whose leaders – replacing prosperous pre-war leaders compromised by their collaboration with the Japanese invaders – had taken to the jungle and to communism. Among the active opponents of the Japanese the largest group had been Chinese and most of these were communist rather than adherents of the Kuomintang, but by the very fact of their racial and doctrinal distinctiveness they could not claim to be a nationalist movement like the AFPFL. Their bid for power was of a different nature.

An initial and premature attempt was checked by the British after some hesitation. The British then tackled the racial problem and proposed a Malayan Union in which citizenship would be obtainable by any person who had lived ten years in the country. The Malays opposed this plan which would have made citizenship, and so political power, available to a large section of the Chinese population. The British thereupon proposed in its place, in February 1948, a Malayan Federation in which the powers of the Malay sultans were greater than in the proposed Union and the opportunities for the Chinese to become citizens were restricted.

In that year the Chinese communist insurrection began and in June an emergency was declared which was to last for twelve years during which the insurgents baffled 50,000 troops, 60,000 police and a home guard of 200,000. In 1950 General Sir Harold Briggs, the Director of Operations, realized that the key to the situation lay in the silent support given to the insurgents, often out of terror, by the great mass of the population, and he therefore made plans to assemble and protect the people in resettlement areas where they would be immune from blackmail and would cease to supply the insurgents with food. General Sir Gerald Templer, who arrived as governor in 1952 in succession to the murdered Sir Henry Gurney, continued this policy and developed at the same time political measures designed to bring the Malay, Chinese and Indian communities together as a prelude to independence. Malaya became independent on 31 August 1957 under a constitution which established a revolving presidency tenable by the Malay sultans in turn. Malaya entered into a defence agreement with Britain but did not become a member of Seato and refused in 1962 to allow Malayan territory to be used by British units which might be called upon to help Thailand in the event of a threat to that country from Laos.

Singapore, with a population three-quarters Chinese, was set on the road to independence by the usual British process. A new legislative council with an unofficial and elected majority was installed alongside a nominated executive council. This machinery of government then evolved into a legislative assembly and a council of ministers under a chief minister, most of whose colleagues were chosen by the assembly, the governor retaining certain reserved powers. Full independence came in 1959 subject to the retention of British rights in the naval base. The prime minister, Lee Kuan Yew, was anxious for closer links with Malaya but since a union would place the Chinese in a majority the Malays were reluctant unless the union were at the same time extended to other and less Chinese territories. Such territories existed in Sarawak, North Borneo and Brunei.

In 1946 the rajah of Sarawak, Sir Charles Brooke, ceded the principality which his family had held since 1841 to the British government and in the same year Britain assumed in North Borneo the rights and responsibilities which had belonged before the war to the British North Borneo Company. Both Sarawak and North Borneo became crown colonies. Brunei, a third territory along the northern side of the island of Borneo (most of which formed part of Indonesia), resumed its pre-war status as a British protectorate.

In 1963 Sarawak and North Borneo (now Sabah) joined Malaya and Singapore to form a Greater Malaysian Union, despite protests from the Philippine Republic which had claims in North Borneo, and from the Indonesian Republic which regarded the scheme as a plan to create a western-orientated state capable of checking Indonesian growth and ambitions. Brunei refused to join at the last moment and a revolt against the sultan, who was believed to favour accession, gave the Indonesian President Sukarno the idea that the federation was unpopular and might be destroyed by inexpensive guerrilla operations, persistence and propaganda; and he might be able to add the rest of Borneo to Indonesia. The ensuing Indonesian confrontation forced Malaysia to appeal for British and Australian military help and frustrusted the British intention of getting out of the region after creating Malaysia. The confrontation abated when Sukarno was demoted by his army in 1965–66, but Malaysia was a contrived constellation whose components had been forced into federation for external and adventitious reasons and upon the assumption that the territories tacked on to Malaya could not exist on their own. After its creation Malaysia's largest ethnic group was Chinese (43 per cent) with Malays the next largest (40 per cent). In the Malayan peninsula Malays were 50 per cent and Chinese 37 per cent of the population.

Brunei had rejected the assumption that the smaller territories in the region could not exist on their own and Singapore rebutted it. *Brunei*, vestigial survival of an empire which had once reached to the Philippines, fabulously rich in relation to its size and population and virtually the private estate of its autocratic sultan, attained internal self-government in 1971 and complete independence from Britain in 1984 when it joined the UN, the Commonwealth and ASEAN (see below). *Singapore* joined Malaysia at its inception and then broke away. Its socialist People's Action Party (PAP) was opposed by the conservative Malayan Chinese Association on the issue, among others, whether Malaysian politics should be conducted essentially on class lines or racial. Both parties were, like the island itself, largely Chinese but the PAP wanted politics throughout the federation to be organized round the needs and interests of economic classes. Across the water in Malaya Tunku Abdul Rahman, who was a conservative Malay nobleman as well as party leader and prime minister, was alarmed by the attitudes of the PAP and its leader Lee Kuan Yew and was determined to ensure that no Chinese Singaporean should become prime minister of the federation. He decided to evict Singapore from it. Lee Kuan Yew, doubting Singapore's independent viability, had no wish to secede but tensions between the two territories and their two leaders convinced him that an early and reasonably amicable divorce was imperative. His doubts about the island's economic prospects quickly dissolved. Sinapore developed an outstandingly successful mixed economy. Foreign capital flowed in; income per head trebled in the first decade after the breach in 1965; and the PAP reaped the benefits by remaining in power for a generation. Singapore had for several years uneasy relations with Indonesia, inflamed by incidents such as the execution in Singapore of two Indonesian soldiers and the refusal to recognize Indonesia's conquest of East Timor in 1975 (see the note at the end of this Part), but disagreements were contained and eased within the framework of ASEAN.

In *Malaysia* – thus constituted with the Malay states, Sarawak and Sabah but without Brunei or Singapore – the principal political problem was relations in the Malay peninsula between the rural Malays, numerically superior, and the urban Chinese, economically predomin-ant. Elections in 1969 were tumultuous and the army had to be used to restore order. The prime minister, Tunku Abdul Rahman, resigned in the wake of this setback to hopes of peaceful communal development. He was succeeded by Tun Abdul Razak who enjoyed the fruits of an impetus to the economy which brought benefits to Malays through economic growth rather than economic redistribution at the expense of the Chinese. Although the second Development Plan (1971–75) made a faltering start and was temporarily upset by the world oil crisis in 1973–74 Malaysia's diverse economy successfully withstood the buffets of the mid-seventies. Politically, the risk of racially polarized conflict was avoided. Tun Abdul Razak began by reviving the United Malayan National Organization (UMNO) which had been created in 1946 as a focus for Malay nationalism against the British and the assertion against the Chinese of the Malay nature of Malaya. Next he reconciled factions within UMNO and coaxed it into alliance with the Malayan Chinese Association (MCA – founded in 1949) and the Malayan Indian Congress (founded in 1954). By the early seventies all parties of consequence in Malaysia were associated in a multicommunal Alliance, in which UMNO was the largest component.

In external affairs Tun Razak modified Malaysia's pro-western stance in the direction of non-alignment. He visited the USSR and China and after 1975 he favoured the inclusion of Vietnam in ASEAN, but he died in 1976. His successor, Dato Hussein Onn, who was prime minister until 1981 when his health gave way, faced economic deceleration, renewed threats to communalism from Malay nationalism (and assertive Muslims), allegations of corruption and fears – unrealized – of secession by Sabah, but economic recovery helped his National Front of ten parties to convincing victory in elections in 1978. His deputy prime minister and successor, Mohammad Matathir, was a more controversial politician who had first made his mark by criticism of Tunku Abdul Rahman and later adopted a robust stand against what he regarded as undue and unnecessary deference to British interests. After becoming prime minister Matathir's political fortunes were erratic. His position was tainted by rumours of financial scandals, in spite of which he won unexpectedly clear victories in federal and all state elections in 1986. In the next year he almost lost the presidency of UMNO and in 1988 the Supreme Court declared UMNO an unlawful organization on grounds of procedural delinquencies, but Matathir circumvented this damaging judgment by going to war with the judiciary. The Chief Justice was suspended and then dismissed; five other senior judges were suspended and two of them dismissed; the Court nevertheless confirmed its original ruling. On the political stage Matathir was opposed by two of his most eminent former colleagues, Tengku Razaleigh Hamzah and Datuk Musa Hitam. The latter accepted an ambassadorial appointment in 1989 and in a general election in the following year Matathir defeated Razaleigh's challenge.

Beyond the British possessions in Burma, Malaya and Singapore lay in

1945 the former Dutch empire in Indonesia to the south and the French empire in Indo-China to the east. When the British returned to South-east Asia after the defeat of the Japanese, their actions were consciously or unconsciously dominated by their decision to leave India. South-east Asia (with the exception perhaps of Singapore) was for Britain an adjunct of India and it was hardly conceivable that the British could for long pursue in South-east Asia policies that were plainly at variance with their chosen course in India. No such considerations affected the Dutch and the French whose positions in Indonesia and Indo-China were not regulated by any other positions in Asia. For them the question was the basic question which the British put to themselves in India – whether to go or to stay – and not the secondary question which confronted the British in Burma – whether to stay in spite of the departure from India; but since the factors affecting the British in India were quite different from those affecting the Dutch and the French further east, the first answer of the latter was also different. The Dutch and French proposed to revert more or less to their pre-war positions and they looked to their British allies to help them.

The return of the Dutch to *Indonesia* was generally assumed – or feared – in 1945 but for purely practical reasons the British supreme commander was unable to undertake extensive operations and dealt directly with the nationalist leader Sukarno in the key island of Java. Dutch forces arrived to take the place of the token British occupation but found themselves opposed by a comparatively well-organized and well-equipped movement under leaders of ability and sophistication whose foreign contacts and travels had given them an insight into the wider forces affecting the continuance of European rule in Asia. In this situation the British tried to mediate and by the Linggadjati agreement of November 1946 the Dutch recognized the *de facto* authority of the self-proclaimed Indonesian republic in Java, Sumatra and Madura and agreed to withdraw their forces from these areas; a union between the Netherlands and Indonesia was to be created by the beginning of 1949. But this curious and cumbrous scheme failed to please anybody, and amid suspicions and disputes the situation degenerated into chaos. In July 1947 the Dutch resorted to force in what came to be called the first police action. In January 1948 a respite was secured by the Renville agreement but fighting soon recurred, the situation was brought before the Security Council, and after a second police action in December the Dutch, who were considerably impeded by the anti-colonialism of the United States and its representatives in Indonesia, found themselves obliged by international pressures to compromise. Independence was conceded in 1949, subject however to the acceptance by the new Indonesian Republic of a shadowy union with the Netherlands (unilaterally abrogated by Indonesia in 1956); to the exclusion of West Irian (western New Guinea); and to a federal constitution of seven

18.2 Indonesia

states, converted into a unitary state a year later, although not without sporadic fighting and abortive secessions from central Javanese control. Under the influence of Nehru the Indonesian Republic, of which Sukarno became president, adopted a non-aligned stance in international affairs and enhanced its standing by playing host in 1955 to the first conference of non-aligned states at Bandung. In south Asia the Bandung conference was regarded as a retort to the previous year's Treaty of Manila whereby the United States seemed to plan to extend the Cold War to Asia and the Pacific. Zhou Enlai's appearance at Bandung helped Indonesia to establish good relations with China and gave Indonesia's non-alignment a communist rather than a western tilt.

At its visionary widest an independent Indonesia had included Malaya, Singapore, North Borneo and New Guinea. More practically, it included all the Netherlands East Indies. West Irian fell into this category but the other half of New Guinea was Australian, either part of the Australian Commonwealth or as a Trust Territory administered by Australia. Fears of the extension of Indonesian power and claims throughout New Guinea caused the Australian government to support the Netherlands' retention of this corner of its empire, but the logic of events – measured in miles from Holland – forced the Dutch to abandon in 1962 a last outpost to which they had succeeded in clinging on the plea that the inhabitants were not Indonesians and were unlikely to get a fair deal from Indonesia. The prolongation of this question for thirteen years after independence kept nationalist spirits on the boil and strengthened the position of Sukarno, the country's most eloquent and popular nationalist, in spite of the gradual collapse of parliamentary democracy under his rule and economic recession (aggravated by the eviction of the Dutch and the nationalization of their enterprises). In 1959 Sukarno, supported by the army and the Communist Party (PKI), transformed the state into what he called Guided Democracy, a euphemism for personal dictatorship and a bravura performance in which however he overplayed his hand. His determination to secure West Irian drove him to closer relations with the USSR and China and earned him therefore the distrust of the United States which regarded him as a conduit through whom the communist powers might get control of South-east Asia's largest state. The PKI encouraged Sukarno in his second major external venture, opposition to the creation of a Malaysian federation which was strongly anti-communist and suspected by Sukarno of being a device for preserving British colonial influence. Sukarno backed a revolt in Brunei in 1962 against its merger with Malaysia – it was suppressed by the British in a few days – and kept up confrontation with Malaysia by operations across its borders and in protests at the UN and other international meetings from its creation in 1963 until the end of his rule.

Indonesia was, by virtue of its size (over 13,600 islands) and potential wealth, a power of a completely different order from any other state in the region of South-east Asia. It could be a counter to Chinese influence and expansion or an adjunct to them. The PKI under its leader K. N. Aidit was one of the most effective in the world and pro-Chinese. There was therefore constant speculation about the balance of power between the communists (who had failed in 1948 to win a monopoly of power by a coup at Madiun in Java) and the army and about the likely outcome of a struggle between the two when Sukarno, frequently reported to be a sick man, should die. In September 1965 a false report of his death became the signal for a communist putsch. Six senior generals were murdered after the cruellest mutilation but others escaped and the coup failed. In a counter-coup, widely believed to have had American aid, something like half a million communists (including Aidit) or supposed communists were killed and the army established its control over Sukarno and the country. Bung Karno, or brother Karno, the creator of Indonesia, was gradually stripped of his powers: he resigned in 1967 and died in 1970. His successor and the ruler of Indonesia for the next two decades, General T. N. J. Suharto, kept vast numbers of his opponents and presumed opponents in detention (they were later transported to a convenient offshore island) but the national economy prospered with American and Japanese help. Although earnings from the export of rubber fell, Indonesia's oil and its enviable variety of other minerals more than redressed the balance and by the seventies and eighties the economy as a whole was growing at the rate of 7–10 per cent a year. This growth was checked in the late eighties by declining revenue from oil and by the rising cost of imports from Japan and debt service to it, and the currency was devalued. Suharto was re-elected president unopposed in 1988 in the expectation that 1993 would see the end of his long, authoritarian but not specially tyrannical rule. In 1989 Indonesia resumed formal relations with China after a breach lasting twenty-four years and Suharto visited Moscow after an equally long period of tepid and distant contacts.

Thailand had the unique experience of escaping the European conquest which embraced the rest of South-east Asia. It was left as a buffer between the British who advanced from India into Burma and the French who advanced from Annam and Tongking into Laos and Cambodia. Unlike Burma, Laos and Vietnam it had no frontier with China and it had succeeded in assimilating a substantial part of its Chinese population of 4 million (12 per cent of the total), but it shared the general apprehensiveness of all South-east Asia concerning the revival of Chinese power and welcomed an American alliance as an insurance. It became the one genuinely Asian member of Seato (the

Philippines and, even more so, Pakistan being but peripheral members of an alliance termed South-east Asian). From 1938 to 1973 Thailand was ruled by a succession of strong men – Marshals Pibul Songgram, Thanarat Sarit and Thanom Kittikachron – with an interlude of civilian rule (1944–46) under Nai Pridi Panomiong who on being worsted by Pibul, retired to China and there revived his wartime Free Thai movement which did not this time amount to much. Rich in rubber, tin, teak and rice Thailand stood in less need of foreign aid than most of its neighbours but it became expensively embroiled in the wars to the east. Threatened in 1962 by communist units on its borders with Laos it was offered and accepted the help of American troops. Two years later it permitted the establishment of American air bases for use in the war in Vietnam, and this counter-aid to the United States was gradually expanded to six major bases accommodating forces of 50,000. By the seventies the strains of war, and the awareness that the war was being lost by the Americans, fostered discontent which was accentuated by the general corruption, inefficiency and the uncertain policies of military rule. The American alliance and the consequent involvement in Vietnam were increasingly criticized and after riots in 1973 civilian rule was restored. This change marked a partial reversal of external policies as well as a desire to clean up public life which had been corrupted by oligarchic government and the inflation and vices attendant on a foreign military presence. The American forces began to leave in the same year but another product of the war remained in the shape of the Patriotic Front which, with some Chinese support, had for ten years maintained guerrilla groups a few thousand strong among the Meo peoples who (numbering in all about 300,000) lived astride the Thai–Laotian border. In 1976 an increasingly bewildered civilian régime was again replaced by the military behind a military–civilian façade, whose main worry was the advent of Vietnamese power to the borders of Thailand.

Vietnam's conquest of *Kampuchea* (Cambodia), for long the buffer state between Thailand and Vietnam, threw thousands of refugees into eastern Thailand and forced Thailand to look for help to counter Vietnamese expansion and restore Kampuchea's independence. Thailand's friends and allies in South-east Asia, less directly involved and linked in an unmilitary alliance (see below), did not provide the kind of support required by Thailand, which turned to China and the United States. Both supplied arms, the latter (by an agreement of 1987) in large quantities and on condition that these arms might be available for use by the United States as well as Thailand. With economic growth around 10 per cent a year, industrial investment and output growing, tourism also growing and external payments in balance, Thailand prospered although it could not rival the economic explosion of Hong Kong or Taiwan. Within its monarchical framework it was governed by a succession of administrations which represented primarily the business community and were headed by generals: in 1988 General Prem Tinsulanonda gave way at the age of 82 to General Chatichai Choonhavan. Kampuchea apart, this respectable stability was dented only by the considerable corruption at the centre and, mainly in the west and south, disturbances of various kinds caused by Muslim or communist insurgents or organized opium dealers.

The *Philippines* (about 700 islands), overrun by the Japanese during the war, were recovered by the United States in 1945 and given their indpendence in the next year. The terms of the transfer of sovereignty included a lease of bases to the United States for ninety-nine years, reduced in 1966 to twenty-five years from that date. The central problem of the new government was authority. The country had become a gangland in which different groups, including the police, had become laws unto themselves. Violence was endemic and rose to a crescendo at or near election times. Prominent among the forces in the state were the Hukbalahaps, originally anti-Japanese guerrillas supported during the war by the Americans but, the war having ended, now expendable or worse: their leader Luis Taruc proclaimed himself a communist. He surrendered in 1974 but his movement persisted in the north where its New People's Army (NPA) governed substantial areas with some support from the local population. The NPA's sphere was near enough to the American air and naval base at Clark Airfield and Subic Bay to cause the United States some uneasiness and ensure support for a series of presidents judged capable of containing the insurgents. There was also dissidence in the south where an established Muslim majority found itself becoming a minority and formed the Moro National Liberation Front. In the capital, Manila, ostentation flourished alongside the debris of war.

In 1962 President Diosdado Macapagal exhumed the Philippines' claim to Sabah (North Borneo) which forms one side of the Sulu Sea, otherwise enclosed by Philippine islands. He broke off relations with Malaya and refused to recognize the new state of Malaysia of which Sabah had agreed to become part. But this issue was allowed to drop by his successor Ferdinand Marcos (president, 1966–86) who, although elected as a reformer, became preoccupied with attempts to retain the presidency beyond the constitutional term and a fabulous enrichment of himself and his family. A referendum in 1973, following the imposition of martial law in 1972, allowed him to prolong his hold on office. Martial law was annulled in 1981 and Marcos unsurprisingly won a presidential election in the same year. His rule was tyrannical and his wife, who became a political personage in her own right, was no better. In 1983 Benigno Aquino, the most eminent opponent of the régime (who had been imprisoned in 1973 to keep him from winning an election and was released in 1979 to seek medical treatment in the United States), was assassinated as he set foot on his native soil from an aircraft, killed by a hired gunman who was himself immediately shot dead. A subsequent inquiry pointed the finger at a group which included the chief of army staff, General Fabian Ver, and two other generals, but they were officially exonerated. With fresh elections due in 1986 and increasing unrest verging on civil war, the Americans were forced to ask themselves whether Marcos was not a rapidly wasting asset, but the more vulnerable he became the more the Americans found themselves trapped between him and what was to them an even more unpalatable, increasingly left-wing alternative. Having lost Vietnam and its base at Camranh Bay to allies of Moscow they were fearful of seeing the Philppines with their even more important bases go the same way. They sustained Marcos until he became unsustainable and then switched their support to Aquino's widow, Corazon, who campaigned against Marcos for the presidency and forced him to decamp two weeks after a further re-election – and the Americans to change sides – under the pressures of huge peaceful demonstrations and a few highly placed desertions to her side. Marcos died in the United States in 1989.

Mrs Aquino, although president by popular acclaim, was none the less dependent on the army, personified by Juan Ponce Enrile and Fidel Ramos. Her vice-president Salvador Laurel had been her rival for the presidency. She inherited a 20-year-old insurrection in the south, an external debt of $25 billion, a debt service which absorbed a third of foreign earnings, declining domestic production and an agreement with the IMF which was on the verge of being abrogated for non-compliance with its terms. She negotiated a new agreement but recovery was sluggish. Discord in the insurgent provinces persisted and discord within the government soon made its appearance, particularly from army officers critical of her inability to repress the NPA and the Moro Front. Forced to dismiss Enrile she found herself the more dependent on Ramos; Vice-president Laurel deserted her for Enrile at local elections in 1987. A series of revolts advertised her uncertain control, prevented her from embarking on much needed land reforms and increased her dependence on American goodwill. In spite of earlier support for those demanding the closure of American bases, she stood by the agreement permitting their presence until 1991 while obtaining Washington's assent to quinquennial reviews, which were a way to raise the rent. She concluded with Reagan an agreement whereby the two presidents undertook to use their best endeavours to ensure payment of $962 million for two years, but the US Congress approved only $365 for one year. Any extension of the bases beyond 1991 would require endorsement by two-thirds of the Philippines' senate and possibly a referendum. The bargaining power of the Philippines was far from inconsiderable since the bases were not wholly replaceable except at staggering cost and their evacuation would impose on the United States a thorough and painful strategic review.

The countries of South-east Asia other than those in Indo-China formed in 1967 the Association of South East Asian Nations (ASEAN). The first members of this association were Indonesia, Malaysia, Singapore, Thailand and the Philippines. They were joined in 1984 by Brunei. Their aims were to attack poverty, disease and other social ills; improve their commercial and economic weight in the world; secure their independence by reducing the sources of domestic upheaval and the temptations to outsiders to meddle in their affairs; and keep foreigners away. There were to be no joint military planning or exercises nor any other kind of military collaboration. This was a mutual aid association, economic and social but not without some silent hopes that it might curb Indonesia's potential capacity to overawe the region.

ASEAN was not the region's first postwar essay in co-operation. In 1961 Thailand, Malaya (as it then was) and the Philippines formed the Association of South-east Asia which, however, disintegrated as a result of the rival claims of the last two to Sabah. In 1963 these two and Indonesia projected a different tripartite association which never came to birth. There were at this period two major obstacles: tensions arising out of the creation of Malaysia (achieved in 1963) and the pro-communist attitudes of Sukarno in Indonesia which was much the biggest, richest and most populous state in the region. The removal of Sukarno by the Indonesian army was a necessary pre-condition for the creation of a broad South-east Asian association, as too was Indonesia's willingness to collaborate. Sukarno's successors were willing. Confrontation between Indonesia and Malaysia (see above) faded away and the quarrel between Malaya and the Philippines, although it produced a diplomatic rupture, also died down after Sabah voted in 1967 to join Malaysia: President Marcos visited Kuala Lumpur a year after his inauguration. Relations were again soured that same year after a mysterious massacre of Muslim soldiers on Corregidor (possibly by their own officers) and by a brief revival of the Philippines' claim to Sabah but the claim was put on ice by Marcos who, although unwilling to take the unpopular step of finally abjuring it, rated it below the new regional solidarity. President Aquino later made a formal reununciation.

The British departure from South-east Asia and the Americans' war in Vietnam tested this solidarity. The announcement in 1968 of imminent British withdrawal from Malaysia and Singapore prompted these two states to conclude with Australia, New Zealand and Britain a new agreement (to which Brunei later adhered) replacing the existing

Anglo-Malayan defence agreement and then in the same year to join their partners in ASEAN in proposing that South-east Asia be declared a zone of peace, freedom and neutrality. If these two steps were barely consistent with each other, the inconsistency was the price paid for transition from one colonial world to a new system of regional co-operation for the better securing of national independence. The American war in Vietnam was an affront to that independence, but after the Tet offensive at the beginning of 1968 the United States began planning the retreat which was eventually assured by the treaties signed in Paris in 1973. For the ASEAN states the most disturbing sequel to the United States' failure in Vietnam was Nixon's *rapprochement* with China and the opening given to China to exercise in South-East Asia the power role abandoned by the United States, with the further problem of deciding whether the prime enemy in the region was now communist China or communist Vietnam. The threat from Vietnam was made the more acute by Vietnam's invasion and domination of Kampuchea.

Members of ASEAN were divided. At the UN in 1970 Malaysia and Singapore had voted to give the Chinese seat in the Security Council to the communist régime in Beijing, the Philippines had voted against and Indonesia and Thailand had abstained. Most members of ASEAN had hoped to add Vietnam to their association in spite of its communist régime, but by invading Kampuchea Vietnam had offended against one of ASEAN's basic tenets – respect for national sovereignty and independence. Vietnam's treaty with the USSR was another count against it since another of ASEAN's tenets was its resolve to keep major powers away. The dilemma was most acute for Thailand. Thailand wished to act in concert with its ASEAN partners but it was more directly threatened than they were by Vietnamese expansion into Kampuchea and was well aware that ASEAN had no military might to oppose to Vietnamese aggression, whereas China had. In fighting terms the anti-Vietnamese effectives were the Khmer Rouge and China. For other ASEAN members on the other hand, in particular Indonesia, China was the main threat to the region in the long term and China's incursion into northern Vietnam in 1979, a sinister omen. In these circumstances ASEAN's survival was a tribute to the statesmanship of its leaders and their perception of its value to them, but the strains within it were not relieved until the Vietnamese withdrawal from Kampuchea and the Russian withdrawal from Vietnam at the end of the decade.

The allies were disturbed by reports during 1989 that Singapore was preparing to grant to the United States the right to establish military bases in breach of ASEAN's commitment to keep the region a zone of peace. They were assured that any such base would be used for repairs and maintenance only.

NOTES

A Korea

The Korean War left North and South deeply hostile to each other and condemned to decades of misrule. The military inferiority of the South was mitigated by American reinforcement and a vastly and ultimately spectacularly better economic performance. The UN voted annually in favour of the reunification of the country by way of free elections but these resolutions were without effect. So were talks between North and South in 1971–73 and in the eighties. In North Korea Marshal Kim Il Sung held uninterrupted sway. Opposition dared not show its head. As he grew older (he was born in 1912) he became more autocratic and intent upon securing the succession for his son King Jong Il. In South Korea Synghman Rhee's ruthless rule, buttressed by a defence treaty of 1953 with the United States, ended in 1960 when he was forced to resign and flee to Hawaii where he died in 1965 at the age of 90. A military coup in 1961 carried General Park Chung Hee to power, and such was the inflexibility of South Korean political life that Park continued in power for nearly twenty unlovely years. They were marked by considerable economic success (checked in and immediately after 1973) and continuous, if ineffectual, protest against harshness and corruption. In 1963 martial law was lifted and Park and his principal colleagues transformed themselves into civilians. Park was elected president in 1963 and again in 1967 and 1971 and sent a contingent to fight with the Americans in Vietnam. In 1971 one of two United States divisions was removed. Martial law was reintroduced in 1972 with such extreme disregard for human rights that President Carter announced that the remaining American division would also be withdrawn – a decision reversed by Reagan when it appeared that North Korea's large armed forces were being made even larger. In 1979 Park was assassinated by the chief of his intelligence services. The new president, Choi Kyu Hwa, bade fair to inject a measure of democracy but was quickly rendered powerless by a group of officers led by General Chon Doo Hwan. Demonstrations which turned into a revolt in Kwangju in May 1980 were isolated and brutally repressed (perhaps 2,000 were killed) and after nine months as a civilian façade for military rule Choi resigned and was succeeded by Chon who was invited by Reagan to visit Washington. In 1983 a bomb, all but certainly placed by North Koreans, killed twenty-one people in Rangoon, including four South Korean cabinet ministers. President Chon, the main target, escaped. This outrage disrupted talks which had begun for the unification of the two Koreas. They were, however, resumed in 1984–85. The results were meagre: a few dozen visits in either direction to see relatives but no reduction in frontier fortifications or military exercises. The choice of Seoul for the 1988 Olympic Games induced North Korea to ask for some participation. The International Olympic Committee offered to hold five events in the North but on terms which North Korea did not accept.

The year 1988 was also the end of Chon's presidency. The succession might be by fiat, coup or election. Chon chose the last and his choice was justified by the event. His chosen successor, Roh Tae Woo, won the election with 37 per cent of a large turnout and against a divided opposition. The imminence of the Games may have helped him inasmuch as South Koreans were anxious to avoid disturbances or bloodshed during the Games and were therefore drawn to the established régime rather than to the uncertainties of change. Six months of extreme violence had preceded the elections, alarming the United States as well as Roh who adopted a conciliatory tone directed particularly to the middle class and middle-aged who had been showing signs of sympathy with the seething indignation of radical youth. After his victory Roh set out to conciliate some of his main opponents. These were three: Kim Jong Pil, an ex-officer who had played a leading part in the 1961 coup but broke with Park in 1975 and re-emerged in 1980 as leader of the New Democratic Republican Party; Kim Young Sam, leader of the Democratic Reunification Party; and Kim Dae Jung, leader of the largest opposition group, the Party for Peace and Democracy. The first two of these accepted amalgamation with Roh's Democratic Justice Party and formed with it the Democratic Liberal Party which represented an attempt by Roh and his new associates to escape from the past.

B *Timor*

Timor, the last major island in the chain stretching between continental Asia and Australia, was divided by the Dutch and Portuguese in almost equal sections. The eastern and Portuguese half was detached from Macao at the end of the nineteenth century to become a separate colony, which it remained after the western half had become part of the Indonesian republic. The overthrow of the military régime in Lisbon in 1974 was expected to lead to the engulfing of eastern Timor in Indonesia, but opposition to Indonesia was manifested by two groups, the one pro-Portuguese and the other demanding independence. The latter was left-wing. Civil war broke out in 1975, the small Portuguese force left and at the end of the year Indonesia invaded the territory, devastating it with modern (American and British) arms and killing some 100,000 of the inhabitants. A further 300,000 were incarcerated in camps. Portugal and Australia implicitly acquiesced. The rest of the world hardly noticed. The president and vice-president of the independence movement FRETELIN were assassinated in 1979.

PART FIVE
AFRICA

19 NORTH AFRICA

THE MAGHRIB

The artificiality of dealing with political and economic affairs in terms of geographical categories is nowhere better illustrated than in Africa. The northern fringe of the African continent has been made by history a part of the Arab-Islamic civilization and has been more conscious of affinities with the Middle East than of its ancient economic or current political links with the rest of Africa. Moreover the European overlordship exercised from Casablanca to Suez through protectorates, unequal treaties, military agreements and direct annexation was different in kind from the colonial empires established by Europeans south of the Sahara. But North Africa is at the same time part of Africa; the ethnic line between the Arab–Berber and Bantu races runs through the Sudan and gives trouble there which other states on either side of the line cannot altogether ignore; Egypt and Morocco have played prominent parts in African affairs and conferences and associations; the more reticent Tunisia had a leading voice in the Congo's early troubles; Libyan ambitions and arms have troubled not only Central but also West Africa. The desert is no longer the barrier that it used to be since the aeroplane and above all the radio have enabled men to transcend it; language is no more a barrier between Arab Africa and Bantu Africa than it is within these two areas; and religion provides points of contact between Muslims and Christians on both sides of the divide. The North therefore, though still distinct from the rest of the continent in special and enduring ways, will be classed here as more African than Asian with the sole exception of Egypt whose postwar African role has been consistently subordinated to its Asian and not the other way round.

In the 1950s and 1960s Africa produced a phenomenon of unparalleled extent – the emancipation from foreign rule of enormous areas in the form of independent sovereign states. This process had worldwide repercussions and overshadowed all other African affairs. It was on the whole unexpected. When the Second World War ended there were only three fully independent states in Africa: Ethiopia,

Liberia and South Africa. The next ten years were a decade of preparation for the liquidation of the French, British and Belgian empires, and a further ten years later most of Africa was free. Since France, Britain and Belgium came to accept with versatile swiftness the need to go, these decades witnessed struggles over timetables rather than principles. Compelled by calculation rather than by force the imperial powers abandoned with unexpected ease vast areas whose governance they had acquired in the previous century with equal facility. The process of decolonization was, however, halted in the southern tip of the continent by the stubbornness of the Portuguese in Angola and Mozambique and by the ruthless determination of the semi-independent white settlers of Southern Rhodesia. The self-preservative resistance of the latter, and the refusal of the former to calculate in the same way as the French, the British and the Belgians, were decisively influenced by the existence still further south of the South African stronghold of white supremacy, where the white minority was comparatively much larger (one in four) than elsewhere in Africa and was at the same time fortified by riches, by modern technical power, by having nowhere else to go, and by a doctrinaire racialism which permitted extremities of repressive injustice and cruelty. There were also other pockets of Portuguese or Spanish rule.

The whole of the North African coast came under European domination – French, Italian, British – during the nineteenth century or soon afterwards. The British sphere in Egypt has been considered elsewhere in this book but the rest of the area, though preponderantly Arab and Muslim, will be considered here in its geographical African context. So too will the Sudan, the country where the dividing line between Arab and African, Muslim and non-Muslim, cultures is most evident.

The French invaded Algeria in 1830 and declared it a part of metropolitan France in 1848. As a consequence of their occupation of Algeria they became involved in the two neighbouring monarchies of Tunisia to the east and Morocco to the west, then under the nominal suzerainty of the Ottoman sultan. By the Bardo Treaty of 1881 they established a protectorate over Tunisia, a poor and relatively small country with a population, in 1945, of only 3 million. In Morocco the evanescence of the Ottoman sultan's power coincided with the decay of the Moroccan sultan's own authority, thus creating an invitation and an excuse for foreign intervention, but French power was not so easily substituted owing to the ambitions of other European states. In the first years of the twentieth century France obtained a free hand in Morocco by conceding the same to Italy and Britain in Libya and Egypt, by defeating a claim by Germany (which accepted compensation in central Africa) and by allowing Spain to appropriate the northern strip whence the Arabs had invaded Spain 1,200 years earlier. The Treaty of Fez with the sultan in 1912 crowned these diplomatic successes and established a protectorate of the same kind as the French protectorate over Tunisia, although the whole country was not brought under effective French control until the 1930s. Tangier became an international zone and a fiddlers' paradise. The Italians reaped the reward of their complaisance when they were allowed in 1911 to take Tripolitania from the Turks on the eve of the Balkan wars.

During the Second World War the whole of northern Africa became a battlefield or, in the case of Morocco, a military rear area. Equally important were the political concomitants of the war, especially the Atlantic Charter, the eviction of France from the Arab countries of Syria and Lebanon, and the appearance on the scene of the Americans, including President Franklin D. Roosevelt himself, who had a much publicized interview with the Sultan of Morocco, Mohammed V ben Yusuf. The Tunisian nationalist leader Habib Bourguiba was released from a French prison in 1943, went to Cairo in 1945 and thence to the United States, and settled in his native country once more in 1949. The Moroccan leader Allal al-Fasi, who had been in prison from 1937 to 1946, also went in 1947 to Cairo and then settled temporarily in Tangier. In 1947 the newly created Arab League established a Maghrib Bureau (Maghrib means 'West' in Arabic; the Maghrib comprises at least Morocco, Algeria and Tunisia, sometimes Tripolitania as well), thus institutionalizing the Arab interest in the affairs of North Africa which was to become deeper and more effective in the coming years.

Both France and Italy had been defeated during the war. Both, however, ended up on the winning side. In North African terms Italy paid the price of defeat while France won the rewards of victory; Italy lost its African colonies while France was reinstated in the Maghrib. In the Maghrib the French, aware of the need for changes, sought modifications within the framework of the Bardo and Fez treaties, but the nationalists aimed to terminate the protectorate status altogether. In all three territories the French had encouraged immigration, so that there was a considerable French population settled on the land or in business alongside the French administrators who ran the government of Algeria and had also come to do much the same in Morocco and Tunisia in spite of the sovereignty of sultan and bey. French education had nurtured an élite which appreciated French culture, as the French intended, but also became attracted to the idea of independence, which the French had not foreseen. These modernizing nationalists found themselves allied, if on this point only, with traditionalist malcontents who resented the French presence from a conservative and Muslim standpoint. Caught between these currents the bey of Tunis wavered ineffectually until he was more or less captured by the French, to his eventual discomfiture, while the much younger sultan of Morocco wavered more purposefully, attached himself to the nationalist movement and was exiled by the French, to his eventual benefit.

The governments of the fourth French republic were all coalitions which contained ministers who wanted to meet nationalist movements more than half-way and other ministers who did not want to make life unpleasant for the settlers. This was an impossible combination which rendered France ineffective, allowed Tunisia and Morocco to achieve their aims and drove the largest group of the settlers, the Algerian, to revolt against the government of France. The first French plan was also the first French failure. The French Union, conceived in 1946, created the new category of Associated States with Morocco and Tunis, and also Vietnam, Laos and Cambodia, in mind, but whereas the Asian trio accepted this new status the African pair refused it. There were, however, reasonable hopes of a settlement with Tunisia after the return of Bourguiba in 1949 and until his arrest early in 1952. Robert Schuman, prime minister of France, spoke in 1950 of the ultimate independence of the protected states, and internal reforms of a democratic nature were seriously discussed; Bourguiba's Neo Destour Party was represented in the bey's government. But many nationalists regarded the reforms as inadequate except possibly as a first step, whereas the French regarded them as a long step with no immediate next step in sight. By the end of 1951 the dialogue had turned into rivalry for the support of the bey who was himself so uncertain of his better course that he appeared sometimes to be a nationalist and sometimes a puppet of the French who were pressing him to accept the projected reforms.

At the beginning of 1962 a tougher line gained ground in Paris. Bourguiba was arrested in January and the prime minister, Muhammad Chenik, was dismissed and arrested in March. The bey accepted the French programme and a number of nationalists fled to Cairo. In Tunisia constitutional changes which had been meant to please the nationalists were imposed by authority against their will. The attempt to reach agreement bilaterally had failed, for the acquiescence of the bey was unimportant by contrast with the disagreement of the nationalists who now carried the debate into the international sphere. The next two years merely confirmed the failure and exposed its consequences. Then in 1954 Pierre Mendès-France, after his blitz peace in Indo-China, insisted that the Tunisian problem must be solved no less radically. He flew to Tunisia accompanied by the right-wing Marshal Juin to propose full internal self-government. He fell from power in February 1955 before his initiative had borne fruit, but his successor Edgar Faure pursued the negotiations and in June Bourguiba accepted the French proposals as a step towards independence and returned to Tunisia. Nine months later, on 20 March 1956, Tunisia became fully independent and concluded a treaty with France which included provision for the stationing of French troops in the country.

The Moroccan case was not very different. A period of genuine negotiation revealed to both sides the gap between the French programme of democratic gradualism and the nationalists' determination to get independence very soon. The principal difference between the Moroccan and Tunisian cases lay in the temper of the ruler. Mohammed V ben Yusuf had shown signs of allying himself with the Istiqlal (Independence) Party at the end of the war, and by so doing he had destroyed the basis of government in Morocco which, during the seven-year term of office of General Noguès as resident-general, had rested upon the good personal relations between the two men – the *dialogue sultan–résident*. A second major factor was the isolation of the French settlers from the outside world during the war years 1940–42, an isolation which had larger consequences in Morocco than Tunisia because the French community in Morocco was also isolated from the surrounding Muslims by Lyautey's pre-war policy of siting new French towns away from the traditional centres of Moroccan life. From 1947 to 1951 Marshal Juin was resident-general, but in spite of his somewhat forbidding presence a new *dialogue* Paris–Fez was initiated and the sultan visited the French capital in 1950. The French, however, believed that they had an alternative to treating with the nationalists, whom they and some Moroccans were tempted to write off as uncharacteristic and irresponsible townees, of less significance than traditional personages like the pro-French, and anti-sultan, pasha of Marrakesh, el Glaoui. The sultan was persuaded – he subsequently said coerced – into signing in 1951 decrees initiating the reforms which the French were prepared to introduce, but the consequent agitation in Morocco and elsewhere in the Arab world caused him to swing away from the French and for a year there was increasing uncertainty and disorder, culminating in December 1952 in violent and barbaric anti-white outbursts in Casablanca. In the following February the sultan was sent into exile. His absence, however, did not serve to restore order or strengthen French rule, while in Spanish Morocco an assembly of notables refused to recognize the exiled sultan's uncle, Muhammad ben Arafa, whom the French had placed on the throne. In 1955, following the settlement with Tunisia, the sultan was brought back and before the end of the year France had agreed to concede full independence. It took effect on 2 March 1956. Both Morocco and Tunisia became full members of the Arab League in October 1958.

By this time the Algerian revolt against France, a far more serious problem, had begun. Hostilities which opened in the Aurès mountains in 1954 were at first regarded as a fresh instalment of familiar colonial troubles but they developed into a war which involved the flower of the French army, the full panoply of military rule and censorship and terrorism and torture, three separate white French challenges to the authority of Paris, the fall of the Fourth Republic and the achievement by Algeria – uniquely in Africa until Zimbabwe – of independence by force of arms. The situation was without any parallel in the rest of Africa. The European population had been a part of the country for much longer than any other settler community, it was nearer to the mother country, and in the main cities it was as numerous or almost as numerous as the Muslims; its services to Algeria were conspicuous. Juridically too the situation was peculiar since Algeria was constitutionally a part of metropolitan France, so that Frenchmen who failed even to envisage a severence were maintaining an unreality which was nevertheless no fiction. The legal position contributed to a stubborn psychological attitude which caused outsiders to wonder why it was that Frenchmen alone in the world were unable to see that their days as rulers in Algeria were numbered. The French, moreover, like the British in the Middle East after the retreat from India, hated the thought of further surrenders after the collapse of their empire in Indo-China; just as Africans were encouraged by the ending of French and British rule in Asia, so in reverse were the French and British influenced in their African policies by their postwar experiences in Asia, making in Algeria and Egypt in particular mistakes of timing and understanding which they might have avoided if they had not felt that their descent from the first rank was proving too hasty for dignity or safety.

In Algeria, additionally, senior French officers developed in the shadow of the defeat in Indo-China a sense of mission so strong that it distorted their sense of proportion and led them in the end to jettison their oaths of allegiance. These officers convinced themselves that they belonged to the gallant and prescient category of the saviour with the sword, that they alone appreciated the full import of the communist threat to civilization, and that theirs was the honourable destiny of leading the resistance to the hosts of darkness and opening the eyes of woolly-minded sluggards to the dangers and responsibilities of the twentieth century. This apocalyptic determinism was accompanied by an almost equally passionate emotion which was local and practical instead of cosmic and visionary. The day-to-day business of administering large tracts of Algeria had become the responsibility of the army, and in the course of governing their localities officers had acquired a proficiency, knowledge and sympathy for the people in their care which, they rightly judged, would not easily be supplied by anybody else.

There was a foretaste of revolt at Sétif in 1945. Like a similar rising in Madagascar in the same year, this revolt was suppressed with brutality and many casualties; France in 1945 was in no mood to do things by halves. The nationalist leader Ferhat Abbas was arrested and the French community was given the incentive and the excuse to arrogate to itself an authority which belonged rightly to the government in Paris. The weaknesses and divisions of the governments of the Fourth Republic allowed this authority to be exercised and enhanced until the return to power of General de Gaulle in 1958 put it to a test which it failed. There was, however, no effective nationalist threat to French rule during the decade between the Sétif rising in 1945 and the revolt in the Aurès mountains at the end of 1954. During these years French ministers and governors-general tried to temper the repression of nationalism with economic advancement and democratic reform, but they failed to mollify the nationalists whose aim was not reform but independence and they antagonized the European community whose preoccupation with repression left little room for anything else.

This dilemma was illustrated vividly during the first stage of the revolt. The defeat of the Faure government in November 1955 had been followed by a general election and the installation of a minority government led by Guy Mollet. The new prime minister attempted to find a way to bring the fighting to an end. Yet when he went to Algiers he was pelted with garbage by Europeans, while approaches to leaders of the insurrectionary Front de Libération Nationale (FLN) were entirely unproductive. Mollet appointed General Catroux, a widely respected and liberally minded proconsul, to the governor-generalship, but Catroux resigned his office within a week and without leaving France. In May 1956 Mendès-France resigned from the Mollet government on the grounds that it was not doing enough, while the prime minister probably felt that if he ventured more boldly he would provoke a trial of strength between Paris and the Europeans in Algeria, which Paris would not win. In October 1956 the weakness of Paris was dramatically illustrated, and its position with regard to the FLN seriously damaged, when five FLN leaders, including Ahmed Ben Bella, were kidnapped when returning by air from a meeting with the sultan of Morocco. The aircraft in which they were travelling, which was registered in France and piloted by a Frenchman although operated by a non-French company, was diverted from its destination to Algiers without the knowledge of the government in Paris. During the next eighteen months political attitudes remained irreconcilable, the French army and the FLN secured positions in which neither could defeat the other, terrorism increased on both sides and spread to Paris and other cities in France, torture became a regular instrument of government and was seen to be, and any lingering intention of applying the new compromise constitution called the Algerian Statute of 1947 was finally abandoned. The impasse seemed to be complete, politically and militarily.

In this same period Morocco and Tunisia were drawn more closely into the conflict. The sultan of Morocco had been deeply offended by the kidnapping of Ben Bella who had been his guest but an hour or two earlier, and Bourguiba was angered when the French, irritated by the FLN's freedom to use Tunisian and Moroccan soil as an asylum where they could rest and refit without fear of attack, delivered an air attack on Sakiet in Tunisia in February 1958 and killed seventy-five people; Bourguiba threatened to stop supplies to French units in Tunisia. The Moroccan monarch and the Tunisian president had met at Rabat at the end of 1957 and had offered to mediate but the French, deceived into optimism by some recent successes in the field, had declined. Bourguiba persisted in his attempts to find a peaceful solution, not without some regard to the increasing links between the FLN and Egypt with which he was on bad terms as a result of an attempt on his life for which he blamed Nasser. There was talk of a Maghribian federation to include an independent Algeria, Morocco and Tunisia.

On 28 May 1958 the last civilian prime minister of the Fourth French Republic, Pierre Pflimlin, resigned, a victim of the Algerian war for which he and five predecessors could find no solution. On 13 May Algiers had rebelled against Paris. On 30 May, so it was planned, this government would seize power in Paris by a coup. Almost the whole of Corsica, the stepping stone, had accepted the rebel régime and half the commanders of the military regions in France were believed to be disloyal. Only one obstacle to success in the capital remained – a Frenchman of enormous prestige and outstanding political skill. On 1 June General de Gaulle was invested with full powers. On 4 June he flew to Algiers.

It is only possible to guess what policy de Gaulle had in June 1958. He may have had no fixed policy but he probably saw the inevitable end. What happened was that, by a mixture of authority and ambiguity, he imposed himself upon the situation and gradually acquired the power to impose a solution upon it. This took him nearly four years. By doing enough to retain the initiative, but not too much to reveal himself, he prevented potentially hostile groups from acting against him until it was too late. He began by patching up relations with Tunisia and Morocco, agreeing to withdraw French forces from both countries (except from the Tunisian naval base at Bizerta). He next moved from Algeria many senior officers who, even were they minded to object to their postings, could not gainsay the legitimacy of an ordr from *the* general. General Salan, a prime rallying point for disaffection and leader of the May *putsch*, was permitted to remain temporarily in his command, but he was relieved of his civilian functions which were now once more divorced from the supreme military command. After these preliminary moves, and with cautious deliberation, de Gaulle prepared his first major statement on the future status of Algeria and made his first bid for peace with the FLN. In September 1959 he formulated a choice (not unlike his offer to France's colonies in western and central Africa in 1958) between independence, integration with France and association with France, the choice to be made within four years from the end of hostilities, defined as any year in which fewer than 200 people had been killed in fighting or by terrorism. This pronouncement precipitated a second white revolt. On 24 January 1960 the European community showed that it would oppose even de Gaulle rather than accept the independence of Algeria. The revolt was a failure. The French government, acting energetically in Algeria and at home, showed in return how the authority and power of Paris had grown during the past eighteen months. But to Algerians de Gaulle's offer in 1959 was no more than a half-way house, a solution short of true independence and by now unacceptable.

Support for de Gaulle within France, more widespread and more positive in 1960 than in 1958, was partly due to a feeling that the war had gone on too long and partly to restiveness over the methods which were being used to wage it. Henri Alleg's book *La Question* focused attention on the use of torture by units of the French army. The trial of Alleg in 1960, followed by the disappearance and (as it was correctly surmised) murder of the French communist university lecturer Maurice Audin, the trial in 1961 of the Algerian girl Djamila Boupacha, protests by the Roman Catholic cardinals occupying French sees, and a manifesto signed by 121 leading intellectuals, all contributed to turn French opinion against the French community and the French army in Algeria. Towards the end of 1960 the leaders of the January revolt were themselves put on trial. But there was still one white rebellion to come. It came in April 1961. It was led by four generals and it lasted four days. Two of the four generals, Salan and Jouhaud, were subsequently sentenced to death *in absentia* and the other two, Challe and Zeller, who surrendered, to fifteen years' imprisonment – all sentences being eventually reduced. Out of the failure of this rebellion rose the Organisation de l'Armée Secrète (OAS) which resorted to terrorism and, by creating among the European population fears of reprisals by an independent Algerian government, provoked – as independence became inevitable – an exodus which deprived the country of much needed skills in administration, education and other public services.

De Gaulle's victory on the white front was not at first accompanied by any improvement in the nationalist quarter. In September 1959 the FLN had proclaimed a provisional Algerian government with Ferhat Abbas as prime minister and the imprisoned Ben Bella as his deputy, and Ferhat Abbas had left Tunisia for Cairo which was to be the seat of government for the time being. De Gaulle, true to his general disposition, temporized after the defeat of the white revolt of January 1960, and this inactivity caused the Algerians to turn for help to Moscow and Beijing. During 1960 moreover it became apparent that the movement of opinion among non-combatant Algerians was towards the FLN and its unequivocal demand for independence and not towards any middle position between the FLN and the Europeans (as de Gaulle may have hoped at the time of his pronouncement of

September 1959). De Gaulle began therefore to move more purpose-fully towards negotiation with the FLN. A first secret encounter at Melun in June was a failure but after discussions between de Gaulle and Bourguiba, between FLN leaders and Georges Pompidou (still at this time a private banker) and between the FLN and Moroccans, Tunisians and Egyptians, a conference opened at Evian in May 1961. But suspicions and difficulties proved at this stage too great; the latter included the FLN's claim to be recognized as a government, the right of the imprisoned Ahmed Ben Bella to appear at the conference, guarantees for the French who might wish to remain in Algeria, continuing French rights in the naval base at Mers-el-Kebir, Saharan oil, and the conditions under which the proposed referendum on the status of Algeria would be held.

This conference failed to reach agreement but in July de Gaulle, in a televised speech, unequivocally accepted Algerian independence. In the same month, however, Franco–Tunisian relations suffered a sharp relapse when Bourguiba, concerned about Tunisian rights in the Sahara, demanded a complete French evacuation of Bizerta (effected in October 1963 after Tunisia had laid its complaints before the United Nations, thus accentuating de Gaulle's dislike of that organization); and the FLN adopted a more assertive line when Yusuf Ben Khedda succeeded the more moderate Ferhat Abbas at the head of the provisional Algerian government, supported Bourguiba over Bizerta, and delivered some forceful speeches at the conference of non-aligned states in Belgrade in September. Still in the same month the OAS made an unsuccessful attempt on de Gaulle's life, OAS activities increased throughout France as well as Algeria, and there were rumours of the proclamation of a dissident French republic under General Salan in northern Algeria. In October Ben Khedda proposed a new round of negotiations.

The second Evian conference took place in March 1962. On 18 March a cease-fire agreement was signed. The conference also agreed on the terms for holding a referendum and, on the assumption that the result would be a vote in favour of independence, further agreed (among other things) that French troops would be withdrawn progressively over three years except from Mers-el-Kebir which France was to be permitted to occupy for at least fifteen years; that France might continue its nuclear tests in the Sahara and retain its airfields there for five years; that France would continue its economic activities in the Saharan oilfields; and that French technical and financial aid to Algeria would continue undiminished for at least three years. On 3 July 1962 Algeria became an independent sovereign state for the first time in history. But its leaders did not hold together. In the ensuring quarrels Ben Bella, returning to the scene after six years' absence in prison, won power but alienated colleagues and followers by moving too fast, by trying to reorganize the FLN on communist lines and by trying to play a leading and radical part in African and Afro-Asian affairs to the neglect of urgent domestic problems. In June 1965 he was overthrown when he was on the point of ousting his minister of defence, Colonel Houari Boumédienne, who succeeded him at the head of the government. Ben Bella remained a fugitive until 1990.

Boumédienne's policies included, in domestic affairs: a new structure of government, state capitalism, the nationalization of natural resources, vigorous exploitation of oil and gas deposits, and industrialization; in external affairs: cautiously good relations with the USSR, continued collaboration with France, a Maghrib entente, and active association with the Arab states against Israel. He ruled through a Council of the Revolution which was created at this point; he himself was its chairman but its further membership was undisclosed. He created in 1968 regional authorities for economic and social affairs and made them elective a year later. Dissatisfaction – sharply evinced by an abortive army revolt led by Colonel Tahar Zbiri – focused on the failure to partition all big estates at once or give workers in industry as much control in management as many of them wanted, but by and large the new government became quickly and firmly established. In the foreign field Boumédienne concluded a series of agreements with France for the development and nationalization of mining and other industries, securing both French aid and Algerian control. He also secured the return to Algeria of 300 works of art removed by the French. In 1967 France evacuated its remaining land bases in Algeria and next year the naval base at Mers-el-Kebir. Boumédienne visited Moscow soon after his accession to power, broke off diplomatic relations with Britain over Rhodesia, declared war on Israel and sent troops to fight it, and broke off relations with the United States. When a first pan-African cultural festival was held in Algiers in 1969 it was attended by the president of the USSR and the French foreign minister as well as a concourse of African and other notables.

Algeria went briefly to war against Morocco in 1963 over their common frontier and as a result of the removal of French control over both of them. The conservative monarchy of Morocco and the socialist Algerian republic were not made to be friends, even in the absence of an ill-defined frontier, but talks between King Hassan and Boumédienne in 1968–70 led to a settlement which fixed the border and also provided for joint exploitation of iron ores at Tindouf on the basis that Tindouf itself was in Algeria. This agreement was distinctly favourable to Algeria. Morocco signed it in the hope of getting Algerian support against Mauritania in the disposal of Spanish Mauritania (Rio de Oro).

Between Morocco and Mauritania there was a common bond so long as Spain retained its African possessions but an underlying conflict over the eventual fate of one of these: Rio de Oro. Spain had ceded Spanish Morocco to Morocco in 1956, retaining however the towns of Melilla and Ceuta and three other small enclaves whose population was mainly Spanish. In 1957 Spain sent troops to Ifni in south-west Morocco but ceded it to Morocco in 1958 as far south as latitude 27° 40'. There remained the Canary Islands, which stayed part of Spain, and Rio de Oro, claimed by both Morocco and Mauritania. These rival claimants were united in opposition to the Spanish presence in a territory where the world's richest phosphate deposits had been found in 1945. Morocco, heavily dependent on the export and therefore the world price of phosphates, would have liked to acquire the whole of Rio de Oro but was prepared to concede a substantial part of it to Mauritania rather than see the creation of a new state, possibly with a Hispanophile monarch and extensive Spanish aid and tutelage. Mauritania wished to thwart the creation of a Greater Morocco. Spain, having announced its departure in 1974, wished for a referendum which would produce a majority for a new independent state. Morocco fought off this prospect by getting the UN to ask the International Court of Justice who had owned Rio de Oro before the Spanish got there. The Court answered in 1975 that the status of Rio de Oro must be determined on the basis of self-determination and not by reference to past history.

While the Court was still deliberating Morocco reached a preliminary agreement with Mauritania over the exploitation of the phosphates and in 1975 King Hassan personally led 350,000 Moroccans a few miles into Rio de Oro in a demonstration designed to force Spain to negotiate with Morocco and Mauritania and not hand over to any third authority. Spain agreed at the end of the year to transfer Rio de Oro to the two African claimants jointly and they, five months later, partitioned it: two-thirds to Morocco and one-third to Mauritania.

Algeria looked askance at a settlement which had been made without its intervention and barred its access to the Atlantic. It resolved to support the Polisario (Popular Front for the Liberation of Saguiet el-Hamra and Rio de Oro) which had been in existence since 1973 and claimed that Rio de Oro should belong neither to Morocco nor Mauritania. In February 1976 a Sahrawi Arab Democratic Republic was proclaimed (in Libya). Morocco and Mauritania joined forces against the Polisario but the latter found the effort too great for its penurious economy and in 1978 the army removed President Ould Daddah and gave up the fight. The war went on because the Polisario's tactics and resources, effective against Mauritania, were not effective against Morocco. Whereas the Polisario was able to inflict on Mauritania military defeats whose economic consequences Mauritania could not take, Morocco was not so easily disposed of. Equally, however, Morocco was not able to drive the Polisario from the field.

The conflict had wider dimensions. The Polisario had Algerian support and Russian arms. Morocco received aid from France and the United States: King Hassan was in American eyes a bastion against communism in north-west Africa. In the period after the fall of the shah of Iran, when Washington's loyalty to its friends was being questioned, the United States judged it expedient to promise the king increased military and other aid, if only to allay this anti-American current. (The promises, once given, were only tardily executed.) The king further courted the west by his readiness to despatch modest forces to troubled areas such as the Shaba province of Zaïre. Algeria on the other hand, although suspiciously left-wing, had the makings of a more solid ally. It was to Morocco what India was to Pakistan in western geopolitical calculation: strategically and economically a worthwhile friend but politically dubious. The death of Boumédienne in 1979 marginally shifted the equation, for Boumédienne's successor was the more cautious Benjedid Chadli who was expected to play Sadat to Boumédienne's Nasser.

Chadli consolidated, in a lower key, his personal position as Boumédienne's successor and sketched a vision of a federated Greater Maghrib. The first instalment was a treaty with Tunisia in 1983 to which Mauritania later adhered. With Morocco, however, Algeria's relations remained difficult on account of the two countries' difference over the western Sahara and were further strained when Colonel Qadafi surprisingly visited Rabat in 1983 and bartered away his support for the Polisario in exchange for a Moroccan promise to keep out of the imbroglio in Chad (see the next section). But Morocco's attempt to detach Libya from the Polisario by placating Qadafi displeased the United States and in 1986 King Hassan denounced his treaty with Libya in order to repair his relations with Washington.

In 1986 Hassan celebrated twenty-five years on the throne of Morocco. He combined ostentatious wealth and unconcealed autocracy with political astuteness. He commanded the trust of his army and exploited the nationalism which animated Moroccans of all parties and classes. All patronage, political and religious, was in his hands. Political parties, which had been allowed from 1977 to take part in elections, accepted nominal democracy at the price of good behaviour. Muslim fundamentalism was curtailed in spite of not inconsiderable popular support. Left-wing parties, when not destroyed, were penetrated by the secret police. His policy in the Sahara was not questioned, but its success encouraged opponents of the royal autocracy whose voices had been muted out of patriotism.

In the Sahara Morocco was chiefly concerned to keep the Polisario away from its Atlantic provinces. Although Hassan rejected a plea by the OAU to talk with the Polisario he appeared willing to back a referendum which, it was assumed, would give him those disrupted areas which mattered to him at the cost of letting others become an independent Sahrawi republic. By the mid-seventies the war was a stalemate in Morocco's favour, for whereas the Polisario made no significant gains Morocco not only contained it but was slowly pushing it back by the inglorious but effective strategy of building walls of sand stretching along 2,000 km of desert. This moving line, punctuated by forts 5 km apart and manned by 100,000 troops, created enclaves which were then peopled by Moroccan immigrants. But the war was ruinously expensive and in 1987 Hassan agreed to a meeting with Chadli in the hope of stemming Algerian aid to the Polisario. The Polisario was allowed to retain its quasi-government in Algiers but lost Algerian funds and by the end of the decade its leaders were split on whether to continue the struggle and, if so, how.

Morocco was simultaneously freed of its anxieties on the Mauritanian front. Mauritania, although it adhered to the Algerian–Tunisian treaty of 1983 and recognized the Sahrawi Arab Republic, was beset with troubles at home and to the south. Economic stringencies, including an encroaching desert, exacerbated ethnic tensions. Mauritania comprised paler (Moorish) and blacker peoples – the former dominant, marginally less numerous, divided within the Arab world between pro- and anti-Libyans, but united against their blacker compatriots. These had kin over the border with Senegal. The government of Colonel Ould Taya, which came to power by force in 1984, failed to establish its authority and in 1989 a massacre of about 1,000 people was followed by the flight of some 30,000 more into Senegal. These refugees were non-Muslims and their arrival in Senegal provoked a counter-expulsion of some 70,000 and created for a while a threat of war. (There were about ten Mauritanians in Senegal for every Senegalois in Mauritania.)

In 1988 a fresh attempt was made by the UN secretary general, Javier Perez de Cuellar, to resolve the Saharan problem. Morocco and the Polisario accepted a UN plan for a cease-fire, to be followed by a referendum to choose between independence and incorporation with Morocco. This agreement was completely without substance. Within a few weeks the fighting had started again and within a year Morocco concluded with Algeria, Tunisia, Libya and Mauritania a treaty for an Arab Maghrib Union which left the Polisario out in the cold. The new union was essentially geographical and not the ideological bloc which Qadafi had from time to time tried to form. Its brittle cohesion was quickly tested when Morocco (like Egypt) responded to the American call for the despatch of troops to Saudi Arabia to confront Iraq's seizure of Kuwait, while Algeria and Tunisia were more critical of the United States and their peoples more openly sympathetic to Saddam Hussein's denunciations of the United States and Israel.

Popular emotions were becoming more open and influential in both countries. In Tunisia, where Zayn al-Abdin Ben Ali succeeded the venerable but senile Bourguiba in 1987, political parties were allowed to emerge, although no specifically religious party might be formed: the government feared Islamic fundamentalists. In Algeria riots in 1988 preceded the formulation of constitutional changes which were put to the people in a referendum and adopted. Political opposition was legalized within limits and civil rights, including the right to strike, were recognized. As in Tunisia and for the same reasons no party devoted to a particular ideology or limited to a certain race or religion might be licensed, although this provision was in practice overlooked with the licensing of the Front Islamique and the Berber Rassemblement. Under the new constitution a party winning half the votes in a (multimember) constituency took all the seats, a party winning less than 10 per cent of the votes got none.

LIBYA AND CHAD

The postwar fate of Italy's North African colonies was to be resolved by the four principal victorious powers by September 1948, failing which the problem would be transferred to the United Nations. The British and Italian governments devised a plan, called after their foreign ministers the Bevin–Sforza plan, whereby an independent Libyan state would come into existence at the end of ten years and during the interval its existing three parts would be under British or Italian tutelage: the Fezzan (which was coveted by the French as an addition to Tunisia) under Italian trusteeship, Tripolitania in the middle under British administration for two years and Italian trusteeship for eight, and Cyrenaica further east under British trusteeship for the whole ten years. This plan was objectionable to the Arabs and to the Russians, who proposed a five-year UN trusteeship (they also proposed UN trusteeships of five and ten years for Eritrea and Italian Somaliland). The political committee of the Assembly accepted the Bevin–Sforza plan but the Assembly itself just failed to endorse it and there followed a period of negotiation and investigation by a UN commissioner (Dr Adrian Pelt), as a result of which the whole of Italy's North African empire was converted into a tripartite constitutional monarchy under the emir of Cyrenaica, Muhammad Idris as-Sanusi, as King Idris of Libya. The new state came into being on the first day of 1952 and shortly afterwards entered into an agreement with Britain which secured essential economic aid and arms to Libya and military rights to Britain in the small post of El Adem. The Americans subsequently established a larger base at Wheelus Field. In 1969 the king was ousted by army officers, who were disgruntled by corruption in high places. Their leader was Colonel Qadafi who disdained the conventions by interfering wherever possible to help (notably the Palestinians) or harry (oil companies, communists, Israel and established governments, especially monarchies). Within the Arab world Qadafi projected a series of unions or federations which were insubstantial and increasingly derided: with Egypt and the Sudan in 1969, extended to Syria in 1970, but never effective; with Egypt and Syria again in 1971, equally without consequence; with Egypt in 1972 upon the eviction of the Russians from Egypt but followed in 1973 by complete diplomatic rupture; with Tunisia in 1974, the most short-lived of these attempts at fusion since it was denounced by Bouguiba two days after it was proclaimed; with Syria in 1980; and with Chad at the beginning of 1981. In the last case union appeared to be a euphemism for at least partial annexation. Qadafi's contempt for conventions led him to organize the killing of political opponents who had fled to foreign countries, even using his diplomatic missions for this purpose.

Within Africa Qadafi not only played a leading part in the troubled affairs of Chad but was suspected of much wider ambitions. Huge, arid and underpopulated (about 4 million inhabitants), athwart the dividing line between Arab and Bantu-speaking Africa, with six international frontiers and presumed wealth in uranium, gold, oil and other precious commodities, Chad was endemically unstable and a standing temptation. Its first president, François Tombalbaye, a representative of the educated southern élite, was unsympathetic towards the Muslims of the north whose opposition to his government he insisted on regarding as banditry. It was also a threat to the tourist traffic which he hoped to encourage. By 1966 he was challenged by FROLINAT, a northern liberation movement with headquarters in Libya. He turned for help to France with which Chad, like other former French colonies, had a defence agreement. (France had some 6,000 troops in West and Central Africa in these years, distributed over thirteen states.) This help began with supplies but expanded in 1968–70 to direct intervention with paratroops and aircraft which secured Tombalbaye's position until 1975 when he was assassinated. His successor Felix Malloum gradually lost the war against FROLINAT. Meanwhile the leaders of FROLINAT's several armies fell out. The French withdrew, Qadafi backed Goukouni Oueddei who was willing to cede – or to promise to cede – the northern Ouzou strip and its supposed uranium deposits to Libya. His rival Hissen Habre formed a brief alliance with Malloum before turning on him and seizing power in the capital Ndjamena in 1979. Libya, the Sudan and Niger engineered a superficial accord between Oueddei and Habre but in 1980 Libya, driving its Russian tanks across the desert with surprising speed and efficiency, enabled Oueddei to put Habre to flight. In 1981 Qadafi and Oueddei announced a union of their two countries. Qadafi then agreed to pull his troops out in return for a French undertaking to do likewise, but when the French withdrew the Libyans nevertheless remained in occupation of the Ouzou strip.

Elsewhere Habre regained and consolidated his position but his impoverished government was weakened by falls in the price of cotton which fuelled popular discontent. A peace conference at Brazzaville in 1984 was unsuccessful but thereafter Habre's fortunes revived, particularly from 1986 when Libya, having failed in a fresh offensive, abandoned Goukouni and Goukouni himself split with one of Habre's other opponents, Acheikh Ibn Ommar. In 1987 Habre's forces won a convincing victory in the north although without recovering the Ouzou strip – thus vindicating President Mitterrand's policy of giving aid to Habre but deprecating large-scale hostilities against Qadafi. After this victory many of Habre's enemies either came to terms with him or fled to the Sudan, but in 1989 a coup against him (which failed) demonstrated the turmoil beneath the surface. The plotters, led by an old and close associate Idriss Deby, resented favours dispensed to erstwhile enemies, personal or tribal, in order to seal this reconciliation and soften some of the asperities of Habre's harsh rule. They had help from Libya and in 1990 they tried again and were successful. France, which had intervened on several occasions to protect Habre, refused to do so again although it had a force of about 1,300 in the country. American patronage and his Israeli guards were not enough to save Habre, who fled to Cameroun.

When Reagan took office in 1981 the new administration in Washington, understandably irritated but extravagantly obsessed by Libya's often outrageous behaviour, sent warships into the Gulf of Sirte and shot down two Libyan aircraft. The United States also imposed economic sanctions and in 1983 and 1984 sent AWACS intelligence aircraft to Egypt to deter Qadafi from adventures in that direction: Qadafi had threatened to march into Egypt and he had a hand in an abortive plot to overthrow President Nimeiry by dropping bombs on Khartoum as a prelude to a coup by Sudanese officers. In 1986 the Americans delivered a massive air and naval attack on Tripoli and Benghazi (see also Chapter 4) which failed to kill Qadafi and probably strengthened his position in his own country. In a smaller attack in 1989 two Libyan aircraft were destroyed after the United States had accused Libya of building a plant for the manufacture of poison gases.

Africans were alarmed by Qadafi's activities and by his visions of a great Islamic Saharan empire which would point a menacing finger at the wealth of Zaïre, overawe the Sudan and Uganda, and cut a swathe westward from Chad through Mauritania, Mali and Niger to the Atlantic in Senegal, the Guinea and Ivory Coasts and the Bight of Benin. The murder of President Luiz Cabral of Guinea-Bissau, the overthrow of President Sangoule Lamizana of Upper Volta, a coup which failed against President Seyni Kountche of Niger (who endured almost annual coups after seizing power in 1974) – all these events in 1980 were ascribed to Libyan machination. So too was an abortive coup in the Gambia which was suppressed by prompt Senegalese intervention. The remoter Central African, Cameroon and Gabon Republics also felt a Libyan current blowing their way and privately wished that France might send troops back to Chad. The Gambia, Senegal, Ghana and Gabon severed relations with Libya and Nigeria threatened to follow suit.

Yet Libya was in no position to create an empire. Its population numbered only 3 to 4 million, its army about 40,000. During the crisis in Chad in 1980 Egypt mustered more than twice that force on its border with Libya alone and breached the frontier with impunity. What Qadafi had was an alarming political style and oil. He used the oil partly to twist the arms of customers to whom he chose to sell at half price or less, and partly to buy Russian arms. But in the 1980s Libya's oil production fell to a quarter of its peak in the previous decade, and although Qadafi turned Libya into the largest *place d'armes* of Russian origin outside the USSR and central and eastern Europe much of this weaponry was either unsuited to his foreign ventures or left inadequately tended in places where it quickly deteriorated. His interventions in Chad were inconsequent. After declaring himself the champion of the Muslims he helped non-Muslims to power. The uranium which he was supposed to covet had no proven existence. (The Ouzou strip had been assigned to Chad by a Franco–British agreement of 1899. An unratified Franco–Italian agreement of 1935 assigned it to Libya. Tombalbaye allegedly sold it to Libya in 1973 by an agreement of which no record has been produced. In 1989 the OAU persuaded both countries to refer their dispute to the International Court of Justice.)

Europeans were interested in Africa long before they occupied it. In the
century after the death of the Prophet Mahomet North Africa mounted
the greatest threat to European Christendom which it has ever faced,
and although that threat was parried by the Frank Charles Martel and
by the Byzantine emperor Leo the Isaurian, Spain remained for
centuries partly under an alien rule buttressed on occasions by fresh
support from Berber Africa. When the Christians finally drove the
Muslims out of the Iberian peninsula, their momentum carried them on
into Africa, and Spanish and Portuguese adventurers, still finding it too
difficult to turn east, explored and circumnavigated Africa and made
Cape Horn a station on a new route to the east. In more modern times
Africa became a place where Europeans got things: slaves for
plantations in the west, food for industrialized countries whose peoples
were leaving the land for the factory, precious minerals like gold and
copper and diamonds and uranium. At first only the coastal areas were
exploited, but later the rumoured wealth of the interior tempted
organized expeditions to follow in the steps of adventurers and
missionaries. Although checked at first by the unexpected strength of
African kingdoms, white power eventually prevailed – especially when
the motives of curiosity and enrichment were reinforced by inter-white
competition. So, in a final phase of European penetration, Africa was
partitioned by official emissaries, part soldiers, part administrators,
making territorial claims and fighting for them because traders
demanded protection and each European state was afraid that others
would take what it did not annex for itself. Areas, large but vaguely
defined, were assigned to adventurers backed by, or acting in the name
of, European states which had been taught by centuries of history to
think first and foremost in territorial terms.

In the last quarter of the nineteenth century it became apparent that
Europe had acquired a great part of Africa in a very short space of time,
and that there was some danger of fights between the European states
concerned as a result of the untidy and uneven distribution of the spoils.
The Europeans proceeded to settle these matters reasonably amicably
among themselves. There were many wars in Africa during the colonial
period, but none of them was fought between European states except as

20.1   North–west Africa (with inset of Nigeria at the time of the Biafra War)

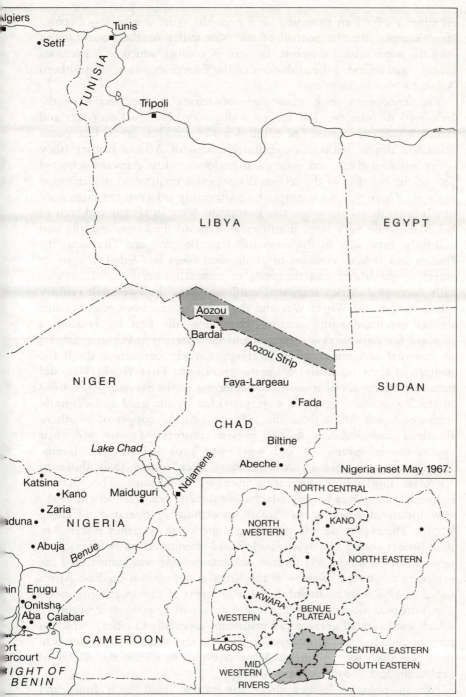

Algiers

Tunis
• Setif

TUNISIA

Tripoli

LIBYA

EGYPT

Aozou

Bardai

Aozou Strip

NIGER

Faya-Largeau

SUDAN

• Fada

CHAD

Biltine

Lake Chad

Abeche

Ndjamena

Katsina

• Kano　Maiduguri

• Zaria

aduna•

NIGERIA

• Abuja

Benue

hin　Enugu

Onitsha
Aba　Calabar

ort
arcourt

CAMEROON

*IGHT OF
BENIN*

Nigeria inset May 1967:

NORTH CENTRAL

NORTH
WESTERN

KANO

NORTH EASTERN

KWARA

WESTERN

BENUE
PLATEAU

LAGOS

MID
WESTERN

RIVERS

CENTRAL EASTERN

SOUTH EASTERN

an adjunct of a European war, and even the most menancing disputes (for example, for the control of the Nile valley or the possession of Angola) were settled without the sort of conflict which in a previous century had attended the ambitions of the European powers in southern Asia and North America.

The Europeans took possession of Africa at the height of the Industrial Revolution. The technical disparity between Europeans and Africans was enormous. The cultural gap was no less great. Europeans remained almost without exception ignorant of African history (they often assumed there was none) and customs, while Africans acquired few of the benefits of the technically superior civilization of their new masters. There was no attempt at a partnership between the races until nearly a century later when the Europeans were in retreat and seen to be. Meanwhile very large numbers of Africans died unnecessarily and painfully, especially in the areas ruled by Belgians and Germans; the French and British versions of civilization were less lethal in spite of wars, forced labour and the pains of mineral concessions. Economically, occupied Africa stagnated until well into the twentieth century when the Second World War and the incipient successes of nationalist leaders produced some startling changes – the first by creating a demand for African raw materials and the latter by making an impact on colonial authorities who, although vaguely concerned about the welfare of their territories from the end of the First World War, did next to nothing about it until the beginning of the Second. Exceptions to this economic stagnation were provided by the gold and diamond mines of South Africa from the 1870s and by the copper of Northern Rhodesia and Katanga in the present century. Towns and their appurtenances sprang up and work was provided (at special non-European wages and in circumstances even worse than those of Victorian England) for increasing numbers of Africans. The effect of industrialization was heavily adverse for the African. The benefit to the new industrial workers was small since industry operated on cheap labour. The expectation of life among miners was low; they returned to their homes young and dying, useless and often infectiously diseased. A new class of migrant was created, the countryside was ruined, and the extremes of poverty were – as the Royal Commission on East Africa noted in 1955 – to be found in the main areas of European settlement. The European occupation had created an appalling economic problem, which itself created grave social problems (especially in cities), which in turn encouraged white observers to despise and shun the Africans. On their side the more indignant Africans began to accuse the whites of exploiting and debauching the blacks.

African political leaders drew inspiration from both India and America. They formed National Congresses in imitation of the Indian National Congress; many of them were attracted by Gandhian ideas of passive resistance; and the independence of India in 1947 had an effect in Africa which had not been foreseen by the colonial powers. From the American continent, and notably the Caribbean, Africans gained confidence and dignity and a habit of meeting together. A first pan-African conference was held in 1900, followed by a second in Paris during the peace conference of 1915. These first meetings were dominated by West Indian blacks but the sixth, held at Manchester at the end of the Second World War, was attended by the principal African leaders – Kenyatta, Nkrumah, Akintola, Nyerere, Banda. It voiced demands for independence which would have seemed totally unreal five years earlier. A mere ten years later West Africa was leading the way to independence from European rule.

In Accra, the capital of the British colony of the Gold Coast, there were riots in 1948 started by ex-servicemen in protest against high prices. The colonial authorities were taken by surprise, and a commission of inquiry produced a radical report which said in effect that the colony's newly proposed constitution was out of date before being introduced: to give Africans a majority of the seats in the legislative council was no longer enough. A new commission of Africans, with an African judge as chairman, was appointed to devise a new constitution. These developments coincided with the appearance of a new nationalist leader, Kwame Nkrumah who, aged probably 38, had returned to his country from the United States in 1947 and was determined to press for independence more energetically than older leaders such as J. B. Danquah. Nkrumah demanded immediate self-government. He seceded from Danquah's party, formed the Convention People's Party, earned the distinction of a prison sentence and won electoral victories in 1951, 1954 and 1956. After the first of these the British governor, Sir Charles Arden-Clarke, summoned him from prison and made him chief minister, thereby adopting the view that the colonial problem was not how to prolong colonialism, but how to make the best use of what time was left, to swim (not drift) with the tide and not uselessly to fight against it.

The British method, in the Gold Coast and elsewhere, was gradually to increase the elective and African elements in legislative and executive councils. Legislative councils in British territories progressed from assemblies dominated by appointed officials to assemblies containing a majority of elected members, and at the same time the governor's executive council was similarly transformed by the introduction into it of the leaders of the main party in the legislature. The governor retained at first extensive reserve powers but at a later stage this association between the colonial authority and nationalist movements was carried a stage further by converting the nationalist leader from the governor's chief minister into a prime minister of a self-governing territory. At this point the territory was on the verge of independence, and when independence was granted the governor disappeared. If the territory decided to remain in the Commonwealth, it might accept the British queen as its titular head with a governor-general as her representative on the spot, or it might become an independent republic within the Commonwealth but without any direct link with the British Crown. The new state would in any event establish diplomatic relations with the British government (as distinct from the British Crown) through representatives called high commissioners if the Commonwealth link were maintained, or ambassadors if it were not.

Given this method, the main problem was to regulate the pace. This was inevitably an uneven exercise in compromise between an irresistible flood and a removable power. The Gold Coast became self-governing in 1955, independent under the ancient name of Ghana in March 1957 and a republic in 1960. It led the way for Africans into the Commonwealth. Nkrumah, influenced by India's example, calculated also that the Commonwealth association would be a help to new states coming naked into international society.

The second West African state to become independent was French Guinea (1958). The French had been slower than the Spaniards or the Portuguese to enter Africa and less successful at first than the British or the Dutch. When in the seventeenth century they followed the new fashion their motive was emulation rather than any large expectation of gain. In the eighteenth century, however, they were participating in the slave trade on a big scale, extracting at one time as many as 100,000 slaves in a year, and after the abolition of the trade in 1815 and of slavery itself in 1848 (fourteen years after a similar prohibition in the British territories) French merchants turned from human goods to ivory and rubber and French explorers and missionaries began to penetrate inland and so stimulated ambitious dreams of a vast and compact empire stretching from the west coast to the Nile and from Morocco to the equator. In the event France acquired 3 million sq. km. by the end of the century, something between a fifth and a quarter of the whole continent. Almost the whole of the great African bulge came under French rule; it was formed into the governor-generalship of French West Africa in 1895 and comprised eventually eight separate colonies and, after 1945, the two trust territories of Togo and Cameroon. Four equatorial territories were similarly federated in 1910. Only in the valleys of the Niger and the Nile were the French worsted by the British. In 1900 French advances from Morocco in the north, from Senegal in the west and from the Congo in the south, where the great explorer de Brazza left his name, converged at Lake Chad. France also acquired in the First World War the enormous island of Madagascar; most of the German Cameroons, leaving a small slice which passed to the British who administered it with the eastern province of Nigeria; and half of Togoland, which was also originally German and was divided in 1919 between France and Britain as the owners of the adjacent territories of Dahomey and the Gold Coast.

After the fall of France in 1940 French West Africa opted for Vichy until the invasion of north-west Africa by the Americans and the British in 1942. An attempt by the Free French and the British to seize Dakar, the capital of Senegal, in 1940 failed. In Equatorial Africa, however, the governor-general Félix Eboué, a native of the Caribbean, took the Gaullist side in August 1940 and introduced a number of imaginative social and political reforms. At a conference at Brazzaville in 1944 the Africans were promised more participation in mixed Franco–African councils, more decentralization and a wider franchise.

The first French constitution of 1946 was liberal from the colonial point of view but it was rejected by the French people and the second constitution of that year was less far-reaching. It created the French Union, comprising the French Republic, Associated States and Associated Territories (there were also Overseas Departments and Overseas Territories, which were part of the French Republic). All the West and Equatorial African territories became Associated Territories with representatives in the French National Assembly and the Council of the Republic. Representative assemblies were also established in each territory with a grand council at federal level. From 1947 to 1954 France had a succession of predominantly conservative governments, but in 1956 the Mollet government, which included Gaston Defferre as minister for overseas territories, introduced a *loi cadre*, which was intended to lead to a substantial degree of internal autonomy by way of universal franchise, elected councils and the Africanization of public services. The *loi cadre* marked the abandonment of the policy of integration or assimilation in favour of a freer federation in which the African territories, while still associated with France, would increasingly order their own affairs and develop their own services and personalities. The *loi cadre* was elaborated by a series of decrees in 1957 which endowed the twelve West and Equatorial African territories with assemblies elected on a common roll and with councils of government elected by the assemblies. Considerable powers were reserved to the governors, the West or Equatorial high commissioners, or the metropolitan government, but nationalist demands had secured the elimination of special votes for whites and every constituency in every territory had a majority of black voters. The Rassemblement Démocratique Africain, the principal nationalist party which operated throughout French West Africa, won the ensuing elections in Guinea, Soudan, Ivory Coast and Upper Volta.

These political changes were, however, offset on the economic side where French policy remained integrationist and, in return for French aid and guaranteed markets in France, proposed to make French Africa a highly protected area serving French metropolitan economic interests. In the following years Africans became increasingly restless about economic policy in the franc zone. They claimed that a system which allowed free trade in the zone but erected barriers round it profited the stronger members rather than the weaker, impeded economic growth in the African territories, and prevented them from diversifying their economies. In addition the *loi cadre* accentuated differences among African leaders. Some, of whom Félix Houphouet-Boigny of the Ivory Coast was representative, seemed well satisfied with the French proposals, while others, among whom Sekou Touré of Guinea was the most eminent, suspected the *loi cadre* of being not a stage to sovereign independence but a device to postpone it indefinitely.

When de Gaulle returned to power in 1958 he faced the West Africans and Equatorial Africans with a choice: either autonomy within a *communauté* in which France would clearly retain control of the economic levers, or independence – which was a polite term for expulsion into a francless world. All but Guinea made the first choice. Guinea became an independent sovereign state in October 1958, humiliatingly discarded by its French mentors and forced to look to communist powers for the wherewithal to sustain its independence. The association was not a happy one and Touré was forced to change course (see Chapter 24) before he died in the United States in 1984 after a heart attack, his position already undermined by discontent which came to a head in a coup which put Colonel Lansana Conte in his place to cope with a legacy of repression, corruption and bankruptcy. Conte's position was strengthened by the failure of a counter-coup but he faced persistent popular grievances grounded in tribal rivalries and the standard IMF medicine administered to impecunious countries and swallowed with revulsion by its chief victims, the poor.

France's other West African colonies, which had chosen autonomy within the projected *communauté*, did not long remain content with their status. In 1959 Senegal, Soudan, Upper Volta and Dahomey decided to federate under the name of Mali and ask for independence. The two latter changed their minds under French pressure and although Senegal and Soudan persisted the resulting federation lasted only a couple of months, after which Senegal too withdrew leaving Soudan with the new name of Mali; it moved into the Guinea–Ghana orbit. The idea of a Mali federation had been unpopular not only in Paris but also among French African states further south, especially in the Ivory Coast where Félix Houphouet-Boigny riposted by forming with Niger and the detached Upper Volta and Dahomey an association called the Council of the Entente. The Entente then asked for independence by the beginning of 1960, which was conceded. Houphouet-Boigny wished to fortify the Entente by introducing dual nationality in it, but it was weakened by coups in Upper Volta and Dahomey in 1961 and by persistent suspiciousness in these and other states (including Togo which joined in 1966) of Houphouet-Boigny who was regarded as unduly hostile to Nkrumah and too partial to Tshombe in the Belgian Congo (see the next chapter). The net result of these centripetal and centrifugal forces was to solidify the several French colonies as independent sovereign states.

The independence of the Entente countries in 1960 deprived the *communauté* of any meaning although in theory it continued to exist as an association comprising France, Madagascar and the Equatorial states. These latter – Gabon, Chad, Ubangi-Shari and French Congo (the last two renamed the Central African Republic and Congo-Brazzaville) – produced a plan for a federation which was however abortive; they too became independent as separate sovereign states in 1960. In 1963 the Senegal River states (Senegal, Mali, Guinea and Mauritania) planned an association which was however frustrated by political differences: the notion was revived in the late sixties. The enduring association was the much bigger and looser OCAM (see Chapter 5).

The huge British territory of Nigeria also became independent in 1960, followed in 1961 by Sierra Leone, the British colony wedged between Guinea and Liberia, and in 1965 by the Gambia, the northernmost and last remaining British territory in West Africa, a narrow enclave within the embrace of Senegal. Of the trust territories in West Africa the French Cameroons and French Togoland became independent republics, while the British Cameroons and British Togoland were attached to Nigeria and Ghana respectively.

Spain and Portugal were slower to divest themselves. The Spanish island of Fernando Po in the Bight of Biafra – renamed Macias Nguema island – together with Rio Muni, an enclave in Gabon, became the independent state of Equatorial Guinea in 1968 and shortly thereafter a family autocracy. The Portuguese islands of Príncipe and São Tomé, 200 miles west of Gabon in the Gulf of Guinea, became independent in 1975. In Portuguese Guinea, or Guinea-Bissau, a liberation movement (PAIGC: African Party for the Independence of Guinea and the Cape Verde Islands) founded in 1956 by Amilcar Cabral, started a rising in 1959 and full-scale war in 1963, in the course of which the Guineans gradually established their control over the greater part of the country. In 1970 Portugal was implicated in an invasion of the neighbouring state of Guinea where PAIGC had its headquarters. An inquiry by the UN found that 350–400 invaders had been landed by ships manned by white men; the Security Council censured Portugal. In 1973 Cabral was murdered in the Guinean capital, Conakry. Guinea-Bissau and the Cape Verde islands became separate states in 1975 with plans for a union which was not consummated. The islands, ten of them 320 km from the mainland, provided sustenance for no more than a third of their inhabitants. They were isolated and kept politically stable by the tight control of a ruling group.

Each of these West African states experienced after independence one or more military coups. The tale of these coups is depressing. Twenty years after the main emancipation year (1960) the only original rulers still in power were Leopold Senghor in Senegal, Sekou Touré in Guinea and Houphouet-Boigny in Ivory Coast. Senghor – poet and scholar (the first African *agrégé*) before he was a statesman, a Christian leader of an overwhelmingly Muslim country, a leader in whom charisma was an addition to and not a substitute for intelligence, a president who abdicated voluntarily and peacefully after twenty-one years in power – made way in 1981 for Abdou Diouf who was confirmed in his position by a convincing electoral victory two years later but failed to stem sectarian rivalries, to escape the control of elderly and conservative local bosses, or to retrieve an economy overburdened by unwanted groundnuts and afflicted by drought. Unemployment rose, living standards fell, regional feuds and Islamic fundamentalism reared their heads. External debt charges rose to approximately half the national income, recourse to the IMF entailed painful austerity, and ventures such as phosphate plants, the Dakar shipyards and the Senegal River Plan languished. Diouf won further elections in 1988 by hook or crook but the disorders which followed obliged him to impose martial law. Senegal's relations with its neighbours Mauritania and the Gambia were uneasy, leading in the first case to undeclared war (see the preceding chapter). The Gambia was a stranger neighbour since it was entirely embraced within Senegal. This smallest of the British colonies in West Africa led at first an equable existence after independence. With an economy which enabled it to dispense with British aid after 1967, the Gambia experienced nothing worse than rubs in its attempts to work an 'association' with Senegal, but in 1981 President Dawda Jawara was saved from eviction only by the humiliating move of calling on Senegalese troops and by accepting confederation with Senegal – by which the Gambia hoped to have the benefits of independence and of partnership with a larger economy. But relations were soured by the prevalence of Gambian smuggling and Senegalese suspicions of Gambian intrigues among malcontent tribes in Senegal's southern province of Casamance. Disorders in this province, amounting to civil war, appeared to have also support from Mauritania and the adjacent Guinea-Bissau. In 1989 Senegal renounced plans for the integration of Senegal and the Gambia.

South of Senegal and south again of the Guinea Coast (Guinea and Guinea-Bissau) Sierra Leone was ruled by the brothers Margai until 1966 – Sir Milton until his death in 1964 and the more radical Sir Albert until his plans for constitutional changes cost him the elections of 1966. The army intervened briefly, chiefly in order to keep Siaka Stevens from power, but in 1968 Stevens became prime minister and in 1971 president of the newly proclaimed republic of Sierra Leone. Stevens turned the country into a one-party preserve, an economic catastrophe and a paradise for corrupt tycoons who sucked it dry while waiting for the aged Stevens to depart. He resigned in 1985 after seventeen years' rule and was succeeded by General Joseph Momoh with promises to end the corruption and misrule which had characterized the government of which he had himself been a member for over a decade. Momoh had difficulty in dissociating himself from the unsavoury pillars of the old régime, while the business world became a battlefield between old-established Lebanese operators and immigrant Israelis (backed in some cases by South Africa).

The eccentric history of Liberia, virtually an American preserve, was disrupted in 1980 by the violent removal of the dominant Tolbert family and the ruling True Whig Party by Sergeant, later General, Samuel Doe. Doe's support was tribal and although he survived for ten years, protected by an Israeli-trained guard and the Israeli secret service, he failed to establish his authority throughout the country. Economic disaster supplemented tribal animosities and in 1990 invasion from the north-east started a chain of massacres and civil war which culminated in Doe's capture and summary execution. The United States, which deplored Doe's demolition of the Tolbert régime but came to terms with him and used Liberia as an intelligence centre, cold-shouldered him when his rule became blatantly tyrannical and his prospects dim. Five West African states assembled a military force, predominantly Nigerian but commanded at first by a Ghanaian officer, to stop the fighting between the rebels and Doe beleaguered in the capital, and between rival sections of the rebel forces which were fighting one another. But the West African force failed to protect Doe who was seized and killed after taking refuge with it, and it then became involved in the fighting between the rival rebels. Protracted civil war caused anarchy and famine.

Ivory Coast, Liberia's neighbour, was by contrast the most successful of all West African states in the first decades after independence. Superposing good management on good fortune (a benign climate and no real desert) its government designed, first and foremost, to intensify and diversify the rural sector; secondly, to give measured encouragement to industrialization, including opportunities for private enterprise within a state-controlled system and assurances to foreign capitalists wishing to invest and earn a fair profit; and thirdly, to avoid heavy spending on defence and other forms of ostentation. As a result the national product grew steadily at the rate of 3 per cent a year and the average annual income of the country's 8 million people rose from less than $100 before independence to about $800 by 1980. But this average increase owed more to the rapid enrichment of the few than to the spread of prosperity to the many, and after 1980 growth faltered. Oil began to flow in 1984 but with limited effect on the economy, offsetting recession rather than enhancing growth. Collapsing cocoa prices, due to over-production worldwide, undermined the commodity which still in the eighties provided (with coffee) half of Ivorian foreign earnings, and this shortfall combined with high borrowing at high cost to create an economic crisis. In 1987 Ivory Coast suspended payment on its foreign debts (which amounted to 150 per cent of GDP) and exports of cocoa; two years later it halved the price paid to cocoa growers. Private businesses were owed more than $1 billion by the state and private banks were collapsing. Loans from the World Bank expiring in 1989 were not renewable and the country was not poor enough to qualify for special debt remissions. Cuts in public services and wages – the IMF demanded cuts up to 75 per cent in salaries in the public sector – provoked strikes and demonstrations but failed to rectify the country's deficits. As Houphouet-Boigny, confessedly 80 but nearer to 90, approached the end of his natural span he took few steps to ensure an orderly succession. A constitutional amendment introduced in 1980 had designated the vice-president as heir but nobody was appointed to that office and five years later Houphouet-Boigny announced that he would remain in office until he died. In 1990 he so far bowed to domestic anxieties and to the new wind of change in Africa as to sanction the formation of more than one political party, but his main concern in his declining years was the construction at unconscionable cost of a vast church in his native village and getting the Pope to sanctify it, which the Pope did. Houphouet-Boigny was re-elected president. Some two dozen parties, newly established, contrived to field only one candidate who nevertheless received 18 per cent of the votes cast in elections held under the control of, and not without manipulation by, the ruling party.

In Ghana, the pioneer of West African liberation, the personal leadership of Nkrumah turned into a febrile autocracy which passed step by step beyond a struggle to maintain the unity of the new state and a struggle to modernize it, and became perverted into a struggle to assert and preserve the authority of Nkrumah himself. Upon the attainment of independence Nkrumah had three principal aims. He wished to propagate his vision of African unity by accelerating the independence of other territories and consolidating the energies of Africans and Africanism in the service of African dignity and African effectiveness in the world; but his methods and his personality did not always commend him to other African leaders, whose own pan-Africanism was filtered through their several national experiences and ambitions. Like Nasser's pan-Arabism, Nkrumah's pan-Africanism was suspect. The exuberance and vigour which had contributed so much to make him the first ruler of a sub-Saharan African republic were drawbacks in a new situation which demanded the arts of diplomacy rather than the *élan* of leadership.

Nkrumah's second ambition was to make Ghana an efficient centralized and prospering state. This ambition was impeded by a complex of regionalism, conservatism and political jealousies and also by a serious drop in the world price of cocoa, Ghana's principal source of revenue. The Convention People's Party, whose main strength was in the coastal areas, was opposed by chiefs whom it regarded as a divisive and reactionary force and by the United Party led by K. A. Busia and J. E. Appiah. Nkrumah's increasingly dictatorial and suspicious manner alienated opinion at home and abroad. The illiberality evidenced, for example, by the removal of the chief justice after the delivery of an unpalatable verdict in a treason trial, coupled with increasing corruption and spendthriftness in the administration, destroyed Nkrumah's attempts to get foreign friends and finance and created a new opposition to him in the army which, by a bloodless coup in 1966, unseated him while he was away on a visit to China.

Thirdly, in the world at large Nkrumah wished to follow a policy of non-alignment. His circumstances were exceptionally favourable. Upon independence Ghana's resources and reserves – at £200 million the latter were larger than India's – gave it a material base for a measure of independence which might the more easily be maintained since the Cold War had not at that date reached Africa. But in practice Ghana under Nkrumah never achieved non-aligned status in the eyes of outsiders. For half of the period 1957–66 it appeared pro-western, for the other half pro-eastern. In the first years Nkrumah sought and got western capital for development, notably for the Volta River dam. Ghana remained in the Commonwealth and was visited in 1961 by Queen Elizabeth II, but the crisis in the Congo and particularly the murder of Lumumba, for which he blamed the west, turned Nkrumah against the western world, while the elaboration in theory and practice of his 'scientific socialism' with the inauguration in 1962 of a one-party system turned the western world against him. In contradistinction to Nasser's evident pragmatism, Nkrumah became increasingly ideological and illogical, evolving a form of economic planning akin to communist models but nevertheless dependent on western capital for its success.

Nkrumah wasted Ghana's enviable heritage and belied his own vision and ideals. He reduced the country to bankruptcy and initiated the corruption which no subsequent régime proved able to master. With one two-year interlude his fall was followed by four military governments of varying incapacity. The first of these, led by Colonel Ankrah, found that Nkrumah's extravagances had run the reserves down to £4 million and the external debt up to £279 million. Ghana also had a deficit on external account of £53 million. Colonel Ankrah and his colleagues made some improvements to this dismal tale before relinquishing power in 1969, but economic growth remained below 1 per cent a year, the population was increasing at an annual rate between 3.5 and 4 per cent, the standard of living had been cut by a severe devaluation and the first attempts of the new prime minister, Dr Kofi Busia, to secure an alleviation of the external debt were only moderately successful. By the beginning of 1972 Busia had been defeated by his predecessors' legacy, by an imprudently liberal policy which permitted an inflow of foreign goods which crippled the balance of payments, and by a drastic devaluation which doubled the external debt at a stroke. He was ousted while away in London and succeeded by any army committee calling itself the National Redemption Council under the chairmanship of Colonel I. K. Acheampong. This well-intentioned group struggled, not always harmoniously, with economic problems which were being aggravated by steep rises in the price of oil and other essential imports and by consequent rises in the cost of living. Ghana's creditors gave it some relaxation on the repayment of debts but not as much as it hoped for. By 1978 Acheampong's rule had become corrupt and ineffective. He was ousted by General F. W. K. Akuffo, who lasted less than a year against a rising tide of indignation. He too was removed and, together with Acheampong and six others, executed after a coup led by Flight-Lieutenant Jerry Rawlings, who promised to end corruption, reverse economic decline and restore civilian rule. In his three months in power he succeeded only in the last, completing an electoral process which had already been set in motion and which installed Dr Hilla Liman as president of a country with a collapsing economy and aggravated social tensions. At the end of 1981 Liman was ousted and Rawlings returned, struggled against the economic slide and sporadic plots and riots, pulled away from his more radical associates and introduced substantial deflation and a number of devaluations in order to get help from the IMF. Having attacked Liman for being willing to deal with the IMF and having failed to get economic aid elsewhere Rawlings switched to a policy of IMF-led growth and had some qualified success: inflation fell from 100 to 20 per cent, the budget was balanced and growth reached 6 per cent. But revenues from cocoa and timber declined (gold sales, however, went up); foreign debt remained a throttling burden; the cost of imported oil, which had quintupled in the decade preceding Rawlings's return, absorbed nearly half the country's foreign earnings; the devaluation of the cedi in 1983 from 2.75 to 1.62 to the dollar caused great distress; promises of an early return to civilian rule and of popular consultation were not kept; the ruling Provisional National Defence Council was a clique with good intentions but no sound constitutional standing; opposition in politics or in the administration became a road to jail but this treatment did not deter Rawlings's enemies at home and abroad (mostly in Ivory Coast and Togo) from keeping up their intrigues against him. The justification for these tribulations and stringencies would be the attraction of foreign capital but the issue – and the outcome therefore of Rawlings's economic strategy – remained uncertain. He had forfeited the support of radicals, introduced measures which hurt the many more than they hurt the few at the top, and risked the disgruntlement of junior officers which had kindled more than one coup in Ghana's history. Such a coup in 1989, although unsuccessful, was the more ominous for coming from his own Ewe people.

In Togo, where the first president Sylvanus Olympio was assassinated in 1963 and the second Nicolas Grunitzky displaced a few years later, Gnassingbe Eyadema maintained himself in power against substantial – largely regional and ethnic – unpopularity and frequent plots, some of which may have been invented for tactical purposes. In adjacent Dahomey, renamed Benin in 1972, a country living under the shadow of Nigeria and without jobs or resources, the military were in and out of government, displacing one civilian president and installing another until in 1970 they forced three past presidents to work together on a rota system which proved to be no more than a two-year interlude before military rule. In 1972 Colonel Matthieu Kerekou seized power, survived a series of attempts against his life – including one in 1977 allegedly launched from Togo with French, Moroccan and Gabonese help – was re-elected in 1984 and (narrowly) in 1989, made a tour of communist capitals including Beijing (1986) and then turned cautiously back to the French connection. The opposition to his rule, was divided, consisting of young people without jobs, junior officers without promotion, unions, and ethnic rivals in the south. He saw his country become a small exporter of oil and also an entrepôt for drugs from Asia to the west. But by 1990 his days seemed numbered.

Behind the arc of relatively small states stretching from the mouth of the Senegal River almost to the mouth of the Niger lay three large, arid and landlocked countries: Mali, Burkina Faso (formerly Upper Volta and the smallest of the three) and Niger. In Mali Modibo Keita, one of the architects of the abortive Malian federation, was ousted in 1968 by General Moussa Traore who in his search for foreign aid vacillated between the communist states of Europe and Asia (which he visited in 1986) and the readier, if unpalatable, succour of the IMF. Part of Mali's pre-independence inheritance was a border dispute with Burkina Faso which was aggravated after Captain Thomas Sankara took power there in 1983 (ousting a three-year-old cilivian régime which had succeeded the earlier military régime of General Saye Zerbo). Sankara was attractively young and honest but his authority rested on an amalgam of discordant elements. He developed good relations with Benin and projected a union with Ghana but this trend alarmed Mali which launched a small, short and ill-conducted war in 1985. Two years later Sankara was murdered and succeeded by a close friend and colleague Blaise Compaore, less radical than Sankara and more autocratic. Besides its troubles with Burkina Faso, Mali had troubles to the north from the Tuaregs, Berber desert-dwellers who lived also in Niger, Algeria and Libya and entertained dreams of secession from Mali which led to fighting in 1963–64 and again in 1990.

Niger too suffered plots and disorders, generally instigated by military dissatisfaction with the efficiency or honesty of civilian rule. These coups were effected with the minimum of violence and amounted to an accepted, if not very satisfactory, way of changing a government which had failed but which had no ready-made successor in a one-party state without adequate machinery for changing the government in any other way. Niger's first ruler, Hamami Diori, had won his position with strong French help against a rival, Djibo Bakary, who leaned rather to the left and also to the Islamic north of the country. During the civil war in Nigeria Diori supported the central government in defiance of France's support for Biafra and he paid the price in 1974 when the army turned him out: a drought in the previous year, extreme even by Niger's standards, had weakened his position. His successor Seyne Kountche remained president until his death in 1987. He was followed by Colonel Ali Seybou who would, it was hoped, display a less offensive life style than Kountche but did not. Niger's uranium made it a cynosure of persistent French attention so long as uranium was believed to a scarce mineral.

Skipping for the moment West Africa's most important country, Nigeria, the southward route leads to three more ex-French colonies and another landlocked empire. In Cameroun – a relatively successful adjuster of linguistic and ethnic tensions – France intervened to sustain the friendly government of Ahmadu Ahidjo against a revolt whose causes were mainly economic. Ahidjo resigned suddenly in 1982, to be succeeded by Paul Biya who proved to be disappointingly ineffective. Sharp falls in the prices of Cameroun's principal exports – coffee, cocoa, cotton – produced crippling debt, left public servants unpaid, encouraged corruption and smuggling, dictated recourse to the IMF and austerity, and stimulated political in-fighting which Biya failed to master.

In Gabon high hopes turned to disillusion. Potentially one of the richest states in Africa Gabon was ruled by President Leon M'Ba (deposed in 1963 but restored by French troops) and Albert Bongo (1967–90), who changed his first name to Omar upon converting to Islam in 1973 and completed the country's transition to a one-party state. In spite of its natural wealth Gabon was struck by economic crisis in the seventies and eighties, so that the government had to levy a forced loan on salaries and re-schedule its foeign debts as the only way to avoid default. Serious riots in 1990 forced Bongo to introduce a multiparty system faster than he would have liked. After elections in which his party, the Parti Democrate Gabonais, comfortably outpaced its challengers he formed a new government of six parties, the PDG retaining the principal ministries but taking only a minority of places in the cabinet.

In Congo-Brazzaville the first president, Fulbert Yalou, was overthrown by revolution, France refusing to intervene to save him in a situation which it recognized as one of genuine and well-founded popular indignation. Alphonse Massemba-Debat and then Marien Ngouabi took the country to the left but the latter was assassinated in 1977 and the former shortly afterwards executed. President Denis Sassou-Nguesso of the Parti Congolais du Travail kept both pro-Chinese and pro-Russian parties down but not wholly out. His ill-planned use of public funds and extravagant spending on projects of little merit, coinciding with falls in oil production and the oil price, debilitated the economy, encouraged a self-defeating drift to the towns, exacerbated ethnic rifts and increased imports and foreign debt. When the army refused to quell riots in 1985 the presidential guard had to be used and created a number of martyrs in the course of saving the president.

In the landlocked Central African Republic a coup by Colonel Jean-Bedel Bokassa, similar in its origins to military coups in Burkina Faso, Benin and Niger, led however to enormities when the colonel declared himself emperor and went to insane lengths of ostentation and cruelty. France, after becoming embarrassingly closely associated with one of the period's most indecent tyrannies, assisted with its overthrow in 1979. An attempt by Bokassa in 1983 to return failed.

Nigeria, huge and diverse, was a twentieth-century creation. The colonies of Lagos and South Nigeria were united by the British in 1906. The former was the home of the Yoruban whose society was based partly on tribal chiefs and partly on cultivated cities. The dominant people in the latter were the Ibo who had neither chiefs nor cities but were therefore the more easily united as a nation and displayed a thrusting vigour which carried many of them long distances from their homes in eastern Nigeria and into the western and northern parts of the federation created by the British when, in 1914, they joined northern Nigeria to the two southern colonies.

The north was in a state of flux when the British reached it at the end of the nineteenth century. Early in that century the Islamicized Fulani had established their authority over a medley of pre-existing Hausa states of very varying size and had so created the empire of Usuman dan Fodio and his descendants. Conflict between Fulani and Hausa and others persisted and the British assumed the task of mastering it as a prelude to uniting all their territories in this part of the world, but the federation which they created was an uneasy amalgam of states and cultures without a national consciousness or unity. After the Second World War the southern half of the country pressed for independence, while the north hesitated for fear of being reduced to dependence on the south with its coastal windows on the outside world's commerce, skills and manners. The north even toyed with the idea of a separate state with access to the sea either down a river corridor along the Niger or through Dahomey or the Cameroons on the one side or the other. Before independence, riots with racial and religious overtones gave manifest warning of the dangers which the new state would run, but the advantages of unity seemed to make the experiment worthwhile and in 1960 Nigeria became independent with a constitution based on three regions. The federal premiership went to a northerner, Sir Abubakr Tafewa Balewa. The eastern leader, Namdi Azikiwe, became president and his party co-operated with the principal northern party in the government at the centre. It was Azikiwe's belief that a country as big and heterogeneous as Nigeria could only be governed by a coalition of all its main groups within a federal structure, but the western leader, Chief Obafemi Awolowo, preferred to form an opposition in the federal parliament.

The accord between east and north did not last long, nor did the cohesion of the west. The Iboe annoyed their northern partners by trying to win parliamentary seats in the northern region. In the west Chief Akintola challenged Awolowo and succeeded in getting him and other leaders tried and imprisoned. Akintola was not satisfied with Awolowo's policy of forming an opposition at the federal level. He preferred a policy of alliance with the north, displacing the Iboe and getting for his own people a share in the power, perquisites and finances of central government. In 1963 a fourth, mid-western region was formed. In 1964 a census showed a total population for the whole country of 55.6 million, of which 29.8 million were in the north – more than half. This demographic preponderance of the north increased the attractions of an alliance with the leaders of that region and, together with charges that the census had been faked, also increased political tensions. Elections in the western region in 1965 produced allegations of flagrant malpractice and fighting. In the next year more serious fighting began in the north.

In January 1966 a group of young Ibo officers rebelled, partly in protest against bad government and partly as a demonstration against the north and its allies in the west. The federal and northern prime ministers, Sir Abubakr Balewa and the Sardauna of Sokoto, were murdered along with Chief Akintola and many more, but senior officers stepped in quickly to arrest further developments and the junior officers. A comparatively senior officer, General Johnson Ironsi, was proclaimed head of state with the mission of keeping the country from breaking up and providing competent and honest administration. General Ironsi was an Ibo. He was well intentioned but not otherwise well equipped for the delicate task of holding the country together and when in July he incautiously suggested that a unitary constitution might be better for Nigeria than a federal one, northern fears of attempted Ibo dominance flared up into another coup and he was murdered in his turn. He was replaced by Colonel Yakubu Gowon, a northern Christian, who released a number of imprisoned civilians, including Awolowo, and expressed the usual hopes for an early return to civilian rule. In September a conference at Lagos agreed on a loose fourfold federal structure, but it coincided with a counter-massacre of Iboe in the north (there had been a similar, though less severe, massacre in May) and the flight of the survivors back to the eastern region.

After the first coup in 1966 Lieutenant-Colonel Odumegwu Ojukwu had been appointed military governor of the eastern region. He now concluded that the salvation of the Iboe could only be secured by secession from Nigeria. Dissuaded from taking this step at a conference in January 1967 at Aburi in Ghana, he nevertheless proclaimed in May the independent state of Biafra and civil war began. Attempts at mediation by the OAU (at Kinshasa in 1967, Algiers in 1968 and Addis Ababa in 1969) all broke down. The federal army, expanded from 10,000 to over 200,000 men, gradually prevailed in spite of the toughness of Biafran resistance. While Britain and the USSR supplied arms to the federal government, France supplied Biafra (thereby perhaps somewhat prolonging the war) and two of France's closest African associates, Ivory Coast and Gabon, recognized the secessionist state – as too did Zambia and Tanzania – in attempts to stop the killing. The suffering in Biafra, overcrowded and virtually besieged, was appalling and widely reported throughout the world. By January 1970 it had become decisive. In that month Biafra was forced to capitulate and, as such, ceased to exist. Gowon proved a statesmanlike victor. He preached reconciliation and practised it. Nigeria's economic growth was resumed at a great pace. It became one of the world's largest producers and exporters of oil, besides being rich in coal, tin and other minerals, and in agriculture. But the government was none the less overspending its revenues and internal problems were not washed away by this wealth. The rich got richer and the poor mostly stayed poor or, with inflation, got poorer. The huge army and a large police force of 30,000 became notorious for corruption, as did the more affluent sectors of civilian life. There were strikes and unemployment. The constitutional problem was unsolved. After the civil war the country was divided into twelve states (later increased to nineteen) but Gowon incautiously indicated that there might be more, on an ethnic basis which, if seriously applied, could produce up to 300–400 states. The census of 1973 returned a total population of 79.76 million, a growth of 43.5 per cent since 1963 and an average annual increase double that of the fastest growing populations in the world. Nobody believed the figures although some people in some areas liked them. The fact that increases varied widely and suspiciously from state to state forced Gowon to say that they would not be used as a basis for any political decisions. By 1974 it was announced to the relief of many Nigerians that the return to civilian rule promised for 1976 would be postponed. Gowon's too evident inability to grasp the nettle of corruption led to his displacement in 1975 while he was out of the country. He was allowed to go with his family to England. His successors Generals Murtala Mohammed (assassinated after a few months) and Olesugun Obasanjo were more vigorous in their attacks on corruption and other problems. The latter promised to restore civilian rule in 1979 and after prolonged constitutional debate which produced the bulkiest constitution in the world Alhaji Shehu Shagari became president of a new federation of nineteen states.

Nigeria was a giant among African states in more than size. It had wealth. It was among the first half-dozen oil producers in the world and had a GNP at the end of the seventies of about $35 billion ($460 per head) and a growth rate of 6–7 per cent a year. At its peak in 1974–76 oil production exceeded 2 million barrels a day. But this bonanza engendered an orgy of activity which got out of control. Nigerian oil, exceptionally expensive to produce, happened to come into world markets in large quantities in the same period as Alaskan and North Sea oil, with the result that demand slackened, the price had to be cut and production held back to 1.5 million barrels: the balance of payments, which had shown a surplus of over 4 million naira in 1974, went suddenly into the red in 1977, reserves fell by two-thirds and inflation rose to 40 per cent a year. But Nigeria's credit remained high and it was able to borrow large sums to put it back on to sounder courses. Its basic problem was not how to balance its books but how to apply its enviable revenues. It was at this stage an immensely wealthy country whose inhabitants nevertheless saw nothing of this wealth but continued to live in a colonial, mainly agricultural, society which was using no more than half its cultivable land and, as a result of neglect, inefficiency and incompetent investment, was importing food instead of exporting it. The country was also frighteningly lawless and blatantly corrupt; its ethnic divisions and mistrusts had not evaporated; its army (although reduced from 230,000 to about half that number in 1980) was an expensive and unsettling legacy of civil war. But it was a measure of the new civilian government's resources and optimism that it felt able to produce a five-year plan for 1981–85 which aimed to make Nigeria self-sufficient in food and manufactured goods by the end of that period.

Both the outgoing military régime and its civilian successor intended Nigeria to play a positive part in African affairs, perhaps in world affairs too. It forced its way on to the Security Council in 1976 against the candidature of a fellow African state (and neighbour) nominated by the OAU. It put a lot of energy and money into the 1976 Festival of African Arts in Lagos, a prestige jamboree which partially rebounded because of organizational chaos and scandals about overspending. It so dominated the Economic Organization of West African States (ECOWAS) that this organization would have been boneless without Nigeria. Lagos became a necessary port of call for British, American and other politicians trying to resolve the Rhodesian crisis. As a member of the OAU, the Commonwealth and OPEC, as well as the UN, Nigeria was active in a unique sample of international organizations.

On the last day of 1983 the army returned to power. Major–General Mahommad Buhari became head of state in place of President Shagari. There were many reasons for an upheaval which displeased few Nigerians: blatantly rigged elections in the previous August; even more blatant corruption; soaring food prices; an economy no longer buoyed up by oil whose price had been cut by 10 per cent and production by nearly 25 per cent; interminable constitutional wrangles; religious disorders in the north, notably in Kano where thousands were killed in suppressing riots by the Muslim Maitatsine at the end of 1980 and again in Borno and Gongola states in 1982 and 1984 respectively. The new government was akin to its predecessor, conservative and pledged to produce prosperity without corruption. For some, including junior officers waiting their turn and Muslims of a puritan turn of mind, it was too like the Shagari régime with too many of the same businessmen and chiefs in the seats of federal and provincial power. It was threatened within a few months by rumours of fresh coups which were suspected by some of being fabricated in order to enable the government to forestall action from within the army's middle ranks, dissatisfied by dilatory measures against the profiteers of the previous régime. When the government did take action it bungled. The most notorious of the alleged profiteers, Umaru Dicko, had taken refuge in London where he was kidnapped by three Israelis and a Nigerian with ill-concealed Nigerian government involvement and more than a little suspicion of official Israeli participation: this coup was foiled when British police extracted Dicko from a packing case in which he was about to be flown to Nigeria.

The Buhari government was an all-round failure. It denounced corruption without abating it, savaged criminals without reducing crime, intensified economic austerity without any countervailing benefits and forwent needed aid from the IMF (to bolster its foreign creditworthiness) by refusing to devalue the naira. To its neighbours it was no improvement on its predecessor. Both expelled large numbers of immigrants who had flocked to Nigeria to find work and both reduced ECOWAS to near inanition: ECOWAS was either a way of sharing wealth and enterprises in the region or it was nothing, and a few improvements in transport systems and freer trade did not suffice to alter the complexion of the area as a cluster of separate and disparate economies whose inequalities and inefficiencies could not be improved by a dominant Nigeria beset by political and economic instability. Further afield the Buhari government irritated its partners in OPEC when, like Britain and Norway, it cut its oil prices but without giving OPEC notice in advance: oil revenues had sunk to half their 1980 value and the Buhari government was nervously aware of the part played by oil in the decline and destruction of the Shagari government. Within two years Buhari was evicted by one of the principal members of his governing council, General Ibrahim Babangida, a recurrent figure in Nigeria's political crises but one who had hitherto avoided the first place and its responsibilities.

Babangida's main tasks were to rescue the economy, restore civilian rule within a reasonable time and prevent Nigeria's regional conflicts from turning into a religious war between north and south, Muslims and Christians. Nigeria's economic problems arose not from lack of resources but from its over-optimistic use of a single source of wealth (oil) whose value had suddenly plummeted for reasons outside Nigeria's control. The collapse of the oil boom stunned Nigeria the more forcibly because it had been riding so high on the crest of the wave that was now spent. With the end of the boom the naira was floated and lost 70 per cent of its value. Inflation, wage freezes and penal interest rates hit both the poor and the flocks of *nouveaux riches* born of the boom. Average income per head dropped in five years from over $1,000 to $250. Babangida needed to restore confidence within Nigeria and to recapture international confidence and funds, but his attempts to do so evoked strong criticism from those – including Obasanjo – who inveighed against an economic policy which made the poor poorer and gamblers richer without reversing industrial recession. As a prelude to the restoration of civilian rule a constituent assembly was elected in 1987 with, however, strictly limited competence: it was precluded from considering the federal principle, the two-party system, the ban of former politicians, or religion. Babangida's confidence in himself was shown by two striking acts in 1989. When an electoral commission approved six political parties from which the government would select two, Babangida rejected all six and licensed two others of his own devising. Secondly, he intervened decisively in the succession in the sultanate of Sokoto. The death in 1988 of the aged sultan provoked a politico-religious tangle which developed into an issue in relations between the sultanate and the federal government. A son of the deceased sultan was proclaimed sultan in his father's place but the government interposed a veto and appointed instead an eminent Muslim, Ibrahim Dasuki, a direct descendant by a junior line of Usman dan Fodio. No less disturbing than these economic, constitutional and religious problems was one other: demography. A population of 118 million in 1990 was projected to reach more than twice that total within thirty years in the absence of birth controls, of which there was only the most modest prospect. This was a problem widespread in Africa but peculiarly alarming in Nigeria which would on existing trends become one of the most crowded countries in the world and drastically short of food, schools, hospitals and other crucial services.

A quarter of a century of political instability, economic disaster and misrule left West Africa with the independence which it had won from the colonial powers but few of the anticipated fruits of independence. Spirits were low, expectations reduced, disappointments bitter, tempers frayed. A number of the states of West Africa hoped to alleviate their economic plight through federal associations among themselves. Sixteen of them created in 1975 an Economic Community of West African States (ECOWAS), a halfway house between national sovereignties and the continental OAU. The first aims were to increase trade between the members and to fund co-operative developments in agriculture, communications and education, with further economic co-operation to follow. Nigeria's affluence gave the members hope but Nigeria's power gave them pause, more especially the francophone members, six of which created a community within a community: CEAO – Communauté de l'Afrique de l'Ouest. (CEAO had counterparts in Central Africa in CEEAC – Communauté Economique des Etats de l'Afrique Centrale – and UDEAC – Union Douanière et Economique de l'Afrique Centrale – whose names sufficiently indicated their ambitions. All six members of the latter belonged to the former, whose ten members included English and Portuguese states as well as French speakers.) France established with its former colonies a special relationship from which they derived some economic stability and France a continuing influence. France underwrote the new states' currencies by undertaking to exchange them at the fixed rate of 50 to 1, but with time the French franc became on this basis extravagantly undervalued, labour became more and more expensive, French investment was diverted to anglophone countries where real rates of exchange prevailed, and a busy trade grew up in smuggling goods to francophone countries in return for local currencies convertible into French francs at the fixed rate. As the cost of supporting ailing economies in this way became unacceptable France considered discarding the system in favour of closer links with Nigeria and ECOWAS.

The members of both ECOWAS and CEAO concluded also defence

agreements: ECOWAS in 1981, Mali, Guinea-Bissau and Cape Verde abstaining; and CEAO by stages from 1977, Togo joining the original six. The signatories of CEAO's defence pact were divided between some who regarded it as a first step to getting rid of French troops from West Africa and others who were far from ready to approve such a step. These defence arrangements were of much less consequence than economic agreements. The economic agreements were on the other hand hampered by the inescapably worldwide nature of the problems which they addressed.

West Africa's political problems were largely home grown and blamed on the new rulers. The colonial past bore some responsibility, but a receding one. Colonialism had by its very nature destroyed the ruling class and its institutions. Even where the colonial rulers practised indirect rule and so made use of the indigenous system, this system and its protagonists were downgraded. Moreover the new nationalists who led the successful campaigns for independence – unlike the leaders of the National Congress in India which had been founded in the nineteenth century – had minimal experience of government and precarious authority. Their authority was personal. It derived from charisma or rank, so that the choice for the people, so far as they had a choice, lay between the demagogue and the general. Some were good and some were bad, but all lacked systematic political backing and they were obliged therefore to rely on their wits or their swords. The natural outcome was either an entrenched tyranny or constant shifts. In West Africa, which was in this respect distinct from most of the rest of the continent, there was more instability than tyranny. Freedoms were curtailed or abused on the plea that the autocrat or the one-party state would be more efficient, but such régimes failed to deliver the goods.

West Africa – and in this respect its lot was repeated through most of sub-Saharan Africa – saw a modest economic advance in the sixties, checked in the seventies and reversed in the eighties. In the course of the twentieth century Africa's population was multiplied by nearly ten (from 100 million to an expected 1,000 million or not much less) and it moved into cities. The demand for food created by the first of these trends was magnified by the second, as the migrants became non-producing consumers of food. The countryside became denuded, the cities insanitary and dangerous. The food deficit was further aggravated by the post-independence view that the road to prosperity was industrialization. The application of this nostrum created more debt than success, exposed the lack of adequate managers and fanned the corruption inherent in a chase after contracts. Aid was misused and often the misuse was encouraged by ignorant or greedy donors. Industrial and commercial failures were visited on other sectors: roads, schools and universities decayed and health deteriorated. Only half the children went to school; half the teachers were unqualified. Corruption in business was barely severable from corruption in government which extended to bullying the judiciary and the press. Wars, drought, famine and adverse terms of trade in a world governed by the wealthier countries made matters worse. Foreigners turned their backs on investment in Africa and ignored its tourist attractions. Yet much of the continent possessed excellent agricultural land, valuable minerals and plentiful sources of energy. The economic balance sheet was not wholly negative but the remedies for centuries in an economic backwater, followed by decades of bad policies and bad government, required harsh sacrifices which must fall mainly on the numerous poor, making them not only poorer but also ill-disposed to trust their governments. The IMF's and the World Bank's recipe for salvation was two-edged. On the one hand these institutions provided funds but on the other they required devaluation of currencies, liberalization of trade and increases in productivity which more often than not could be achieved only by sacking people, raising prices and cutting services. This was medicine which cured the community by killing its members. Plans to offset the painful side-effects were, again more often than not, either feeble or sidestepped. The World Bank, in a review in 1989 of the well-known ills of poor agricultural performances, industrial decline and excessive debt, noted their political as well as their economic sources – the precariousness of the rule of law, the absence of a free press – and the Bank edged towards a policy of paying more attention to competence and democracy in the allocation of loans. Such observations are applicable to many countries outside Africa. Analogies may be found in every continent but the African case stands out both because of Africa's wide extent and because of the disheartening chasm between the hopes and experiences of so many people in the aftermath of their independence. As the last decade of the century dawned new trends appeared. The end of the Cold War blunted American interest, never strong, in Africa; tribal mistrusts, half suppressed for a generation, became more obtrusive; and one party rule was losing ground although with what effect on standards of living and behaviour remained uncertain.

21 FROM CONGO TO ZAÏRE

West Africa became independent without anything that could be called an international crisis. East Africa was to follow suit in the next few years. But the independence of the Belgian Congo produced not only internal chaos and civil war but also one of the principal international crises of the postwar period, in which major powers were brought to the brink of a confrontation. African states were divided among themselves, and the United Nations was called upon to play expected and unexpected roles in the course of which it was attacked by some of its principal members, its secretary-general was killed and its very existence was called in question. The sources of this catastrophe were, first, the hurriedness with which the Belgians took their departure from a colony which they had hardly at all prepared for independence; secondly, the very great size of the Congo and its ethnic and tribal diversity; thirdly, the revolt immediately after independence of the Force Publique or army, whose mutinous conduct left the new central government powerless; next, the attempt to detach the rich southern province of Katanga and make it a separate state; and finally, the fact that the United Nations was required to perform a multiplicity of barely consistent tasks and was hampered in them by the inadequacies of its own machinery and by the hostility and independent actions of certain governments, notably the Russian and the British.

The Congo is a large country of over a million square miles inhabited by many different tribes, some of which constitute tribal federations. The most prominent of these are the Bakongo in the west, including the capital of Leopoldville, and also in the neighbouring territories of Angola and Congo-Brazzaville; the Baluba in southern Kasai and northern Katanga; and the Balunda in southern Katanga. In spite of its great size the Congo touches the ocean only at the end of a corridor between Congo-Brazzaville and Angola, and its modern history begins with the ventures of explorers along the Congo River. It became famous as a result of H. M. Stanley's expedition in 1874 and was at once an object of international competition among the principal European powers. Britain, already well-endowed and also busy elsewhere, did not enter the lists on its own account but pushed the claims of its old friend, Portugal. France and the three-year-old German empire were not so altruistic and in 1876 an international conference reached a temporary compromise by creating the International African Association which was to act as a sort of composite cultural mission to enlighten the darkest heart of Africa and find out what was there. This conference met, not by accident, in Brussels and was convened by the Belgian king Leopold II.

The International African Association did not eliminate the ambitions and manoeuvres of the European powers, and in the early 1880s there was widespread fear of war as a result of their jealousies and claims in West Africa from the Niger down to the Congo. In 1884 a conference in Berlin, engineered and presided over by Bismarck, sorted things out on the basis that there was enough for everybody and no need to fight: Europeans would do best to recognize one another's possessions and tacitly sanction in advance further acquisitions of anything not yet under a European flag. The Congo was handed over to the Congo International Association which was the International African Association under a new name, and in effect Leopold II in person. The king thus became the largest private estate owner in the world, although he did not yet know how rich his property was. His obligations were to extirpate the slave trade, permit free trade and secure free passage for all on the Congo River. He defaulted in his first obligation until an outcry in Britain and elsewhere compelled him to abolish the trade – and to resort to forced labour instead. His administration of his estate became one of the most notorious scandals since Cicero's denunciation of the proconsulship of Verres, and in 1908 the Congo was transferred from Leopold to the Belgian state which despatched a governor-general to rule with the help of a Belgian civil service. The interests of Africans were to have priority over the exploitation of the domain but this principle was not in practice found to involve any advancement for Africans or any but the most rudimentary mingling of the races.

Shortly before the First World War the mining of copper in Katanga began and brought with it two potent changes. Katanga gradually became twice as rich as the whole of the rest of the Congo; should the Congo ever become independent the Katangans would be in a position to demand first place in the state or to leave it and set up on their own. The second and more immediate change was the transformation of the territory into a booming partnership between the administration, Belgian finance houses and the Roman Catholic Church. And so it remained for nearly half a century. Some attention was paid to the economic well-being of the Africans but no political activity was tolerated and education above the elementary level was reserved for very few. In so far as Belgians thought about the future they imagined a slow advance by Africans to a level at which a new form of association might have to be devised, but a transfer of power to Africans did not enter into their calculations and so no steps were taken to train even an élite. So far as any practical man needed to see the Congo would remain as shut off from the rest of the world as Japan before the Meiji restoration.

This view began to be questioned in the fifties. The missionaries became alive to the pressures of nationalism and uneasy therefore about the assumptions on which the territory was being ruled by the church and its associates. In Brussels, where a left-wing coalition came to power in 1954, the liberation of French and British territories could not be ignored; de Gaulle's offer of autonomy in 1958 was made at Brazzaville just across the river from Leopoldville. African leaders, some of whom met one another for the first time at the Brussels Fair of 1958, began to espouse independence in place of a somewhat less gradual evolution, and in December 1958 many of them attended the Pan-African Conference in Accra where they received encouragement from fellow Africans and were reinforced in their determination not to get left behind. A few days after the end of the Accra conference there were riots in Leopoldville.

The Belgians had recently appointed as governor-general Maurice van Hemelrijk who believed that an acceleration was the only possible policy. He advocated a parliament for the Congo by the end of 1960 and independence in 1963 (reduced, by the end of 1959, to independence in 1960). but van Hemelrijk was forced by conservative protests in Belgium to resign in September 1959. His successor, Auguste de Schryver, found he had to go even faster. Tribal fighting began before the end of the year and in January 1960 the Belgians assembled in Brussels a conference at which, to their surprise, the Africans unitedly asked for immediate independence. The Belgians agreed to leave the Congo at the end of June. Never had so much been conceded so quickly. The frontiers of the new state were to be the same as those of the colony, and when Sir Roy Welensky suggested that Katanga should leave the Congo and join the Rhodesian federation, the Belgian government was much displeased. The internal structure of the new state, whether it should be military or federal, was however left undecided, while the distribution of top posts was also unsettled pending elections which were held in May. The Belgians made some attempt to remedy their sins of omission by running a crash training programme in Brussels for Africans and by enlisting Ghanaian help in the training of more Africans in the Congo.

At this time the most prominent of the Congolese politicians, and the favourite of the Belgians, was Patrice Lumumba, one of the founders in 1958 of the Mouvement National Congolais which was the main non-tribal party in the Congo. Lumumba and his principal associates, who included Cyrille Adoula and Joseph Ileo, demanded the Africanization of public services and professions with a view to ultimate independence. At the Accra conference Lumumba struck up a friendship with

Nkrumah and, although he became more extreme in his demands during 1959 and was eventually imprisoned, he retained his good standing with the Belgians until the eve of independence. He wanted a strong centre rather than a diffuse federation, in contradistinction to his opponents who were essentially the modern equivalents of tribal and local chieftains: Joseph Kasavubu, the more sedate and aristocratic leader of Abako which was founded in 1950 among the Bakongo with the aim of restoring the old Kongo empire but which became converted to the idea of a Congo state provided it was a federal one; Moise Tshombe, the rich middle-class *évolué* and leader of Conakat through which the Balunda aimed to exercise power in Katanga either within a federal Congo or independently; and Jason Sendwe, whose Balubakat eyed the Balunda to the south with considerable suspicion and prevented Conakat from speaking for the whole of Katanga. Lumumba's tendency to quarrel with other leaders in his own party, and a change of attitude in Brussels, led to attempts to create an anti-Lumumba front, but the attempts failed, Lumumba's party emerged from the elections as the biggest and Lumumba was installed as prime minister of a broad coalition government with Kasavubu as president.

Independence was proclaimed on 30 June 1960 and the official celebrations lasted for four days. Forty-eight hours later there occurred the first mutinies in the Force Publique which sparked off a train of terrible disasters. The soldiers seem to have expected that independence would instantly improve their pay and open their way to the officer grades, which were entirely filled by white men. When nothing happened, they decided to replace their officers. This indiscipline was accompanied by a certain amount of violence and some rapes, much multiplied in the telling. An African sergeant, Victor Lundula, was appointed commander-in-chief and the situation seemed to have been brought under control in a couple of days. But fresh mutinies and more serious violence quickly followed; there was, however, no killing until after Tshombe's proclamation of the independence of Katanga on 11 July.

The mutiny of the Congolese army was the source of all the Congo's woes. It deprived the Congolese government of power and authority. It caused a panic among Europeans, and the Belgians announced that, with or without Congolese consent, they would return to protect their nationals. Tshombe unilaterally asked for Belgian help and declared Katanga independent. The long-term consequences of this action will be examined below. The immediate consequence was to humiliate and infuriate Lumumba who became suspicious of a Katangan–Belgian plot to subvert the independence of the new state and disrupt it by detaching its richest province. Subsequent events successively strengthened his suspicions. Although he remained for a time willing to discuss with the Belgians the maintenance of law and order, he was not willing to do what Tshombe had done and ask for their help in suppressing the mutinies. Since there was no other force immediately available to him, this rift between Lumumba and the Belgians enabled the mutinies to spread and take hold. At the same time the rift between Lumumba and Tshombe made Lumumba more anxious to maintain than to disarm the Congolese army with the result that when UN forces arrived to restore order Lumumba dissuaded them from taking the essential step of disarming the mutinous units.

These were not the only consequences. The Belgians, who occupied Leopoldville with parachute troops on 11 July, in effect abrogated their recently signed treaty of friendship with the Congo and switched to Tshombe, whom they provided with a Belgian armed force and commander-in-chief. They thereby annulled not only the Belgian–Congolese association but also the unity of the Congo. This unity was already precarious and the attempts to re-establish it form one of the two principal strands in the complex story of the next three years. The other strand is the conflict over the powers and duties of the UN forces which began to arrive in Leopoldville on 14 July to restore order and displace the Belgians – but without agreement on whether the restoration of law and order included the subjection of Katanga to the authority of the central government.

On the domestic political front Lumumba and Kasavubu began working in harmony, but in September they broke with each other and Kasavubu dismissed Lumumba and appointed a new government. The parliament supported Lumumba who maintained, with some justice, that the president's action was illegal. In the ensuing crisis Hammarskjöld's representative in Leopoldville, Andrew Cordier, closed airports and radio, thereby giving an advantage to Kasavubu by denying to the more popular Lumumba the opportunity to state his case in different parts of the country or make his voice heard on the air. This action was bitterly resented within the Congo and beyond and led to fierce Congolese attacks on the UN with Russian support. Lumumba remained in Leopoldville in his official residence. Cordier's successor, Rayeshwar Dayal, refused to assist him, and he became in effect not the prisoner but the protégé of the UN (which was now attacked for being pro-Lumumba) until he fled from Leopoldville at the end of November, hoping to reach Stanleyville by car. He was overtaken a few days later with the help of aircraft and was lodged in gaol in Thysville, whence he fled to the Katangan capital of Elisabethville on 17 January, only to be captured again and murdered.

Shortly after the Lumumba–Kasavubu rift in September power in Leopoldville was seized by Colonel Joseph Mobutu, the chief of staff of the army (the commander-in-chief, Victor Lundula, was not in the capital). Mobutu ejected both the parliament and the Russian and Czech embassies and, when attempts to reconcile Lumumba and Kasavubu failed, declared for Kasavubu who acquiesced in the colonel's virtual usurpation. Mobutu was the principal ruler in the capital until the end of the year. He introduced a new constitution and some degree of order and efficiency, but although supported by the west he failed to establish the sort of military régime which other soldiers were successfully establishing in Asian and Arab states at this time. The provinces did not respond and the resources available to him – communications, trained personnel – were totally inadequate. Moreover the army itself was divided; General Lundula and the forces in Orientale province remained pro-Lumumba, as did many politicians and, so far as was ascertainable, the popular favour.

In February 1961 it was apparent that the Mobutu–Kasavubu team had failed and a new government was appointed under Ileo. It lasted six months until August when Ileo was succeeded by Adoula, who remained prime minister until 1964. During this period the Lumumbists, led by Antoine Gizenga in Stanleyville, and the Katangans, led by Tshombe and Godefroid Munongo in Elisabethville, were separate and often separatist factors in the situation. Various attempts were made to bring all three sections together but hopeful moves in the direction of Stanleyville usually caused Elisabethville to shy away, and vice versa.

The Stanleyville secession was never formalized in the same way as the Kantangan. It developed after the break between Lumumba and Kasavubu and gathered strength after the murder of Lumumba when the Russians seemed to be on the verge of recognizing the Stanleyville party as the government of the Congo and of supplying it with arms. But if the Russians were expected to secure a foothold in Africa by exploiting the emotions roused by Lumumba's death, they miscalculated; their faces were as white as any Belgian's, their intervention was in principle as unwelcome, and instead of pleasing they shocked Africans by the ruthlessness with which, upon their arrival in Orientale, they proposed to set about the anti-Lumumbists. They were seen off by a small party of UN troops, having badly damaged their reputation in Africa. Gizenga meanwhile equivocated over his relations with Ileo, watching the state of Ileo's relations with Tshombe, but when he was appointed deputy prime minister to Adoula he accepted the post on the understanding that Adoula would use force to put an end to the Katangan secession. He accompanied Adoula to the conference of non-aligned nations in Belgrade in September 1961. The failure of the operations against Katanga, about to be related, revived his suspicions and he returned to his own base in Stanleyville, thereby re-creating the tripartite pattern. Attempts to induce him to return to the capital having failed, he was brought there under arrest in January 1962, lodged in jail and expelled from the government.

The Katangan secession was a formal, if illegal, state of affairs with a precise beginning and a precise end. It was proclaimed by Tshombe on

11 July 1960 and renounced by him on 21 December 1961. Its inception thus coincided with the mutiny of the Force Publique and Belgian intervention, and it was accompanied by an appeal to Belgium and a refusal to allow Kasavubu and Lumumba, the federal president and prime minister, to go to Elisabethville. As a result of these moves Katanga was for the time being protected from the chaos developing in other areas, and while the UN was trying to re-establish order in Leopoldville province the Belgians did so in Katanga. They also provided Tshombe, at his request, with administrative services, and – the most important aspect of the partnership – they ran the mines and paid royalties to Tshombe instead of to the central government. These payments were a direct breach of the pre-independence agreement (the *loi fondamentale*) which had been signed by the Belgian government and accepted by, among others, Tshombe; but they enabled Tshombe to enlist and pay an army of foreigners with which to oppose his Congolese adversaries and, if need be, the UN. One of the most pregnant eventualities of the first weeks of independence was this alignment of Katanga – wealthy, relatively isolated, strongly led and able to command Belgian aid – against the rest of the Congo and its UN supporters.

The UN came to the Congo in response to three appeals by Kasavubu and Lumumba on 10, 12 and 13 July 1960. They appealed first for technical aid, including aid in the organization and equipment of security forces. In their second and third messages they appealed for help against Belgian aggression. Hammarskjöld, taking the initiative under article 99 of the Charter, on 13 July asked the Security Council to consider technical aid for the Congo and the problem of law and order. The Council authorized the despatch of military aid to the Congolese government with the proviso that force should not be used by UN troops except in self-defence. The council was divided on whether to require the Belgians to withdraw, Britain, France and China abstaining from the vote. Hammarskjöld immediately asked African states north of the Congo for military and other help, an appeal later extended to certain European and Asian members. The first troops reached the Congo on 14 July and four days later a force of 4,000 had been assembled. The airlift was provided by the United States, Britain and the Soviet Union. Differences of opinion about the functions of the UN troops arose at once. General Alexander, in command of the Ghanaian contingent, immediately began disarming the mutineers of the Force Publique. Had he been allowed to continue to do so, all might have been very different, but Lumumba insisted on stopping the process, partly because he was suspicious of outside interference and partly because he wanted to use the Force Publique against Katanga.

The Security Council met again on 20 July and resolved unanimously that the Belgians should withdraw and that other states should refrain from aggravating the situation; it confirmed the authority already given to Hammarskjöld and commended what he had done. The Belgians began to withdraw on the 20th and by the 23rd they had left the Congo again – except Katanga. Ghana and Guinea then threatened to withdraw their troops from the UN force and place them at the disposal of the Leopoldville government in order to help evict the Belgians from Katanga and force the province to accept the authority of the Kasavubu–Lumumba régime. Consequently the UN had to consider most urgently whether its own force was entitled to enter Katanga to achieve these objects and, if not, whether it should now be empowered by new resolutions to do so. Hoping to bypass this difficulty Hammarskjöld flew to Brussels and the Congo to secure the entry of UN units by negotiation and announced on 2 August that a first contingent would do so in three days' time. But the Katanga authorities said they would resist and Ralph Bunche, despatched to Elisabethville to discover if they really would, advised postponing the move. Rather than use force, and uncertain whether he was empowered to in these circumstances, Hammarskjöld returned to New York to seek further instructions from the Security Council. This check was accounted a victory by the Katangans. It further infuriated Lumumba who decided that the UN had let him down and that he should seek African support for a campaign against Katanga.

The Security Council's third meeting took place on 8 and 9 August and (France and Italy abstaining) repeated the injunction to the Belgians to leave immediately, authorized the entry of UN forces into Katanga and said once more that these forces were not to be used to influence the internal conflict. The last part of the resolution was but doubtfully consistent with the second, since the essence of the conflict was the authority of Leopoldville over Elisabethville, and the entry of UN troops into Katanga, even if designed only to compel the departure of the Belgians, could not fail to have an effect on the balance of domestic Congolese forces which were in conflict. Hammarskjöld, fortified by this resolution, returned to the Congo and to his policy of getting UN forces into Katanga bloodlessly. He entered Katanga with a token force but refused to take a representative of Lumumba with him, thus further antagonizing Lumumba who became convinced that the secretary-general was embroiled in a plot against him. For his part Hammarskjöld became convinced that Lumumba's main aim was to get rid of the UN presence. Tshombe meanwhile used the breathing space afforded by these quarrels to consolidate his position. A fourth meeting of the Security Council on 21 August produced an ominous sign when a resolution of strong support for Hammarskjöld was opposed by the Soviet Union and Poland.

Throughout August the situation in the Congo deteriorated with every prospect of a clash between the Congolese and Katangan armies.

A conference of thirteen African states in Leopoldville failed to give Lumumba the support he wanted and advised against an attack on Katanga, but Congolese troops were taking matters into their own hands and contrived a massacre of Baluba who were trying to establish a state of their own between the two principal river forces. (They had already suffered a massacre by the Balunda since Tshombe could not establish his predominance in Katanga as a whole without this radical alteration of the numerical balance.) At this point Kasavubu's resolve to get rid of Lumumba, whose unpredictability had grown alarmingly and whose reputed pro-communism was, though unfounded, embarrasing, gave Tshombe a second breathing space; the projected attack on him was called off, and his Belgian troops took the opportunity to move north and establish a second secessionary state in Kasai under the short-lived presidency of Albert Kalonji. A separate state backed by the Belgians had come into existence in the south, while in the north-east the Russians were beginning to play with the idea of another separate state backed by themselves.

The Congo seemed to be about to break up into three large and warring units, two of which would be foreign bases, and a number of smaller ones. The situation was aggravated upon the opening of the UN General Assembly in September, when Khrushchev arrived in person to attack the secretary-general and two rival Congolese delegations competed with each other for seats in the Assembly and the ears of its members.

This session of the Assembly was notable for the admission of seventeen new African members, and for the part they played. They refused to support the Russian attack on Hammarskjöld and joined with the western bloc to isolate the communist states. But they did not agree with prevailing western views on the Congo, nor did they remain solidly united among themselves. In Britain, France and the United States the Katangan case, propagated by an active and lavishly supplied promotion lobby which tended to put the interests of its clients before the truth, made many converts in political and business circles on the plea that Katanga was an oasis of peace and sanity in an otherwise barbarous and increasingly communist Congo. This thesis found no acceptors among Africans who unanimously condemned Tshombe and his ways, while being divided on what to do. One group turned against the UN and reverted to Lumumba's plan for a joint African invasion of Katanga. Another group remained attached to the idea of UN action, though dissatisfied with the action apparently contemplated; this group became a pressure group at the UN with the object of persuading the secretary-general and other members that a policy of reducing Katanga by negotiation was hopeless and should be replaced by direct action. A third group of Africans, consisting of recently emancipated French colonies, placed its faith for a time in the Mobutu–Kasavubu alliance and the gradual radiation of law and order from Leopoldville out into all the provinces. The decline of Mobutu, the murder of Lumumba and the installation of Ileo provided a depressing background to events in the last months of 1960 and the beginning of 1961, during which successful attempts were made by Hammarskjöld to get the Russians and the Belgians to stop their independent bolstering of Stanleyville and Elisabethville.

On 21 February 1961 the Security Council explicitly authorized the UN forces to use force in the last resort to prevent a civil war. It did not, however, authorize the use of force against Katanga, or for the removal of the Belgians, or to secure a political solution. This development marked a return to better relations between Hammarskjöld, the independent African states and the west – or at any rate the United States where Kennedy had just assumed the presidency – but it alienated not only Tshombe but also the Kasavubu–Ileo government which suspected the UN of being in western pockets, disliked any increase in its pretensions and now began to draw closer to Tshombe. At a conference at Tananarive in March Tshombe persuaded Ileo to accept a plan for a loose confederation of sovereign Congolese states. No Lumumbist had attended the conference, whose proceedings they regarded as a western ruse to give legitimacy to Tshombe by manipulating the ex-French colonies in his favour. Ileo, however, quickly repented of having moved so far in the direction of Katanga, set about repairing relations with Gizenga and the UN and, at a further conference at Coquilhatville, ordered and effected the arrest of Tshombe.

In July the Congolese parliament assembled at Lovanium, the university town near Leopoldville, in order to patch up a grand coalition. Tshombe was released, Ileo gave way to the honest and respected manager of men Adoula (a sort of Congolese Eisenhower), and Gizenga joined the government. On the UN side the replacement of Dayal, who was weighed down by the unhappy past, by the Tunisian Khiari and the Ghanaian Gardiner helped to improve relations between the government and the UN. But the grand coalition was not achieved. Tshombe was now odd man out.

There followed the military operations against Katanga. By now Katanga was in African terms a formidable power, equipped since the beginning of the year with men, supplies and even aircraft from Belgium, France, South Africa and Southern Rhodesia. A few specified Belgians had been removed as a result of laborious negotiations, but the course of these discussions and of events convinced UN representatives on the spot that Tshombe was only playing for time and had no real intention of dismissing the Belgian and other mercenaries or of coming to terms with Leopoldville. These suspicions received blatant confirmation at the end of August. UN forces seized about 100 foreign officers who had been declared to be undesirable aliens by the Adoula government. Tshombe acquiesced but the local UN representative, Conor Cruise O'Brien, agreed that in order to minimize personal affronts the details should be handled by the Belgian consul in Elisabethville, who guaranteed the voluntary departure of the officers but then failed to honour his word. Moreover other foreign officers not in Elisabethville remained untouched. This attempt to evict some officers was doubly unfortunate for the UN since its failure encouraged Katangan obduracy while its legality was strongly attacked by British representatives in the Congo and New York and Britain became for a while as useful an ally for Katanga as Belgium or France.

In the face of this rebuff the UN had to decide whether to take further steps or to acquiesce. Khiari and O'Brien, believing that Munongo was the real kernel of resistance, hoped to separate Tshombe from Munongo and to get Tshombe to Leopoldville where Hammarskjöld would come to talk him into a more amenable and reasonable frame of mind. But Tshombe refused to be enticed and O'Brien, believing that he had Khiari's authority to use force to round up the foreign officers in Katanga and put an end to the Katangan secession, planned a second military operation, which included the virtual kidnapping of Tshombe. It failed. The Katangans were better prepared and the British government, by refusing to allow Ethiopian jet aircraft to fly over Rhodesia to the Congo, presented the Katangans with a decisive advantage. UN forces captured the post office and radio station at Elisabethville, but Tshombe took refuge with the British vice-consul and then in Rhodesia. The UN operation had produced bloodshed which, much exaggerated in the reporting, shocked and antagonized those who thought that a peace force must achieve peace without force, and Tshombe had been left slip. Hammarskjöld arrived in Leopoldville to find an utterly unexpected situation – confusion and stalemate in Katanga, stubborn and effective hostility from Britain and, if in smaller degree, from the Belgian and American governments also. He determined to seek out Tshombe and talk to him. He left for Ndola in Rhodesia by air on 17 September and was killed when his aircraft crashed *en route*.

This appalling calamity – for Hammarskjöld was one of the half-dozen outstanding personalities in postwar international affairs – was followed by a cease-fire and the return of Tshombe to Katanga. After the appointment of U Thant to serve the rest of Hammarskjöld's term of office, the Security Council returned to its familiar dilemma: whether to try to reconcile Adoula and Tshombe or to bring the latter to heel. On 24 November the Council, Britain and France abstaining, authorized the new secretary-general to use force to expel foreign mercenaries and political advisers from Katanga, thus implicitly endorsing O'Brien's policy although he himself was removed from the scene. UN forces were still in Elisabethville but they were awkwardly placed since Tshombe's mercenaries were manifestly keen to provoke a next round of fighting, in which they would surround and destroy the UN forces. The UN representatives in Katanga decided to take action in order to prevent their scattered units from being picked off piecemeal before the arrival of reinforcements, but they were again handicapped by Britain which, having promised to deliver a supply of 100-lb bombs, succumbed to right-wing pressures and cancelled its undertaking. Fighting was inconclusive and when Tshombe agreed to meet Adoula, U Thant ordered a new cease-fire. On 21 December 1961, at Kitona, Tshombe renounced secession, and the Kitona agreement was endorsed by the Katangan assembly two months later.

But the troubles of the Congo were not so easily assuaged. During most of 1962 Adoula and Tshombe were engaged in a series of fruitless discussions concerning the implementation of the Kitona agreement, which was opposed in Katanga by Munongo and European secessionists. Tshombe, who interspersed his meetings with Adoula with secret visits to Welensky in Rhodesia, seemed unable to make up his mind. He eventually departed for a prolonged stay in Europe. Although Adoula took three Katangans into his cabinet in April 1963 no genuine reconciliation was brought about. The central government continued to be oppressed by problems of economics and law and order, and early in 1964 a more serious revolt broke out in Kwilu under the leadership of Pierre Mulele, who had recently made a trip to China. This outbreak was the more ominous because the UN troops were departing. The last planeload left at the end of June, the fourth anniversary of independence.

The balance sheet of these four years of international endeavour, sometimes co-operative and sometimes competitive, is not easily struck. At the very beginning the UN, through sticking to the letter of the law, desisted from disarming the mutinous Force Publique, a major source of continuing disorder. There were also mistakes and misunderstandings in the handling of relations with the legally appointed, if personally difficult, prime minister Patrice Lumumba, and the resulting suspiciousness affected not only the UN's own standing and operations but also relations among African states and relations between them and other states. Given the circumstances, however, the misunderstandings could easily have been worse. In the Katanga operations the UN earned the hostility of certain powers and suffered from the criticism that UN forces had come to secure order but had shed blood in the name of peace. Apart from the fact that all police operations must envisage the use of force as an ultimate sanction, the blame for the ambiguities over Katanga belonged primarily to the members of the Security Council whose instructions were not at first sufficiently precise; the reverses suffered by the UN in terms of public sentiment demonstrated above all the need to provide the secretary-general with more effective consultative and executive machinery. In the last resort, however, a joint operation such as the UN operation in the Congo was bound to run into difficulties as soon as there appeared among the members any serious discrepancy of aim.

The successes of the UN were considerable. It achieved almost immediately its first aim of displacing (except from Katanga) the Belgians who had returned when the Force Publique mutinied. Its intervention also prevented intervention by individual states on their own account and enforced in one case, the Russian, a retreat; fears that Africa would become a new theatre for the Cold War were allayed. The UN also succeeded to a remarkable degree in keeping the Congolese economy going, providing elementary administrative services, and preventing famine and epidemics. It could take credit for staving off civil wars in the Congo which would almost certainly have been worse but for the UN presence and became worse when that presence was removed. Finally, when the UN forces departed in June 1964 Katanga had not seceded. But it was still, as it was bound to be, richer than the whole of the rest of the country, economically so dominant that its leaders were in a position either to play a separatist hand or to claim a dominant position in the central government.

The central government's lack of authority became patent immediately after the departure of the UN forces. Civil war started again. The Adoula government was first reconstituted and then replaced by a new administration under Tshombe, who returned from Europe as the UN departed. Tshombe tried to form a broad coalition and to enlist the support of the OAU, but Gizenga (whom, among others, he released from prison) formed a new opposition party and the OAU – in spite of creating a reconciliation commission under Kenyatta's chairmanship – failed to find a remedy for the Congo's ills. Tshombe was too greatly disliked to be able to control the situation except by arms and he began, soon after his return, to enlist a new force of (mainly) Belgian and South African mercenaries. This force was quickly successful and the rebels, who had taken Stanleyville in August, found themselves threatened with the loss of all their principal strongholds. They had meanwhile taken hostages, and in an attempt to rescue these hostages Belgian parachute troops were flown in October in American aircraft from the British island of Ascension to Stanleyville, which was recaptured from the rebels. About 200 hostages were killed in spite of this operation (or, as some maintained, because of it), in addition to some 20,000 Congolese who lost their lives in the furies of this rebellion. Africans outside the Congo were divided between those who took the easy course of denouncing the Belgians, Americans and British as imperialist recidivists and those who, stifling their dislike of Tshombe, defended the right of the Congolese government to ask for outside help if it wanted to. Tshombe, who had already in July been refused an invitation to the OAU's conference of heads of state in Cairo, was kept out of the conference of non-aligned states in the same city in October. Upon his arrival in Cairo he was escorted to a hotel and kept there until he decided to return to Leopoldville.

Both in Leopoldville and in Stanleyville, the Congolese leaders were divided among themselves. Rebel unity did not survive reverses and President Kasavubu's appointment of Tshombe as prime minister had not betokened any real reconciliation. Although Tshombe was successful in elections in April 1965, Kasavubu shortly afterwards dismissed him. The president failed, however, to construct a new government without Tshombe and in November the army, in the person of General Mobutu, stepped in, dismissed the president and established military rule. With this revolution the army, which alone had had real power since independence, assumed responsibility as well. Mobutu, who had once been a Lumumbist, defeated Mulele's revolt in 1966 and next year survived an attempt, assisted by mercenaries, to restore Tshombe. He broke up the political map by reducing the number of provinces from twenty-one to twelve and then to eight, and he reduced the likelihood of secession by nationalizing the assets of the Union Minière. He repaired relations with Belgium, which he visited in 1969, concluded financial and technical agreements and played host to King Baudouin in Kinshasa. Although he had to imprison large numbers in the process, he brought a semblance of peace and some prospect of economic improvement to an exhausted country. In 1970 he became president for seven years. He felt strong enough at home to give his attention to wider African problems, meeting President Ngouabi of Congo-Brazzaville (relations between the two countries began a much needed improvement) and also Presidents Kaunda and Gowon. He introduced civilians and younger men into senior government posts in place of Adoula who fell ill and Bomboko and Nendaka who were sacked. He consolidated his personal power, renamed the country Zaïre and set about turning it into the Iran of Africa with himself as its shah.

In 1977 the Lunda peoples of Zaïre and neighbouring Angola, organized as the Front de Libération Nationale Congolaise (FNLC), staged a revolt in Shaba (ex-Katanga). The west assumed that Cubans, who were helping to train refugees from Zaïre in Angolan camps, had promoted the revolt but Castro swore that he had on the contrary tried to restrain it and there was no evidence to gainsay him. The wealth of the province – cobalt, uranium, diamonds and copper – made it a matter of concern to the outside world and in spite of the embarrassment of going to the aid of a régime as corrupt as Mobutu's France transported, largely at Saudi Arabian expense, 1,500 Moroccan troops to stiffen a Zaïrean army which was widely regarded as useless.

A year later a second revolt took place. One hundred and thirty Europeans were killed and in order to save further lives 700 French and 1,700 Belgian paratroopers were flown to Zaïre in American aircraft. Having evacuated 2,500 Europeans they were replaced by a mixed African force recruited from Morocco, Senegal, Ivory Coast, Togo and Gabon. This African intervention was to be coupled with a wider international effort to rescue Zaïre from the bankruptcy into which it had been plunged by the collapse of the world price of copper, the closing of its principal rail outlet (to Benguela in Angola) and Mobutu's malpractices. But aid from the IMF and the EEC was dependent on internal reforms and resident IMF supervision, and since Mobutu postponed the one and cold-shouldered the other the plans came to nothing. Some sections of the economy prospered but the state piled up huge debts and was shored up by western countries which valued its minerals and superficial stability. Over a quarter of a century in which Mobutu ruled most Zaïreans became progressively worse off and the life of the average Zaïrean ended at 40, while Mobutu himself and his family became prodigiously and ostentatiously rich. For most of this period Mobutu seemed irremovable but suddenly appearances changed. By 1990 bazaars and universities were seething, the economic infrastructure collapsing, prices soaring and civil servants striking for a fivefold increase in their salaries. Serious disorders culminated in a massacre at Lubumbashi. Mobutu espoused a multiparty system and dozens of parties appeared, from which Mobutu proposed to pick and legitimize three.

THE SUDAN

The history of the Sudan in modern times is an alternation of subjection and self-rule. From 1820 to 1881 it was a part of the Ottoman empire in name and of its autonomous Egyptian pashalik in fact. From 1881 to 1898 it was ruled by the Mahdi and his successors. (The Mahdi – Muhammad Ahmad Abdullah, who proclaimed himself Mahdi in 1881 – died in 1885.) From 1899 to 1955 it was subject in theory to an Anglo-Egyptian condomium, in practice to Britain. In 1956 it became an independent state, and then a member of the Arab League and the United Nations.

The Anglo–Egyptian condominium reflected no Anglo–Egyptian agreement about the Sudan. The administering powers agreed in little and did not bother to co-operate. After the Anglo–Egyptian treaty of 1936 the British allowed a greater degree of Egyptian penetration, but although the Sudan was coveted by Egyptian governments it attracted few Egyptian administrators. Sudanese nationalism gathered strength in the 1930s under the leadership of Ismail al-Azhari who became secretary of the Graduates General Congress, formed in 1938. Owing to the active role of Britain and the comparatively negative role of Egypt Sudanese nationalism was at first more anti-British than anti-Egyptian and indeed looked to Egypt to help displace the British. This predominantly anti-British streak was intensified during the Second World War when nationalists raised the issue of the Sudan's postwar status and received unsympathetic answers from the British who were fully occupied with present and pressing realities in the campaigns against the Italians in Ethiopia and against the Italians and the Germans in North Africa. The Egyptians sensed the opportunities in this situation and welcomed the formation by Azhari of the Ashigga party which aimed at the union of the Sudan with Egypt. He had the support of Ale el-Mirghani, one of the Sudan's two principal religious leaders. As a direct response a second party, the Umma Party, was created to work for the independence of the Sudan under the leadership of the Sudan's other principal religious leader, Abd al-Rahman al-Mahdi, the posthumous son of the famous Mahdi of the 1880s. The Umma Party

22.1 The Horn and East Africa

was suspected, or at any rate accused, by its opponents of dreaming of a revival of the Mahdist monarchy with British help.

The conflict between Britain and Egypt, which existed independently of the Sudan, was intensified by these moves and when the British administration took a step towards Sudanese self-government by creating an advisory council for the northern Sudan, the Egyptian prime minister, Mustafa al-Nahhas Pasha, resurrected the slogan of the unity of the Nile valley. The British also antagonized both the northern and the southern Sudan by omitting the south from the new councils; the south was affronted, while the north suspected Britain of a plan for detaching the south and annexing it to Uganda. This conflict, which was to lead to severe fighting on the eve of independence, was partly religious, partly racial and partly economic, but fundamentally cultural in the broadest sense. The south comprised the three provinces of Bahr al-Ghazal, Upper Nile and Equatoria with a population of rather more than 3 million out of a total population of 10 million. These three provinces, bordering upon five African states (the Central African Republic, Congo, Uganda, Kenya and Ethiopia) looked to their African neighbours rather than to the Arab north. The inhabitants, although they included some 40 per cent of Muslim Africans, were predominantly negroid and pagan; some of the tribes continued to display the weaknesses inflicted by slavers from the north who had systematically removed the best men and women; the poverty of the south was worse than the poverty of the north. After the war the British, who had in the past been open to the charge that their administration accentuated the divide between north and south, adopted a policy of unification, but a conference held in 1946 contained no southern representatives and gave the south cause to complain that unification was really subordination. After a further conference at Juba in 1947 northerners claimed that the south had agreed to unification, while southerners denied this interpretation and continued to ask for separation from the north or a form of federation with guarantees.

This internal dispute was, however, partly obscured by the larger dispute between Egypt, insisting on the unity of the Nile valley, and Britain, insisting on the Sudan's right to decide for itself after a period of self-government under the British aegis. In 1947 Egypt accepted the principle of self-determination in the mistaken belief that it would produce a union of the two countries, but Britain and Egypt were still unable to agree on the immediate constitutional changes and in 1948 Britain introduced a new constitution without Egyptian concurrence. Legislative and executive councils covering the whole of the Sudan were established but the elections for them were boycotted by the pro-Egyptian parties. After anti-British demonstrations Azhari was arrested. Egypt was at this time embroiled in the Arab–Israeli war and its immediate aftermath.

In 1951 the British governor appointed a commission to consider further constitutional advances. The Sudan was plainly moving fast along the road through self-government to self-determination, and Egypt thereupon carried out a threat, uttered in 1950, to abrogate the condominium agreement of 1899 and the Anglo–Egyptian treaty of 1936. King Farouk was declared king of Egypt and the Sudan. But in 1952, as a result of the revolution in Egypt, he became king of neither.

A few months earlier Britain had produced a self-government statute for the Sudan which provided for the creation of a council of ministers, a house of representatives and a senate, and reserved to the governor only external affairs and ultimate emergency authority in domestic affairs. The new Egyptian government, whose chief, General Neguib, was half Sudanese, accepted the self-government statute, improved it (from the Sudanese point of view) and persuaded all the principal Sudanese parties to issue a pro-Egyptian declaration. The modified statute curbed the governor's authority by introducing a five-man international commission and by reducing special powers originally reserved to him in the south. It was embodied in the Anglo–Egyptian agreement of February 1953 and was intended to lead to independence not later than January 1961. Elections, preceded by vigorous Egyptian campaigning, were held at the end of 1953 and gave an overwhelming victory to Azhari's refurbished party, now called the National Unionist Party. Azhari became prime minister at the beginning of 1954. At the end of the same year Neguib was out.

The disappearance of Neguib was not the only cause of the ebbing of the pro-Egyptian tide in the Sudan. The tide had in fact not been flowing as strongly as it seemed, since the voting in 1953 had been more anti-British than pro-Egyptian. Two years after the elections the Sudan shook off both the British and the Egyptians and declared its independence, but before doing so it experienced mutiny and rebellion in the south. Disappointed by the new government's allocation of posts and by the persistent rejection of its demand for secession or a federal association, the south exploded in August 1955 as the result of an incident in which an army section turned upon its Arab officer. Disaffection spread rapidly and was only mastered when the prime minister invoked the aid of the British governor and moved substantial forces from the north into the south. The south, submitting, claimed that it had done so in reliance upon British mediation and was subsequently let down. Repression was certainly thorough and probably brutal. Southerners were executed in their hundreds and deported to the north in their thousands and fled to neighbouring African territories in their tens of thousands. The south became a closed area whence reliable information was difficult to obtain and was replaced by gruesome reports.

The revolt accelerated independence which was claimed by Azhari before the end of the year and inaugurated on the first day of 1956. It was followed by the break-up of Azhari's party, a coalition under him and then a coalition without him. New parties formed. Abdullah Khalil, who succeeded Azhari in 1956, grappled for two years with economic problems (lightened by an aid agreement with the United States in 1958) and with reviving fears of Egypt. In 1958 Egypt sent troops into two disputed areas on the Egyptian–Sudanese border, but this tactless demonstration recoiled on Cairo at elections in the same year which gave the Umma Party the largest number of seats. Nevertheless Khalil was afraid of an alliance between Azhari and Nasser and he was suspected of being privy to an army coup by which he and his government and the constitution were all swept away. General Ibrahim Abboud took power with a supreme council of officers.

Military rule lasted for six years, during which the situation in the southern provinces deteriorated drastically. The Sudanese government pursued a policy of Arabization and looked with extreme suspicion on the foreign Christian missionaries whom it suspected of being not merely anti-Muslim but also active agents of a western policy of separatism. The Missionary Societies Act of 1962 restricted their activities and induced a number to leave; the surviving 300 were expelled in 1964 after the resumption of full-scale insurrection by the separatist Anya Nya movement and brought with them to the outside world tales of extensive massacres by government troops. In October 1964 General Abboud's military régime was overthrown and after a few weeks during which General Abboud ruled in conjunction with a civilian administration he himself resigned. Ser el-Khatim Khalifa formed a transitional coalition of intellectuals and re-emergent politicians which was replaced early in 1965 by a more normal coalition of politicians in which the Umma Party had the largest voice – a position which it confirmed and enhanced at elections in April. A southerner, Clement Ngoro, held the ministry of the interior and north–south negotiations took place both in the Sudan and in Nairobi with a number of leading southern exiles. A further conference planned for February at Juba was postponed owing to a refusal by the Anya Nya to surrender in advance, but discussions were resumed in Khartoum in March. With the south demanding a federal constitution and northern politicians inveighing against separatist plots little was achieved. Fighting continued and southern opinion moved increasingly away from federation and towards independence with both sides seeking support from neighbouring states. The Sudanese government exerted itself to improve its relations with Ethiopia, Uganda and the Central African Republic, and the Sudanese African National Union appealed to African opinion through the Organization for African Unity and its Liberation Committee in Dar-es-Salaam.

In 1969 a group of military officers led by General Gaafar

Mohammad Nimeiry seized power and established a more left-wing and pro-Egyptian government. The coincidence of similar coups in Somalia and Libya gave rise to projects for a union of all these countries with Egypt and the creation therefore of an Arab bloc of north-east African states. In 1970 this plan was further expanded to attract South Yemen and Syria, thus linking it with the defunct union of 1958 with Egypt as the central point and common factor, but these foreign schemes came to nothing. In the Sudan they were attacked by critics who argued that they were diverting attention from more urgent domestic problems, especially the dissatisfied south, where civil war dragged on until 1972. Nimeiry survived a series of attempts to unseat him which, in 1975 and 1976, were at least assisted, if not instigated, by Libya and Ethiopia. In 1977 the Sudan moved close to war with Ethiopia as a result of the help which it was giving to the Eritrean revolt against Addis Ababa. At home a reconciliation between Nimeiry and his principal opponent Sadiq al-Mahdi, marked by the latter's election to a vice-presidency of the Sudanese Socialist Union, brought Muslim fundamentalists into the government and thereby split the Muslim Brotherhood between those prepared to share power in this way and others who insisted on holding out for the imposition of comprehensive theocratic rule. The coalition crumbled in 1979. Nimeiry refused to sever relations with Egypt after Camp David.

Throughout the early eighties Nimeiry's fall was confidently predicted. His troubles in the south revived, his economy went from bad to worse, students and other malcontents demonstrated against him, his suppliers – mainly Saudi Arabia and the United States – began to ask themselves whether they would not be better without him; and his borders were crossed by hordes of destitute and starving refugees from Ethiopia and Chad. He reacted by imposing and savagely implementing Islamic laws and penalties, calling himself Imam (although a third of his countrymen and women were not Muslims) and by granting valuable concessions to Saudi and other tycoons. Sadiq al-Mahdi opposed the severity of the application of the Shar'ia and was put in prison in 1983 but released the next year. By 1985 about a fifth of the population was starving, maladministration had brought public services and basic works (irrigation, for example) to a standstill, the special security police were justly loathed, the foreign debt service exceeded the value of exports, foreign loans were obtainable only at ruinous cost, the south was again in arms against Khartoum and to all intents and purposes autonomous. In April Nimeiry, away on a visit to the United States, was removed by the army after what amounted to a strike by the professional classes – a pre-emptive coup by the military to forestall more radical action. The succeeding military government proved only a stop-gap while traditional political parties argued their way to a civilian coalition with Sadiq al-Mahdi as prime minister. But al-Mahdi, weak and inconsistent, gave hostages to fortune by espousing (contrary to his campaign rhetoric) Islamic fundamentalist policies and fell out with his allies of the Democratic Unionist Party by failing to stop – or not trying hard enough to stop – the war in the south. He was accused of sabotaging peace moves. The DUP left his government in 1988 and he became dependent on the National Islamic Front. The army feared defeat in the south, was impatient with his dithering and fearful of economic collapse. The war, resumed in 1983, had cost at least half a million dead and 1.5 million refugees. The external debt had risen to $7 billion; discussions with the IMF broke down; food riots became frequent. In 1989 the army resumed overt power under General Omar al-Bashir, a more circumspect but hardly less convinced Islamicist than his predecessor. War in the south went on, famine overtook large areas in the north and sympathy for Iraqi attitudes in Middle East affairs impaired Sudan's relations with Saudi Arabia.

THE HORN

The ancient Ethiopian kingdom, an amalgam of races, languages and religions, retained its independence even in the nineteenth century and therewith a certain immunity from the modernizing trends which normally accompany both colonialism and anti-colonial movements. Subjected for only five years in the twentieth century (1936–41), it resumed its hallowed way of life under its astute monarch Haile Selassie, who had first mounted the throne in 1930 at the age of 38. The emperor was a cautious innovator whose reforming proclivities were in advance of the landed feudatories and wealthy churchmen who were the most eminent and ultimately the most powerful people in his realm. An attempted coup at the end of 1960, followed by army mutinies in March 1961 and a reported conspiracy in August of that year, suggested the existence of some discontent among the educated young and junior officers who looked to Prince Asfa Wossen for more spirited progress, but the emperor re-established his control with awe-inspiring ease and continued his policy of slow internal advance. He also cultivated good relations with the emerging states of Africa (perhaps as an insurance against traditional Muslim hostility towards his predominantly Christian empire); in 1958 his capital became the headquarters for the UN Economic Commission for Africa and in 1963 the Organization for African Unity came to birth there. For both these organizations the emperor caused spacious quarters to be built.

Ethiopia's special external concern was with the neighbouring and non-Bantu Somalis who, unlike the Ethiopians, were not only conquered by Europeans in the nineteenth century but also partitioned among them. The Somalis, Muslims but not Arabs, appeared in the Horn of Africa towards the end of the European Middle Ages and subsequently joined in Muslim attacks on the Christian kingdom of Ethiopia. They were subjected in the latter part of the nineteenth century, first by the French in the sixties and then by the British and the Italians (who also took Eritrea flanking the Red Sea to the north of Ethiopia) in the eighties. The British colony of Kenya extended northwards over a predominantly Somali area, and Ethiopia appropriated in its Ogaden province territory to which the Somalis laid claim. Relations between Ethiopia and the Somalis were therefore inherently bad and British relations with both were uneasy, since the Ethiopians suspected Britain of partiality to Somali claims against Ethiopia, while Somalis found Britain unsympathetic to their claims against Kenya.

In 1935 the Italians, dissatisfied with the barrenness of their part of Somaliland and their imperial pretensions in general, exploited an incident at Wal Wal in the disputed Ogaden in order to conquer Ethiopia. They were suspected of toying with the idea of a Greater Somalia which would annex British Somaliland, but their defeat by the British in 1941 revived the independent Ethiopean empire (to which was added Eritrea in 1952 after a period of British trusteeship) and left the Somalis still subject and divided. At the end of the war Ernest Bevin proposed at one moment a Greater Somalia consisting of British and Italian Somaliland and parts of Ethiopia, but this notion antagonized Ethiopia without profiting the Somalis. Discussions on the Ethiopian–Somali frontier proceeded sluggishly until 1959 when a conference in Oslo with Trygve Lie as arbitrator produced a compromise agreeable to neither side. In 1960 Italian Somaliland, to which the Italians had returned in 1950 to administer a ten-year trusteeship, became independent, and as this date approached the British, who had become nervous of Egyptian interference in British Somaliland, hurried their own colony forward so that it could be joined with Italian Somaliland to make the independent republic of Somalia – large but poor, racially mixed, ill-prepared, and distrusted and menaced by its Ethiopian and Kenyan neighbours.

At the Lancaster House conference on Kenya in 1962 the Somalis asked unsuccessfully for a plebiscite in the Northern Frontier District of Kenya (an area of over 260,000 sq km) and its union with Somalia. Later in the same year Kenyan politicians discussed with Somalis an East African federation which would embrace not only Somalia and the British East African territories but also Ethiopia; in the event of such a development the Kenyans made it plain that they intended to keep the whole of the Northern Frontier District for themselves. In

December a boundaries commission recommended that the district be divided into two regions, both to be included in the new Kenyan state. This recommendation, which was accepted by the British government, produced riots and a rupture of diplomatic relations by Somalia. Kenya was able to get other African states on its side and a Kenyan delegation walked out of an Afro-Asian conference at Moshi in Tanganyika in February 1963 when the Somalis raised the border issue. At a further conference in Addis Ababa in May a number of Africans chided the Somalis for again raising the question.

In the same year open hostilities broke out between Somalia and Ethiopia. The Somalis did not accept the treaty of 1897 by which Britain had ceded part of British Somaliland to Ethiopia; between Italian Somaliland and Ethiopia there was no established border. On independence the Somalis had refrained from challenging a neighbour which possessed American equipment. Ethiopia too, conscious of the racial divisions within its own borders, avoided a clash. But the Somali claim against Kenya alarmed Ethiopia owing to its affinity with Somali claims on Ethiopia's Ogaden province. Fighting developed unofficially along the border during 1962. In the next year the Somali prime minister, Abdirashid Shermake, visited the USSR, Egypt, India, Pakistan and Italy. He got little help or encouragement. Kenya's independence at the end of that year saw also the formal conclusion of a pre-arranged Kenyan–Ethiopian defence treaty, and a few months later open fighting began between Ethiopia and Somalia. The Russians offered their mediation and a deputy foreign minister of the USSR went to Mogadishu, thereby evincing Russian concern, if not for the Somalis, at any rate about possible American or Chinese influence in the Horn. More effective mediation was proffered by the president of the Sudan and the king of Morocco, and after talks in Khartoum hostilities were suspended. But the underlying problem was not resolved and further discussions between Kenya and Somalia in 1965 were abortive. Sporadic fighting continued until 1967 when a new Somali government asked President Kaunda to mediate. Diplomatic relations were restored the next year.

In French Somaliland a movement in favour of amalgamation with the Italian and British territories was circumvented by a vote in the assembly at Djibuti to continue as an Overseas Territory of the French Union, but in 1975 France decided to leave (retaining only a small armed force) and in 1977 the independent Republic of Djibuti came into existence. It included the port of Djibuti and the west shore of the Bab el-Mandeb, was coveted by Somalia and vital to the external commerce at Ethiopia, and was divided between Afars who had kin in Ethiopia and Issas who were Somalis.

The Horn of Africa, besides its regional feuds, acquired international significance in the context of the Cold War. It provided at the southern end of the Red Sea a bridge from Africa into Asia hardly less important than the complementary passage through Sinai, and eastward it faced the wider waters of the Indian Ocean. The United States established influence and bases in Ethiopia. The USSR responded in Somalia where it supplied arms for the Somalis to use against their neighbours in return for storage and communications facilities, intelligence posts and a large air base. In 1974 these manoeuvres were inflamed and transformed by revolution in Ethiopia.

The Ethiopian emperor Haile Selassie had been pressed by friends and relatives to abdicate in 1973 when he reached the age of 80. He was old and much burdened – his heir had a stroke in 1973; his alliance with Israel crumbled in that year of war in the Middle East; American cordiality was waning; students were rioting and workers striking – but he refused to resign. He made a move to loosen the lid which he had clamped on his country but the past blew up in his face. A group of army officers mutinied. This mutiny led to a further revolt by privates, NCOs and junior officers, to the dethronement of the emperor (who later died in prison, possibly murdered or maltreated) and to numerous political assassinations. The deadening influence of the aged, if once noble, emperor had produced intolerable strains (between regions and classes and even within the army), conspiracies, corruption, misgovernment and stagnation, all of which were worsened by the drought and famine which afflicted much of Africa in the early seventies and by the contrasting affluence of the court and nobles. The first mutiny was followed by a series of shortlived governments and by the formation of a loose amalgam of groups called the Dergue (or Committee) whose membership seemed to be fluid and was largely unknown but which became the real power in the capital.

The dominant figure in the new régime was Colonel Haile Mariam Mengistu, a clever manoeuvrer who defeated his main rivals in the Ethiopian People's Republican Party with the help of the socialist Meison which he then routed. Mengistu and his Alyotawi Seded secured control in Addis Ababa but not over the whole country and, most particularly, not in Eritrea in the north nor in the disputed lands in the south. For the next fifteen years and more Mengistu was at war on several fronts, and without foreign help he would have lost one or all of these wars. He got help from the USSR and its Cuban surrogates when, in 1977, Moscow decided to back Mengistu, jeopardizing and forfeiting its alliance with Somalia in order to displace the United States in Ethiopia. Cuban arms saved Harar and Diredawa for Ethiopia and repulsed the Somalis who had been on the verge of conquering the Ogaden. This relief enabled Mengistu to hold his own against the Eritreans until, once more with Russian and Cuban help, he could mount a counter-offensive. For the time being Mengistu was saved –

and the USSR committed to supporting the Christian Amharic empire of Haile Selassie in its new colours under the Dergue. Besides his conflicts with Eritreans and Somalis Mengistu faced revolts in Tigre in the north-west and by the Oromo or Galla peoples of the south (the latter constituting about half the country's population).

Somalia was switched by these events from Russian to American protectorship. But it too was a gravely divided country. Colonel Said Barre, who won power by a coup in 1969, belonged to the Marehan clan which was a section of the Darode peoples who were sandwiched between Issas to the north and Hawieh to the south. Barre benefited from an Ethiopian attack in 1982 which induced his rivals to close ranks against the national enemy but he was seriously injured in a car crash in 1986 and his new term of office, which began a few months later, was bedevilled by intrigues over the succession. An attempt to remove him in 1988 failed, but an Issa incursion from Ethiopia (brutally repressed) and murderous riots in 1989 (two Roman Catholic bishops were killed and order restored only by grisly executions) exposed the country's fragility. Progressively in 1988–90 Barre lost control of the north, the south and finally the central zone and the capital and in 1991 he fell.

In Ethiopia Mengistu's government was able to cow the Western Somali Liberation Front and to check, but not defeat, the Eritrean People's Liberation Front (EPLF). Sudan and Saudi Arabia tried to unify minor Eritrean groups – three of which signed an agreement in Jeddah at the beginning of 1983 – as a prelude to a broader accord with the EPLF whose leftward inclination they distrusted, but these moves were ineffectual and the EPLF demonstrated its vitality by inflicting serious defeats on Ethiopian government forces in 1983 and again in 1988. The United States reclassified the EPLF as a democratic liberation movement instead of a Marxist insurrection. The revolt in Tigre waxed and waned with the fortunes of the Eritreans and the government suffered serious defeats in Tigre in 1989. Russian aid was tapering off and Mengistu felt obliged to offer Eritrea autonomy in a federation. A coup against him misfired but the army, on which he depended, had had enough of war and pressed for any agreement with Eritrea short of independence. Talks began in 1989 with the former President Carter as intermediary. For all the peoples of this region the horrors of seemingly endless wars were compounded by famines so lethal that the outside world put them at the top of the news and was briefly stirred to raise its support for impossibly overworked and underfunded relief agencies. As the Cold War receded the superpowers found themselves at one in wishing to end the wars and reduce the other horrors of the region by promoting a loose federation of Eritrea with Ethiopia which might be expanded to include Djibuti and Somalia, possibly also the Sudan, Uganda and Kenya – all of them members of the International Authority for Drought and Development.

UGANDA, TANZANIA, KENYA

The preponderant power in east and south central Africa had been the British, but the first Europeans to arrive were the Portuguese. Diaz touched land in East Africa on his journey from the Cape to India and back again. On this coast the Portuguese came in touch with the Arab world, establishing ports of call and repair where Arabs were already trading: Kilwa, Zanzibar, Mombasa, Malindi. The nature and extent of Portuguese rights were vague and fluctuating, and they were gradually reduced by the Arabs and then by the British and the Dutch until only the territory of Mozambique remained to them.

The British interest in East Africa has been twofold. To the dominant power in the Indian Ocean the coastal territories were a natural bait, while Britain also became a continental African power in the course of establishing control over inland regions which were deemed necessary to safeguard British strategic interests at the Cape and in the valley of the Nile. A northern thrust from the Cape bypassing the Boer republics and continuing into Rhodesia combined with a southern thrust from Egypt and the Sudan to create the strategic importance of Uganda and the route of access to it through Kenya. In a particularly colourful chapter of the history of exploration and great power competition Britain acquired Uganda and Kenya at the end of the nineteenth century, adding Zanzibar in 1890 (in exchange for giving Heligoland to Germany) and Tanganyika in 1919 as a mandated territory after Germany's defeat in the First World War.

British power was not at first territorially deployed. Preferring, as usual, the indirect approach Britain chose to exert influence on the coast through the Sultan of Zanzibar, an Arab potentate who was also Sultan of Muscat in Arabia but had moved his capital to Zanzibar in 1840. (Zanzibar and Muscat were separated again in 1861, two sons of a deceased sultan setting up separate states and dynasties as the result of mediation by the Viceroy of India, Lord Canning.) Inland, British governments left the business of expansion to commercial concerns until the last quarter of the nineteenth century when the failure of the companies chartered to exploit parts of Africa (found to be only doubtfully rewarding), coupled with the competitive expansion of European powers in Africa, induced Britain to shift to policies of territorial annexation. The failure of the British East Africa Company, for example, led Lord Rosebery's cabinet to endorse a British protectorate over Uganda, the prime minister's doubting colleagues being overpersuaded by strategic arguments about the intentions of other European powers, particularly Italy and Belgium, in the regions of the headwaters of the Nile. After the capitulation of the Italians at Adowa in 1896 to the Emperor Menelek II, Britain feared that Ethiopia would make an alliance with France or with the Mahdists in the Sudan, and Lord Salisbury pressed the construction of the Uganda railway as an adjunct of his policy of reconquering the Sudan. No less important was the contest with Germany, whose determination to become an African power had been made manifest at the Berlin Conference of 1884–85.

The Germans had staked out claims in South-West Africa and then in East Africa to the embarrassment of Britain, which disliked German expansion in Africa but was in need of Germany's friendship in Europe and elsewhere during the period of bad Anglo–French relations from 1880 to 1904. Britain consequently acquiesced in the German occupation of South-West Africa, while taking the precaution of securing Bechuanaland against possible German (or Boer) aspirations which might interfere with the railway from the Cape northwards. In East Africa Britain likewise acquiesced in a German presence and gave up using the Sultan of Zanzibar to make things difficult for the Germans in Tanganyika, while at the same time leasing from the Sultan in 1887 a coastal strip 16 km long (including Mombasa) and developing British power in Uganda and Nyasaland so that the emerging German empire might be contained within limits compatible with essential British interests. The First World War eliminated the German factor, but the early part of the twentieth century also saw, in Britain's more northerly colony of Kenya, an enterprise which was later to produce its own problems. This was the development of Kenya by white settlers. While the removal of great power complications enabled the Foreign Office to dismiss East Africa from its mind, the emergence of new complications of a different nature does not seem to have troubled the mind of the Colonial Office until too late, for whereas the Devonshire Declaration of 1923 had affirmed the primacy of African interests, the settler community assumed, and was allowed to go on assuming until the eve of independence, that its own powers and privileges were not threatened within the foreseeable future. Even in the 1950s both races believed that a white government's devotion to the principles of self-determination and majority rule would stop short at putting a substantial white community under black rule.

East African independence followed West African but – partly because it came later – was achieved by a telescoped sequence of the established pattern of evolution from nominated to mixed councils and so to the fully elected parliaments which accompanied self-government and presaged independence. Tanganyika became independent in December 1961, Uganda in October 1962 and Kenya in December 1963, but in spite of their geographical closeness the circumstances of the three territories were very different.

The special features of Uganda's progress to independence were provided by the composite political structure of the country. The Uganda protectorate included a number of monarchical entities, of which the most important was Buganda under the rule of its kabaka, Frederick Mutesa II. Others were Bunyoro, Toro, Ankole and Busogo. Moreover, between Buganda and Bunyoro there was a territorial feud of long standing. One consequence of the existence of these principalities was that Uganda had a relatively strong nationalism of a traditionalist kind which was antagonistic both to British colonial rule and to the more democratic and anti-monarchical forms of nationalism. The comparative weakness of these latter strands tended to cast the colonial administration for a progressive role in opposition to the conservatism of the kabaka, who was concerned to preserve his traditional powers and the separate identity of his principality. In 1953 a British minister let fall in London an ill-timed remark about an East African federation which was taken by the kabaka – and many other Africans – to betoken a British scheme to create a large new political unit for the better preservation of white rule. A central African federation was being formed at this time and East Africans feared that the white settlers in Kenya were to be given throughout East Africa the powers which Southern Rhodesia's white minority was in the process of confirming in its own country and extending to Northern Rhodesia and Nyasaland. A quarrel ensued between the kabaka and the governor, Sir Andrew Cohen, and the kabaka was despatched into exile for failing to observe the Uganda agreement of 1900, by which he was obliged to accept British advice on certain matters.

The kabaka's exile lasted until 1955. A commission under Sir Keith Hancock worked out a new constitution which the kabaka accepted by the Namirembe agreement and by which he agreed to turn Buganda into a constitutional monarchy and recognize it as being an integral part of Uganda; the Buganda parliament or lukiko was to send representatives to sit in the Uganda parliament (though it began by refusing to do so). The kabaka was thus restored, but the principality to which he returned was a budding democracy within a larger democracy and the British aim to create an independent Uganda which was a unitary parliamentary democracy and not a federation had been significantly advanced.

Britain failed, however, to resolve Buganda's quarrel with Bunyoro. This quarrel went back to 1893 when the British under Lugard and the then kabaka had made war on Bunyoro. Buganda had taken from Bunyoro five counties and two parts of counties and this transfer had been sanctified by Britain in the Uganda agreement of 1900, since when Britain had turned a deaf ear to all Bunyoro complaints. In 1961, however, Britain appointed a commission of privy councillors (the Molson Commission) to try to resolve the quarrel before independence. The commission recommended a compromise which was only partially implemented by the British authorities. Buganda was confirmed in its possession of four counties which were allotted to it by the commission, but a decision on the rest of the disputed territory was postponed. In 1964, after independence, the government of Uganda conducted the plebiscite which had been recommended by the Molson Commission and which conclusively restored these areas to Bunyoro.

Constitutional change in Uganda had begun in 1950 when the legislative council was given an equal number of official members (that is, colonial servants) and unofficial members. Of the latter eight were African, four Asian and four European in recognition of an ethnic problem which did not, however, impede the advance to independence owing to the fact that the European settlers were too few to think of retaining political power and the Asians judged it expedient at an early date to conciliate rather than antagonize the African majority. A similar balance of official and unofficial members was established in the executive council in 1952. In 1954 the size of the legislative council was doubled. In 1961 Uganda was given self-government and Benedikto Kiwanuka became its first prime minister, but Bugandan separatism continued to delay full independence. The lukiko, which had petitioned the British Crown in 1957 for greater autonomy and refused in the following year to play its allotted role in a general election, even declared Buganda independent. The Uganda People's Congress, which had been formed by Milton Obote to fight for independence, entered into an alliance with the Bugandan home rule party, Kabaka Yekka, in order to win a parliamentary majority. Obote took Kiwanuka's place. Independence followed in October 1962. In the following year Uganda became a republic in the Commonwealth and the kabaka accepted the ornamental office of president. But the alliance between Obote and the kabaka did not last. Early in 1966 rumours of scandals in high places threatened to weaken Obote's position. He set up an inquiry and then assumed emergency powers, dismissed and arrested a number of his ministers and dismissed the president. Two months later he introduced a new constitution which precipitated a fresh clash between himself and the lukiko and made himself president. Recurrent rumours of Bugandan plans to resort to force induced, or enabled, him to act first. The kabaka's palace was sacked and the kabaka, barely escaping, was driven once more into exile.

Tanganyika followed in form a similar course through official–unofficial partnership in government to self-government and independence, but the British authorities tried to give a special multiracial twist to events by espousing the equality of races as opposed to the equality of individuals. This concept was enshrined in a constitution of 1955 which provided that the electors in each constituency should all elect one member of each of the three races, but a party formed to apply it, the United Tanganyika Party, never secured much support and was eclipsed by the Tanganyika African National Union (Tanu) formed by Jullius Nyerere in 1954. In 1957 Nyerere, who had been asking for independence in twenty-five years' time, was appointed a member of the legislative council together with Rashid Kawawa, but he soon resigned in order to press the pace and urge independence by 1969. In elections spread over a period in 1958–59 Tanu won all the seats which it contested, and in 1960 it extended its victories throughout the country. The multiracial experiment was given up after a change of governor and of colonial secretary in 1959, and Tanganyika attained independence in 1961. It chose to be a republic and a member of the Commonwealth.

One of the most important elections in the history of British decolonization was held not in any colony but in Britain itself. In 1959 Harold Macmillan was returned to power by the British electorate and one of his first undertakings after this refreshing experience was a journey through Africa which made manifest a new attitude to colonial affairs. Macmillan had felt the 'wind of change' and had determined to let it blow him along. His new colonial secretary, Iain Macleod, was immediately faced with the most difficult of all the East African situations, Kenya.

In Kenya unofficial members of the legislative council began to be given ministerial appointments immediately after the end of the Second World War. They were, however, not black but white, representatives of the British settlers who had been coming to Kenya since the beginning of the century and had been acquiring and developing, in good faith and with intelligent toil, the excellent agricultural land in what came to be called the White Highlands. This community became also politically powerful. It hoped either to rule Kenya in lieu of the colonial authorities or to share in governing a multiracial state on a scale appropriate to its wealth and sophistication rather than to its numbers. It was in other words an aristocracy with scant prospects in a democracy and it was suddenly faced with the problems, more familiar to historians than to farmers, of the aristocracy which is required by events to come to terms with a non-aristocratic future.

In 1953 this community and the colonial régime were faced with a savage outbreak in the Kikuyu tribe which lived in and around Nairobi and had long nourished grievances against the white settlers. Overtly the Kikuyu were represented by Jomo Kenyatta, one-time student of anthropology at London university and president of the Kenya African Union, who had returned to Kenya in 1947. In addition the Kikuyu had formed about 1948 a secret society called Mau Mau, whose activities – known to the authorities but not made much of – were the militant expression of a deep-seated nationalist or xenophobic movement. Mau Mau administered oaths and performed secret rites and cherished apocalyptic fancies, all of which were anti-European and anti-Christian.

With time the society became extreme in its ambitions and barbarous in its practices. It took to murder – mostly of other Kikuyu – and finally developed a campaign of violence and guerrilla warfare. The government declared an emergency, called for military reinforcements from neighbouring territories and from Britain, arrested thousands of Kikuyu including Kenyatta (who was sentenced in 1954 to seven years' imprisonment for organizing Mau Mau), and gradually suppressed the rising. It also initiated a programme for the psychological reorientation of the detainees, although in other departments it succumbed to the infectious passions roused by the Mau Mau and became responsible for ugly beatings of detainees, notably at the Hola camp where gross inhumanities and murders were disclosed at a coroner's inquest in 1959. The African victims of Mau Mau numbered some 8,000; the number of Europeans killed was sixty-eight.

The British government realized that Mau Mau could not be made an excuse for abandoning constitutional advance and in 1956, the year of the termination of the emergency, it introduced changes in the legislative council. The guiding principle was that of multiracialism or partnership between the races, a theory of government which found almost no support among the Africans who demanded a majority in the legislative and executive councils and refused to accept parity with the European elected members in the former or a minority of seats in the latter. To Africans multiracialism was a device for giving the whites unfair shares. The Africans also insisted on being given a date for independence, whereas the British government, unwilling to accept the evidence of an accelerating tempo throughout Africa or to affront the Kenyan settlers by naming a date acceptable to Africans, tried to proceed towards independence at an unrevealed pace without losing control of the situation. In 1959 this policy was abandoned (along with the current colonial secretary) and Kenyatta was conditionally released; in 1961 he was given full freedom of movement and then allowed to stand for and be elected to the legislative assembly.

A constitutional conference was held at Lancaster House in London in 1960 and shortly afterwards the leader of government business in the assembly, Ronald Ngala, was upgraded to chief minister. But the African political leaders, who were now clearly destined to take power in the near future, were divided among themselves. Many of them represented tribes rather than a nation and they failed therefore to create the single unified independence movement which was characteristic of other emergent African countries. The weaker tribes combined to oppose the stronger Kikuyu and Luo and to press for a federal constitution in which important powers would reside in regions rather than with the central government. Constitutional conferences became contests between the Kenya African Democratic Union (Kadu), the proponents of regionalism led by Ngala, and the Kenya African

National Union (Kanu), which objected that too much regionalism would make the constitution unworkable and that Kenya had neither the money nor the trained administrators to be able to afford the complications and duplications of a federal system. The advantage lay with Kanu, under the leadership of Kenyatta, who became prime minister in June 1963, and the British government was even forced to amend in September constitutional proposals of a federal nature which had earlier been accepted by all parties. Kanu's success in elections in May enabled it to face the British government with the choice between revising the constitution on the eve of independence or seeing it changed immediately afterwards. The British preferred to give way in the hope of sparing Kenya a constitutional crisis on the morrow of independence, even though the cost of concession was a not implausible charge of bad faith from Kadu. Kenya became independent on 12 December 1963. It became a republic in 1964, whereupon Kenyatta swiftly removed the constitutional safeguards for minorities and regional rights and, by absorbing Kadu into Kanu, created a centralized one-party state. In 1969 it lost the ablest of its younger leaders when Tom Mboya was assassinated. Before this Kenyatta had removed his principal left-wing rival Oginga Odinga from the vice-presidency and then put him in detention.

Kenya's delayed independence had been a source of anxiety in Tanganyika and Uganda. Kawawa and Obote went to London in 1963 to try to persuade Britain to hurry Kenya into independence. In June the leaders in the three countries declared their intention to federate. Uganda, however, had reservations about a federation since Obote feared that Buganda would insist on being a full member of such a union instead of a component part of Uganda. Kenyatta subsequently disclaimed any serious intention to federate, declaring that the plan had been no more than a means of pressing Britain to hasten Kenya's independence. Perhaps Nyerere alone was wholehearted. The proceedings were certainly dilatory. Obote failed to attend a meeting held in Nairobi in September to discuss the scheme, and the Kenyans established an awkward system of being represented by Kanu at one meeting and Kadu at the next. There were also genuine difficulties such as the location of the federal capital, the choice of a federal president (the promotion of Kenyatta, the obvious candidate, would unleash an inopportune contest for the Kenyan presidency), the division of powers and other constitutional matters, opposition from Ghana to any regional associations likely to hamper Nkrumah's pan-African schemes, and Tanganyika's trend to the left in its domestic and its external policies. In the end Tanganyika, regretfully but firmly, insisted on a decision and the scheme thereupon collapsed.

The three East African territories made some attempts to integrate their economies. Under British rule they had had a common currency and certain common services (for example, posts, railways, medical services) and had constituted a common market. Tanganyika and Uganda complained, at intervals and with some justice, that Kenya took the lion's share of the resulting benefits and in 1960 the Raisman Commission was appointed to report on these dissensions. It recommended that the links should be retained subject to some reorganization in favour of Tanganyika and Uganda. In 1964 Kenya offered further concessions in order to prevent the disruption of this partial union and in 1968, after a fresh inquiry and report by a Danish expert, the three states signed a Treaty of East African Co-operation. It became a dead letter as the three partners pursued divergent social and economic policies and their relations became strained, and it was finally dissolved in 1977.

Kenya under Kenyatta became a relatively stable country run by a progressively more corrupt black élite. Nairobi became a magnet for the rural unemployed who congregated in shanty towns which were sporadically destroyed by the authorities. Kenya's relations with its neighbours deteriorated. Its rumbustious capitalism grated with Tanzania's possibly more salubrious but less successful socialism and these ideological differences turned in the seventies into bickerings, mutual expulsions and the closing of the frontier. With Uganda a border dispute initiated by Idi Amin, followed by charges of Kenyan complicity in the Entebbe rescue operation (see below: the Israeli rescuers used Nairobi on their way back) almost led to war. Kenya's traditional friendship with Ethiopia against the Somalis temporarily lost its charms when the Dergue deposed the emperor Haile Salassie. Kenyatta's senescence was another source of worries. His family and familiars were expected to make a bid to retain power and affluence when he died and prepared to do so, but in the event (1978) Vice-president Daniel Moi stepped smoothly into his place with promises of continuing the country's good fortunes and erasing its less estimable features.

Moi displayed unexpected authority and gave Kenya a second instalment of comparative political stability. He withstood a semi-covert challenge from Charles Njonjo (one of Kenyatta's more ebullient colleagues and a standard-bearer of the Kikuyus) and he survived an attempted coup in 1982, but his position was sapped by unappeased Kikuyu resentment at his elevation and by economic recession. He transformed Kenya into a one-party state, harassed independent bodies (lawyers, for example) and resorted to strong-arm rule, imprisonment and torture, while he himself became a flagrantly rich man surrounded by mediocre cronies. Kenya's ambition to be the Ivory Coast of the east – a thrustingly successful capitalist state – lost its momentum, unemployment rose, wages fell, landless cultivators flocked to the capital which became one of the more dangerous as well as one of the more corrupt cities in Africa, and by the mid-eighties this corruption had led to financial scandals, collapsing banks and secret police intrigue. The importance of Kenya's ocean coast (a tropical paradise) attracted the United States which built bases there, dispensed lucrative contracts and provided funds for strategic and less serious ancillary services. Kenya's relations with its neighbours were poor, particularly with Uganda: each country harboured refugees from the other. In 1990 the foreign minister, Robert Ouko, a possible successor to Moi, was murdered by Moi's police.

Tanganyika became Tanzania by an act of union with Zanzibar concluded in 1977 but foreshadowed by earlier events. In Zanzibar, still a British dependency, the Afro-Shirazi Union staged a successful coup at the beginning of 1964. This party, which represented the bulk of the African population of about 200,000 (the Arabs numbering some 44,000) had suffered a setback in elections in 1961 which had given control to a coalition of the Zanzibar National Party and the Zanzibar People's Party; and in 1963 the British, ignoring warnings from Tanganyika, had transferred power to the sultan and the Arab minority with the result that Zanzibar had carried into independence an inbuilt racial conflict in which the scales had been artificially tipped in favour of a minority. The Afro-Shirazi Union wanted neither the sultan nor any kind of Arab dominance. Its leaders – Abeid Karume, Abdullah Hanga, Othman Shariff – led what was essentially an African, anti-Arab revolt and proclaimed a republic with the first two as president and vice-president. Their allies in this reversal of power included a minor Arab party, the Umma Party led by Abdul Rahman Muhammad Babu, the local correspondent of the *New China News Agency*, and a curious soldier of fortune styled Field-Marshal John Okello, who was said to have fought in Cuba but was soon sent into exile when the value of his services proved less than the embarrassment of his presence. The Afro-Shirazis and their friends were quickly branded by a startled world as tools of China.

Alarm was felt in Dar-es-Salaam too and on 17 January Nyerere, remembering perhaps Nasser's anti-communist pre-emptive action in Syria in 1958, sent his home minister and some armed police to Zanzibar, thus acquiring control of the situation. On 20 January troops in Dar-es-Salaam mutinied; a second mutiny occurred at Tabora in central Tanganyika on the following day. Similar acts of insubordination took place in Uganda and Kenya on the 23rd and 24th. In all these places order was restored with the help of British troops who were still stationed in Nairobi (they were not due to leave until the end of the year). The mutineers asked for better pay and the replacement of British officers by Africans. They were using violence to protest to their leaders, not attempting to overthrow them. But in the light of events in Zanzibar rumours circulated of a widespread communist plot, reinforced by Okello's presence in Dar-es-Salaam on the eve of the first disturbance. The British left a week after their arrival. In April Tanganyika and Zanzibar were joined together to make the new state of Tanzania with Nyerere as president and Karume as senior vice-president. The association proved most unhappy for Nyerere. He was denied all influence in Zanzibar and even access to it. Karume established an autocratic régime which, whether or not it was under Chinese control, certainly produced some extreme scandals such as the much publicized forcing of teenage girls into marriage or concubinage with the island's new élite. In 1969 Karume was able to exact from Nyerere the return to Zanzibar of political enemies who were thereby consigned to their deaths. This humiliating concession to brutality by a statesman of an uncommonly humane nature may have been due to Nyerere's fear that Zanzibar might add to his other current troubles, for he was facing discontent in the south, among former members of trade unions (which he had suppressed) and from women's organizations, junior officers and disappointed civil servants. Karume was assassinated in 1972. The formal unification of Tanganyika with Zanzibar and Pemba was effected in 1977. Tanzania's stability (despite poverty) and its influence in African affairs (for example, in the protracted Rhodesian crisis) were due to the character and intelligence of President Nyerere who remained in office until 1985 but bequeathed to his successor, Ali Hassan Mwinyi, an economy which, partly by bad management and partly from bad luck and its own inherent weaknesses, was faced with famine, rationing, a declining standard of living and unpayable foreign debts.

Although Nyerere resigned the presidency he did not retire from politics and he remained chairman of Tanzania's ruling party, Chama cha Mapindusi; he was re-elected to this post in 1987 for a further five years. He criticized his successor's economic policies. Mwinyi turned for help to the IMF and secured large credits at the price of devaluing the currency by 50 per cent and accepting the standard IMF package of funds in return for austerity – the policy which Nyerere had always opposed. Mwinyi also had problems in Zanzibar. He had been president of Zanzibar from 1984 when he succeeded Aboud Jumba until he became president of Tanzania a year later. Zanzibar's new president, Abdul Wakif, was a figurehead and the Zanzibaris feared outright annexation; they took to the streets and people were killed. After elections in 1990 Mwinyi appointed a new prime minister, John Malecela, who became thereby the outstanding contender for the presidency in succession to Mwinyi.

Kenyatta and Nyerere brought stability, if of different kinds, to their countries – virtually unchallenged in office, the former becoming more remote and unpredictable with age and giving rise to some apprehension about what would happen when he died; the latter continuing to guide Tanzania along the road of self-reliance proclaimed by the Arusha Declaration which in 1967 pledged the country to a village socialism and participatory democracy within the framework of a single-party state. In Uganda things were different. Obote was overthrown by an army coup while he was attending a Commonwealth conference in Singapore in January 1971. In coming to power he had antagonized many traditionalists, particularly in Buganda; he had then scared the property-owning classes by mildly left-wing pronouncements, and intellectuals by authoritarian scorn. After surviving at attempt on his life in 1969 he tried to curb the power of the army and its commander, Idi Amin, but failed to do so. Amin took his place. Hailed at first as a good sound army type (and boxing champion) with a respectably British background, Amin instituted a reign of terror, especially after an unsuccessful attempt by Obote in September 1972 to invade Uganda from Tanzania with a force of about 1,000 men. (Obote had gone first to the Sudan but had had to leave as a result of the pacification of the south by Nimeiry.) Amin was not reluctant to play a part in international affairs. He proclaimed himself a friend of Israel but then changed sides and became a strong partisan of the Palestinians. In 1976 Uganda became a centre of world attention when an Air France airbus, hijacked at Athens by the Palestinian PELP in an attempt to secure the release of Palestinians from Israeli and other jails, landed at Entebbe. After its 150 non-Israeli passengers had been released, the remaining 100 were rescued in a spectacularly daring and efficient Israeli commando operation.

Amin made a particular stir by giving notice to Uganda's 70,000 Asians to leave the country within three months, though he later exempted those of them who were Ugandan citizens. Since most of them were British citizens Amin's move greatly embarrassed the British government which, having foolishly failed to take up an earlier offer by Obote to discuss this problem, now found itself caught between its evident obligation to allow British citizens into Britain and the clamour against allowing them in if they were numerous and black. Amin also evicted the British military mission and High Commissioner whom he accused of complicity in Obote's attempted counter-coup. In the following year he began the take-over of hundreds of foreign, mostly British, businesses while throughout the country the roll of Ugandans, distinguished and undistinguished, who disappeared increased gruesomely, to 500,000 by the time he was overthrown in 1979. Amin was what ordinary people call mad. (Coincidentally 1979 saw the disappearance of two other mad monsters, the emperor Jean-Bedel Bokassa of Central Africa and President Macias Nguema of Equatorial Guinea.

All three had received more support than was decent from the three antecedent colonial powers.)

Amin's fall was effected by a Tanzanian invasion, the only practical step by any African state to rid the continent of a barbarous tyranny. A Tanzanian force, accompanied by a Ugandan National Liberation Army, seized the capital without difficulty and installed a provisional government under a former vice-chancellor of Makerere university, Dr Yusufu Lule. After a mere two months Lule was deposed by his National Consultative Council and was replaced by Godfrey Binaisa, a lawyer who had held ministerial office under Obote. Binaisa was himself deposed by the army and placed in detention while a pro-Obote Council took over the government of the country. These changes, together with Nyerere's known partisanship of Obote who soon reappeared in Uganda, presaged the latter's return to power, and at the end of 1980 his popularity in the northern half of the country and the active support of the civil and military authorities carried him back to the presidency by a narrow and disputed margin. His rule, which lasted until 1985, was disastrous and hardly, if at all, less bloody than Amin's. With ethnic feuds unabated and the army out of hand, mass slaughter was reduced only by mass flight – mainly to Sudan and Zaïre. Those who ousted Obote were soon fighting one another. The ultimate victor was the National Resistance Army of Yoweri Museveni which, having defeated Obote's forces and the succeeding military government of Tito Okello, put an end to organized opposition by the defeat of General Basilio Okello in the north (but mopping up continued for three years). Museveni became the new president at the age of 40 with a reputation for decency and political acumen, an appalling legacy of savage destruction and no obvious way to convert foreign sympathy into economic aid.

THE LEGACY OF CECIL RHODES

Towards the end of the nineteenth century the British presence in Cape
Colony, hemmed in and menaced by the German occupation of South-
West Africa on the one hand and the Boer republics across the Orange
and Vaal rivers on the other, caused the British to venture northwards
in order to rule out a junction between these two potential enemies and
to secure a passage for a railway to the north through British territory.
In 1844 the British government declared a protectorate over Bechuanaland, a huge and largely desert area to the north of Cape Colony,
but for the rest of the century it was a British citizen rather than any
British government who directed the British advance in this sector.
That citizen was Cecil Rhodes and one of the principal reasons why he
was able to direct policy was the fact that he was able to finance it.

Rhodes struck north from the Cape Colony into Bechuanaland with
his eyes on the Zambezi River – and possibly even the Nile. His
company, the British South Africa Company, was chartered by the
British government in 1889 to administer Bechuanaland and he lost no
time in pushing on. In 1896–97 he fought and conquered the Matabele
and the Mashona and so became the ruler of what was later to be called
Southern Rhodesia, but also in 1896 the failure of the Jameson raid into
the Transvaal wrecked his ambition to rule in Johannesburg too and
resulted in a gradual reassertion of British governmental control over
policy towards the Boers: in 1899 it was the British government and
not Rhodes who made the Boer War. From Southern Rhodesia he
continued across the Zambezi and, by questionable methods and with
questionable legality, won concessions from the sovereign or litunga of
Barotseland and other African chiefs. (Lewanika, the litunga of
Barotseland, had given a concession to a fortune-hunter in Johannesburg who sold it to the company. He then gave further concessions to
the company in the hope of enlisting British support against the
Matabele monarch, Lobengula. It seems very unlikely that the parties to
the concession agreements were talking about the same things and
accordingly the agreements would, in English law, be void.) Rhodes's
empire was now considerable and there was no reason to suppose that it

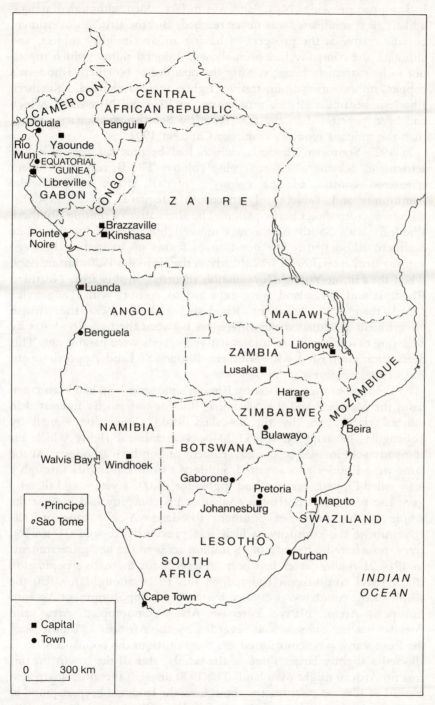

23.1 Equatorial and southern Africa

had stopped growing. Nyasaland was in fact added, although Katanga, a likely next candidate, was never reached. But the British government became restive at the prospect of having an over-mighty subject, and although the company had been allowed mineral rights (which turned out to be extremely lucrative after the opening of Northern Rhodesia's copper mines) its administrative rights were restricted. Northern Rhodesia became a British protectorate in 1924 and Nyasaland, which had been penetrated in the first place by Scottish missionaries rather than the militant pioneers from the Cape, in 1907.

In 1923 Southern Rhodesia, which had become an area of white settlement, became a self-governing colony. The British government transfered control of the colony's internal affairs to its white community and, subject only to certain safeguards and reservations, withdrew from direct participation. The alternative of uniting Southern Rhodesia with South Africa was mooted but rejected by the white Southern Rhodesians. The question of forms of association between various British territories was already in the air in the 1920s but in 1929, when the Hilton Young Commission reported on this area, Northern Rhodesia and Nyasaland were expected to consort with Tanganyika rather than with Southern Rhodesia, and in 1930 the British government accentuated the differences between the two Rhodesias by declaring that in the protectorates native interests were paramount. This declaration contrasted with Southern Rhodesia's Land Apportionment Act of the same year.

At the time of the conquest by Rhodes's pioneers land had been taken from the Matabele and the Mashona. Rhodes was chiefly interested in mineral rights and, by the so-called Rudd Concession signed by Lobengula, he acquired for £1,200 a year mineral rights which his company sold in 1933 to the government of Southern Rhodesia. At the same time Rhodes also acquired, indirectly from Lobengula through a man called Lippert, certain 'land' rights for £1,000 a year – and thereby gave rise to a long controversy whether his company had bought the whole of the surface of Southern Rhodesia. At the time of self-government the company, which had previously re-sold 31 million acres, transferred a balance of 45 million acres to the new government. In 1914 21 million acres had been 'reserved' for the native population and a royal commission had judged this to be enough. In 1930 the whole of the country was divided by the Land Apportionment Act into European Areas, Native Purchase Areas, Unoccupied Areas and Forests, but the division was regarded by the Africans as unjust since the Europeans, who constituted less than a fifth of the population, were allotted a slightly larger share of the whole, and all the towns; in this area no African might own land. The 1930 division therefore sharpened instead of allaying resentments about how the land had been acquired in the first place, and showed that in Southern Rhodesia native interests would be anything but paramount. The principle of racial division of the land was also a foretaste of further racial irritants on a similarly unjust and discriminatory basis.

After a preliminary conference of officials from the two Rhodesias at Victoria Falls in 1936 the Bledisloe Commission was appointed in 1938 to consider closer union between them and Nyasaland. The commission rejected the idea on the grounds that divergences in native policies and the hostility of the Africans made it impracticable. It recommended no more than a Central African council consisting of the governors of the two protectorates and the prime minister of Southern Rhodesia to co-ordinate matters of common concern. This pale and tepid council was created in 1944. But the protagonists of closer union were neither discouraged nor defeated and in nine years they secured the creation of the Central African Federation. Throughout these years Southern Rhodesia was pursuing a policy of association with Northern Rhodesia after having rejected the alternative of association with South Africa. It was not contemplating a separate existence on its own, although there was among the whites a group which wanted dominion status for Southern Rhodesia within the Commonwealth.

The white leaders in Northern and Southern Rhodesia realized that their interests were not the same and were wary of each other. Roy Welensky in the north, where the riches lay, suspected Godfrey Huggins in the south of wishing to take over Northern Rhodesia for the benefit of the more numerous white population of Southern Rhodesia. On the other hand Southern Rhodesia, although poorer, was freer in terms of British control over its internal affairs; it had a quasi-independence which the whites in Northern Rhodesia (excluding the colonial administrators) coveted for themselves and wished to secure through the Southern Rhodesian back door. These attitudes were clearly to the fore at a conference at Victoria Falls in 1949 which, with no African present, became a tussle between Huggins and Welensky, with the latter falling back on the position that there should be no federation without a referendum. The northerners were at this stage suspicious of the federal idea, but the conference put it on the map and made it the central talking-point of the next few years. This conference was followed in 1951 by a conference in London of officials from the three territories and the two British departments of state concerned (the Colonial Office and the Commonwealth Relations Office). Their report, while again recognizing African opposition to federation, hoped that it would evaporate under the impact of the economic advantages which they listed. At a further conference in the same year at Victoria Falls the politicians (who included the two British secretaries of state as well as the two governors), senior officials and white Rhodesian leaders accepted the greater part of the officials' arguments. This conference was also attended by Africans from Northern Rhodesia and Nyasaland, but they were less impressed by the economic advantages of a federation than by the fear of coming under the rule of the white minority in Salisbury.

A change of government in London from Labour to Conservative shifted the balance of forces in favour of federation. Whereas Labour ministers had come to look favourably on federation but were unwilling to go forward with it without first discovering more about the wishes of the African population, Conservative ministers were more emphatic in their approval, considered that it was impossible to discover what the Africans really thought, ascribed African opposition to irascible and ignorant factiousness, and believed that it was in any case the duty of government to do what was best even if some people did not yet see how good it was. Yet another conference assembled, this time at Lancaster House in London (the maternity ward for emergent constitutions). It was boycotted by the Africans of the two northern territories, though the Southern Rhodesian delegation included Joseph Savanhu and Joshua Nkomo who acted as uneasy camp-followers until the end of the conference. The outcome was a federal constitution with temporarily significant reservations. The federation was to have three separate territorial administrations and assemblies as well as a federal government and parliament, the retention of the British protectorate over the northern territories, the proviso that the federation should not be granted dominion status without the consent of a majority of the population, and the creation of an African Affairs Board with blocking powers designed (unsuccessfully as it proved) to prevent racially discriminatory legislation. The federation came into being on 1 August 1953. Huggins became the first federal prime minister with Welensky as his deputy and a cabinet of six; Huggins also became the leader of a newly formed Federal Party with branches on both sides of the Zambezi. In Southern Rhodesia Huggins was succeeded by Garfield Todd as prime minister and leader of the United Party.

The Central African Federation lasted ten years. It was accepted with misgiving by some whites in Southern Rhodesia who feared cheap black labour and rightly opined that the connection with the British protecting power in the north would act as a drag on their plans for dealing with the racial situation. But on the whole federation was welcomed by the whites who believed that within it they would conserve their privileged standards of living, excitingly expand the material things which they were already doing well, and somehow find a way of fitting a small African middle class into the existing order. The idea of partnership, which was written into the constitution and salved a lot of uneasy consciences in London, meant at best a half share in power for Africans in a barely discernible future. Like the Belgians in the Congo they regarded the African as an economic man who could be satisfied with a material competence (however assessed) and, apart from a few over-educated eccentrics and professional trouble-makers, had no real interest in politics. Nationalism they grievously underestimated, and also the force of human indignation over inequality and injustice. Ideas were not their stock-in-trade and so they failed to realize that ideas were at the root of the refusal of the Africans to accept their rule. From the prime minister downwards they insulted and humiliated their black fellow citizens with remarks about living in trees and with the practical application of segregation in public places like post offices and restaurants, and so quickly confirmed the Africans' conviction that partnership was to be not an endeavour but a pretence.

The life of the federation was violent as well as short. The Africans began the violence. Most of them were never interested in the economic aspects of federation or never understood them; the more sophisticated among them understood and saw that they were largely bogus. Despite a distinct current of non-violence, in the African national movements the partisans of violence, aided by circumstances and by exaggerated white reactions, became increasingly prominent. An incident provoked by thieves in the night at Cholo in Nyasaland in August 1953 caused the death of eleven Africans and injuries to many more and led the authorities to magnify the prevalence of hooliganism and subversive activities. It was also a curtain-raiser for more significant events in Nyasaland.

Nyasaland was included in the federation because the British insisted, unwilling to keep it on their hands as a separate dependency with little hope of becoming anything but a drain on the British exchequer. It was an African country with a white population of only 1 in 500, no settlers or industry, its people dependent on Southern Rhodesia and South Africa for the jobs which did not exist and had not been created in their own country. It had been nurtured by the Church of Scotland in much the same way as Paraguay by the Jesuits. It had also a charismatic figure beyond the horizon in Dr Hastings Banda who had spent most of his life learning and practising the profession of medicine in the United States, Scotland, Liverpool, Tyneside and Ghana.

Dr Banda arrived in Nyasaland in 1958 to lead an anti-federation crusade in conjunction with nationalists of a younger generation who were glad to enlist and serve under this more famous elder figure. As in many similar cases certain differences of aim and outlook were easily submerged by the single paramount objective of seceding from the federation and establishing an independent sovereign state. In January 1959 there occurred a secret and apparently confused palaver between nationalist leaders which was afterwards represented as a murderous conspiracy to kill a number of Europeans and seize power. Banda was not present at this meeting and either knew nothing of it, or did not mind what happened at it, or knew all about it and chose to turn a blind eye. Banda himself was a man of considerable, even violent, oratorical powers who preached non-violence, but the situation was one of growing violence and jumpiness and in February the governor of Nyasaland asked for Rhodesian troops to help keep order. The government of Southern Rhodesia sent 3,000 troops and took the opportunity to declare a state of emergency in its own territory. The governor of Nyasaland followed suit a week later. Between 2,000 and 3,000 Africans were rounded up in the federation, the African National Congresses in all three territories were dissolved and Banda and his chief associates were among those lodged in jail. The British colonial secretary, Alan Lennox-Boyd, said that he had evidence of an impending massacre.

These dramatic events evoked some scepticism as well as alarm, and the British government appointed a commission under a High Court judge, Sir Patrick Devlin, to verify the allegations with which these emergency measures had been justified. The commission was unable to find evidence of any murder plot and specifically exonerated Banda. It found that the governor of Nyasaland had got into a position where he had either to abdicate or reach for emergency powers and troops, and that in consequence Nyasaland had become temporarily a police state in which it was unsafe to express approval of the policies of the Congress to which the great majority of Africans adhered. This report, by exploding a myth propagated by authorities in London as well as Salisbury, gave a fillip to the anti-federation campaign and discredited the bona fides of their opponents. Shortly after its appearance the Colonial Office was placed in the charge of a more liberal member of the Conservative government, Iain Macleod, and the prime minister, Harold Macmillan, began a series of devious moves designed to give British colonial policies a leftward shift. These moves were to include his tour of Africa, his 'wind of change' speech at Cape Town during that tour, the appointment of the Monckton Commission, and Macleod's first visit to Kenya – all in 1960.

The federal constitution of 1953 had left the territorial constitutions untouched. It had also made clear that the federation could not hope for independence or dominion status until they were touched. In 1958 there were elections for the federal and the Southern Rhodesian parliaments. In the former Welensky, who had succeeded Huggins (now Lord Malvern) in 1956, scored an overwhelming victory; few of the qualified Africans bothered to register or vote, partly because they disliked the existing two-roll franchise and partly because they were afraid of the police. In Southern Rhodesia Todd was forced to resign by his cabinet colleagues, who refused to accept a wage increase for Africans which had been recommended by the Labour Board. More important, they regarded the comparatively liberal Todd as an electoral Jonah and although he was allowed a seat in the new cabinet formed by Sir Edgar

Whitehead he was soon dropped and in the elections his new United Rhodesia Party won no single seat. Whitehead scraped in, although the Dominion Party led by Winston Field, campaigning in favour of independence by 1960, got more votes. This eclipse of Todd was in part a white reaction to the reanimation of the African National Congress by George Nyandoro and Robert Chikerema in 1957 and was also the first of a series of moves which placed the premiership in the hands of ever more extreme politicians who were gradually forced to be more explicit about the basic white demand for independence from Britain as the only way of ensuring that power would remain in white hands for as long as anybody cared to look into the future. In Northern Rhodesia a new constitution preceded elections in 1959 which gave victory to the United Federal Party (the new name for the local version of the Huggins–Welensky party); the party was, however, almost universally rejected by Africans in spite of the support it received from the whole press. These elections showed that the enchantments of federation were not working even before the alleged murder plot and the judgements of the Devlin Commission.

From about 1960 there was in effect a race between the forces which wanted to extract independence for the federation out of the British government and the forces which wanted to break up the federation and establish black rule in its several parts. The British government, caught in this crossfire, resorted to the expedient of sending a commission to look into the situation. Welensky opposed this manoeuvre in private but acquiesced in public. The Africans boycotted it, as did the British Labour opposition. The commission, presided over by Lord Monckton, an eminent Queen's Counsel and former Conservative minister, produced an ambivalent report in which a majority extolled the principle of federation but judged it unworkable. The nature of the commission's work inevitably raised the question of the right to secede from the federation, although the white leaders in Rhodesia and their friends in Britain hotly contended that the commission had no power to consider the matter and that the British prime minister had promised that it would not be raised; a majority concluded that there was no legal right to secede but that, as a matter of practical politics, the issue should be placed on the agenda of a federal review conference and that Britain should declare its willingness to permit secession after the passage of a defined trial period of federation. This was the commission's most important recommendation since it placed federation on probation. The commission's report marked in fact the turning of the tide in favour of the break-up of the federation, even though the commission gave more attention and space to reforms designed to make it work (such as parity between Europeans and Africans in the federal parliament, a broader franchise, and immediate advances towards self-government in Northern Rhodesia with an

African majority in the legislative council and an unofficial majority in the executive council).

A federal review conference assembled in London at the end of 1960. The federal constitution did not require such a conference at this date but in the judgement of the British government it had become necessary. Yet it achieved nothing and was adjourned *sine die*, to be followed by a Northern Rhodesia constitutional conference which produced bitter backstage fighting in which Welensky (who, like Cecil Rhodes, relied partly on a group of members of the Westminister parliament) was worsted by Macmillan and Macleod. Each side suspected the other, perhaps correctly, of being about to use force and Welensky called up troops. The constitutional proposals which escaped from this mêlée would have made it impossible for Welensky to secure control of the Northern Rhodesian parliament. But the proposals, when embodied in a White Paper, were not allowed to pass unscathed and the British government made some slight concessions to Welensky. In so doing it angered Kenneth Kaunda and other leaders of the United National Independence Party (Unip) who accused the British of tinkering behind the scenes with the agreed outcome of the conference. There were violent demonstrations in Northern Rhodesia and the proposals were reversed. These swingings and swayings reflected the divided mind of the British Conservative Party and cabinet; it was by this time reasonably clear that the federation was doomed, although nobody was prepared to say so; and although Welensky and his white followers had fervent friends in London, there was a growing body of opinion in the party which recognized the greater expediency of being friends with Kaunda and the many African states which stood behind him. A third set of proposals was eventually propounded which ensured that neither Unip nor the Federal Party could get a parliamentary majority and was in any case too complicated to be understood by anybody but a constitutional maniac. It was rejected by Kaunda.

During this same period another conference went through similar travail to produce a new constitution for Southern Rhodesia. Its proposals, which guaranteed a larger minority parliamentary representation to Africans but also removed nearly all the residual powers of the British government, were accepted by Nkomo at the conference but repudiated by him immediately afterwards because he came to believe, again probably correctly, that if he accepted the increased number of seats, the British government would immediately grant independence to Southern Rhodesia under its white rulers who would then either arrest or even reverse the advance towards African majority rule. The British government had hoped to find a formula containing a large enough element of agreement to enable it to give independence with a good conscience and get out of a hopeless situation, but African insistence on the magic formula of majority rights – echoed after all by many in Britain itself – baulked its efforts and kept it on the hook.

The following year, 1962, saw an abortive British Plan to carve up Northern Rhodesia by elevating Barotseland into a separate state under its traditional and conservative ruler, the litunga, and by giving a further slice of it to Southern Rhodesia. The only effect of this bizarre and anachronistic notion was to create bad blood between the nationalists and traditionalists. R. A. Butler was then appointed to a special office of Central African Affairs. His business was to assuage the internal feuding in the Conservative Party and to wind up the federation. By the end of the year Nyasaland had been promised self-government and the right to secede from the federation. In Northern Rhodesia Unip was asked to join the government in 1962 and the right to secede from the federation was acknowledged in 1963. With the secession of Northern Rhodesia there was no federation left. It expired on the last day of 1963.

Nyasaland and Northern Rhodesia, independent from July and October 1964, became the republics of Malawi and Zambia (both of them within the Commonwealth) and with Banda and Kaunda as their presidents. Banda, born before the turn of the century, developed into a conservative dictator, intolerant of opposition but successful both in surviving threats of civil war and in developing Malawi's agricultural economy to the point where he was able to raise in 1978 a Euroloan of £14 million. Under a plausible plea of economic necessity he made a commercial agreement (1967) and established conventional relations with South Africa and he supported Renamo in Mozambique until about 1986. Autocratic, sharply anti-communist, morally intolerant, Banda had some of the traits of the South African Nationalists. As age dimmed his wits – he was a little older than the century – his authority passed to Cecilia Kadzamisa and her uncle John Tembo who became Banda's heir apparent in a situation of deepening uncertainty.

Zambia's fortunes were diametrically different. Zambia became independent with healthy resources and exports and a favourable balance of payments. First among its assets was copper, but it was rich also in other minerals, water and agriculture. A boom in the later sixties fortified hopes for prosperity together with progress in education and other social services; but the seventies were a bitter disappointment particularly after the closing of the frontier with Rhodesia in 1973. The Tanzam railway (see Chapter 24) failed to come up to expectations. Copper prices slumped in 1975; some mines became unprofitable; whites began to leave the Copperbelt; blacks lost their jobs and their troubles were compounded by a shortage of maize. Kaunda's popularity waned and there were plots or at least rumours of plots against him. With the ending of the war in Rhodesia it became apparent that Zambia's misfortunes could not wholly be blamed on that war.

One of Africa's potentially wealthier countries and the recipient of a fair share of western financial and technical aid, Zambia had lapsed into perilous economic straits because development had been grievously mismanaged. The poor got poorer and lacked basic goods; agriculture was neglected while city building and an élite of city dwellers flourished. Kaunda, his personal rectitude unsullied, was none the less criticized for picking mediocre advisers, for refusing to face economic facts and for presiding over a saddeningly inept decline in his people's fortunes. To secure re-election in 1978 he resorted to disqualification of rivals in advance and in 1980 he took emergency measures against an alleged conspiracy to overthrow him. To secure essential foreign credits through the IMF he cut subsidies on foodstuffs with the inevitable result that prices soared and there were serious riots in the Copperbelt in 1986. Whether or not these riots were inflamed by South African agents South Africa applied economic and military sanctions against Zambia which had become a principal headquarters and base for the ANC. Economically Zambia's dependence on South African routes and ports had been intensified by disorders in Mozambique and Angola which atrophied the alternatives. In 1987 the South African air force attacked Lusaka and killed a number of Zambians and in 1989 Kaunda restricted the ANC's presence in Zambia, disowned its militant tactics and embarked on a dialogue with South Africa's in-coming president F. W. de Klerk. Mounting popular discontent, allied with growing uneasiness in the army and the churches, forced Kaunda to abandon in 1990 his opposition to the multiparty system which he had abrogated early in his rule. Parties had in fact sprung up and the one-party system was dissolving of its own accord.

In Southern Rhodesia the constitution of 1961 had left only one political issue between the Southern Rhodesia and British governments: independence. Winston Field had envisaged an independent Rhodesian dominion consisting of Southern Rhodesia and most of Northern Rhodesia, with Barotseland and Nyasaland as separate states under high commissioners appointed by the United Kingdom, but this unlikely scheme had been overtaken by events. In 1963 he began negotiations with Britain on the bare issue of independence for Southern Rhodesia and was confronted with five conditions: unimpeded progress towards majority rule in Southern Rhodesia; guarantees against regressive amendments of the 1961 constitution; an immediate improvement of African rights; an end to racial discrimination; and a basis for independence acceptable to the people of the country as a whole. Ian Smith, who ousted Winston Field in 1964, tried to meet the last and most intractable of these conditions by assembling an *indaba* of chiefs who, having been fêted by the government and even given nice trips abroad, said exactly what was expected of them – but without convincing anybody in Britain that this was a demonstration of the popular will. The advent of a Labour government in London at the end of 1964 caused despondency among whites in Salisbury and increased the demand for a unilateral declaration of independence, but the new British government, beset by a major economic crisis and possessing only the thinnest parliamentary majority, decided to keep talks with Salisbury going for the sake of talking and gaining time. There was, however, no basis for agreement since the British government was pledged to conditions which ran counter to the fundamental demand of the great majority of the white community in Rhodesia: the indefinite preservation of their minority rule. As a last resort the British government proposed the appointment of a royal commission under the Rhodesian chief justice, Sir Hugh Beadle, to examine ways of testing the popular will but this proposal was rejected by Smith and on 11 November 1965 the Smith government declared the country independent. The government was thereupon dismissed by the governor, Sir Humphrey Gibbs. It remained, however, the effective government of Rhodesia within its borders.

The British government was determined not to use force except in the event of a major breakdown of public order. Superficially the situation was one in which previous British governments had not hesitated to use force, but the Rhodesian case was in substance different in two decisive ways: first, because Rhodesia, although technically a colony, had been administered and in effect governed by its own white population for more than forty years and not by Whitehall, and secondly because the rebellious government was white and not black, so that a recourse to force in what the Rhodesian whites had made a racial issue would bitterly have divided opinion in Britain and could even have faced British army officers with a test of obedience which they might not have passed. The British government was left therefore with two courses, negotiation and economic coercion.

For a year it pursued both courses with the emphasis on the first. It immediately took fiscal measures against Rhodesia, imposed oil sanctions and secured the passage of a Security Council resolution against the supply of arms to Rhodesia and requesting an international economic boycott. Over forty countries besides Britain complied with this request. In April 1966 the Security Council, at British request, authorized the use of force to implement oil sanctions and in December, again at British request, it imposed mandatory sanctions over a wide assortment of commodities. Eighteen months later this ban was made total. But despite hardships, which took time to take effect or become apparent, the Smith régime was able to maintain itself thanks to the South African government (which supplied credit and goods and facilitated the export of Rhodesian products), thanks to Rhodesia's capacity to retaliate economically against Zambia (which was dependent on Rhodesia for coal for its copper mines and in other ways), and thanks also to the British government's reluctance to intensify its economic measures so long as it could go on hoping for a negotiated settlement. Rhodesia's exports were substantially blocked, its reserves were depleted, its government had to resort to internal loans, it became virtually a dependency of South Africa, but the régime was not compelled to capitulate and the economy, though damaged, adjusted itself.

In applying sanctions Britain was intent not on destroying the Rhodesian economy or even the Smith régime but on forcing Smith to come to terms. These tactics and aims did not commend themselves to most of the Commonwealth which suspected the British government of being bent on a deal with Smith even to the extent of betraying its predecessor's and its own pledges. At a Commonwealth conference in Lagos in June Britain succeeded in buying time but not in retrieving the trust of its African partners in the Commonwealth, and at a further conference in London in September Britain was obliged, by a nearly unanimous show of resolution by members from all continents, to promise to ask the Security Council to apply selected mandatory sanctions if negotiations between London and Salisbury did not produce a return to legality by the end of the year. By the first anniversary of the unilateral declaration of independence the futility of these negotiations had become manifest, and Britain faced a lengthy economic battle which, if pursued, was bound to develop into a contest between the overwhelming majority of the United Nations on the one hand and South Africa and (less resolutely) Portugal on the other hand, whose policy was to keep the battle going until Rhodesia's opponents got bored and gradually ceased to enforce sanctions. Two attempts to exorcise the problem by personal negotiations between Harold Wilson and Ian Smith – the one on board HMS *Tiger* in 1966 and the second on board HMS *Fearless* in 1968 – failed, principally owing to the obduracy of Smith (or his more extreme lieutenants), but the return of the Conservatives to power in Britain in 1970 revived the prospect of a settlement – and rekindled the mistrust of the rest of Africa.

An initial and unofficial exploration of the chances for a settlement by Lord Alport produced a pessimistic answer but Sir Alex Douglas-Home, back at the Foreign Office in London, opened a dialogue with Smith through Lord Goodman and produced a plan for a return to constitutionality subject to his being satisfied that it was acceptable to the people of Rhodesia as a whole. A commission under Lord Pearce went to Rhodesia in 1972 to find the answer to this question and reported that the majority of Africans rejected the plan. The British government retired once more into the background. Inside Rhodesia guerrilla operations, which had been prematurely and unsuccessfully started a few years earlier, increased but were contained by Smith's forces with South African help. Attempts by the OAU to heal splits among black Rhodesian leaders were unsuccessful but the collapse of Portuguese rule in Mozambique transformed the situation by dealing strategic and psychological blows to the white Rhodesians (the frontiers to be defended became several hundreds of miles longer) and by posing new policy problems for South Africa. The leaders of neighbouring countries – Zambia, Botswana, Mozambique, Zaïre, Tanzania – wanted the overthrow of Smith without a war. They were willing to talk, and to try to persuade black Rhodesians to talk, about a short transitional period before majority rule and about guarantees for the lives and property of whites. They were encouraged by the shift in South African policies, notably by a speech at the UN in which the South African representative spoke plainly about the existence of *apartheid* in South Africa, deplored it and looked forward to a time (unspecified) when it would be removed. This surprising statement was subsequently qualified, presumably for internal consumption, by Vorster, who said that it did not mean one-man-one-vote or a black parliament. Vorster's balancing act was plain for outsiders to see and Kaunda was not deterred from sending an envoy to talk with Vorster who seemed as keen as Kaunda and his colleagues to compass a change of régime in Rhodesia without bloodshed. In December 1974 Smith released the two principal detained nationalist leaders, Joshua Nkomo and Ndabaningi Sithole, as a preliminary to a cease-fire and a possible constitutional conference, and in the following September Smith, at Vorster's prompting, attended a conference with nationalists on a bridge over the Victoria Falls, Vorster and Kaunda themselves also attending. The conference was a failure, technically because of a dispute about the terms of reference already agreed between Vorster and Smith, substantially because Smith was not prepared to discuss any constitutional proposals except his own, which did not then include a transfer of power to the majority. The notion of a constitutional conference was kept alive by Smith and Nkomo but the prospects were dimmed both by white intransigence and by renewed splits among black leaders who had been temporarily persuaded into a show of unity. The collapse of the Vorster Kaunda initiative left little in prospect except war. In Rhodesia the stalemate continued but around it two big changes had occurred. For Vorster the Rhodesian situation represented a wolf at the door, but the wolf had changed its colour. The failure of the Victoria Falls conference completed the alienation of Vorster from Smith. The main danger for South Africa was no longer the disappearance of white rule but its persistence in hopeless circumstances and the manner of its eventual undoing. Smith was no longer a shield but an Achilles' heel. Secondly, Russo-Cuban intervention in Angola must bring the United States too into a field of forces from which nevertheless it would have preferred to keep out. The chief American concern, besides the removal of Cuban armies from Africa and checking the spread of Russian influence, was stability which in Rhodesia was unachievable without the eclipse of white power.

Smith did not see the writing on the wall. In the first place economic sanctions were a farce. The Beira naval patrol, which was maintained by the British for ten years (until Mozambique became independent in 1975) at a cost of at least £100 million, prevented the delivery of crude oil to Rhodesia through Beira, but nothing was done to stop the supply of refined products through Lourenço Marques or by other routes. Portugal and South Africa made little secret of their assistance to Smith to circumvent sanctions. American compliance was imperfect: the import of Rhodesian chrome and other minerals was legalized in 1971. And it subsequently became clear that Smith was plentifully supplied with oil, mainly by British and associated companies which were assiduous in devising means to help Smith – in which they were able to count on the benevolence of British officials and ministers who turned a blind eye to traffic which was too bulky to be invisible. (Even when this discreditable story became public knowledge no prosecutions were launched against companies or individuals who, in breach of the law, had conducted a foreign policy at variance with their government's commitments and ostensible objectives.)

Smith was also encouraged by the dissensions among his black adversaries. His tactics were to exploit these differences with the aim of saving white control through a deal with one or more of the black leaders, preferably Nkomo. It was a classic policy of divide and rule. But Smith aimed too high, clinging too long to white minority rule and then, when forced to come to terms with Bishop Muzorewa and others, drove a bargain too good to stick.

The failure of the Victoria Falls conference was followed by negotiations between Smith and Nkomo. These broke down by the early part of 1976, mainly as a consequence of Smith's obdurate rejection of majority rule. During these months guerrilla operations, although still relatively ineffective and confined to border areas, increased and Robert Mugabe emerged as the one leader whom most guerrillas trusted: he alone was uninterested in wheeling and dealing with the whites. Mugabe eschewed the politicking which was second nature to Smith and he also divined, correctly as it turned out, that the conflict was one which would be settled by other means. Smith, unable to distinguish one kind of left-winger from another, was over-confident of his ability to represent Mugabe as a Muscovite stooge and over-contemptuous of the guerrillas.

The collapse of Portuguese rule and the Russo–Cuban intervention in Angola obliged the United States to review its policies. These had been predicated on a stability which no longer existed. Kissinger's first look at southern Africa in the early seventies had led him to the conclusion that Washington should and could improve its relations with both black and white régimes in order to prevent the USSR from doing likewise; and he assumed that the régimes which he saw there would remain there. The collapse of Portuguese rule undermined this policy. By cutting all but the South African outlets for Rhodesia's commerce it rendered Rhodesia both more dependent on South Africa and less attractive to South Africa as an ally; it dramatically reduced Smith's chances of survival. To the east it not only closed Rhodesia's routes to the sea but also opened a new guerrilla front. To the west it created in Angola an international crisis by which the USSR secured a toehold in southern Africa. The immediate American ripostes, all of them misconceived, were to switch aid from the Portuguese to the two Angolan liberation movements which failed and to instigate a South African invasion which also failed. When Kissinger returned to Africa in 1976 he announced a surprisingly sharp pro-black turn by declaring himself in favour of majority rule not only in Rhodesia but in Namibia and South Africa too. This pronouncement was, however, only the rhetorical prelude to an uneasy alliance with South Africa to put pressure on Smith. Vorster stopped military aid to Smith and allowed his surviving economic channels to the outside world to become clogged. Kissinger went to South Africa for a tense meeting with Smith who was forced to yield to superior power. He accepted majority rule within two years together with a transitional plan which included a black majority in the cabinet and a black prime minister.

Within Rhodesia the guerrilla war became a major factor during 1976. It spread beyond the borders into the heart of the country; its strains on the economy and manpower became visible and painful; it gave a boost to white emigration. But in his own mind Smith was far from surrender. He insisted on interpreting majority rule to mean not black but responsible majority rule; that is to say, he rejected one-man-one-vote. While announcing the end of white rule he contrived to give the impression that white control would continue. He succeeded in tearing up the Kissinger plan. Kissinger had implied to both sides more than had been agreed by either. He allowed Smith to think that the details which he sketched had been affirmed by the African Front Line presidents and by the guerrillas' leaders, when this was not the case. The Front Line presidents complained in their turn that they had been misled by Kissinger; they and the Patriotic Front regarded as negotiable terms which Smith held to be part and parcel of the bargain which had been forced upon him by Kissinger. It was therefore easy for Smith to declare himself released from that bargain unless no letter of it were altered. The Kissinger plan was exposed as a set of imprecise undertakings which fell far short of agreement. A conference of all interested parties in Geneva failed to rescue the plan. So did a subsequent British diplomatic trot round the continent.

At this point the deadlock seemed worse than ever but the guerrilla leaders had meanwhile agreed to co-operate, militarily and politically, as the Patriotic Front. Brittle though it was this alliance was to win the war. Nor were external powers prepared to remain inactive. Britain, the United States and South Africa were committed to replacing the Smith régime by something else. So too were the Front Line presidents, whose countries, – particularly Zambia and Mozambique – were suffering severely from the economic consequences of the war and from Rhodesian retaliatory strikes against guerrilla camps in their territory.

On assuming office in 1977 President Carter appointed Andrew Young to handle African affairs. London too had in David Owen a new foreign secretary, and after a joint tour of African capitals these two produced a fresh plan for ending UDI by the transfer of power to the black majority after a very brief resumption of British authority and elections to be held under international supervision. The plan failed chiefly because Smith was outraged by its provision for one-man-one-vote and the prospect of losing white control of the armed forces and security. Smith flew to a secret meeting with Kaunda, once more in search of an alliance with Nkomo – which again eluded him. He turned therefore to a second best version of the same tactics: a deal with other African leaders, an alternative way of pre-empting a victory for Mugabe. After acrimonious bargaining Smith, Muzorewa, Sithole and Chief Jeremiah Chirau were able to announce agreement on a scheme for sharing power between whites and blacks. Smith now accepted one-man-one-vote but secured the white position by entrenched rights in the constitution. It was a political move to defeat the militant Patriotic Front. Britain and the United States endorsed it with a reservation which made nonsense of it: they approved it provided the Patriotic Front were brought in. But it was a plan to keep the Patriotic Front out.

After much heart-searching the Rhodesian whites approved the new constitution in a referendum in 1979. Elections with a commendable turnout gave Muzorewa the victory and he became prime minister of the aptly named Zimbabwe-Rhodesia. But this settlement was unconvincing. The whites remained obviously in control for an indefinite period and the new government failed to introduce even eye-catching reforms to alleviate, much less remove, racial discrimination.

Fortuitously the Rhodesian elections coincided with the elections in Britain which returned the Conservatives to power under a prime minister suspected of having rather more sympathy for Smith than most British politicians. Mrs Thatcher appeared from her public statements to favour recognition of the Muzorewa government and the immediate removal of sanctions. But British pragmatism prevailed. The Patriotic Front was by now too effective to be affronted lightly; it could even be said to be the winning side. At a Commonwealth conference in Lusaka Britain continued to withhold recognition from the Muzorewa–Smith settlement until one more attempt could be made to reconcile the warring parties. Britain prepared a new constitution, purged of the more blatant pro-white provisions of the 1978 document, and presented it to both sides at a conference in London at the end of 1979 on a take-it-or-leave-it basis. The new foreign secretary, Lord Carrington, was able to threaten to recognize Muzorewa if the Patriotic Front did not accept his constitution, while on the other side Mugabe and Nkomo, the rival of leaders of Zanu and Zapu, were under strong pressure from the Front Line presidents to reach agreement. This combination prevailed. The whites and Muzorewa, although bitterly disappointed and angry, had no alternative to acceptance because what they had constructed was unsound. The conference, contrary to initial expectations, reached agreement. A British governor went to Salisbury for four months. Elections, fair and free in the view of some, the reverse in the view of others, gave Mugabe and Zanu a decisive and overall majority and he became the prime minister of the independent state of Zimbabwe.

Independence disposed of the conflict between black and white but sharpened that between the Shona and the Ndebele, personified by Mugabe and Nkomo. The next few years deepened the personal and tribal rifts. Nkomo was expelled from the government in 1982 and the Ndebele, far from being reconciled to a junior partnership in the new state, were progressively alienated and alarmed: disorders were met by methods which were certainly ruthless and seemed racial. After elections in 1985 which confirmed Zapu's hold over Matabeleland Mugabe, intent on firm one-party rule, initiated a reconciliation with Nkomo which was, however, barely more than superficial. Hopes of moulding Zimbabwe into a truly united state crumbled as the Ndebele minority became permanently alienated and mistrustful, numerous enough to disrupt the country but too few to create on their own a constructive society in a hostile environment. The hopes invested in Mugabe himself were clouded as internal violence led to illegal detentions without trial, rampages by army units and the diversion of food from, and consequent starvation in, politically selected areas. Not all Mugabe's senior colleagues withstood the temptations of power and in 1988–89 scandals forced five ministers to resign and one to kill himself. Mugabe's unconcealed preference for state socialism in a one-party state was unpopular not only with western opinion and governments but also within his own party where each section feared that in a one-party state another section of the party would become the single ruling group. An impressive economic plan which initially attracted international (specifically western) support was rendered precarious by drought, political instability, poor transport and distribution, a flight from the land to overcrowded towns with inadequate housing and no jobs, an intolerable foreign debt service, declining foreign revenues as world prices fell, and inflation which went up and down but a national product which went only down: all of which weakened the personal position of the man whose pre-eminence had made him peculiarly vulnerable to the twists and turns of fortune.

Two special factors aggravated this situation. The first was war in Mozambique. Zimbabwe formed in 1982 a Special Task Force to defend the oil pipeline to Beira on the Mozambican coast against the Renamo guerrillas, and this comparatively modest venture led Zimbabwe deeper into Mozambique's civil war. In 1986 Renamo declared itself at war with Zimbabwe, thus bringing hostilities to Zimbabwe's eastern province of Manicaland and leading to the creation in 1989 of the Zimbabwean Unity Movement by disgruntled members of Zanu – chief among them Edgar Tekere whom Mugabe had dismissed from his government. Secondly, discontent was nourished by the sluggishness of the land settlement programme, one of the major promises of independence. Families evicted from their lands after 1890 – the more massive evictions had taken place in the period 1930–60 – were promised recovery, but the new state also undertook to pay compensation in foreign currency to evicted white owners at a rate applicable to sales between a willing seller and a willing buyer. In spite of British contributions to this programme the cost was burdensome and progress slow. A first plan to settle 162,000 families in five years reached only a third of its target, partly because of practical difficulties such as the need to make new roads, partly because too little land was made available for the landless, and partly because the government insisted that newcomers must first renounce their title to land (if any) which they were leaving – and they were reluctant to do so. In 1989 the government announced that it intended to proceed more vigorously, which however it could do only by watering down its obligations to white owners and introducing some form of compulsory purchase.

SOUTH AFRICA

Bantu peoples reached the southern tip of the African continent in the eighteenth century and there met the Dutch, clashed with them and were gradually subdued and turned into hewers of wood and drawers of water. The Dutch, who had followed the Portuguese to the Cape and were at first confronted only by the Hottentots, enjoyed a brief dominance until, their home country having become a part of the French revolutionary empire, they became fair game for the British in the Napoleonic wars and lost their base at Cape Town which they had founded in 1652. In the 1830s they packed up and trekked and set up new independent states – successfully beyond the Orange River and the Vaal but unsuccessfully in Natal where, although they defeated the Zulus, they were again pushed on by the expanding British who annexed Natal in 1843. The British colony of the Cape grew politically, economically and demographically; it was granted constitutions in 1853 and 1872, receiving on the latter occasion the right to a prime minister of its own.

In the latter part of the nineteenth century South Africa achieved an entirely unexpected prominence in British thinking for two quite separate reasons. The first of these was the discovery of its wealth – diamonds in the sixties and gold in the eighties. The second was the conviction that South Africa was a vital link in Britain's imperial communications and that therefore Britain must keep firm hold not only of Cape Town and Simonstown but also of the hinterland. This second preoccupation turned the Dutch, or Boers, into potential enemies, since they might invite other European powers to occupy the sensitive hinterland or cause trouble for the British in Cape Colony by creating an alliance with their kinsmen in the colony. Moreover attempts by the Boers to reach the coasts in Portuguese territory and to trade with the outside world through Portuguese ports were a further source of friction since these activities threatened the monopolistic profits of British traders at the Cape. The British therefore began to expand more purposefully than before. They took Basutoland from the Boers and made it a colony in 1868. They annexed Kimberley, the diamond city, in 1871 and the Transvaal in 1877. Brought up against the Bantu they fought a series of wars (notably the Zulu War of 1879) and in 1880–81 they went to war with the Boers, whom they incidentally accused of maltreating the Bantu. A British Liberal government, perplexed at this same time by the graver practical and moral dilemmas of the Irish question, was divided about the right attitude to adopt towards the Boers, and after the battle of Majuba in 1881 adopted a policy of conciliation, restored the Boer republics of the Transvaal and Orange Free State and so implicitly recognized the existence of a separate and valid Boer nationalism.

Cecil Rhodes became prime minister of Cape Colony in 1890 and for a few years his voice rather than London's was the decisive one. Within the colony his policy was one of co-operation with the Boers for the paternal rule of the Africans, but any extension of this policy to form an Anglo–Boer entente in a wider field was prevented by British fears about the political and commercial policies of the Boer republics. Rhodes developed and paid for the Cape–Bechuanaland–Zambezi axis which put the Boer republics in jeopardy, countered the German threat from South-West Africa and forestalled a possible anti-British alliance between the Germans and the Transvaal. In 1895 he over-reached himself. With the connivance of a part of the British government he

Key to Homelands

1 Qua-Qua
2 Swazi
3 Gazankulu
4 Kwazulu

Bophuthatswana
Ciskei
Transkei
Venda

Lebowa

NAMIBIA

BOTSWANA

TRANSVAAL

• Pretoria
Johannesburg

SWAZILAND

ORANGE

FREE

STATE

LESOTHO

NATAL

Durban

CAPE

PROVINCE

Cape Town

0   400km

23.2   South Africa and the Homelands

stimulated a rising against President Kruger of the Transvaal and sent
Dr Jameson raiding into Boer territory to sustain it. The result was a
rebuff for the raiders and also for the British government when the
German emperor sent Kruger his moral support by telegram. But
although Kruger triumphed and Rhodes fell, the British government,
which now resumed the dominant role, adopted Rhodes's basic thesis
that the first British aim must be to prevent the emergence of a Boer
South African republic comprising the Boer republics and the British
colonies. By fighting and winning the Boer War in 1899–1901 Britain
postponed this eventuality but did not succeed in scotching it, for it
came to pass in 1961. Britain also earned the hatred of the wounded
Boers but failed to appreciate its depth.

After the Peace of Vereeniging in 1902 the British pursued two barely
compatible lines of policy. On the one hand they busied themselves
being fair and generous to the defeated Boers, often forgetting the

Africans in the process. The Transvaal and Orange Free State were granted self-government in 1906–7, and the constitution of 1908 provided for an all-white parliament which, while meant as a symbol of Anglo–Boer reconciliation, looked in retrospect more like a pledge of African exclusion. On the other hand the British had entrenched the policy of British supremacy by insisting on the extinction of the sovereignty of the republics and the dominance of the English language, so that the Boers planned for the day when the balance of power in South Africa would shift in their favour and they would be able then to turn the tables on the British. By creating the Union of South Africa in 1910 the British government tried to confederate the two self-governing Boer republics and the two British colonies as an independent dominion within the British empire, but this South African dominion was fundamentally if unperceivedly different from the three other old dominions by reason of the persistent non-British culture of the Boers (or Afrikaners) and the existence of an African majority in the shadows. When the European war broke out in 1914 the dominion joined in hostilities and sent forces overseas; the Boers however revolted, refusing – as they were to refuse again in 1939 – to be counted simply a part of a South African nation. They saw themselves as a people or Volk and not as a state.

The persistence of a distinct Afrikaner nationalism which ultimately triumphed through the electoral victories of the Nationalist Party was accompanied by the growth of an African nationalist movement was was frustrated by the Afrikaners. The Afrikaners had to resort to increasingly stringent measures and extreme ideologies in order to preserve and justify their newly won supremacy, and by the middle of the century South Africa had become an oligarchy ruled by a particular racial group without the consent of the majority of the governed who – to make matters worse – were a different colour.

The Afrikaners' attitude to colour was an extreme instance of a common prejudice. It had played a part in their decision to trek out of Cape Colony, where the British were putting more liberal ideas into practice and where the coloureds (the offspring of white alliances with black servants) were given the vote in 1853 subject to certain educational tests – a right which they retained until 1956. But the African was an essential factor in the state since his labour was needed in industry and could be had cheaply owing to the scarcity of work in the native reserves (which, comprising one-tenth of the surface of the state, were supposed in theory to accommodate all the Africans but were incapable in fact of supporting more than half of them). Colour became therefore equated with economic degradation; a black man was a labourer who must and could be had for a low wage. And economic degradation led to social degradation as the Africans were crowded into slummy locations which bred self-disgust and crime. Whereas in

Europe the victims of the Industrial Revolution were the more unfortunate members of society, in South Africa the revolution which exalted mining and heavy industry above agriculture found its victims in a separate society, alienated and increasingly hostile. Natal possessed an additional element in the Asians who first migrated there in search of work in the middle of the nineteenth century.

The Nationalist Party was built up by General James Hertzog who was supported by the Labour Party (the representatives of white labour) and opposed by the British section of the electorate and by the moderate Afrikaners led by Louis Botha until his death in 1919 and then by Jan Smuts. Hertzog was prime minister from 1924 to 1939. He and Smuts joined forces in a coalition government in 1933 but upon the outbreak of war in Europe in 1939 they again separated and Hertzog drifted back towards D. F. Malan who had founded a new Nationalist Party rather than follow Hertzog into alliance with Smuts. The Nationalists refused, however, to ally themselves with the fascist Ossewa Brandwag led by Oswald Pirow. In the first postwar elections, held in 1948, the United Party was ousted by the Nationalist Party, which embarked on an extended period of power under a series of prime ministers – Malan, J. G. Strijdom, H. F. Verwoerd, B. J. Vorster, P. W. Botha – who turned South Africa into an independent republic outside the Commonwealth and a police state based on racial discrimination.

The policies of the Nationalist Party were based partly on the fears and hatreds of a minority faced by a majority of a different race and colour, and partly on a theory which was elaborated in this context. To the Afrikaner the African, especially the urban African, was an uncivilized barbarian unfit for public responsibility or private inter-course; or alternatively the African, especially the rural African, was a tame, happy and rather lazy servant whose chief desire was to remain in his undemanding, if servile, state. The mingling of the races moreover was biologically evil. Logic therefore, as well as prejudice, dictated the attempts to separate the races which collectively amounted to the policy of *apartheid*. Although the races must remain in some contact with one another for a transitional period, the aim was the segregation of the black Africans in separate territories – dubbed Bantustans – which would be racial enclaves, economically self-sufficient, within a single South African polity. This theory and its elaboration were equally flawed. Scientists, including South African scientists, rejected the biological assertions at the basis of the policy of *apartheid*; economists demonstrated that the native areas could never become viable except at a cost unacceptable to the white population, and that the white community could not do without black labour: the African was to be returned to a semi-industrialized countryside while the white urban centres nevertheless craved for his services. The theory also overlooked the strength of human feelings of righteous indignation, and the political awareness of Africans who knew what was happening elsewhere in Africa. Finally, many of the protagonists of *apartheid* probably underestimated the extent to which their policies forced them to rule by violence and fraud and would attract worldwide attention and condemnation. Prisons filled, floggings became an habitual part of the process of government, executions took place at the rate of one a day, the mail ceased to be private, spies and informers multiplied, an inevitably brutalized police became a law of assault unto itself, and the régime felt itself obliged to build up a white citizen army with a potential strength of 250,000 in addition to a part-time commando force of 50,000 (based on four years' compulsory service) and a police force of 20,000 and police reserve of 6,000.

On the other side the African nationalist movement also took to violence. A Native Nationalist Congress, later renamed the African Nationalist Congress, had been formed in 1912. The object of its first leaders – chiefs and then lawyers – was to secure a place for the black African in South African society without upsetting any applecarts, but both the leaders and the rank and file began to have doubts about their prospects during the Hertzog period. The Nationalist victory in 1948 sharpened African apprehensions. The Congress leaders pursued a policy of strikes and civil disobedience to draw attention to demands which they formulated in 1955 at a conference at Kliptown. The government's response to the Kliptown Charter was to charge the leaders with treason. One hundred and fifty-six persons were indicted in a trial which lasted four years and ended with the acquittal of all the accused. In 1957 an increase in bus fares produced a wholesale bus boycott in which Africans, by trudging long miles to work every day, demonstrated their poverty and their discipline, but violence also began to grow and in 1958 outbreaks in the Transvaal were fiercely repressed. In 1959 a section of the African National Congress broke away to form the Pan-Africanist Congress led by Robert Sobukwe.

On 21 March 1960 a crowd of Africans, probably 3,000–4,000 strong but subsequently inflated by reports to much larger dimensions, converged on the police station at Sharpeville. It was one of a number of similar crowds which were doing the same thing all over the country in protest against the pass laws which required adult Africans always to have their identity documents upon them. In organizing this demonstration Robert Sobukwe had told Africans to leave their passes behind and present themselves at police stations in an orderly manner and unarmed. Newspaper reporters said afterwards that the crowds at Sharpeville and elsewhere were in cheerful holiday mood. At Sharpeville, where a small police force of seventy-five was nervously on duty, somebody fired a gun and within minutes dozens of Africans had been killed and many more wounded; the wounds of the victims were, according to hospital testimony, almost all in the back. At Langa in Cape Province there was a similar scene and altogether that day eighty-three Africans were killed and about 350 wounded. Sharpeville became a household word throughout the world. Statesmen of all colours denounced the bloodshed, flags were flown at half mast and formal tributes of silence were paid to the dead. In South Africa a state of emergency was declared as the protests against the pass laws continued, the militia was called up and thousands of Africans were apprehended and put in prison.

Nevertheless the principal African leaders – Chief Albert Luthuli (shortly afterwards awarded the Nobel Peace Prize), Nelson Mandela, Walter Sisulu – continued the struggle by non-violent means. A successful three-day strike in 1961 was followed by preparations for wholesale non-cooperation throughout the country and Mandela went underground in order to organize the campaign. The government was gradually placing most of the responsible leaders behind bars. As their leaders, their activities and their organizations were proscribed both Congresses produced more militant offshoots in the Sword of the Spirit and Poqo (founded in 1961 and 1962 respectively, the latter using murder as a weapon). In 1963 the government arraigned Mandela, Sisulu and others in a further mass trial at Rivonia and sentenced them to long terms of imprisonment.

The government did not hesitate to use force in return but it preferred, like any government, to provide its actions with legislative cover. Its legislative programme was extensive and cannot be considered in detail here. Its principal features, although framed within a single grand design, may be reviewed under separate headings.

In the first place there were a number of statutes affecting the individual in his private capacity. Sexual relations between Africans and Europeans had been a criminal offence since 1927. In 1950 this prohibition was extended to relations between Europeans and coloureds, and in 1949 the Prohibition of Mixed Marriages Act (unlike many other Acts) did precisely what its title indicated – not without reference to the marriage of Seretse Khama of the Bamangwato to an English girl. Also in 1950 the government enacted the Popular Registration Act, described by Malan as the basis of *apartheid*, which prescribed registration and classification by race. The position of the individual before the law was also affected by the Native Laws Amendment Act 1957, which gave the authorities power to exclude Africans from such places as churches on the grounds that they might cause a legal nuisance (the Dutch Reformed Church protested and then complied); by the Separate Amenities Act 1953, which declared that separate amenities for blacks and whites need not be equal, as the courts had tended to insist; by the General Law Amendment Acts of 1961, 1962, and 1963 which stringently reduced the rights of the individual against the police, introduced house arrest for periods up to five years and sanctioned the indefinite detention of suspects; and by the Bantu Laws Amendment Act 1963, which legalized the eviction of any African from any urban area no matter how long he had lived there and turned him into a squatter on sufferance who was allowed to work but not to settle.

A second category of statute fortified and formalized Nationalist control over the machinery of state. In 1949 separate Indian representation in parliament was abolished and the government then launched its attack on the coloured franchise in the Cape province. Its Separate Representation of Voters Bill 1951, removing the Coloured voters from the common roll to a separate one, was declared unconstitutional by the courts because it took away rights which were entrenched by the South Africa Act 1909, and could not therefore be validly removed without a two-thirds majority of the two houses of parliament sitting together. The government thereupon brought in the High Court of Parliament Bill 1952 to give a committee of members of parliament power to override a decision of the Court of Appeal, but it too was voided by the courts. Malan then dissolved parliament, increased his majority but failed to win the two-thirds majority necessary for his purposes. He won over some United Party members in the lower house but not enough and then summoned a joint session of the two houses of parliament to consider a bill to amend the South Africa Act. This move also failed in spite of a measure of United Party support and Malan was then replaced by J. G. Strijdom who abandoned Malan's legalistic tactics in favour of packing the judiciary and altering the constitution of the senate. By these means he secured, first, the passage by the requisite two-thirds majority of the South Africa Act Amendment Act 1956 (which validated the ill-fated Separate Representation of Voters Act 1951) and, secondly, judicial endorsement of the Senate Act 1956.

This long tussle stimulated extra-parliamentary but still mainly non-violent opposition to the government among liberal whites as well as among Africans. The Torch Commando, the Black Sash movement and the bus boycott were its principal manifestations; but the principal consequences were the extinction of the lesser opposition parties (the Liberal and Progressive Parties), the increasing resort to house arrest and detention without trial, and a vigorous use of the communist bogy to brand all opponents of *apartheid* as subversive agents of an international conspiracy. The South African Communist Party had, after some internal disagreement, taken up the cause of the black worker which the Labour Party refused to espouse, but the communists had been as much hampered in South Africa as elsewhere by the twists and turns of Moscow and they had not greatly prospered. In 1950, however, the Malan government secured the passage of the Suppression of Communism Act which was important, not because it proscribed communist activities and the relatively feeble Communist Party, but for its definition of communists and for the powers given to the executive to deal with such people. A communist was defined as any individual whom the minister of justice chose to call a communist, and in so determining the minister was to take the widest possible view since any person seeking to promote political, industrial, social or economic change by unlawful acts or omissions, or the threat of them, was to be considered a communist, as were various other broad categories of people. The Act was in fact an instrument for eliminating every kind of opposition in parliament, trade unions, schools, universities and elsewhere, and at the same time a piece of propaganda meant to exaggerate the communist menace and so win support for the Nationalist régime.

In the field of labour Africans had been forbidden to form unions since 1937. A ban on strikes imposed during the war remained in force after it, and the Native Labour (Settlement of Disputes) Act 1953 repeated these bans on unions and strikes and kept labour relations under white control.

A further category of statute was concerned with the special subject of education. The Bantu Education Act 1953 showed the government's awareness of the crucial fact that children do not naturally adopt racial antagonisms (juvenile loves and hates being otherwise motivated), and also of the crucial need to give Africans a qualitatively different education if they were to form a permanently separate and inferior community in a society under white minority control. The Act created a new division of the Department of Native Affairs which was to direct and finance Bantu education and which would displace the religious missions which were running most of the schools for Africans. Some churches handed over their schools willingly, others unwillingly; the Anglicans preferred to close their schools in the Transvaal and the Roman Catholics decided to carry on and bear the cost themselves. In the new nationalized schools education was geared to the place of the African in South Africa; that is, an unskilled worker in industry or a docile rustic in the special territories to be allotted to him. A further Bill to permit the exclusion of Africans from universities had to be withdrawn in 1957, but two years later the university college of Fort Hare was taken over by the state and separate (but well-equipped) university colleges for Africans were created. Africans remained entitled to apply for admission to white universities if they could show that they were qualified to attend courses not available elsewhere, but in practice such pleas were always found by the authorities to lack substance and the liberalism of the universities themselves was thwarted by executive action.

The kernal of the Nationalist programme was the territorial separation of the races. In this field the Group Areas Act 1950 prescribed racial segregation in terms of residence, business and ownership of land. One of its immediate effects (completed by the Natives Resettlement Act 1954) was the wholesale removal of Africans from areas of Johannesburg which were needed by the whites. Some of these areas were slums, others were not; to the Africans they were areas where they had been able to own property. This Act was followed in 1951 by the Bantu Authorities Act which sought to re-create chieftainship as a basis for the management of the African population. Chiefs, appointed and paid by the government, were to exercise authority in tribal areas, which would be grouped in regions, which would be grouped in territories, over which the Minister for Native Affairs would have ultimate control. This scheme was carried a stage further by the Promotion of Bantu Self-government Act 1959, which (besides depriving the Africans of the right to elect whites to represent them in parliament) consolidated the African reserves into eight Bantustans. Six territorial authorities were established by the end of 1962, including one for the Transkei (an economically non-viable area of 40,000 sq km with a population of 2 million in the north-east of Cape province) which was equipped with a cabinet of six under Chief Kaiser Matanzima and a legislature of four paramount chiefs, sixty chiefs and forty-five elected members. Meanwhile the Tomlinson Commission, appointed by the government, had reported in 1955 that the cost of implementing the Bantustan policy would be £104 million spread over ten years and that the African population in 1960 was likely to be 21.5 million. The government promised £3.5 million for the development of the Bantustans and established in 1959 a Bantu Investment Corporation with a capital of £500,000 to develop Bantu industries.

These affairs in South Africa engaged the attention of the outside world because other Africans, backed by Asians and white sympathizers, made it their business to force them into the foreground of debate at the United Nations, and also as the result of particular episodes such as the treason trial and the Sharpeville shootings.

It so happened that the Sharpeville calamity fell shortly before a meeting of Commonwealth prime ministers at which South Africa intended to seek assurances that it would be accepted as a continuing member of the Commonwealth if it became a republic. This change of status had been a prominent item in the Nationalist programme and it had not been expected to give rise to any difficulties, since the Commonwealth had already adapted itself to the presence of republics. Formally, however, the change required endorsement and there were in the Commonwealth a number of members to whom South African racial policies were so repugnant that they might grasp at an excuse to withhold their assent. Verwoerd, who had succeeded Strijdom as prime minister in 1958, was unable to attend the conference owing to an attempt on his life by a white farmer, and South Africa was therefore represented by its minister for external affairs, Eric Louw. The question of *apartheid* was with difficulty kept off the formal agenda on condition that individual prime ministers might express themselves to Louw in private. Louw, so far from making the impression which he had hoped to make on his colleagues, was forced in these conversations to appreciate the strength of their feelings and to accept a final communiqué which hinted that an application to remain in the Commonwealth, unaccompanied by reform of South African racial policies, would be rejected. Ghana, which had already voted by referendum to become a republic, was accepted as a continuing member. The Commonwealth therefore sidestepped the unpleasant and unprecedented step of expulsion and left the initiative with South Africa. A referendum was held later in the year with the expected republican result and South Africa thereupon left the Commonwealth.

Sharpeville also had repercussions at the United Nations. The General Assembly had been concerning itself with *apartheid* for some years. During its 1952–53 session it had appointed a commission to consider the racial situation in South Africa and this commission had reported that the situation was harmful to peaceful international relations. In succeeding sessions the Assembly regularly passed resolutions asking South Africa to review its policies in the light of the UN Charter and deploring its failure to do so. After Sharpeville the Security Council resolved that the situation in South Africa might endanger international peace and security, called on South Africa to mend its ways and instructed the secretary-general, in consultation with the South African government, to take measures to uphold the Charter. Hammarskjöld went to South Africa in January 1961 but his visit was as fruitless as the Assembly's resolutions. The Assembly repeated its censures in 1961 and then in 1962 asked members to break off diplomatic relations with South Africa, close their ports to South African shipping and their airports to South African aircraft, prevent their own ships from calling at South African ports, boycott all South African products and suspend exports to South Africa. The Assembly also appointed a special committee to keep the situation under review. This committee produced a series of reports and in August 1963 the Security Council recommended the suspension of all sales of military equipment. Throughout these proceedings the African members were pressing for UN action partly out of genuine attachment to the idea of collective international action as embodied in the Charter and partly because they had no prospect of achieving anything effective on their own against the vastly superior military and economic strength of South Africa. They were the more embittered by the refusal of Britain and other powers which were capable of exerting economic pressures but reluctant to do so.

The campaign for economic sanctions against South Africa developed in the sixties as the wave of independence came up against its most formidable obstacle in Africa's deep south. Here was a white minority fortified by an authoritarian and non-egalitarian theology totally different from the secular libertarianism and egalitarianism which, even if subconsciously, formed the policies of the principal European colonial powers. This minority moreover was strong and rich, and it was not a colonial offshoot but a people at home with no thought of going anywhere else. The new African states found themselves powerless to do anything about a problem to which they had given an absolute priority. They were compelled therefore to turn to those who could do something about it – in the first place Britain and secondly the United States. They hoped that these countries would be not only outraged by the enormities perpetrated by the South African régime but also convinced that *apartheid* was a danger to international peace; they wanted international economic sanctions which would either force the Nationalists to parley with the Africans and give them a share of political power, or would cause a disintegration of the régime and the emergence of something new which could in no event be worse.

The British and Americans were not prepared to agree that the practices of *apartheid* were a threat to international peace within the meaning of article 39 of the Charter. Their reasons were many. Both countries were preoccupied with problems which seemed to them more urgent. The United States gave unhesitating priority to Vietnam and to Latin American affairs at least. Britain was more intimately involved because of the old Commonwealth connection and Britain's much longer acquaintance with Africa, but in Britain's financial situation even the relatively small profit on trade with South Africa could not lightly be forgone; British exports to South Africa earned about £150 million a year, 4 per cent of total British exports, while imports from South Africa cost £100 million, 2 per cent of the import bill, leaving a favourable balance of about £50 million. In addition about two-thirds of South Africa's gold went into western reserves and was largely handled, at a profit, by the London market. In both Britain and the United States there were vested financial interests and pressure groups which, though they might not be so influential with government as was sometimes supposed, were nevertheless marginally effective owing to the articulate assiduity with which they made the case against intervention. British investments in South Africa were valued at about £1,000 million. Britain was also held back by fears of reprisals against its dependencies of Bechuanaland, Basutoland and Swaziland, by the residual importance of the right to use the naval base at Simonstown, and by a postwar mood of getting out of things rather than into them. Public opinion was largely unaroused; the committed minorities were believed to be too small to have electoral significance.

The most weighty of these various considerations was the existence of other absorbing international commitments which made both London and Washington hope that an upheaval in South Africa could be postponed, but almost equally important were doubts about the effectiveness of sanctions, about their legality in the circumstances which had arisen, and about the immediate consequences of applying them. The South African economy had not only been expanded rapidly but had also become more self-sufficient; at the same time oil and other materials had been accumulated. There was no agreement among experts on the period during which South Africa would stand a virtual siege, nor was there agreement on the degree of effectiveness of the naval blockade which would be necessary for a short, and possibly for a long time. On the legal side it was argued that the preconditions for such action laid down in article 39 of the Charter (namely, a threat to international peace) existed and had indeed been acknowledged by the members of the Security Council who formally resolved in 1963 that the policies of the South Africa government 'disturbed' international peace. But the substitution of the word 'disturb' for the word 'threaten' was a precise gauge of the political temperature, for it enabled members of the Council to say one thing and yet avoid the consequences of their words. Britain and the United States could no longer bring themselves to deny the substance of the allegations made by the African states but they were determined all the same not to be embroiled with South Africa and so they insisted on using a word which was not part of the language of article 39. Nor was this simply hypocrisy, although it may have been unwise in as much as it postponed an issue which was getting worse and not better. It was not simply hypocrisy because those who had the power were unwilling to use it so long as they could see so little of its probable effects. Sanctions would require a blockade and a blockade would lead to a war. Within South Africa the collapse of the régime could produce an anarchic situation, bloodshed and misery. Ought they to take this responsibility? Since they did not want to anyhow, the question was not too difficult to answer.

The refusal of the British and Americans to be moved by the arguments in favour of sanctions on the grounds that *apartheid* constituted a threat to peace was, however, not the end of the matter. South Africa was also vulnerable on a completely different count. It was the mandatory power in South-West Africa and was accused of violating the mandate agreement by, among other things, introducing *apartheid*. If this charge could be established, South Africa could be required to mend its ways in South-West Africa or expose itself to legitimate intervention upon its failure to comply; and *apartheid* would be condemned in at any rate one context. The Africans went to law.

South-West Africa, huge, rich and under-populated, the most barren expanse in Africa except for the Sahara, came under German rule at the end of the nineteenth century because nobody else wanted it. In the 1870s the Cape Colony had expressly considered and rejected annexation and even the great Berlin share-out of 1884 left South-West Africa as *res nullius*. In the concluding years of the century, however, the Germans moved in, first as allies of the Bantu Herrero against the Nama (an aboriginal people second in antiquity only to the Bushmen) and then as settlers and farmers. Rebellions by the Herrero and later by the Nama led to savage repressions amounting to genocide, and by 1907 the territory had been devasted, subdued and handed over to German farmers together with the surviving Africans who became little better than slaves. In the First World War it was conquered by General Botha and a South African army in a matter of weeks, but after the war it was – together with all other conquered German possessions outside Europe – placed under international mandate instead of being treated as the spoils of the conqueror. The mandate was entrusted by the Principal Allied and Associated Powers to King George V to administer through his government in South Africa but without any transfer of sovereignty. The mandate agreement provided, among other things, for the suppression of trade in slaves, arms and liquor; prohibited the establishment of military bases and the military training of Africans; guaranteed freedom of religion; and required the mandatary to submit annual reports to the Permanent Mandates Commission of the League of Nations and to forward to the League complaints and petitions from the inhabitants. In its execution of the mandate the South African government treated the new order as tantamount to annexation. Attempts were made to convert South-West Africa into a fifth province of South Africa and although these attempts were successfully resisted by the League the character of the territory was profoundly altered by an influx of white South Africans who acquired land cheaply and became a ruling class complete with an elected parliament. In the north areas were reserved for Africans. White immigration was prohibited in these areas which were ruled by a governor-general appointed by South Africa acting through African chiefs who received salaries if they were complaisant but were deposed if they were not.

After the Second World War Smuts repeated pleas for the integration of the territory with South Africa on the grounds of propinquity and economic advantage; he denied that, as the mandatary, South Africa was under an obligation to negotiate a trusteeship agreement with the United Nations; and he argued that the inhabitants of the territory were happy and prosperous and wanted to be part of South Africa. Smuts was obliged to drop his attempt to secure integration and he agreed to submit to the UN reports on conditions in the territory, but after 1948 the Nationalist government stopped the reports and also allotted six seats in the South African lower house and four in the senate to representatives of South-West Africa's 53,000 European inhabitants (the non-Europeans numbered 400,000).

The International Court of Justice ruled in 1950, in an advisory opinion (which was elaborated on subordinate points in further opinions of 1955 and 1956), that the mandate was still in force, that South Africa was not obliged to place the territory under trusteeship, but that it was obliged to submit reports and transmit petitions. From this time the Herrero, Nama and Damara tribes made their views known to the world through their spokesman, the Rev. Michael Scott, who presented on their behalf a picture of their conditions and wishes very different from the official South African line. South Africa offered to negotiate with the United States, Britain and France, as the survivors of the Principal Allied and Associated Powers of the First World War, an agreement to place South-West Africa under the administration of the International Court, but this novel idea was rejected by a special committee of the United Nations and was withdrawn in 1955. In 1957 the UN appointed a good offices committee of three (Britain, the United States and Brazil) which visited Pretoria the next year and recommended that either the Trusteeship Council or a new body consisting of former League members should receive reports from the mandatary, but South Africa maintained that the mandate had lapsed and that it was gratuitously continuing to administer the territory in the spirit of the mandate. South Africa next suggested a partition whereby the southern part of the territory would be annexed to South Africa and the northern part (where there were no whites) would be under South African trusteeship and administratively part of South Africa. The General Assembly rejected this scheme. The territory was in practice progressively absorbed into South Africa's administrative system and became subject also to the politics and practices of *apartheid*.

In 1959 a report by the UN Committee on South-West Africa comprehensively condemned South Africa's execution of the mandate and in the following year the Organization for African Unity decided to initiate a substantive case before the International Court, claiming that the mandate agreement had been violated. Ethiopia and Liberia, former members of the League and the senior independent states of the continent, thereupon petitioned the court accordingly and engaged an eminent American lawyer, Ernest Gross, to argue their case at The Hague. In 1960 the court accepted jurisdiction by the narrow margin of eight judges to seven. After protracted and expensive proceedings the court in July 1966 non-suited the plaintiffs and, in spite of its preliminary decision in 1960, ruled by the president's casting vote (making eight against seven) that they had no standing in the matter before the court. This refusal to entertain the substance of the case caused universal astonishment and was considered all the more unsatisfactory in that the outcome was plainly due to accidents of death and ill-health, without which the judgment on this point would have gone the other way. The immediate effect, besides jubilation in South Africa and some discrediting of the role of law in international affairs, was to return the South-West African issue to the arena of politics (where it was bound to end up in any case).

In October 1966 the General Assembly, brushing aside the notion of further recourse to the court, resolved by 114 votes to 2 with two abstentions that the mandate was terminated and the UN must assume the administration of the territory. A special committee was appointed to consider how the second part of this resolution could be made effective. Essentially the majority in the Assembly was searching for a course of action in which Britain (which had abstained on the resolution) and the United States (which had voted for it) would participate. The committee and a subsequent special meeting of the General Assembly in 1967 were divided between those who asserted, without contradiction, the enormity of South Africa's proceedings and those who asked, without reply, what was to be done about it. In 1968 the UN created a Council for Namibia (as the territory was henceforward called). This Council was not in a position to do anything. In 1970 the Security Council declared South Africa's occupation of Namibia illegal on the ground that it contravened the terms of the mandate. In effect the UN annulled the mandate. The Council's western members abstained but cast no veto.

While the case before the International Court was still in progress the South African government had appointed the Odendaal Commission to make recommendations about South-West Africa. This move was prompted by more than international interference, for in 1960 a South-West Africa People's Organization (Swapo) had been formed and had declared itself at war with South Africa, initiating disorders in the territory of unpredictable consequence. The Odendaal Commission reported in 1964 in favour of dividing the territory into one white and ten black areas and spending £80 million over five years on communications, water and other schemes. The black areas would have certain local government powers but matters such as defence, internal security, frontiers, water and power would be reserved to the central authorities. The habitable land and the known minerals fell within the white area. The consideration of this report was postponed pending the decision of the International Court.

The collapse of the judicial offensive against South Africa and the increasingly evident refusal of major powers to enter on an economic war with it coincided with the aggravation of the Rhodesian independence crisis and also with the granting of independence to black régimes in Britain's three protected territories of Bechuanaland, Basutoland and Swaziland which lay on or within South Africa's borders. South Africa was simultaneously strengthened and faced with problems of external policy. The South African government aimed to preserve white supremacy by economic and military power and did not doubt its ability to do so. It had to consider whether white supremacy could be preserved beyond its own borders and, secondly, how it should conduct relations with established black states. White supremacy was strengthened by the waning of the old feud between the Afrikaner and English-speaking minorities. The Afrikaner Nationalist victory at the elections of 1948 seemed to have become irreversible. Moreover the rapid growth of the South African economy blurred the old dividing line between an Afrikaner country party and an English urban one. Afrikaners, while continuing to constitute a country party, were also penetrating in larger numbers into the upper reaches of the industrial plutocracy and sharing the bounding standard of living enjoyed by that class. This change in the fortunes of a part of the Afrikaner commuity created a possible dilemma for the future, when the affluent Afrikaners might have to choose between the rigour of their racial doctrines and the maintenance and the expansion of this standard of living by consenting to the lifting of job reservations. This prospect gave some comfort to the more optimistic liberals who hoped that economic pressures would enforce a gradual abandonment of the practices of *apartheid*. Externally the South African government appeared to conclude that white rule in Rhodesia and the Portuguese territories could not be indefinitely maintained and that the weaker black states could be induced by necessity to respond to a show of amicability and so breach the unanimity of black Africa's hostility. South Africa supported the illegal Smith régime in Rhodesia not so much because it believed in the permanence of white rule in that territory but because of the force of South African white popular sympathy for it and in order to show that the economic measures threatened against South Africa could not work even against the very much weaker Rhodesian economy. At the same time Verwoerd and Vorster pressed Smith to come to terms with Britain. Vorster at least hoped that the creation of a moderate black régime would forestall the victory of black nationalists friendly to the ANC, but he misjudged the obduracy of the Rhodesian whites. In the longer view South Africa, like the USSR after 1945, strong but beleaguered, would look out towards a hostile world over an expanse of satellites which would one day include also a black Rhodesia, Angola and Mozambique. The model was Malawi.

In the late sixties the Nationalist Party was strong enough to afford internal dispute without risking the loss of power. A hard-line or *verkrampte* section took issue with the enlightened or *verligte* wing (a comparative term) but was severely defeated at the polls. The *verligte* majority proceeded to develop its economic relations with African states, concluded an economic agreement with the Malagasy Republic in 1970 and was encouraged by the response of such diverse African leaders as Houphouet-Boigny and Busia, Kenyatta and Bongo. South Africa also saw in 1970 an opportunity to gain credit by obtaining from the new British government a badge of respectability in the form of a reversal of the Labour government's refusal to sell it arms. Vorster perceived and played on the Conservatives' continuing vision of world affairs in primary Cold War colours and their reluctance to consummate Britain's withdrawal from military vantage points in Asia and the Indian Ocean.

This British withdrawal from the world beyond Europe had continued during the sixties. Partly because of the natural reluctance to withdraw and partly too because the British were filling a gap which the Americans were in no hurry to man, British military power had remained in evidence in the arc stretching from the Red Sea to Singapore. But after the departure from Aden in 1968 the retention of forces in the Persian Gulf seemed more than ever anomalous and transient, and in 1968 economic stringencies led the British Labour government to announce that British forces in the Gulf, and also east of it, would be withdrawn as early as 1971. This acceleration of earlier intentions alarmed Malaysia and Singapore. Singapore's prime minister, Lee Kuan Yew, went to London to contest it: he got a little money and a nine months' extension. Discussions, hitherto largely academic, for a defence agreement between Malaysia, Singapore, Australia and New Zealand were begun.

The British decision to withdraw in 1971 instead of a few years later seemed at the time precipitate. Yet in another sense it was a belated recognition of the obvious and its significance rested more in the delay than in the haste, for the delay ensured that it should coincide with the growth of Russian naval power. Thus a British withdrawal which, earlier, would have forced the Americans, Asians and Australasians to fill the gap now offered the alternative prospect of Russian naval power taking the place of British naval power in the east. Although impeded by the closing of the Suez Canal by the 1967 war, the Russians were able to extend their gains in the Middle East to the Indian Ocean where a small Russian naval force became a familiar feature, supported by bases in Socotra, Mauritius and as far east as the Andaman Islands in the Bay of Bengal. Whether or not this extension was prompted by conflict with China or by a natural tendency of major powers to be active everywhere, it redoubled American opposition to the British withdrawal and caused Britain itself, which saw withdrawal as humiliating rather than sensible, to look around for a different policy. It cast east-of-Suez strategies into a Cold War, anti-communist mould.

During the British election campaign of 1970 Sir Alec Douglas-Home, the putative foreign secretary, said that a Conservative government would reverse the Labour government's policy of not selling arms to South Africa. Conservatives were not partisans of *apartheid* but wished to be friends with South Africa in spite of *apartheid* and because they could see no state nearer to the Indian Ocean that was both strong and anti-communist. After the Conservative victory one of Sir Alec's first acts was to repeat and set about implementing this declaration. He was supported by the new prime minister, Edward Heath, who resisted all arguments against this course, largely, it seemed, on emotional grounds: that election promises must be kept and that British policy decisions must rest in British hands (a proposition that nobody had denied). While Heath treated arguments by African leaders as attempts to push Britain around, Douglas-Home treated African politics as a department of the anti-communist Cold War. On the other side it was argued that a Russian naval threat, should it develop, could not in any event be met by a relatively small British–South African naval force; that the focus of such a threat, essentially a threat to the oil traffic, would not be in the southern oceans but round and about the southern shores of the Middle East; and that the British alignment with South Africa – a political demonstration – would create for the Russians political opportunities in Africa far greater than any military benefits likely to accrue to the anti-Russian side. Just as conflict in the Middle East and the ensuing arms race in that area and the American attachment to Israel had created a Russo–Arab front, so would a British alliance with South Africa throw African countries, however reluctantly, into the arms of the USSR; the USSR could look forward in the seventies not merely to a growing role on the high seas but in addition – and one more because of western mistakes – to a political windfall on the African continent. Within South Africa these external arguments kept alive the illusion that South Africa would be welcomed into a southern counterpart of Nato in a global anti-communist strategy. Yet South Africa, mainly for technological reasons, was becoming unnecessary for any such strategy and, mainly for political reasons, was an unacceptable ally. The Anglo–South African agreement for the use of the Simonstown naval base (1958) was allowed by the British to expire in 1975.

For South Africa the seventies were a decade of alarms surmounted. At the end of them South Africa appeared stronger and more independent in spite of the collapse of Portuguese rule in Mozambique and Angola, the transfer of Rhodesia to black rule and the abrupt cessation of Iranian oil supplies. At home a boom in the price of gold gave South Africa a windfall. But race relations, including the special problem of the control of black labour, remained unresolved and apparently unresolvable.

The decisive event of the decade was the dissolution of Portugal's empire in Africa. The Portuguese record in Africa and Asia was first in, last out: the first colonizers and the last imperialists. This small European country first ventured into strange continents 500 years ago and it acquired in Africa an estate twenty-three times its own size. Bartolomeo Diaz rounded the Cape of Good Hope in 1487, followed by Vasco da Gama in 1498. The Guinea trade, of which Portuguese Guinea was a relic, flourished during the sixteenth century but the Portuguese were gradually pushed out of West Africa by the Dutch, the British and the French, and they were to find their biggest prizes further south. Luanda, the capital of Angola, was founded in 1576 by a grandson of Diaz; it was held by the Dutch for a short time in the seventeenth century but was recaptured by the rich Brazilian adventurer Salvador de Sá who became its governor and restored Portuguese rule. In the seventeenth and eighteenth centuries Angola provided slaves for Brazil. The trade was abolished in 1836 and the institution of slavery itself supposedly from 1858. During the intensest phase of the European scramble for Africa Portugal was supported sporadically but ineffectually by Britain, but by nobody else. Germany coveted Portuguese territories and hoped to succeed to them by lending Portugal more money than it could repay and then foreclosing. A Portuguese dream of linking Angola with Mozambique by a land strip never materialized. Although Mozambique was settled in the twenty-five years before the First World War, the Portuguese evinced only tepid interest in Africa, while their laxity in the suppression of slavery earned them a scandalous notoriety, especially after the publication in 1906 of H. W. Nevinson's *A Modern Slavery*.

Major risings in Angola in 1922 and 1935 were ruthlessly suppressed but also nurtured nationalist movements. Lisbon began to see that its rule was threatened less by white home-rulers than by black nationalism, even though the nationalists were in the short term hopelessly hampered by illiteracy, tribal divisions and the overwhelming might of the Portuguese policy and army. In 1952 Portugal's colonies were renamed overseas provinces and the fifties saw a burst of material progress in the shape of public works and development plans. The change of name enabled Portugal to claim that it was under no obligation to submit reports to the UN under article 73(e) of the Charter, Angola and Mozambique having become not non-self-governing territories but provinces of Portugal. In this contention Portugal had the support of its American and British allies and its Brazilian kinsmen, but in 1963 a resolution of the General Assembly urging Portugal to accelerate self-determination was supported by the United States and Britain; only Spain and South Africa voted against it; France abstained.

The Portuguese practised a policy of assimilation as a means of gradually expanding the franchise, but increasing immigration from Portugal in the mid-fifties altered social and economic patterns, reinforced the colour bar and reduced many Angolans to unemployment or semi-employment. Tens of thousands of Angolans were in exile, mostly in the Congo, by 1960, and the nationalist movements established their headquarters in Leopoldville. Confidence was shaken by a dispute over the election of a northern chief, in which the Portuguese authorities acted in accordance with the letter of the law but with dubious wisdom and probity. The emancipation of the British and French West African colonies and of the Belgian Congo brought the modern African problem to Portugal's Angolan doorstep and in February 1961 there were riots in Luanda, partly stimulated by the adventures of a Captain Galvao, who seized the liner *Sta Maria* and was expected in Luanda to appear off the coast in the role of liberator. These riots were suppressed but in March there were further disorders in the north and an invasion from across the Congolese frontier. The Portuguese were taken by surprise, suffered casualties of about 1,400 in killed and wounded and disastrously responded to barbarities with further barbarities. African casualties were of the order of 20,000 and a stream of hideously wounded refugees – 20,000 in 1961 and a further 150,000 in the next three years – into the Congo blackened the Portuguese name, while the cost of Portuguese authority became a serious strain on Portugal's economy.

In Mozambique a guerrilla liberation movement, Frelimo, began an armed rising in 1964 and secured control over parts of the country, but it suffered in 1969 the assassination of its leader, Dr Eduardo Mondlane. The economy was hit by the blockading of Beira to implement sanctions against Rhodesia, but the Portuguese showed no signs of giving up. They embarked instead on a vast scheme to develop Mozambique's economy in association with South African, European and American concerns (which would thereby acquire a vested interest in Portuguese rule). This scheme, which centred round the building of a hydro-electric barrage at Cabora Bassa, would also entail the addition of a million persons to the white population. The political nature of the plan was barely concealed and, considering that Mozambique already had six hydro-electric schemes and needed no more, hardly could be. The political implications and lobbying by African states caused some of the participants to think again and – in the cases of Sweden and Italy – to withdraw.

By 1970 Portugal's colonial wars had forced it to allot half of its budget and over 6 per cent of its gross national product to military spending, to raise the largest armies ever raised in Portugal's history and to conscript its young men for four years. The absence of a politically active public opinion shielded the government from what had been one of the strongest, perhaps the strongest, of the decolonizing forces in London, Paris and Brussels, but ten years of costly and unsuccessful fighting in three widely separated territories sapped the will of the Portuguese armies. The liberation movement had survived and grown, winning popular support, extending their geographical control and getting arms from abroad. In response the Portuguese tried bombing and barbed wire, but bombing was inefficient against guerrillas and barbed wire failed to separate them from the populace because the latter (unlike their counterparts earlier on in Malaya) were on the side of the former. In Guinea-Bissau the governor, General Spinola, becoming convinced of the hopelessness of the struggle, resigned in 1973 and went back to Lisbon as an outspoken opponent of continuing colonial rule. His actions and writings contributed to the overthrow by the army in 1974 of the military dictatorship founded in 1926 and the Armed Forces Movement which won control in Lisbon declared itself in favour of independence for Portugal's African colonies. This was immediately achieved in Guinea-Bissau and Mozambique, Vorster, bowing to the accomplished facts, publicly accepted Frelimo's victory and wished the new government well. Both he and Samora Machel, Mondlane's successor and first president of the new state, knew that a quarter of the black labour in South Africa's mines consisted of Mozambican migrants, a constraint upon both governments. In Angola there was no single equivalent to Frelimo and when on the eve of independence Holden Roberto's FNLA attacked Agostinho Neto's MPLA South Africa clandestinely invaded Angola in support of a third movement, Jonas Savimbi's Unita. But Neto appealed for help to Fidel Castro and the South Africans were forced for the time being to retreat.

Angola's independence gave Namibia a frontier with a sovereign black state, gave Swapo bases within easy reach of that frontier and reanimated international concern over the territory. Since growing disorder inside Namibia would oblige South Africa to make its occupation ever harsher and so exacerbate foreign criticism and the threat of international sanctions, South Africa abandoned its policy of annexation for the alternative of transferring authority to an anti-Swapo alliance likely to be responsive to South Africa's needs and susceptibilities. Discussions in the Turnhalle in Windhoek during 1975–77 led to the formation of the Democratic Turnhalle Alliance (DTA), an interracial association of racially based parties. It was opposed by the multiracial Namibian National Party (a coalition of five parties) and by white segregationists. The Turnhalle conference produced a plan for transition to independence at the end of 1978 together with a draft constitution so complex, and a fragmentation of the territory so excessive, that it sharpened suspicions that its main object was to leave all effective power in Pretoria. The plan, whose essential aim was to put an acceptable Namibian government in place before elections and before independence, was stillborn because it was unacceptable to the UN which was concurrently elaborating other plans. Vorster, having abandoned annexation, abandoned the Turnhalle alternative. He substituted no new policy but formally annexed the port of Walvis Bay, which had never been part of the mandated territory, and twelve offshore Penguin islands.

The initiative passed to the UN which, by Security Council resolution 435 of 1978, adopted its own programme and also established a 'contact group' consisting of the United States, Canada, Britain, West Germany and France to negotiate with South Africa. The UN programme required a cease-fire, release of prisoners, return of fugitives to Namibia but retention of Swapo guerrillas in their bases in Angola, withdrawal of all but 1,500 of the 20,000 South African troops, the despatch of a UN force, elections for a constituent assembly, supervision of the whole process by a Special Representative of the UN and by a UN Transitional Assistance Group (UNTAG), and so to independence on the last day of 1978. South Africa accepted this plan provided that Walvis Bay were expressly excepted, and an effective cease-fire supervened before the withdrawal of South African forces began. Swapo was worried by the deployment of the remaining South African forces which it wished to see concentrated in the south, and about the ill-defined co-operation between the South African and UN representatives. While discussion on these points was still in train South Africa delivered heavy attacks on Swapo's bases in Angola and Swapo broke off the talks. The murder of Chief Clemens Kapuuo, an enemy of Swapo and pillar of the DTA, and the South African Administrator's harsh repression which followed, all but wrecked the negotiations. They were however resumed after strong Zambian and Tanzanian pressure on Swapo to keep talking and the UN was able to convoke a conference of all interested parties in Geneva at the beginning of 1981. Besides the protagonists – South Africa and Swapo – the five western and six black African states attended as observers. The conference was brought to nought by South African design. Namibia's independence was further delayed by two changes: the succession of P. W. Botha to the leadership of South Africa and the arrival of Ronald Reagan in the White House in Washington. Botha conducted for some years a more vigorous regional policy than his predecessor; Reagan tied progress in Namibia to the removal of the Cubans from Angola.

In 1978, partly as a result of half-veiled scandals and partly because he was ill, Vorster moved to the presidency of the South African Republic and was succeeded as prime minister by Botha. Vorster had ruled for twelve years. He was heir to an insoluble problem and handed it on unresolved but not unchanged. The task of South Africa's leaders was to defend not a state but a state-within-a-state and a racial system hated by many at home, reviled throughout the continent and abhorred in the world at large. Vorster tried to shift South Africa's regional and global positions but did not significantly improve them. In terms of power these two positions were diametrically different. Regionally South

Africa was a dominant power but globally it was of secondary importance at best. Even at the height of the Cold War South Africa failed to persuade more than a handful of conservatives (mostly in Britain and the United States) that South Africa mattered more to them than they did to it. South Africa was rich in resources but dependent on the outside world for capital to exploit these resources, vulnerable therefore to financial pressures or sanctions, and geographically and strategically more marginal than it liked to think. So long as defending South Africa meant defending *apartheid* South Africa found few friends and those whom it did find were not so much genuine as (Israeli and Taiwanese arms dealers, for instance) merely mercenary. Vorster perceived the hopelessness of trying to ally white South Africa with the principal western powers and addressed himself to the region, particularly after the abdication of Portuguese power in Angola and Mozambique and the collapse of white rule in Rhodesia exposed his landward flanks. In an attempt to come to terms with the transition in Rhodesia he sought the co-operation of President Kaunda to pre-empt a victory for the armed guerrillas in Rhodesia and he offered independent Mozambique friendship and economic aid. But in Angola he made war. He did so ineptly. His invasion of Angola in 1975 had no clear political or military aims and if, as seems probable, he counted on western support because of the Cuban presence he was wrong or at least easily deceived about the extent and decisiveness of (mainly American) help. South African casualties, although not severe, shocked South Africans who had not been told that they were engaging in war. This setback was compounded in 1977 when other clandestine operations of a different kind came to light. The government's Department of Information had been authorized to engage in deception and bribery in order to win friends and disarm criticism and in the course of its campaigns much of the money provided for these purposes had been misued or appropriated by officials of no mean standing.

Finally in the Vorster years, a special event both symbolized South Africa's bedevilled situation and further soured its relations with the west. It became a nuclear power, but its added military might was irrelevant to its particular problems and alienated its potential friends. In 1977 preparations for a nuclear test in the Kalahari desert, about which the United States was informed by the USSR, led to strong protests from the principal powers. South Africa denied that the Kalahari site was designed for a nuclear explosion but the denial was not widely believed and South Africa continued to refuse to adhere to the Nuclear Non-Proliferation Treaty. The United States, which had been supplying South Africa with enriched uranium, adopted in 1978 legislation prohibiting such sales to any state which did not permit inspection by the International Atomic Energy Authority. (Reagan later found ways of circumventing this ban.) In 1979 a phenomenon inexplicable except as a nuclear explosion was observed by an American intelligence satellite over the ocean between South Africa and the Antarctic. In 1987 South Africa abruptly changed its attitude to the Non-Proliferation Treaty and agreed, under threat of expulsion from the IAEA, to adhere to the treaty. By this time it was clear that South Africa had at least the capacity to make and use nuclear weapons, even though it had no rational use for them. Against its neighbour they were unnecessary, against its own townships and internal enemies unusable.

Botha inherited therefore a situation which was not only intrinsically daunting but also tarnished by recent failures within and beyond South Africa's frontiers. He ruled (1978–89) for nearly as long as Vorster. He won the leadership by a narrow margin and would not have got it at all if his principal rival and Vorster's obvious successor, Connie Mulder, had not been eliminated by the scandals and divisions which precipitated Vorster's retreat. Botha appeared relatively a soft-liner but more in the sense of having doubts and hesitations than in the sense of having firm policies of his own. He was a politician from the Cape and not from the boilerhouse of Afrikanerdom in the Transvaal. He had held the defence portfolio for eleven years and had the respect and confidence of the military; although victorious within the Nationalist Party he was not strong enough to offend the hard-liners. Stubborn and cautious but increasingly domineering, he was determined that South Africa should know the firm smack of government and should stand on its own feet rather than being beholden to allies who laced their friendship with offensive homilies about its internal affairs. Serious riots in Soweto in 1976 (met with brutal police reaction) and the emergence of the Black Consciousness movement led by Steve Biko until he was beaten to death by police in 1977 showed that the will to live dangerously and fight against fearful odds had not been extinguished. These trends illuminated the refusal of a new generation to come to terms with the whites; here were two communities with no way of talking to each other and not much wish to do so. Nevertheless Botha accelerated the abatement of petty *apartheid*: football teams and audiences, for example. He toured the Homelands or Bantustans (see the note at the end of this Part). He hoped to conciliate and detach from the black majority a small black bourgeoisie with a marginal share in the country's prosperity – an exercise in the use of economic resources for political ends – and tried also to prevent Indians and Coloureds from making common cause with the black peoples by offering the former limited internal autonomy. Separate assemblies of whites, Indians and Coloureds would be created; a mixed electoral college with an overall white majority would choose a president who would appoint three prime ministers, who would pick their own cabinets; and there would be also a multiracial council of ministers with a white majority. There was no place for black Africans in this scheme since their numerical preponderance would have destroyed the commanding position which, on arithmetical principles, the whites were able to use against the Indians and Coloureds. But these were gestures which changed nothing of substance. The Homelands had become evidently nonsensical and the constitutional tinkering was first spurned by Indians and Coloureds and then only half-heartedly accepted.

Other varieties of federal and confederal solution were canvassed. They were more academic than practical. Talk of partition into a black state and a white was revived, but no line of demarcation conceivably acceptable to both sides could be devised; fairness, in terms of an equitable division of wealth, could not be achieved in any way likely to secure peace between them. Chief Gatsha Buthelezi, who had revived the Inkatha movement (founded in 1928) and aimed to turn it into a vehicle for negotiating a non-violent settlement with the whites, proposed a National Convention to discuss non-violent progress towards majority rule in a unitary state and under a constitution accepted by all four racial groups. This proposal had the merit of all plans which prefer talking to fighting, but it seemed to offer little prospect of agreement between blacks and whites in their prevailing moods. Nor was it clear how far Buthelezi, a Zulu chief, could speak for non-Zulus or for the younger generation.

In elections in 1981 Botha lost votes but not seats; his plans were checked but not abandoned. In the following year the right wing of the Nationalist Party, led by Dr Andreas Treurnicht, having failed to gain control of the party left it, leaving Botha freer to proceed with his constitutional changes. These were approved by the white electorate by a 2–1 majority in a referendum at the end of 1983 and accepted, after some hesitation, by the Coloured and Indian communities who were thereby embraced in the new tricameral legislature with 85 and 45 representatives to 178 whites. The blacks were entirely excluded but were promised some relaxation of the minor indignities of *apartheid* and some participation in the local administration of their own communities. The black response was overwhelmingly cynical, as was that of the outside world. The banned ANC intensified its activities both within South Africa and on its borders.

In regional affairs Botha was as ambivalent as Vorster. He liked to show the flag and did not shrink from firing the gun. On the other hand he resuscitated the concept of an association of all states in southern Africa. Verwoerd had toyed with the prospect of an African commonwealth stretching up to (and even possibly including) Zaïre and under South African economic control. Botha's version was called a 'constellation' but it was too nebulous to attract serious attention and was regarded by black states as no more than a design to increase their economic dependence on South Africa. South Africa's economic strength served to scare rather than unite the area. Distrust and indeed aversion to South Africa were profound and black states were more intent on lessening their dependence on an overmighty neighbour than on going into partnership with it. They created therefore a countervailing Southern African Development Coordinating Council (SADCC) of nine black states which, at conferences at Arusha in 1979 and Lusaka and Maputo in 1980, evolved ambitious plans for regional economic cooperation and secured promises of $670 million from outside sources – priority being given to husbandry and communications. SADCC was an essay in regionalism by sovereign states with a population of 60 million, considerable natural resources but inadequate capital, technology or managerial skills. Its members suffered from sporadic drought, direct attacks from South Africa, increasing defence expenditure and an overall decline in output of 15–20 per cent in the first half of the eighties. First steps were modest but the organization gained international regard and at its fifth congress in Harare in 1986 thirty-seven states were represented.

South Africa's main aim in the region was to destroy or disable the ANC. Aid to Lesotho was tied to the eviction of 3,000 alleged members of the ANC. With Mozambique South Africa played a double game. It concluded in 1984 at Nkomati an agreement whereby it undertook to cease supplying the insurgent Renamo (or MNR) and end its economic warfare in return for Mozambique's abandonment of the ANC, but in spite of a confirmation of these promises later in the year Renamo continued to receive aid from South Africa. President Botha (as he had become under the new constitution) had an interest in stifling the ANC and in pacifying southern Mozambique but no interest in inhibiting Renamo's activities further north so long as these did not force President Machel back into the arms of the USSR. Pretoria's approaches to Mozambique before the Nkomati agreement were prompted both by the presence of the ANC there and by generally worsening relations which had provoked talk of war and visits of Russian warships. For South Africa Renamo was a useful thorn in Machel's side. But in spite of aid from South Africa and from Portuguese sympathisers it failed to create anything like a rival government. Equally, however, Machel's government failed to suppress it and this failure was due not only to outside aid to Renamo but also to the unpopularity of Machel's government which rode roughshod over traditional customs and culture in its headlong attempts to modernize the country by fiat and dogma. Machel was killed in an air crash in South Africa, probably accidental, in 1986. His successor Joaquim Chissano was, at 49, a representative of a younger generation which criticized many in Frelimo's old guard for military incompetence and personal corruption. Chissano preferred diplomacy to war, if only because his government might contain Renamo but could not extinguish it so long as South Africa chose to sustain it. On the government's side morale and discipline were low as the cost of living rose and the pacification of the country appeared to be out of reach. Under the impact of the interlocking problems of civil war and economic collapse Chissano steered a reforming course, away from communist centralism and towards a multiparty system, with elections promised for 1991. Communist Mozambique abandoned the one-party state sooner than its non-communist neighbours in Malawi, Zambia and Tanzania.

In Angola Dr Jonas Savimbi's Unita, more openly and lavishly armed by South Africa, succeeded in making itself the effective ruler of a substantial part of the country. Here the situation was complicated by Pretoria's involvement in Namibia and by Washington's determination to secure the removal of the Cubans – a determination which, particularly after the transfer of office from Carter to Reagan, overrode the desire to pacify Angola or help Namibia to independence. In Namibia there was stalemate. The DTA was flagging, its leader Dirk Mudge resigned from the council of ministers, and a new association of anti-Swapo groups – the Multi-Party Conference (MPC) – came into being. In 1984 South Africa declared itself ready to give independence to a government of national unity but a conference in Lusaka attended by Swapo and the MPC produced no unity, Swapo refusing to co-operate with the MPC except upon the basis of a precise timetable for independence. In 1985 South Africa devolved some powers to a transitional government but the key to the situation was outside the territory in Angola where South Africa, although continuing to give unstinted aid to Unita, was also engaged in a series of discussions with the Angolan government. This twin strategy reflected the confusion of separate issues. By reinforcing Unita South Africa undermined Angola's ability to dispense with the Cubans. Pretoria was both negotiating with President dos Santos of Angola and helping Unita to throttle him. Militarily South Africa's incursions were again dubiously valuable to it. Tracts of Angola were occupied, devastated and then abandoned. But in 1985 Angola, fortified by fresh Russian military equipment, took the offensive against Unita, and South Africa accepted the challenge to rescue it at the cost of escalating the conflict. Both sides failed. South Africa suffered another rebuff. A joint Unita–South African air onslaught on the strategic base at Cuito Cuanavale in 1987–88 was thwarted and the South African air force humiliated. But Unita, although battered in the south, was re-established in Zaïre by the United States, partly with the use of Saudi money. Angola could not get free of its enemies.

Botha switched to an apparent readiness to mollify the USSR and abandon his forward policy in Angola. He was under pressure from the United States to seize the opportunity for a comprehensive multinational deal which would entail the departure of the Cubans. Talks began in London in 1988 between South Africa, Angola and Cuba with American assistance (but Unita was left out in the cold) and were continued in Brazzaville where agreement was reached on the withdrawal of South African and Cuban troops from Angola, the exclusion from Namibia of armed members of Swapo, a joint military patrol of the Angolan border with Namibia, and implementation of Resolution 435. South African forces left Angola during 1989, as did half the Cubans; the remainder were due to leave by mid-1991. In the same year dos Santos and Savimbi were briefly reconciled at a meeting at Gbadolite in Zaïre, but their accord did not last long and the war between them in southern Angola was resumed. Angola's gradual advance to international favour was marked by a re-scheduling of its debts to the west and the USSR, membership of the World Bank and the IMF, and a substantial Brazilian loan. Elections in Namibia, also in 1989, gave Swapo 57 per cent of the vote and 41 out of 72 seats in the constituent assembly, fewer than the two thirds which would have given it virtually unbridled power in framing the constitution. The DTA got 29 per cent of the vote and 21 seats. The remaining seats were divided between small and resentful offshoots of Swapo which had defected or been driven out during the years in exile (when dissidents had been treated with deplorable severity and cruelty). A constitution was quickly adopted in 1990 and Swapo's leader Sam Nujoma was elected Namibia's first president.

For most of the eighties South Africa lacked settled policies. In spite of its military and economic dominance in the region it displayed little more than a patchwork of inconsistent expediencies. The Nkomati agreement with Mozambique was initially ambivalent and then dead; the forward policy in Angola was abandoned, resumed and abandoned again; none of Pretoria's shifts in Namibia advanced its interests. Displays of strength had incommensurate results. They coincided with disappointments and half-measures at home. The Homelands, most of them still on paper, had became a monument to dogmatic inflexibility pointing down a dead end; the brutality of the police was failing to quell protests or riots and was fuelling outrage abroad; constitutional changes in 1984 were criticized by whites on both of Botha's flanks as well as being rejected by non-whites; and the president himself wobbled between going forward and going back to pure repression. He announced in 1985 a relaxation of the rules of *apartheid* governing sex and marriage but not the restrictions imposed by such centrepieces of *apartheid* as the Group Areas Act or the Bantu Education Acts. He envisaged some devolution of authority to blacks locally but was adamantly opposed to any black share in power at the top, even in the restricted form conceded to the Coloureds and Indians. As violence led to scenes reminiscent of Sharpeville in 1960 and Soweto in 1976, South

Africa's principal trading partners – including this time the United States – took fright and began once more to talk about economic sanctions. Western capitalists began to run down their investments, the rand collapsed temporarily and the white business community in South Africa expressed forthright dismay when Botha's riposte was more rod than olive branch.

In 1985 South Africa seemed to be on the edge of an explosion. It had so often been there before that there was a stubborn insistence, among whites and their foreign friends, to regard the crisis as exaggerated: white power could be preserved by superior force, superior intelligence and changes which would include no concessions on the Group Areas Act, the Reservation of Separate Amenities Act or the constitutional dominance of the white vote. Yet there was by this date a new situation which was being fashioned by more than the steady accumulation of pressures and discomforts, and the greatest change was the public acceptance – albeit by a small section of the whites – that there must be negotiation with the ANC. The biggest obstacles to this change of mind had been, first, the almost universal (white) belief that there was no need to talk to the ANC or any other black body and, second, the equally widespread belief that the ANC was merely a stalking horse for the communists and black power a prelude to rule from Moscow. The second belief, buttressed by the presence among the ANC's leaders of a sizeable minority of communists, remained strong but the first had become a subject for discussion. During 1985 white leaders of industry and banking held a formal meeting with ANC leaders outside South Africa and at the end of the year the creation of a new Congress of South African Trade Unions emphasized the government's problems in retaining control over organized labour. The government imposed censorship over the reporting of black riots and police counter-brutalities but although these measures impeded foreign journalists they did not stop the disorder or render the principal black townships less ungovernable. The banned ANC and the precariously legal United Democratic Front were the principal beneficiaries of these cracks in white solidarity and government confidence, although they themselves, being amalgams of groups of different origin and temper, were not unmarked by suspicions and jealousies which might be expected to increase as the black cause gained in strength and optimism. Nevertheless the overriding change of these years was the arrival at the top of the political agenda of the questions how, when and within what limits to treat with the blacks.

This shift owed something to the internationalization of the affairs of Africa's deep south – the internationalization which was anathema to white South Africans and reluctant on the part of governments of major white states which would have been happy to leave South Africa to order its own affairs if they had thought it capable of doing so. But as the white state-within-a-state lost moral authority and relied more and more on force, as the whites themselves became more nervously divided, and as the blacks remained capable only of harassing the white régime and incapable of supplanting it, so chaos seemed a not impossible prospect. For countries which looked to South Africa for valuable minerals or corporate profits chaos had to be avoided. Mouthing abhorrence of *apartheid* was not enough. Nor were partial or token economic sanctions. The UN had imposed in 1977 a mandatory ban on the supply of arms to South Africa (which fostered South Africa's manufacture of relatively small weapons but left it dependent on clandestine suppliers of heavier equipment and advanced technology). Otherwise Mrs Thatcher and to a lesser degree President Reagan espoused a policy of business as usual on the assumption that prosperity would soften racial asperities and enable the whites to keep control of a situation which, if it was deteriorating under white rule, would deteriorate faster without it. From this standpoint Reagan was able to see Unita and Renamo as romantic freedom fighters, but in 1985 the US Congress approved additional sanctions and it seemed probable that the next president, whoever he might be, would not veto severe measures adopted by the Congress. Thatcher, who saw the ANC as nothing more than a terrorist organization, tried to thwart but succeeded only in snubbing her Commonwealth partners when they voted in favour of tougher economic measures. (She was again isolated at a later Commonwealth conference in 1989.) By way of compromise the Commonwealth despatched an Eminent Persons Group to South Africa. Simultaneously, but perhaps not coincidentally, South African attacks on Botswana, Zimbabwe and Zambia scotched any usefulness which it might have had, and a mission by the British Foreign Secretary, Sir Geoffrey Howe, in the following year met blunt and resentful rebuff: both missions hoped to set a diplomtic ball rolling by securing the legalization of the ANC and PAC and the release of Nelson Mandela, imprisoned since 1963. Nevertheless, South Africa's efforts to extinguish the ANC having failed, a new international agenda which included discussion and accommodation with the ANC was necessarily taking shape.

So too, painfully, slowly and arguably too slowly, were minds changing within the white South African community. Broadly speaking the seventies had witnessed a surprising level of confidence; the eighties questioned this confidence. In the seventies whites, who had become used to facing external criticism, fancied that they saw the threats to their position diminishing. The ease with which economic sanctions against Rhodesia were defeated by western corporations with governmental connivance reduced to insignificance the threat (never strong) of similar action against South Africa. The late seventies saw too an economic recovery unforeseen a few years earlier. Growth exceeded forecasts, partly export-led but also nourished by domestic consumer demand. The boom in the price of gold filled the country's coffers and enabled it to pay off foreign debts; taxes were cut; the balance of payments improved. South Africa was not merely surviving but prospering in spite of internal tensions and external vilification. It was becoming less of a 'windfall' economy (although the gold boom belonged to that category), more self-sufficing and independent. Its principal weaknesses were its dependence on imported capital and fuel, shortage of skills, and the uncertainties surrounding the black labour force. Capital continued to flow in spite of the political risks, and the development of oil from domestic coal advanced so rapidly that the cessation of critical supplies of oil after the Iranian revolution of 1979 imposed no more than minor restrictions on private consumption. But the labour market, skilled and unskilled, posed more serious problems. The shortage of skills compelled the abandonment of many promising projects and increased unemployment. The unionization of black labour was potentially a source of effective militancy, by strikes or violence; it was unclear how the whites could keep control of black labour. Whether unemployed or organized in labour unions the black urban proletariat could become allied with traditional black nationalism.

The eighties darkened this side of the picture. GDP declined; foreign investment virtually ceased; inflation rose above 20 per cent a year; the economy was ceasing to generate profit to finance its future; the reserves were running down. Discontent was manifested in five by-elections in 1985 when the ruling party lost votes to the hard right in very different constituencies. The ANC had been badly harmed without being smashed: the raids on neighbouring countries which were designed to scare them into disowning and expelling the ANC did not do so. Attempts to control the black townships by tens of thousands of arrests and the declaration of a state of emergency shook confidence, particularly the confidence of the business community. Even South Africa's undoubted military strength was less reassuring than it had seemed in earlier years. South Africa, although neither a world power nor a superpower, was a fully modernized power capable of spending about 2,000 million rand (about £1 billion) a year on defence and vulnerable only to a direct attack assisted by a superpower, or to a prolonged guerrilla war assisted by a major internal rebellion. Yet it was dependent on outside sources for the maintenance and further development of its more sophisticated equipment; its expanding forces were short of officers, NCOs and instructors; and its perimeter was uncomfortably long.

To retain the goodwill, or negate the ill will, of the west South Africa boasted invaluable minerals which, it believed, the west could not do without. These minerals were not only remarkable in themselves but, in a number of cases, irreplaceable except by recourse to the USSR as the only other known major repository. In manganese, essential and irreplaceable in steel making, South Africa dominated world production and reserves; in vanadium it was a major producer and possessed enormous reserves; in uranium it had considerable reserves and although other countries also had reserves most of these had no exportable surpluses, so that western Europe and Japan could be seriously upset by any cut in supplies from South Africa (and Namibia); in platinum, whose diverse uses embraced the chemical, electrical, glass and petroleum industries, the United States was dependent on South Africa. To some extent this dependence might be lessened by stockpiling and the search for substitutes but the haphazardness of nature in endowing these two areas – southern Africa and the USSR – with such large shares of the world's known deposits of a variety of strategic minerals was a significant factor in international affairs and in the way in which white South Africans assessed their prospects in the world.

In these confused and dangerous cross-currents two facts stood out. The Afrikaner political and intellectual élites were losing their faith in the *apartheid* which had sustained them since the Nationalist Party came to power in 1948. They were less dogmatic, more flexible. But although they shed their ideology they were not ready to shed power – or, in so far as some of them foresaw the need to loosen their monopoly on power, were restrained by an electorate which envisaged no such loss. The blacks on the other hand were unimpressed by a shift in attitude which seemed to them to betoken no change in the realities of everyday life or the realities of power. Events spoke louder than the conferences where a few leaders on both sides were beginning to know one another. The death of Steve Biko was only the most flagrant and famous of a stream of incidents which were creating martyrs for the black cause and making a peaceful settlement less and less likely. Each martyr was a figure to whom his surviving compatriots owed a debt which they felt could not be compromised. The generation of the under-thirties equated South African capitalism with exploitation, *apartheid* and police rule; and it was uninterested in any dialogue with the whites, even liberal whites.

This situation was changed by one man: F. W. de Klerk. Botha's political failings, his unattractive personality and ill health combined to embolden his senior colleagues to get rid of him. Of the candidates to succeed him de Klerk was the most conservative but he transformed the political atmosphere. He stopped trying to appease the hard white right; he set out to curb the security forces, military and police, which were acting as though they were a law unto themselves; he stressed, in contra-distinction to Botha's style, the role of cabinet and parliament; he abandoned the policy of destabilizing governments in neighbouring states; he permitted protests and orderly demonstrations; he initiated secret talks with Nelson Mandela; he released from jail Walter Sisulu and other incarcerated black leaders; and he released Mandela himself. These measures indicated a determination, probably irreversible, to negotiate in effect a treaty with black South Africans, represented first and foremost by the ANC, and to give South Africa a new constitution.

Nelson Mandela was an even more striking figure. With Oliver Tambo and Walter Sisulu he had been one of a trio of black youth leaders. In 1963 he had been sentenced at the Rivonia trial to imprisonment which seemed likely to last as long as his life. He was vice-president of the ANC, the president being Tambo who had escaped imprisonment but was at this date seriously ill in Sweden. The ANC was the creation of a liberal black élite. Although its popular base expanded in the fifties and onwards its leaders remained select, urban and middle class. It looked to the USSR for financial help and became closely associated with the South African Communist Party in spite of some distrust of that white organization. It preferred non-violent tactics but endorsed violence when non-violence got it nowhere. Unlike, for example, Black Consciousness (a product of the hopeless seventies), the ANC did not disdain white support and was not dogmatically anti-white. On emerging from prison after twenty-seven years Mandela was revealed as a man of extraordinary composure and dignity. If de Klerk had created a new situation, Mandela was the man without whom their new starting point would most likely be of no avail.

Both men had the task of finding common ground for working out a new constitution. Both realized that beginning to talk was an initial portent and the merest prelude to an eventual agreement which might lie some way ahead. Both had the no less daunting problem of securing adequate consent, each from his own constituency, by marginalizing extremists. The ANC was insistent upon one man one vote. The government had to find a way of reconciling this recognition of democratic majority rights with safeguards for the apprehensive white minority, part of which was viciously hostile to any relaxation of white rule. The ANC accepted a multi-party system and a mixed economy (so too did the SACP) but was wedded to much more government control over the economy than white politicians or businessmen approved. Public order was an immediate issue. De Klerk tried to get Mandela and the ANC to forswear violence, which they were unwilling to do so long as the only actual changes in the country were the release of Mandela and others and the president's evident sincerity and willingness to talk. The ANC agreed, however, in 1990 to suspend violence in return for the gradual release of all political prisoners and the termination of the state of emergency which gave the authorities extensive powers of arbitrary arrest and indefinite detention. The government limited its removal of the state of emergency by excepting

Natal which was the scene of violence of a special kind – violence between blacks. While the ANC was countrywide the undoubted representative of the black community as a whole, in Natal this position was contested by the Inkatha, the movement led by the Zulu chief Gatsha Buthelezi. Inkatha had solid support in rural Natal but was losing ground in the towns to the ANC (or, before the ANC was legalized, to the United Democratic Front which was the ANC in disguise). The resulting contest took the form of hideous violence between Zulu and Zulu in which thousands were killed. The violence spread beyond Natal, in particular to the Transvaal where it pitted Zulus against non-Zulus. The ANC complained with more than a little plausibility that the police were helping Inkatha at least negatively by standing by instead of intervening to keep or restore order, even perhaps positively by encouraging violence in order to impede the government's talks with the ANC. Police revelations (suspected as a fabrication) of a revolutionary conspiracy between blacks and communists were assumed to have the same disruptive purpose, but de Klerk and Mandela kept to their common purpose. De Klerk declared that membership of the Nationalist Party should become open to blacks, thus creating the prospect of two mass parties – the NP and the ANC (already open to whites) – as the principal political pillars of a non-racial democratic South Africa in which the white minority would not be sequestered in a permanently minor party, thereby promising sweeping abolition of *apartheid*.

The internal evolution of South Africa provided in these years the main focus for the debate on the efficacy of international economic sanctions which, before the Second World War, had been focused on the external threat to Ethiopia from Italy. The more this question was generalized the more intractable did it become since the question itself was intrinsically complex and its several practical applications peculiarly divergent. In general the efficacy of sanctions rested on two entwined sets of calculations: their economic consequences, and their impact on the political will of various groups within the country assailed by them. In the particular case of South Africa sanctions aggravated the existing economic problems of an expanding and sophisticated economy, largely dependent on the international economy, in a period of worldwide economic stringency. Commercially, sanctions obliged South African enterprises to redirect their business, notably away from the United States and towards West Germany and Japan, but this forced search for new markets was in itself no bad thing, and with the aid of subtle and not so subtle evasions of the obstacles imposed by sanctions, South Africa's trade suffered from sanctions no serious net loss. Particular losses were mitigated, if not fully compensated, and South Africa learned to live with the marginal loss at least in the short term. Financially, the withdrawal of foreign companies gave South African companies the opportunity to buy, often at bargain prices, the plants and operations left behind by the departing foreigners; some individuals became rich out of these transactions. More serious, if also more ambivalent, was the reduction in the flow of foreign funds. In common with other countries South Africa experienced in the mid-eighties a payments crisis which it surmounted by rescheduling its debts but which was nevertheless a disturbing reminder of its dependence on foreign capital. In purely economic terms this dependence on foreign creditors was offset by the creditors' knowledge that, if they refused to extend their loans, they risked losing their money and their chief bargaining counters. Psychologically, however, the shock was sharp and one element in it was the feeling that sanctions had aggravated the situation and might do greater damage in the future. This psychological reaction had political repercussions, first among financiers and industrialists and so among politicians who took note of the fact that the white business community needed to participate in the world economy and feared isolation. While the poorer whites might be driven by sanctions to support extreme and racialist policies and parties, the business classes on the other hand were driven by these sanctions in the opposite direction and this trend gave force to arguments outside South Africa for continuing or even intensifying sanctions. Within the space of a few months in the second half of 1989 the OAS, the Commonwealth and the UN not only asserted the efficacy of existing sanctions but also treated them – and the promise of their remission in return for fundamental changes in South Africa – as a major instrument for the social and constitutional reforms which de Klerk seemed irreversibly to have espoused but was introducing with tantalizing slowness.

What the Russians knew about Africa when the Second World War ended was little. A few nineteenth-century travellers in the Nile valley, a comic opera invasion of Somaliland and Ethiopia in the 1880s and some marginal activity by the Orthodox Church were all that tsarist Russia had to put against the stores of knowledge acquired by western traders, explorers, missionaries and colonial governors; and since almost none of Africa was independent Russia had no diplomatic missions to observe and report about it. The Bolshevik revolution gave a spurt to African studies but these were quickly submerged under the pressure of more urgent cares. As the Second World War ended Stalin put in a bid for a share in Italy's conquered colonies, but it failed. In the fifties African studies were expanded, an Africa Institute was founded in Moscow (1959) under the direction of an eminent historian, I. I. Potekhin, and the USSR began to send representatives to Afro-Asian conferences. In 1960 the People's Friendship University, later renamed Lumumba University, was founded in Moscow.

African leaders were by definition anti-colonialist and so anti-western. Most of them also professed to be socialists. This was for Moscow a promising background, but it proved less fruitful than expected for a number of reasons: the anti-colonial struggle was unexpectedly short and peaceable; African leaders, beginning with Nkrumah, espoused non-alignment; the familiar paths to London and Paris remained well trodden; Soviet aid never matched western aid. Even African socialism created no strong association with the socialist Mecca. It was a nebulous concept derived at least as much from western socialism as Russian communism. The principal vehicle had been the French and not the Soviet Communist Party and although the Rassemblement Démocrate Africain (RDA) – established in October 1946 at Bamako – had in Gabriel d'Arboussier a secretary close to communist thinking, its president Felix Houphouet-Boigny was hostile to it. Another founder of the RDA, Sekou Touré, was typically unhelpful to the USSR. Evicted from the French trade union federation of the CGT he had joined its African counterpart the CGTA (later UGTAN), in which communists were in a minority, and he became the first of a number of African presidents to evict Russians from his country.

Moscow's first venture into African politics south of the Sahara was a reaction to an opportunity. Guinea, pitched into independence in 1959 upon refusing to join de Gaulle's '*communauté*', was born in desperate straits. A poor and thinly populated state it had nevertheless a strategic position on the south-west corner of upper Africa, a port nearer than any other to mid-Atlantic, about a third of the world's bauxite and massive grievances against the west. Moscow was quick with diplomatic recognition, credits (140 million roubles in 1959), offers of trade and Czech arms. Sekou Touré was invited to Moscow. Khrushchev promised to visit Conakry and Brezhnev did. Daniel S. Slod, who had served with credit as ambassador to Syria and Egypt, was transferred to Guinea with the purpose of turning Conakry into a centre of Soviet influence and activity in West Africa.

Mali and Ghana fell more or less fortuitously into this picture. Mali (or Soudan, as it still was) was the poor relation of the shortlived union with Senegal which collapsed in August 1960 under the weight of its incompatibilities. Huge, arid and landlocked it had nothing to offer an ally but Modibo Keita, a socialist of the Sekou Touré brand, was brought by Guinea into the Soviet sphere by a similar friendlessness. He was offered credits of 40 million roubles and Bamako airport was made available to Aeroflot. Ghana, already independent three years earlier, was offered 160 million roubles at this time, although Moscow had at first shown only perfunctory interest in Ghana and sent no ambassador there until 1959. Nkrumah was a strong Commonwealth man, candid about his need for western aid and – in Soviet eyes – a typical product of the wrong section of the African bourgeoisie which was ready to do deals with the British. But Nkrumah had also been the first to hold out a helping hand to Sekou Touré, he gave aid and a home to the truly revolutionary Union Populaire du Cameroun, and he became bitterly anti-American after the murder of his friend Lumumba. He was a pendulum swinging in the right direction for Moscow. Like Sekou Touré and Modibo Keita he was to receive the Lenin Prize.

Yet within a few years there was nothing left of this pro-Russian constellation in West Africa. Upon the fall of Nkrumah in 1966 the régime of General Ankrah expelled all Soviet experts (about 1,000 of them), the bulk of the Soviet, Cuban and Chinese diplomatic missions and the entire East German trade mission; relations with the USSR degenerated into a slanging match. Modibo Keita survived until 1968 (when he was removed by the army and kept in prison until he died eight years later) but the Russian connection languished almost from the start, Russian aid came to a full stop and although a Russian group was reported in the seventies to be prospecting for minerals in northern and eastern Mali the common belief was that the USSR was more interested in possible landing grounds for aircraft or paratroopers. The initial, and most promising, association with Guinea turned sour even more swiftly when, in December 1961, Solod was told to pack his bags and leave Guinea, accused of complicity in a communist-inspired conspiracy against Sekou Touré. Moscow sent no less a personage than Anastas Mikoyan to try to patch things up but he failed and in 1962 Sekou Touré took a first step towards a more neutral position by accepting $70 million of American aid. During the Cuban missiles crisis he refused to allow the Russians to use Conakry airport, which they had built. Ironically the first jet aircraft to land there was French.

The main consequence of these Russian failures in West Africa was the fillip which they gave to new thinking in Moscow about Africa. The Russian ventures in Guinea, Ghana and Mali were in origin partly fortuitous and partly ideological. Their principal instrument, however, was economic: money plus expert advice. Russian credits (which were made available on exceptionally easy terms) were to be used to finance mutually approved capital projects, meet the balance on trading accounts so far as Russian imports were not paid for by Guinean bauxite or Ghanaian cocoa, and contribute to the training of West Africans in the USSR. Moscow sought in this way to detach these states from the western economic embrace, to secure control of their exports and to plant Russian experts in them. But the experts turned out to be more numerous than welcome – 3,000 in Guinea alone at their peak. They tended to recommend showy rather than useful works – such as a big stadium and theatre in Conakry – and they promoted collectivization of agriculture which was so unpopular that it led in Guinea to unrest which the government had to suppress. Excessive quantities of Russian goods were imported; bills and resentment piled up.

Worst of all from Moscow's point of view was the growing feeling that the Russians were interested only in driving crassly selfish bargains from a position of strength. This was not entirely fair. Over the sixties as a whole the USSR paid rather more than the world price for Ghanaian cocoa. The USSR was for Ghana an assured and steady purchaser and when world prices fell Russian purchases stayed the fall by reducing the supply to other markets. The Russian contract kept prices in Ghana's traditional markets more buoyant than they would otherwise have been. In Guinea on the other hand the Russian appetite for bauxite ran far ahead of anything resembling generosity or tact. After deposits at Kindia had been prospected by Russian experts a so-called joint company was formed; it was owned and run entirely by Russians. This company's profits were allocated in the first place to a clearing account to offset Guinean purchases of Russian arms and other goods but were juggled in the worst neo-colonial manner. In addition the USSR contrived to pay a beggarly $6 a tonne for bauxite all the way to 1976 when the price was raised to $16 – still a mere two-thirds of the world price. The ill will so generated was compounded by the

Russian refusal to help Guinea build a fishing fleet or to part with any of its own catch in Guinean waters, a foolish niggardliness in sharp contrast with the East Germans and Cubans who were willing to hand over some – in the Cuban case the whole – of theirs. In sum Guinea, Ghana and Mali served no practical Russian purpose and did less than nothing for the USSR's image in Africa.

But they were a testing ground, for in these years Moscow was developing a new, more pragmatic style in the aftermath of Stalin's death in 1953. Stalin's death sanctioned an intellectual ferment which Khrushchev's temperament encouraged. The rigid dogmatic categories into which Stalinist communist thinking had been driven were loosened and Khrushchev, an unintellectual old man in a hurry, was more than willing to stir the pot without caring too much where the spirit of inquiry might lead. Africa, always towards the bottom of any Russian agenda, was not a precipitating cause of this new mood, whose main foreign source was probably the new rulers' determination to find ground for ending the quarrel with Tito. But there were implications for African policy too. The search for friends in Africa need not be confined to leaders whose credentials could pass the tests of Stalinist orthodoxy, which in fact no leading African did. Nationalists, provided they were moving in a socialist direction, became acceptable friends and allies. The path of 'non-capitalism' – a usefully vague phrase which was a favourite with Khrushchev – became respectable. It was in this context that the links with Sekou Touré, Nkrumah and Keita were made without doing violence to basic Russian postulates, and although these particular links led only to disappointment the policies underlying them survived. In consequence Moscow had a vastly broader field for diplomatic manoeuvre.

Moscow was also becoming much better informed. The African Institute was expanded particularly in its economic and social sections, and on the death of Potekhin in 1965 the directorship went to V. G. Solodovnikov, an economist (and, from 1976, ambassador in Zambia). Solodovnikov was also put at the head of a Co-ordinating Council for African Studies, created by the Academy of Sciences in 1966. By 1970 the USSR had 350 scholars working on African ethnography, economics, law, philology, history and geography; twenty-two of them reached the rank of DSc. When Solodovnikov left the Africa Institute its standing was such that he was succeeded by the son of the foreign minister, A. A. Gromyko. There was similar development in Leningrad and in universities in eastern European countries.

Whether or not for these reasons, there was a marked difference in Moscow's handling of the crises and opportunities created by the two big civil wars of the sixties, in the Congo and Nigeria. In the former the USSR began by endorsing UN intervention, partly because Lumumba – Belgium's own choice to lead the new state – fitted

Moscow's identikit of an African socialist of the right sort; but when Lumumba was ousted and later killed Moscow attacked Hammarskjöld's handling of the situation and threatened unilateral military intervention in support of Lumumba's heir, Antoine Gizenga, who, however, lacked adequate support in the country or on its borders (Sudanese hostility sealed the fate of his revolt in Orientale province); his rebellion created a temporary alliance between Kasavubu and Tshombe, which was detrimental to Russian aims; and the final outcome – the establishment of Mobutu, the USA's great black hope – was accompanied by the forcible closing of the Russian embassy in Kinshasa. The USSR retired hurt by its own miscalculations. It had also offended the great majority of the members of the OAU which was brought into existence in 1963 largely as a consequence of this war.

By contrast Moscow considerably strengthened its position in Nigeria during the civil war in that country. This was a victory for pragmatism over ideology. The USSR had been slow to pay attention to Nigeria. Although a Nigerian ambassador went to Moscow a few months after independence in 1960, Moscow did not return the compliment until 1964. Its instinctive sympathies did not lie with the dominant North, or with a general such as Johnson Ironsi who was regarded as a member of a feudal, pro-British class. But disillusion with civilian leaders in West Africa led Moscow to see virtue in military men who might be expected to provide more stable government and to prove themselves more predictable and enduring friends. Theory too accommodated itself to the practical necessities by depicting the military as a popular and progressive force, sweeping away bourgeois capitalist hangovers. Gowon, Ironsi's successor, was not a northerner and showed some signs of making an alliance with Awolowo, whom he released from prison. (Awolowo had found favour in Moscow's eyes immediately after independence when he became the first leader of the opposition in the federal parliament. Moscow now hoped, wrongly, that Gowon might make him prime minister.) Moreover, as Ojukwu moved towards the Biafran secession it became clear than an overwhelming majority of the OAU opposed him. Moscow did not propose to offend them. It decided to back – and arm – Gowon.

The negotiations were carried out quickly, professionally and the more easily because Nigeria was already negotiating with the USSR for economic aid. Nigeria's development plans were so extensive that it could not get all the aid it required from the west and so, overcoming its profound anti-communism, it turned also to the USSR and eastern Europe. In 1967 a small five-man team of Russian experts spent four weeks in Nigeria travelling over many parts of the country and studying possibilities for a steel industry (for which, with other projects, the USSR eventually advanced $140 million at the end of 1968). But with the outbreak of civil war Gowon's problems had been reduced to one: getting arms. Britain and the USA refused to give him what he wanted and he turned to the Russian ambassador, Alexander Romanov, an adept and sensitive negotiator who did not try to drive an over-hard bargain (Lagos was in any case ready to pay cash) and understood that although Nigeria could not be made communist it could be made friendly. Within weeks of the beginning of hostilities Russian and Czech arms began to arrive and Russian support for Gowon persisted firmly and openly. This was a policy which achieved its limited aims. Successive Nigerian governments, all of them strongly anti-communist, preserved the equable relationship with the USSR which was established during the civil war.

For ten years after the end of the Second World War the USSR failed to find a point of entry into northern Africa. Opportunity came in a curiously roundabout way. Nasser wanted arms which he could not get from the west. He did not know Stalin's successors but on his way to Bandung he unexpectedly met Zhou Enlai at Rangoon airport. He explained his predicament and Zhou suggested he try Moscow. Zhou promised to put in a good word for him. After discussions in Cairo and Prague the Russians sent Shepilov to Cairo to give Nasser to understand that he could do what he liked with the Egyptian communists: it would be no part of an arms deal that these should benefit from the pact. When a year later the Americans declined to help with the financing of the Aswan Dam Nasser declared that he would go ahead all the same. He counted on Russian help. This was a chance for the USSR and after some hesitation Moscow plunged to the extent of offering finance for the first stage. When France and Britain encouraged Israel to invade Egypt and joined in the attempt to overthrow Nasser Moscow's position was consolidated.

This marriage of convenience ran smoothly enough so long as it was personified by Nasser and Khrushchev. The USSR provided Nasser with transport for his expedition to Yemen in 1962 and two years later Khrushchev attended the celebrations at Aswan. This was a few months before his fall. Already his colleagues were charging him with undue adulation of Nasser. Doubts were strengthened when Nasser refused to back the USSR against China in the row over whether the former was an Asian power and so eligible to attend a second Bandung Conference. During the Israeli attack on Egypt in 1967 Cairo accused the Kremlin of giving only feeble military and diplomatic support. When Nasser died in 1970 the Russian presence in Egypt had become as uneasy as it was large. In 1972 Sadat demanded the immediate withdrawal of 20,000 Russian advisers and experts. They left in seven days. Sadat appropriated all their installations and equipment.

Nasser and Khrushchev were both exceptionally plain-spoken heads of state. They were able to cut through a lot of the suspicions inevitable in a dialogue between two states so unfamiliar to each other as Egypt and the USSR. Their successors lacked this knack. Sadat suspected the Kremlin of intriguing with Ali Sabry and others of his domestic adversaries. He suspected Brezhnev of wanting to do a global deal with Nixon which would incidentally stop aid to the Arabs from either superpower for the struggle against Israel. He resented having to make two begging trips to Moscow in one year and getting little in return. For his part Brezhnev suspected Sadat, whom he rightly regarded as much less radical than Nasser, of unsavoury transactions with rich Saudis and Americans. In the 1973 war the USSR, swallowing its pride in an attempt to recover lost ground, rescued and rearmed Egypt, but this was only an interlude in Sadat's progression away from Nasser's Russian alliance and to the Camp David powwow with Carter and Begin. In 1976 Sadat abrogated the treaty he had made with the USSR in 1971. The Kremlin had lost its greatest prize in Africa.

The USSR stumbled in the Sudan too. Moscow was prompt to recognize and welcome Sudanese independence; it classified Abboud, when he took power in 1960, as a progressive soldier and was further encouraged by the Nimeiry coup of 1969. Nimeiry gave the communist Mohammad Ahmed Mahgoub a cabinet post, and the coincidence of similar coups in Somalia and Libya created the pleasing illusion of a left-wing bloc of these three countries with Egypt. But the next year Nimeiry expelled Mahgoub from the Sudan and, when he came back and stirred up a revolt, had him executed. This was particularly embarrassing for Moscow, which acclaimed the coup in the belief that it had already succeeded.

More important than Sudan and hardly less alluring than Egypt was Algeria. Mers el-Kebir was almost as attractive a naval base as Alexandria and, by its position westward in the Mediterranean, offered opportunities for outflanking Nato – a counter to Nato's gains when Greece and Turkey adhered to the western alliance. But Russo–Algerian relations were never easy. Moscow was half-hearted about the FLN, whose leaders seemed to stand at the wrong end of the socialist spectrum. It hesitated to offend the French Communist Party and its Algerian offshoot, both of which were hostile to the FLN. It hesitated too to offend de Gaulle so long as he was a thorn in the side of Washington. Russian recognition of the FLN as a government did not come until 1960 (China recognized it in 1958), and Russian backing remained restrained until the failure of the French generals' coup in 1961, followed by the second Evian conference in 1962, set the seal on the FLN's success. Moscow then gave Ben Bella enthusiastic support until his fall in 1965 when, with almost indecent haste, it sought Boumédienne's friendship with equal zeal.

Algeria's problem was to get the best of two worlds, the USSR and France, and to sup with a long spoon with both. It expanded its trade links with the USSR by a series of commercial agreements, sent hundreds of young men to study in the USSR and accepted some 2,000 Russian technicians and as many military advisers. But it employed as many French and other technicians; made a point of honouring heterodox leaders like Tito and Ceausescu; and took the line that both the Russian and American fleets should get out of the Mediterranean. Algeria became a prime example of the USSR's main difficulty in Africa. Ideological sympathies led to military aid but not much else. The Russian and Algerian economies were not complementary; their several needs and resources did not mesh. Morocco could supply the USSR more copiously than Algeria with the phosphates which it needed for its chronically sick agriculture; but Morocco was ideologically opposed to the USSR and also at odds with Algeria.

In East Africa the USSR had an unhappy time. In Tanzania Nyerere made no secret of the fact that he distrusted Moscow as much as Washington. In Kenya the USSR made a bad tactical mistake when it backed Oginga Odinga who, at independence in 1963, seemed to be Kenyatta's favoured number two but overplayed his hand and was disgraced in 1966. Although Kenya had no arms agreement with the USSR, Russian and Czech arms arrived in the country and were found on Odinga's land. Kenyatta accused Moscow of organizing and financing a conspiracy against him and Odinga of being a communist agent. Russian and other communist diplomats were expelled. The best that Moscow could do in these parts was to keep on better terms with Uganda, which it did even with the atrocious Amin (to whose court a deputy foreign minister, Alexei Zakharov, was sent as ambassador in 1972). But Uganda, coastless, was the least promising of East African states in geopolitical terms.

Compensation was found further north. In 1963 the USSR made a first agreement with Somalia, offering credits and grants up to $35 million. The connection was strengthened after the coup of 1969 which brought Colonel Siad Barre to power. The payoff was the development of a naval base at Berbera, an air base at Hargeisa, storage for missiles and other weapons, and facilities for intelligence and telecommunications. In 1972, when the USSR's positions in Egypt and the Sudan were becoming dubious, Marshal A. Grechko, the Russian minister of defence, paid a visit to Somalia. He was followed two years later by President Podgorny, who concluded a ten-year treaty of friendship and collaboration which, among other things, expunged the Somali debt to the USSR – an unusual piece of generosity. By 1977 Russian military aid had reached $250 million, there were 2,000 Russian military technicians in the country and the value of the bases and equipment available for Russian use was about $1 billion. The Russian stake was considerable.

All this had more to do with the Indian Ocean than the continent of Africa. Russian preoccupation with these waters is ancient. Before 1917 Russian access to what is a segment of the world's main maritime highway was blocked by the Ottoman empire and Persia. Thereafter a variety of Arab states, and their western sponsors, stood in the way, until in 1955 the arms deal with Egypt opened a door into the Middle East and so, via the Red Sea, to the Indian Ocean. And in 1971 Aden, at the further end of the Red Sea, became a part of the independent and left-wing state of South Yemen – a strategic outpost of enormous significance if, under Russian tutelage, it could be fitted into a more comprehensive group of client states. As its positions in Egypt and the Sudan degenerated the USSR became commensurately concerned to counter the American dominance in Ethiopia which, since its virtual annexation of Eritrea in 1952, commanded 1,500 km of the coast of the Red Sea (the opposite coast being under the control of Washington's even stauncher friend, Saudia Arabia).

During the sixties moreover the USA evolved the A3 Polaris missile with a range of 4,000 km. If launched from vessels in the Indian Ocean this new weapon would be able to hit Soviet cities. Moscow's first reaction was a proposal to declare the Indian Ocean a nuclear-free zone. When this idea fell flat Admiral S. G. Gorshkov, the father of the modern Russian navy, sent a token force from Vladivostok to the Indian Ocean and established during the seventies a permanent patrol there. Thus the development of Russian naval power, one of the outstanding features of the postwar contest between the superpowers, took effect in waters where much of the United States' imported oil and two-thirds of western Europe's were at risk.

In the mid-seventies events offered Moscow a chance greatly to enlarge its sphere of influence in this part of the world. In 1974 Haile Selassie fell. In the ensuing confusion outsiders moved gingerly. The United States, already shifting from its Ethiopian base at Kagnew to a new strongpoint on Diego Garcia in the Indian Ocean, continued for a while to provide Ethiopia with financial aid, arms and training. The USSR was pulled two ways: its Somali ally was bitterly hostile to Ethiopia, but the chance for Moscow to supplant the Americans there was very appealing. Moscow had long been mindful of Ethiopia's significance. In 1959, when the country was firmly in the American camp, Moscow had sent the head of the African department of the foreign ministry, A. V. Budakov, to be ambassador in Addis Ababa. It had extolled Haile Selassie's part in the creation of the OAU, depicted his antiquated and repressive régime as progressive, and given him a comparatively generous measure of aid. After his fall Moscow found itself possessed of a weapon which Washington did not have. It might arm the new régime: Washington would not.

Arming Ethiopia must put the Somali alliance at risk, but Moscow hoped to have it both ways. In 1977 it resolved to take the plunge. Mengistu had emerged as the man to back but he would have to be backed against foreign as well as internal enemies – in particular against Somalia. Moscow turned to Castro to persuade Siad Barre to drop his quarrel with Ethiopia and join a left-wing constellation to be formed round Ethiopia, Somalia and South Yemen.

Castro's sympathies lay with the Somalis (and the Eritreans) rather than the Ethiopians: there had been a Cuban training mission in Somalia since 1974. Yet he accepted Moscow's charge. But predictably he failed to persuade Barre to forgo the golden opportunity to annex the long-disputed Ogaden from Ethiopia. Castro thereupon obliged Moscow a second time. He placed his armies at the disposal of Moscow and Addis Ababa to defeat his erstwhile Somali friends. First contingents were flown from Cuba to the USSR and thence to Africa. Later units followed by air and by sea from Angola. They saved Harar and Diredawa from capture by the Somalis, halted the Somali advance and then utterly repulsed it. The Russian contribution to these operations was a gigantic airlift via Aden which, beginning in October 1977, comprised 550 T54 and T55 tanks, at least 60 MiG 17s and 21s and 20 MiG 23s, SAM 2 and 3 ground-to-air missiles, BM 21 rocket launchers, 152 and 180 mm. artillery, self-propelling anti-aircraft systems, armoured personnel carriers and much else. For the USSR this was not only a strategic move but also a display of strength, efficiency and confidence. It was all the more remarkable since never before, even to protect its positions in Egypt, had the USSR resorted to the direct use of force in Africa. But having saved Ethiopia from Somali attack the USSR did not permit an Ethiopian counter-attack upon Somalia itself – a measured restraint probably dictated by a determination not to provoke the United States too far and to avoid open superpower confrontation. But even with Russian aid Mengistu could do no more than stave off his enemies and ask for more aid. By the time Gorbachev came to power Mengistu was clearly more expensive than he was worth. He was told that Russian aid and Cuban troops would fade away.

The defeats inflicted on the Somalis enabled Mengistu to hold his own against the Eritreans until, once more with Russian and Cuban help, he could mount a counter-offensive. For the time being Mengistu was saved – and the USSR committed or, as some thought, entangled. Mengistu's Ethiopia, no less than Haile Selassie's, was a patchwork empire dominated precariously by its Christian Amharic minority. Besides its conflicts with Eritreans and Somalis the Dergue was opposed by the Oromo peoples of the south (themselves about half the country's population) and the Tigrayans to the north-west. At the Islamic conference at Taif early in 1981 eleven members of the OAU joined in unanimous condemnation of the repression of Muslims in the

Horn. Neither as an ally nor a dependency was Ethiopia likely to prove a stable asset of Russian world power.

Upon the fall of Salazar in Lisbon in 1974 the USSR sent V. G. Solodovnikov to Zambia as ambassador. Solodovnikov had held no diplomatic post. He was Moscow's leading African academic. He was reputedly given high rank in the KGB. Approachable, genial but a notable absentee from the diplomatic cocktail party round, he had the task of making Lusaka a centre of Russian influence and intelligence such as Cairo and Conakry had failed to become. Solodovnikov was as much concerned with Zapu in Rhodesia and Swapo in Namibia as with Zambian affairs. At the same date the USSR established a surprisingly large embassy in Botswana.

During the rest of the decade the USSR pursued a low-risk policy in southern Africa, in contrast with its forward policy in the Horn. It gave minimal support to insurgent movements in Rhodesia and Namibia, enough to keep them going and keep them sweet but no more. In Angola it contrived to interfere only by proxy. But it became increasingly alert. In 1976 General (later Marshal) S. L. Sokolov travelled as far south as Mozambique in the course of an African tour. Next year a group of no fewer than eleven Russian generals was spotted in southern Angola and another year on General V. I. Petrov visited Angola and Mozambique. The calibre of these explorers was notable. Sokolov was a member of the highest group in the military hierarchy, a group of four. Petrov was the number two in the ground forces, had seen service in the Far East and had been the controlling genius of the operations in Ethiopia and the Horn. The group of eleven included specialists in planning, training, supply, air transport and radio and electronic intelligence; both the ground forces and the air forces were represented. Their surveys led to no operations. They were, however, symptomatic of the Kremlin's awareness that such operations might one day become desirable.

A little earlier, and a little further off the map, a prestigious delegation from the Africa Institute visited (in 1976) Madagascar and Mauritius to testify to Russian interest in these parts. In 1975 Madagascar took a sharp turn to the left with the advent to power of Didier Ratsirake, while in the Comoros Ali Solih (murdered in 1978) also took his country to the left. So did France-Albert René in the Seychelles in 1977.

But the weightiest developments in southern Africa in the seventies were the sequel to the collapse of Portuguese rule. In Mozambique Samora Machel established, against virtually no opposition, a one-party state which was distinctly left-wing in its domestic affairs but non-aligned in relations to external power blocs. In Angola the fight for the succession was more closely contested and produced one of the strangest intrusions in the whole history of the continent: the arrival in force of the Cubans. This astonishing move was prompted by Fidel Castro's personal temperament but would have been impossible without Russian aid and sanction. It gave Moscow a vicarious instrument in a zone where it was reluctant to operate directly and (like Washington) was probably still too ignorant to operate to good effect. It led also to the use of Cuban forces in the Horn.

As a result of American economic sanctions against Cuba Castro had become by this date critically dependent on the USSR: a series of economic disasters on the home front put him at Moscow's beck and call. But Moscow would hardly have called him into Africa if the idea of doing things there had not been his in the first place. Africa always beckoned to Castro. Cuba was too small for him; his attempts to spread his revolution in Latin America were failures; and when he recalled that 'African blood flows in our veins' and spoke of Africans as his brothers and sisters he was expressing something that was real to him, as well as romantic. He wanted to help. Within two years of coming to power he sent instructors to help train guerrillas in camps in Ghana. Two years later, in 1963, a second training mission went to Algeria. But here training spilled over into something more. When Algeria became involved in border fighting with Morocco Castro sent Ben Bella three shiploads and an aircraft load of equipment, accompanied by Cubans who knew how to operate it. These Cubans would almost certainly have become involved in the fighting if it had not stopped just before they reached the firing line. The combat troops were then withdrawn but the training mission remained until the overthrow of Ben Bella in 1965.

Castro was also involved in the Congo. Advisers and a small fighting force of about 200 men with Che Guevara in person went to the aid of Lumumba's heirs, but Mobutu's coup at the end of 1965 put an end to their adventure. A few of the advisers crossed the Congo River to Brazzaville but when, next year, the Cuban mission in Ghana was withdrawn upon the fall of Nkrumah, Castro's African expeditions seemed to have proved as futile as those he sent to Latin America.

But he did not lose interest. The toehold at Brazzaville was matched by another in Conakry – the nearest African capital to the Caribbean and a centre for training guerrillas to fight the Portuguese in Guinea-Bissau. Castro also organized an internal security force and bodyguard for Sekou Touré and others for Presidents Alphonse Massemba-Debat in Brazzaville and Siaka Stevens in Sierra Leone. (In the seventies he branched out into South Yemen, Oman's Dhofar province and the Golan Heights.)

Castro made contacts with liberation movements in all Portugal's African colonies during the sixties. The Angolan scene was peculiarly perplexing. Dozens of movements came into being but these sorted themselves out into three major forces: Agostinho Neto's MPLA, Holden Roberto's FNLA and Jonas Savimbi's UnITA. The FNLA looked consistently the most effective but Roberto was anti-communist and closely linked with Mobutu. He got aid from various quarters: Zaïre, China, Romania, Libya and the USA (which stuck to Portugal to the last minute but switched the bulk of its aid to the FNLA early in 1975). So the USSR backed Neto, but only sporadically; in the year before the fall of Salazar Russian aid had dwindled so far that Neto turned in desperation to Scandinavia and Cuba. But six months after the Lisbon coup Moscow reinstated its aid and, when the FNLA attacked the MPLA in March 1975, in effect saved Neto by rushing supplies and weapons to him by air via Conakry and Brazzaville and also by sea. By October China had retired from the game, unable to match Russian aid to the MPLA which – according to the CIA – had by then received from the USSR and eastern Europe arms worth $80 million. Romania also retreated, but the USA, after some hesitation, persisted and wasted a lot of money.

These successes of the MPLA settled nothing because in October, four weeks before the date fixed for independence, South Africa invaded the country. In November the MPLA declared itself a provisional government; other Africans rushed to recognize it and to denounce the South African invasion and its American sponsors; and Nigeria gave Neto $20 million. Nevertheless Neto's position was precarious. This time he was saved by Castro.

Castro and Neto had become personal friends. Cuban aid had helped to fill the gap when Moscow turned cold on Neto in 1973–74. Several hundred Cuban advisers arrived in MPLA camps in April and September 1975 and when Neto appealed to Castro early in November for combat troops to fight the South Africans he did not appeal in vain. The first unit arrived by air two days later. It consisted of eighty-two men in civilian disguise, the forerunners of what was to become an army of 20–30,000. The first seaborne reinforcements arrived at the end of November and this first ocean crossing of nearly 10,000 km was followed by forty-one more during the ensuing six months of active hostilities. At one point no fewer than fifteen ships were simultaneously at sea on an eastward course, the biggest procession of men and material across the Atlantic since the Americans had sailed to North Africa and Europe to make war on Hitler. The seaborne effort was supplemented by an airlift in which Cuba's antiquated Britannias, after landing at Barbados, flew to Guinea-Bissau and Brazzaville. When the Barbados staging point was cut out, under US pressure, by a refusal to refuel the aircraft, an alternative was improvised in the Cape Verde islands.

The Cuban expedition to Angola was a gamble that, on balance, came off. Its failure would have put paid to the Cuban presence in

Africa and perhaps to Castro's rule in Cuba itself. But success was not complete. The MPLA achieved no final victory over its domestic rivals, particularly UnITA which remained in being in southern Angola. Nor did the expedition develop as Castro intended. He hoped to have his troops back home in six months and was still expecting to accomplish this as late as March 1976. In the event his overseas force, which absorbed a considerable proportion of Cuba's entire army of 160,000, was obliged to remain in Angola indefinitely in order to keep Neto and (after his death in 1979) his successor, José Eduardo dos Santos, in power. Even though the Russians paid the bills, Castro's quixotry imposed strenuous demands and sacrifices on thousands of Cubans – fighting, dying or suffering bereavement back home. Unlike the Piedmontese sent by Cavour to flounder in the mud of the Tchernaya, they could not comfort themselves with the thought that they were paying for the independence of their own country.

Nobody has been generous to Africa, and the Russians have been among the least generous. If economic aid is a major diplomatic instrument, then the Russian use of it has been surprisingly feeble: they have not even kept up with the Joneses. At the end of the seventies the total of Russian overseas development aid was equivalent to 0.02 per cent of estimated GNP. Even Italy did better than that. (The more generous givers were Sweden, the Netherlands, Norway and France, with respectively 0.99, 0.85, 0.82 and 0.6 per cent. Britain managed 0.38, the USA 0.22, Switzerland 0.19 and Italy 0.09 per cent. Although there are conflicting ways of taking these measurements they do not materially affect these relative positions.) Of the net flow of aid to Africa from all sources, national and international, the USSR provided less than 3 per cent. Economic aid therefore was treated by the USSR, not as a major tool, but as a minimum political investment.

On the other hand the effects of Russian aid may have been greater than such figures suggest because it was concentrated in relatively few countries. Certain recipients stood out: Egypt, Algeria, Morocco, Guinea, Somalia. They were picked for political reasons and liable to be dropped for the same reasons. Within them the USSR – like other donors – showed a preference for big industrial projects rather than, for example, rural development: in Egypt, for example, the Aswan Dam, the Helwan steel works, the Nag Hammadi aluminium works. Russian technicians were similarly concentrated; of some 34,000 in Africa in 1977 only 5,000 were south of the Sahara.

The proportion of loans to grants in Russian aid was about 2:1. Rates of interest were low at 2.5 per cent or even nil; but repayment dates were comparatively short, normally ten to twelve years where a western loan would be repayable over thirty or forty years. The USSR proved even more reluctant than other creditors to cancel or reschedule debts, although Somalia was so favoured in 1974. Repayment was normally in goods at fixed prices, a practice which led to much grumbling by borrowers who were thus prevented from reaping the benefits of rising world prices.

In terms of trade the USSR was doing a mere 2 per cent of its trade with African countries, but this insignificant proportion was not entirely inconsequent since the USSR was running a surplus on its trade with Africa which was more than sufficient to offset the deficit on its trade with the west. For Africa the USSR had little commercial importance: only Egypt and Guinea ever did more than 10 per cent of their trade with the USSR.

Military aid fell into two broad categories. There was the provision of material and training given as part of the business of making friends in likely quarters; and there were special efforts made for a particularly strategic gain. The statistics of military aid showed therefore jumps at crucial points. During the seventies, up to and including 1976, Russian and eastern European military aid to Africa averaged $300–350 million a year. It was fairly widely spread: more than half of Africa's air forces acquired Russian aircraft. In 1977, principally on account of Angola, military aid reached $1,500 million and in 1978 a further $1,000 million was expended on Ethiopia alone. These were, in Russian terms, big figures, a reflection of Moscow's preparedness to take a plunge in Africa and pay for it.

Invitations and grants to students are another kind of aid. Its pitfalls are well known. Students are frequently disappointed in their hosts and the Russians were no more successful than westerners in avoiding the slights inflicted by colour prejudice. The USSR opened its arms to foreign students as far back as 1922 when the first Mongolians were welcomed to Moscow, but substantial programmes for students were developed only after the Second World War. In the first postwar decade nearly all of them came from the European satellites but with the decolonization of Asia and Africa, and the Cold War's competition for the goodwill of the Third World, steps were taken to attract students from these countries and Latin America too.

Few knew any Russian. They spent therefore a preliminary year learning the language (for which 4,500 teachers were recruited) and doing a course in 'scientific socialism'. The second half of this programme was sometimes resented but perhaps less so than westerners liked to imagine. When Kenyan students went on strike in Baku in 1965 and asked to be sent home their grievances included indoctrination; but communism was part of what the USSR had to offer and many students approached this course with at least a modicum of initial curiosity. Of the substantive courses the most popular were in medicine and engineering.

Foreign students in the USSR were offered 100 roubles a month –

twice the grant given to a Soviet citizen – plus cheap lodging at about 2 roubles a month, free medical treatment and an annual vacation grant of 100 roubles for spending in the USSR. About half of all Third World students were at the Patrice Lumumba University and more than half of them came from Africa. According to Russian sources there were in these years some 50,000 foreigners studying in universities and technical colleges, not counting others doing vocational courses at lower levels or postgraduate work at higher levels. This total was supplemented by universities and specialist schools in eastern Europe – for example, schools in Budapest and Berlin set up to train Africans in trade unionism and journalism respectively. In purely numerical terms this was a useful and welcome contribution to one of Africa's most urgent needs but (again merely numerically) it was only a minor addition to more familiar educational routes. In the sixties and seventies Britain alone had twice as many African students as the USSR and all eastern Europe combined, and – to take a particular example – at the end of ten years of independence Nigeria had about 15,000 students studying abroad and nearly all of them were in Britain.

The foreign student in eastern Europe, like his domestic fellow, was granted much less freedom than the student in the more permissive west; his daily round was bleaker, although East Germany provided some of the bright lights and carefree style sought by young people who have embarked on a foreign adventure; he was more supervised, even segregated, and experienced more than the usual unpleasantness when claiming the attention of local girls. In 1963 Ghanaian students demonstrated in Moscow's Red Square after the death of one of them in a punch-up, and in a particularly bothersome incident 250 Egyptian students were flown from the USSR to the USA after complaints about their living conditions and indoctrination courses. There was in other words a debit side to the account.

For the immensely larger number of Africans who stayed perforce at home the USSR gradually built up its foreign broadcasts. At the end of the seventies it was broadcasting to the world at large for 2,000 hours a week in eighty languages (China was using only half that number). But Africa, excluding North Africa which was served by the distinct Middle East service, was not a prime target. In 1979 it was allotted 147 hours per week, the same as in 1966. The leading languages in use by the African service were French, Swahili and Hausa which occupied 66.5 hours, leaving 80.5 hours for eleven other languages. Apart from its African service the USSR was broadcasting in English round the clock and many of these programmes could be heard in Africa. Among other eastern Europeans broadcasting to Africa the East Germans were the most prominent. The substance of the programmes was the familiar mixture of news laced with music, but the music was not the latest thing and probably turned more sets off than listeners on. Africans seemed to like rather more western decadence than Russian (or Chinese) broadcasters could bring themselves to provide. The quality of news and feature programmes improved considerably after the fifties when unfamiliarity with the target areas and their culture gave rise to much factual error and poor judgement, but – to the western ear at least – these broadcasts remained crassly slanted and the Russian and Chinese broadcasters devoted a tedious amount of time to abusing one another.

All these general adjuncts of foreign policy reflected the marginality of Africa in the Russian scheme of things. Africa was worth some study and some effort and some expenditure but most of the time it was not a prime or even secondary field of action. The attention devoted to it indicated that Moscow had in mind that one day it might be. There were exceptions – areas and occasions where the effort assumed much more significant proportions (Egypt, Ethiopia) – but the motive in these cases could be found in the Middle East rather than the African continent itself. Meanwhile Moscow accumulated knowledge through its diplomatic missions, its secret services, the journalists of Tass and Novosti, and academic bodies in Moscow and elsewhere. This work coincided with the striking increase in Russian capabilities which characterized the Brezhnev years. Under neither Stalin nor Khrushchev was the USSR a truly world power. Stalin turned it into a nuclear power sufficiently menacing to be a counterpoise to the USA in a bipolar world. Khrushchev inherited this position and, by the failure in the Cuban missiles crisis, demonstrated that Moscow's reach was still limited. But in the seventies the continuing growth of Russian power and technology put the USSR on the map everywhere. Thenceforward the question, in relation to each part of the map, was what it might decide expediently to do there.

Gorbachev saw that what was being done in Africa was both expensive and fruitless. The commitment in Ethiopia, like the commitments in Vietnam and Afghanistan, was a ruinous folly. Military activities cost too much and bought no political gain. Even the relatively small subsidies given to the ANC were money wasted so long as the ANC relied on violence to destroy *apartheid*: the USSR must continue to support the ANC and the South African Communist Party but not necessarily their methods. Gorbachev preferred to put Soviet weight behind the Front Line states. He improved relations with Zimbabwe where his predecessors had made the mistake of backing Nkomo against Mugabe. He reduced the Russian presence to the political, rhetorical and covert, and waited for others to make mistakes instead of making them himself.

Throughout these decades the Chinese played a sporadic *disobligato* to Russian and Cuban performances in Africa. China's achievements in Africa have been prodigiously exaggerated. Africa is even more remote from China than from the USSR. By the end of the seventies China still had no direct link with Africa by air or sea (Aeroflot was flying to twenty-nine African airports). Trade, totalling about $400 million a year, was mutually negligible.

Yet China arrived in postwar Africa not far behind the USSR and at the same point: Egypt, where a Chinese embassy was opened after the Bandung conference in 1955. The main motives – international recognition, admission to the UN and to friends in the Third World – were extraneous to Africa. After the break with the USSR came the desire to make difficulties for Moscow, notably by outbidding its revolutionary fervour at a time when the USSR was shifting towards more pragmatic diplomacy. But the rapid spread of independence undermined Beijing's emphasis on subversion; and although Zhou Enlai visited ten African countries in 1963–64 (the revolts in Keyna, Tanganyika and Uganda curtailed his tour), the Cultural Revolution caused an almost complete withdrawal for a time: in 1966 China's eighteen ambassadors were all recalled. To Africans the Chinese appeared to be nice people from a long way away who behaved more agreeably than Russian or Americans but had much less to offer.

China recognized Sudan and Ghana in 1956 and 1957 but had to wait for three and two years respectively for counter-recognition. It was the first to recognize the FLN as the provisional government of Algeria in 1958. It was prompt to offer aid to Sekou Touré: Guinea is one of the few states in Africa with a sizeable Chinese population (4,000 – the others are Mauritius, Madagascar and South Africa). But Chinese credits for Guinea ($26 million), Ghana and Mali ($19.5 million each) were a long way short of Russian offers. Terms, however, were extraordinarily generous: no interest, repayment over long periods, even (in the case of Kenya in 1961) no repayment at all. But when the Cultural Revolution reduced aid to a trickle only about 15 per cent of Chinese credits had been taken up. They were even more marginal than the Russian.

To the smiling face of communism was added revolutionary zeal. From Conakry China supported a group of Ivorian exiles and, until his assassination in 1960, Felix Moumié's exceptionally savage Union des Populations du Cameroun. China gave Lumumba £1 million, supported Gizenga until he joined the Adoula government and then helped to train guerrillas for Mulele and Soumaliot. In 1963 it intervened in Burundi's troubled waters where Tutsi refugees from Rwanda were plotting a return to their country. The Chinese backed the feudal Tutsi but the expedition was a disaster and the Burundi, suspicious of Chinese meddling in their own hardly less turbulent politics, evicted the newly arrived Chinese diplomatic mission. A bigger mission in Congo-Brazzaville, established in 1964, also came to grief after a military coup there in 1966.

China's steadiest friend in Africa was Tanzania. The Chinese arrived there by the back door as a result of the revolution in Zanzibar in 1964. One of its leaders, Mohammad Babu, had good enough connections with China to raise a loan of $14 million and when Zanzibar was united with Tanganyika (paradoxically Babu opposed the union) the Chinese won the goodwill of Nyerere who, ever cynical about Moscow and Washington, happened at this time also to be on cool terms with Britain. Zhou Enlai and Nyerere exchanged visits in 1965 and the head of the African department of the Chinese foreign ministry was sent to Dar-es-Salaam as ambassador. Then came the Tanzam railway, China's showpiece in Africa.

There were at independence no rail links between Tanganyika and Zambia. Kaunda was particularly anxious to create a passage for Zambian minerals avoiding Portuguese territory, and both he and Nyerere saw the railway as a means to develop neglected areas in their two countries. China, which in 1964 offered aid for building railways inside Tanzania, next year extended the offer to an international line. Both African presidents were seeking western aid and turned to China only when they failed to get it. A first agreement was signed in 1967 after a visit by Kaunda to Beijing. Final agreement followed in 1970 and work began that year.

The Tanzam railway is a single-line track of nearly 2,000 km with ninety-one double-line stations. It was finished two years ahead of schedule and on completion became the property, in equal shares, of the Tanzanian and Zambian governments. Fifteen thousand Chinese were employed in its construction. They set a good example at work and behaved themselves when off. There was some propaganda byplay but after complaints by the African governments this was restricted to handing out the works of Mao – a latterday version of the distribution of Bibles by Christian missionaries. The building of the railway did the Chinese a lot of good for a time, but maintenance was poor, services degenerated and the Dar-es-Salaam terminal became clogged. For these shortcomings the Chinese were not responsible but their repute suffered none the less when the railway ceased to be one of the wonders of the modern world.

Chinese penetration of Africa was facilitated by French recognition of the communist régime in Beijing at the beginning of 1964. Most of francophone Africa followed suit. On their return to Africa after the Cultural Revolution the Chinese quickly took over embassies previously occupied by the régime on Taiwan, often in countries where entry could have been difficult if the Taiwanese had not got there first. Chinese broadcasts to Africa, which began in Arabic at the time of the Suez crisis in 1956, were gradually expanded but did not match the Russian either in hours per week or in their range of languages. In the sixties and seventies the Chinese instigated no revolutionary change, largely because they picked the wrong people to support or supported them too feebly; a guerrilla leader in search of arms was better advised to ask Moscow for them. But China showed interest in Africa and established a presence unlikely to be expunged. In 1982, nearly twenty years after Zhou's continental tour, a new prime minister, Zhao Ziyang, visited ten African states but Africa remained in Beijing a marginal and specialist concern.

NOTES

A *Rwanda and Burundi*

Rwanda and Burundi, formerly German colonies, were placed under Belgian mandate after the First World War. The population consisted of the Hutu, a Bantu people, and the Tutsi, Amharic warriors who arrived in the sixteenth century and became a semi-divine ruling caste. In 1959 the Hutu in Rwanda revolted. The Tutsi monarch, or mwami, who had succeeded upon the mysterious death of his half-brother in 1959, was deposed in 1961 and fled in the following year to Uganda. A republic was proclaimed under President Kayibanda. In the same year the Belgian mandate was terminated, Rwanda and Burundi ceased to be jointly administered, Rwanda became an independent republic and Burundi an independent monarchy. During the upheavals which followed the revolt of 1959 very many Tutsi fled to Burundi, Uganda and the Congo. Raids by some of those exiled led in April 1964 to a frightful massacre of Tutsi in Rwanda on something like a genocidal scale. In 1965 a similar onslaught was made by the Hutu on the Tutsi of Burundi who, unlike their cousins across the border, had retained their power. In 1966 the monarchy in Burundi was overthrown but the Tutsi kept power. In 1972 the Hutu rose and were slaughtered or fled to Tanzania where, numbering about 200,000, they posed a threat to Burundi similar to the threat posed to Rwanda by the Tutsi in Uganda. In 1987 a new president in Burundi, Pierre Buyoya, embarked on a conciliatory policy, allowing the Hutu a bare majority in his cabinet and the office of prime minister. He may have hoped by these concessions to improve his case for foreign aid but he risked sowing discord in both the Tutsi and Hutu communities – in the former where the Tutsi (a mere 16 per cent of the population) feared that concessions were the edge of a slippery slope, in the latter where many Hutu branded the Hutu prime minister and his colleagues as collaborators in the bad sense of that term. In 1989 Buyoya survived both an attempt on his life from within the country and an invasion of Hutu from Tanzania. In 1990 President Juvenal Habyarimana of Rwanda survived an invasion by the Tutsis in Uganda.

B *The Malagasy Republic and the Indian Ocean*

The island of Madagascar, lying off the Mozambique coast, came under French rule at the end of the nineteenth century. In 1947 a serious revolt against the postwar restoration of that rule was rudely repressed, but independence was nevertheless not long delayed. Within the island there was a conflict of interest between the Hova dominant minority, which wanted independence at the earliest possible moment, and a larger nationalist group under the leadership of Philibert Tsirinana, which preferred a short delay in order to be sure of gaining power for itself and not for the Hovas. This group succeeded in its aims. Madagascar became the Malagasy Republic in 1958, remaining in the French Union. Tsirinana became president and full independence followed in 1960. Tsirinana steered a pro-French course and became a prominent supporter of black dialogue with South Africa. Although re-elected in 1972 he was forced that year to hand over real power to General Gabriel Ramanantsava, the nominee of the army, to whom he resigned the presidency after a referendum which approved the army's action. Ramanantsava was displaced three years later by Colonel Richard Ratsimandrava who was assassinated within a week and succeeded by Captain Didier Ratsiraka. French troops left the island in 1973. Ratsiraka nationalized French concerns without compensation and disputed with France the ownership of the Iles Glorieuses, Juan de Nova, Bassas da India and Europa in the Mozambique Channel. The riots which removed Tsirinana in 1972 were repeated and savagely defeated in 1985. Asians were indiscriminately assaulted and many fled. Outside the capital mob rule prevailed. Elections due in 1988 were postponed to the end of 1989 when Ratsiraka retained the presidency but grave riots broke out again. The Malagasy Republic was loved by the IMF but few others.

At the northern end of the Mozambique Channel lie the Comoros. Mayotte, the southernmost of them, remained by its own choice French territory when the rest of the group became independent in 1976. Their first president Ali Soilih, a man of the left, was murdered two years later and the islands became a base for right-wing mercenaries and their Belgian commander Bob Denard, dubiously styled colonel, who gained control of this small fiefdom after various adventures in Africa and Asia and maintained his rule by useful contacts with French and (increasingly) South African covert agencies, by the ruthless savagery of his small private army and by adopting the Muslim faith. The Comoros became a staging post for the supply of South African and Saudi military aid to the insurgent Renamo guerrillas in Mozambique less than 300 km away across the water. Denard removed Soilih's successor President Ahmed Abdallah in 1975, restored him in 1978 and had him killed in 1989.

To the north-east of the Comoros is the British island of Aldabra, famous for its giant tortoises, and beyond that the Seychelles. This group, about 1,500 km from the African coast and twice as far from Bombay, was a British colony from which Britain detached the Aldabra and Chagas groups (mostly uninhabited) to form in 1965, for strategic purposes, a new colony called the British Indian Ocean Territory (BIOT). The rest of the Seychelles were given a constitution in 1967, revised in 1970, and became in 1976 a member of the Commonwealth. In return for the islands detached to the BIOT, Britain built on Mahé, the capital island, an airport to help the Seychelles to become a tourist area. The first president of the new state, James Mancham, was soon ousted by his prime minister, Albert René, more to the left and in external affairs non-aligned. René survived an invasion by white mercenaries connived at by South Africa in 1980. A second such attempt in 1983 was, however, stopped by South Africa. In 1986 René pre-empted a coup fostered by the CIA with British and

South African assistance. He subsequently improved his relations with these enemies, chiefly in order to expand the islands' tourist industry.

Yet further to the north-east and nearer to the Asian shores of the ocean the Maldives – 1,200 small islands rising only a few feet above water and lying some 1,300 km south of Sri Lanka – became independent of Britain in 1965, granting to Britain a lease for twenty-six years on Gan where the British were building an air base. Britain also bought the island of Diego Garcia from its colony of Mauritius (east of Madagascar) before giving Mauritius independence in 1966. In 1970 Britain and the United States resolved to build a joint naval base on Diego Garcia and in 1971 the island was secretly leased to the United States and most of its inhabitants were removed. A few years later Mauritius laid claim to Diego Garcia. The claim was subsequently toned down but not abjured. Mauritius was a French-speaking British colony with a racially mixed population in which Indians were in a majority. Originally acquired in order to pre-empt France, it was turned into a sugar plantation when its strategic importance evaporated and was worked by imported Indian labour. In time Indians came to own more than half the land and were opposed politically by French-speaking creoles who had the support of a small Chinese minority (about 3 per cent of the population). Mauritius was an economic success and it hoped to increase its prosperity by economic links with the Seychelles and the Malagasy Republic. It was wary of its neighbour Réunion, still a French dependency, and of French plans for a francophile association of Réunion, Mayotte and the Comoros. An attempt in 1988 against the life of the prime minister Aneerood Jugnauth, a low-caste Hindu, failed.

C Botswana, Lesotho, Ngwane

The three territories of Bechuanaland, Basutoland and Swaziland became protectorates of the British Crown in 1884, 1868 and 1890 respectively. Their transfer to South Africa, which had been envisaged in the South Africa Act 1909, was mooted by Malan during the Commonwealth conference of 1949, during a visit to South Africa by the Commonwealth relations secretary, Patrick Gordon-Walker, in 1950, again in 1951, 1954 and 1956. But the developing policy of racial *apartheid* and the intensification of police rule in South Africa eliminated such possibility as there might have been for British compliance. The Tomlinson Report included all three territories among South Africa's Bantustans but Tomlinson himself acknowledged a few years later that there was no likelihood of their transfer. In 1960 a transfer under the terms of the South Africa Act became an impossibility, since that Act required an order by the king in council upon the receipt of addresses from both houses of the South African parliament – an impossible procedure after South Africa became a republic. More important, the British parliament had been given assurances, frequently repeated, that there would be no transfer without a debate at Westminster and consultation of the wishes of the inhabitants.

But Britain's neglect of the territories had left them economically dependent on South Africa; Britain's traditional predilection for conservative chiefs retarded the advance of self-government without reconciling the traditionalists who, fearful of the newer type of nationalist, found some attractions in South

African schemes for separate African territories based on the authority of chiefs. British weakness in regard to South Africa was demonstrated when Seretse Khama, the hereditary chief of the Bamangwato in Bechuanaland, married an English girl in 1949. Under pressure from the outraged South Africans the British banished both Seretse and his uncle, the highly talented and efficient Tshekedi Khama, on the plea that the tribe was split on the question whether to accept Seretse with a white wife as chief. Seretse remained in exile until he renounced in 1956 his claims and those of his descendants. He subsequently formed the Bechuanaland Democratic Party and after a general election in 1965 (held under a new constitution introduced in 1961) became prime minister. Bechuanaland – huge, underpopulated and largely desert – became an independent state under the name of Botswana in 1966 but its nominal independence was even more constricted than that of most poor countries, for its poverty made it dependent either on outside aid or on its big neighbour, and in the absence of substantial aid it seemed doomed by past neglect and present stringency to become a satellite of South Africa with all the consequent threats to the moderate and democratic rule which Seretse and his party hoped to give it. Under Seretse, president until his death in 1980, Botswana allowed the Rhodesian guerrillas to set up training camps and joined the group of Front Line states whose aim was to secure majority rule in Rhodesia with the least possible extension of violence.

In Basutoland, entirely engulfed in South Africa, the paramount chief Constantine Bereng, who succeeded to his office in 1960 at the age of 38 after an English education, led a moderate nationalist party (the Maramotlou Freedom Party) but was sandwiched between the traditionalists in the Basuto Nationalist Party led by Chief Leabua Jonathan and the more forthright nationalism of the Basuto Congress Party led by Ntsu Mokhehle. In elections in 1965 the Nationalists narrowly defeated the Congress but then appeared from the evidence of by-elections to lose ground. The opposition parties, suspicious of Nationalist links with South Africa where Chief Jonathan was regarded as the lesser evil, pressed Britain to strengthen the powers which the paramount chief would have as monarch after independence and to conduct fresh elections before independence, but the British government was unmoved by these pleas and in 1966 Basutoland became independent Lesotho with a narrow balance of domestic political forces and a tenseness in the political atmosphere which boded ill for Chief Jonathan's government and suggested that if it ran into difficulties in maintaining its authority it would have no choice but to ask South Africa for help. Riots which occurred at the end of the year gave Jonathan the opportunity to exact from King Moshoeshoe II a pledge to keep out of politics and to confine him to his palace. In 1968 some chiefs who had sided with Jonathan appeared to be switching their allegiance to the king and when Jonathan seemed to be losing the elections held in that year he cancelled the proceedings, suspended the constitution and so kept for the time being his office of prime minister. The king retreated into exile but returned in 1970. Jonathan survived until 1986 by which date South Africa, concluding that Jonathan was no longer the best bet from its point of view, applied economic pressures and encouraged the army to take over. General Justine Lekhanya, who had been dismissed by Jonathan in 1964, put an end to the twenty-year rule of the Nationalist Party. The new government was more cautious in relation to South Africa, less accommodating to the ANC. In 1990 the king was virtually dispossessed in a military takeover. Swaziland, the smallest of the three territories and the last to attain independence, had an elderly paramount chief, Sobhuza II, who was advised by a singularly conservative council. Between 1960 and 1973 he experimented with a modest degree of democracy. At elections in 1964 his Mbokodo Party formed an alliance with the United Swazi Party, the organ of the white farming and business community of 10,000, and routed an assorted opposition of divided and ill-prepared nationalists. Under the constitution prepared for independence in 1968 the monarch was given a dominant position: he could nominate enough members of the parliament to block measures which he did not like, he was not bound to act on ministerial advice in all matters in which a constitutional monarch is normally so bound, he was given control over Swaziland's principal asset (its minerals) subject only to advice from his traditional council and not from his minister, and his party was entrenched in power by an electoral system in which the towns, and therefore the nationalists, were submerged in large rural constituencies. Control over the minerals was, however, taken away from him on the eve of independence. Opposition was weakened because a number of nationalists joined the Mbokodo Party for opportunist reasons. The death of Sobhuza II in 1982 at the age of about 83 was followed by multiple intrigues in and around the royal family and by a regency under a queen mother who was quickly deposed in favour of another queen mother. Under South African pressure the ANC was proscribed. A new king, Mswati III, aged 18, was installed in 1986. He opposed partisans of democracy and the ANC but when he tried to repress his adversaries by widespread arrests and treason trials he was rebuffed by the acquittal of those indicted.

D The Homelands or Bantustans

By 1990 four Homelands had been established and six more were projected:

Transkei: a geographically almost coherent agglomeration of 2.5 million Xhosa-speaking peoples, self-governing from 1963 and 'independent' in 1976; 45,000 sq km of (largely neglected) agricultural and timber-bearing land; 1.7 million Xhosa-speakers outside the Homeland lost their South African citizenship. Transkei broke off relations with South Africa – it had none with any other state – over the latter's refusal to incorporate East Griqualand in the Homeland and over the dumping of unwanted Xhosa-speakers in it. In 1979 South Africa stopped the main source of this forcible migration: the bulldozing of Crossroads in Cape Province.

Bophuthatswana: a Homeland for about half of the Tswana peoples not in Botswana which, since the migrations to the goldfields in the nineteenth century, has contained only a minority of them; 'independent' in 1977; over 40,000 sq km in seven different segments without a capital but with the world's largest platinum mines.

Venda: an almost coherent Homeland of 6,500 sq km incapable of supporting its 1.3 million Vhavenda (kin of the Shona); an area of poor agriculture but, being only 10 km from Zimbabwe, some strategic importance; 'independent' in 1979.

Ciskei: a poor and unruly area of 5,500 sq km and 500,000 Xhosa-speakers who crossed the Kei in the nineteenth century; claimed by Transkei; self-governing from 1972. The Ciskei and the 'white corridor' leading to East London (where the jobs were) were mutually dependent – and hostile.

The designated Homelands comprised *Kwazulu*: a Homeland intended for 4 million of the 5.5 million Zulus and comprising 31,000 sq km in ten (originally forty-eight) segments; includes one-third of Natal, of which the Zulus claim the whole. Chief Buthelezi, the outstanding Zulu personality (although formally inferior in rank to King Goodwill Zwelithin), refused to accept independence. *Lebowa* and *Qwagwa*: for the North and South Sotho; small and arid; the former self-governing from 1972. *Kangwane*: north of Ngwane; 3,700 sq km in two segments for 250,000 Swazis (one-third of the total). *Gazankulu*: 6,300 sq km in four segments for 350,000 Shangaan; arid but possibly covering minerals. *South Ndebele*: extracted from Bophuthatswana; the North Ndebele, destined for Lebowa, might join it.

In 1990 all four established Homelands were demonstrating their rejection of government policy and support for the ANC. In Bophuthatswana there were demonstrations against President Lucas Mangope. In Venda President Frank Ravele was forced out of office. In Ciskei Lennox Sebe, president for life, was ousted by the local army which renounced independence and aligned itself with the ANC. In the oldest of the Homelands, Transkei, a similar coup had removed two chief ministers in 1987. The embryonic Homelands also renounced their projected independence and, including even Kwazulu, declared their support for the ANC.

PART SIX
AMERICA

25 CANADA

Canada, the world's third largest country, played a singularly benign part in international affairs. The Second World War shifted it perforce from one primary setting to another – from its attachment, historical, political and sentimental, with Great Britain to attachment, economic, strategic and geographical, with the United States. This shift, like most Canadian processes, was effected unostentatiously. It was accompanied by a resolve to participate in world affairs through multilateral bodies such as the UN and the Commonwealth. The closer association with the United States was grounded in and publicly recognized by the Ogdensburg Declaration of joint responsibility for the security of North America and was followed by the wider commitments entailed by membership of Nato. The Nato connection led to further bilateral Canadian–United States undertakings: Canada's participation in the Early Warning System designed to nullify surprise Soviet missile attacks on North America, and in the North American Defence Command (NORAD) established in 1958. Yet further afield Canada sent troops to the Korean War in what was then the orthodox western view of the war as a necessary operation to contain communist, more specifically Russian, aggression. In economic matters postwar Canada prospered in old and new ways: in grain, lumbering and established mineral (chiefly nickel) undertakings, and additionally in electronic and chemical industry, petroleum research and extraction, and the exploitation of radium deposits which enhanced a nuclear programme initiated during the war. These activities were on such a scale that Canadian capital did not suffice for them and was supplemented by money from the United States to the point where control of half Canada's manufacturing, mining and carbon fuel industries passed into US hands. For the United States Canada was a neighbour of vast space and unmeasured, untapped resources, which might replace United States resources in food and raw materials that were threatening to become inadequate through natural exhaustion and population increase. The United States might the more easily concentrate its economic efforts in the manufacturing sector if it were assured of supplies of Canadian primary products. For Canadians on the other hand the flow of US capital was unwelcome as well as welcome. Economically it was not only welcome but essential. Yet it was also a source of resentment and apprehension for those Canadians who complained of a loss of control over their own assets and even scented a loss of national identity. But this imbalance began to be reduced in the seventies and by 1986 Canada was the fourth largest investor in the United States – behind Japan, Britain and the Netherlands. Each country was the other's biggest trading partner and the two together constituted the world's biggest bilateral trading partnership. A free-trade treaty which came into force at the beginning of 1989 provided for the elimination of all tariffs and other obstacles to trade by 1999. If, as was supposed, President Taft had coined in 1911 the expression 'special relationship' to describe the US–Canadian relationship, he was not far wrong.

Canadians evinced a forthright championship of international organizations, played a mediatory role in them and championed social alongside strategic policies. With India Canada was a principal founder of the Commonwealth to replace the British empire. In the Commonwealth it worked to mollify the asperities created by the British assault on Egypt in 1956 and the tensions caused by *apartheid* in South Africa (when these proved irresoluble Canada aligned itself with those members who judged that the Commonwealth would be better off without South Africa than with it). Of the white members of the Commonwealth Canada took the most pains, and most successfully, to understand the needs and feelings of the newer members, particularly those in the Caribbean. In the formation of Nato Canada's was the main voice in insisting that the new organization should be committed, by article 2 of the North Atlantic Treaty, to economic and political purposes as well as military. It was also a prominent supporter of the abortive provisions in the UN Charter for an international force and a military staffs committee.

The rapid increase in Canadian prosperity posed a special problem in Quebec, the seat of Canada's French heritage and culture. Four-fifths of the inhabitants of the province were French-speakers, most of them rural conservatives. In spite of their numbers they owned, however, only one-fifth of its productive economy and their average income was substantially below that of English-speakers. From 1944 to 1959 the province was dominated by Maurice Duplessis (prime minister also in 1936–39) who presented himself as a traditional Québecois while associating also, and not always openly, with English-speaking Canadian and US capitalists who were contributing to Quebec's economic transformation. He was succeeded in office by the Liberal Jean Lesage who espoused the modernization of Quebec with a more determined policy of securing the benefits for the French-speaking majority, but in 1966 the Liberals were unexpectedly defeated, losing working-class voters who had come to the conclusion that modernization was benefiting the middle classes only. A visit by de Gaulle in 1967

25.1 North America

enthused French separatists and in 1968 a new party, the Parti Québecois (PQ), was formed to campaign for independence for Quebec upon the premise that it could not hope for a fair deal within a predominantly English federation. In the same year a Quebec Liberal, Pierre Trudeau, became prime minister at Ottawa, determined to maintain the federation. More extreme than the PQ, the Front de Libération de Québec (FLQ) advocated and practised violence in order to win the independence which the PQ aimed to win peacefully. The FLQ consisted of a tiny handful of men and women who, invoking Che Guevara and Mao Zedong, committed a number of bank robberies and other acts of violence without attracting widespread support or, until 1970, much attention. In elections in that year the PQ won a quarter of the votes cast but only seven seats out of 108: the winners were the Liberals under Robert Bourassa. The FLQ resorted to more serious violence, kidnapping the British Trade Commissioner James Cross and the province's Minister of Labour Pierre Laporte, whom they strangled. The central government applied the War Measures Act and outlawed the FLQ but gave the kidnappers a safe exit to Cuba in return for the release of Cross after two months' confinement. The security forces, whose ineffective intelligence had allowed the FLQ a surprisingly long lease of life, succeeded in extinguishing it by 1972. The separatists' cause became entirely limited to the non-violent route which however got them nowhere. After winning fresh elections in 1976 the PQ introduced a series of measures giving the French language a special status in the province (the federation as a whole had been declared officially bilingual by an Act of 1969). In a referendum in 1983 proposing negotiations for a 'sovereignty association' 60 per cent of those voting opposed such negotiations.

But Quebec's nationalism impinged on federal politics in a way which revived the demand for independence. In 1984 the Conservative leader in Ottawa, Brian Mulroney, wooed Liberal voters in Quebec by supporting a movement for constitutional change (the Meech Lake amendment) to increase the influence of provincial governments in senior judicial and senatorial appointments, immigration and financial affairs. In provinces other than Quebec, however, the amendment was not popular and it failed to win the necessary endorsement of a majority of the provinces. Mulroney's failure had the effect of repelling the Québecois and for the first time a poll in Quebec showed a majority in favour of sovereign independence.

South America in the nineteenth century was isolated from world politics not – as were Africa and much of Asia – by the muffle of European imperialism but by the heritage of post-colonialism. At the same time the South American republics were largely isolated from one another as well as from the rest of the world. The twentieth century witnessed an accelerating reversal of this pattern, accompanied and complicated by spasmodic attempts to assimilate the democratic and industrial revolutions which were the hallmark of the experiences, and to some extent the successes, of western Europe and the United States of America: to implant, that is, democratic political forms and democratic social values in resistant, narrow oligarchies, and to develop manufacturing industries where trade in primary products had hitherto sufficed for the needs of the ruling classes.

In a century and more after independence South America had become a byword for political instability and could, but for widespread ignorance of its affairs, have become no less a byword for social immobility. It was notorious for civil wars, revolutions, coups, political assassinations and shortlived constitutions, while at the same time it entrenched extreme social and economic injustice. Its basic needs were the reverse of its experience; namely, political stability and social and economic change. It was in these respects not unique but its ills had been aggravated by time until they posed a daunting dilemma: was it possible to get social and economic change without revolution? Was it possible to get political stability without perpetuating social and economic stagnation? The underlying conflict between the few and the many was not mediated by a middle class such as had tided western Europe over the bar of oligarchy without intolerable violence.

The government of South America after the end of Spanish rule devolved upon a social élite consisting of big landowners supported by the Roman Catholic Church and by a military caste aspiring to the same social status. By 1945 the traditional power of the upper classes had been destroyed nowhere south of the Panama isthmus and ten years later only in Bolivia (1952). Nevertheless the oligarchy's props were weakening. Within the religious and military establishments there were growing doubts about the immutability and propriety of its monopoly

26.1 South America

of power and profit and some concern, expressed with varying degrees of success and sincerity, over the plight of the rural poor, the growing urban proletariat and the suppressed Indians. An awareness of gross inequalities was stirring consciences and fears and so enlisting in the service of the underdog those two powerful political forces, indignation and the recalculation of expediencies. Churches began to shift their attention and their political weight somewhat to the left, and there appeared in the armed forces officers with some of the instincts of populists and a taste for demagogy.

Through South America a great part of the population was extremely poor, illiterate, unproductive and virtually outside the state. Many states were not merely run by an oligarchy but also owned by it in the sense that the land and what grew on it and what lay beneath it were the private property of a small number of individuals: in various countries 60 to 90 per cent of agricultural land was owned by a tenth of the population. Quite apart from abstract notions of fair or unfair shares, this distribution was the cause of great inefficiency. Many landowners, possessing more land than they needed to cultivate, left much of it untilled and untended, but were firmly opposed to any redistribution to other proprietors who might be more disposed to cultivate it. (Forcible redistribution produced the opposite evil of a multitude of economically intractable plots: in Colombia, for example, more than two-thirds of the land was uncultivated while much of the cultivable area had been broken down into holdings of a few acres.) Bountifully supplied with cheap labour the big landowners had no need to invest their profits in their land, modernize their methods or increase production.

The rural poor remained poor to the verge of destitution and beyond, and either endured short lives of useless and hopeless misery or drifted to towns where they were not much better off, since they were not fitted to take jobs. Public education in South America as a whole was so meagre that less than a tenth of the population completed a primary course and illiteracy rates of 50 per cent were not uncommon, 90 per cent not unknown. If they were Indians, the peasants who went to the towns invited incomprehension and ridicule by their strange speech and attitudes. Moreover, if the peasants had little to offer, the towns too had little to offer on their side. Industry cannot flourish in places where half the population is too poor to buy its products. South American industries were handicapped by the lack of a domestic market with the result that the South American countries continued to import goods which they could have been making for themselves. Hence the towns to which the peasants migrated, so far from needing their labour, already contained unemployment; in some of them a third of the inhabitants might be unhoused. And this unemployment was growing not only for economic reasons but also because the population explosion was greater than anywhere else in the world: the population was in the process of doubling itself in periods of a quarter century.

There existed therefore in most parts of South America a revolutionary situation. This situation was accentuated by awareness of it, since an assumption that a pattern cannot last much longer is itself a potent factor for change. The forces making for change were the relatively passive rural and urban proletariats and the active leaders who might emerge from the established social groups or the nascent middle class and who, out of dissatisfaction with the existing state of affairs, might make common cause with the masses some or all of the way towards revolution.

The growth of a South American middle class had been stunted by the slow pace of industrial development just as industrial development had been stunted by the self-sufficiency of a ruling class capable of maintaining its standard of living by exporting primary products and using the proceeds to import all the necessities and luxuries which it wanted from the outside world. This economic pattern had social and political consequences, since a small middle class is less likely than a large one to adopt distinctive social habits and political aims of its own, and in South America the small middle class, imprisoned within the oligarchic system, was relatively effortlessly seduced into gravitating into and so preserving the upper reaches of a system which it had no power to subvert. Here again South America was not unique, except perhaps in degree. The standing of the middle class was, however, altered by the Second World War which deprived South America of its habitual imports and so promoted industrial development. After a pause in the immediate postwar years the demands created by the Korean War gave a fresh fillip to industrial expansion. These wars, events external to the sub-continent's own affairs, thus altered its economic course, although they did not do so to the extent of seriously altering its social hierarchy. The industrial middle class prospered in some centres, notably in Brazil, but for the most part it came nowhere near to supplanting the traditional ruling class in the exercise of political power.

The rise of a middle class is commonly associated with the growth of democracy as the middle class, annexing a part of the power wielded by a landed aristocracy, points the way to a yet further expansion of the political system. This process was reinforced in South America by a strand in its history of European origin. While South America owed its independence to the circumstances of the Napoleonic Wars which sundered it from Spain and Portugal as well as France, and whereas the waging of wars of liberation favoured the establishment of autocratic and military rule, the revulsion from European dominion also carried with it ideas of the Enlightenment so that liberated South America was imbued with a rejection of autocracy as well as rejection of distant,

foreign rule. But this was not a dominant theme, and it succeeded only
sporadically in making serious modifications to a quasi-feudal pattern
which was supported by the most powerful element in the state, the
armed forces.

After the wars of liberation early in the nineteenth century the new
South American states engaged in few wars among themselves and
faced no enemy threat from beyond the sub-continent. Their armies
assumed therefore a domestic political role rather than the function of
national defence. Officers, with the conservatism natural to their caste
and the social ambitions which became a substitute for more serious
military employment, saw themselves as the guardians or godfathers of
the state – and the state as the same as the status quo. Unduly inefficient
or corrupt politicians would be replaced by others or by a period of
direct military rule, and in the exericse of this regulative function the
officer class pictured itself as acting for the public weal, a habit of mind
which could lead to surprising results if the army's interpretation of the
public weal should change. And around the middle of the twentieth
century there were indications of such a change. As armies expanded,
they acquired officers from somewhat different backgrounds, so that
the awareness of the need for social change and mild support for it
found their way into the military establishment. The consequences of
this shift were, however, ambivalent. On the one hand the insemina-
tion of a radical element into the military mind was an encouragement
for the proponents of change, but on the other hand an establishment
ready for no more than a small dose of change could easily be
frightened back into a more rigid conservatism, if the pace of change
began to outstrip the progressive officers' own cautious assessment of
the need. The addition of a military element to the progressive forces
could affect the pace of change in one of two ways: either by increasing
it and so alienating progressive officers and bringing on a clash with the
forces of conservatism, or by reducing it to a level acceptable to these
officers and so alienating the more intrepid elements and producing a
clash at a different point along the political spectrum.

Alongside this regrouping of domestic forces old and new, whose
outcome was likely to differ from one state to the next, there was a
search for new models, for political forms to replace the existing forms
which were being judged and found wanting. This search led the more
inquiring minds to consider two foreign models, each of which seemed
to have something to contribute: western democracy with its emphasis
on freedom and human rights, and communism with its reputation for
economic growth. The South American intellectual who could discover
how to get the best from both these two worlds would perhaps have
found the synthetic short-cut to prosperity and justice. But he too was
faced with a multiple dilemma. He knew that, for economic reasons,
South America needed foreign aid; he knew that, for historical reasons,

South America wanted to steer clear of foreign aid; and he had to face the fact that if, in his search for the synthetic short-cut, he looked for aid and inspiration to both the western and the communist strongholds, he would be met in each with the argument that the two models were antithetical and that he must make up his mind between them before expecting help from the guardian of either. Like Asians and Africans, although for different reasons, he would need to be non-aligned while soliciting the favours of those whose line he refused exclusively to take.

South America's approach to the outside world reflected the needs of countries whose economies were in a process of transition without adequate domestic resources or machinery, against a background of ill-regulated foreign aid in a previous generation. Towards the end of the nineteenth century and at the beginning of the twentieth the principal capitalist nations had lent money to South America to excess and at very high rates of interest to the mutual dissatisfaction of both sides – of the South Americans who felt that they had been exploited, and of the lenders who resented many a subsequent default and the expropriation of a number of enterprises which they had built up. But South America could not do without foreign capital if it was to implement development programmes, close trade gaps and meet its large (and largely short-term) foreign debts. The capital required was not being produced at home. The poor were too poor to save and were getting poorer, the rich frequently invested or banked their wealth abroad, and domestic banks and other financial institutions had not developed the habits or the mechanisms for providing credit for industrial expansion. The reformers, who appreciated the need for foreign aid but were required by their environment to be anti-foreigner as well as anti-establishment, hoped to be extricated from this dilemma by getting aid from international agencies instead of foreign governments, but these agencies proved disappointing since they applied strict financial rules to their lending, insisted on currency stabilization and a reasonable prospect of profit as preconditions, and hesitated to come to the aid of petitioners with limited financial credentials and limited economic expertise: the postwar years in South America were peppered with too many economic blunders as wartime profits were dissipated on luxuries and industrialization was pursued fitfully and without discrimination.

Washington held therefore a commanding position. Washington wanted to encourage democracy, social progress and stability, it was opposed to communism and, on the whole, to revolution. It adopted, notably in the Alliance for Progress, a gradualist policy in a revolutionary situation on the assumption that lavish aid could promote democracy and social progress in South America and at the same time ward off revolution and stifle communism. This was a very large assumption to which it was objected that in Latin America's predicament aid of this kind could hasten revolution but not prevent it, while communism was bound to be an unexorcisable element in the reform movement, as impossible to eradicate as it was in France. Washington's assumptions and policies in the middle of the century were of undeniable importance but uncertain import. They were largely influenced by the Monroe Doctrine and by special, if local, concern over the Caribbean and Central American republics which lay like a hyphen between the northern and southern blocks of the American continent.

South America differed from North America not only by its Latinity but also by its fragmentation. While South America became divided into many states, North America did not. From the days of the Liberators, when the sub-continent was Balkanized by post-imperial wars and politics, there were hankerings for the sub-continental solidarity of the great Spanish viceroyalties. A surviving cultural community and a certain geographical compactness and isolation promoted in time an inter-American system, which was enlarged in turn into a pan-American (as opposed to a Latin American) organization. But the contrast between south and north could not be eradicated. In the north the United States had shown an amazing capacity to accommodate a hotch-potch of races and preserved its unity in spite of the disruptive social and economic forces which produced the Civil War, while Canada succeeded in keeping its British and French populations under a single political roof. These two states therefore were much bigger and more powerful than any South American state, and the South Americans became fearful of US preponderance and imperialism. Canada, which might have served as a makeweight, was reluctant to join any organization which might involve it in the conflicts between the United States and the Latin states.

The United States fed Latin American fears and suspicions. During its years of expansion the United States was uncertain of its attitudes towards its neighbours in Central America and the Caribbean, and during its years of emergence as a great power it frequently acted as though these states were something less than sovereign. Just as Britain in the twentieth century found it hard to think of Middle Eastern countries as independent or deserving independence, so the United States in an overlapping period felt much the same way about a group of states which were supposed to have a special impact on North American vital interests. When President Monroe forbade the expansion of European territorial dominions in the New World, Spain and Portugal had already lost theirs; the British, French and Dutch, who had arrived too late to get more than the pickings left over from the Hispano–Portuguese partition, had little interest in challenging Monroe's unilateral declaration and the one serious attempt to do so – France's attempt to turn Mexico into a new Habsburg empire during the American Civil War – was a catastrophic failure. By this time the United States had itself annexed one-third of Mexico, had evinced interest in an isthmian canal and was about to toy with the idea of acquiring the large islands of Cuba and Hispaniola (the latter containing the Dominican and Haitian republics).

The Monroe Doctrine, enunciated in 1823, was the basis of a policy of turning America into an island by purchases (Louisiana, Florida, Cuba, Alaska) and by barring all European powers from recovering their possessions or extending their influence in the continent. It was inspired equally by fears of Russia in the north-west and other Europeans to the south-east. For more than a century the doctrine required little exertion on the part of the United States, mainly on account of the state of Anglo-American relations, and it was not seriously called in question until, in the 1960s, the Russians dared to raid in the southern area where Monroe and his cabinet had originally feared British or Spanish activity. Britain made no attempt to enlarge its West Indian empire. During the decades after the breach between Britain and the new United States British naval power served to buttress rather than to challenge the doctrine. Geography has placed no islands between the British Isles and the seaboard of the United States, so that the initial post-independence period was one of estrangement but not of conflict; it is hard to believe that conflict could have been avoided, especially during the Civil War, if the North Atlantic had been dotted with islands which the two powers would have competed to occupy. In the event the possession of a common language and common traditions was not countered by territorial disputes (except over Canada which, illuminatingly, failed to get very robust support from London), and when by the end of the century the power of the United States had grown to significant proportions, the goodwill between the two countries prevailed over occasional conflicts and led in the next century to an alliance which pulled Britain out of a European and into an American orbit. This alliance might not have been achieved but for Britain's abnegation of the role which it had once been in a position to play in central America.

In the middle of the nineteenth century, when the United States first began to think of a canal across Nicaragua to link the Atlantic and the Pacific, British assent and co-operation seemed essential. Britain had territories and claims along the nearby coast (in British Honduras, the Mosquito Coast and the Bay Islands); the United States negotiated favourable treaties with Nicaragua and Honduras. From these positions the two countries negotiated the Clayton–Bulwer Treaty of 1850 whereby they agreed that neither should acquire exclusive control over any canal or special privileges in it; and further that neither should occupy or fortify or colonize or assume or exercise any dominion over any part of Central America. This treaty, concluded at a time when the United States was the weaker of the two parties, became an obstacle to later plans to go ahead with the construction of a canal without British collaboration and to acquire dominion over its course and banks, but by the end of the century British interest in this part of the world was small compared with British interest in the Middle East and southern Asia and in 1901 the Clayton–Bulwer Treaty was replaced by the Hay–Pauncefote Treaty which reaffirmed the principles of neutrality and free and undiscriminating use, but otherwise removed the limitations set by the earlier treaty. The United States then entered into discussions with Colombia for a grant of territory at Panama. A treaty was negotiated but rejected by the Colombian senate, whereupon in 1903 the United States promoted a revolt at Panama and the secession of the area from Colombia. A new Panamanian republic was created and, for $10 million and an annual rent of $250,000, granted to the United States perpetual sovereignty over the area to be called the Canal Zone and also the right to intervene in Panama's internal affairs. The United States made use of this right by despatching troops on a number of occasions.

More important to the United States than Panama was the large island of Cuba, closer to the United States than any other Latin American country with the sole exception of Mexico. For strategic reasons the United States tried on various occasions in the nineteenth century to buy Cuba from Spain but without success. In 1868 the Cubans rose against Spain and waged war for ten years. They were defeated but rose again in 1895. Feelings in the United States were enraged by the cruelty which the Spanish authorities used to defeat the revolt and by concern for American investments, but the government took no action until, in February 1898 and in circumstances which have remained unexplained ever since, the battleship USS *Maine* was sunk in harbour at Havana. Washington delivered an ultimatum and, although the terms were largely accepted and the war virtually over, declared war on Spain. Fighting, which extended to the Pacific, lasted three months and ended with the complete defeat of Spain and the cession to the United States by the treaty of Paris of the Philippine Islands, Guam and Puerto Rico in return for $20 million. Cuba passed in effect under the tutelage of the United States and so remained until 1933. In 1901 the United States asserted by the Platt Amendment (an amendment to the Army Appropriation Bill) that it would not withdraw its military forces unless its right to intervene for the preservation of good government were embodied in the Cuban constitution. US forces were stationed in the island in 1906–9 and 1912–13 in support of corrupt military régimes, and a naval base was built at Guantanamo.

Within a few years of the Cuban War the United States intervened in 1905 in the Dominican Republic. Fearful of European intervention as a consequence of the default of the Dominican government on its debts, President Theodore Roosevelt formulated the Roosevelt Corollary to the Monroe Doctrine, by which the United States arrogated to itself the right to intervene in Latin American countries in order to keep governments in order. US forces reappeared in 1916 and for the next eight years the country was under the direct military rule of the United States with a US officer as president. A similar occupation of the neighbouring Haitian republic, also intended to forestall European creditors, lasted from 1915 to 1934. On the mainland the United States intervened openly in the Mexican revolution and civil war by a naval bombardment in 1914 and an unsuccessful army expedition in 1916–17; and US forces, sent to Nicaragua in 1911 to support a favoured president, kept the liberal opposition quiet until 1933 when, upon their departure, the dictatorship of Anastasio Somoza was inaugurated.

This US policy of direction and control, sustained by sporadic military descents, was abandoned by President Franklin D. Roosevelt and his Secretary of State, Cordell Hull. In his first inaugural address Roosevelt promulgated a good neighbour policy based on non-intervention, and his undertaking was repeated at the Pan-American Conference of 1936 at Buenos Aires. The Platt Amendment was repealed. The right to intervene in Panama's internal affairs was abrogated by treaty. The withdrawal of US marines from Haiti was accelerated. The president accepted the right of the Mexican government to nationalize oil properties within its territory. Latin American hopes were also raised by the passing of the Reciprocal Trade Agreements Act of 1934 which gave the president power to reduce tariffs by as much as 50 per cent, and by the establishment in the same year of the Import-Export Bank for the lending of US public funds to foreign governments.

But this amelioration of the intra-American atmosphere did not produce all that Washington desired. Before the Second World War, as after it, the United States wanted to enlist Latin American sympathies and support for wider matters, but largely failed. Before the outbreak of war Hull, mindful of Germany's attempt in the First World War to get Japan to attack the United States through Mexico, tried but failed to persuade Latin America that Nazism and fascism were present dangers against which the whole American continent should take joint precautions. At Havana in July 1940 the American states agreed that no non-American state should be allowed to take over any piece of American territory, but this new and anti-German enunciation of the Monroe Doctrine was to be upheld by joint American action; the United States was given no invitation to intervene on its own against any external threat, but rather to supply its neighbours with the arms and equipment to do so. Consequently, one result of Washington's fears for the defence of the hemisphere was the strengthening of the military class throughout the area. Small Brazilian and Mexican forces were sent overseas during the war, but American military supplies affected the structure of politics within Latin America far more than they affected the course of the war.

After Pearl Harbor, Mexico, Colombia and Venezuela broke off relations with Japan, Germany and Italy, and all the Central American and Caribbean republics declared war. When the end of the war was in sight the American states, meeting at Chapultepec in Mexico in February 1945, declared themselves in favour of collective defence against internal as well as external threats (this arrangement was placed on a more permanent footing by the Inter-American Treaty of Reciprocal Assistance, concluded at Rio de Janeiro in 1947), but Washington's concern to create a continental anti-communist alliance or defence system found little response among states which were still used to thinking of the United States and not the USSR as the prime intervenor in their internal affairs and were much more worried by postwar economic problems than by communism. The military classes, which were the most immediately affected by joint defence schemes, were less interested in co-operation than in strenthening their own forces. They looked to the United States for more, and more modern, equipment. The United Sates on the other hand became increasingly concerned with communism and increasingly trapped between policies of pre-empting communism by economic aid to its neighbours and interfering in their affairs to suppress communists or anybody who looked like a communist from Washington.

In 1951 the Mutual Security Act was extended to Latin America and from 1952 the United States concluded a series of bilateral defence agreements. If the United States (and Latin American civilians) had qualms about this further reinforcement of armies which operated most often as domestic political forces, Washington felt itself constrained by the veiled threat that armies unable to satisfy their needs in the United States might go shopping elsewhere. An inter-American police academy was established at Fort Davis in the Canal Zone in 1962 for the study and practice of techniques of counter-insurgency, but otherwise inter-American military co-operation was not noticeably fruitful or popular.

The conferences at Chapultepec and Rio were the seventh and eighth in a series of inter-American conferences which had been inaugurated in Washington in 1889. The ninth of these meetings was held at Bogatá in 1948 and created new institutions and continuing machinery for pan-American consultation and action (Canada still, by its own wish, excluded until 1989). Obstensibly pan-American, but in some minds a Latin counter-weight to northern power, the Organization of American States had for its objects the maintenance of peace within the area of its members, the peaceful settlement of their disputes, joint action against aggression and co-operative development of economic, social and cultural interests. For Latin America this association with the United States was welcome chiefly on account of the prospect of an economic outpouring like the Marshall Plan for Europe, but the prospect proved a mirage since Washington saw Europe and Latin America in a completely different light: Europe had been ravaged by war, was in danger of immediate economic collapse and was believed to be a defenceless bait for further Russian advances. These arguments to the hearts and heads of US policy-makers applied little or not at all to Latin America, even had these policy-makers been as much concerned with good neighbourliness as Franklin D. Roosevelt in the thirties. Latin America had not a high priority in postwar Washington. Disenchant-ment grew on both sides. When war broke out in Korea, in Washington's eyes an anti-communist war in which all should be prepared to stand up and be counted, Colombia alone sent troops. The Korean War sharpened Washington's global anti-communist suscep-tibilities and clarified its priorities in Latin America where it abetted and organized the overthrow of the left-wing President Jacobo Arbenz Guzman (see Chapter 27) and so showed how much more importance it attached to the suppression of communism than to the principle of non-intervention or to good relations with its Latin neighbours. Washington also displayed its belief that its actions in the southern half of the continent need not be trammelled by great power considerations: the reaction of the USSR could be regarded, at this date, as minimal or impotent. The final lesson of the Guatemala affair was, or should have been, the impossibility of drawing a line between radical programmes which were social and therefore good and radical programmes which were communist and therefore malignant. The United States evicted in Guatemala a reforming administration whose actions were not in themselves noxious but whose motives and further intentions were suspect. Latin America did not accept the anti-communist justification put forward in Washington.

In 1958 Vice-President Richard Nixon, on a tour of Latin American countries, was received with insults and even violence which en-lightened official and popular opinion north of the Rio Grande about some Latin American attitudes towards the United States. In two of the countries in his itinerary, Peru and Venezuela, dictators had recently been displaced, but not before they had received from President Eisenhower the Legion of Merit: Nixon found himself the target of popular indignation against the US approval of dictators. In 1960 Eisenhower himself undertook a Latin American tour as part of a calculated attempt to improve relations. In the interval between the two visits the United States agreed to the creation of an inter-American Bank and an inter-American Fund for Social Development (the latter to finance unprofitable schemes which the World Bank was debarred from helping); Washington had previously frowned on these institutions. Although the eleventh inter-American conference, due to be held at Quito in 1959, was postponed, the foreign ministers of the American states met once in that year at Santiago and twice in the following year at San José. The first of these meetings was mainly devoted to denouncing Trujillo and Batista, matters on which it was not difficult to get a wide consensus. In 1960 a Venezuelan allegation that Trujillo had instigated an attempt to murder President Betancourt produced an inquiry, a condemnation of Trujillo and the eviction of the Dominican Republic from the OAS, but when the United States proposed economic sanctions and internationally supervised elections in the Dominican Republic its associates drew back for fear of setting a precedent for intervention in their own affairs (Trujillo was himself murdered in 1961). There was also a clash between the United States and the rest on whether Cuba had become decently or dangerously left-wing. The conference was on the whole anti-Cuban but was not prepared to express itself at all directly. A proposal for inter-American mediation between the United States and Cuba gained no ground. Nevertheless the Organization of American States was functioning and seen to be functioning and the discords within it were not acute, although on the perennial problem of economic co-operation an attempt by President Kubitschek of Brazil to obtain United States aid for an 'Operation Pan-America' had produced little response in Washington.

The next year, however, President Kennedy sounded a new note. Addressing himself to Latin America as no president of the United States had done since Franklin D. Roosevelt, Kennedy proposed an Alliance for Progress, massive and long-term co-operation between the United States and its Latin neighbours for the improvement, at the expense of the United States, of their economies on condition that they would also introduce certain fundamental reforms. The United States would provide $20 billion over ten years to pay, in effect, for economic and social reform. Although Latin American governments preferred bilateral to multilateral aid, and although they presumably preferred aid without strings to aid tied to reform, the Alliance for Progress was the sort of intervention which they had been seeking ever since the inauguration of the Marshall Plan for Europe, as opposed to the sort of intervention which they habitually feared or said they feared. Later in the same year, at Punta del Este in Uruguay, all the members of the OAS except Cuba subscribed a charter giving effect to Kennedy's proposals.

The Alliance for Progress was a bold psychological stroke, important for its impact upon the citizens of the United States as well as on the peoples further south, but it was imperfectly thought out in advance and the practical results had proved disappointingly meagre by the time of its author's death. The reasons for the disappointment were many. First, Kennedy's death came all too soon after his inauguration; there had been little time to get results. But, secondly, there were more material reasons. The sum pledged was large but it was questionable whether even this sum could do more than hold a deteriorating situation. It was expected moreover that government funds would attract private spending, but the volume of the private spending did not come up to expectations, and some of the government funds had to be diverted to unforeseen short-term purposes owing to a fall in Latin American revenues from primary products. Thirdly, there was some confusion about the purposes and priorities of the Alliance from Washington's point of view. Was it designed primarily to alter social structures, or to alleviate immediate poverty, or to promote a state's economic progress, or to facilitate interstate economic integration, or to combat communism? Unless priorities were established it was difficult to know where to begin or what to approve. Finally, there were misunderstandings and pitfalls. The misunderstandings transpired when the question was put whether funds were to become available immediately or only conditionally upon the introduction of social changes. The pitfalls were disclosed when the question arose of giving aid to a reactionary or unconstitutional régime. Cutting off aid meant damaging the hopes of the blameless poor. Continuing aid might mean condoning unconstitutional violence instead of promoting constitutional reform, financing backward régimes instead of encouraging progressive ones.

Brazil, the fourth largest country in the world and second in the Americas only to Canada, became an independent state as an empire which lasted from 1822 to 1889 when the second emperor was displaced by a bloodless revolution led by a professor of mathematics. It possesses enormous natural resources, occupies one-third of Latin America and accounts, with Mexico and Argentina, for nearly two-thirds of its products. According to the census of 1970 its population had grown by a third in ten years and had reached more than 93 million. Thanks to its vast and varied resources it was able to make economic progress both during and after the First World War. In 1930 Getulio Donnelles Vargas, a mild liberal, was put in power by the army which was dissatisfied with the traditional conservative oligarchy. He began the modernization of Brazil. He strengthened the central government, nurtured industry and introduced state economic planning. He became both more autocratic and more popular. The army grew suspicious of him on both counts. It feared his new power base in the poorer classes and in 1945 he was forced out of office. But he was returned to power in 1950 by popular vote and with the support of a new type of younger army officer. The army, hoping to control him and reluctant blatantly to flout a fair election, allowed him to take office but by 1954 it had had enough of him and was about to evict him – on the grounds of incompetence – when he committed suicide.

The next decade saw the running down of the Vargas era under three presidents. The election of 1955 was won by Juscelino Kubitschek with Julio Goulart as his vice-president. The armed forces, divided in their attitudes towards this result, interposed no objection and indeed acted to allow the successful pair to take over. They thereby demonstrated the new president's dependence upon them, and he in return tacitly acknowledged the relationship by raising pay and providing funds for more and better military equipment. Some officers, like their counterparts in other countries, wanted more than this and hoped for a mildly reforming administration which would attack corruption, incompetence and the grosser manifestations of social injustice, but they were not willing to endorse any very radical measures nor – in the Brazilian case – did they have the satisfaction of observing a good administration at work, for President Kubitschek embarked on extravagant enterprises (such as the building of the new capital, Brasilia) and in the course of an energetically misguided administration opened up huge new opportunities for private speculation.

At the next election, in 1961, Jânio Quadros, with Goulart still as vice-president, succeeded, but he resigned after seven months leaving Goulart to take his place under the eyes of a divided and increasingly dubious army and a solidly conservative navy and air force. In these circumstances President Goulart's powers were strictly limited and he quickly reached the limits. Where Quadros had preferred to quit, Goulart chose to forge ahead; he rode for a fall. He proposed a wide extension of the franchise, land reform and a neutralist foreign policy. He appealed to the people against the armed forces and congress, accepted communist support at home, established relations with the USSR and opposed the eviction of Castro's Cuba from the OAS (but joined the United States naval blockade of Cuba during the missile crisis). These measures won him some popularity but also evoked fear and hatred, enabled communists to infiltrate into central and state administrations and trade unions and, as different provinces lined up on different sides, produced a threat of civil war, at which point the army intervened.

Having evicted Goulart the army leaders forced the congress, after a pause in which constitutional propriety was observed by recognizing the president of the chamber of deputies as president, to install General Humberto Castelo Branco as president for the remainder of Goulart's term. The general was succeeded by Marshal Costa e Silva and he by Generals Garrastazu Medici, Ernesto Geisel and João Batista de Oliveira Figuieredo. Political parties were banned with the exception of two new ones of no independent vitality. The régime turned a hard face towards trade unions, peasants and students. It made little progress with land reform and halted literacy programmes which seemed to it dangerous: Brazil remained a country of unused land and unused talent. Faced with growing opposition it resorted to strong-arm methods, including wide-spread and appalling cruelty to the political prisoners who were thrown in increasing numbers into the jails.

On the other hand the military régime claimed credit for its handling of the economy. Having inherited galloping inflation it not only reversed the trends of the lean sixties but achieved for a while (1968–74) a growth rate of 10 per cent a year, much in excess of anything seen in the previous twenty years. The main instrument was exports, which were quadrupled, assisted by heavy borrowing from foreigners impressed by Brazil's natural resources and disciplinary government. But 1974 was a year of reckoning in Brazil as elsewhere in the world. The healthy world markets which had taken Brazil's exports became unhealthy. Internal developments financed from abroad slowed down and Brazil turned to import controls and import substitution. The beneficiaries of the boom began to grumble, its victims to assert themselves. The latter were numerous. In spite of the boom nearly half the population was worse off than before – 40 per cent were sharing less than 10 per cent of the national income. Regional as well as class tensions were aggravated, as the under-privileged north-east waxed indignant about the fat cats in the south. With the advent in 1979 of President Figuieredo the government set about the dual task of restructuring the economy and at the same time humanizing the régime. Censorship was greatly relaxed, torture probably diminished and a wide, though not total, amnesty decreed for political prisoners. In the economic sphere special effort was put into the search for alternatives to foreign oil: prospecting for off-shore oil (which proved disappointing), the search for substitutes and a nuclear programme. The last raised the usual questions about whether Brazil had it in mind to develop nuclear military power as well as a nuclear-powered economy.

Brazil in the seventies was not the leader in nuclear development in South America. Its old adversary Argentina was ahead. Brazil had not signed the Nuclear Non-Proliferation Treaty but had signed, with reservations, its regional equivalent, the Treaty of Tlatelolco (1967). Argentina signed neither. (Mexico, also in the nuclear race, signed both.) In 1975 Brazil, after a rebuff from the United States, turned to West Germany for help in accelerating its nuclear programme. In return for part-payment in Brazilian uranium, Bonn agreed to supply Brazil with eight reactors, a fuel-processing plant and uranium enrichment technology. Brazil's aim was to have no less than seventy-three reactors by the end of the century. Although the main purposes of this programme were industrial and civilian, the processing plant and the technology to be supplied by West Germany pointed to a military capability. The safeguards embodied in the agreement were stringent but, in the nature of the case, less than total. Brazilian and Argentinian programmes created the possibility of a nuclear arms race in South America similar to those between India and Pakistan or Israel and Iraq.

But Brazil's attitude to its traditional opponent was not bellicose. Brazil's great size, undeveloped resources and comparatively stable government allowed Brazilians to look forward to the day when one of South America's classic feuds would be ended for ever by Brazil's irreducible superiority. Questions remained about the buffer lands of Paraguay and Uruguay but so far as Brazil was concerned these were matters which could be confronted with assurance and left to time.

Brazil's size made it a giant among Latin American states. Its potential wealth made it a potentially mighty giant. Its Portuguese background differentiated it from its Spanish-speaking neighbours and gave it a more cosmopolitan flavour which was accentuated by its awareness of its African origins. Brazil was both a part of South America and turned its back on South America. It was no less detached from North America, determined to assert its independence from the United States and not to play second fiddle to Washington, even when the two countries shared conservative and capitalist outlooks. It sought closer links with the rising stars of Africa and Asia – Nigeria and Japan – and also with Iraq, another country with well-grounded ambitions and the supplier for the time being of the greater part of Brazil's imported fuels. Its weak points lay in the excessive growth of its population and its foreign debts, conducing the one to social, the other to economic nightmares, to grave unemployment and unrest and to inflation. As the dreams of the seventies turned thin, congressional and provincial elections in 1982 gave the government unaccustomed reverses; the IMF insisted in 1983 on painfully classic measures as conditions for its help; and in 1985 the military deemed it prudent to take a back seat after twenty-three years of political power. Tancredo Neves was elected president but immediately collapsed and died, leaving a little-known deputy and successor, José Sarney, to cope with daunting economic and social problems. Sarney abandoned the monetarist recipe for economic rehabilitation, partly because its purely economic dictates were bound to foment misery and likely to create a revolution, partly because Brazil's inherent strengths enabled it – or seemed to enable it – to negotiate with its creditors for relief and with the IMF for funds to support a moderately expansionist economic plan. In spite of its huge debts Brazil was able to pay the interest on them punctually. It was also able to imply that without outside aid the Sarney régime would founder, leaving the creditors without hope of interest or the repayment of their capital and confronting the world with the abhorrent possibility of either a reversion to military rule or a régime much to the left of Sarney's. But Sarney lacked political anchorage. His government was a coalition in which the largest partner, the Brazilian Democratic Movement, gave the president full support only when he least needed it. The Movement scored an overwhelming victory in federal and provincial elections in 1986 and then, with the introduction of painful economic measures, bickered with Sarney. These measures excited opposition without stemming inflation which was running at 200 per cent a year and growing to astronomic four-figure proportions. Elections in 1989 gave a clear majority to Ferdinando Collor de Mello who, at the age of 40, won nearly twice as many votes as his main rival and introduced severe measures which curbed inflation at the price of curbing everything else too. Bank accounts were frozen for eighteen months, thus removing about $70 billion from the economy; a new currency was introduced; public services were drastically reduced; tax changes shifted money from the private to the public sector. Unemployment soared, businesses collapsed and the weaker classes were driven to penury and despair.

Argentina, the second in extent of South America's major states, achieved its independence from Spain at the cost of losing territories which formed the new states of Uruguay, Paraguay and Bolivia. It was only gradually and painfully unified but from the latter part of the nineteenth century it prospered with the development of its lands, largely by immigrants from Europe. The government was in the hands of upper-class conservative and moderately radical politicians who competed for power and sporadically permitted an admixture of democracy, especially between 1916 and 1930. The country's population, its agriculture and its railways expanded steadily and with the introduction of refrigeration it became one of the world's major exporting countries before the First World War; but it lacked minerals and the capacity to develop industry alongside agriculture and commerce. It was severely hit by the slump of 1929 and suffered, partly in consequence, a revolt in 1930 in which army officers (including a 35-year-old Juan Domingo Perón) had the support of the possessing and the dispossessed classes. This event was followed by a period of autocratic conservative rule, buttressed by the army and by renewed prosperity. At the same time urbanization and immigration were producing a more politically conscious and socialist working class.

During the war the presidency was held by the ultra-conservative Ramón Castillo, first as acting president from 1940 to 1942 and then as president for a further year. Castillo refused to break off relations with the Axis powers, partly because he had fascist leanings himself and partly in despite of the United States, towards which Argentina's governing classes were traditionally hostile. In 1943 the army again intervened in politics, this time in order to remove the reactionary régime of landowners whose tenure of power since 1930 had proved that they had learnt nothing. The revolution was more than a transfer of power. Its leaders had a programme, or at least a series of general aims, which epitomized powerful desires in one section or another of Argentine society and mentality. One of these aims was Argentina for the Argentinians: a rejection of the role of foreigners in the Argentine economy who promoted useful enterprises but took all the profits away, and a rejection too of the Argentine ruling class itself which aped foreign, mainly French, fashions and spent half its time in Paris. Another aim, going beyond the assertion of Argentine pre-eminence in the sub-continent, was to make Argentina not only an independent power in the world but a great one whose voice would be heard and heeded in international affairs generally. And thirdly, the new men – or many of them, including Perón – wanted social justice at home, by which they meant a less blatant maldistribution of wealth and a less extreme concentration of power in the capital at the expense of the provinces.

A series of generals occupied the presidency in the next two years. In 1944 Argentina broke off relations with Germany and Japan, less out of a change of heart than from a well-calculated need to stand well with Washington as the war in Europe approached its end. In the next year Argentina declared war. (All the independent states of South and Central America and the Caribbean declared war on Germany and its associates between 1941 and 1945. Argentina was the last to do so.) During this period Perón held a number of official positions, developed good relations with union leaders and great popularity with the *descaminados* (the shirtless or destitute), but earned the jealousy of many of his brother officers. Dismissed in 1945 he created a new political party which won elections in 1946. Perón became president partly through this expression of the popular will but no less through the wave of extra-parliamentary enthusiasm displayed by the crowds of *descaminados* who invaded the political arena. Throughout this contest Perón was openly and vituperatively opposed by the US ambassador.

Perón ruled for nine and a half years which were crammed with legislative and other measures designed, mainly by authoritarian methods, to turn Argentina into a modern and just country. Banks and other enterprises were nationalized, foreign concerns were bought out with wartime profits, public services and popular education were expanded, industrialization was accelerated, the centralized buying and selling of agricultural products was introduced in order to cushion the effects of price fluctuations. But the pace was too hot for the economy and for the propertied classes, and Perón also gave grave offence to the Church. Although the programme was trimmed in the later years Perón made too many mistakes and too many enemies, and in June 1955 the navy and the air force, with the Church in the background, tried to bomb him out of the presidency. The army, however, not only remained loyal to him during the abortive coup but did not feel obliged to replace him by any other leader after it. Perón dismissed some of his ministers who were most obnoxious to the conservatives and set about safeguarding his position by organizing and arming the *descaminados*. This latter move alarmed the army which turned against him and, in September 1955, removed him by a coup which placed another general in his place.

The oligarchy had closed ranks in order to put an end to economic policies which were harming the country and social reforms which were harming themselves. They had the support of intellectuals who, although they might approve Perón's social aims, disapproved of his authoritarian methods, particularly censorship; for Perón's advocacy of social reform did not include freedom of expression. The fall of Perón halted the reform movement and, as in Brazil, raised the hopeless question of what to do when the need for reform is urgent but the readiness of the powers that be for change is restricted. The supporters of Perón – and of the vivacious Eva Duarte, whom Perón had married just before his triumph in 1942 but who had died of cancer in 1952 – did not disappear. They represented a force which, if it could not be wooed away to some other movement, must either be disfranchised or be allowed to resume the *peronista* course.

Meanwhile the army ruled. It first installed General Eduardo Lonardi in the presidency, in which he was later succeeded by General Pedro Aramburu pending elections in 1958. In that year Arturo Frondizi, a representative middle-class politician, became president with army consent. The persistence of *peronista* feeling was demonstrated at elections in 1960 when, with the *peronistas* barred from putting up candidates of their own, one million abstentions were recorded. In 1962 the *peronistas* were allowed to vote once more, Frondizi gambling on his ability to win them to his side. The gamble failed conspicuously. Officers of the three services, angered by Frondizi's miscalculation, discarded him and took council among themselves on the basis that the first article of government was the continued exclusion of Perón (in exile in Spain) and his like. The navy, Perón's stoutest opponents, insisted on the simple course of not having elections, and they were supported by a section of army officers known as the *gorillas*. Other army officers, however, backed by the air force, preferred to revert to the system of holding elections as required by the constitution but with the *peronistas* disfranchised. Fighting ensued and the latter group won. New elections were held but could not disguise *peronista* strength which could always be manifested either by pro-*peronista* votes or by abstentions. In the next year the moderate army group made Arturo Illía president. The armed forces had refused to accept the electoral verdict of 1962 and had failed to find a constitutional way of excluding

Perón. They had therefore resorted to unconstitutional manoeuvres and had in the process further exposed the divisions in their own ranks. In 1966 they removed Illía and substituted Juan Onganía. In 1970 they removed Onganía and substituted Roberto Levingston who was removed in his turn in 1971 to make way for General Alejandro Lanusse. None of these governments could master inflation or keep order. Disorder increasingly took the form of kidnapping for publicity and ransom – for example, the seizure and murder by a Trotskyist group of Fiat's Director-General in Argentina.

In 1972 Perón, now 77 years old, returned amid speculation and apprehension. His arrival was undramatic and his stay short. He endorsed the candidacy of Hector Cámpora in the approaching presidential election and went back to Spain after a few weeks. Cámpora won the election in 1973 with 49.6 per cent of the vote and his party – the Frente Justicialista, alias *peronista* – won twenty out of twenty-two governorships and control of both parliamentary chambers. But Cámpora was unable to control the violence and kidnapping by groups which claimed a share of the Peronist mantle but were disavowed by the Frente, and after a brief interval Perón reappeared, Cámpora resigned, the Frente nominated Perón and his second wife for the presidency and vice-presidency and they received 61.8 per cent of the vote. Perón introduced heavy taxes, bearing specially on the rich but also – in the case of a VAT at 16 per cent – on other classes too. He died in July 1974, leaving his widow to face the problems of inflation and public order, in dealing with which she was no more successful than her predecessor. She and her government were removed in 1976 by the army which put General Jorge Rafael Videla in her place but could think of nothing more useful to do than imprison and kill its critics.

The military régime, which continued under the presidencies of Generals Roberto Eduardo Viola and Leopoldo Galtieri, lasted until 1982 when it was undone by the humiliating outcome of the Falklands War. Under its aegis and by its agents some 30,000 Argentinians were tortured and killed, many of them being dumped alive into the sea out of aircraft. Inflation exceeded 250 per cent a year, the foreign debt was sextupled, production and industry collapsed. Galtieri hoped to redeem this record by capturing the Falkland Islands on the 150th anniversary of their occupation by Europeans. After talks at the UN early in 1982 which perpetuated the Anglo–Argentinian stalemate, Galtieri sent a civilian unit, under naval protection, to South Georgia in the Antarctic to dismantle a disused British whaling station and then proceeded to invade the Falklands. The Argentinian expedition, which landed on 1 April, was immediately successful and Galtieri himself visited the capital, Port Stanley, three weeks later. But the British despatched a force to regain possession of South Georgia and then attacked the

Argentinians on the Falklands in a war for which Argentina was militarily and psychologically unprepared.

Over the ownership of the Falklands there has been a long dispute which neither bilateral diplomacy nor international machinery has been able to dispel. The islands were discovered by John Davis at the end of the sixteenth century and named over a century later after Lucius Cary, Viscount Falkland, one of the most illustrious victims of the English Civil War. The French colonized East Falkland in 1764, the English West Falkland in 1765. The Spanish bought the former and seized the latter a few years later but then yielded West Falkland to the British who promptly abandoned it. The Spanish subsequently abandoned East Falkland. In 1829 a new colony was established in the name of the United Provinces of Rio de la Plata, successors in title to the Spanish empire in South America and predecessors of the Argentine republic. Britain registered a verbal protest. It had established in 1820 a symbolic presence which was destroyed in 1833 by the United States, whereupon the British came back, evicted the few remaining Argentinians and established a colony embracing both East and West Falkland. Argentine persistently challenged the British title which Britain offered on several occasions to submit to the International Court of Justice, an offer always rejected. Argentina also claimed sovereignty over South Georgia, the South Orkneys and other territory in the South Pacific and Antarctica. This claim clashed with Chilean as well as British claims, of which the latter dated from early in the twentieth century.

In 1979 the British Foreign Office, uneasily but not urgently alive to the dangers, elaborated a plan for relinquishing sovereignty over the Falklands and leasing them back. This plan was presented to a committee of the cabinet which gave it scant attention although the approach of the 150th anniversary of the British reoccupation in 1833 was a likely source of trouble: a full-scale invasion was not envisaged even after General Galtieri's promotion to the presidency at the end of 1981 was followed by rumours and suspicious acts. After bilateral ministerial talks in New York at a relatively low level in the following February the Argentine government issued a brusque declaration which the talks' pallid conclusions did not seem to warrant, and in the next month a party of Argentinian scrap dealers was sent to South Georgia under naval protection to dismantle an abandoned British station. This probe was not unconnected with the well-advertised withdrawal in the previous year, on grounds of expense and against the advice of the Foreign Office, of the British survey vessel *Endurance* – a symbol of the British presence whose removal led Argentinians to believe that Britain's position throughout the South Pacific was no longer greatly prized in London. Two weeks after the arrival of the scrap dealers in South Georgia Argentina seized the Falklands, undeterred by last-minute attempts by the United States to prevent this blatantly illegal act of aggression. President Galtieri was able to make a triumphant visit to Port Stanley, the islands' capital.

The British government's failure to assess Argentinian intentions until too late left it with few choices. These were negotiation from a position of weakness or war. Ostensibly it professed to be using force to secure negotiation but once a naval armada had been assembled and despatched there was little prospect of anything except war: peace-makers were up against a time limit and entrenched national obduracies. The British government may have toyed with the notion of a deal whereby – provided the invading Argentinian force was voluntarily removed – Britain would reintroduce its rule for a short time only and then transfer sovereignty to Argentina; but the dominant British resolve was not to treat with the enemy but to beat him, and in this mood negotiation – and all third-party negotiators – tended to appear as impediments. The outcome upon which the British government was resolved was a clear-cut victory, and negotiation is apt to produce something much less satisfying. The British expedition was sent into action swiftly but only precariously protected – its air cover was inferior to that provided for any British squadron since the *Prince of Wales* and *Repulse* had been sunk by the Japanese in 1941. It won a resounding victory, but by a whisker and not without grievous loss. It recovered the Falklands, caused the fall of a hateful dictatorship and saddled Britain with the defence of the islands for an indefinite future and at greatly increased cost.

In the aftermath of this victory one episode stood out. This was the sinking of the Argentinian cruiser *General Belgrano* on 2 May. The reasons were various: the loss of life (368 dead); the circumstances in which the action was authorized; the consequent suspicion, in Britain, that the specially constituted war cabinet had not exercised proper control over naval operations; and the allegation, again in Britain, that the torpedoing of the *Belgrano* was an item in the determination to torpedo current peace negotiations. The last two charges appear to be mutually incompatible. The ensuing controversy was of little interest outside Britain.

The attempts to keep the peace while the British force was sailing south consisted, first, of some hectic diplomacy by the United States secretary of state, Alexander Haig, whose main aim was to persuade President Galtieri (and his associates in the military junta) that the British force was no mere bluff and would recover the Falklands by force if no agreement was reached between the adversaries before the expedition reached the islands. This attempt had failed by 29 April and the chief consequences of the failure were two: the United States, which had failed to condemn Argentinian aggression as the UN Charter required, abandoned its neutrality and came out in Britain's favour; and secondly, the war cabinet in London abated its opposition to the Royal

Navy's pleas for more hostile action. For professional but also political reasons (the economic axe was threatening the navy more severely than the other services) naval chiefs wished to demonstrate their unique value to the nation. Proposals for an attack on South Georgia having been rejected, the navy wanted to bag a scalp in the shape of a major Argentinian warship, preferably the aircraft carrier *25 de Mayo* or alternatively the *Belgrano*. The collapse of the first stage of Haig's diplomacy cleared the way and on 2 May the war cabinet, at a strangely slapdash meeting at Chequers, changed the rules of engagement laid down earlier and so authorized an attack on either vessel. By the prevailing rules Britain had publicly given notice that it would engage and sink any Argentinian vessel within a 12 mile 'exclusion' zone round the Falklands. On 2 May this rule was changed to permit action anywhere outside Argentinian territorial waters although, unlike the defining of the exclusion zone, the new rule was not made public until 7 May.

The sinking of an enemy ship in war is not normally an event to cause surprise. The sinking of the *Belgrano* became controversial on two grounds: first, because it was allegedly unnecessary, and, second, because it destroyed the second of two attempts to preserve the peace, Peruvian diplomatic intervention.

The case for the sinking of the *Belgrano* was that it posed a threat so long as it was at sea and regardless of its position or course. The case against the sinking was that the *Belgrano* was known to have changed course for port, was not – as the defence secretary and the prime minister told the House of Commons and the prime minister repeated a year later – closing rapidly on the British force, and had ceased to pose any threat. (In a strange volte-face seven months later the chief of defence staff said that the only threat came from the *25 de Mayo*.) By a stream of contradictory and sometimes false statements British ministers dug pitfalls for themselves, revealing a disconcerting ignorance of important details and some tardiness in correcting mistakes after the true facts had become available.

The second matter of controversy was the connection, if any, between the sinking of the *Belgrano* and the proposals for peace which were being canvassed by the government of Peru. Alexander Haig subsequently wrote that both he and the Peruvian president, Fernando Belaunde Terry, had received from both belligerents general approval of these proposals before the sinking of the *Belgrano* and were working on the details, all of which were known to British officials. The British government denied this account. The British foreign secretary, Francis Pym, flew to Washington on 1 May and reported to London on the state of negotiations late on 2 May, after the sinking. That negotiations were in progress was known to all. That the sinking of the *Belgrano* put an end to them is sufficiently evident. That the British war cabinet welcomed or – far worse – instigated the sinking as a means to abort them has not been proved and is inherently less plausible than the supposition that London was sceptical about them and paid them little attention.

Three days after final British victory in June Galtieri was dismissed. Civilian rule was restored after a short interval and the ensuing elections were won by the Radical Party, whose leader Raoul Alfonsin became president with the tasks of repairing the economy, investigating the disappearance of thousands of victims of the military régime, keeping the military in order, and repairing relations with Britain without abandoning Argentina's claim to the Falklands.

Alfonsin had decency but little else in his favour in politics. He was distrusted by the military whose overweening style survived the Falklands fiasco; by the Church, by the unions and eventually by the populace which had acclaimed him but turned away from him when prices began to double every month. He survived scattered military mutinies at the cost of giving in to demands to abandon trials of officers accused of enormities against civilians during the military régime. At mid-term elections a revived Peronist party won sixteen out of twenty state governorships and in the presidential election of 1989 the Peronist candidate Carlos Menem, a flamboyant campaigner of Syrian extraction, easily won the popular vote. During his campaign Menem praised Castro and Stroesser indiscriminately; deployed the familiar Peronist rhetorical style; made extravagant promises to the poor but seemed to have no idea how to redeem these promises; and was fierce in his resolve to recover the Falklands. The economic state of the country on the morrow of the election was so alarming that Alfonsin was persuaded to resign in order that Menem might be inducted in June instead of November. He quickly authorized exploratory talks for the resumption of diplomatic and commercial relations with Great Britain (which proceeded slowly in the face of British lack of enthusiasm) and embarked on an economic programme similar to that of President Collor in Brazil. He ditched controls over prices and wages; the former rose steeply and the latter were halved. Businesses and employment collapsed. So too did the currency. Retailers took to pricing their goods in US dollars whose value quintupled in two months. Hyperinflation was reduced to inflation at about 60 per cent a year but then rebounded into the thousands per cent. Menem tried to sell off state enterprises but had difficulty in finding buyers. His government could raise no money by issuing bonds since nobody would or could buy the bonds.

Chile's history in the nineteenth century had been one of progress only briefly interrupted by civil war in 1891 and based on rich mineral resources and successful wars against Peru and Bolivia. In the twentieth century Chile had its share of political instability and inflation, its difficulties being accentuated by competition from artificial nitrates. The landed oligarchy lost its hold on power after the revolt of 1891 and thereafter Chile moved painfully towards a more democratic order. In 1938 elections gave power to a popular front which included communists and was not debarred from taking office by the armed forces. A period of orderly civilian government, conservative rather than radical, followed. In 1964 two progressive forces competed for the succession to President Jorge Alessandri – a popular front led by the socialist Salvador Allende and a Christian Democrat Party led by Eduardo Frei Montalva. The latter won and established a progressive, anti-communist government, overtly akin to the Christian Democrat parties of Europe but obstensibly more radical.

By the end of his term Frei had to his credit a considerable advance in education, a noticeable drop in illiteracy, some industrial development and new housing, and the introduction of graduated taxes. But inflation was not mastered, wages remained low, the number of landless peasants high – so high that they began to occupy lands, from which many were evicted by force and some killed. Conscious of the size of his economic problem Frei tried to avoid a direct clash with the oligarchy or the United States, but his gradualism offended on the one hand the more militant elements and on the other the more chauvinist. In 1970, in a three-cornered presidential election, Frei's designated successor, Radomiro Tomic, came bottom of the poll and amid general surprise Allende narrowly defeated the conservative Alessandri. Allende was the leader of a coalition which embraced socialists, communists and other groups on either side of these. During the campaign he played up his friendship with Castro. Although he did not win an absolute majority of the popular vote the Chilean parliament, to which the decision passed, followed the usual rule and installed him in office. Attempts to instigate an army coup to prevent him from taking over were without effect, although the commander-in-chief was assassinated by right-wing extremists for keeping the army out of politics.

Allende's government began by nationalizing copper, nitrates and other minerals and the principal banks and by extending the programme of agricultural reform initiated by Frei. These measures were all but universally popular. The expropriation of US copper companies evoked no Chilean protest and the prosecution of land reform was entrusted to the expert who had prepared Frei's scheme. But Allende ran into a variety of troubles, some of his own making. Against the advice of his more cautious communist allies he wanted to press on with nationalization as fast as possible and without pausing to consolidate his first measures. He alienated the large class of medium proprietors. He also refused publicly to disavow wilder groups who were using the language of the tumbril or to insist on the disbanding of private armies, thereby laying himself open to the charge of being either fearful of or indulgent to the revolutionary left. He further alienated opinion by a style of living which was out of keeping not only with socialism but also with a usage observed by Frei, Allesandri and other presidents who had followed the Chilean tradition of living as simply in office as out of it. Allende had too a piece of bad luck. If the world price of copper had kept up he might have weathered the storms that came upon him, but the price fell and inflation rising to 300 per cent a year turned criticism and apprehension to open resistance. In the coup which followed in 1973 Allende committed suicide and Chile was given over to the very untender mercy of a right-wing autocracy under General Augusto Pinochet Ugarte, helped to power by United States agencies. In 1980 Pinochet secured by referendum the extension of his rule for a further eight years after its expiry in 1981. But churchmen were uneasy about their association with an appalling régime; military and police chiefs were uneasy about keeping order against rising indignation and outrage; businessmen wondered whether they might not do better without Pinochet than with him. The threat to Pinochet came from these diverse groups who wanted Pinochet's Chile without Pinochet.

In 1988 Pinochet failed in a referendum to obtain a renewal of his rule beyond its term in the next year when therefore elections were held. Some twenty parties entered the lists. The centre and left united round Patricio Aylwin Azocar, himself a man of the centre-right, and defeated a splintered right. Aylwin, who assumed office early in 1990, inherited a foreign debt of $16 billion, a decline in the price of copper which accounted for half of Chile's foreign earnings, and discontent among a population which had seen the gap between rich and poor widen over Pinochet's sixteen years in power and wages halved.

One item which Aylwin did not inherit was Chile's ancient quarrel with Argentina at the southern tip of the American continent where the Beagle Channel leads from the Atlantic Ocean to the Pacific. The question between them was where the one ocean begins and the other ends. Their dispute concerned islands lying at the eastern, or Atlantic, end of the channel. In 1977 an arbitral award gave these islands to Chile but Argentina refused to accept the award and staged naval and air demonstrations, to which Chile responded in kind. In 1979 both sides agreed not to prosecute their claims by force and to accept the mediation of the Vatican. In 1980 Chile again sent armed forces to the disputed area. The quarrel was settled in 1984, substantially in Chile's favour.

The three major states of South America, while occupying almost the whole of the south and east of the sub-continent, left room for seven other successors of the Spanish empire (joined in 1966 by the new state of Guyana – see the note at the end of this Part). In the north-west, where Bolivar had hoped to create a single grand Colombia, three states resulted: Colombia and its two offshoots, Venezuela and Ecuador. Colombia and Venezuela possessed exceptional wealth in two very different forms, cocaine and oil. To the south Peru and Bolivia (formerly Upper Peru) also possessed considerable mineral wealth: Bolivia lost its coastal regions to Chile in the nineteenth century. Yet the region as a whole was as notable for strife – partly racial, partly class – and for economic disaster which neither its civilian élites nor its military castes were able to master. Southward again Paraguay and Uruguay provided the chief examples of personal autocracy and democracy.

During the fifties there was a clatter of falling dictators throughout South America beginning with the fall of Perón in 1955. The following three years saw the withdrawal of President Manuel Odria in Peru and the displacement of Presidents Gustavo Rojas Pinilla and Marcos Perez Jimenez of Colombia and Venezuela. The trend in these years was for the military to retire from sight. They could not abdicate real power since power inevitably was theirs. The exercise of that power in politics had become a habit partly because, with no conceivable military enemy in view, they had nothing else to do and partly because of the defects of the rich ruling classes. The officer who is not required to prepare for a war can either opt for society or for politics. Many opted for the best society and nothing more; others for society and also for a share in the political dominance of the upper classes (to whom fundamentally the armed forces were essential); others again, having opted for politics, became dissatisfied – and, although they might despise democracy, wished to make the conduct of public affairs more efficient and less corrupt and to make a modest start with social reform. This last group came to be dubbed *nasseristas* and it was their influence which, with as yet unpredictable results, was felt in the late fifties and sixties and spread the notion that both national politics and national armies should become more professional. But if the first impact was the destruction of old-style dictators and a diminution of the prestige of old-style officers, it did not follow that government by civilians was to be the new rule, for the civilians might either fall short, in efficiency or integrity, of what was desired of them, or exceed expectations and tolerance by going ahead too fast with social reforms. In either event the military would return. The personal autocracy of the caudillo, interested only in his own power and unencumbered with ideology of any kind, came to be represented south of the Panama Canal only by Alfredo Stroessner of Paraguay who survived until 1989 in a backwater, a secluded fiefdom of Brazil which got electric power from Paraguay and was concerned above all to see it quiet. Elsewhere newer varieties of military rule – or military–civilian coalitions – sought to combine conservative discipline and their class interests with social and economic programmes. But in no event would revolutionaries be persuaded that either the military or the dominant civilian castes would make adequate reforms. In all the countries of the northern arc of South America, from Venezuela to Peru, new governments were challenged by revolution.

The first of these challenges came in *Venezuela* where the dictatorship of Perez Jimenez was followed by a short interlude under the young and progressive Admiral Wolfgang Llarazabal, but many of the dictator's enemies deserted Llarazabal as soon as they had got rid of Perez Jimenez and elections in 1959 and 1963 gave large majorities to the cautious Accion Democrática of Presidents Romulo Betancourt (president also in 1945–48) and Raul Leoni. On the expiration of Leoni's term in 1968 a Christian Democrat, Rafael Caldera, won on a split vote and raised hopes of moderate reform along the lines pursued by President Frei in Chile, but the Accion Democrática remained the largest party in the Congress and a bulwark against measures unpalatable to the comfortable classes. Less easily satisfied elements, which had taken the lead in the overthrow of Perez Jimenez and had no use for the Accion Democrática, turned to revolution. After the Cuban revolution of 1959 they received encouragement and some help from Castro and a few years later scattered risings began. Risings begot repression and vice versa. After initial failures various groups – communists, non-communists and dissident army officers – formed a joint Liberation Army, but unity was precarious and the communists in particular disliked guerrilla methods. From 1965 these groups were openly divided. At the end of Caldera's term in 1973 the Accion Democrática returned to power with Carlos Andres Perez as president. In a fifth successive peaceful election in 1978 the Accion Democrática was beaten by the Social Christian Party, COPEI, led by Luis Herrera Campins, but recovered power in 1984 with Jaime Lusinchi and, once more, Perez. Venezuela was exceptional for its wealth (chiefly oil) as well as its political orderliness and the two may have been not unconnected, but from the mid-seventies increased revenues from increased oil prices tempted governments into bigger spending and bigger borrowing accompanied by corruption and strains on the balance of payments. In the eighties half of foreign earnings were being consumed by interest on foreign debts while oil revenues were halved in the years 1983–89. The possibility of a default in a country as wealthy and assumedly dependable as Venezuela alarmed United States and international institutions far more than similar threats from the likes of Peru: Venezuela had become to the outside world a model, from which such action was not expected. From 1959 a two-party civilian system had put in power by ballot five successive presidents, all of them men of ability who, although coming from different parties, were cast in a liberal bourgeois mould. The common explanation of their phenomenon was that Venezuela, being the richest country in the sub-continent, could afford democratic politics and make them work, but since stability and tolerance are not the common experience of all rich countries, further explanations have to be sought. Besides its natural resources Venezuela had a manageable population (12 million), a minimum of racial conflict, and the good fortune to possess and the good sense to elevate men with the brains and the moral standards needed to make the most of these advantages.

Before the Second World War *Colombia* enjoyed a reputation for political stability and measured economic progress. The latter was based on cocoa, a variety of manufacturing enterprises and a manageable foreign debt. The ruling class was divided into two political parties, conservative and liberal, and shared power on a roster system until menaced by left-wing insurgents and the dictatorship of Rojas Pinilla (1953–58). In the forties and fifties ferocious violence – the *violencia* – achieved the assassination of the progressive president Jorge Gaitán; and in 1949 the province of Marquetalia, not many kilometres south-west of Bogotá, declared itself independent and was recovered in the sixties only with the help of the United States. The Cuban revolution led to hopes of aid for the flagging revolutionaries, but these hopes were falsified and the Colombian insurgents fared only marginally better than their Venezuelan comrades. At elections in 1974 the liberal candidate, Julio Cesar Turbay Ayala, beat the conservative and an assortment of candidates of the left. He was narrowly re-elected in 1978. Four years later the conservative Belisario Betancur beat a divided opposition but was reduced by further elections in 1983 to governing with a hostile parliament. Facing the Caribbean and Central America as well as the Pacific and South America, Colombia was drawn into the politics of the area to its north and drifted into measured criticism of Reagan's policies in and around Nicaragua. By formal agreements with rebel forces Betancur put an end to civil wars which had been going on for thirty-six years but his pacific policies did not command universal approval and a spectacular attack on the Supreme Court, in which many were killed before the attackers were forced to surrender or kill themselves, was variously interpreted as a last act of desperation by the insurrectionary M-19 movement or the recrudescence of civil war on a fiercer scale.

A more serious threat appeared in a different quarter. The trade in cocaine became Colombia's most successful enterprise and its chiefs established themselves not only as men of enormous wealth ostentatiously displayed but also as a state within the state in the north-western parts of the country, including the cities of Medellín and Cali where they ruled with the help of Israeli, British and other mercenaries and provided more jobs and better pay than did the government in its own sphere of competence. The economic empire of these drug barons depended on their markets in the United States where, for a time, US agencies were less alive to the dangers of flooding the market with poisonous drugs than to the opportunities of taking part of the profits to finance US policies against Nicaragua: many blind eyes were turned until the murder in 1989 of Luis Carlos Galan, likely to be the next president of Colombia, concentrated attention on the slide, not into anarchy, but to the capture of the state by a sinister cartel whose single aim was money. President Virgilio Barco promised tough action and President Bush promised lavish help, but the former was reluctant to accept the latter's offer of military support which was distasteful to many Colombians. Some 12,000 persons were arrested but hardly anyone of much consequence. The United States pressed for the extradition of senior malefactors but the barons replied with a threat to kill judges, magistrates and children for every operator extradited. Since more than fifty judges had been murdered the threat was plausible. In 1987 the Supreme Court of Colombia invalidated an extradition treaty of 1979 with the United States. In elections in 1990 the main themes were appeals for better prices for cocoa and other exports and promises to do no deals with drug barons. The winner was the young Liberal candidate Cesar Gaviria whose protestations on the last issue seemed unlikely to survive the harsh test of practical choices.

Southward from Colombia the Andean republics of Ecuador, Peru and Bolivia displayed the troubled swings between civilian and military rule. *Peru* combined great riches with some of the worst rural poverty, urban slums (full of workless migrants from a waterless countryside neglected by absentee landowners), illiteracy and starvation in the continent. The dominant oligarchy paid no taxes, ignored the masses, obstructed government intervention in the country's economic and social affairs and allowed foreign capital to acquire the succulent heights of the economy. Peruvian politics were a contest between the upper classes and the army on the one hand and APRA, a party founded in the twenties with a semi-socialist programme, on the other. APRA had been outlawed after elections in 1931 which were conducted with bloodshed, but José Luis Bustamente of APRA ruled as president from 1946 to 1948. He was then ousted by General Manuel Odría and his party was once more outlawed; its leader, Víctor Raúl Haya della Torre, took refuge in the Colombian embassy where he remained for several years before departing into exile in Italy. General Odría held power for eight years and then allowed elections to be held in 1956, as a result of which the presidency passed to Manuel Prado, a conservative politician who had held office in the thirties. During his period in office peasant risings began to occur. The poor were driven by want either to move to Lima and the coast and stage riots there or to seize lands in the interior. Their risings were scattered and easily suppressed. Once again the leaders were disunited and the communists in two minds about whether to support guerrilla action – in this case partly because the most notable guerrilla chief, Hugo Blanco, was a Trotskyist and partly because they were themselves divided into pro-Russian and pro-Chinese factions, each more occupied in eyeing the other than in fighting the established order. In elections in 1962 no candidate secured enough votes to win.

There were three: Haya della Torre, Odría and Fernando Belaúnde Terry, by profession an architect. The army vetoed the accession of Haya della Torre or of Odría, declared the elections fraudulent for no adequate reason, and installed a committee of four to rule pending fresh elections in 1963. The re-run election was won by Belaúnde who, although no conservative, was a safe man from the army's point of view and had had occasion to observe the president's dependence on the army's will. He proceeded to enlist the army's support for his progressive measures, which were all the more measured in consequence. Fresh risings occurred in 1965. By 1968 Belaúnde had few friends. His government was tarnished by scandals rising out of the devaluation of the currency, flagging over promised agricultural reforms (which were opposed by the land-owning class) and squeezed between the *aprista* opposition pressing for more reform and the army which was beginning to find him a burden and despatched him out of the country by air. The new régime of General Juan Velasco Alvarado proceeded to expropriate United States sugar and oil interests and to promise votes for all, including illiterates. It thus proclaimed its hostility to foreign capital and a policy of social reform from above. It seemed prepared to affront the oligarchy in order to pre-empt a revolution by the dispossessed. For the United States there appeared to be a choice between taking sanctions against the expropriation of US corporations and accepting the notion of a military-reformist régime which might do some good in Peru and might turn to the USSR or China if the United States showed ill will.

The Peruvian course from 1968 was an experiment, under strongly centralized and military direction, to introduce economic planning and a measure of social reform within a capitalist framework (from which however foreign capital had been extruded) with the emphasis on technological and managerial innovation in the service of industry and exports. Velasco himself was a nationalist hostile to US penetration of Peru, a man of the mild right but born outside the dominant oligarchy. A number of his army and civilian colleagues and supporters were radicals as hostile to the oligarchy as to the United States. The régime had therefore an innate instability which afflicted it when its first achievements gave way to ideological division and were clouded by economic strains. In spite of initially broad agreement on a programme of nationalization (which included the International Petroleum Company) and land reform, Velasco quickly lost the support of the principal political groups which had helped him to power and felt compelled to seek instead a popular base outside the political establishment. His government moved therefore to the left. In doing so Velasco lost more than he gained, particularly because land reform, although far from insignificant, fell short of expectations and so prevented him from winning peasant and student suffrages. In 1973 both these groups were joining in riots against the government which stiffened their right-wing enemies within it. Conservatives, encouraged by the Pinochet coup in Chile in September, were further alarmed by the economic consequences of world recession which, in 1974, hit Peru at a time when the president fell seriously ill. The piling up of foreign debt in earlier years and a sharp deterioration in the balance of payments were countered by disagreeable measures which were blamed on left-wing incompetence. A bloodless conservative coup removed Velasco in 1975 and promoted his prime minister General Francisco Morales Bermudez to the presidency. But the military were tiring of grappling with the tasks of government and taking the blame for its failures. A return to civilian rule seemed expedient and after an election in 1980 Belaúnde returned to the presidential palace from which he had fled twelve years earlier. Not much had changed in the interval. Belaúnde failed to curb inflation or the insurgent Sendero Luminoso (a small army of about 5,000 recruited chiefly among the rural poor) and in 1985 APRA captured the presidency and Peru announced that it would limit debt-service charges to a fixed percentage of the national product – an innovation likely to be noted by debtor nations all over the world. The new president, Alan Garcia, set a centre-left course flavoured with anti-Washington gestures at home and in Central America. But the filthy war went on with multiple murders, torture and unaccountable 'disappearances' of people whom the army or police did not like. Economic distress went on too: inflation at 100 per cent a year, a large budget deficit, and the suspension by the World Bank and the Inter-American Bank of their lines of credit to the Peruvian government. Garcia was soon at odds with the army. He proposed to give it one instead of three places in his cabinet, to reform military administration and cut the army's share (40 per cent) of government spending, and to investigate the massacre of 300 persons in a Lima prison allegedly by the army. The armed forces and the political right, with covert United States support, undermined Garcia's government and then overthrew it.

Elections in 1990 turned into a contest between a well-known man of letters and an unknown businessman of Japanese descent. Mario Vargas Llosa, who had moved from communism to the far right, was expected to win but lost at the second round to Alberto Fujimoro whose tasks were to gain control of runaway inflation, rectify a huge budget deficit, reverse falling production, and end a ten-year civil war which had cost 20,000 lives. By reversing Garcia's refusal to honour foreign debts the new president secured enough new foreign money to pay the interest on them.

Bolivia's social configuration was rather different from its neighbours' because Victor Paz Estenssoro, after an unsuccessful attempt in 1943, had led in 1952 a successful revolt in which non-communists, communists, Trotskyists and junior officers, appalled by corruption and inefficiency, injustice and poverty, had participated. His régime nationalized Bolivia's extensive tin mines, broke up large estates, introduced universal suffrage and elementary social services, and attempted to diversify the economy in order to reduce the country's dependence on mining. The régime quickly ran into economic trouble by trying to do more than its resources permitted and was forced to adopt severe stabilization measures which cut down its programmes and so produced political trouble in the form of disputes between the different components within the new order. But it ran none of the risks which undid President Arbenz because land-locked Bolivia was not so close to the United States as Guatemala and its possessing classes were not American corporations.

President Paz, who was succeeded by Hernán Siles Zuazo in 1956, returned to office in 1960 but was exiled in 1964 after a coup by General Alfredo Ovando Candia. In 1967 the existence of guerrilla activities was admitted and made world famous by the arrest and trial of the French Marxist writer, Regis Debray (committed to prison for thirty years) and the death in Bolivia of Che Guevara. The government was weakened by splits and by conflict between Ovando and the titular president René Barrientos. In 1969, a few months after the death of Barrientos, Ovando took power, installed a purely military régime and embarked on policies partly borrowed from General Velasco's populist military régime in Peru. A year later an abortive right-wing coup assisted by the United States was followed by a coup from the left led by General Juan Torres, but in 1971 the pendulum swung again as Colonel Hugo Banzer displaced Torres. Banzer's rule was a stereotype of military repression, censorship and brutality but it observed constitutional forms to the extent of permitting an election in 1978 for the succession to Banzer. The army's candidate, Juan Pereda Asbun, was unexpectedly defeated by the veteran Siles, who then went on hunger strike when he was not allowed to take over. The Bolivian Congress annulled the election but a military rising brought about the premature retirement of Banzer and the installation of Pereda in his place. Pereda, however, lasted only five months and in a re-run election in 1979 Siles defeated Pereda, Banzer and a number of other candidates. Siles offered the army a series of concessions and guarantees but he was not allowed to take office. After a two-week interlude when Colonel Alberto Natusch Busch seemed to have gained control, Lidia Gueiler Tejida became the country's first female president. She was expelled in her turn in 1980 by a coalition of right-wing officers and prosperous drug traffickers who, with Generals Luis Garcia Meza Tejada and Celso Torrelio Villa as presidents, inaugurated a fresh régime of terror and torture. Fifteen years of military rule ended in 1982 with the return to power of Siles, half-heartedly applauded by the United States.

In *Ecuador*'s milder political climate the military seized power in 1976 but held it only briefly, making way in 1979 for a left coalition led by the 38-year-old Jaime Roldos Aquilera who was killed two years later in an air crash. A brush with Peru occurred in 1981 over disputed territory assigned to Peru by an agreement of 1942. A left-wing guerrilla movement made its appearance in the eighties.

Throughout the seventies the guerrilla activity characteristic of South America in the previous decade declined. The death of Che Guevara had been a blow to morale. The development of anti-guerrilla techniques under the surveillance of US officers enabled governments to defeat movements which had never been numerically strong and were only fleetingly united. Protest found different and less romantic forms. The guerrilla *foco* was replaced by urban kidnappers – the Uruguayan *tupamaros* and their like who in Argentina, Brazil and elsewhere, specialized in the capture of diplomats as hostages. One of the most notable exploits of the *tupamaros* was the capture of the British ambassador in Montevideo, but although they held him for eight months they gained nothing by doing so. Urban tactics were no improvement on the *focos*. In elections in *Uruguay* in 1971 the Frente Amplio or broad left ran third to the two traditional parties of Blancos and Colorados and after intricate and disputed calculations Colonel Juan Bordaberry of the latter party was installed president in 1972. Like his precursors he was confronted with the task of finding for Uruguay, once rich on its exports of wool, an economic future in a world which had invented rayon. He was, however, unseated by the military in a country which had for long vaunted its addiction to civilian rule. In 1980 the Uruguayans, with unexpected temerity, rejected the new constitution proffered to them by this régime in anticipation of a more obedient vote. In 1985 twelve years of military rule ended with the installation of a civilian president, Julio Sanguinetti, who was peacefully succeeded in 1989 by the Blanco candidate, Luis Lacalle.

Whereas in earlier decades the politics of South America oscillated between military dictatorship and government by competing political parties, the trend of the late seventies was to one-party rule, whether military or civilian or mixed. This was a search for stability, closely identified with the status quo, by forces opposed both to revolution and to liberal parliamentarism. Two things had failed. Violent revolution, rural or urban, had achieved no success outside Cuba. Equally thwarted were those who hoped for the advance of the bourgeois liberal or social democracy familiar to Europeans of the nineteenth and twentieth centuries. Developments of this kind, though espoused by a small cosmopolitan intellectual élite, had too few roots in the political soil of South America where the enduring tradition was that of pre-Napoleonic Spain. South America did not revolt against Spain. Napoleon's subjection of Spain had simply caused Spanish power in the New World to evaporate. The liberators were therefore successors rather than liberators and they assumed, for themselves and generations to come, the centralist powers and attitudes which the Spanish Crown had exported to Spanish presidencies and vice-royalties in South and Central America. This was an autocratic tradition, often liberally interpreted, but not a democratic one. The new men of the second half of the twentieth century, most but not all of them military, were with rare exceptions not concerned to alter the system. They were concerned to take for themselves the positions of power and direction which had hitherto been monopolized by a different ruling class.

Economically and culturally most of South America remained in the shadow of foreign domination. Industrialization was weak or delayed for many reasons: ruling élites opposed import tariffs and quotas which infant industries needed but rich consumers did not like; the several domestic markets were too small and attempts to combine them rudimentary; industries which arose tended to excess capacity, their products to high costs; technology was either local and behind the times or foreign and therefore strange and expensive. Transport and other public services were poor or non-existent except near big cities. Half the population was drawn into cities of 20,000 or more, over-crowded, dirty, violent and a prey to property speculators. The economic gap between town and country was widening. The land provided status, wealth and a way of life for the few; the towns failed for the most part to become engines of new economic activity. The need for land reform was manifest and a number of countries passed relevant laws, but little practical action followed except in the wake of revolutions. Workers on the land were ill paid, under-employed and growing in numbers in spite of the drift to the towns. Without credit or adequate communications or, in many areas, water, small proprietors would get neither seeds nor fertilizers nor machinery for what was economically productive land.

Mexico, like Canada, is a country which may be destined for ultimate embrace in a North American economic zone dominated by the United States. Between Mexico and the United States, however, there is an historic feud which is more easily forgotten in the latter than in the former. Mexico lost Texas to the United States in 1836. Ten years later US troops occupied Mexico City. Half of what was then Mexico became the south-western United States. In 1862 a French debt-collecting expedition (with British and Spanish encouragement) turned into an imperial adventure and created a shortlived Mexican empire with an Austrian archduke as emperor. This régime was followed after a short interval by the dictatorship of Porfirio Diaz which lasted from 1876 to 1910 with only one four-year interlude. His remorseless, modernizing rule ended in revolution and seven years of civil war in which the United States intervened on the side of counter-revolution, and a war between Mexico and the United States was only narrowly avoided. The long dictatorship of Diaz was eventually succeeded by the even longer rule of a single party called, after 1946, the Partido Revolucionario Institucional (PRI) and committed to social mobility and economic reform. But the years eroded the party's revolutionary zeal, it never grasped the nettles of taxing the rich and reforming a notoriously inefficient agriculture, and it became the political vehicle of the well-to-do. In 1938 President Lazaro Cardenas nationalized oil reserves and the oil industry. Presidents succeeded one another decorously and constitutionally and by the end of the Second World War Mexico was a stable country under civilian rule. Relations with the United States had proceeded to a dignified wariness.

Mexico declared war on Germany, Italy and Japan in 1942 and sent an air contingent to the Philippines. After the war it played a leading part in establishing an inter-American security system: by the Treaty of Chapultepec (which is in Mexico) the American states agreed to mutual consultation if the borders of any one of them were infringed and envisaged joint action up to and including the use of force; the Treaty of Rio in 1947 made more precise provision for the peaceful settlement of disputes and collective defence; and these agreements culminated in the creation in 1948 of the Organization of American States (OAS).

Foreign leaders paid attention to Mexico. All United States presidents from F. D. Roosevelt onwards visited it and so did all French presidents from de Gaulle onwards. In regional affairs Mexico ostracized Cuba in 1962 but reversed this attitude in 1975; it joined Venezuela and other American states in attempts to restore Cuba to inter-American respectability and to settle the war in Nicaragua; it condemned Pinochet's Chile and sympathized – sometimes sided – with left-wing movements in Central America; its professed aims included the reduction of United States and Russian influence south of the Rio Grande; it refused to accept a US military mission (1951) and openly criticized US actions and judgments in Guatemala, Cuba and Nicaragua; it was a sponsor of the Treaty of Tlatelolco in 1967 which essayed to ban nuclear weapons in the sub-continent; and, principally as a consequence of its oil wealth, it established links with other oil producers, notably Nigeria, while refusing characteristically to become a member of OPEC.

But Mexico's weight in the world or the region was difficult to assess. It had become an oil giant producing 2.5 million barrels a day by 1980 and possessing proved reserves of 60 billion barrels, perhaps three or four times as much; it was exporting more than half of its production (half of it to the United States) and expanding its economy by 8 per cent a year. On the other hand its population was growing faster than almost anywhere in the world, and with half the working population unemployed or underemployed the stability which it had enjoyed since about 1971 could no longer be taken for granted. Opposition voiced by hungry workers or indignant students was more savagely repressed the more open it became and the grisly defeat of the young who staged demonstrations during the Olympic Games in Mexico City in 1968 gave the world an inkling of hidden ills. Successive governments applied themselves to economic growth – if necessary with US capital, unpopular though this was – in order to please the rich and salve the poor and then in the seventies placed their desperate hopes in oil and borrowed lavishly, gambling on future expectations. The gamble failed. Debts exceeded expectations. When in 1982 Miguel de la Madrid Hurtado was elected president at the age of 47 this gifted politician and economist faced a collapsing peso, rising unemployment, clamps on public capital spending and oil-fed corruption. He was able to strike a bargain with the IMF which secured to Mexico a loan of $3.4 billion and the rescheduling of half of its external debt of $96 billion, but Mexico failed to meet the conditions attached to the agreement and the IMF was about to rescind it when in 1985 an earthquake of appalling force struck Mexico City and made any tightening of the screws temporarily inopportune. Even with half its debt rescheduled Mexico would need for the rest of the century about $6 billion to cover interest on, and piecemeal repayment of, the other half – sums which

27.1 Central America

would have to come, by agreement or default, from foreign creditor banks in so far as oil revenues failed to provide them. Relief, assessed at $3.6 billion a year for thirty years, was provided by an agreement reached with its creditors in 1990 under the so-called Brady Plan (see Chapter 5). President de la Madrid was succeeded in 1988 by Carlos Salinas de Gortari who had the misfortune to see the ruling party lose a provincial governorship for the first time in more than half a century.

As Mexico narrows southward almost all of its land border is shared with *Guatemala*. (British Honduras, independent as Belize from 1981, has a short border with Mexico as well as a longer, disputed border with Guatemala.) Of three republics of comparable size in Central America Guatemala lies to the north, Nicaragua to the south and Honduras marches with both. For over a hundred years (1838–1944)

Guatemala was ruled by four military dictators with short intervals of civil governments in between. In 1944 the army was divided and a group of junior officers supported a comparatively left-wing candidate, Juan José Arévalo, who was president until 1950. During this period the division in the army continued and was represented by the rivalry between two majors, Francisco Xavier Arana and Jacobo Arbenz Gúzman. The former was assassinated in 1949 and the latter won the election of 1950. This victory caused alarm in the United Sates where the new régime was regarded (disputably) as pro-communist or a forerunner of communism and therefore as presenting a threat to the Panama Canal; and also (correctly) as an enemy of foreign capitalists and especially of the United Fruit Company which, as the owner of a tenth of the country's land, exercised even more economic power in Guatemala than the Anglo-Iranian Oil Company in Iran, and stood in the way of essential land reform.

The Guatemalans, mostly of Indian stock, suffered from extremes of poverty, disease and social inattention, which were rendered the more intolerable to the thinking section of the people by the prosperity of a small minority and by the economic omnipresence of foreign enterprises which owned not only an abundance of land but also the railways, docks and public utilities. President Arbenz accelerated his predecessor's reform programme; he nationalized uncultivated land and supported strikes against foreign concerns. These moves were interpreted in Washington as the beginnings of a fully fledged communist policy, notwithstanding that communists were greatly outnumbered by anti-communists in the Guatemalan government, parliament and civil service and that power lay with an anti-communist army. At the tenth inter-American conference at Caracas in March 1954 Dulles tried to get a condemnation of the Arbenz régime but discovered that no other state accepted Washington's interpretation of events in Guatemala. The conference passed a general resolution condemning communist domination of any American state but refused to single out Guatemala for special mention, and Dulles thereupon left Caracas abruptly and turned to conspiring with disaffected Guatemalans who were preparing to invade their country from Honduras and Nicaragua. These two countries, having complained of communist incursions from Guatemala, were themselves provided with arms from the United States, while Washington tried to prevent Guatemala from getting arms by appealing to its allies not to supply them and by trying to intercept communist shipments from Europe. The invasion took place in June and was successful. The Guatemalan government appealed to the Security Council but was frustrated by a proposal to refer the matter to the OAS. This attempt to deflect the matter was vetoed by the USSR but a week later President Arbenz was forced to resign. The leader of the invasion, Colonel Carlos Castillo Armas, succeeded him and retained office until he was assassinated in 1957. The annual rate of growth of the Guatemalan economy fell from 8.5 per cent (over 1944–54) to 3 per cent and under Castillo's successors Guatemala lived in a state of suppressed civil war.

Castillo was succeeded by General Miguel Ydígoras Fuentes. In an election in 1957 Ydígoras came second, but after some disorder and a second election in 1958 he was duly installed. His power was confirmed by a fraudulent election in 1961 but riots, repressed by the army, demonstrated a dependence which he was not wise enough to acknowledge. Military opinion turned against him on the grounds that he spent too much money on himself and too little on the armed forces. In 1962 the army defended him against an attempted coup by the air force, but he then fatally antagonized the army by allowing ex-president Juan Arévalo to return to Guatemala and campaign for the presidency. Arévalo, who seemed certain to win a fair election, was regarded as a reincarnation of Arbenz, and in 1963 the army under Colonel Enrique Peralta ejected Ydígoras and suspended the constitution. In 1965 the army tolerated the election of a comparatively liberal president, Julio Cesar Mendez Montenegro, but he was no more able than his more oppressive predecessors to pacify the country. A motley and frequently divided opposition, consisting of communists, Trotskyists and guerrillas who were neither, staged unsuccessful risings and resorted to murder and kidnapping when their risings failed. US forces helped the government. A US ambassador was among those assassinated.

In the seventies nominal control was shared between the army and civilian parties with left-wing parties proscribed. A number of officers went into business and became rich, thus earning the jealousy of other officers and attracting charges of corruption. Guerrillas who had been operating since the sixties were not suppressed. Elections in 1974 were contested by three candidates, of whom the youngest – Colonel Efraim Rios Montt, a passionate Protestant – won but was shouldered out of the way by his elders. The military were divided between hardliners who saw only guerrillas and on the other hand a more enlightened minority who saw also widespread poverty and injustice and, at the centre, corruption. Faction was added to violence, corruption and economic collapse. Abuses of power became so gross that in 1977 Carter stopped US aid (it was resumed in 1981 by Reagan who had other priorities and values). Elections in 1978 gave the presidency to Romeo Lucas Garcia, a right-wing general of peculiar brutality who eradicated villages but not guerrillas. He was ousted in 1982 by Rios Montt who promised to end private murder, civil war and financial scandals but was himself ousted in the next year with these promises unfulfilled. He was followed by General Oscar Mejis Victores who devoted himself to the suppression of the left in his own country but showed less interest in conflicts beyond his borders, for which indeed Guatemala had limited resources to spare. A nominal reversion to civilian rule in 1985 left the army unfettered, President Vinicio Cerezo being little more than a figurehead who might be saddled with the blame for economic chaos and be charged with attempts to get foreign aid. Internally Cerezo's ability to stop the rot was constrained by his inability to improve miserable standards of living. The guerrillas, who had dwindled to about 2,000 against an army of 40,000, continued to deny the government control of many rural areas. In international affairs Cerezo edged away from Washington's stark anti-Sandinista policy in Nicaragua and collaborated with other Central American presidents in seeking peace with the Nicaraguan régime, reconciling President Duarte of Salvador with President Ortega of Nicaragua and ending the Contras' use of Costa Rica as part of a pincer attack on Nicaragua. In the elections of 1990 a dozen presidential candidates took the field, ranging from centre-right to extreme right. Rios Montt, declared constitutionally ineligible by the Supreme Court, backed Jorge Elias Serrano who came second in the first round and was elected on the second. The voters, fewer than half the electorate, hoped that he would prove to be the man to end civil war, rampant crime and corruption.

On the Pacific coast of Central America south of Guatemala the small and once wealthy state of *El Salvador* was wrecked by civil strife. A standard military dictatorship under General José Maria Lemus was modified in 1961 by the installation of a middle-of-the-road government under General Julio Rivera which adopted a programme of social reform and economic investment which, if inadequate in the eyes of the left, nevertheless made a substantial step away from the narrow conservatism of past rulers. But the modest hopes raised by this change proved illusory and during the seventies extreme violence erupted between the government and left-wing guerrillas of the Farabondo Marti Liberation Front (FMLF), the militant arm of a broad political left. The inauguration in 1977 of President Carlos Humberto Rovero was boycotted by the clergy in protest against the violence and torture practised by the régime itself and in 1979 a coup by junior officers installed a new government pledged to moderate agrarian reform and the nationalization of selected financial and commercial concerns. But this mildly right-wing government failed to control extreme right-wing terrorism. The murder in 1980 of the archbishop of San Salvador typified growing anarchy and a polarization to extremes which left the government stranded in the middle. The United States, fearing that the extreme left might prevail, supported the government as a lesser evil and tried to persuade Guatemala and Honduras to agree to intervene should the government collapse and the extreme left take power but neither country was keen to denude its domestic position by sending troops abroad.

With the election of Reagan in 1980 El Salvador became a piece in a positive, even obsessive, US policy of overthrowing the government of Nicaragua in particular and helping any Central American government of the right. The FMLF was stigmatized as a terrorist organization and Reagan certified, in the face of ample evidence to the contrary, that the Salvadorean government's record in human rights was satisfactory and that its army was under government control – an equally implausible statement. But in spite of increased American aid President Napoleon Duarte was unable to suppress the Front. He was also unable to break free from the extreme right which in elections in 1982 won more seats than the president's party of the less ferocious right. Robert d'Aubuisson was elected president but was persuaded under pressure from Washington to give way to the more respectable and neutral Alvaro Mangana. Another election two years later was similarly indecisive as between Duarte and d'Aubuisson. Mounting guerrilla successes during 1984 were countered by more American aid in money, helicopters and miscellaneous weaponry. If, as seemed to be the case, Duarte genuinely wished to treat with the insurgents and introduce some reforms he was thwarted by continuing civil war of a peculiarly nasty kind in which the greater proportion of the killings were the work of right-wing squads belonging to the army or more loosely connected with it. In 1985 Duarte prevailed over the extreme right and so won room to manoeuvre for peace with the left, provided the terms were acceptable to the holders of ultimate power, the army. But he remained uncomfortably wedged between two extremes, hardly an independent force, his authority more nominal than real, a spent force (in health as well as politically) and the ineffectual arbiter of a war which had cost his small country 70,000 lives. The guerrillas, in spite of maintaining a threat, failed to incite a broad popular revolt and were reduced to a few thousand against an army boosted to 50,000 with US aid amounting to $1 million a day. The military and political wings of the left were divided on whether to negotiate with Duarte; on the right the military and their paramilitary accessories or death squads were out of control and perpetrated indiscriminate massacres. Attempts from 1986 to arrange a cease-fire came to nothing. Elections in 1989 were won by d'Aubuisson's Arena Party which installed Alfredo Cristiani as president. The death squads were no more responsive to Cristiani than they had been to Duarte. US aid was increased but failed to ensure either of its professed aims – stability or democracy.

Internationally much the gravest commotion in Central America occurred in *Nicaragua* following the collapse in 1979 of the dictatorship of the Somoza dynasty which had lasted for nearly fifty years. The

Somoza dynasty stemmed from General Anastasio Somoza Garcia who seized power with the help of the United States in 1930. He and his son Luis, who succeeded him in 1956, ruled in alliance with the prosperous landowning and business classes but after the latter's death in 1967 his brother, Anastasio Somoza Debayle, alienated and even scandalized these allies by the brutality and corruption of his rule, notably his appropriation of large sums out of foreign aid sent to Nicaragua after a serious earthquake in 1972. Armed resistance had begun in 1961 by guerrillas calling themselves the Sandinista Front after Colonel Augusto Cesar Sandino, assassinated in 1934 afer leading a rising which was suppressed with the help of troops from the United States. The Sandinistas remained for many years few in number since they failed to win widespread support among the peasantry or the urban working class, but Anastasio II's misrule earned them more sympathy among the professional classes and the Roman Catholic clergy and the murder in 1978 of the editor of Managua's principal newspaper *La Prensa* was the signal for serious attempts to put an end to one of Latin America's most outrageous dictatorships.

President Peres of Venezuela took the lead and tried to persuade President Carter to intervene. Carter was torn between, on the one hand, his revulsion against the tortures and other abuses prevailing in Nicaragua and his fears that Somoza's excesses would lead to the opposite extreme and a second Cuba in Central America; and, on the other hand, his reluctance to intervene in the internal affairs of a neighbouring sovereign state, particularly to intervene with force. While these issues were being debated and various forms of economic pressure discussed, the chance to replace Somoza by a moderate and democratic régime slipped by. Washington's indecision hardened the determination of the Sandinistas and their allies, domestic and external (Cuba supplied arms through Costa Rica), and in 1979 Somoza was forced to flee.

The victorious alliance began immediately to fall apart. Promises to hold quick elections and install a multiparty system were shelved. The Sandinistas' clerical and professional allies dribbled away. President Reagan began a covert war which eventually put about 12,000 men – the Contras – into the field against the new government. These Contras, dubbed by Reagan Freedom Fighters, consisted of old and newer opponents of the Sandinistas reinforced by mercenary bandits of no fixed political views except that they were anything but democrats. Their main bases were in Honduras where the United States built a large air base and increased its aid to the Honduran government tenfold. These exertions failed, however, to overthrow the Nicaraguan government; provided it with excuses to maintain and tighten its authoritarian régime and further postpone the promised elections; alienated anti-Sandinista elements which reprobated Reagan's support for the Somozistas in Honduras and Florida; and gradually converted Nicaragua's neighbours from auxiliaries in Reagan's war to active proponents of a peace which would include the recognition of the Sandinista government.

The attack on Nicaragua, although mainly directed from Honduras in the north, had also a pincer arm in Costa Rica in the south. The former's enthusiasm for aiding the US cause waned towards the end of the eighties, more particularly after the election in 1989 of Raffaello Leonardo Callejas who wanted to get out of the war. On the Costa Rican front the principal figure was Eden Pastora, a social democrat who had joined forces with the Sandinista Front in the early seventies, quickly changed his mind and broke with it, was then persuaded to rejoin it in 1976, became its commander-in-chief under the sobriquet of Comandante Zero two years later, again defected soon after the victory of 1979 to become leader of the anti-Sandinista forces in Costa Rica, and finally in 1988 abandoned his opposition to the Sandinista government out of disgust with Reagan's tactics. His shifts and changes symbolized the confusion and perplexities among anti-Somozistas who were half disenchanted with the Sandinistas but no less disheartened by United States policies. The governments of other Central American countries oscillated in the same way. Anything but left-wing, they nevertheless came round to preferring the Sandinistas to Reagan's war.

Washington's rooted dislike of any left-wing government in Central America was sharpened in the case of Nicaragua by the fact that, however exaggerated Washington's propaganda about their links with Cuba and the USSR, the Sandinistas both needed and got arms from Cuba. This Cold War aspect of the upheavals following the fall of Somoza became a ruling, and to some considerable extent a blinding, element in the United States after the advent of Reagan. The Reagan administration took office resolved to give high priority to Central America as a critical zone in the global conflict of the superpowers. Its endemic troubles, economic and political, had been exacerbated during the preceding decade. Its economic growth, which had been nurtured on an expanding middle class, was brought to a halt by the general world recession with the result that this class became divided in its political allegiances and the poorer classes became poorer: the middle class was drawn on the one hand to the old oligarchies which represented, even when they could no longer command, the settled order dear to middle-class enterprise and money-making but, on the other hand, this class was alienated from the oligarchs by their selfish brutality and by the suspicion that their days were numbered. The poor had been emboldened by glimpses of a juster order and hardened by the renewed hardships of the late seventies. The consequent upheavals were, however, regarded in Washington as something more sinister and any inclination by liberal America to welcome Central America's belated revolutions was overlaid by the conviction that they were more than half provoked and extensively supplied by communist Cuba and the USSR. Nicaragua was seen as a Soviet satellite in the making, all the more dangerous than Cuba for being on the mainland. Reagan was therefore easily persuaded that he must ensure the defeat of the guerrillas in El Salvador, stifle any other leftish movement which might arise in the area and above all overthrow Nicaragua's Sandinista régime. The means were military, covert and open, and they failed. Besides organizing, training and paying for anti-Sandinista forces in Honduras and Costa Rica, the United States navy staged demonstrations off the Nicaraguan coasts in 1983 and in the next year mined Nicaraguan ports on the Atlantic and Pacific oceans; this mining in contravention of international law was censured by the Security Council (but the United States vetoed the resolution) and condemned by the International Court of Justice. Further hostile action was impeded by the US Congress which refused funds requested by the president for the Contras – a refusal circumvented by a number of subterfuges such as selling arms to Iran and diverting the proceeds or part of them to the Contras with, it can hardly be doubted, the connivance of the president.

In 1983 four states – Mexico, Venezuela, Colombia, Panama – formed the Contadora Group, an outer ring of states concerned about the manifold disorders in Central America. Their purpose was to bring about a general pacification in Central America on the basis of recognition of all governments actually in place, self-determination and the reduction of armaments, but the group was distrusted in Washington on account of its even-handedness which would recognize and probably validate the position of the Sandinistas in Nicaragua. Under pressure from Washington, Honduras, Guatemala and El Salvador refused to attend a conference which the group proposed to convene in 1985. But the group persevered and produced in 1986 a detailed programme (the Carabellada Declaration) for talks between Central American governments. This programme was irremediably opposed to Reagan's insistence that peace must be achieved through talks between the Sandinistas and the Contras and that the former must first introduce political reforms within Nicaragua. To all appearances Reagan put the removal of the Sandinistas above peace, while the Contadora Group envisaged a pacification which might leave the Sandinistas in power. Washington described the Contadora proposals as a threat to the region and to the United States.

But Reagan recoiled from the open military intervention which alone could achieve what he wanted and his support for the Contras was hampered by the revelation, on the eve of mid-term elections in 1986, of the Iran arms deals. The United States was able to keep the Contras in the field in Honduras but in spite of a strength of 15–20,000 and of lavish modern equipment they took no sizeable town in Nicaragua.

Honduras, which harboured them and was well paid for doing so, received no support from any other Central American government, while on the southern front Costa Rica abandoned the war. The misgivings of the outer ring had reached the inner ring.

Costa Rica had been a commitedly pacific state which, after a century and more of peculiar turbulence, had gone to the lengths of abolishing its army in order to have more to spend on public services and utilities. But it remained poor and dependent on the United States and after the Sandinista victory in 1979 it responded to Washington's appeal to play a part in containing and eradicating communists in Central America. This attitude was, however, reversed when in 1986 Alberto Monge was succeeded by Oscar Arias who produced a plan (for which he was later awarded the Nobel Prize for Peace) which was subscribed by five Central American presidents including Nicaragua's. It proposed that presidential, national and local elections should be held in Nicaragua in February 1990, preceded by the removal of press censorship and of obstacles to multiparty political activity. This scheme was viewed askance in Washington and with premature optimism elsewhere. Nicaragua took quick action by releases from jail, by allowing *La Prensa* to reappear and by annulling its state of emergency and its ban on political parties – but it was criticized for not doing more. Other signatories squabbled over whether they too had done what was required of them in their countries. Nevertheless the Arias plan was a portent, if only because it pointed in a direction which doomed Reagan's policies and forced his successor George Bush to review and ultimately slide away from them. In 1989 the five presidents pressed their initiative by demanding the disbandment of the Contras and their reintegration into Nicaraguan society.

In 1990 Nicaraguans were allowed their first elections since 1984. Then they had given the victory to the Sandinistas, but this time they did not. Although the Sandinistas remained the largest single party they were beaten by a coalition led by Mrs Violeta Chamorro, widow of the murdered editor of *La Prensa*. Although the US attack by means of the Contras had been an expensive failure, US sanctions had wrecked the Nicaraguan economy and Nicaraguans wanted a new government which would end the sanctions and ensure them a decent standard of living. Moreover, the Sandinistas' good record in such matters as health and education was offset by economic incompetence, corruption and in a broader sense by the mournful consequences of taking on the United States in a war which had cost tens of thousands of lives. Although over half the land and over a third of the principal industries remained in private hands government had nationalized the banks and taken control of wages, prices and imports with disastrous results. Foreign aid, most of it from the USSR and East Germany, was considerable but wasted. Real wages fell during the eighties by nine-tenths of their value, industrial output declined by a fifth each year and domestic product per head sank to $300 a year, the lowest in the region. Mrs Chamorro formed a government in which place was found for some Sandinistas but none for any of the Contra leaders. Her election coinciding with Reagan's departure from the White House allowed the war to come to an end. Throughout Central America the Gorbachev revolution in the USSR – Gorbachev's policies of retrenchment and the ending of the overriding confrontation of the superpowers – was inducing the United States to take a more relaxed view of the left in Central America and to look less indulgently on the excesses of its right-wing associates. And communism began to seem a lesser menace than cocaine.

In *Panama* President Arnulfo Arias Madrid set a record of three depositions from office (1941, 1951, 1968). His successor on the third occasion was Colonel Omar Torrijos Herrera, a popular mestizo who had army support and engineered a boom by encouraging foreign banks to do business in Panama and foreign commerce to make the fullest use of its free port. He negotiated the treaties of 1977 by which the United States agreed to hand over the Panama Canal in 1999 on condition that it be permanently neutral and that the United Sates have permanently the right to defend it. US troops would be withdrawn in the year 2000. The canal was becoming less strategically important to the United States but remained economically vital to Panama whose economy rested on the rent paid by the United States, the commerce of the free-trade zone, the traffic in flags of convenience, and offshore banking in the Canal Zone. In 1981, after he had relinquished office but was still commander-in-chief, Torrijos was killed in an air crash. From 1982, following a military coup, a sequence of lustreless generals ruled and power accumulated in the hands of General Manuel Noriega Morena, second in command of the army. Noriega was a likely president, but in 1984 Arias was re-elected against the wishes of the army. Funded by the CIA in spite of his known role in the drug trade, hailed in the United States as a democrat, Noriega remained in the background organizing the torture and murder of his opponents, enjoying an income said to be $100 million a year from making Panama the chief channel for the traffic in drugs between Colombia and the United States, and rising to be chief of the army. He was dropped by the United States when scandals became too open and he was publicly accused of drug trafficking, electoral frauds and murder. In 1988 Washington urged President Eric Delvalle to dismiss Noriega from his army post, whereupon Noriega dismissed Delvalle from the presidency. In the next year he cancelled the election which had all but certainly elected Enrico Endara to that office. He was indicted on drug charges in the United States and Washington tried also to bribe him to leave Panama and live in Spain, but he refused to go. All else having failed Bush resolved to invade Panama and seize Noriega, which he succeeded in doing in an operation which – depending on the point of view – was either hilarious or humiliating. Noriega was taken to jail in the United States.

The island of Cuba, the largest of the Antilles, thrusts its western end into the jaws of the Gulf of Mexico almost midway between the peninsulas of Florida and Yucatan, from which it is separated by channels about 160 km wide. Cuba is therefore of all the West Indian islands also the nearest to the mainland of north and central America. Its affairs were a special concern of the United States from the middle of the nineteenth century onwards. Its liberation from Spain at the end of the century proved (like the liberation of Arab lands from Turkish rule after the First World War) to be no more than a change of masters, and it entered upon a period of colonial rule without the benefits of a colonial administration. Far ahead of its Caribbean neighbours in educational standards and facilities, and as well-endowed with a middle class as the most advanced Latin American country, it endured nevertheless a record of bad government uninterrupted from its liberation up to and including the Castro régime. The abrogation in 1933 of the Platt Amendment coincided with the end of the corrupt and odious rule of Gerardo Machado, which had rested to some extent on US support. Machado had just transferred the presidency to Manuel de Cespedes but a revolt by non-commissioned officers (including Sergeant Fulgencio Batista) and students overturned the régime and inaugurated a period of twenty years during which a number of presidents held office. Batista, who ruled from 1940 to 1944, refrained at first from infringing a constitution which prescribed four-year terms with a ban on immediate re-election, but in 1952 he made himself permanent dictator and introduced a reign of terror. On 26 July of the next year, a date which gave its name to a movement, Fidel Castro led an attack on the Moncada barracks in an unsuccessful attempt to supplant Batista. After eighteen months in prison Castro emerged to prepare in Mexico a second attempt, and in December 1956 he led an invasion band of eighty-four which was swiftly defeated. The survivors, who numbered only twelve, escaped to the Sierra Maestra, where they turned from the tactics of a *coup de main* to guerrilla warfare which they waged for two years. In March 1958 Batista attacked the growing forces of rebellion, but his campaign was a failure and served

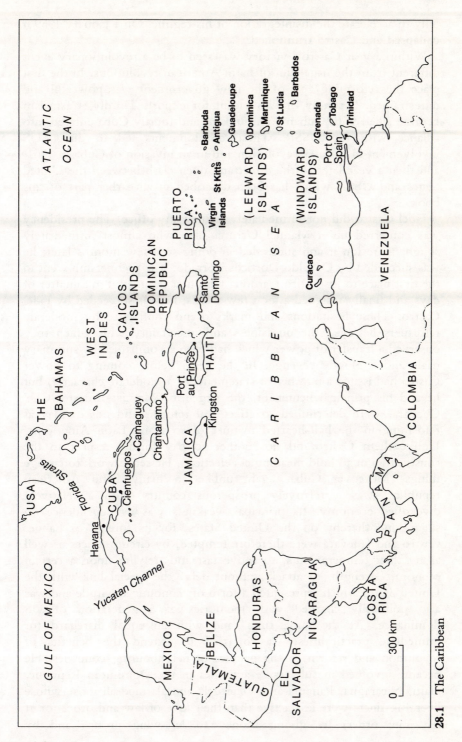

28.1 The Caribbean

only to accelerate the disintegration of his régime. On 1 January 1959 it collapsed and Castro triumphed.

Within a year Castro's victory was seen to be a revolutionary event different from the usual run of Latin American revolutions. In the first place the reforming zeal of the new government was powerful and unrestrained. Secondly, it was meant for export. Thirdly, Castroism became allied with Cuban communism, and fourthly Cuba entered into alliance with the USSR. These developments led to direct US involvement in counter-revolution and in an invasion of Cuba in 1961, and then a year later to the direct and open clash between the United States and USSR which has been described in an earlier part of this book.

Fidel Castro did not immediately assume any office. The presidency was conferred upon Manuel Urrutia Lleo who almost immediately sought to resign it and succeeded in doing so a few months later; he was succeeded by Osvaldo Dorticós Torrado. The premiership went in the first place to José Miró Cardona who first resigned it in a matter of days and finally resigned after a few weeks; he was succeeded by Fidel Castro. These hesitations and marks of no confidence by moderate reformers betrayed the uneasiness and uncertainty with which they observed a transfer of power which had been accompanied by summary trials and a bloody revenge. In the years before coming to power Castro had issued a number of statements of a moderate character, but he and his principal lieutenant, the Argentine Marxist Ernesto 'Che' Guevara, were determined to effect real reforms and not to play at reforming in the half-hearted manner of so many Latin Americans. Unlike them Castro did not bother to pay formal respect to the constitution or to hold meaningless elections. He set to work to change things. Moreover Cuba, again unlike so many Latin American republics, was a relatively prosperous country with a relatively diversified economy. Its principal weakness was its dependence on sugar, and thereby on the United States, for its foreign exchange. Castro and Guevara were therefore tempted, by circumstances as well as by thier temperaments, to move fast and, relying upon a certain economic strength, to attack without delay the special link with the United States which represented a form of economic servitude and was also politically charged with memories of a generation of US dominance. At the same time, and with an equal disregard for immediate practicalities, Castro tried to extend the benefits of revolution and reform to the peoples of neighbouring countries. He became involved in subversive activities in the Dominican Republic, Haiti, Nicaragua, Panama and Venezuela and alarmed all those whose liberal instincts were less active than their love of law and order (or at any rate order) by giving money to left-wing groups and by broadcasting to Latin America a Castroist message as disturbing as the voice of Nasser in the Middle East.

Castro's economic policy called for foreign aid and credits and for foreign customers to replace the United States. He made the obvious move. In February 1960 Mikoyan visited Havana and concluded a trade agreement with Cuba which, among other things, enabled Cuba to buy Russian oil. Later in the same year Guevara made a tour of eastern European countries. In May Cuba established diplomatic relations with Moscow and in June it began buying arms from the USSR and other communist governments. At the same time Castro attacked the US rights in the Guantanamo naval base and its economic influence through the sugar trade. In June US and British refineries refused to refine Russian oil, thereby giving Castro an excuse to take them over. The Eisenhower administration in Washington, which had been watching events with restraint, hoped to bring joint American pressure to bear but at San José in August an inter-American conference of foreign ministers, while condemning Russian and Chinese intervention in Latin America, refused to refer to Cuba by name. Washington decided to act on its own. It stopped further purchases of Cuban sugar and, after Castro had retaliated by nationalizing US property, imposed a complete commercial boycott and in January 1961 severed diplomatic relations.

From early in 1960 the United States had been helping and encouraging Cuban refugees in two places, both under the aegis of the Central Intelligence Agency. In Florida exiled politicians were formed into a political committee which hoped to become a government of Cuba; it included men of very different views who were only held together by their common opposition to Castro and by their US managers. In Guatemala a force was being trained against the day when it would return to Cuba in small bands and start guerrilla warfare; at first there was no thought of US military participation in the adventure, but as time went on the original tactics were transformed from piecemeal infiltration to a single invasion thrust with US air cover, and the exiles were further allowed to assume that the United States would back their ground operations with force rather than let them fail. When Kennedy was apprised of these activities immediately after his successful campaign for the presidency, he was troubled by them, but between that date in November 1960 and the launching of the attack on the night of 14/15 April 1961, he never translated his doubts into prohibition. The operation was already in train; the chiefs of staff, his most awe-inspiring advisers, were in favour of it; he did not want to let down several hundred Cubans, with whom he sympathized, nor did he know what to do with them if they were to be disbanded; the expectation that Castro would soon have Russian jet aircraft would make it very difficult, if not impossible, to sponsor such an invasion at a later date. Kennedy reaffirmed the ban on the involvement of United

States forces but overrode the opposition of Senator William Fulbright and a few other civilian advisers who advocated the containment of Cuba in preference to direct action which would be contrary to the charter of the OAS and all too consonant with Washington's reputation for imperialism and hypocrisy in its dealings with its southern neighbours.

The invasion was a complete failure. A force of 1,400 men – nine-tenths of them semi-trained civilians – supported by B–26 bombers operating from Nicaragua with Cuban pilots landed in the Bay of Pigs only to discover that, contrary to the assurances of the CIA, the US administration was not prepared to back them up and that expected risings in Cuba itself were not materializing. The Cuban government's riposte was more effective than had been anticipated and after forty-eight hours all was over. For good measure Castro imprisoned several thousands of his fellow citizens, thus seizing the opportunity to silence, demoralize and in some cases extinguish his opponents. His prestige beyond Cuba was greatly increased.

Nevertheless his position was in other respects unhappy. The economic measures taken by his government had, by its own admission, been ill conceived. A modish passion for industrialization led to the construction of factories for the manufacture in Cuba of articles which could be imported from abroad at less cost than the cost of the raw materials for their manufacture. In the countryside peasants displayed the worldwide dislike of their kind for co-operatives, the nationalization of land, and the enforced cultivation of crops destined for sale at fixed low prices. The middle class, which had been a more active ingredient in the revolution than the peasantry or the urban working class, became antagonized when nationalization was extended from foreign to domestic enterprises, and when the new régime took to the bad old ways of its predecessors in putting political opponents away in noisome jails. By 1962 there was an economic crisis, a general refusal to work by the peasants, food rationing and widespread disillusion, discontent and poverty.

At the end of 1961 Castro declared himself a Marxist. The Cuban Communist Party was a distinct entity which had at the outset little or nothing to do with Castro's 'July 26' movement. It was not a party with mass support and in the Batista period it had preferred back-stage political manoeuvres which secured it a humble position on the periphery of the ruling constellation. Before the Castroist victory in 1959 there were in both the Castroist and the communist camps some who encouraged a *rapprochement* or even a fusion and others who opposed any such move. During 1961 the former groups prevailed and the parties effected a considerable degree of integration. Cuba became in consequence a part of the communist world in terms of international politics, but Castro did not become either an orthodox communist (he seemed to care little about communist teaching) or a captive of a communist machine. As independent in his way – and within the limits imposed by Cuba's need for foreign friends – as Mao or Tito, he also remained domestically the leader of a government and a movement which were only partly communist. Leaders of the Cuban Communist party were promoted to office and influence but in March 1962 the most eminent of them, Anibal Escalante, was dismissed and fled to Czechoslovakia shortly before Castro set out for an extended visit to the USSR. The two parties had fallen out, the Castroists prevailed and Moscow backed the winners.

Moscow's support for Castro had become an economic burden with exciting political and strategic possibilities. Keeping Castro afloat economically was probably costing the USSR more than it had bargained for in financial terms; keeping Castro afloat politically in the face of the US determination to destroy him could be an even more costly and risky policy, but it was also an exceptionally tempting once since an effective alliance between the USSR and Cuba would give the Russians a foothold in Latin America with all its unpredictable revolutionary possibilities, and a base within 160 km of the United States to offset the bases with which the USSR was ringed by its antagonists. According to Cuban – and Chinese – sources the idea of sending to Cuba the missiles and jet aircraft which were first observed by United States reconnaissance in October 1962 was Khrushchev's. However that may be Cuba, which Castro had made an economic and political ward of the USSR, was converted by Khrushchev into an armed pawn. Whereas Castro had wanted to equip Cuba to defend itself against a second attack like the one in the Bay of Pigs, Khrushchev despatched weapons of an altogether different significance. The upshot has already been described and discussed. In the narrower Latin American context the results were that the OAS (which had expelled Cuba from its ranks at the beginning of the year) approved the deployment of force by the United States against the approaching Russian ships; that a number of Latin American states contributed to the blockade of Cuba instituted by the United States; that Cuba was left out of the reckoning as Kennedy and Khrushchev moved to resolve the crisis; but that Castro was given an outstandingly splendid reception when he revisited Moscow in April 1963 and won assurances of continuing Russian favour and support.

The crisis of 1962 involved for Castro a threat of extinction inasmuch as the rebuff to the USSR might carry with it an implicit freedom for the United States to work its will in Cuba and remove a government which had connived at, or even possibly instigated, an attempt to alter the balance of power in the American hemisphere more radically than at any time since the eighteenth century. But time seemed to show that

Kennedy's triumph over Khrushchev was not to be so interpreted. Castro himself felt secure enough against renewed intervention by the United States to engage, towards the end of 1963, in a plot against the government of Venezuela (for which the OAS in July 1964 declared him an aggressor and recommended the severance of diplomatic and commercial connections, a step which only Mexico then refused to take); and Castroism was also one of the ingredients in a rising in Andean Peru in 1965 in which desperate underdogs tried, with the help of Castroist and communist supplies and moral support over the radio, to force their plight upon the attention of their government. But the ostracism of Castro in 1964 was a reminder that he was still there to be ostracized, and if he was still there part of the reason was that his state was under the protection of a major power.

The Russians had been physically beaten out of the Caribbean but they retained a protective or intrusive capacity of another order. The assertion of the Monroe Doctrine had revealed its limitations. There were to be no foreign bases in the American continent but the American hemisphere's politics could no longer be sealed off from wider international politics. The United States had been harping for some time on the dangers of international communism in Latin America, but this ideological approach had missed the main point which was the opening of Latin America to the processes of non-ideological international politics, in much the same way as the Middle East and the rest of Asia and then Africa had become international magnetic fields as soon as both the major world powers decided to exercise there the powers which nobody could prevent them from exercising. In the first postwar decades it had been assumed that two areas in the world were immune from this interplay: Latin America in the penumbra of the United States, and Moscow's satellite empire in Europe in the irresistible tow of the USSR. The Cuban crisis showed that this assumption was at least an exaggeration. In the case of Latin America Khrushchev, with Castro as his eye-opener, scented that the time had come to question the unquestionable. This capacity was one of his strengths as a politician. Characteristically, however, he followed his instinct with more enthusiasm than caution and so exposed himself to a stinging tactical defeat. Characteristically too Washington, with the restraint which democracy imposes on action and even sometimes on thinking, had not come within sight of any comparable policy in Europe, thus avoiding any comparable defeat. But the principal implication of the Cuban crisis was the demolition of the theory that major powers have back gardens round which it suffices to put up notices against trespassers. Although interference in such areas remains preternaturally hazardous, the areas themselves are not enclosures where special conditions are bred, but areas where the various winds of international politics blow in different force. This revelation marked a stage in Latin America's international history as well as in the appreciation of great power politics.

For Cuba itself the experience was bitter. During the period of United States dominance up to 1933 Cuba had been a quasi-colonial territory which was permitted to contract no foreign alliances and harbour no foreign bases. Castro reversed this situation to the extreme extent of making an alliance with the USSR and turning Cuba into a Russian base. He did so on a calculation of Cuban interests which turned out to be a miscalculation, since the USSR showed by retreating in the face of Washington's challenge that Cuba's interests played very little part in Moscow's calculation of its own interests and possibilities in the western hemisphere. Although the USSR had defied the Monroe Doctrine it had not done so in support of Cuban nationalism or Cuban ambitions. Castro, who had hoped to become the Latin American equivalent of Tito, Sukarno and Nasser, at once the personification of a new national dignity and the regional leader of revolution, found himself instead the ruler of an island which had become an international curiosity rather than an international fulcrum and which was beginning to look rather bedraggled as a consequence of economic and administrative muddle. For Guevara, the Argentinian pan-American for whom Cuba's revolution (not Mexico's or Bolivia's) was to have been the real beginning of Latin America's revolution, the reassessment recessitated by the Russian retreat was even bitterer than it was for Castro, and in the course of it the two men fell out and Guevara disappeared, taking with him much of the Cuban revolution's international favour which he tried to inject into South America until he met his death in Bolivia in 1967.

Castro's adventures in Africa have been described in Part Five of this book. They increased and publicized his dependence on the USSR and they coincided with the global inflation and recession of the late seventies. In the first part of that decade the Cuban economy expanded at the rate of 10 per cent a year, but this rate fell to 4 per cent for the rest of the seventies. Food, housing and transport became scarce and dear; the price of fuel became prohibitive for large numbers of people; many workers were having to travel four hours a day to and from their work. Stricter regulations against small businesses created a large and economically stranded sub-proletariat. Nepotism, inequalities and stifling controls unaccompanied by commensurate benefits aggravated its plight. In 1979 a cyclone added its toll, the sugar crop failed and the tobacco crop was badly blighted. The weight of Washington's economic blockade was increasingly felt. In April 1980 10,000 Cubans invaded the Peruvian embassy in Havana demanding to go to Peru – and hoping to go to the United States. Some of them were common criminals or would-be political refugees, but the bulk were Cubans who had had enough of being in Cuba. Castro made the best of a bad job by allowing them to go, but they were a startlingly bad advertisement for his conduct of his country's affairs. His plight worsened a few years later when Gorbachev, who visited Cuba in 1989, cut Russian aid and aid from eastern Europe ceased altogether.

Apart from Cuba and the neighbouring large island of Hispaniola (divided between Haiti and the Dominican Republic) the Caribbean was colonial, mainly British, ground until after the Second World War. Decolonization was the main topic of the first postwar decades. A federation of British colonies in the Caribbean had been under discussion since the middle of the nineteenth century. Such a federation was created in 1958 but came to grief in 1961. There have been divergent views about the causes of this failure. On the one hand it has been alleged that the delay in bringing it into being after the end of the Second World War allowed animosities to develop between the islands and that the blame for this delay rested upon the British government which, regarding West Indian leaders as much more left-wing than in fact they were, slowed down the pace towards independence and therefore federation. On this view there was a genuine desire for federation, at the popular as well as the political level, despite the acknowledged difficulties – great disparities in the size and wealth of the different islands and the great distances between them. The alternative view is that, except perhaps in the smaller islands, there was no popular interest in federation or support for it and that the federation of 1958 rested therefore on a narrow base of political and trade-union leaders who were liable to be undermined by a popular revulsion; and that such a revulsion was in the event stirred up by other leaders who saw in it a way to take power. This view stresses the ways of thinking of the Caribbean peoples, islanders with a keen sense of belonging to their particular islands but little sense of community with others beyond the horizon (a habit accentuated by the fact that under colonial rule each colony had been treated by the British Colonial Office as a distinct object in a series of bilateral relationships with Britain).

Shortly after federation, and before its economic benefits had had a chance to make their impact, the prime minister of Jamaica, Norman Manley, was challenged by his rival, Alexander Bustamente, to hold a referendum to see whether Jamaicans wished the federation to continue or not. The result was a narrow defeat for Manley and the federation, which Jamaica left in January 1962. Trinidad-Tobago followed suit. Both became independent members of the Commonwealth and the OAS, as did Barbados in 1966. The smaller islands became associate members of the Commonwealth, self-governing except in relation to foreign and defence policies in which Britain retained a share of responsibility. There were six of these associates: Antigua with Barbuda which progressed to independence and UN membership in 1981;

Grenada which became an international celebrity in 1983 (see p. 52); Dominica; St Lucia; St Vincent; and St Kitts–Nevis–Anguilla. The last proved unhappily assorted and Anguilla rebelled against the government on St Kitts. It achieved a *de facto* separation which Britain, despite some sympathy with Anguillan complaints, refused at first to endorse but accepted in 1980 when Anguilla became formally a separate state, Britain assuming responsibility for its defence, foreign affairs and internal security with a say in its senior appointments. Four British colonies remained colonies: Montserrat, the British Virgin Islands, the Turks and Caicos Islands and the Cayman Islands – some of which became favoured haunts of tax-evading bankers and their Third World equivalents in the drug business. On the mainland British Honduras, which changed its name to Belize in 1973, moved only slowly to independence under the shadow of Guatemala's claim to the whole territory. It became in 1981 an independent member of the Commonwealth protected by a small British force.

In 1968 a fresh and more modest co-operative venture was launched under the name of Carifta (Caribbean Free Trade Association). It was joined by all Commonwealth states and territories except British Honduras and the Bahamas. The former joined three years later, and in 1973 changed its name to Belize. The weaker members claimed that Carifta benefited the stronger members more than themselves. All were worried by British accession to the EEC since they had, under the Commonwealth Sugar Agreement and similar schemes, an assured market and stable prices for their sugar, fruit, rum and other produce. With the exception of the solitary oil producer. Trinidad and Tobago, they were harder hit by rising oil prices in the seventies which aggravated endemic unemployment and anti-government sentiment. In 1973 four states – Trinidad and Tobago, Guyana, Jamaica and Barbados – created a Caribbean Community (Caricom), membership of which was open to all Commonwealth countries which chose to join within a year. The participation of Jamaica, which had torpedoed the federation of 1958, was vital. This new association, which replaced looser meetings of heads of government, had a small population but was nevertheless economically overpopulated: its two largest members, Jamaica and Trinidad (whose perennial prime minister, Eric Williams, died in 1981), counted only half a million people between them but a quarter of the population of working age was unemployed and the average income was less than $500 a year.

Much the largest of the British possessions was Jamaica. In 1961 Jamaicans, asked to choose in a referendum between independence and a West Indian federation, chose independence. This was the policy of the Jamaica Labour Party (JLP) led by Alexander Bustamente – and subsequently by Donald Sangster, Hugh Shearer and Edward Seaga. The pro-federation People's National Party (PNP) of Norman Manley (in office 1957–62) resigned and the JLP governed for the next ten years. This was a period of largely unhappy post-colonial reconstruction. The economic base was broadened from its traditional reliance on sugar to embrace also tourism, bauxite and manufacture, but the shift from agriculture to manufacture increased unemployment to 20–30 per cent of the working population at a time when the habitual escape – emigration to Britain – became all but barred. Hence pressures and conflicts, notably in overcrowded Kingston, and discontent directed against the economic establishment: a small oligarchy, foreign capital and – in the commercial field – Lebanese, Syrian and Chinese minorities. Discontent mounted to violence not far short of civil war (major riots in 1968) and a helpless JLP government lost the 1972 election. The PNP now led by Norman Manley, Jr., returned and remained in office until the end of 1980. Like Castro, Manley wanted to break away from Washington's economic stranglehold and, in rebellion also against the terms on which the IMF did business with impecunious developing countries, to get aid from the USSR and eastern Europe. As a result he got himself a bad name in the west without compensating benefits from the east. The island was also hit by declining revenues from bauxite and other exports. In 1980, in an election which claimed at least 500 lives, the comparatively right-wing JLP triumphed with an economic recovery programme based on conventional capitalist remedies with US approval. The new prime minister, Edward Seaga, made a quick tour of Washington and other western capitals and closed the Cuban embassy but he was not able to stem the slump in Jamaica's main exports – sugar, bananas, bauxite – or reduce a foreign debt which was eating up half of Jamaica's export earnings. With the economic infrastructure collapsing and the poor getting poorer Manley won the elections of 1989. He secured fresh loans from the IMF but had to agree to cut subsidies, devalue the currency and keep inflation below 9 per cent a year. The soaring prices occasioned by the first part of this programme led to high wage-claims which endangered the undertaking on inflation and therefore the whole package.

For a generation after independence Trinidad and Tobago, besides being at the other end of the Caribbean, presented a contrast to Jamaica in its style and fortunes. Its two principal communities, of African and East Indian origin, coexisted without serious conflict. It pursued unselfish policies of lending to its neighbours and subscribing for World Bank loans. But after 1980 declining oil revenues and high interest rates dented its prosperity and stability. Meanwhile it had lost its status as a developing country, while its attempts to diversify its economy and reduce its dependence on oil and sugar ran into protectionist obstacles from the United States and the European Community. As world prices for its exports collapsed, unemployment rose, a series of devaluations forced up prices, wages were frozen, and crime and disorder increased.

In these circumstances the rule of the People's National Movement came to an end in 1986 when the National Alliance for Reconstruction, led by Robbie Robinson (of African origin), won a convincing victory. The new government accepted the standard IMF remedies.

With the exception of Jamaica and perhaps Trinidad the several new states of the Caribbean had electorates of eighteenth-century proportions to go with their constitutions of twentieth-century design. Consequently elections were all too easily conducted with threats and promises – a promise to abolish taxes, for example. This circumstance did not make for good or stable government. It also robbed electoral verdicts of much significance, so that generalizations about a leftward or rightward trend were uncommonly deceptive and misleading. The poverty of so many of the islands, coupled with Castro's appeal and meddling, favoured parties with radical programmes. Nevertheless, where a valid distinction could be drawn between right and left, there was in the seventies a tendency to choose the more right-wing parties. In Antigua, for example, Vere Bird's Labour Party recovered in 1976 the power it had lost in 1971 to a more radical rival; but its return was facilitated by its promise to abolish income tax and by its predecessor's too extreme corruption. In the same year J. M. G. Adams's Barbadian Labour Party defeated the more left-wing party of Errol Barrow, and in Trinidad and Tobago the comparatively conservative Eric Williams won another term of the office which he had held since 1956. In 1979 St Vincent and St Kitts–Nevis also shifted to the right and so perhaps did Dominica, where the government of Patrick John was forced to resign after revelations concerning peculiar dealings with South Africa. Many of these small states were obliged to search for unorthodox sources of revenue but Patrick John's scheme for leasing a substantial part of his island to the South African government was too eccentric and portentous to pass muster.

The contrary left-wing trend, supported by Cuban aid and inspiration, won some success in Grenada where Eric Gairy's United Labour Party, re-elected in 1976, failed to cope with the island's economic distress or to maintain a semblance of honest government. It was removed by force by Maurice Bishop, an admirer of Castro. Other Caribbean parties sympathetic to Castroism remained in the wings, their fortunes still latent but their presence significant enough to induce Washington to quadruple its financial aid to the region between 1975 and 1980. A scare in 1980 over the supposed arrival in Cuba of a Russian brigade reinforced this beneficence and also the feeling that the Caribbean was being drawn once more into world politics as it had been at the time of the Cuban missiles crisis in 1962. The election of Reagan added a touch of gunboat diplomacy to the prevailing dollar diplomacy, its most notable exploit being the invasion of Grenada in 1983.

Bishop had begun his rule by making overtures to the United States but he was snubbed in Washington and found his development plans blocked by US votes in international financial institutions. He obtained nevertheless favourable mention from the World Bank in 1982 for his rural schemes and extensions of public services and he released in the same year some of the political prisoners whom he had put in jail upon coming to power. His party, the New Jewel Movement, was an amalgam of two roughly equal sections, the one led by himself and the other by Bernard and Janet Coard who were regarded as closer in temperament and ideology to Castro (or even, in the eyes of their enemies, to Pol Pot). By 1983 these two groups had become openly hostile and were murdering each other. Bishop was assailed from two sides – his more left-wing colleagues on the one hand and, on the other, the United States which had decided to unseat him and was using blatantly exaggerated propaganda against him. The Coard faction murdered him. A US force landed and destroyed the Coards and their adherents, using a variety of excuses to cover a rehearsed operation: that the airport being built by British contractors was not, as alleged, intended to boost tourism but to serve the purposes of Castro and his allies; that the lives of a group of US nationals engaged in research in Grenada were at risk; and that a substantial Cuban military force was already on the island. In spite of being rehearsed the United States adventure was bungled; intelligence was poor; the invaders took ten days to conquer a small defenceless island and suffered over a hundred casualties, inflicted mostly on themselves. There were no Cuban forces on Grenada and official statements were embarrassingly and blatantly untrue. But the operation was far from unpopular. Washington secured endorsement of its action from neighbouring Caribbean governments, although most Commonwealth governments, including the British, were piqued by what they regarded as an illegal and politically unnecessary act. Washington got away with it because the operation was brief, welcome to the inhabitants of Grenada and in tune with prevailing anti–left-wing sentiments. A new political party was put together under Herbert Blaize and captured in 1984 all seats in the parliament except one. Blaize died in 1989 and in elections a few months later the ruling National Democratic Congress failed by one seat to secure a majority of the parliament's fifteen members. Relics of Bishop's party won no seat and a mere 2 per cent of the vote. Nicholas Braithwaite became prime minister in an unstable situation.

Haiti's independence was won by slave revolts against Revolutionary and Napoleonic France after being a French colony from 1697. French rulers set an example of atrocious behaviour which was not lost on their wards and successors. Until 1843 the island of Hispaniola comprised a single state but in that year it was divided into Haiti and the Dominican

Republic. Haiti was occupied by the United States from 1915 to 1934. Society and politics revolved round a black majority and a mulatto élite which, after briefly combining to get rid of French rule, treated one another with savagery. Dictators were common but not always or entirely vicious. The main characteristics of the régime of Colonel Paul Magloire (1950–56) were extravagance, jollity and corruption. His place was taken by François Duvalier (Papa Doc) who had been in hiding in Magloire's time but emerged to win an election in 1957 and survived, first, by being a better plotter than his rivals and, secondly, by recruiting the fearsome Tontons Macoute. He had also support from the United States until Washington connived at a ludicrously incompetent invasion by his enemies in Florida. After this fiasco Washington switched back to Duvalier. His rule became rough, ruthless and crazed. He died in 1971 and was succeeded by his son Jean-Claude (Baby Doc). Whereas Papa Doc had been the leader of a black middle-class coterie which hijacked the state and treated it as private property while at the same time extolling negritude, the national voodoo religion and the cruder ideas and practices of European fascism, Baby Doc found his friends among the rich mulattos. He was less intelligent than his father and perhaps less ruthless but he was evicted in 1986 after over-straining the indulgence of the Roman Catholic Church, the professional classes and the young (here, as in many countries, habitually referred to as students). The Duvalier régime was followed by instability, two elections in 1987 and 1990 marred by violence, and the eviction in 1990 of another strongman, Prosper Avril. A third post-Duvalier election gave Father Jean-Bertrand Aristide a convincing victory after a campaign in which he promised to make life better for oppressed and undernourished underdogs and the electorate allowed itself to hope that he might be allowed to do so.

At the northern edge of the Caribbean, north-east of Cuba and south-east of Florida, the Commonwealth of the *Bahamas*, an independent member of the Commonwealth from 1973, flourished as a principal ancillary of the seamier side of international finance and of the drugs trade. Sir Lynden Pindling, chief minister 1967–73 and prime minister from 1973, rose to power as the champion of the black majority against the white merchant élite (the Bay Street Boys). His governments were periodically assailed by scandals, notably in 1984 which he survived and in 1987 when he felt obliged to call an election which his Progressive Liberal Party won after a confused and ill-tempered contest which, however, was adjudged by US observers to be fair enough. The opposition Free National Movement, accused of being equally corrupt and élitist to boot, won a few seats from the PLP but Pindling won 31 out of 49. He enjoyed the support, with diminishing enthusiasm, of the United States.

NOTE

Guyana

Guyana, once British Guiana, is an almost equally divided bi-racial country in which the descendants of Indians imported by the British (after the abolition of slavery in 1838) slightly outnumber the Africans while a small Roman Catholic minority with European origins can in these circumstances be electorally important. The Indians are predominantly rural, the Africans urban. The postwar leaders of these two groups were at first divided more by temperament than policy. The Indian leader, Cheddi Jagan, a Rooseveltian liberal with a socialist American wife, joined forces with Forbes Burnham, a shrewd politician of African descent. Both men moved to the left but the former moved faster than the latter. While Jagan allowed himself to be pushed by conflict into more extreme attitudes, Burnham exercised more self-control and successfully subordinated the expression of opinions to the capture of power. They became therefore the leaders of opposing parties, separated at first by tactical considerations but increasingly racial in their confrontation. In 1961 Jagan won an election, but his radicalism, and especially his plans to unionize labour, alarmed the European planters, while local American interests were reporting him to be a dangerous communist. This view of Jagan's impact on the colony was sharpened by riots necessitating the despatch of British troops and by Jagan's leanings towards Castro's Cuba, an inclination partly temperamental but partly also economic: Cuba was one of Guyana's principal markets for its surplus rice and this market had been cut off after Castro's revolution.

With independence in the offing the United States and to some extent Britain were anxious to ensure the victory of Burnham over Jagan. Burnham cultivated the small Roman Catholic party and won the election of 1964 after the British had conveniently altered the constitution by introducing proportional representation. On a straight vote Jagan could and almost certainly would win; under proportional representation he could not. This election was followed in 1966 by independence, whereupon British Guiana became Guyana and joined the UN but not, owing to a border dispute with Venezuela, the OAS. In the next few years the victorious Burnham began to move to the left, impelled chiefly by the needs of the urban unemployed Africans and by general anti-American and anti-planter ideological imperatives. Burnham's perennial rival, Cheddi Jagan, and his People's Progressive Party suffered a series of defeats too overwhelming to be credible and the alternative opposition, the Working People's Alliance, retired from the elections of 1980 after its leader was assassinated. A new constitution in 1978 established a presidential form of government. Burnham died suddenly in 1985. His successor Desmond Hoyte maintained the dominant position of Burnham's People's National Congress, subject however to increasingly trenchant accusations of sharp electoral malpractice and a steep decline in the country's economic fortunes. Revenues from sugar and bauxite flagged, the currency was devalued, food and electric power became scarce, wages were cut.

East of Guyana Surinam became independent of the Netherlands in 1975. From 1980 to 1988 it experienced military rule which was reasserted in 1990 by a coup which Surinam's neighbours in South America and the Caribbean deplored and denounced. French Guyana remained a Department of France. a thousand miles westward of Surinam the Netherlands Antilles and Aruba were, by an agreement of 1986, promised independence in 1996.

INDEX

Notes
1. Where there are several page references major entries are shown in **bold** figures.
2. References to maps are shown in *italic* figures.
3. Entries with country names in brackets refer generally to organizations or political parties.

Muslims *see* Islam
Mussolini 10, 213, 296
Mutesa II, Frederick 546
Mutual and Balanced Force Reduction 53–4
Mutual Defence Agreement 75
Muzorewa, Bishop 570, 572–3
Mwinyi, Ali Hassan 553
Myanmar *see* Burma

Nadir Shah, Ahmed 423
Nagy, Ferenc 235
Nagy, Imre 27, 242–3, 258
al-Nahas Pasha, Mustafa 297, 535
Nairobi conference (1976) 160
Najibullah, Muhammad 428
Nakasone, Yesuhiro 80
Namibia 51, *129*, *557*, 571, 589, 595, 596, **601–2**, 606, 620
Namirembe agreement 546
Nassau meeting (1962) 203–4
Nasser, Colonel Gamal Abdel 27, 505, 693, 697
    and 1952 revolution 296, 298–9
    and Suez Canal dispute 302–6, 310
    disputes and wars with Israel 302–4, 313–18, 321
    and economy 323
    and India 300
    and Iran 386
    and Muslim Brotherhood 387
    and neutralism 146, 238
    and Saudi Arabia 374
    and Sudan 537
    and Tunisia 482
    and USSR 142, 615–16
    and Yemen 377
    death 322, 325
Nasser Mohammed, Ali 380
Natal 578
National Alliance for Reconstruction (Jamaica) 701
National Congress (India) 391–3, 399, 407, 413, 415–18, 516
National Congresses in West Africa 496
National Democratic Congress (Grenada) 702
National and Democratic Congresses, Nepali 407
National Front (Czechoslovakia) 235, 247
National Front (Malaysia) 461

National Independence Front (Hungary) 235
National Islamic Front (Sudan) 538
National League for Democracy (Burma) 436
National Liberal Party of Chamoun (Lebanon) 335
National Liberation Army (Uganda) 555
National Party (Namibia) 595
National Party (Zanzibar) 552
National People's Congress (China) 120
National Planning Commission (China) 93
National Police Reserve (Japan) 75
National Redemption Couincl (Ghana) 506
National Resistance Army (Uganda) 555
National Salvation Front (Romania) 263
National Unionist Party (Sudan) 536
Nationalist Party (South Africa) 577–87 *passim*, 590, 598–9, 606, 608
Nato
    and Africa 592, 616
    and Canada 637, 638
    and Communist Europe 229, 240, 250, 261
    and Indo-China 445
    and Middle East 298, 344
    and Southern Europe 213–14, 216–17, 218, 221, 223, 225, 227
    and southern Europe, Cyprus 276, 278, 279, 281
    and superpowers (USA & USSR)
        arms race 34, 35, 39, 46, 49, 50, 51–2, 53–4, 56–7
        Cold War 19–21, 22, 25–6, 28
        depreciation 60, 61–2, 64
    and Third World 139, 142, 155
    and United Nations 125
    and Western European recovery 175–7, 178, 180–1, 182, 185, 204, 207
Natusch Busch, Colonel Alberto 675
Navarre, General 441
navies 48–9, 194, 591–2, 648
Nazimuddin, Khwaja 398
Ndebele people 573
Nedelin, Marshal 29
Nefa (North-East Frontier Agency of India) 402, 406, 408

AUG 2 3 1995